MOTIVATION, EMOTION, AND COGNITION

Integrative Perspectives on Intellectual
Functioning and Development

The Educational Psychology Series

Robert J. Sternberg and Wendy M. Williams, Series Editors

Marton/Booth • *Learning and Awareness*

Hacker/Dunlovsky/Graesser, Eds. • *Metacognition in Educational Theory and Practice*

Smith/Pourchot, Eds. • *Adult Learning and Development: Perspectives From Educational Psychology*

Sternberg/Williams, Eds. • *Intelligence, Instruction, and Assessment: Theory Into Practice*

Martinez • *Education as the Cultivation of Intelligence*

Torff/Sternberg, Eds. • *Understanding and Teaching the Intuitive Mind: Student and Teacher Learning*

Sternberg/Zhang, Eds. • *Perspectives on Cognitive, Learning, and Thinking Styles*

Ferrari, Ed. • *The Pursuit of Excellence Through Education*

Corno, Cronbach, Kupermintz, Lohman, Mandinach, Porteus, Albert/The Stanford Aptitude Seminar • *Remaking the Concept of Aptitude: Extending the Legacy of Richard E. Snow*

Dominowski • *Teaching Undergraduates*

Valdés • *Expanding Definitions of Giftedness: The Case of Young Interpreters From Immigrant Communities*

Shavinina/Ferrari, Eds. • *Beyond Knowledge: Non-Cognitive Aspects of Developing High Ability*

Dai/Sternberg, Eds. • *Motivation, Emotion, and Cognition: Integrative Perspectives on Intellectual Functioning and Development*

MOTIVATION, EMOTION, AND COGNITION

Integrative Perspectives on Intellectual Functioning and Development

Edited by

David Yun Dai
University at Albany, State University of New York

Robert J. Sternberg
Yale University

 LAWRENCE ERLBAUM ASSOCIATES, PUBLISHERS
2004   Mahwah, New Jersey   London

Lawrence Erlbaum Associates, Inc., Publishers
10 Industrial Avenue
Mahwah, New Jersey 07430

Cover design by Sean Trane Sciarrone

Library of Congress Cataloging-in-Publication Data

Motivation, emotion, and cognition : integrative perspectives on intellectual development
and functioning / edited by David Yun Dai and Robert J. Sternberg.
    p. cm. — (The educational psychology series)
Includes bibliographical references and index.
ISBN 0-8058-4556-9 (c : alk. paper) — ISBN 0-8058-4557-7 (pbk. : paper)
    1. Intellect. 2. Motivation (Psychology). 3. Emotions and cognition. I. Dai, David Yun.
II. Sternberg, Robert J. III. Series.

BF431.M72 2004
153.9—dc22
                                     2003049396
                                          CIP

Printed in the United States of America
10 9 8 7 6 5 4 3 2 1

Dedicated to the memory of Richard E. Snow,
who envisioned and championed integrative
approaches to intellectual phenomena

DYD
RJS

Contents

III.   Intelligence and Personality:
From Psychometrics to Personal Dynamics

IV.   Development of Intellectual Competencies

V.   Intellectual Functioning and Development
in Social and Cultural Contexts

Preface

What enables us to function effectively in society, to acquire and generate knowledge, to develop intellectual prowess and high-level expertise, to create and invent? Psychologists have attempted to answer this question for generations. Historically, intellectual functioning and development have been largely viewed as cognitive phenomena, to be explained in terms of cognitive capacity, structures, and processes. Motivation and emotion are often seen as peripheral or epiphenomenal in that regard, or worse, as potentially detrimental to reason and sound judgment. We call this view a cognitive-reductionistic perspective. We argue that an exclusive emphasis on cognition misses some essential components of intellectual functioning and development. We wonder whether such a narrow focus has started to yield diminishing returns in generating viable accounts of various intellectual phenomena.

In this volume, we pursue a different tack, an integrative approach, which views motivation, emotion, and cognition as inextricably related, for good or ill, in intellectual functioning and development. This road has been less traveled but holds the promise of providing insights as to how people operate and adapt themselves intellectually in real functional contexts instead of just performing laboratory tasks. An emphasis on integration naturally brings the enactive person as a whole to the forefront. In other words, such an emphasis puts perception and cognition back in the context of human adaptive efforts to effect changes in their environments as well as in themselves, and related emotional reactions and affective experiences.

Specifically, this volume represents integrative efforts along four lines of psychological research.

In terms of cognitive processes, we see how motivation and emotion alter, channel, or otherwise direct cognition in significant ways, rendering an exclusive focus on cognitive architecture or pure cognitive system problematical.

In the tradition of differential psychology, we see a movement from a static view of human intelligence to a dynamic, contextualized view of intellectual functioning that integrates many facets of personhood and personality that are motivational and emotional in nature.

From a developmental perspective, we see how the role of motivation and emotion should be reinstated in accounting for the development of intellectual competencies and expertise.

Along with theoretical traditions that highlight the importance of social and cultural contexts, we see that intellectual functioning and development are necessarily embedded in social interaction and enculturation processes, which have profound cognitive, self-evaluative (affective), and motivational ramifications.

Contributors to this volume are from diverse psychological backgrounds. Indeed, one of the purposes of this volume is to combat compartmentalization in psychology and to generate cross-talk among people of different theoretical and research traditions and affiliations. However, under this apparent diversity one also finds a common vision—to broaden a largely exclusive focus on cognition to include constructs of motivation and affect or emotion, and situate cognition in its functional context to reveal its adaptive (or, at times, maladaptive) character.

We intend this volume to be of interest to both psychologists and general audiences who have an interest in the nature of intellectual functioning and development. Although the volume mainly addresses theoretical rather than practical questions, educators and other practitioners whose main charge is to enhance intellectual functioning and human performance will find integrative perspectives promising and productive. For these perspectives tend to view intellectual functioning as contextual, dynamic, and varying with situations and domains, rather than fixed and invariant, thus opening doors for interventions.

We thank two anonymous reviewers for their constructive comments on our book proposal. We also thank Naomi Silverman and Erica Kica for their editorial assistance. This book project was also made possible in part by a grant from the National Science Foundation to the first author (#0296062) and grants from the National Science Foundation (REC-9979843) and U.S. Department of Education (R206R000001) to the second author.

David Yun Dai
Robert J. Sternberg

P.S. As this volume just went to production, we heard of the untimely passing of Paul Pintrich, one of our contributors. Paul contributed much during his career to integrative approaches represented in this volume. We cherish the memory of him as a great colleague as well as his scholarly legacy of going beyond "cold cognition" in understanding intellectual functioning and development.

I

INTRODUCTION

1
▼▼▼▼▼▼▼

Beyond Cognitivism: Toward an Integrated Understanding of Intellectual Functioning and Development

David Yun Dai
University at Albany, State University of New York

Robert J. Sternberg
Yale University

> Long separation inevitably leads to reunion, and vice versa.
> —Chinese proverb

> *It takes time for the human to bring all that he or she knows about a problem at hand, and it never completely happens . . . The peaks of rationality always rise up on the temporal horizon just another ridge or two away. Much real behavior takes place on the foothills of rationality . . . Cognitive psychology—I should say modern experimental psychology—has located itself at immediate behavior and only gradually moves up the scale. Such movement, then, becomes an indicator of putting it all together.*
> —Allen Newell (1988, p. 428)

In late January and early February, 2003, Kasparov, arguably the best chess player in the world, had another human-machine face-off with computer chess, not Deep Blue this time, but its more academic cousin, Deep Junior. The six-game match led to a draw, and a much happier Kasparov (Kasparov, 2003).

Although the human player and computer chess seem neck-and-neck in generating strong moves, there are distinct differences as to how they do it. The human relies more on experience-based and knowledge-based perceptions and intuitions, the machine on its speed and capacity of computation (literally three million moves per second!). Human thinking is more fuzzy and flexible and the machine is more precise and rigid. Kasparov got annoyed but his opponent, a cold, calculating machine, never did, even as Kasparov tried

3

desperately to create situations that would make Deep Junior uncomfortable (whatever that means!). The human player would anticipate future occurrences and get surprised or feel push-backs (i.e., counter-moves), but the machine, like an autistic savant, was totally immersed in its own monologue of calculation. Kasparov got tired and Deep Junior never did.

Despite the marvelous achievement of artificial intelligence in the second half of the 20th century, several limitations of Deep Junior are quite striking. The programmers of Deep Junior still felt that they had to intervene regarding a draw offer by Kasparov instead of allowing the machine to make a decision on its own (e.g., setting a fixed threshold point in evaluation for rejecting or accepting a draw offer). The learning ability of Deep Junior, if any, is very limited. After each game, the programmers of Deep Junior had to serve as a metalevel control and fine-tune the machine based on the information from the previous games. When all is said and done, Deep Junior was still a data-crunching program, executing instructions as it had been programmed to do.

What lessons can we learn from this human–machine comparison? For decades in the early 20th century, we did not have a proper language to describe what is going on inside the black box of the human mind. The emergence of the computer changed things, giving rise to the metaphor of the mind as an information processing device (Baars, 1986). The computer metaphor has given us a powerful language to describe how the mind might work. Ironically, a half century later, the unfolding of artificial intelligence gave us a new window through which to look back at the human mind and human intelligence. It became clear, based on the previous comparisons, that human intellectual functioning and development[1] are subject to a different set of constraints compared to machine intelligence.

Limitations of Cognitivism

The computer metaphor provides an approximation of the mind to a certain point. After all, the designers of the standard computer clearly attempted to mimic the way humans process information (von Newmann, 1958). However, when the mind is reduced to merely a symbolic processing device, we get

---

[1]The term intellectual functioning is often used to refer to complex, higher-order forms of cognition such as reasoning, problem solving, and decision making. We use the term to denote: (a) any act of generating or utilizing knowledge or strategies, or both, for practical or purely intellectual purposes by an intentional system; and (b) the effectiveness of such an act in achieving specific desired outcomes. Defined as such, it distinguishes itself from mere cognitive operations. In other words, intellectual functioning and cognitive functioning belong to two levels of analysis; the former is at the intentional level, and latter is at the operational level, to use the terminology of activity theory (Leont'ev, 1978; see also Oerter, 2000). Defined as such, intellectual functioning subsumes, but cannot be reduced to, cognitive functioning.

a lopsided image of how the mind functions. In the following section, we discuss some problematic aspects of this approach to intellectual functioning and development. In providing a critique of what might be called cognitivism,[2] we are not negating the possibility of the potential of computational modeling to simulate the mind in all its richness and complexity, including intricacies of human motivation and emotion, as Tomkins (1963) envisioned decades ago. Rather, we are referring to a general tendency in cognitive psychology to build formal cognitive models of intellectual functioning and development that do insufficient justice to the role of emotion and motivation in specific functional contexts.

The first limitation of such cognitivism is its assumption of a pure cognitive system of perceiving and thinking, free of emotion and motivation (or treating them as peripheral or epiphenomenal). As Norman (1980) pointed out, what is conspicuously missing in this account is the regulatory aspect of the mind such as motivation and emotion. The result is an account of thinking as fully disembodied, objective, mechanical, rational, and cold (Labouvie-Vief, 1990). However, as Neisser (1963) pointed out a long time ago:

1. human thinking always takes place in, and contributes to, a cumulative process of growth and development;
2. human thinking begins in an intimate association with emotion and feelings which is never entirely lost;
3. almost all human activity, including thinking, serves not one but a multiplicity of motives at the same time (p. 195).

Overcoming this limitation means restoring the adaptive nature of intellectual functioning and development. What has contributed to Kasparov's immense intellectual prowess in chess is not only his reasoning or pattern-recognition capacity but also his motivation to win, and his emotional capacity to feel, his metacognitive capacity to self-regulate, his ability to learn and make self-corrections.

---

[2]The term cognitivism represents a broad movement in psychology in the second half of the 20th century known as the cognitive revolution (Baars, 1986; Gardner, 1985); it manifests itself in many ways and does not have a simple definition (see Smith, 2001; see also Haugeland, 1981). Yet the main thrust of this movement was to treat the computer, a mechanical computational device, as a model of the human mind, and its main tenet is rule-based symbol manipulation. For a detailed critique of cognitivism, see Johnson and Erneling (1997). Cognitivism should not be confused with cognitive sciences, which represent interdisciplinary efforts to understand the mind, and cover all spectrum of cognitive, affective, and motivational issues, including the nature of consciousness, intentionality, intersubjectivity, and self (see Wilson & Keil, 2001).

The second limitation of such cognitivism, related to the first one, is its exclusive focus on the constraints of what is called cognitive architecture on performance, independent of various supporting (and sometimes enabling) or debilitating emotions and motivations in functional contexts. To be sure, findings of cognitive psychology about attentional bottleneck (Simon, 1994), working memory capacity (G. Miller, 1956), or schemata (Rumelhart, 1980) are some of the most important scientific breakthroughs in the history of psychology. Indeed these findings have profound implications for intellectual functioning (e.g., progressive deepening: Newell, 1990), emotion (the violation of schematic anticipation and surprise: Kagan, 2002), and task motivation (e.g., the regulatory control of attention: Simon, 1967, 1994). However, Broadbent had every reason to be unhappy that his innovative ideas regarding short-term memory got picked up quickly but his main message of how stress might influence cognitive performance was ignored (Broadbent, 1958, 1971). In real life, levels of intellectual functioning are typically not an invariant property of a cognitive system, but depend on one's motivational and emotional states. This is why while G. Miller (1956) was figuring out the magic number 7 plus/minus 2 (short-term memory capacity), Bruner (Bruner, Matter, & Papanek, 1955; see Bruner, 1992) contemplated a more functionalist question of whether motivational states such as hunger might narrow the scope of information search, or even create a tunnel vision. Kasparov (2003) felt a great deal of pressure in the face of the daunting machine, which was poised to beat him and undermine his premier reputation as the world chess champion. Such a high-stakes functional context is stressful and anxiety-provoking yet energizing for Kasparov but does not change Deep Junior's behavior in any conceivable way. Such a performance condition also tests the human capacity for harnessing one's emotional energy in the service of goal strivings, while controlling distracting, interfering, or otherwise debilitating emotions and feelings, and ego concerns unknown to classical cognitive models of human problem solving (e.g., Newell & Simon, 1972).

The third limitation of cognitivism is its inability to include human phenomenological (i.e., subjective) experiences as a legitimate (and often essential) force for higher-order mental functions. Labouvie-Vief (1990) quite cogently characterized this omission as thinking without the thinker. What is missing in a typical cognitivist approach is the role of consciousness, intentionality, and reflectivity. Snow (1986) described these properties of the mind as part and parcel of human intelligence:

> Persons (including psychologists) not only feel, strive, and know, but also *know* that they feel, strive, and know, and can anticipate further feeling, striving, and knowing; they monitor and reflect upon their own experience, knowledge, and mental functioning in past, present, and future tenses. (pp. 133–134)

As Kasparov (2003) pointed out, Deep Blue not only was unaware of the fact it was playing a world champion, but had no self-awareness that it was winning or losing. Such lack of self-awareness and consequent emotional reactions would be potentially devastating for human players, because this crucial piece of information would motivate adaptive strategic adjustment (e.g., to fight back).[3]

The failure to consider subjective experiences also creates blind spots such as how a thinker's values, attitudes, dispositions, self-understandings, and beliefs guide his or her thinking. Because cognitivism focuses on the formal or syntactic aspect of symbol manipulation (Smith, 2001), and neglects mental or semantic contents of one's directed consciousness or intentionality (Searle, 2001), what gets obscured is the entire issue of how the culture, with its rich historical legacy, enables our thinking through language and other conceptual tools working seamlessly but potently in an intersubjective world, without which most of what we call intellectual development is simply out of the question (Gardner, 1985; see also D'Andrade, 1981, 1995, for a discussion of differences between computer programs and cultural programs of cognition). The very Kasparov phenomenon (or the phenomenon of Deep Junior, for that matter) cannot be understood without the proper context of cultural values, incentives, tools, and resources (including a body of the codified chess knowledge, coaching, tournaments) supporting the development of chess expertise.

The Trend Toward Integration

What we have witnessed since about 1990 is, to paraphrase Bruner's (1994) comments, a "renewed respect for a rather classical form of functionalism" (p. 277) that tries to situate perception and cognition in a broader functional context of human adaptation. Such a change logically calls for a more integrated understanding of intellectual functioning and development. As Newell (1988) pointed out, cognitive psychology started with elementary cognitive processes, and only gradually shifted its focus to higher levels of purposive behavior. Such a shift necessarily brings the whole person and functional

---

[3]There is a debate as to whether computational models are capable of derived intentionality, albeit the fact that it cannot produce real conscious experiences (e.g., Dennett, 1991; Searle, 1990). G. Matthews (personal communication, May 12, 2003) pointed out that consciousness and intentionality are beyond the computational metaphor, but many of the functional attributes of conscious states may not be. Our focus is how the human mind works. Whether computational models can simulate functional properties of mental states and acquire derived intentionality is another question. To the extent Deep Junior does not have a functional property resembling human emotional reactions to an imminent loss or win, we can say the system is not embodied.

contexts to the forefront. Indeed, efforts for integrating motivation, emotion, and cognition have been made by those pioneers of cognitive psychology (e.g., Bruner, 1986; Norman, 1980; Simon, 1967, 1979, 1994). Yet, much remains to be desired. Kintsch (1998) lamented that "an all too narrow focus on cognition places intolerable restrictions on cognitive science" (p. 13). He predicted that future progress would depend on the ability to reintegrate the cognitive and emotional-motivational aspects of human behavior (see also Bransford, Brown, & Cocking, 2000; Bruner, 1994; Gardner, 1985; Hilgard, 1980; Hoffman, 1986; Norman, 1980; Resnick, 1989; Shuell, 1996; Simon, 1994, for a similar position).

In the rest of this introduction, we provide an overview of different perspectives on intellectual functioning and development, and highlight and preview some of the issues discussed in the ensuing chapters. Specifically four general perspectives are discussed:

1. *Cognition in motivational and affective contexts.* We present three basic approaches to integration: neurobiological, psychological-behavioral, and phenomenological.

2. *Intelligence and personality.* We discuss how the field of differential psychology moves toward a more dynamic, multidimensional approach to understanding intellectual functioning.

3. *Development of intellectual competence.* We discuss the emergent role of personal agency, and in what way personal agency helps develop high levels of expertise through learning and development.

4. *Intellectual functioning and development in social cognitive and cultural contexts.* We discuss social contexts as integral part of intellectual functioning and culture as an important modulator of intellectual functioning and development.

Due to the scope and nature of the topic at hand, our introduction is schematic, illustrative, and occasionally speculative.

COGNITION IN MOTIVATIONAL AND AFFECTIVE CONTEXTS: FUNCTIONAL-DEPENDENCY PERSPECTIVES

The notion that basic mental processes such as attention, perception, cognition, and memory never occur as neutral events containing raw data of whatever is registered or encoded, but rather colored with motivational and affective[4] overtones, is not new (e.g., Bartlett, 1932). In the early years of the cognitive revolution, Abelson (1963) challenged cognitive simulation researchers to simulate hot cognition, cognition with an affect or attitude. In the following sections, we discuss several approaches that treat human beings as living systems that are capable of higher-order mental functions, not just pieces of cognitive machinery (Ford, 1992).

Integration of the First Order: Neurobiological Approaches

Broadly defined, neurobiological approaches attempt to elucidate the biological and neuro-chemical substrates of mental processes. As integration efforts, they are concerned with how affect and motivation support or impede higher mental functions at the brain level. Interestingly, neurobiological approaches to higher mental functions share similarity with cognitive approaches in that both deal with mental architecture. However, by reintroducing biology (the architecture of the brain) into mental affairs, neurobiologists and neuropsychologists can reinstate emotion and motivation as having a significant regulatory impact on cognitive processes and serving important adaptive functions (Damasio, 2001; Edelman, 1989).

As a systematic integration effort, Tucker and Derryberry (1992) proposed that the interaction of cognitive processes of the frontal cortex and more elementary emotional evaluation (e.g., anxiety) and motivational control (i.e., regulatory control of attention) provided by limbic and subcortical structures may be necessary for planning (e.g., sequencing actions, evaluating significance of events, and future-oriented processing) and self-control (e.g., inhibition). They further suggested that recruiting and maintaining an appropriate affective edge (i.e., certain levels of arousal) facilitate persistent efforts in planning and critical analysis. In this vertical integration of brain functions, the limbic system has some regulatory power over the cortical areas, by narrowing or broadening the breadth of attention and by directing attention selectively to specific sources of information, for good or ill (Derryberry & Tucker, 1994), rather than always the other way around (see also Panksepp,

---

[4]The terms affect and emotion are often used interchangeably, but one can still make a distinction in terms of their referents. Some argue that affect refers to subjective feelings, without necessarily being accompanied by autonomic arousal or visceral activity; the latter is often seen as necessary for *real* emotions. Affect also seems to carry more general evaluative overtone, indicating positive and negative valence of transactional experiences with certain situations, while emotions often refer to more specific reactions to situations vis-à-vis one's needs and wishes (e.g., excitement or frustration). This is why affect is often used more inclusively, encompassing emotion, attitude, and value (see Mandler, 1989a, for a discussion).

1998). This perspective sheds a new light on the old debate over cognitive versus emotional primacy (Lazarus, 1984; Zajonc, 1980).

While Derryberry and Tucker (1994) tend to emphasize the important bottom-up role of the limbic system (and anxiety) in what they call attentional orientating, other researchers focuses on top-down attentional control. Allman and his colleagues (Allman, Hakeem, Erwin, Nimchinsky, & Hof, 2001) proposed, based on a bulk of neuroscientific evidence, that the anterior cingulate cortex is responsible for emotional self-control, focused problem solving, error recognition, and adaptive response to changing conditions, all essential to intelligent behavior. The anterior cingulate is also the focus of Posner and colleagues' (Posner & Peterson, 1990; Posner & Rothbart, 1998) work on neuronal networks of attention and self-regulation. Consistent with their hypothesis of executive control of attention, Drevets and Raichle (1998) found that, when subjects were performing attention-demanding cognitive tasks, their cerebral blood flow decreased in areas controlling emotions and increased in areas responsible for cognitive functions. This pattern implicates an activated inhibitory mechanism at the brain level (although one can alternatively hypothesize that the conscious allocation of attention to task-relevant information and suppression of certain emotional reactions can also lead to the observed reduced blood flow).

Complex neurochemical mechanisms for effectively dealing with the complexity and novelty of a task have also been explored. For instance, Ashby, Isen, and Turken (1999) combined several lines of research on humans and animals and proposed a theory that dopamine mediates the effects of positive affect on cognitive flexibility in creative problem solving through its neural pathways to impact brain structures (e.g., the anterior cingulate) responsible for maintaining cognitive flexibility. Similarly, Kagan (2002) suggested that the amygdala, among other brain structures, get activated when one encounters an unexpected or discrepant event (i.e., novelty), creating a state of surprise. As we see in later discussion, such a mechanism is essential for learning.

Although the previously mentioned research programs have different emphases in terms of positive and negative contributions to intellectual functioning, taken together, they suggest that: (a) the infrastructure of the brain that supports various higher-order mental functions can be localized to some extent; (b) cognitive and emotional processes are intricately related, structurally as well as functionally, at the brain level; and (c) there are neurochemical mechanisms for the interplay of affect and cognition (e.g., dopaminergic activity: Ashby et al., 1999), which are typically neglected or unobservable in the psychological research. Thus, although still in their infancy, neurobiological approaches provide a unique window for an integrated understanding of biological constraints for intellectual functioning that otherwise cannot be achieved.

Integration of the Second Order:
Psychological-Behavioral Approaches

We call the second type of approach psychological-behavioral because the focus is no longer on brain mechanisms but rather on mental-behavioral functions. Compared with the previous more or less molecular approach, psychological-behavioral approaches operate distinctly at a molar level of description. Various motivational, emotional, and cognitive constructs, such as surprise, schematic reaction, volition, intention, expectancy, planning, are molar-level constructs. For instance, whereas Derryberry and Tucker (1994) used the term motivation to denote a regulatory function of the limbic system, motivation at the molar level is a mental construct that can only be understood in a functional context (e.g., to win a game or solve a math problem). Tolman (1932) described molar behavior as integrated responses that have their own emergent properties, such as forward-reaching or goal-directedness, means–end readiness, or goal–situation pairing. Thus they represent the higher-level organization of mental and behavioral functions that serve adaptive purposes, and cannot be reduced to molecular-level analysis.

Directional Influences of Motivation on Cognitive Processes.   Broadly defined, motivation is indicated by the intensity (or energy), direction, and persistence of a goal-directed behavior or action. Dweck's work on goal orientation (Dweck, 1999; Dweck, Mengals, & Good, chap. 2) clearly emphasizes the direction aspect of motivation. In other words, motivation does not just kickstart a mental act, with the rest of the action carried out by cognitive processes. Goal orientation (whether the attentional focus is on the self or on the task to be learned, and what is the implicit or explicit purpose of engaging in the task) frames the mindset, and can significantly influence the allocation of attentional resources, effort expenditure, and emotional reactions to difficulties, and persistence in the face of setbacks.

The Quality and Valence of Affect on Cognition.   Dweck's theory is predicated on the assumption that motivation is cognitively based (i.e., goal-directed), and subsequent emotional responses to task demands and performance are derivative of one's belief systems and goal orientation. Linnenbrink and Pintrich (chap. 3), in contrast, attempt to show that positive or negative affect may influence cognitive functioning. This approach echoes the research tradition of mood dependent memory and other cognitive processes (Eich, Kihlstrom, Bower, Forgas, & Niedenthal, 2000). There is a growing body of research on the role of affect on intellectual functioning, with a particular focus on the affective valence, for example, Fredrikson's (1998) Broaden-and-Build model of positive emotions (see Linnenbrink & Pintrich, chap. 3, for a review). The role of affect in problem solving in mathematics and sciences has also become a research focus (e.g., Goldin, 2000; Gruber, 1995; McLeod, 1989; Thagard, 2002).

Integration of the Third Order: Phenomenological Approaches

We label the third type of approach as phenomenological because the focus here is on a person's subjective, conscious experiences, including bodily sensations and mental images, and other perceptions and cognitions, such as desired outcomes, current concerns, personal epistemologies, intentionality, and the self. Although emotion, cognition, and motivation are all related to human consciousness, treating consciousness as a domain par excellence is a relatively recent event (e.g., Meltzinger, 2000). Ironically, it is mainly philosophers, linguists, and neurobiologists who had attempted an integrated understanding of the mind from a first-person perspective (e.g., Edelman, 1989; Merleau-Ponty, 1962; Polanyi, 1966), before it became a legitimate topic in the community of psychology (e.g., Apter, 2001; Varela, Thompson, & Rosch, 1993). The psychological effects of having consciousness and self-awareness of feelings and emotions are obvious but often get neglected. The most obvious one is what is called the self-reference effect (Rogers, Kuiper, & Kirker, 1977; see Symons & Johnson, 1997, for a meta-analysis). When subjects were shown adjectives and asked whether these adjectives described them, they performed better on ensuing recall tasks. Events that have personal relevance show distinct patterns of brain activation (i.e., event-related brain potentials [ERP]; see Johnson, 1986; see also Dweck et al., chap. 2). We also suspect the involvement of limbic system that enhances the basic function of memory. However, the ramifications of having consciousness and self-awareness are much broader and deeper than simple recall.

The Mind–Body Issue Redefined: Embodied Cognition. Discontent with the classic mind–body dichotomy has been evident at least in philosophy. Polanyi (1966) challenged the long-held Cartesian position: "Our body is the ultimate instrument of all out external knowledge, whether intellectual or practical. In all our waking moments we are relying on our awareness of contacts of our body with things outside for attending to these things" (pp. 15–16). Damasio (2000) framed this argument more formally, "Knowing begins as a feeling because its substrate is built from body signals" (p. 117). In other words, knowing is a visceral as much as a frontal matter; the feeling of what happens is just as important as the thought of what happens. Indeed, the two cannot be completely separated (Neisser, 1963). This establishes, first and foremost, that knowing is never a completely detached, unperturbed, pure rational process, but rather a dynamic sense-making that defines an intimate encounter between an enactive person and an impinging environment, be it children's conceptions of kinds or categories (Carey, 1999), or learning of mathematics (Schoenfeld, 1992).

The Centrality of Meaning-Making in Intellectual Functioning.   Due to unique self-awareness and conscious experiences of personal import, meaning takes on subjectivity. Rather than seeing meaning as a list of features about a category or propositional statements people use in an impersonal way to represent the surrounding world, Eldelman (1989, 1995) sees meaning as based on the functional value for the person and growing with the history of remembered body sensations and mental images. Similarly, Glenberg (1997) suggested that meaning is fundamentally embodied:

> An embodied account of meaning suggests that meaning is not independent of human functioning and that a sentence cannot have a universal meaning separate from the people doing the comprehending. Instead, embodied meaning is intrinsically embedded in human functioning. Rather than abstract meaningless elements, basic elements of embodied meaning reflect human capabilities, goals, emotions, and perception. (p. 509)

Consider text comprehension as an act of meaning (Bruner, 1990). It involves construction of a coherent mental model out of discrete elements of a textbase (Kintsch, 1998). Such a process cannot be objective, but rather is filled with mentally simulated actions. Thus Wineburg's (1991) historians would go to great lengths to set up an ad hoc mock reader in order to understand social persuasion embedded in the discourse represented in a historical document. Dai (2002a) also showed how such an act of meaning can break down when personal beliefs (e.g., "knowledge is simple and certain") are incommensurable with the complexity of discourse in the text.

Engagement of the Whole Person.   Integration through consciousness goes a step further from molar approaches, by blurring the distinction between cognitive, emotional, and motivational constructs. Bruner (1994) argued that separation of emotion and cognition is likely a theoretical assumption rather than existing in the immediate phenomenology of human experiences. Merleau-Ponty (1962) also argued that cognitive life cannot be separate from the life of desire or perceptual life, subtended by an intentional arc, which unifies our experience. *Interest* is one of those phenomena where the boundaries between motivation, affect, and cognition are blurred. To be interested in something is to have a subjective feeling for it (affect), to be drawn to it (conation), and to have some degree of knowledge about the object or activity in question (cognition). Because interest is an emergent property of a rather dynamic relationship or union between a person and an object or activity that frames the significance and meaning of the object or activity to the person, decomposing it is difficult, if not impossible (Hidi, Renninger, & Krapp, chap. 4). However, in Hidi and colleagues' exposition, primacy seems to be given to affect rather than cognition, a position consistent with Zajonc (1980). Precisely due to its ambiguous status, the psychological nature of interest appears elusive, although its functional significance for intellectual development is well recognized (e.g., Allport, 1961; Dewey, 1913; Izard, 1977; Tomkin, 1962). We suggest that interest can be better understood in the context of embodied meaning-making in transactional experiences. We are particularly interested in what Berlyne (1954) called epistemic curiosity or a desire for knowledge, and what Prenzel (1992) called epistemic interest. These constructs are closely associated with exploratory behavior, essential for intellectual development and personal growth. They also provide clues as to why interest and knowledge have a reciprocal relationship, and why the depth of knowledge tends to be associated with qualitative changes in the nature of interest (see Alexander, chap. 10; Tobias, 1994).

Extended Consciousness and Selfhood. Edelman (1989) distinguished between primary and extended or higher-order consciousness. The extended consciousness is based, not on ongoing experience, as is primary consciousness, but on the ability to model the past and the future (see also Tulving, 2003). Extended consciousness naturally leads to an important dimension of intellectual life: personal history. To illustrate the importance of the extended consciousness and its temporal dimension, think of scientists trying to formulate some new theories. Based on a thorough investigation of the evolution of Einstein's theory, Holton (1981) argued that what underlies scientific imagination is not merely some disembodied logic, but rather themes or what he called themata (e.g., symmetry, continuum, unity). Themata cannot be derived from observation or pure rational thinking, but must grow over time as deep convictions about the fundamental properties of the universe in the consciousness of individual scientists (e.g., think about Einstein's comments on Heisenberg's uncertainty principle: "I shall never believe that God plays dice with the universe"; Einstein, 1971, p. 91).

Extended consciousness inevitably leads to the phenomenon of the self. To paraphrase Gazzaniga (2000), we are constantly running an autobiographic narrative. This is not trivial for intellectual development in that mental stock-taking is essential for knowledge integration. Damasio (1999), Edelman (1995), among others (e.g., Zajonc, 1980), suggested the self is shored up not only by extended consciousness but also by emotion and feeling, a position reminiscent of James (1997), who described the phenomenal self as a person's emotional center. James (1997) commented a century ago that, "All we know is that there are dead feelings, dead ideas, and cold beliefs, and there are hot, and live ones; and when one grows hot and alive within us, everything has to re-crystallize about it" (p. 219). Such recrystallizing has a direct bearing on a wide range of intellectual activities, from the development of new scientific theories (e.g., Darwin's evolutionary theory; see Gruber, 1981) to conceptual change in classroom (Sinatra & Pintrich, 2003).

Summary

We have described three types of approach to integration: neurobiological, psychological-behavioral, and phenomenological. They attempt to explain the same intellectual phenomena but at different levels of description. As we shall see in the following sections, individual differences, developmental, and contextual approaches all resort to these three levels of description and explanation (for alternative frameworks, see Newell, 1990, and Pylyshyn, 1984). We also argue that an ultimate understanding of intellectual functioning and development depends on integration of all the three levels of analysis.

INTELLIGENCE AND PERSONALITY: FROM PSYCHOMETRICS TO PERSONAL DYNAMICS

Differential perspectives on intellectual functioning has enjoyed a long history, reflecting a deep-rooted assumption in the West about individual differences in intellectual potential (e.g., Galton, 1883). It is worth noting that this mode of thinking is population based; that is, it focuses on different levels of individual functioning relative to population norms (e.g., within-species variations; see Lohman, 2001). Interestingly, the definitions of intelligence in the formative years of intelligence theory were highly functional rather than structural. For example, Binet (Binet & Simon, 1916) emphasized direction, adapation, and criticism (an equivalent of reflection or metacognitive control in today's language), a distinct process view of intelligence that combines conative and cognitive dimensions. Spearman (1927) suspected that intelligence has to do with mental energy, and thus is conative as well as cognitive (see Messick, 1996 for a discussion). McDougall (1923) seemed to foresee some of the problems of interpreting what is intelligence in later years: "Intelligence is essentially the capacity for making new adaptations; it cannot be described in terms of structure" (p. 379). Wechsler (1950) also insisted on the inclusion of conation and other nonintellective factors in the definition of intelligence. It is only when factor analytic technique perpetuated a more structural view of intellectual competence that the construct of intelligence became hardened and lost more juicy and dynamic aspects of its meaning.

With the rise of cognitive psychology, major theoretical and research efforts have been attempted to explain psychometric intelligence in terms of underlying cognitive processes (e.g., the componential subtheory of the triarchic theory of intelligence: Sternberg, 1985; see also Deary, 2001 for a most recent synthesis of the literature). This represents a reductionistic route to the nature of intelligence. In contrast, nonreductionistic approaches consider the role of noncognitive factors such as motivation and personality (Deary, 1999), and experience and context (e.g., the experiential and contextual subtheories of the triarchic theory: Sternberg, 1985). Integration efforts obviously belong to the latter.

Performance Versus Competence

Ackerman and Kanfer (chap. 5) make a critical distinction between maximal performance and typical engagement. Essentially, this proposition echoes the distinction made between competence and performance in the developmental and cognitive psychology literatures (see Chierchia, 1999). The only difference is that here competence means putative individual differences in what levels of performance one can potentially attain, given optimal conditions. Ackerman and Kanfer (chap. 5) argue that ability testing often elicits maximal performance due to its high-stakes nature (a condition of sufficient motivation; see Simon, 1994 for a similar view for experimental conditions). In daily life, however, people have their own characteristic ways of engaging in intellectual activities based on their inclinations, knowledge, and positive or negative experience, among other factors.

Disposition Versus Capacity

The notion of typical performance opens the door for dispositional factors to intervene in otherwise purely cognitive processes (assuming maximal motivation in testing conditions). It is an important step toward integration because the distinction between maximal and typical performance bridges the gap between traditional, purely structural views of intellectual functioning and more contextual, process-oriented views, between two branches of psychometric research: intelligence and personality. New neuroscientific evidence seems to support the typical engagement argument. For example, Davidson (2001) consistently found two distinct responses to the same stimuli: positive, approach-related affect and negative withdrawal-related affect. He labels this individual difference affective style. These approach and avoidance tendencies seem to reflect quite stable temperamental differences with neurobiological underpinnings, and mediate how individuals respond emotionally to environmental events. This is where Ackerman and Kanfer (chap. 5) started their inquiry about typical engagement as more of a dispositional than capacity issue.

Perkins and Ritchhart (chap. 13) ask when is good thinking, thus placing intellectual functioning squarely at the interface of a person and a situation. Their argument is that task-on-demand testing conditions rarely tap into one's typical intellectual functioning in a specific situation. In their triadic conception of thinking, including sensitivity, inclination, and the ability to think through about a problem, only the last corresponds to what is assessed in intelligence tests. However, they emphasize sensitivity as a bottleneck of intellectual functioning, rather than attentional capacity (Simon, 1994), working memory capacity (Just & Carpenter, 1992), or reasoning ability (Kyllonen & Christal, 1990). This view is consistent with findings that in knowledge-rich domains, as well as everyday situations, thinking shortfalls are often caused not by the constraints of working memory but by information uptake, that is, whether one detects relevant, critical information (Saariluoma, 1992; see also Vicente & Wang, 1998). Sensitivity threshold is likely determined by the level of affect triggered by a situation or message (Simon, 1979). Inclination, on the other hand, indicates a person's disposition to act, mentally or physically, a distinct conative construct (Snow, 1992). The ability to think through takes persistence as well as the cognitive ability to reach a satisfactory solution. Such a dispositional view of thinking integrates motivational, affective, and cognitive processes, and indicates the personal organization of behavior vis-à-vis situational demands in general (i.e., personality functioning).

Trait Complexes Versus Dynamic Processes

An important step of integration from psychometric perspectives is the postulation of trait complexes, a constellation of traits across cognitive, affective, and conative trait families (Ackerman & Kanfer, chap. 5; Cronbach, 2002). The purpose of positing such a construct as a unit of analysis is to provide a richer description of human functioning vis-à-vis a task environment. Population-based thinking is still at the core of the construct, but it becomes multivariate rather than univariate. The multivariate approach implies that each dimension is relatively independent of others yet interrelated, and when combined with other traits, has added or multiplicative importance; in other words, the whole is larger than the sum of its parts (Ackerman & Heggestad, 1997). In a similar vein, when Salovey and Mayer (1990) proposed the construct of emotional intelligence, they argued that there is another layer of intellectual competence untapped by traditional definitions of intelligence. Instead of replacing traditional definitions of intelligence, emotional intelligence simply enriches a multivariate matrix of intellectual competence (Mayer, Salovey, & Caruso, 2002). Furthermore, instead of treating emotional intelligence as a structural property of mind, they have attempted to elucidate underlying processes responsible for the observed performance differences in emotional intelligence measures (see Brackett, Lopes, Ivcevic, Mayer, & Salovey, chap. 7).

A different tack can be seen in Matthews and Zeidner's (chap. 6) work on personality functioning. Here, intellectual functioning is cast in a unified framework of personal adaptation to the environment. What is unique about this approach is that the authors go beyond the traditional trait or state accounts of personality and unpackage personality to reveal the motivational, emotional, and cognitive component processes, the trilogy of mind, that support specific behavioral tendencies. Moreover, such a process account of personality (instead of state-level or trait-level descriptions) opens new avenues for understanding how complex personality processes either enhance or weaken certain aspects of intellectual functioning depending on task demands and preferred coping mechanisms (e.g., see Matthews & Zeidner, chap. 6, on extroversion vs. introversion).

Summary

Although population-based thinking still underlies the integration efforts from differential perspectives, we have witnessed a trend toward a more process-based, rather than structural, explanation of individual differences in intellectual functioning. Constructs such as typical intellectual engagement, problem-based and emotion-based coping, and emotional and motivational biases in cognitive processing start to help us understand personality-related constraints on intellectual functioning. Putting intellectual functioning in the context of personality functioning is a step further from putting cognition in motivational and affective contexts discussed in the previous section. It sheds light on some unique system-wide functional properties of the individual mind that are typically not addressed by the research with an exclusive focus on the interplay of motivation, emotion, and cognition itself.

In addition, we have also witnessed a trend toward a developmental approach within the differential tradition. This is probably due to a fundamental realization that intellectual competences are dynamic and changing, rather than static and fixed (McCall, 1981), and that the development of intellectual competences involves a prolonged period of cognitive investment, and thus takes commitment, perseverance, and emotional coping (Ackerman, 1999; Ackerman & Kanfer, chap. 5).

DEVELOPMENT OF INTELLECTUAL COMPETENCES: THE EMERGENT ROLE OF PERSONAL AGENCY

Differential perspectives are based on the assumption of characteristic ways individuals function. In contrast, developmental perspectives on intellectual functioning focus on the ontogeny or developmental course of motivational, affective, and cognitive functions and their dynamic integration as adaptations to environmental demands and opportunities, facilitated or constrained by transactional experiences and activities, and maturation.

Developmental Variability Versus Invariance

Traditionally, intellectual development is considered *normative* and *invariant*, a more-or-less, sooner-or-later matter. Piaget's structuralist view of intellectual development clearly has perpetuated this conception. In all fairness, Piaget (1967, 1981) also considered affect and motivation as indispensable for intellectual functioning and development. Piaget (1967) asserted that "there is a constant parallel between the affective and intellectual life throughout childhood and adolescence. This statement will seem surprising only if one attempts to dichotomize the life of the mind into emotions and thoughts. But nothing could be more false or superficial" (p. 15). According to this parallellist view, affect provides energy and the valuation of an activity (what he called energetics), and cognition provides structure. Thus affect may accelerate cognitive development, but it never changes the cognitive structures, which are considered invariant in their developmental trajectories. However, Piaget also seemed to espouse another competing view of the interplay of affect and cognition in his explication of cognitive disequilibrium. According to this view, affect or emotion is epiphenomenal to cognition (Piaget, 1952; see Cicchetti & Hesse, 1983 for a discussion). This is simply the recurrent issue of the primacy of cognition versus emotion at the developmental level. Either way, developmental variability in intellectual functioning in terms of divergent paths is not within the purview of Piaget's theory.

The Emergent Intellectual Agency

The central issue of intellectual development is how to describe and explain the emergent intellectual agency, broadly defined, of the developing person. Piaget (1950, 1952), arguing from an epistemological point of view, provided a plausible account of the development of scientific thinking during childhood and adolescence. In a neo-Piagetian tradition, Pascual-Leone and Johnson (chap. 8) attempt to provide a rich account of the emergent agency in terms of cognitive and affective schemes (i.e., action patterns), self-motivation, reflective consciousness, and the self. What they delineate is an emergent architecture of human agency booted by both biological maturation and social-contextual experiences. It is worth noting that neurobiological perspectives and evidence are heavily enlisted for this purpose. What emerge from this architecture are various mental operations and functions (i.e., the integration of second order discussed earlier), as well as primary and extended consciousness, intentionality, and the self (i.e., the integration of third order). The construct that holds three levels of analysis together as the center of gravity in their model is M-capacity, the developing mental capacity. What is the most striking is their painstaking efforts to delineate specific forms or structures of various mental functions of the cognitive, motivational, and affective nature. Such a task is often neglected by psychologists (Kagan, 2002) and can be most appropriately addressed from a developmental point of view.

Bruner (1983) pointed out, based on the infant research, that various forms of human agency, in terms of symbolic capability, means–ends sensitivity, self-awareness, and concern with evaluative standards, all appear at the end of the second year of life. Similarly, Labouvie-Vief and Gonzalez (chap. 9) discuss the emergence of extended consciousness and the reflective self during the same period of development. Different from an exclusive focus on representative intelligence as Piaget did, these authors attempt to extend the Piagetian tradition. They explicate how affective experiences and motivation shape the way individuals interact with the environment, and how the process is constrained by both organismic and contextual factors, including aging (see also Zimmerman & Schunk, chap. 12, for a social-cognitive view of the development of the self-regulatory agency).

Maintaining Self Versus Expanding Self

Labouvie-Vief and Gonzalez (chap. 9) elaborated on the legacy of the Piagetian notion that developmental transformation occurs as a result of a dynamic interplay of relatively reactive equilibrium-maintaining (assimilation) and relatively proactive, disequilibrating (accommodation) strategies. What is novel in their argument is that in order for new cognitive structures or competencies to take hold, they need to be validated by feeling and rendered meaningful and integrated at a personal level (or appropriated; see Ferrari & Elik, 2003, on conceptual change). However, in the process of cognitive-affective integration, one can overaccommodate, resulting in cognitive or knowledge structures purely derived from others and not firmly affirmed by affective experiences; one can also overassimilate in an attempt to maintain positive affect, resulting in cognitive rigidity and the failure of differentiation, hampering chances for intellectual growth. Such formulation breaks loose of the normative doctrine of intellectual development, and thus is poised to explain the phenomenon of developmental variability and divergence not adequately addressed by Piaget (Bidell & Fischer, 1992).

As Bidell and Fischer (1992) pointed out, Piaget never resolved the tension between two main tenets of his theory: his constructivist view of knowledge as the product of self-regulated functional activity in specific contexts, and his abstract structuralist stage theory. It is not coincidental that Pascual-

Leone and Johnson (chap. 8) and Labouvie-Vief and Gonzalez (chap. 9) carry over the Piagetian legacy of the former, not the latter. This makes perfect sense if we take notice of the fact that Piaget's stage theory was an attempt to present a psychologically plausible (but not necessarily realistic in the sense of how individuals actually develop) account of genetic or developmental epistemology (Lourenço & Machado, 1996). Such a theory, by nature, has a philosophic overtone, addressing the normative structure of human intelligence (the Kantian question of how knowledge is possible), rather than explaining manifestations of diverse intellectual development in reality (Zigler, 1986). A constructivist approach, on the other hand, looks into actions that connect the whole person to a functional context, thus making intellectual development fully grounded in psychology.

Besides, both chapters postulate higher-order self-regulatory agency, as well as lower-order attentional and working-memory resources, as supporting or constraining motivation (see also Guttentag, 1995). Both chapters raise the issue of style or characteristics ways of dealing with environmental challenges, reminiscent of Matthews and Zeidner's (chap. 6) cognitive-adaptive view of intellectual functioning, wherein affect, coping (by a self-regulatory agent), and cognitive engagement are inextricably related in intellectual functioning.

Development of Biologically Secondary Competencies

While the Piagetian and neo-Piagetian traditions bring insights into how intellectual functioning and development can be understood in the context of personal adaptation and self-organization, the research on expertise, an emergent branch in cognitive psychology, has forced us to consider another set of constraints for the development of intellectual competencies. As Matthews (1999) pointed out, adaptation to real-life pressures and demands often depends on acquired skills rather than fundamental components of information processing.

The learning perspective on intellectual development brought in by the expertise research and other traditions (e.g., information processing approaches; Siegler, 2000) raises several interesting points about intellectual functioning and development (Canfield & Ceci, 1992). First of all, it has established domain-specific knowledge as a legitimate ingredient of intellectual functioning (Estes, 1986). Chi (1978), for example, demonstrated that children with chess expertise recalled more chess pieces than adult novices when the meaningful positions were presented; however, the opposite is the true when chess pieces are arranged in a random fashion. In fact, most domains of intellectual functioning, including everyday cognition, can be characterized as semantic-rich or knowledge-rich rather than knowledge-lean (Simon, 1979; see Alexander, chap. 10, for an illustration of the distinction).

Based on Geary's (1995) distinction between biologically primary and secondary abilities, and Greenough's distinction experience-expectant and experience-dependent learning in terms of differing brain mechanisms (see Greenough, Black, & Wallace, 1987), it is likely that various biologically primary abilities and dispositions are co-opted to learn specific skills valued in a culture. The question becomes what constellation of cognitive and affective traits would support the development of expertise in a specific domain, an issue addressed by Ackerman (1999; Ackerman & Kanfer, chap. 5).

Aptitude Versus Deep Engagement. While traditional psychometric perspectives tend to emphasize high IQ, among other factors, as a necessary aptitude factor for the development of expertise (see Ackerman & Kanfer, chap. 5), some researchers suggests that IQ and expertise are unrelated; rather, expertise reflects dedicated mechanisms specific to domains (Ceci & Liker, 1986; Hirshfeld & Gelman, 1994). Ceci and Ruiz (1993) questioned a typical conception of intelligence (presumably under the influences of Spearman and Piaget) as the general mental power for abstract thinking, which would show through in any domain-specific learning. Ceci and Liker (1986) found that people who gave mediocre performance on adult intelligence tests can perform marvelous intellectual feats when it comes to their domain of expertise (e.g., highly sophisticated reasoning on the racetrack gambling). The implication is that deep engagement in a domain counts much more than some general mental power for the development of expertise, a position consistent with ecological theories of intelligence (e.g., Pea, 1993) and expertise (Vicente & Wang, 1998). More recently, talent accounts of expertise have also been challenged (Howe, Davidson, & Sloboda, 1998).

Similarly, according to Ericsson (Ericsson, Krampe, & Tesch-Romer, 1993), a key mechanism for the development of expertise is deliberate practice, a form of practice that is highly focused and intensive. The logic is as follows: if the achievement of expertise takes thousands of hours of deliberate practice, and the pay-off of these efforts is often remote, then, what may ultimately distinguishes those who became experts from those who did not is not their initial abilities, but their motivational characteristics, such as determination and commitment (see also Charness, Tuffiash, & Jastrzembski, chap. 11). However, the variables of aptitude[5] and deep engagement or deliberate

_____

[5]It is important to distinguish between psychometrically defined aptitudes such as IQ or music aptitude tests, and aptitude as a theoretical construct. Snow's (1992) definition of aptitude as the inclination or readiness to respond to a certain class of situations already implies a selective tendency for deep engagement in certain activities.

practice are often confounded in real life, due to the inherent self-selection process wherein individuals may opt out as the result of repeated failures (Sternberg, 1996).

Knowledge, Interest, and Strategies Underlying the Development of Expertise. Cattell (1971) saw the development of intellectual competences as a response to cultural concerns as well as individual inclinations. He also saw developed skills and interests as reciprocally related (an isomorphism in his words). Alexander (chap. 10) carried out this line of inquiry further by exploring how advances in domain-knowledge, the development of a deeper interest, and deep strategic processing may support one another and create a functional synergy. Ackerman and Heggestad (1997) also found a several cognitive abilities, personality traits, and interests tend to converge in an adaptive way to support specific career paths. Formulated as such, deep engagement cannot be solely a function of the willingness to exert mental efforts (i.e., deliberate practice) but involves a developmental process of personal identification reflected in intrinsic or individual interests (see also Hidi et al., chap. 4).

What Develops and How: Two Forms of Embodiment

The learning perspective also brings to focus the question of what exactly is learned, and how it supports further learning in a domain. Kagan (2002) suggested two basic forms of knowledge: schematic and semantic. They are embodied in different ways.

It was Tolman (1932) who first postulated learning as the development of expectations and a cognitive map of the causal texture of the environment in question. Charting a new territory or learning the landscape becomes a powerful root metaphor for knowing (Greeno, 1991). De Groot (1978), in his now classic book on chess, introduced Selz's concept of schematic anticipation as a key to understanding the nature and development of expertise (see also Neisser, 1967 for a similar proposition). The acquired anticipatory structure is conative as well as cognitive in that it suggests where the action should be. Development of such anticipatory structures may be associated with the development of what Damasio (1994) called somatic markers, experience-based secondary emotions that trigger emotional states and gut feeling that serves as a top-down processing heuristic for problem solving and decision making in familiar situations. As Damasio (2001) pointed out, "appropriate learning can pair emotion with all manners of facts (for instance, facts that describe the premises of a situation, the option taken relative to solving the problems inherent in a situation, and, perhaps, most importantly, the outcomes of choosing a certain option, both immediately and in the future)" (p. 105). To illustrate Damasio's point, think of Kasparov contemplating a move in response to the move made by Deep Junior. See also Barnes and Thagard (1996) for an extension of somatic-marker hypothesis based on Thagard's (2000) coherence theory.

In order for schematic anticipation to function adaptively, not only some somatic-markers have to be in place to alert the conscious agent of the probability of success of an action based on the past experience, a mechanism sensitive to even a subtle violation of expectations in the perceptual input also needs to be in place (a surprise effect; see Kagan, 2002) so that discrepancy, anomaly, and novelty can be detected and effectively dealt with, and the whole system reconfigured and reorganized accordingly.

In contrast to schematic knowledge, semantic knowledge involves meaning-making. According to Kagan (2002), when conflicting messages are encountered, individuals will experience uncertainty and the ensuing desire to resolve cognitive conflicts. Similar views on cognitive motivation can be found in Piaget's (1950) notion of disequilibrium, and Festinger's (1957) cognitive dissonance theory. As discussed earlier, meanings are embodied in one's experienced affect, beliefs, and values (Glenberg, 1997). Whether they cohere, to use Thagard's (2000) theory, determines whether the emotional center of the self holds. Thus, seeking the certainty of meaning in a largely uncertain world (whether in everyday encounters or philosophic discourse) constitutes a major developmental task for the self (Labouvie-Vief & Gonzalez, chap. 9).

Summary

Significant advances have been made in understanding intellectual development both in the Piagetian and cognitive psychology traditions. The former focuses on the dynamic integration of affect, motivation, and cognition through the transactional experiences with the world, and the latter focuses on mastering skills valued in a culture, and how the process involves affect and motivation. The consensus seems to be that intellectual development is not preordained, thus open to experiences and opportunities, and subject to external and internal constraints. Both individual biological selectivity (values and aptitudes) and cultural modulation may play a role in shaping one's developmental trajectory given sufficient opportunities to explore various developmental possibilities. Knowledge is embodied through acquired emotions and feelings as well as beliefs, values, and personal meaning systems.

INTELLECTUAL FUNCTIONING
AND DEVELOPMENT IN SOCIAL
AND CULTURAL CONTEXTS

So far all discussion of integrated understanding focuses on the individual person. It may leave an impression that integration of cognition, emotion, and motivation is very much an intra-personal process, and has little to do with social and cultural contexts. However, from Vygotsky's (1978) and other socialcultural theories, not only emotions, and motivation, and intentions but higher cognitive functions such as reasoning and conceptual learning are socially constructed and enculturated. Integration of motivation, emotion, and cognition is necessary precisely because of the at least partially *situated* nature of cognition. The person is engaged in an often socially structured and culturally sanctioned activity that has personal significance and consequence.

Piaget (1950), who is often criticized for neglecting social factors in intellectual development (see Lourenço & Machado, 1996), questioned the likelihood of maintaining a coherent system of thoughts and beliefs by oneself alone. He had this to say:

> In fact, it is precisely by a constant interchange of thought with others that we are able to decentralise ourselves in this way, to co-ordinate internally relations deriving from different viewpoints. In particular, it is very difficult to see how concepts could conserve their permanent meanings and their definitions were it not for co-operation. (Piaget, 1950, p. 180)

The last statement sounds almost Vygotskian! What is implied in the message is that social interaction is not only a necessary condition for the emergence of more complex forms of intelligence, it also provides a necessary shared symbolic platform on which the individual mind can operate intellectually.

Social Context as Integral Part of Intellectual Functioning

Building on the legacy of Piaget, Hatano (1988) saw dialogical interaction as a necessary condition in engendering cognitive incongruity in the form of surprise, perplexity, and discoordination (i.e., variations of disequilibrium, to use Piaget's term), and motivating comprehension activity which, in turn, leads to conceptual development. In this formulation, both motivational and cognitive processes are socially engendered (see also Hatano & Inagaki, 2003). What is unique about Hatano's approach is that he sees the means–end structure of a socially organized activity as inherently determining the motivational and cognitive conditions for learning. For example, Brazilian children peddling in streets requires semantic transparency; that is, they need to explain to their customers the computational procedures used are mathematically correctly. This requirement engenders the need for conceptual understanding, which leads to adaptive expertise. In contrast, Japanese children learning abacus in school are simply engaged in routine exercises; no inquiry is necessary about the justification of specific procedures. The end result is routine expertise. With this highly contextual view of intellectual functioning, Hatano seemed to part company with Piaget and makes himself more aligned with the school of situated cognition and learning (e.g., Greeno, 1989; Lave, 1988). By the same token, children learning to play *pokemon* with peers operate under very different motivational, emotional, and cognitive conditions in comparison with their learning of rules of phonemes or grammar in school.

Effects of Beliefs, Values, and Affect on Intellectual Functioning and Development

Mandler (1989b) cogently pointed out that we live in a world of artifacts, not only in terms of tools we invented, but in terms of folk beliefs and values shared in a community of culture or subculture. These folk beliefs and values can be just as powerful a regulator of emotion as biological needs. He discussed why math anxiety is a cultural phenomenon, and how playing math idiot can be a strategy of mental disengagement. Similarly, cross-cultural differences in implicit theories of intelligence (Sternberg & Kaufman, 1998) and of learning (Li & Fischer , chap. 14) reflect what is perceived as essential for effective functioning and what is important in the subjective culture of a community (Triandis, 1989). Steinberg (1996) found fault with the popular myth of intelligence as a fixed entity, possibly perpetuated by the IQ movement, which is detrimental to motivation and learning for many school-age children in the United States. From a functional point of view, the findings that Western folk conceptions of learning place more emphasis on cognitive processes than do Eastern ones (Li & Fischer, chap. 14) may reflect an instrumental and technical orientation (i.e., what it takes to get the job done). In contrast, Chinese folk conceptions of learning, which put more emphasis on character building and personal perfection, might well be a cultural strategy to ward off negative emotions and debilitated motivation in the face of setbacks, failures, and difficulties. Also, in collectivist cultures such as China and Japan, emphasis is given to interdependence, reliability, and proper behavior, whereas in individualistic cultures such as the United States, characteristics such as independence and creativity are rewarded (Triandis, 1989). These cultural differences have profound ramifications for intellectual development, including the development of self (Dai, 2002b; Markus & Kitayama, 1991, 1994).

Lest culture be reified as an entity independent of people who share canonical cultural experiences, folk beliefs and cultural values are like currencies: they are as valid as people are still carrying them around. Individuals and culture are mutually constitutive of each other (Rogoff, 2003). However, more than just sharing, one can conceive of generative characteristics of intersubjective processes whereby beliefs and values are taking shape, migrating, propagating, amplifying, and transforming in an intersubjective space of a community of people (Brown & Campione, 1994), very much in the same way McClelland (1961) conceptualized the socialization of achievement motivation in youth development.

On the positive side, such generative characteristics of social communication indicates an intellectually stimulating environment. There can also be a tension, however, between individuals and cultural establishments along the process. For example, the essential tension that presumably leads to scientific revolution (T. Kuhn, 1977), and even the very notion of paradigm, can only exist in the intersubjective world of a scientific community. Thus, an act of creativity does not just occur in a solitary mind, but is inherent in generative social interaction and intersubjectivity (Csikszentmihalyi, 1992; Runco, 1994; Sternberg, 2003). On the negative side, social structures and dynamics can also hamper instead of facilitate intellectual functioning and development, as in the case of groupthink in a conformity-inducing environment (Janis, 1972) and or mind control in extremely inhibitory social conditions such as a cult (Zimbardo, 2002). Under such conditions, intellectual functioning degenerates, individually and collectively.

The Nature and Nurture of Habits of Mind

Dewey (1933) remarked that "the real problem of intellectual education is the transformation of more or less casual curiosity and sporadic suggestions into attitudes of alert, cautious, and thorough inquiry" (p. 181). Dewey clearly did not underestimate the difficulty of the task. It is not unusual that people get entrenched in my-side biases (Perkins & Ritchhart, chap. 13) or rely on heuristics rather than more principled ways of thinking (Kahneman, 2003; Tversky & Kahneman, 1974). Indeed, less than optimal intellectual functioning can even be attributed to natural habits of mind, a biological constraint. In everyday life, humans are cognitive misers, spending just enough energy to get the job done (see Kanfer, 1987, for a discussion of an effort–utility function for motivation). People can often get by with sloppy thinking, but sometimes a slight slip in thinking can cause disasters of the global magnitude (e.g., the Chernobyl Nuclear Accident; see Byrne, 1997 for details). According to Dewey (1933), education as a process of enculturation is to develop mindfulness and a caring for thinking or thoughtfulness. Bereiter (1995) found teaching for understanding often insufficient for the productive use of knowledge on the part of students. He proposed a dispositional view of knowledge transfer wherein teaching that nurtures the habit of thinking scientifically or the value of acting according to moral principles.

Perkins and Ritchhart's (chap. 13) exposition of dispositions rather than capacity as critical for intellectual functioning is in line with Dewey's concern. In the same vein, Zimmerman and Schunk (chap. 12) discuss model self-regulated, reflective learners, and Li and Fischer (chap. 14) discuss culturally defined ideal learners. What is common among these chapters is that intellectual functioning is treated at two levels: one is empirical, concerning what is (i.e., its nature and manifestations); the other is normative, concerning what ought to be (Simon, 1969). The former is descriptive and objective, and the latter is prescriptive and value-laden, a matter of cultural desirability. Dewey (1916) apparently thought that the education of minds capable of critical thinking is crucial for a viable democracy. Thus, we can meaningfully discuss how to inculcate intellectual values (D. Kuhn, 2002) and build intellectual character (Bereiter, 1995; Perkins & Ritchhart, chap. 13; Ritchhart, 2002) along the way of teaching subject matters.

We can conceptualize intellect as a two-fold phenomenon, with a knowledge component (e.g., deep understanding of principles of a domain, be it academic or practical, tacit or explicit) and a personal component (e.g., values, dispositions, personal epistemologies, identity). Indeed, in an embodied mind, these two dimensions are fully integrated and thus cannot be separated (Polanyi, 1958). If education only focuses on the former, it is an incomplete education, to say the least. Precisely because it is difficult to maintain such habits of mind, the notion of a community of learners committed to a common goal of self-improvement in pursuing knowledge, and who push one another to work at the edge of each's competence, gains currency (Bereiter & Scardamalia, 1993; Brown, 1997).

Summary

Social and cultural contexts are not some additional factors to be reckoned with on top of individual characteristics. Rather, they are an integral part of individuals' intellectual functioning and development. There are theoretical differences as to whether personal factors and social-contextual factors can be understood as separate constituent components of a complex person-environment system. Whatever the case, cultural values and beliefs shared by people of a community have a direct bearing on individuals' intellectual functioning and development. Education as a force of enculturation can have a significant impact on the development of a person's values, beliefs, and dispositions as well as knowledge and skills.

CONCLUSION

In this introduction chapter, we attempt to make a case that intellectual functioning and development never occur as solely cognitive events but involve motivation and emotion, or the whole person vis-à-vis adaptive pressures and challenges. Going beyond cognitivism does not imply that motivational and emotional issues are more important than or as important as cognitive processes and mechanisms. Rather, our point is that without taking into consideration the motivational and emotional aspects of intellectual functioning and development, we cannot even properly understand cognitive processes involved. Reducing intellectual functioning and development to merely cognitive matters is simply no longer tenable both on theoretical grounds and in light of empirical evidence. Going beyond cognitivism follows the same principle of moving up closer to the peaks of rationality, according to Newell's (1988) vision of the progressive and evolving nature of human intellectual functioning.

Snow (1992) envisioned integration efforts as going through a process from something like a patchwork of several different languages to something of seamless fabric. We are far from the state of seamless fabric, if there is such a thing. However, we have started to weave together different pieces, indeed sometimes seemingly incompatible or discrete ones. We attempt to provide a relatively unified framework so that a certain degree of commensurability can be achieved between and among different perspectives and approaches. What unifies a discipline is not its methodology, but its phenomena (Sternberg & Grigorenko, 2001). Division of labor is still necessary to tackle different aspects of a phenomenon at different levels of description; yet it should be recognized as such. We will probably never reach a complete reunion, the ultimate truth that we can all agree upon. Just as Newell (1988) said, the peaks of rationality are always one or two ridges away in the temporal horizon of our intellectual journey. At a minimum, biologically inclined and socially oriented psychologists, differential and developmental psychologists, psychologists specialized in motivation and emotion, and those in cognition, can sit and talk to each other without feeling awkward as if they live in completely different planets and speak drastically different languages when it comes to intellectual functioning and development. More optimistically, they will complement each other in attaining an ever enriched and deepened understanding of the issue at hand. "The goal is not to choose among alternative paradigms, but rather for them to work together ultimately to help us produce a unified understanding of intellectual phenomena" (Sternberg, 2001, p. 410). Our main charge is to make a comprehensive yet coherent account, based on the totality of evidence, of the nature and development of human intelligence, expertise, and creativity, as exemplified by Kasparov or the programmers of Deep Junior, while leaving the job of how Deep Junior or Deep Senior functions (or ought to function) to AI researchers.[6]

ACKNOWLEDGMENTS

We thank Gerald Matthews, David Perkins, Michael Posner, and Dan Rea for their thoughtful comments on earlier drafts of this article.

This work was made possible by a grant from the National Science Foundation to the first author (#0296062), and grants from the National Science Foundation (REC-9979843) and Department of Education (R206R000001) to the second author.

REFERENCES

Abelson, R. P. (1963). Computer simulation of "hot" cognition. In S. S. Tomkins & S. Messick (Eds.), *Computer simulation of personality: Frontier of psychological theory* (pp. 277–298). New York: Wiley.

Ackerman, P. L. (1999). Traits and knowledge as determinants of learning and individual differences: Putting it all together. In P. L. Ackerman, P. C. Kyllonen, & R. D. Roberts (Eds.), *Learning and individual differences: Process, traits, and content determinants* (pp. 437–460). Washington, DC: American Psychological Association.

Ackerman, P. L., & Heggestad, E. D. (1997). Intelligence, personality, and interest: Evidence for overlapping traits. *Psychological Bulletin, 121*, 219–245.

Allman, J. M., Hakeem, A., Erwin, J. M., Nimchinsky, E., & Hof, P. (2001). The anterior cingulate cortex: The evolution of an interface between emotion and cognition. In A. R. Damasio, A. Harrington, J. Kagan, B. S. McEwen, H. Moss, & R. Shaikh (Eds.), *Unity of knowledge: The convergence of natural and human science* (pp. 107–117). New York: The New York Academy of Sciences.

Allport, G. (1961). *Pattern and growth in personality*. New York: Holt, Rinehart & Winston.

Apter, M. J. E. (2001). *Motivational styles in everyday life: A guide to reversal theory*. Washington, DC: American Psychological Association.

---

[6]This is not to say computational modeling cannot be done to simulate human mental processes, as long as such simulations provide psychologically viable accounts of mental processes involved in intellectual functioning, including affective ones (e.g., Picard, 1997). Our point is that advances in artificial intelligence and computational modeling provide no direct evidence as to how human intelligence works because the isomorphism between the two should not be assumed. Building a successful chess program like Deep Blue or Deep Junior does not provide a clear understanding of how Kasparov made his way to chess stardom. Likewise, how Deep Blue makes a move does not intrinsically provide any insights into the mind of Kasparov, although their levels of performance are comparable. In other words, making claims about human intelligence and intellectual functioning purely based on empirical evidence from computational simulation without sound theoretical justification and corroborating human data is problematic. This is where the Turing test fails (see Chomsky, 1997 for a similar position; see also Searle, 2001, for a description of the Chinese Room Argument and the Turing test).

Ashby, F. G., Isen, A. M., & Turken, A. U. (1999). A neuropsychological theory of positive affect and its influence on cognition. *Psychological Review, 106*, 529–550.

Baars, B. J. (1986). *The cognitive revolution in psychology.* New York: Guilford.

Barnes, A., & Thagard, P. (1996). Emotional decisions. In Cognitive Science Society (Ed.), *Proceedings of the eighteenth Annual Conference of the Cognitive Science Society* (pp. 426–429). Mahwah, NJ: Lawrence Erlbaum Associates.

Bartlett, F. C. (1932). *Remembering.* Cambridge, England: Cambridge University Press.

Bereiter, C. (1995). A dispositional view of transfer. In A. McKeough, J. Lupart, & A. Marini (Eds.), *Teaching for transfer: Fostering generalization in learning* (pp. 21–34). Mahwah, NJ: Lawrence Erlbaum Associates.

Bereiter, C., & Scardamalia, M. (1993). *Surpassing ourselves.* Chicago: Open Court, HC.

Berlyne, D. E. (1954). A theory of human curiosity. *British Journal of Psychology, 45*, 180–191.

Bidell, T. R., & Fischer, K. W. (1992). Beyond the stage debate: Action, structure, and variability in Piagetian theory and research. In R. J. Sternberg & C. A. Berg (Eds.), *Intellectual development* (pp. 100–140). Cambridge, England: Cambridge University Press.

Binet, A., & Simon, T. (1916). *The development of intelligence in children* (E. S. Kite, Trans.). Baltimore: Williams & Wilkins.

Bransford, J. D., Brown, A. L., & Cocking, R. R. (2000). *How people learn: Brain, mind, experience, and school.* Washington, DC: National Academy Press.

Broadbent, D. E. (1958). *Perception and communication.* New York: Pergamon.

Broadbent, D. E. (1971). *Decision and stress.* New York: Academic Press.

Brown, A. (1997). Transforming schools into communities of thinking and learning about serious matters. *American Psychologist, 52*, 399–413.

Brown, A. L., & Campione, J. (1994). Guided discovery in a community of learners. In K. McGilly (Ed.), *Classroom lessons: Integrating cognitive theory and classroom practice* (pp. 229–270). Cambridge, MA: The MIT Press.

Bruner, J. (1983). *In search of mind: Essays in autobiography.* New York: Harper & Row.

Bruner, J. (1986). *Actual minds, possible worlds.* Cambridge, MA: Harvard University Press.

Bruner, J. (1990). *Acts of meaning.* Cambridge, MA: Harvard University Press.

Bruner, J. (1992). Another look at new look. *American Psychologist, 47*, 780–783.

Bruner, J. (1994). The view from the heart's eye: A commentary. In P. M. Miedenthal & S. Kitayama (Eds.), *The heart's eye: Emotional influences in perception and attention* (pp. 269–286). San Diego, CA: Academic Press.

Bruner, J. (1997). Will cognitive revolution ever stop? In D. M. Johnson & C. E. Erneling (Eds.), *The future of the cognitive revolution* (pp. 279–292). New York: Oxford University Press.

Bruner, J. S., Matter, J., & Papanek, M. L. (1955). Breadth of learning as a function of drive level and mechanization. *Psychological Review, 62*, 1–10.

Byrne, R. M. J. (1997). The coming of age of the psychology of thinking and reasoning. In R. Fuller, P. N. Walsh, & P. McGinley (Eds.), *A century of psychology: Progress, paradigms and prospects for the new millennium* (pp. 207–223). London: Routledge & Kegan Paul.

Canfield, R. L., & Ceci, S. J. (1992). Integrating learning into a theory of intellectual development. In R. J. Sternberg & C. A. Berg (Eds.), *Intellectual development* (pp. 278–300). Cambridge, England: Cambridge University Press.

Carey, S. (1999). Sources of conceptual change. In E. K. Scholnick, K. Nelson, S. Gelman, A., & P. H. Miller (Eds.), *Conceptual development: Piaget's legacy* (pp. 293–326). Mahwah, NJ: Lawrence Erlbaum Associates.

Cattell, R. B. (1971). *Abilities: Their structure, growth, and action.* Boston: Houghton Mifflin.

Ceci, S. J., & Liker, J. (1986). A day at the races: A study of IQ, expertise, and cognitive complexity. *Journal of Experimental Psychology: General, 115*, 255–266.

Ceci, S. J., & Ruiz, A. (1993). Transfer, abstractness, and intelligence. In D. K. Detterman & R. J. Sternberg (Eds.), *Transfer on trial: Intelligence, cognition, and instruction* (pp. 168–191). Norwood, NJ: Ablex.

Chi, M. T. H. (1978). Knowledge structures and memory development. In R. S. Siegler (Ed.), *Children's thinking: What develops?* (pp. 73–96). Hillsdale, NJ: Lawrence Erlbaum Associates.

Chierchia, G. (1999). Linguistics and language. In R. A. Wilson & F. C. Keil (Eds.), *The MIT encyclopedia of the cognitive sciences* (pp. xci–cix). Cambridge, MA: The MIT Press.

Chomsky, N. (1997). Language and cognition. In D. M. Johnson & C. E. Erneling (Eds.), *The future of the cognitive revolution* (pp. 15–31). New York: Oxford University Press.

Cicchetti, D., & Hesse, P. (1983). Affect and intellect: Piaget's contributions to the study of infant emotional development. In R. Plutchik & H. Kellerman (Eds.), *Emotion: Theory, research, and experience* (Vol. 2, pp. 115–169). New York: Academic Press.

Cronbach, L. J. (Ed.). (2002). *Remaking the concept of aptitude: Extending the legacy of Richard E. Snow.* Mahwah, NJ: Lawrence Erlbaum Associates.

Csikszentmihalyi, M. C. (1992). Motivation and creativity. In R. S. Albert (Ed.), *Genius and eminence* (pp. 19–33). Oxford, England: Pergamon.

Csikszentmihalyi, M. (1996). *Creativity: Flow and the psychology of discovery and invention.* New York: HarperCollins.

Dai, D. Y. (2002a, April). *Effects of need for cognition and reader beliefs on comprehension of Narrative Text.* Paper presented at the annual meeting of the American Educational Research Association, New Orleans.

Dai, D. Y. (2002b). The self in cultural context: Meaning and valence. In D. M. McInerney & S. Van Etten (Eds.), *Research on socialcultural influences on motivation and learning* (Vol. 2, pp. 3–21). Greenwich, CT: Information Age Publishing.

Damasio, A. R. (1994). *Descartes' error: Emotion, reason, and the human brain.* New York: Avon Books.

Damasio, A. R. (1999). *The feeling of what happens: Body and emotion in the making of consciousness.* New York: Harcourt Brace.

Damasio, A. R. (2000). A neurobiology for consciousness. In T. Metzinger (Ed.), *Neural correlates of consciousness* (pp. 111–120). Cambridge, MA: The MIT Press.

Damasio, A. R. (2001). Emotion and the human brain. In A. R. Damasio, A. Harrington, J. Kagan, B. S. McEwen, H. Moss, & R. Shaikh (Eds.), *Unity of knowledge: The convergence of natural and human science (Annals of the New York Academy of Sciences, Vol. 935)* (pp. 101–106). New York: The New York Academy of Sciences.

D'Andrade, R. G. (1981). The cultural part of cognition. *Cognitive Science, 5,* 179–195.

D'Andrade, R. G. (1995). *The development of cognitive anthropology.* Cambridge, England: Cambridge University Press.

Davidson, R. J. (2001). Toward a biology of personality and emotion. In A. R. Damasio, A. Harrington, J. Kagan, B. S. McEwen, H. Moss, & R. Shaikh (Eds.), *Unity of knowledge: The convergence of natural and human science* (pp. 191–207). New York: The New York Academy of Sciences.

Deary, I. J. (1999). Intelligence and visual and auditory information processing. In P. L. Ackerman, P. C. Kyllonen, & R. D. Roberts (Eds.), *Learning and individual differences: Process, traits, and content determinants* (pp. 111–133). Washington, DC: American Psychological Association.

Deary, I. J. (2001). Human intelligence differences: Towards a combined experimental-differential approach. *Trends in Cognitive Sciences, 5,* 164–170.

de Groot, A. D. (1978). *Thought and choice in chess* (2nd ed.). The Hague: Mouton.

Dennett, D. C. (1991). *Consciousness explained.* Cambridge, MA: Bradford/MIT Press.

Dennett, D. C. (1996). *Kinds of minds: Toward an understanding of consciousness.* New York: Basic Books.

Derryberry, D., & Tucker, D. M. (1994). Motivating the focus of attention. In P. M. Miedenthal & S. Kitayama (Eds.), *The heart's eye: Emotional influences in perception and attention* (pp. 167–196). San Diego, CA: Academic Press.

Dewey, J. (1913). *Interest and effort in education.* Boston: Riverside Press.

Dewey, J. (1916). *Democracy and education.* New York: The Free Press.

Dewey, J. (1933). The process and product of reflective activity: Psychological process and logical forms. In J. Boydston (Ed.), *The later works of John Dewey* (Vol. 8, pp. 171–186). Carbondale, IL: Southern Illinois University Press.

Drevets, W. C., & Raichle, M. E. (1998). Reciprocal suppression of regional cerebral blood flow during emotional versus higher cognitive processes: Implications for interactions between emotion and cognition. *Cognition and Emotion, 12,* 353–385.

Dweck, C. S. (1999). *Self theories: Their role in motivation, personality, and development.* Philadelphia: Psychology Press.

Edelman, G. M. (1989). *The remembered present: A biological theory of consciousness.* New York: Basic Books.

Edelman, G. M. (1995). Memory and the individual soul: Against silly reductionism. In J. Cornwell (Ed.), *Nature's imagination: The frontiers of scientific vision* (pp. 200–206). Oxford, England: Oxford University Press.

Eich, E., Kihlstrom, J. F., Bower, G. H., Forgas, J. P., & Niedenthal, P. M. (2000). *Cognition and emotion.* New York: Oxford University Press.

Einstein, A. (1971). *Barn–Einstein correspondence.* New York: Walk.

Ericsson, K. A., Krampe, R. T., & Tesch-Romer, C. (1993). The role of deliberate practice in the acquisition of expert performance. *Psychological Review, 100,* 363–406.

Estes, W. K. (1986). Where is intelligence? In R. J. Sternberg & D. K. Detterman (Eds.), *What is intelligence? Contemporary viewpoints on its nature and definition* (pp. 63–67). Norwood, NJ: Ablex.

Ferrari, M., & Elik, N. (2003). Influences on intentional conceptual change. In G. M. Sinatra & P. R. Pintrich (Eds.), *Intentional conceptual change* (pp. 21–54). Mahwah, NJ: Lawrence Erlbaum Associates.

Festinger, L. (1957). *A theory of cognitive dissonance theory.* Stanford, CA: Stanford University Press.

Ford, M. E. (1992). *Motivating humans: Goals, emotions, and personal agency beliefs.* Newbury, CT: Sage.

Forgas, J. P. (1995). Mood and judgment: The affect infusion model (AIM). *Psychological Bulletin, 117,* 39–66.

Fredrickson, B. L. (1998). What good are positive emotions? *Review of General Psychology, 2,* 300–319.

Galton, F. (1883). *Inquiries into human faculty and its development.* London: Dent.

Gardner, H. (1985). *The mind's new science: A history of the cognitive revolution.* New York: Basic Books.

Gazzaniga, M. S. (2000). Cerebral specialization and interhemispheric communication: Does the corpus callosum enable the human condition? *Brain, 123,* 1293–1326.

Geary, D. (1995). Reflections of evolution and culture in children's cognition. *American Psychologist, 50,* 24–37.

Glenberg, A. M. (1997). Mental models, space, and embodied cognition. In T. B. Ward, S. M. Smith, & J. Vaid (Eds.), *Creative thought: An investigation of conceptual structures and processes* (pp. 495–522). Washington, DC: American Psychological Association.

Goldin, G. A. (2000). Affective pathways and representation in mathematical problem solving. *Mathematical Thinking and Learning: An International Journal, 2,* 209–219.

Greeno, J. G. (1989). A perspective on thinking. *American Psychologist, 44,* 134–141.

Greeno, J. G. (1991). Number sense as situated knowing in a conceptual domain. *Journal for Research in Mathematics Education, 22,* 170–218.

Greenough, W. T., Black, J. E., & Wallace, C. S. (1987). Experience and brain development. *Child Development, 58,* 539–559.

Gruber, H. E. (1981). *Darwin on man: A psychological study of scientific creativity* (Rev. ed.). Chicago: University of Chicago Press.

Gruber, H. E. (1995). Insight and affect in the history of science. In R. J. Sternberg & J. E. Davidson (Eds.), *The nature of insight* (pp. 397–431). Cambridge, MA: The MIT Press.

Guttentag, R. E. (1995). Mental effort and motivation: influences on children's memory strategy use. In F. E. Weinert & W. Schneider (Eds.), *Memory performance and competences: Issues in growth and development* (pp. 207–224). Mahwah, NJ: Lawrence Erlbaum Associates.

Hatano, G. (1988). Social and motivational bases for mathematical understanding. In G. B. Saxe & M. Gearhart (Eds.), *Children's mathematics* (pp. 55–70). San Francisco: Jossey-Bass.

Hatano, G., & Inagaki, K. (2003). When is conceptual change intended? A cognitive-sociocultural view. In Sinatra (Ed.), *Intentional conceptual change* (pp. 407–427). Mahwah, NJ: Lawrence Erlbaum Associates.

Haugeland, J. (1981). The nature and plausibility of cognitivism. *Brain and Behavioral Sciences, 1*, 215–226.

Hilgard, E. R. (1980). The trilogy of mind: Cognition, affection, and conation. *Journal of the History of the Behavioral Sciences, 16*, 107–117.

Hirschfeld, L. A., & Gelman, S. A. (1994). Toward a topography of mind: An introduction to domain specificity. In L. A. Hirschfeld & S. A. Gelman (Eds.), *Mapping the mind: Domain specificity in cognition and culture* (pp. 3–35). New York: Cambridge University Press.

Hoffman, M. L. (1986). Affect, cognition, and motivation. In R. M. Sorrentino & E. T. Higgins (Eds.), *Handbook of motivation and cognition: Foundations of social behavior* (pp. 244–280). New York: Guilford.

Holton, G. (1981). Thematic presuppositions and the direction of scientific advance. In A. F. Heath (Ed.), *Scientific explanation* (pp. 1–27). Oxford, England: Clarendon Press.

Howe, M. J. A., Davidson, J. W., & Sloboda, J. A. (1998). Innate talents: Reality or myth? *Behavioral and Brain Sciences, 21*, 399–442.

Izard, C. E. (1977). *Human emotions*. New York: Plenum.

James, W. (1950). *The principles of psychology* (Vol. 1). New York: Dover Publications.

James, W. (1997). *Selected writing (The varieties of religious experience)*. New York: Book-of-the-Month Club.

Janis, I. L. (1972). *Victims of groupthink*. Boston: Houghton Mifflin.

Johnson, D. M., & Erneling, C. E. (Eds.). (1997). *The future of the cognitive revolution*. New York: Oxford University Press.

Johnson, R. (1986). A triarchic model of P3000 amplitude. *Psychophysiology, 23*, 367–384.

Just, M. A., & Carpenter, P. A. (1992). A capacity theory of comprehension: Individual differences in working memory. *Psychological Review, 99*, 122–149.

Kagan, J. (2002). *Surprise, uncertainty, and mental structures*. Cambridge, MA: Harvard University Press.

Kahneman, D. (2003). A perspective on judgment and choice: Mapping bounded rationality. *American Psychologist, 58*, 697–720.

Kanfer, R. (1987). Task-specific motivation: An integrative approach to issue of measurement, mechanisms, processes, and determinants. *Journal of Social and Clinical Psychology, 5*, 237–264.

Kasparov, G. (2003, February 16). Man vs. machine: A new era in computer chess. *The Wall Street Journal*, Editorial Page. Available: http://www.opinionjournal.com/extra/?id=110003081

Kintsch, W. (1998). *Comprehension: A paradigm for cognition*. Cambridge, England: Cambridge University Press.

Kuhn, D. (2002). A multi-component system that constructs knowledge: Insights from microgenetic study. In N. Granott & J. Parziale (Eds.), *Microdevelopment: Transition processes in development and learning* (pp. 109–130). Cambridge, England: Cambridge University Press.

Kuhn, T. S. (1977). *The essential tension: Selected studies in scientific tradition and change*. Chicago: University of Chicago Press.

Kyllonen, P. C., & Christal, R. (1990). Reasoning ability is (little more than) working-memory capacity? *Intelligence, 14,* 389–433.

Labouvie-Vief, G. (1990). Wisdom as integrated thoughts: Historical and developmental perspectives. In R. J. Sternberg (Ed.), *Wisdom: Its nature, origins, and development* (pp. 52–83). Cambridge, London: Cambridge University Press.

Lave, J. (1988). *Cognition in practice: Mind, mathematics and culture in everyday life.* Cambridge, England: Cambridge University Press.

Lazarus, R. S. (1984). On the primacy of cognition. *American Psychologist, 39,* 124–129.

Leont'ev, A. N. (1978). *Activity, consciousness, and personality.* Englewood Cliffs, NJ: Prentice-Hall.

Lohman, D. F. (2001). Issues in the definition and measurement of abilities. In J. M. Collis & S. Messick (Eds.), *Intelligence and personality: Bridging the gap between theory and measurement* (pp. 79–98). Mahwah, NJ: Lawrence Erlbaum Associates.

Lourenço, O., & Machado, A. (1996). In defense of Piaget's theory: A reply to 10 common criticisms. *Psychological Review, 103,* 143–164.

Mandler, G. (1989a). Affect and learning: Causes and consequences of emotional interactions. In D. B. McLeod & V. M. Adams (Eds.), *Affect and mathematical problem solving* (pp. 3–19). New York: Springer-Verlag.

Mandler, G. (1989b). Affect and learning: Reflections and prospects. In D. B. McLeod & V. M. Adams (Eds.), *Affect and mathematical problem solving* (pp. 237–244). New York: Springer-Verlag.

Markus, H. R., & Kitayama, S. (1991). Culture and the self: Implications for cognition, emotion, and motivation. *Psychological Review, 98,* 224–253.

Markus, H. R., & Kitayama, S. (1994). The cultural construction of self and emotion: Implications for social behavior. In S. Kitayama & H. R. Markus (Eds.), *Emotions and culture: Empirical studies of mutual influences* (pp. 89–130). Washington, DC: American Psychological Association.

Matthews, G. (1999). Personality and skill: A cognitive-adaptive framework. In P. L. Ackerman, P. C. Kyllonen, & R. D. Roberts (Eds.), *Learning and individual differences: Process, traits, and content determinants* (pp. 251–270). Washington, DC: American Psychological Association.

Mayer, J. D., Salovey, P., & Caruso, D. (2002). *Mayer-Salovey-Caruso Emotional Intelligence Test (MSCEIT), Version 2.0.* Toronto, Canada: Multi-Health Systems.

McCall, R. B. (1981). Nature-nurture and the two realms of development: A proposed integration with respect to mental development. *Child Development, 52,* 1–12.

McClelland, D. C. (1961). *The achieving society.* New York: Van Nostrand.

McDougall, W. (1923). *Outline of psychology.* New York: Scribner's.

McLeod, D. B. (1989). The role of affect in mathematical problem solving: A new perspective. In D. B. McLeod & V. M. Adams (Eds.), *Affect and mathematical problem solving* (pp. 20–36). New York: Springer-Verlag.

Meltzinger, T. E. (2000). *Neural correlates of consciousness: Empirical and conceptual questions.* Cambridge, MA: The MIT Press.

Merleau-Ponty, M. (1962). *Phenomenology of perception.* Boston: Routledge & Kegan Paul.

Messick, M. (1996). Human abilities and modes of attention: The issue of stylistic consistence in cognition. In I. Dennis & P. Tapsfield (Eds.), *Human abilities: Their nature and measurement* (pp. 77–96). Mahwah, NJ: Lawrence Erlbaum Associates.

Miller, G. A. (1956). The magical number seven, plus or minus two: Some limits on our capacity for processing information. *Psychological Review, 63,* 81–97.

Neisser, U. (1963). The imitation of man by machine. *Science, 139,* 193–197.

Neisser, U. (1967). *Cognitive psychology.* New York: Appleton-Century-Crofts.

Newell, A. (1988). Putting it all together. In D. Klahr & K. Kovovsky (Eds.), *Complex information processing: The impact of Herbert A. Simon* (pp. 399–440). Hillsdale, NJ: Lawrence Erlbaum Associates.

Newell, A. (1990). *Unified theories of cognition.* Cambridge, MA: Harvard University Press.

Newell, A., & Simon, H. A. (1972). *Human problem solving.* Englewood Cliffs, NJ: Prentice-Hall.

Norman, D. A. (1980). Twelve issues for cognitive science. *Cognitive Science, 4,* 1–32.

Oerter, R. (2000). Activity and motivation: A plea for a human frame motivation. In J. Heckhausen (Ed.), *Motivational psychology of human development: Developing motivation and motivating development* (pp. 57–78). Amsterdam: Elsevier.

Panksepp, J. (1998). *Affective neuroscience.* New York: Oxford University Press.

Pea, R. D. (1993). Practices of distributed intelligence and designs for education. In G. Salomon (Ed.), *Distributed cognitions: Psychological and educational considerations* (pp. 47–87). Cambridge, England: Cambridge University Press.

Piaget, J. (1950). *The psychology of intelligence.* London: Routledge.

Piaget, J. (1952). *The origins of intelligence in children.* New York: International Universities Press.

Piaget, J. (1967). *Six psychological studies.* New York: Random House.

Piaget, J. (1981). *Intelligence and affectivity: Their relationship during child development.* Palo Alto, CA: Annual Reviews Inc.

Picard, R. W. (1997). *Affective computing.* Cambridge, MA: The MIT Press.

Pintrich, P. R., Marx, R. W., & Boyle, R. A. (1993). Beyond cold conceptual change: The role of motivational beliefs and classroom contextual factors in the process of conceptual change. *Review of Educational Research, 63,* 167–199.

Polanyi, M. (1958). *Personal knowledge; Towards a post-critical philosophy.* Chicago: University of Chicago Press.

Polanyi, M. (1966). *Tacit dimension.* Garden City, NY: Doubleday.

Posner, M. I., & Peterson, S. E. (1990). The attention system of the human brain. *Annual Review of Neuroscience, 13,* 25–42.

Posner, M. I., & Rothbart, M. K. (1998). Attention, self regulation and consciousness. *Philosophical Transactions of the Royal Society of London B, 353,* 1915–1927.

Prenzel, M. (1992). The selective persistence of interest. In K. A. Renninger, S. Hidi, & A. Krapp (Eds.), *The role of interest in learning and development* (pp. 71–98). Hillsdale, NJ: Lawrence Erlbaum Associates.

Pylyshyn, Z. W. (1984). *Computation and cognition: Toward a foundation for cognitive science.* Cambridge, MA: MIT Press.

Resnick, L. B. (1989). Introduction. In L. B. Resnick (Ed.), *Knowing, learning, and instruction* (pp. 1–24). Hillsdale, NJ: Lawrence Erlbaum Associates.

Ritchhart, R. (2002). *Intellectual character: What it is, why it matters, and how to get it.* San Francisco: Jossey-Bass.

Rogers, T. B., Kuiper, N. A., & Kirker, S. W. (1977). Self-reference and the encoding of personal information. *Journal of Personality and Social Psychology, 35,* 677–688.

Rogoff, B. (2003). *The cultural nature of human development.* Oxford, England: Oxford University Press.

Rumelhart, D. E. (1980). Schemata: The building blocks of cognition. In R. J. Spiro, B. C. Bruce, & W. F. Brewer (Eds.), *Theoretical issues in reading comprehension* (pp. 33–58). Hillsdale, NJ: Lawrence Erlbaum Associates.

Runco, M. A. (1994). Creativity and its discontents. In M. P. Shaw & M. A. Runco (Eds.), *Creativity and affect* (pp. 102–123). Norwood, NJ: Ablex.

Saariluoma, P. (1992). Error in chess: The apperception-restructuring view. *Psychological Research, 54,* 17–26.

Salovey, P., & Mayer, J. D. (1990). Emotional intelligence. *Imagination, Cognition, and Personality, 9,* 539–551.

Schoenfeld, A. H. (1992). Learning to think mathematically: Problem solving, metacognition, and sense making in mathematics. In D. A. Grouws (Ed.), *Handbook of research on mathematics teaching and learning* (pp. 334–370). New York: Macmillan.

Searle, J. R. (1990). Is the brain's mind a computer program? *Scientific American, 262*, 26–37.

Searle, J. R. (2001). Chinese Room Argument. In R. A. Wilson & F. C. Keil (Eds.), *The MIT encyclopedia of the cognitive sciences* (pp. 115–116). Cambridge, MA: The MIT Press.

Shuell, T. J. (1996). Teaching and learning in a classroom context. In D. C. Berliner & R. C. Calfee (Eds.), *Handbook of educational psychology* (pp. 726–764). New York: Simon & Schuster.

Sieberg, D. (2003). Kasparov: "Intuition versus the brute force of calculation." *CNN/ACCESS.* Retrieved February 24, 2003 from http://www.cnn.com/2003/TECH/fun.games/02/08/cnna.kasparov/index.html

Siegler, R. S. (2000). The rebirth of children's learning. *Child Development, 71*, 26–35.

Simon, H. A. (1967). Motivational and emotional controls of cognition. *Psychological Review, 74*, 29–39.

Simon, H. A. (1969). *The sciences of the artificial.* Cambridge, MA: The MIT Press.

Simon, H. A. (1979). Information processing models of cognition. *Annual Review of Psychology, 30*, 363–396.

Simon, H. A. (1994). The bottleneck of attention: Connecting thought with motivation. In W. D. Spaulding (Ed.), *Nebraska Symposium on Motivation, Vol. 41: Integrative views of motivation, cognition, and emotion* (pp. 1–21). Lincoln, NE: University of Nebraska.

Sinatra, G. M., & Pintrich, P. R. (Eds.). (2003). *Intentional conceptual change.* Mahwah, NJ: Lawrence Erlbaum Associates.

Smith, R. C. (2001). Computation. In R. A. Wilson & F. C. Keil (Eds.), *The MIT encyclopedia of the cognitive sciences* (pp. 153–155). Cambridge, MA: The MIT Press.

Snow, R. E. (1986). On intelligence. In R. J. Sternberg & D. K. Detterman (Eds.), *What is intelligence? Contemporary viewpoints on its nature and definition* (pp. 133–139). Norwood, NJ: Ablex.

Snow, R. E. (1992). Aptitude theory: Yesterday, today, and tomorrow. *Educational Psychologist, 27*, 5–32.

Spearman, C. (1927). *The abilities of man.* New York: Macmillan.

Steinberg, L. (1996). *Beyond the classroom: Why school reform has failed and what parents need to do.* New York: Simon & Schuster.

Sternberg, R. J. (1985). *Beyond IQ: A triarchic theory of human intelligence.* Cambridge, England: Cambridge University Press.

Sternberg, R. J. (1996). Costs of expertise. In K. A. Ericsson (Ed.), *The road to excellence: The acquisition of expert performance in the arts and sciences, sports and games* (pp. 347–354). Mahwah, NJ: Lawrence Erlbaum Associates.

Sternberg, R. J. (2001). Intelligence. In R. A. Wilson & F. C. Keil (Eds.), *The MIT encyclopedia of the cognitive sciences* (pp. 409–410). Cambridge, MA: The MIT Press.

Sternberg, R. J. (Ed.). (2003). *Psychologists defying the crowd: Stories of those who battled the establishment and won.* Washington, DC: American Psychological Association.

Sternberg, R. J., & Grigorenko, E. L. (2001). Unified psychology. *American Psychologist, 56*, 1069–1079.

Sternberg, R. J., & Kaufman, J. C. (1998). Human abilities. *Annual Review of Psychology, 49*, 479–502.

Symons, C. S., & Johnson, B. T. (1997). The self-reference effect in memory: A meta-analysis. *Psychological Bulletin, 121*, 371–394.

Thagard, P. (2000). *Coherence in thought and action.* Cambridge, MA: The MIT Press.

Thagard, P. (2002). The passionate scientist: Emotion in scientific cognition. In P. Carruthers & S. Stich (Eds.), *The cognitive basis of science* (pp. 235–250). New York: Cambridge University Press.

Tobias, S. (1994). Interest, prior knowledge, and learning. *Review of Educational Research, 64*, 37–54.

Tolman, E. C. (1932). *Purposive behavior in animal and men.* New York: The Century Co.

Tomkin, S. S. (1962). *Affect, imagery, consciousness, Vol. 1: The positive affects.* New York: Springer.

Tomkins, S. S. (1963). Simulation of personality: The interrelationships between affect, memory, thinking, perception, and action. In S. S. Tomkins & S. Messick (Eds.), *Computer simulation of personality: Frontier of psychological theory* (pp. 3–57). New York: Wiley.

Triandis, H. C. (1989). The self and social behavior in deffering cultural contexts. *Psychological Review, 96*, 506–520.

Tucker, D. M., & Derryberry, D. (1992). Motivated attention: Anxiety and the frontal executive functions. *Neuropsychiatry, Neuropsychology, and Behavioral Neurology, 5*, 233–252.

Tulving, E. (2003, August). *What makes mental time travel possible?* Invited address presented at the 111th annual convention of the American Psychological Association.

Tversky, A., & Kahneman, D. (1974). Judgment under uncertainty: Heuristics and biases. *Science, 185*, 1124–1131.

Varela, F. J., Thompson, E., & Rosch, E. (1993). *The embodied mind.* Cambridge, MA: The MIT Press.

Vicente, K. J., & Wang, J. H. (1998). An ecological theory of expertise effects in memory recall. *Psychological Review, 105*, 33–57.

von Newmann, J. (1958). *The computer and the brain.* New Haven, CT: Yale University Press.

Vygotsky, L. S. (1978). *Mind in society: The development of higher psychological processes.* Cambridge, MA: Harvard University Press.

Wechsler, D. (1950). Cognitive, conative, and non-intellective intelligence. *American Psychologist, 5*, 78–83.

Wilson, R. A., & Keil, F. C. (Eds.). (2001). *The MIT encyclopedia of the cognitive sciences.* Cambridge, MA: The MIT Press.

Wineburg, S. S. (1991). On the reading of historical texts: Notes on the breach between school and academy. *American Educational Research Journal, 28*, 73–87.

Zajonc, R. B. (1980). Feeling and thinking: Preferences need no inferences. *American Psychologist, 35*, 151–175.

Zigler, E. (1986). Intelligence: A developmental approach. In R. J. Sternberg & D. K. Detterman (Eds.), *What is intelligence? Contemporary viewpoints on its nature and definition* (pp. 149–152). Norwood, NJ: Ablex.

Zimbardo, P. G. (2002). Mind control: Psychological reality or mindless rhetoric? *APA Monitor, 33*(10), 5.

II

COGNITION IN MOTIVATIONAL AND AFFECTIVE CONTEXTS

II

2

▼▼▼▼▼▼▼

Motivational Effects on Attention, Cognition, and Performance

Carol S. Dweck
Jennifer A. Mangels
Catherine Good
Columbia University

Why should cognitive psychologists be concerned with motivation? In the typical cognitive psychology formulation, motivation is not a theoretically interesting or important variable. The assumption typically made is that motivation simply involves caring about a task or wanting a successful task outcome—and that once individuals care about the task they will display the cognitive processes (and hence the intellectual performance) of which they are capable. In this view, motivation is a quantity that people have in varying degrees and, if they have enough of it, their intellectual performance will fully reflect their cognitive abilities.

Our perspective challenges this assumption and in doing so casts motivation in a much more interesting light. In place of the view of motivation as a simple amount of caring, it proposes that there are qualitatively different motivational frameworks, driven by people's beliefs and goals, that affect basic attentional and cognitive processes. By doing so, these motivational frameworks can substantially change intellectual performance even among individuals who care very much about succeeding.

In this chapter, we review research showing how the motivational beliefs and goals people hold affect their attentional processes, cognitive strategies, and intellectual performance, particularly in the face of challenge and setbacks. We present evidence from laboratory studies (including electrophysiological studies), field studies, and educational interventions. We hope to demonstrate the powerful effects of these motivational variables, their dynamic and malleable nature, and the striking changes in performance that can result from brief, but targeted interventions.

BELIEFS AND GOALS THAT AFFECT PERFORMANCE

In our research, we have examined the impact of two classes of goals (perform-ance goals vs. learning goals) and of the beliefs that give rise to them (students' fixed vs. malleable theories about their intelligence). A performance goal is the goal of validating one's ability through one's performance, that is, the goal of looking smart and not dumb.[1] In contrast a learning goal is the goal of increas-ing one's ability, that is, the goal of getting smarter. These goals create very dif-ferent mindsets, which we will see, have many ramifications.

Although both goals can be important in achievement settings, some stu-dents are overly concerned with performance goals, while others focus pre-dominantly on learning goals. Why might this be? We have found that stu-dents' theories about their intelligence orient them toward one class of goals or the other (see Dweck, 1999; Dweck & Leggett, 1988). When students be-lieve that their intelligence is a fixed trait (an entity theory of intelligence), it becomes critical to for them to validate their fixed ability through their per-formance. In contrast, when students believe that their intellectual skills are something that they can increase through their efforts (an incremental theory of intelligence), they become less concerned with how their abilities might be evaluated now, and more concerned with cultivating their abilities in the longer term.

In some of the studies described below, we used measures of students' goals or theories of intelligence to predict their cognitive strategies and intel-lectual performance. In other studies, we manipulated students' goals or the-ories of intelligence to produce different patterns of cognitive strategies and intellectual performance. Let us now turn to the studies.

MOTIVATIONAL EFFECTS ON COGNITIVE STRATEGIES

In a study by Farrell and Dweck (1985), junior high school students were taught a challenging new unit in their science class. Before beginning the unit, we assessed, for each student, whether he or she had chiefly performance goals or learning goals for the unit. Those who endorsed performance goals agreed that their goal was to look smart or avoid mistakes, whereas those

---

[1]Performance goals are sometimes defined as competitive goals (wanting to outdo others) or as simply seeking successful outcomes (such as high grades). We and others have not found these other goals to create the same vulnerabilities as the performance goal of validating ability (Grant & Dweck, 2003; Harackiewicz & Elliot, 1993; Kanfer & Ackerman, 2000). Throughout this chapter we use the term performance goals to refer to the goal of validating ability through performance.

who endorsed learning goals agreed that their goal was to learn new things, even if they might get confused, make mistakes, and not look smart.

The unit dealt with a scientific principle that cut across several types of problems (i.e., pulleys, inclined planes, etc.). For the task itself, students were trained on one type of problem (e.g., pulleys) and then given a transfer test to see whether they could apply the same principle to another type of problem (e.g., inclined planes). Looking at students with learning goals versus performance goals, we found that even though both groups of students learned the material equally well, students with learning goals: (a) produced significantly more written work during their attempts to transfer, (b) tried more different transfer strategies, and (c) were more successful in transferring the principle to the new task. Transfer of training is a key part of intellectual functioning (and creativity). This study showed that students who are in a learning mind-set are more likely to search for and to find successful transfer strategies than are those with concerns about validating their ability.

In another study of students' ability to display effective strategies in the face of difficulty, Elliott and Dweck (1988) instilled different goals in late grade-school students as they embarked on a challenging concept-formation task. In addition, half of the children were led to believe they had high ability and would probably do well on the upcoming task, whereas the other half of the children were led to believe they had lower ability at the task. The concept-formation task was one that allowed the researchers to assess the sophistication of students' problem-solving strategies on each trial and so allowed them to monitor changes in the sophistication of their strategies as students encountered a series of more difficult problems, ones that were somewhat too difficult for children their age (see Diener & Dweck, 1978; cf. Gholson, Levine, & Phillips, 1972).

Regardless of whether students had been given learning goals or performance goals, they performed equally well on the initial trials, prior to the difficulty. However, the students with learning goals were able to maintain or even improve their problem-solving strategies over the failure trials—regardless of whether they believed they had high or low ability at the task. In contrast, unless they believed they had high ability, those with performance goals showed a steep decline in the sophistication of their problem-solving strategies over the failure trials, with many of them falling into entirely immature and ineffective strategies. Thus students with equivalent abilities and metacognitive strategies on the early trials, diverged sharply in the level of strategy they were able to use on a more difficult task.

Do students with different goals differ in the strategies with which they approach difficult course material? Much literature suggests they do (Ames & Archer, 1988; Elliot, McGregor, & Gable, 1999; Graham & Golon, 1991; Pintrich & Garcia, 1991). In a recent study, Grant and Dweck (2003) tracked college students during their introductory Chemistry course, the entry course for the pre-med curriculum. Thus it was a highly important course for most students, and it was a difficult one, with the average exam grade equaling a C+. Grant and Dweck found that the more that students held learning goals, the more they reported engaging in deep processing of course material (e.g., outlining the material, relating different concepts to each other, attempting to integrate the material across units). The tendency to engage in deep processing was predictive of higher course grades, and this tendency mediated the positive relation between learning goals and course grades.

Do learning goals confer benefits mainly on learning tasks, or are these benefits apparent on tasks that tap existing intellectual abilities? Mueller and Dweck (1998) looked at the impact of students' goal on their performance on the Raven's Progressive Matrices Task (Raven, Styles, & Raven, 1998), often considered to be a nonverbal IQ test. In this study, late grade-school students succeeded on the first set of moderately difficult problems and then, through the type of praise they were given, were oriented toward learning goals or performance goals. They then encountered much more difficult problems. How did they fare?

Those oriented toward learning goals not only performed better on the difficult problems, but carried over their benefit to a third set of problems (i.e., equivalent in difficulty to the first set), doing significantly better than the performance goal-oriented students on the third set as well. In fact, those with performance goals, after encountering difficulty, performed worse on the third set than they had on the first.

These findings were replicated across a series of studies using diverse populations, and show how, through goal manipulations, we can take children of equal intellectual ability and make them look quite different on tests of intellectual ability.

MOTIVATIONAL EFFECTS ON ACADEMIC PERFORMANCE

In two studies, students making the often-difficult transition to junior high school were followed (Dweck & Sorich, 1999; Henderson & Dweck, 1990). In these studies, we measured their theories about their intelligence and their academic (learning or performance) goals at the beginning of seventh grade and then tracked the grades they received. In both studies, the motivational variables were significant predictors, over and above prior achievement, of the grades students earned. For example, in the Dweck and Sorich (1999) study, students with an incremental theory earned steadily increasing math grades over seventh and eighth grades, while those with an entity theory earned steadily decreasing math grades, even though they entered with equivalent math achievement test scores.

Interestingly, the incremental theorists' grade advantage was mediated partially through their learning goals and partially through their greater belief in the efficacy of effort, both of which led to more vigorous, mastery-oriented strategies in the face of difficulty. These strategies constituted the final route to grades.

MOTIVATIONAL EFFECTS ON ATTENTION AND COGNITIVE PROCESSING: EVIDENCE FROM AN ELECTROPHYSIOLOGICAL APPROACH

Thus far, we have described a model in which different motivational goals, guided by beliefs in fixed or malleable ability, influence how information is processed in challenging learning situations. Recently, in an attempt to understand more precisely how underlying attentional and cognitive processes are affected by these goals we have incorporated electrophysiological measurements into our studies.

What guides goal-related attentional and cognitive processes? The cognitive mechanism that ensures goals are met can be seen as an executive control network responsible for directing attention toward goal-relevant information and away from goal-irrelevant information (e.g., Botvinick, Braver, Barch, Carter, & Cohen, 2001; Posner & DiGirolamo, 1998; Shallice & Burgess, 1996). Selective attention toward goal-relevant information is typically evidenced as an increase in the speed, accuracy, or depth of information processing of that information. Given that entity and incremental theorists hold contrasting goals, we would expect that the executive control network would direct their attention to different information and this difference might have consequences for how quickly, accurately or deeply different types of information are processed.

For students with an entity theory of intelligence, this executive control network may bias attention and conceptual processing toward information that speaks to the adequacy or inadequacy of their intellectual ability (performance goal-relevant information) and not toward information that provides new knowledge that could help them improve. For example, after providing an answer to a general knowledge question (e.g., What is the capital of Canada?), students with an entity theory may allocate more attention to feedback indicating whether they are correct or incorrect (i.e., ability-relevant feedback), than feedback indicating the correct answer (i.e., learning-relevant feedback), even when that information could help them learn. For students with an incremental theory, however, control processes may direct attention more equally across ability-relevant and learning-relevant information because both types of information are consistent with their learning goal of increasing their knowledge.

Recently, we conducted an exploratory study in which we used electroencephalography (EEG) to noninvasively monitor brain activity associated with students' attention to ability-relevant and learning-relevant feedback during a challenging general knowledge retrieval task. In this task (see also Butterfield & Mangels, in press), subjects' answers to general information questions were followed first by feedback indicating the accuracy of their response (i.e., ability-relevant feedback: red if incorrect, green if correct), and then by the correct answer to the question (i.e., learning-relevant feedback). Each type of feedback was also preceded by a brief waiting period, thereby providing a period during which we could assess anticipation of the different kinds of information. To extract patterns of brain activity consistently associated with the processing of these different types of feedback, we constructed event-related potentials (ERPs) that were time-locked to presentation of the feedback. Previous research has delineated a set of ERP waveforms that are correlated with anticipatory vigilance and orienting, including the stimulus-related negativity (SPN; Brunia & van Boxtel, 2001) and frontal-P3 (Friedman, Cycowicz, & Gaeta, 2001). Our analysis revealed that these ERPs differed as a function of students' theories of intelligence in a pattern that was very much in line with our predictions.

When waiting for an event of motivational or affective significance that will occur in the near future, a state of anticipatory vigilance is entered. This type of anticipatory vigilance has been shown to elicit an SPN, a slow negative waveform that typically starts about one second before stimulus onset and increases in amplitude as the significant event looms closer (e.g., Brunia & Damen, 1988; Damen & Brunia, 1994; Ruchkin, Sutton, Mahaffey, & Glaser, 1986; Simons, Ohman, & Lang, 1979). It is especially prominent in anticipation of performance feedback (Chwilla & Brunia, 1991; Damen & Brunia, 1994; Kotani & Aihara, 1999), or stimuli with a strong positive (e.g., Simons, et al. 1979) or negative valence (e.g., Bocker, Baas, Kenemans, & Verbaten, 2001). Recently, it has been suggested that the SPN reflects an attentional process that is tied to a motivational-affective system in which the anterior cingulate cortex plays a major role (Bocker, et al., 2001; Brunia & van Boxtel, 2001; Peterson, et al., 1999). Thus, we predicted that the SPN would be modulated differently by the different motivational goals of the entity and incremental theorists.

We found that both students with entity and incremental theories generated an SPN prior to the ability-relevant feedback suggesting that both were motivated to generate a state of vigilance for this information. In contrast, the SPN prior to the learning-relevant feedback (correct answer) was significantly larger in students with an incremental theory compared to students with an entity theory. Indeed, the SPN in students with an entity theory did not differ from baseline, suggesting that they were not motivated to attend to this information. Perhaps once their performance goals had been met by processing the ability-relevant feedback, they felt no need to attend to the learning-relevant feedback. Interestingly, an SPN to the learning-relevant feedback was lacking in these individuals even when they had just been presented with negative feedback, and therefore, could have used the learning-relevant feedback to correct their error. In contrast, for incremental theorists, an SPN to the learning-relevant feedback was present even when they had gotten the answer correct in the first place, suggesting an intrinsic interest in feedback that provided learning relevant information whether that information was new or simply provided a verification of what they knew.

In addition, although this electrophysiological evidence suggests that students with an entity theory and students with an incremental theory were similarly motivated to attend to the ability-relevant feedback prior to its presentation, they appeared to evaluate the valence of that feedback differently once it was presented. Specifically, students with an entity theory appeared quicker than students with an incremental theory to orient toward information indicating a lack of ability (i.e., feedback that their response was incorrect). This was indicated by the significantly shorter peak latency of an anterior (frontal-maximal) P3 waveform, an ERP component that has been associated with the involuntary orienting of attention to information that does not match expectations (Butterfield & Mangels, in press; Comerchero & Polich, 2000; Friedman, et al., 2001; Knight, 1984; Knight & Scabini, 1998). In contrast, entity and incremental theorists did not appear to differ in their latency to orient to feedback indicating a correct response; the latency of the anterior P3 to correct responses was the same in both groups.

Differences in latency of the anterior P3 as a function of feedback valence underscore the dynamic relationship between executive control and attentional allocation. Control processes are not only important for selecting a goal-relevant channel of information but also for monitoring that channel for information which conflicts with the goals it is trying to maintain. Furthermore, when conflict is detected, the executive control network may attempt to modify the allocation of attention and strategic processes in a way that attempts to realign them with the goals (Fernandez-Duque, Baird, & Posner, 2000; Nelson & Narens, 1994). For students with an entity theory, ability-relevant feedback (goal-consistent information) informing them that they have made an error is not good news about their success in achieving their goal of high performance. Thus, the shorter latency of the anterior P3 to negative performance feedback in entity theorists may index the enhanced saliency of this type of feedback, arising because it conflicts with, and perhaps even threatens, their goal of proving their ability. Students with an incremental theory, on the other hand, may value both negative and positive ability-relevant feedback equally for their function of informing them about the status of current knowledge.

In summary, entity and incremental theorists allocated their attentional resources differently and in accord with their different goals. Students with an entity theory entered a state of vigilance for ability-relevant information and oriented particularly quickly to negative ability-relevant information. They did not, however, generate a state of vigilance for the learning-relevant information that followed. In contrast, students with an incremental theory entered a state of vigilance for both the ability-relevant and the learning-relevant information, which could inform them of the state of their current knowledge and lead to increases in knowledge. Moreover, they vigilantly awaited the learning-relevant information, even when their answer had been correct.

These initial results demonstrate how electrophysiological measures can complement self-report and behavioral measures of attention and strategic processing by providing an observable window into the moment-to-moment changes in internal neurocognitive processes that students engage during academic tasks. We have found EEG–ERP to be particularly useful because of its ability to monitor the fast, dynamic neural changes that occur when processing different types of stimuli in rapid succession. In addition, given that both attention and depth of processing are positively related to successful encoding into long-term episodic memory (e.g., Craik, 2002; Craik, Govoni, Naveh-Benjamin, & Anderson, 1996), we are now carefully evaluating whether these ERP measures of attention are correlated with students' success at correcting (improving) performance when those items initially answered incorrectly are presented on a subsequent retest. Thus, we hope to determine whether effects of different goals on attention and conceptual processing account, in part, for overall differences in learning success over time.

EDUCATIONAL INTERVENTIONS

What are the implications of the motivational findings for educational intervention? For example, by changing students' beliefs, can one change their academic performance? Three recent studies have addressed this question directly (Aronson, Fried, & Good, 2002; Aronson & Good, 2002; Blackwell, Dweck, & Trzesniewski, 2003). The first study (Aronson et al., 2002) was conducted with students from an elite university (Stanford), and was concerned with: (a) the issue of why African-American students with strong academic skills nonetheless underperform in such settings (see Steele & Aronson, 1995), and (b) whether providing these students with an incremental theory about their intelligence would prove beneficial.

Although the incremental theory was predicted to prove beneficial to White students as well, there was reason to believe that it could provide an extra boost to African-American students, who are often the object of negative stereotypes concerning their intellectual abilities. There is a wealth of recent research on stereotype threat showing the degree to which being the object of a negative ability stereotype can undermine performance on intellectual tasks (Aronson et al., 1999; Good & Aronson, 2001; Inzlicht & Ben-Zeev, 2000; Quinn & Spencer, 2002; Spencer, Steele, & Quinn, 1999; Steele & Aronson, 1995). In this context, an entity theory might be especially pernicious. A negative stereotype is a belief about fixed lower ability, and the entity theory simply underscores the idea of fixed ability. In contrast, an incremental theory may defuse the power of the stereotype by portraying intellectual skills as acquirable over time. It can thus make any current judgment less important. Moreover, the incremental theory, by giving students control over their intellectual growth, may make them value, enjoy, and pursue their studies more.

In the Aronson et al. (2002) study, both African-American and White participants were randomly assigned to one of three groups. The first group received training in the incremental theory. They saw a highly compelling film depicting the way in which the brain forms new connections and literally changes every time you learn something new. To fortify this message, they also participated in a pen-pal program in which they wrote a letter to a struggling junior high school student. They were encouraged to emphasize in their letters the idea that intelligence is expandable and increases with mental work. At the end of the semester, the researchers assessed participants' enjoyment of academics, their valuing of academics, and their grade point averages.

There were two control groups. One received no treatment, but the other was given a belief about intelligence that was expected to provide some benefit. They were taught the idea that there are many forms of ability that one can have. Thus, they were told, students should not worry if in their studies they find that they lack one kind of ability; they may still have other important ones. This group also participated in the pen-pal program and wrote a letter that emphasized the theory they had learned.

The two control groups did not differ and the group receiving the incremental intervention looked significantly better than both. Those who had received training in the incremental theory reported greater enjoyment of their academic work (e.g., studying, test-taking) and greater valuing of academics in general. In addition, this group showed a clear gain in grade point average over the other groups. The gains were largest for the African-American students, but they were also apparent for the White students.

In the second study, Aronson and Good (2002) designed an in-depth intervention to investigate whether teaching junior high students about the malleability of intelligence could be used to reduce their vulnerability to stereotype threat and increase their standardized test performance. Specifically, seventh-grade students from a low-income, predominantly Hispanic school enrolled in a year-long computer skills class as part of their junior high curriculum and were mentored by college students who taught them study skills, helped them design a web page, and also delivered the intervention message. The mentoring occurred primarily via e-mail throughout the year but also included two in-person visits.

For the students in the experimental group, the mentors conveyed that intelligence is expandable, and helped each student design a web page that advocated this view. This message was fortified throughout the year in the e-mail correspondence between the mentor and the student and via a web space that the student could surf to learn more about the intervention message. The control group received a different constructive message (an anti-drug message) and performed similar activities vis-à-vis this message.

At the year's end, the two groups' math and reading performance on a state-wide standardized achievement test was compared. Results indicated that the students in the incremental group received higher standardized test scores in both math and reading than students in the control group. Although the incremental manipulation helped all students, it was particularly beneficial to females in math. In the incremental condition, the gender gap in math, evident in the control group, disappeared. Thus, these two studies provide good evidence that interventions directed at students' key motivation-relevant beliefs can pay off by boosting intellectual performance.

In the third study, Blackwell et al. (2003) designed an intervention for at-risk minority students coping with the difficult transition to junior high school. Both the experimental group and the control group received an eight-session intervention, replete with excellent information, including a unit on the brain and how it works, study skill training, and a unit on how people limit themselves by applying trait labels or stereotypes to themselves. However, for two of the units, the experimental groups received training in the incremental theory (while the control group received information about mnemonic devices that could help them in their schoolwork.) In the incremental theory units, students read and discussed an article that, as in the Aronson et al. (2002) intervention, depicted how the brain grows and changes with use and conveyed the idea that they were in charge of their intellectual growth. They also performed a variety of activities that explored this concept and its ramifications.

At the end of the semester, math teachers (who did not know which group any given student was in) were polled to determine whether they noticed any motivational changes in their students. They singled out significantly more of the students in the incremental group for comment, offering comments like the following about students in the incremental group:

Lately I have noticed that some students have a greater appreciation for improvement in academic performance . . . R. was performing below standards . . . He has learned to appreciate the improvement from his grades of 52, 46, and 49 to his grades of 67 and 71 . . . He valued his growth in learning Mathematics.

L., who never puts in any extra effort and often doesn't turn in homework on time, actually stayed up late working for hours to finish an assignment early so I could review it and give him a chance to revise it. He earned a B+ on the assignment (he had been getting C's and lower).

M. was [performing] far below grade level. During the past several weeks, she has voluntarily asked for extra help from me during her lunch period in order to improve her test-taking performance. Her grades drastically improved from failing to an 84 on the most-recent exam.

Students' final grades in math, however, were the major dependent variable. Math was chosen because it would provide the most rigorous test of the hypothesis. For example, the grading is less subjective than in other subjects and deficits in math are difficult to rectify. Nonetheless, although students in the experimental and control groups had earned identical grades the previous semester, in the semester of the intervention, the incremental group earned significantly higher grades than their peers in the control group.

In summary, these studies dramatically demonstrate that a motivational analysis has exciting implications for education and indeed for any endeavor involving skilled performance. Moreover, the studies suggest that cognitive interventions alone may often not be appropriate or sufficient. For instance, the Stanford students in the Aronson et al. (2002) study were not lacking in cognitive expertise. In addition, in the Aronson and Good (2002) study and the Blackwell et al. (2003) study, the students in the control group were taught study skills and memory strategies, to little avail. Instead, in all three cases, it appeared that a motivational intervention was needed to spur the effective use of the existing cognitive skills.

MOTIVATIONAL EFFECTS ON VULNERABILITY TO STEREOTYPE THREAT

The underperformance of stereotyped individuals on an intellectual task has often been attributed to a lack of motivation. For example, often times females' poorer performance in math compared to males' has been blamed on their lower interest in and motivation to excel in math. However, recent research on stereotype threat has argued that the burden of having to perform under the specter of a negative stereotype can undermine performance on a challenging task. Ironically, it is often those who care most and are most mo-

tivated to excel who are the most vulnerable to the impact of negative stereotypes. The studies we have described, however, demonstrate that changing
negatively stereotyped students' motivational frameworks can alleviate their
vulnerability to negative stereotypes and thus, increase their grade point averages (GPAs) and standardized test scores.

How is stereotype threat related to theories of intelligence? Aronson and
his colleagues have argued that individuals targeted by ability-impugning
stereotypes may adopt the same motivational mindset as entity theorists
when faced with a challenging academic task in which they are negatively
stereotyped. That is, stereotyped individuals may adopt performance goals in
an effort to disprove the stereotype about their group. Consistent with this
reasoning, past research has shown that stereotype threat elicits many of the
hallmark responses of entity theorists. For example, stereotype-threatened
individuals tend to choose tasks that ensure success (Good & Aronson,
2001), experience more performance pressure and anxiety (Blascovich, Spencer, Steele, & Quinn, 2001; Steele & Aronson, 1995), and underperform in the
face of challenge (Aronson et al., 1999; Good & Aronson, 2001; Inzlicht &
Ben-Zeev, 2000; Quinn & Spencer, 2002; Spencer et al., 1999; Steele &
Aronson, 1995).

The performance goal mindset that stereotype threat elicits disrupts performance, perhaps because of its effects on attention and cognition. For example, Steele and Aronson (1995) found that African-American students under stereotype threat conditions had more race-related thoughts than did
African Americans under no-threat conditions. These intrusive thoughts may
have directed attention away from the task at hand, resulting in decreased
performance. Furthermore, stereotype threat may interfere with cognitive
abilities in much the same way that an entity theory does. In a study by Quinn
and Spencer (2002), men and women completed a math test under stereotype
threat and no-threat conditions and their problem solving strategies were
coded. The results showed that under stereotype threat, women not only performed worse than men on the math test, but also suffered from an inability
to formulate useful problem solving strategies. In contrast, the women in the
no-threat condition performed as well as the men and did not differ in their
problem solving strategies. Quinn and Spencer (2002) argued that women under threat conditions may have tried to suppress the stereotype-related
thoughts that stereotype threat elicits, thereby experiencing an increase in
cognitive load. Furthermore, the increased cognitive load decreased cognitive
resources available to generate useful problem solving strategies, thus resulting in decreased performance.

The abundance of research on stereotype threat clearly illustrates its dele-
terious effects on performance. As Aronson et al. (2002) argued, these effects
may be due to the entity theory motivational mindset that the stereotype elicits, complete with all the hallmark responses of holding an entity theory: mis-

directed attention, disrupted cognitive resources, and decreased performance. However, encouraging stereotyped individuals to view intelligence as malleable and to adopt learning goals rather than performance goals, may begin to reduce the race and gender gaps in school achievement and standardized test performance.

CONCLUSION

In this chapter, we have demonstrated the important effects that motivation can have on attentional and cognitive processes, on the effective use of cognitive strategies, and on intellectual performance, both on laboratory tasks and in educational environments. These effects are apparent even across students with equivalent cognitive skills. The findings we have presented, like many of the findings now emerging from cognitive neuroscience (Ochsner & Lieberman, 2001), speak to the ways in which motivation, emotion, and cognition work together to produce intellectual performance and to the idea that studying cognition in isolation from its sister processes cannot yield a full or valid picture of the workings of the mind.

ACKNOWLEDGMENTS

The research reported in this chapter was supported in part by grants from the National Science Foundation, the Department of Education, the National Institutes of Health, the W. T. Grant Foundation, and the Spencer Foundation.

REFERENCES

Ames, C., & Archer, J. (1988). Achievement goals in the classroom: Students' learning strategies and motivation processes. *Journal of Educational Psychology, 80*, 260–267.

Aronson, J., Fried, C., & Good, C. (2002). Reducing the effects of stereotype threat on African American college students by shaping theories of intelligence. *Journal of Experimental Social Psychology, 38*, 113–125.

Aronson, J., & Good, C. (2002). *Reducing vulnerability to stereotype threat in adolescents by shaping theories of intelligence.* Unpublished manuscript.

Aronson, J., Lustina, M., Good, C., Keough, K., Steele, C., & Brown, J. (1999). When white men can't do math: Necessary and sufficient factors in stereotype threat. *Journal of Experimental Social Psychology, 35*, 29–46.

Blackwell, L. S., Dweck, C. S., & Trzesniewski, K. (2003). *Implicit theories of intelligence predict achievement across an adolescent transition: A longitudinal study and an intervention.* Unpublished Manuscript, Columbia University, New York.

Blascovich, J., Spencer, S. J., Quinn, D., & Steele, C. (2001). African Americans and high blood pressure: The role of stereotype threat. *Psychological Science, 12,* 225–229.

Bocker, K. B. E., Baas, J. M. P., Kenemans, J. L., & Verbaten, M. N. (2001). Stimulus-preceding negativity induced by fear: A manifestation of affective anticipation. *International Journal of Psychophysiology, 43,* 77–90.

Botvinick, M. M., Braver, T. S., Barch, D. M., Carter, C. S., & Cohen, J. D. (2001). Conflict monitoring and cognitive control. *Psychological Review, 108,* 624–652.

Brunia, C. H., & Damen, E. J. (1988). Distribution of slow brain potentials related to motor preparation and stimulus anticipation in a time estimation task. *Electroencephalography Clinical Neurophysiology, 69,* 234–243.

Brunia, C. H., & van Boxtel, G. J. (2001). "Wait and see." *International Journal of Psychophysiology, 43,* 59–75.

Butterfield, B., & Mangels, J. A. (in press). Neural correlates of error detection and correction in a semantic retrieval task. *Cognitive Brain Research.*

Chwilla, D. J., & Brunia, C. H. (1991). Event-related potentials to different feedback stimuli. *Psychophysiology, 2,* 123–132.

Comerchero, M., & Polich, J. (2000). P3a, perceptual distinctiveness, and stimulus modality. *Cognitive Brain Research, 7,* 41–8.

Craik, F. I. M. (2002). Levels of processing: Past, present . . . and future? *Memory, 10*(5/6), 305–318.

Craik, F. I. M., Govoni, R., Naveh-Benjamin, M., & Anderson, N. D. (1996). The effects of divided attention on encoding and retrieval processes in human memory. *Journal of Experimental Psychology: General, 125,* 159–180.

Damen, E. J., & Brunia, C. H. (1994). "Is a stimulus conveying task-relevant information a sufficient condition to elicit a stimulus-preceding negativity?" *Psychophysiology, 31,* 129–139.

Diener, C. I., & Dweck, C. S. (1978). An analysis of learned helplessness: Continuous changes in performance, strategy and achievement cognitions following failure. *Journal of Personality and Social Psychology, 36,* 451–462.

Dweck, C. S., & Leggett, E. L. (1988). A social-cognitive approach to motivation and personality. *Psychological Review, 95,* 256–273.

Dweck, C. S., & Sorich, L. (1999). Mastery-oriented thinking. In C. R. Snyder (Ed.), *Coping* (pp. 232–251). New York: Oxford University Press.

Dweck, C. S. (1999). *Self-Theories: Their role in motivation, personality and development.* Philadelphia: Taylor and Francis/Psychology Press.

Elliot, A. J., McGregor, H., & Gable, S. (1999). Achievement goals, study strategies, and exam performance: A mediational analysis. *Journal of Experimental Social Psychology, 91,* 549–563.

Elliott, E. S., & Dweck, C. S. (1988). Goals: An approach to motivation and achievement. *Journal of Personality and Social Psychology, 54,* 5–12.

Farrell, E., & Dweck, C. S. (1985). *The role of motivational processes in transfer of learning.* Unpublished manuscript, Harvard University, Cambridge, MA.

Fernandez-Duque, D., Baird, J. A., & Posner, M. I. (2000). Executive attention and metacognitive regulation. *Consciousness and Cognition, 9,* 288–307.

Friedman, D., Cycowicz, Y. M., & Gaeta, H. (2001). The novelty P3: An event-related brain potential (ERP) sign of the brain's evaluation of novelty. *Neuroscience and Biobehavioral Reviews, 25,* 355–373.

Gholson, B., Levine, M., & Phillips, S. (1972). Hypotheses, strategies, and stereotypes in discrimination learning. *Journal of Experimental Child Psychology, 13,* 423–446.

Good, C., & Aronson, J. (2001). *The development of stereotype threat and its relation to theories of intelligence: Effects on elementary school girls' mathematics achievement and task choices.* Unpublished manuscript.

Graham, S., & Golon, S. (1991). Motivational influences on cognition: Task involvement, ego involvement, and depth of information processing. *Journal of Educational Psychology, 83,* 187–194.

Grant, H., & Dweck, C. S. (2003). Clarifying achievement goals and their impact. *Journal of Personality and Social Psychology, 85,* 541–553.

Harackiewicz, J. M., & Elliot, A. J. (1993). Achievement goals and intrinsic motivation. *Journal of Personality and Social Psychology, 65,* 904–915.

Henderson, V., & Dweck, C. S. (1990). Achievement and motivation in adolescence: A new model and data. In S. Feldman & G. Elliott (Eds.), *At the threshold: The developing adolescent* (pp. 308–329). Cambridge, MA: Harvard University Press.

Inzlicht, M., & Ben Zeev, T. (2000). A threatening intellectual environment: Why females are susceptible to experiencing problem-solving deficits in the presence of males. *Psychological Science, 11,* 365–371.

Kanfer, R., & Ackerman, P. L. (2000). Individual differences in work motivation: Further explorations of a trait framework. *Applied Psychology: An International Review, 49,* 470–482.

Knight, R. T. (1984). Decreased response to novel stimuli after prefrontal lesions in man. *Electroencephalography and Clinical Neurophysiology, 59,* 9–20.

Knight, R. T., & Scabini, D. (1998). Anatomic bases of event-related potentials and their relationship to novelty detection in humans. *Journal of Clinical Neurophysiology, 15,* 3–13.

Kotani, Y., & Aihara, Y. (1999). The effect of stimulus discrimination on stimulus-preceding negativities prior to instructive and feedback stimuli. *Biological Psychology, 50,* 1–18.

Mueller, C. M., & Dweck, C. S. (1998). Intelligence praise can undermine motivation and performance. *Journal of Personality and Social Psychology, 75,* 33–52.

Nelson, T. O., & Narens, L. (1994). Why investigate metacognition. In J. Metcalfe & A. P. Shimamura (Eds.), *Metacognition: Knowing about knowing* (pp. 1–25). Cambridge, MA: MIT Press.

Ochsner, K. N., & Lieberman, M. D. (2001). The emergence of social cognitive neuroscience. *American Psychologist, 56,* 717–734.

Peterson, B. S., Skudlarski, P., Gatenby, J. C., Zhang, H., Anderson, A. W., & Gore, J. C. (1999). An fMRI study of Stroop word-color interference: Evidence for cingulate subregions subserving multiple distributed attentional systems. *Biological Psychiatry, 45,* 1237–1258.

Pintrich, P. R., & Garcia, T. (1991). Student goal orientation and self-regulation in the college classroom. In M. L. Maehr & P. R. Pintrich (Eds.), *Advances in motivation and achievement, Vol. 7: Goals and self-regulatory processes* (pp. 371–402). Greenwich, CT: JAI.

Posner, M. I., & DiGirolamo, G. J. (1998). Executive attention: Conflict, target detection, and cognitive control. In R. Parasuraman (Ed.), *The attentive brain* (pp. 401–423). Cambridge, MA: MIT Press.

Quinn, D., & Spencer, J. (2002). The interference of stereotype threat with women's generation of mathematical problem-solving strategies. *Journal of Social Issues, 57,* 55–71.

Raven, J. C., Styles, I., & Raven, M. A. (1998). *Raven's progressive matrices: SPM plus test booklet.* Oxford: Oxford Psychologists Press.

Ruchkin, D. S., Sutton, S., Mahaffey, D., & Glaser, J. (1986). Terminal CNV in the absence of motor response. *Electroencephalography and Clinical Neurophysiology, 63,* 445–463.

Shallice, T., & Burgess, P. (1996). The domain of supervisory processes and temporal organization of behaviour. *Philosophical Transactions of the Royal Society of London Series B* (Biological Sciences), *351*(1346), 1405–1411; discussion 1411–1412.

Simons, R. F., Ohman, A., & Lang, P. J. (1979). Anticipation and response set: Cortical, cardiac, and eletrodermal correlates. *Psychophysiology, 16,* 222–233.

Spencer, S., Steele, C., & Quinn, D. (1999). Stereotype threat and women's math performance. *Journal of Experimental Social Psychology, 35,* 4–28.

Steele, C. M., & Aronson, J. (1995). Stereotype threat and the intellectual test performance of African-Americans. *Journal of Personality and Social Psychology, 68,* 797–811.

3

▼▼▼▼▼▼▼

Role of Affect in Cognitive
Processing in Academic Contexts

Elizabeth A. Linnenbrink
The University of Toledo

Paul R. Pintrich
The University of Michigan

With the exception of the plethora of research on test anxiety (Hill & Wigfield, 1984), the link between affect and cognitive processing in academic contexts has been largely ignored (Pekrun, Goetz, Titz, & Perry, 2002). Thus, although there are recent theoretical advances in our understanding of the relation between affect and cognitive processing generally (e.g., Forgas, 2000c), we know very little about how affect influences cognitive processing for specific academic tasks. Therefore, in this chapter, we apply current social psychological theories linking affect and cognition to the academic context. We begin by providing an overview of general theories linking affect to cognitive processing. We then review the limited research linking affect and cognitive processing in academic contexts, focusing in particular on our work in the areas of conceptual change in science understanding as well as learning mathematics, and apply the more general theories to academic contexts using the empirical research as a guide for our suggestions about directions for future research.

TOWARD A MODEL OF AFFECT
AND COGNITIVE PROCESSING

There are many separate models of affect and cognition, but few models that attempt to integrate affect and cognition. Any attempt to link affect to motivation or cognition requires that the constructs be clearly defined. Affect itself has varied and broad definitions. While there is not universal agreement among affect researchers regarding the way in which affect is defined, it is necessary to provide a working definition for any analysis regarding the links between affect and cognitive processing. Accordingly, in this chapter we follow Rosenberg's (1998) definition of affect in which affect is defined in terms of affective traits and states. This definition is somewhat narrow in that it does not include general preferences or sentiments and thus leaves out motivational aspects of affect such as interest.

Affective traits refer to stable ways or predispositions to emotional responding (Rosenberg, 1998). However, in this chapter we focus on affective states, namely on moods and emotions, as this is more closely linked to research from social psychology on affect and cognitive processing (e.g., Bless, 2000; Forgas, 2000b) and recent work on academic emotions and cognitive processing (Pekrun et al., 2002). Moods and emotions are distinct in terms of intensity and duration (Rosenberg, 1998; Schwarz, 1990; Schwarz & Clore, 1996). Moods tend to be longer lasting than emotions, which are characterized by short, intense episodes. However, while emotions tend to be intense or rather short-lived, they may also fade into general mood states over time. In addition to intensity and duration, Schwarz and Clore (1996) also note that mood states do not have a particular referent; the source of the mood is unclear. In contrast, emotions tend to be a reaction or response to a particular event or person. This distinction between moods and emotions is not used by all (for alternative perspectives, see Batson, Shaw, & Oleson, 1992; Morris, 1992); however, for the purpose of this discussion, we define moods as longer lasting general affective states without a particular referent and emotions as short, intense affective episodes with a specific referent.

Typically, research on affect and cognitive processing fails to consider the arousal or activation dimension of affect and instead focuses almost exclusively on the valence dimension, positive versus negative (Revelle & Loftus, 1990). This is due, at least in part, to the focus of social psychological research on the relations between moods and cognitive processing. Since moods are typically less intense, they usually do not differ in terms of arousal whereas emotions often tend to vary in terms of arousal. However, it is important to note that a number of researchers and theorists (e.g., Cacioppo, Gardner, & Berntson, 1999; Russell & Feldman Barrett, 1999; Tellegen, Watson, & Clark, 1999; Thayer, 1986; Watson, Wiese, Vaidya, & Tellegen, 1999), who focus on the nature or structure of affect, have developed models distinguishing between valence and arousal–activation.

Although the proposed models differ somewhat, they share the same basic dimensions including high–low engagement, pleasantness–unpleasantness, high–low positive affect, and high–low negative affect. The latter dimensions reflect a mixture of arousal (or engagement) with valence (pleasant–unpleasant). In this way, engagement and pleasantness may be distinct but they may also be related such that arousal (high engagement, neutral pleasantness) differs from enthusiasm (high engagement, high pleasantness), which differs from contentment (high pleasantness, neutral engagement). While we acknowledge that these distinctions among valence and arousal are important, especially in terms of emotions, this distinction is not made by the prominent social psychological theories we review and attempt to apply in this chapter. Therefore, we focus primarily on the valence component of affect and refer to this as positive and negative affect rather than pleasantness/unpleasantness, as this more closely mirrors the terminology used by social psychological theories examining affect and cognitive processing. However, we do note when differences in arousal may alter the cognitive processing and consider this to be an important direction for future research.

In terms of cognitive processing, we adopt a general cognitive perspective that highlights the importance of prior knowledge and the processing and understanding of new information and knowledge. This perspective is compatible with social cognitive models of affect and cognition (see Forgas, 2000c) as well as more general cognitive psychological models of memory, learning, thinking, and problem solving (Miyake & Shah, 1999; Sternberg, 1985). These models stress the role of working memory and executive functioning processes as individuals attend, comprehend, and act upon different information and knowledge available to them. In addition, our perspective on cognition highlights the role of various cognitive or metacognitive strategies that individuals might use to regulate their comprehension and learning as they engage in various academic tasks (Pintrich, 2000). This emphasis on cognitive processes is compatible with our general functional and process view of emotions and moods, which makes integration easier.

PREDICTING COGNITIVE PROCESSING AS A RESULT OF AFFECT: THEORETICAL APPROACHES

In recent years, research in social and cognitive psychology has focused on how cognitive processing influences affect as well as how affect influences cognitive processing (for reviews, see Dalgleish & Power, 1999; Forgas, 2000b). Based on this research, two different types of theories regarding affect and cognitive processing have emerged. First, appraisal theories (e.g., Boekaerts, 1993; Scherer, 1999; Smith & Lazarus, 1990) consider how cognitive appraisals of one's situation influence the emotions experienced. That is, the focus is on how cognition influences affect. Given our emphasis on the role of affect as a precursor to cognition, we do not discuss appraisal theories in this chapter.

A second line of research focuses on how affect influences cognition, which is more compatible with the focus of our chapter. Within this second line of research, there are two major approaches. The first examines how affect influences the storage and retrieval of information from long-term memory (e.g., Bower, 1981; Forgas, 2000a). The second area focuses more specifically on how affect influences the way in which information is processed and the way in which one approaches a particular situation. For instance Ellis and Ashbrook (1988), Schwarz (1990), and more recently Bless (2000) and Fiedler (2000) proposed theories suggesting that people in a positive versus negative mood may process information either analytically or heuristically based on their mood. In addition, Fredrickson (1998) examined the role of positive emotions and suggested that positive emotions help to broaden and build one's resources. Given the complexity and breadth of this research on affect and cognitive processing, we focus on how affect influences the way in which information is stored and processed, as we feel this has the most profound implications for how affect influences learning and achievement in academic settings (see Boekaerts, 1993; Pekrun, 1992; Pekrun et al., 2002, for a general review of the influence of affect on learning in academic settings).

Affect and Storage–Retrieval
From Long-Term Memory

Research relating long-term memory and affect has been seminal in incorporating affect into cognitive processing (Forgas, 2000b). The original research in this area conducted by Bower investigated how mood influenced both the encoding and retrieval of information from long-term memory. More specifically, Bower (1981) proposed an associative network theory suggesting that mood was associated with information stored in long-term memory. Accordingly, one would expect that a person's current mood helps to activate information that is congruent with this mood, thus making that information more accessible (mood congruency effect). For instance, if a person is in a positive mood, he is more likely to retrieve positively valenced information. In addition to mood congruency effects, Bower also proposed that a match between mood during encoding and retrieval (state-dependent hypothesis) would facilitate recall. Bower's associative network theory was tested in a variety of studies, many of which did not consistently find results in line with the associative network theory (Bower & Mayer, 1991; Forgas, 2000a).

In an attempt to reconcile the disparate findings regarding the relation of mood to the retrieval of information from long-term memory, Forgas (1995, 2000a) proposed the affect infusion model (AIM). According to this model, mood is only infused into a person's thinking under situations where elaboration and construction of knowledge is required. That is, one only recalls mood congruent information from long-term memory when open, constructive processes are required; thus the recall of mood congruent information will only affect social judgments (and presumably other types of cognition) under specified conditions. More specifically, the influence of mood on the content of one's thoughts varies based on the types of cognitive processing used. Two types of processes, direct access and motivated processing, do not result in mood congruent effects, while two other types of processing, heuristic and substantive processing, do.

Forgas (1995) proposed that neither direct nor motivated processing allows for the infusion of mood into thinking because neither type of processing requires open, constructive processing. That is, with direct processing, information is quickly recalled from long-term memory. This does not call for any construction of knowledge; therefore, there is no opportunity for mood to infuse thinking. With motivated processing, there are predetermined search patterns associated with motivational objectives, which again do not provide an opportunity for mood to infiltrate thinking. Motivated processing here refers to specific situations where there is pressure for a particular judgment to occur; this does not necessarily refer to instances where one has a particular goal (e.g., a goal to learn and understand).

In contrast, both heuristic processing and substantive processing are open and constructive, thus allowing mood to influence the content of judgments and thinking (Forgas, 1995). Forgas (2000a) described heuristic processing as involving minimal effort. This type of processing is used for simple or typical tasks of little relevance to the person. For heuristic processing, Forgas proposed that mood would infuse thinking because people would mistake their current mood as an evaluative reaction to the situation. This is in line with Schwarz and Clore's (1996) idea that affect serves as information about one's surroundings.

Substantive processing occurs when people are faced with novel tasks requiring them to learn new information or link prior knowledge to new information (Forgas, 2000a). The constructive nature of substantive processing allows one's current mood to infuse the thought process. That is, with the building and constructing of new information, a person is more likely to draw on cues from the environment including mood. Mood should also activate information in long-term memory, making the mood-related information more accessible in the constructive meaning making of the situation. These effects are more pronounced when extensive processing is required by the task or situation.

In addition to changing the content of thinking, AIM also suggests that affect can influence how one thinks (use of heuristic, top-down strategies versus attention to detail and the situation). These differences in how information is processed are consistent with the theories of both Bless (2000) and Fiedler (2000), which are discussed in the following section; therefore, details regarding the infusion of affect into how one thinks or approaches a situation will not be discussed in relation to the AIM model.

Affect and Processing of Information

A number of theories have been proposed relating moods to differences in how information is attended to and processed. Two predominant theories that serve as the basis for many current conceptions are the resource allocation model (Ellis & Ashbrook, 1988), which makes hypotheses regarding differing cognitive capacities based on affect, and the affect-as-information model (Schwarz, 1990), which makes hypotheses regarding motivational reasons for the differential effects of mood on cognitive processing.

The resource allocation model focuses on differences in cognitive capacity based on affect. This theory was initially developed to consider the effect of depressed mood on cognitive processing (Ellis & Ashbrook, 1988); however, the results have been replicated for both positive and negative moods (Ellis, Seibert, & Varner, 1995). The theory suggests that cognitive capacity is limited when one is in a depressed or happy mood state. In essence, being in a positive or negative mood results in task-irrelevant processing that clutters working memory, making it more difficult to attend to the current task. Thus, according to the resource allocation model, both positive and negative moods result in increased task-irrelevant thoughts, which in turn overload working memory functioning. The detrimental effects of mood on cognitive processing are expected for complex tasks that require high levels of cognitive processing; simple tasks that do not require extensive use of working memory should not be affected by one's current mood state. While the resource allocation model does not consider arousal in addition to valence, the suggestion that affect is only detrimental for tasks that require high levels of cognitive processing is consistent with Revelle and Loftus' (1990) argument that arousal facilitates working memory functioning for low-load tasks and hinders processing for high-load tasks. Therefore, we might expect that it is important to consider both arousal and valence in examining the way in which affect relates to cognitive processing.

More recent research regarding the relation of affect and cognitive processing has challenged the resource allocation model, particularly the idea that positive affect is detrimental to cognitive processing (e.g., Bless et al., 1996). That is, Bless et al. (1996) found that people in a positive mood used more heuristic processing and, as a result, actually performed better on a secondary task. This suggests that positive moods may actually be adaptive in terms of working memory functioning rather than maladaptive as is suggested by the resource allocation model. Bless et al. (1996) did not consider arousal, so it is not clear whether Revelle and Loftus' (1990) ideas regarding arousal are also brought into question.

A second prominent theory regarding the effect of mood on cognitive processing is Schwarz's (1990) affect-as-information theory. According to this theory, a negative mood state signals that there is a problem that needs to be addressed, which in turn leads to a focus on details (Schwarz, 1990; Schwarz & Clore, 1996). In contrast, a positive mood indicates that everything is fine resulting in heuristic processing of information. In other words, when a person is in a negative mood, he is more motivated to respond to the situation and is more likely to pay attention to the details in the situation whereas when a person is in a positive mood, he is less motivated to attend to the situation and will therefore use less effortful strategies such as general knowledge structures or schemas to interpret and react to the situation. This reliance on general knowledge structures under a positive mood is a result of an evolutionary bias suggesting that effort is not needed under a positive mood. Similar to the resource allocation model, the affect-as-information theory is not able to account for recent empirical findings (e.g., Bless et al., 1996).

More recently, researchers studying affect and cognition have sought to develop integrated models that account for the rather inconsistent results (Forgas, 2000b). In particular, two theories regarding the role of moods in cognitive processing present a more nuanced view, which can account for the diverse set of findings in the literature: Bless' (2000) mood-and-general-knowledge theory and Fiedler's (2000) dual-force model. As with the older theories in this field, both of these theories focus on the processing of information during a short, clearly defined situation. Furthermore, they focus exclusively on valence and do not consider the effect of arousal or the interactive affects of arousal and valence.

Bless (2000) developed his mood-and-general-knowledge theory based on the affect-as-information model and the failure of this model to fully explain empirical findings. The basic relation of moods to cognitive processing is the same as the affect-as-information model. Positive moods are associated with heuristic, top-down processing while negative moods are associated with more systematic, situation-specific processing. A major difference between these theories, however, is that Bless' theory does not assume, as does the affect-as-information theory, that people in a negative mood are motivated (and thus use adaptive processing) and those in a positive mood are unmotivated (and thus use maladaptive processing). Rather, Bless (2000) suggested that a positive mood signals that it is acceptable to rely on general knowledge structures because these structures are usually useful in benign situations. In contrast, a negative mood suggests that there is a problem and problems usually differ from the norm; thus, a negative mood indicates that one should focus on the specific situation and not rely on general knowledge structures. As this reliance on general knowledge structures under a positive mood is not due to lack of motivation, the individual is likely to use those saved resources for processing other aspects of the situation. Bless (2000) also suggested that although a happy mood leads to reliance on general knowledge structures such as scripts, when a person detects that information is not consistent with the script, she will focus on the inconsistent information. That is, the mood-and-general-knowledge theory suggests that students working on a task in a positive mood will use general knowledge structures when they are adaptive, but that they can be flexible in their thinking and focus on the details of the situation when necessary.

Another theory, which makes similar predictions regarding the potential benefits of positive mood, is Fiedler's (2000) dual-process model. Fiedler based this model on Piaget's notions of accommodation or assimilation; with accommodation processes focusing more attention on the external environment and information available there and assimilation giving priority to the use of internal knowledge structures to understand new information. In terms of the dual-process model, accommodation is associated with negative moods and a general aversive or avoidance set while assimilation is associated with positive moods and a more appetitive or approach set. The basis for this distinction parallels the original affect-as-information model (Schwarz, 1990) as well as a revised mood-and-general-knowledge account (Bless, 2000), in that accommodation is associated with a focus on the specific details of the current structure (i.e., stimulus driven) while assimilation is associated with general knowledge structures (i.e., knowledge driven).

Fiedler (2000) suggested that every cognitive process can be described as involving accommodation, assimilation, or both. With accommodation, the focus is on the stimulus input from the environment. In this case, it is more important to attend to the external stimulus information in order to adapt appropriately. Negative moods signal that adaptation or regulation is not progressing appropriately and that there may be a need to attend to the environmental stimulus or external information more carefully in order to adapt appropriately. In other words, the internal knowledge structures may not be sufficient to guide adaptation and that some change is needed based on external information. Assimilation, on the other hand, focuses on applying internal prior knowledge structures to the world. In this sense, the individual moves beyond the stimulus provided by the environment by applying prior knowledge and actively generating new ideas based on the prior knowledge. In this case, a positive mood signals that adaptation is proceeding smoothly and that internal knowledge is appropriate for generating action. In order to understand how positive versus negative moods might impact performance on a particular task, it is important to understand whether accommodation or assimilation processes are needed to complete the task. A negative mood should be beneficial for tasks requiring more accommodation processes while a positive mood should be beneficial for tasks requiring more assimilation processes.

Within the field of social psychology, there has been a large emphasis on the role of negative affect in cognitive processing. And, while current theories consider the role of both positive and negative affect on cognitive processing, many of these were originally designed to account for the effects of depressed mood on cognitive processing (e.g., Ellis & Ashbrook, 1988). Other social psychologists have focused more exclusively on the role of positive affect and cognitive functioning. For instance, Isen (Isen, 1984; Isen, Daubman, & Nowicki, 1987) conducted a number of studies examining how positive mood influences problem solving and cognitive processing. More recently, Fredrickson (1998, 2001) proposed the broaden-and-build model of positive emotions in which positive emotions are associated with a broadening of both thought and action. Accordingly, we briefly describe the broaden-and-build model of positive emotions and consider links among this recent conception of positive emotions, Isen's work on positive affect, and current models linking affect more generally to cognitive processing.

Fredrickson's (1998, 2001) broaden-and-build model was designed to account for positive emotions. In particular, she argued that positive emotions are associated with the broadening of possible thought-action repertoires. That is, positive emotions should be associated with the pursuit of novel, creative, unscripted thoughts and actions. For instance, joy is associated with the urge to play and explore. Play and exploration are associated with a broad variety of action tendencies and therefore are associated with the broadening of possible thought-action tendencies. Furthermore, Fredrickson argued that play helps to build cognitive, physical, and social skills. Thus, joy, as well as other positive emotions such as interest, love, and contentment, broadens one's thought-action repertoire and builds cognitive, physical, and social resources. In line with Fredrickson's predictions, Pekrun et al. (2002) found that positive academic emotions such as enjoyment and hope are associated with more effort, deeper cognitive engagement, more self-regulated learning, and less irrelevant thinking in academic settings.

Fredrickson's (1998, 2001) model in which positive emotions serve to broaden one's thoughts is also consistent with Bless' (2000) notion that a person in a positive mood relies on general knowledge structures. The broaden-and-build model also parallels Fiedler's (2000) suggestion that positive mood and assimilation processes can lead to active generation of new ideas. Finally, the broaden-and-build model of positive emotions ties in nicely with Isen's (e.g., Isen et al., 1987) work linking positive moods to more creative problem solving. That is, if a person experiences a positive emotion such as joy, which is linked to exploration and play, it seems probable that a person experiencing joy would also be more likely to generate novel solutions to various situations, thus enhancing creative problem solving. Recently, Isen and her colleagues (Ashby, Isen, & Turken, 1999) suggested that positive affect is associated with increased dopamine levels and that the differences in cognitive processing associated with positive affect may be a result of the increased dopamine. Thus, there may also be some biological basis for the links be-

tween affect, particularly positive affect, and cognitive processing. Furthermore, Ashby et al. (1999) suggested that the relation of negative affect to cognitive processing does not involve the same underlying biological basis. This
adds further support for the differentiation in the way in which positive versus negative affect relates to cognitive processing, as suggested by the recent
revisions to the theories reviewed here.

IMPLICATIONS FOR ACADEMIC CONTEXTS

Thus far we have discussed theoretical models linking affect and cognitive
processing. These models, however, were primarily developed using typical
cognitive and social psychology experimental tasks and may not be readily
applicable to academic contexts. For instance, in his development of the
mood-and-general-knowledge theory, Bless (2000) drew from studies conducted in a variety of paradigms including mood and stereotyping (e.g.,
Bodenhausen, Kramer, & Susser, 1994), mood and dual processing (e.g.,
Bless et al., 1996), and mood and heuristic processing (e.g., Mackie & Worth,
1989). These tasks do not closely resemble academic tasks.

For instance, in one experimental study, Bodenhausen et al. (1994) induced college students into positive and neutral moods and examined how
mood influenced their social judgments. More specifically, participants were
asked to read a paragraph-long case (involving either a student assault in a
dorm room or cheating incident) and make a judgment about the guilt or in-
nocence of the perpetrator (who was portrayed as either representing a stereotyped group or a neutral group). Another experimental study conducted by
Bless et al. (1996) examined the effect of mood on heuristic dual processing.
In this study, participants completed two tasks simultaneously. For one task,
they were given a worksheet with several rows of the letters "d" and "p" with
different numbers of dashes. They were instructed to circle the d every time it
appeared with two dashes. They completed this task while also listening to a
tape-recorded story about a common occurrence (e.g., a call from a public
telephone booth) that had typical and atypical features. After a break, they
were tested on their recall of the features of the story. Similarly, Mackie and
Worth (1989) examined the effect of mood on heuristic processing using a
persuasion paradigm. Participants were induced into a positive or neutral
mood and were exposed to a persuasive speech (24 lines long) with either a
strong or weak argument about governmental controls to limit acid rain.
They were either given 65 seconds to read the speech or given unlimited time
to read the speech and then asked to complete a questionnaire assessing their
attitudes about acid rain and recall as much information as they could about
the speech. Although students do read texts and are asked to recall them,

most of these tasks differ in a number of ways from the types of tasks used in academic contexts.

The other theories reviewed here also tend to rely on tasks that are fairly far removed from typical academic contexts. For instance, in addition to the emphasis on social psychological paradigms, Bower (1981), Ellis and Ashbrook (1988), Fiedler (2000), and Forgas (2000a) all relied, at least in part, on research involving the recall of word lists under different experimentally induced mood conditions. These examples of the types of tasks and the contexts for the experiments suggest that there may be some difficulty in applying the research conducted in social psychology settings to students' learning in school. First, most of the studies were conducted in laboratories and may not necessarily translate to unstructured classroom contexts. Second, most of the studies were conducted with college students and may not account for developmental differences. Third, and most importantly, the tasks are fairly different from the tasks that students are typically asked to complete in academic settings. For instance, while students may be asked to read persuasive arguments or to recall a story or even to recall word lists in some classrooms, the school tasks are typically much longer in duration than the social psychology tasks. In addition the learning, instruction, and assessment sessions often occur over the course of several weeks rather than the typical 30–60 minute psychology experiment session. Finally, the academic tasks are often focused on content domains where students will have at least some familiarity with and some relevant prior content knowledge.

Unfortunately, few educational psychologists have attempted to apply these affect and cognitive processing theories based on the social psychological research to typical classrooms. Aside from test anxiety, the relationship between affect (moods and emotions) and cognitive processing for academic tasks has been largely neglected (Pekrun et al., 2002). Accordingly, in our attempt to suggest implications for classroom learning, we focus on some preliminary work conducted in our laboratory regarding the relation between affect and cognitive processing on two types of tasks: (a) conceptual change in science understanding and (b) mathematics. For each type of task, we then review relevant research linking affect and cognitive processing in these two domains. Finally, we analyze this research based on the social psychological models discussed previously.

In describing our work, we focus on affect more generally and do not differentiate between moods and emotions. This decision was made because the measures were taken to assess affect during the task, suggesting that emotions were measured rather than mood because there was a specific referent; however, our measures assessed general valence (positive/negative) and not specific emotions making it difficult for us to talk about these in terms of specific emotions. In terms of arousal, some of our measures assessed both low and high arousal in the same measure (e.g., the conceptual change studies and graphing study). These measures do not allow us to distinguish between activation and valence. In another study, we included separate measures for valence and arousal allowing us to consider whether arousal is an important predictor of cognitive processing. However, in interpreting these later results, it is important to keep in mind the theories reviewed do not adequately account for arousal differences.

Affect and Conceptual Change in Science Understanding

Conceptual change in science is a specific and narrow aspect of science learning. Nevertheless, consideration of the role of affect for conceptual change in science understanding may be useful in applying the theories discussed previously to a specific academic context. That is, considering how affect relates to conceptual change in science understanding can help us to understand and evaluate the usefulness of the theories in understanding the role of affect for cognitive processing in academic contexts.

In our laboratory, we have conducted a number of studies linking motivation to conceptual change in college students' understanding of projectile motion. As part of this work, two studies (Linnenbrink & Pintrich, 2002b) investigated the relation between affect and students' learning as a result of reading a passage on Newtonian physics designed to alter their prior misconceptions about projectile notion. In particular, we asked students to report on their affect while reading the passage and then examined the relation of this affect to their change in understanding of projectile motion (as indexed by a pre and post assessment) and the types of strategies that they used while reading the passage. The affective measures distinguished between positive and negative valence but included both high and low activation items on each scale.

In terms of conceptual change, there was a significant positive correlation between positive affect and performance on the post-test exam ($r = .22, p < .05$) for study 1; however, further regression analyses with pre-test exam included as a control revealed that positive affect was not significantly related to post-test exam performance ($\beta = .06, p > .05$). Furthermore, for study 2, the correlation between positive affect and post-test exam was not significant ($r = .11, p > .05$), nor was there a significant relation once pre-test exam was included as a control ($\beta = .04, p > .05$). This suggests that while positive affect may be associated with enhanced achievement on the post-test, it is not linked with increased conceptual change. That is, feeling positively while reading the physics passage was not associated with a significant change in understanding of Newtonian physics.

We also examined how positive affect related to adaptive strategy use in order to gain a broader picture regarding the links between positive affect and cognitive processing (Linnenbrink & Pintrich, 2002b). For elaborative strategy use, there was a significant positive relation for study 1 (r = .20, $p <$ .05); however, the correlation was not significant for study 2 (r = .16, $p >$ .05). Similarly, metacognitive strategy use was not significantly related to positive affect in study 1 (r = .13, $p >$ .05) but there was a significant positive relation for study 2 (r = .33, $p <$ .001). Thus, the findings linking positive affect to strategy use were somewhat small and inconsistent between the two studies.

For negative affect, we found that students with negative affect consistently scored worse on the post-test measure of physics understanding (study 1: r = −.21, $p <$ .05; study 2: r = −.36, $p <$ .001, Linnenbrink & Pintrich, 2002b). However, it was not clear whether negative affect was related to conceptual change. In particular, additional regression analyses designed to examine the change in understanding of Newtonian physics (pre-test score included as a control) showed no significant relation between negative affect and the post-test measure of physics understanding for study 1 (β = −.05, $p >$ .05) but did show a significant negative relation for study 2 (β = −.34, $p \le$ .001). Thus, while the findings suggest that negative affect may be detrimental for conceptual change in physics, further investigation is needed to clarify these findings. In terms of strategy use, negative affect was unrelated to metacognitive (study 1: r = −.03, $p >$ .05; study 2: r = −.06, $p >$ .05) and elaborative strategy use (study 1: r = −.10, $p >$ .05; study 2: r = −.10, $p >$ .05). Thus, while negative affect did not seem to change the types of strategies that students used, it was associated with poorer performance on the post-test measure of understanding projectile motion and seemed to be associated with lower levels of conceptual change.

We are unaware of other empirical research linking affect to conceptual change in science understanding. Therefore, we focus on the interpretation of the results from our laboratory. Overall, we found that positive affect was unrelated to conceptual change but was at least moderately associated with adaptive strategy use and processing. Furthermore, negative affect was either unrelated or hindered conceptual change but did not seem to alter students' strategy use.

However, before we interpret our findings based on the theoretical models, it is important to keep a few limitations in mind. First, our measure of affect was not clearly a measure of moods or emotions. Therefore, we need to use some caution in evaluating the efficacy of the psychological models based on mood to our findings. Second, our reliance on self-report measures to assess affect does not parallel much of the experimental work used to develop these models in which mood was manipulated. It is possible that students may not accurately report on their own affect or that their reports are altered by their performance on the post-test exam such that students who felt they did poorly may report that they had higher levels of negative affect during the task when in fact the high levels of negative affect emerged as they completed the exam. The use of self-report measures is also problematic when linking affect to strategy use in that some of the shared variance may be due to the common methodology (self-report) rather than a relation between affect and strategy use (Winne & Perry, 2000). Finally, similar to social psychology research, our studies were conducted with college students for a relatively short time period (approximately 30–45 minutes). However, unlike the social psychology research, our work examines students' learning of an important concept taught in schools, that of Newtonian physics. Given the scarcity of research linking affect to cognitive processing in academic domains, it seems worthwhile to examine the findings in light of the different theoretical approaches despite the aforementioned limitations.

We begin by considering whether our findings are consistent with the cognitive processing theories of affect and cognition and then consider how the relation between affect and storage of information might play out in a conceptual change context. The first cognitive processing theory we consider is Bless' (2000) mood-and-general-knowledge theory. Overall, the results are not entirely in line with what might be expected based on Bless' model. Bless (2000) suggested that under a positive mood, a person would use heuristic processing unless she detects a difference between the information being taken in and her general schema. In this specific instance, the person would then attend to the new information making it more likely that a change in the general schema based on the new information would occur because the general schema is already activated and the person is attending to the difference between the new information and the existing schema. This activation of the prior schema coupled with attention to new information should facilitate conceptual change. However, our empirical results do not provide evidence to support this claim.

Nevertheless, there is some support for Bless' (2000) theory in terms of cognitive strategy use and positive affect. Our results for elaborative strategy use suggest that students with positive affect are broadening their perspective, which is also in line with Bless' theory. In addition, the positive relation between positive affect and metacognitive strategy use for study 2 supports Bless' idea that positive affect does not signal a lack of motivation, as was suggested by earlier theories (e.g., affect-as-information). Rather, students with positive affect seem to be willing to engage in effortful strategies; they report actively planning, monitoring, and evaluating their understanding of the reading and also report experiencing positive affect. The relation of positive affect to strategy use but not conceptual change suggests that affect plays a role in motivated processing. Positive affect may enhance students' willingness to persist and engage in a task, which may lead to the use of higher levels strategies. It is unclear, however, why positive affect did not enhance conceptual change when it was associated with higher-level strategies, as one would expect that the use of higher-level cognitive strategies should enhance conceptual change.

In terms of negative affect, Bless (2000) suggested that a negative mood focuses the person on the details of the situation and does not activate a general schema making it unlikely that the new information would be related to prior schemas. Thus, while a person in a negative mood may be more likely to process the new information because they are focused on the details of the situation, it is not clear whether this would relate to conceptual change in that prior knowledge structures are not activated and may therefore be less likely to be altered based on the new information. Nevertheless, the empirical findings from our laboratory suggest that negative affect may be detrimental for conceptual change. Furthermore, we found that negative affect was not related to strategy use. This questions the assumption that a negative mood leads to higher levels of processing. However, given the mixed nature of our findings, these results must be replicated before drawing strong conclusions regarding the relation of affect to conceptual change in science.

Our findings can also be interpreted using Fiedler's (2000) model, which stresses accommodation and assimilation processes and parallels the research on these processes for conceptual change. Fiedler (2000) suggested that assimilation, which is associated with positive affect, involves the application of internal knowledge structures to the external environment. In this sense, a person in a positive mood should use prior knowledge (including prior misconceptions) to interpret new information, which may lead to the incorporation of new information into existing knowledge structures rather than the altering of knowledge structures. In this sense, one would not expect positive affect to be beneficial for conceptual change and it might be detrimental. This interpretation is somewhat consistent with our finding that positive affect was unrelated to conceptual change in physics understanding, although we might have expected a negative relation.

In contrast, accommodation processes are associated with negative moods and could lead to more conceptual change or revision of internal knowledge structures. In fact, one of the key instructional strategies suggested for fostering conceptual change in much of the conceptual change literature is the induction of cognitive dissonance, which generates at least some modicum of negative affect, as students are shown that their prior knowledge cannot help them understand the phenomena. However, the two studies conducted in our laboratory suggested that negative affect was either unrelated or negatively related to conceptual change. This discrepancy between theory and empirical data needs to be further considered in future research in order to better understand the role that negative affect plays in the conceptual change process.

Finally, the results for positive affect can be interpreted based on the broaden-and-build perspective (Fredrickson, 1998, 2001). If positive affect broadens a student's perspective, the student should be more open to changing her understanding. That is, the positive emotions may signal that broad, expansive processing is appropriate and thus make the student more open to accepting new information. Indeed, the results suggest that students in a positive mood may have been more likely to elaborate on the information, suggesting a broadening of one's perspective. Nevertheless, we would have expected that positive affect would also lead to conceptual change based on Fredrickson's model and our results do not support this idea.

Overall, while the three theories presented here (broaden-and-build, mood-and-general-knowledge structure, and dual-process model) differ somewhat in terms of predictions regarding conceptual change, there are important similarities to consider as well. For instance, all three theories suggest that positive affect leads to more expansive, broader thinking. However, they differ somewhat in terms of the simultaneous activation of prior knowledge and attention to external information, which is important to stimulate conceptual change. For instance, Bless' (2000) theory suggests that prior knowledge is activated under positive affect but that prior knowledge can also be linked to external information, especially when a discrepancy is detected. In contrast, Fiedler's (2000) theory suggests that external stimuli are attended to under negative affect but that this may also relate to some links with prior knowledge. In this way, different predictions regarding conceptual change can be made based on the mood-and-general knowledge structures theory versus the dual-processing theory. However, given the inconsistent nature of our findings, it is difficult to provide support to one theory over another in terms of explaining the relation of affect to conceptual change in science understanding.

Additional research examining conceptual change and affect could help to clarify some of these ideas. In conducting this research, it will be important to consider the possibility that positive affect is useful for general concept learning but may not be useful for conceptual change due to the reliance on assimilation rather than accommodation. In this way, both Fiedler's (2000) and Bless' (2000) theories could be accurate. It could be that positive affect is generally beneficial but that under situations requiring conceptual change, positive affect may both enhance (based on the mood-and-general-knowledge structure theory) and hinder (based on the dual-process theory) cognitive processing resulting in no clear relation between positive affect and conceptual change, as was found in our studies.

In addition to considering how affect relates to cognitive processing for conceptual change in science understanding, it is also important to consider how affect might be linked to the storage and retrieval of information for conceptual change in science understanding. Although we are unaware of any research speaking directly to this issue, we use Forgas' (1995, 2000a) AIM model to discuss how affect might infuse thinking during the conceptual change process. As noted earlier, Forgas (2002a) suggested that mood may be encoded during storage of information when heuristic or substantive processing is used. It seems likely that conceptual change may involve substantive processing; that is, a student who is undergoing conceptual change is likely to be processing information from a novel or new task (designed to initiate conceptual change) and will therefore be building and constructing new knowledge, as well as linking this to or altering prior knowledge. Forgas (2002a) argued that when new knowledge is constructed, it is more likely that a mood state would be encoded along with the relevant information. Therefore, a congruency between the mood state of encoding and one's current mood state should facilitate retrieval.

Overall, for conceptual change in science understanding, it is likely that affect plays a role both in encoding and retrieval of information as well as the way in which information is processed. For encoding and retrieval, a match between encoding state and retrieval state should facilitate retrieval as new knowledge is constructed and may thus include an affective component (Forgas, 2000a). In terms of processing information, it seems that a positive mood may facilitate conceptual change in that students may be more likely to try to alter their schemas when they are not successful in applying them (Bless, 2000) and because positive affect promotes broad, heuristic processing (Bless, 2000; Fredrickson, 2001), which may facilitate the learning of larger concepts as opposed to small, unconnected, discrete facts or pieces of information. However, it also seems plausible that the tendency to rely on prior knowledge when in a positive mood (Fiedler, 2000) may hinder the conceptual change process as new information may be interpreted based on existing knowledge structures. For negative affect, the picture is also unclear. For instance, negative affect may interfere with the conceptual change process by focusing students on the details of the task (Bless, 2000). However, it also seems plausible that negative affect may enhance conceptual change by stimulating accommodation rather than assimilation (Fiedler, 2000). It is clear that additional research on the way in which affect influences conceptual change is needed.

Affect and Learning Mathematics

In this section, we focus on learning mathematics, as this represents a somewhat different process than conceptual change in science understanding. In particular, we review findings from our laboratory on the links between general affect and learning mathematics for upper elementary and middle school students (e.g., Linnenbrink & Pintrich, 2003). We also discuss a number of studies that link affect to mathematics understanding and problem solving from the extant literature. Finally, in addition to considering the way that affect is linked to the processing of information for mathematics learning, we also consider how affect is linked to memory processes.

In a study conducted with middle school students, we examined the relation between students' affect and their scores on a computer math activity (Linnenbrink & Pintrich, 2003, study 1). In particular, middle school students worked in groups to learn how to solve number sequences. They then completed a similar series of math problems on the computer for 15 minutes. Immediately following the completion of the math problems, they reported on their current affect using single item indicators (sad–happy, tense–calm, tired–excited). Finally, after completing a series of word-recognition tasks, students were asked to report on their effort regulation and cognitive regulation during the computer math task.

Interestingly, the three indicators of affect (sad–happy, tense–calm, and tired–excited) were unrelated to students' scores on the math exam. However, affect was significantly related to students' effort and cognitive regulation during the math exam. For effort regulation, students who reported being more excited than tired reported higher levels of persistence even when they did not want to work on the task ($\beta = .22, p < .001$). For cognitive regulation, students who reported feeling more happy than sad ($\beta = .13, p < .05$) and more excited than tired ($\beta = .16, p < .01$) also reported that they planned, monitored, and checked their work as they completed the number sequences on the computer. What is interesting about these findings is that both valence (sad–happy) and arousal (tired–excited) were predictors of students' cognitive regulation while only arousal (tired–excited) significantly predicted effort regulation. This may mean that arousal is important in terms of motivation to engage in the task while both valence and arousal are important in terms of the quality of engagement (e.g., using higher level strategies). It is somewhat surprising, however, that the other measure of arousal, calm–tense, was unrelated to either type of regulation.

When interpreting these results, it is important to keep in mind that there were several limitations in the methodology used in this study. First, the affect measure was designed to assess students' affect while working on the computer math activity, but their affect may have changed as they completed the computer math test as a result of how well they perceived they were doing on the math problems. Second, the use of self-reported affect and self-reported regulation leaves one open to the possibility of a method bias, where shared variance may have more to do with similarities in measurement than with similarities in the underlying constructs (Winne & Perry, 2000). Third, the use of bipolar affect measures may be problematic if both ends of the scale (e.g., sad and happy) relate in the same way to the outcome. For instance, if both sadness and happiness are negative predictors of math performance, the use of a bipolar measure would not be able to detect a significant relation and would instead suggest that sad–happy and math performance were unrelated.

This third limitation was of particular concern in the current study in that all three measures of affect were unrelated to students' math performance. However, when we split the sample based on the bipolar indicators so that the scale assessed either end of the bipolar measure (e.g., neutral to happy or neutral to sad) for each of the three affect measures, the correlations between the affect measures and math performance were not significant suggesting that the use of the bipolar measure did not limit our ability to detect a significant relation. Nevertheless, it is important to note that for sad–happy, while the correlation was not significant, the correlations for sad and happy were both in the negative direction; this suggests that future studies may want to avoid using bipolar measures, especially when examining the relation between affect and math performance.

In another study conducted with upper elementary students (fifth and sixth graders) during a 6-week math unit on reading and interpreting graphs, we investigated the relation between students' affect and their learning during the unit (Linnenbrink & Pintrich, 2003, study 2). In order to examine how affect during the entire unit related to how much students learned in the unit, we regressed their post-test math score on self-reported positive and negative affect during the 6-week math unit. The measures of positive and negative affect included both high activation (e.g., energetic, agitated) and low activation (e.g., calm, sad) indicators of affect and asked students to rate how they felt during the entire mathematics unit. Therefore, they serve as indicators of valence but not arousal. The scales were initially designed to assess both valence and arousal, but the four dimensions did not separate in exploratory factor analyses, suggesting that younger children have a difficult time differentiating, or at least reporting, valence versus arousal. We also examined the relation of affect reported at the post-test to a follow-up measure of achievement given 6 weeks after the end of the unit and two self-reported measures of strategy use (effort and cognitive regulation).

Surprisingly, students' reports of both positive affect ($\beta = -.24, p < .01$) and negative affect ($\beta = -.30, p < .01$) were negatively related to how much students learned during the math unit and how much they retained 6 weeks later (positive affect: $\beta = -.22, p < .01$; negative affect: $\beta = -.41, p < .001$). For strategy use, positive affect was associated with higher levels of effort regulation ($\beta = .22, p < .01$) and cognitive regulation ($\beta = .53, p < .001$) while negative affect was unrelated.

It is somewhat surprising that positive affect was linked to higher levels of effort and cognitive regulation during the math unit, but this association did not seem to be beneficial for how much students learned during the math activity. In fact, positive affect was related to lower levels of achievement at the end of the unit and lower levels of retention 6 weeks later. One possibility is that the findings for strategy use may be influenced by the methodology used since both strategy use and affect were assessed using self-report measures. However, it is also possible that positive affect has a different relation with effort and cognitive regulation versus actual learning and achievement. For instance, positive affect may serve as a motivational tool, such that students who feel positively are more willing to engage and persist and even more willing to use effortful strategies such as those required for cognitive regulation. However, there may be another component of positive affect that is detrimental for learning mathematics in that it interferes with the storage or processing of the information. In this way, positive affect may help with engagement and strategy use, but if it interferes with cognitive processing, it will still hinder learning. This possibility needs to be explored in future research where either affect is experimentally manipulated or effort and cognitive regulation are not assessed with self-report measures in order to eliminate the possibility that the findings are based on a mono-method bias in assessment.

In summary, our work on the relation between affect and students' learning of mathematics material is consistent for effort and cognitive regulation but not for math performance or learning (Linnenbrink & Pintrich, 2003). As noted previously, it is possible that the discrepancy in the findings may be linked to the differences in the measurement of affect, although follow-up analyses indicated that this was not the case suggesting that we must consider other possibilities. For instance, the discrepant findings may have occurred because the tasks used were very different and the duration and context of the study differed.

Given these differences, it is somewhat surprising that affect did not alter students' performance on the math exam in study 1 since it was more similar both in terms of the task and the design to typical social psychology experiments. That is, students were tested outside of the regular classroom and asked to respond to tasks in an atypical manner (using a computer to record responses). Furthermore, the task was relatively short in duration, lasting 15 minutes. In contrast, study 2 was more similar to a typical classroom. The study took place during a 6-week math unit and students completed the posttest and follow-up tests as part of their regular classroom work. Furthermore, the affect measure was more general in that it was designed to assess affect during the 6-week math unit and examine the effects of that general affect or mood on their learning during the unit. In this sense, the relation of affect to learning was expected to take place over a longer time period and may not have influenced cognitive processing at the same level as was assessed in the first study. We consider these differences in applying the theoretical models to our findings.

It is also interesting that while study 1 and study 2 differed greatly in duration, the findings for engagement, as measured by effort regulation and cognitive regulation, were similar. This suggests that the differences in findings between the studies may have had more to do with the types of tasks and processing of the information than students' motivation or willingness to engage. This similarity across studies in terms of engagement but discrepancy in terms of learning and performance needs to be more closely examined in future research.

Given the discrepancy in our work and some of the methodological limitations, it is important to consider other work on the relation between students' affect and learning in mathematics. Although there is not extensive research in this area, a few studies are relevant. For instance, Bryan and Bryan (1991) conducted a series of studies with upper elementary students with and without learning disabilities. They induced half of the students into a positive mood and half received no mood induction. Students were then asked to work on 50 subtraction and addition problems for 5 minutes. They found that students in a positive mood completed more problems correctly than students in the neutral mood. There was, however, no significant difference in the number of problems completed between the positive mood group and the control group. The authors replicated the first study with junior and senior high school students and found a similar pattern of results. Thus, the results from this study suggest that positive mood is beneficial for mathematics performance, at least in terms of computation. However, in a similar study, Yasutake and Bryan (1995) induced middle school students into a positive mood versus a neutral mood and asked them to complete a mathematics calculation subtest of the Woodcock–Johnson battery for 15 minutes. They found no significant effect of the mood condition on students' performance. Thus, the findings from the Bryan and Bryan (1991) study were not replicated, suggesting that the pattern linking positive affect to computation is not entirely consistent or may vary based on the length of the study (5 vs. 15 minutes).

Two studies also examined middle students' learning of shapes and symbols. While these tasks are not directly related to mathematics computation, they seem relevant in terms of understanding geometry and are therefore discussed here. In the same study described previously, Yasutake and Bryan (1995) compared middle school students' performance, working under a positive versus neutral mood condition, on a 2-minute task in which they needed to learn combinations of symbols and shapes and then make associations (Coding subtest from the Performance section of the WISC-R). The authors found that students in the positive mood condition outperformed students in the neutral mood condition. Masters, Barden, and Ford (1979) conducted a similar study examining how 4-year-old children performed on a shape discrimination task under three different mood conditions (positive, neutral, negative) and two different activation levels (active, passive). Children worked on the shape discrimination task until it was mastered (they could attempt up to 10 trial blocks consisting of 12 problems each). Preschool children induced into a positive mood learned the shape-discrimination task more quickly than children in a negative or neutral mood, as did those induced into an active rather than passive state. There was also an interaction of valence and arousal, with children in the negative mood condition taking longer to master the task when they were induced into a passive rather than active state. Taken together, these results suggest that positive moods are beneficial for learning shape discrimination tasks whereas negative moods are detrimental, especially when arousal is high.

Finally, given the large emphasis on problem solving as part of the mathematics curriculum, research relating problem solving and mood seems relevant to this discussion. For instance, Isen et al. (1987) examined college students' performance on creative problem-solving tasks. In a series of studies, participants completed two types of creative problems solving tasks, Duncker's (1945) candle task and the Remote Associates Test, both of which lasted between 10 and 15 minutes under a variety of induced mood conditions. The results from these studies suggest that positive mood facilitates creative problem solving in comparison to a neutral or negative mood, but there are not differences in problem solving between negative and neutral moods. Finally, some of the studies included an arousal condition (exercise). Students in the positive mood condition scored higher than those in the arousal condition, while there was no difference between the arousal condition and the neutral mood condition. This suggests that valence, but not arousal, is important in terms of students' creative problem solving.

In summary, the research relating positive and negative affect to mathematics learning is not consistent. This may be due in part, however, to the broad range of tasks that fall under the purview of mathematics education as well as the context of the study, including the duration of the task. Therefore, in attempting to apply social psychological theories, we consider that the different tasks may require different processes and, accordingly, positive and negative affect may hinder or enhance cognitive processing in different situations. We also discuss whether differences in the contexts and lengths of tasks may help to account for the discrepancies in the results.

Bless (2000), Fiedler (2000), and Fredrickson (2001) all suggested that positive moods should result in broad, heuristic processing. Fiedler (2000) further suggested that positive affect is beneficial when active generation occurs. In terms of mathematics learning, we would therefore expect positive affect to enhance learning and performance when tasks require a broad perspective or active generation. For instance, learning and distinguishing shapes may require a broader perspective in that considering the whole shape rather than focusing on details of particular aspects of the shape may enhance performance. Furthermore, this information needs to be linked to prior knowledge, so Fiedler's suggestion that positive affect helps to activate prior knowledge should also enhance performance. Therefore, the empirical research suggesting that positive affect enhances shape discrimination (Masters et al., 1979; Yasutake & Bryan, 1995) lends support to these theories. In addition, consistent with Isen et al.'s (1987) findings, positive affect should enhance problem solving, particularly creative problem solving in that positive affect should help students move away from the details of the task and take a broader, perhaps more creative perspective.

In addition, we would expect that positive affect would enhance the interpretation or reading of graphs. That is, when interpreting graphs, students are often asked to look at general patterns, a process which should be facilitated by positive affect. However, the results from our research (Linnenbrink & Pintrich, 2003, study 2) suggest the positive affect hinders students' reading and interpretation of graphs. This unexpected finding may be because students in our study may have needed to use both heuristic and detailed-processing, as the types of tasks falling under the purview of graphing our quite broad. However, if this were the case, we would have expected positive affect to be unrelated to learning, as it might have enhanced learning for some aspects and hindered it for others.

Another possibility, is that our study assessed affect during a 6-week unit and looked at learning over 6 weeks while the prior studies and the studies on which the theories were developed assessed affect during a relatively short duration. Furthermore, we used measures of self-reported affect while prior research has manipulated mood. Thus, while our results regarding the relation between positive affect and graphing cannot be easily interpreted under the existing theories, they also differ in a number of ways from prior research suggesting that a variety of factors may account for the discrepancy. Nevertheless, we should note that our study on mathematics and graphing examined student learning in real school contexts; thus, in trying to understand how affect influences learning in school, the results may be quite relevant.

The results for computation and number sequences are also difficult to interpret in terms of the affect and cognitive processing theories, in part, because the findings are not consistent. In particular, Bryan and Bryan (1991) reported that positive moods enhanced performance on computation problems while Yasutake and Bryan (1995) and Linnenbrink and Pintrich (2003, study 1) found no relation between affect and performance on solving number sequences. One possible explanation for these discrepancies is the duration of time spent on the task. Participants in Bryan and Bryan's (1991) study had 5 minutes to complete the task while participants in the other two studies had 15 minutes. While time does differ among these studies, it seems unlikely that a 10-minute difference could account for the discrepant findings. Based on the theories presented in this chapter, it also seems plausible that the results might be mixed or inconsistent. That is, for typical number sequences or computation problems that follow the general patterns students have previously seen in math, positive affect may be beneficial in that students can activate the basic script for solving the problem (Bless, 2000) and it may be easier for students to access basic number facts to aid in solving the problems (Fiedler, 2000). Furthermore, the use of basic scripts should reduce the cognitive load making it easier for students to complete a series of numbers in the sequence or solve multi-digit computation problems in working memory. A positive mood may not, however, be beneficial when the number pattern does not follow the basic pattern that matches the activated schema or when a computation problem is unfamiliar. In this case, the student may take longer to solve the pattern because she must first try the pattern or solution suggested by the schema and then try other patterns when this one was not successful.

The relation of negative affect to mathematics learning and performance should also vary depending on the type of task involved. For instance, we would expect negative affect to be beneficial for detail-oriented tasks, as negative affect should focus students on the appropriate aspects of the task. That is, both Fiedler (2000) and Bless (2000) suggested that negative affect should focus students on the details of a particular task or situation and Fiedler further noted that negative affect is beneficial for processing new stimuli.

In terms of mathematics, we would expect that negative affect might be particularly beneficial for computation problems, in which students must focus on the details of processing each aspect of the problem. For instance, a student in a negative mood may be more successful on unusual, atypical number patterns as he will begin by focusing on the details of the pattern and may easily detect the pattern based on this focus. This notion is not clearly supported by the empirical data; however, the findings also do not clearly refute this idea. That is, Bryan and his colleagues (Bryan & Bryan, 1991; Yasutake & Bryan, 1995) did not examine how negative mood conditions related to computation, and Linnenbrink and Pintrich (2003, study 1) found no significant relation between negative affect and performance on number sequences. One possibility is that while negative affect may focus students on the details, there is a cost to this focus that may be detrimental for overall performance. That is, a focus on details may overwhelm working memory as suggested by Ellis and Ashbrook (1988). Indeed, in a study conducted with college students, we found that negative affect was associated with lower levels of working memory functioning (Linnenbrink, Ryan, & Pintrich, 1999).

Negative affect should be detrimental for tasks such as problem solving and shape discrimination in that a focus on details may distract students from the broader perspective. While this idea is supported in terms of shape discrimination (Masters et al., 1979), it is not supported by Isen et al.'s (1987) study on problem solving in which the negative and neutral mood conditions did not significantly differ. For graphing, a focus on details may be beneficial in certain situations, such as plotting data on graphs, calculating statistics, or interpreting misleading graphs. In addition, if students do not have prior experience with graphs, a focus on the new stimuli, which Fiedler (2000) suggested is associated with negative moods, should facilitate learning. In this case, it is not necessary to link the new information to prior information, as students may not have relevant prior information to which they would link the new information. However, our research suggests that negative affect is negatively related to reading and interpreting graphs (Linnenbrink & Pintrich, 2003, study 2). As noted previously, however, our tasks were rather complex and occurred over a 6-week period, which may help to explain why our findings our not consistent with the theoretical predictions.

Finally, similar to our results for conceptual change in science (Linnenbrink & Pintrich, 2002b), we found that while positive affect did not enhance performance in mathematics, it was related to high levels of effort and cognitive regulation during the solving of number sequences and during graphing. This provides further support for the notion that positive affect does not signal a lack of motivation (Bless, 2000).

It is also important to consider how the storage and retrieval of information is linked to affect for mathematics learning. Based on Forgas' (2000a) model, we would expect affect to be relevant to long-term memory under certain conditions. For instance, it seems likely that computation tasks, where students are simply retrieving strategies or number facts from long-term memory and applying them, should not be influenced by affect. That is, this type of processing involves direct retrieval, a type of processing in which affect should not infuse thinking. In contrast, other mathematical tasks such as problem solving, graphing, and shape discrimination may involve more substantive processing. Students engaged in these tasks may be learning new information or trying to link new information to prior knowledge. In these situations, it is likely that the affective state is encoded along with the relevant mathematical material. Therefore, this may be a situation in which a congruency between the encoding and retrieval states will facilitate recall. However, none of the studies reviewed in this section tested this idea.

In summary, the research relating affect to cognitive processing in mathematics presents a varied and complex view of the way in which affect influences performance and learning. This is due in part to the wide variety of tasks that fall under the domain of mathematics. Nevertheless, even within a type of task, the results are not consistent, making it difficult to clearly analyze the findings based on the proposed social psychological models of affect and cognitive processing. We have suggested that part of the discrepancy in the findings may be due to the duration of the task, in that affect may have different effects on students' processing depending on whether they must work on the task for a long or short period of time. Other possible sources for the discrepant findings are the complexity of the task (whether it requires both heuristic and detail-oriented processing) and the manipulation of mood versus self-reported affect. Finally, the few studies that examined arousal versus valence provide a mixed view of whether it is important to consider both dimensions of affect. Therefore, we urge researchers to conduct carefully designed experimental and correlational studies that directly examine how mood influences cognitive processing, keeping in mind that the type of task, the duration of the task, the way in which affect is measured or induced, and the distinction between arousal and valence may be important variables to consider.

CONCLUSION

Despite the advances recently made in studying the relation between affect and cognitive processing, there are still several theoretical and empirical limitations to this work. First, almost all of the theories discussed focus on the impact of moods on cognitive processing and largely ignore the impact of emotions. Although there are likely many parallels between positive moods and positive emotions as well as negative moods and negative emotions, research specifically examining how various emotions such as anxiety versus anger might differentially influence cognitive processing is essential in understanding how the relation between affect and cognitive processing might play out in educational settings. As a side note, Forgas (1995) suggested that the AIM model applies to both moods and emotions. However, he notes that emotions may initiate motivated processes rather than heuristic or substantive processing suggesting that in those cases, the emotions would not infuse one's thinking.

In thinking about emotions, we must make sure that we consider relevant emotions for academic contexts. For instance, Pekrun and his colleagues (2002) have developed a scale to measure academic emotions. Prawat and Anderson (1994) also specifically examined the different emotions that emerge during mathematics learning. If we want to move forward in our understanding of how emotions are linked to cognitive processing, we must take this work into account, realizing that certain emotions may be more prominent in educational settings.

Finally, the consideration of emotions in addition to moods underscores the necessity of distinguishing between the valence and arousal dimensions of affect, which is largely ignored by the social psychological theories presented in this chapter. While a few of the studies reviewed assessed these dimensions separately and found mixed results, it is important that research be conducted in which both dimensions of affect are examined. Further, if arousal is determined to be an important predictor of cognitive processing, it may be necessary to revise or extend some of the current social psychological theories on affect and cognitive processing to include both valence and arousal. This may closely parallel extensions or revisions based on the examination of specific emotions, as emotions are more readily classified in terms of both valence and arousal in contrast to more general mood states.

Second, the theories reviewed are largely derived from research using typical social psychology paradigms. For instance, most of the researchers developed their theories based on experiments conducted on group processes and stereotypes in laboratory settings (e.g., Bless, 2000; Fiedler, 2000; Forgas, 2000a). In contrast to many academic tasks, these laboratory tasks are often rather short in duration (lasting for the experimental session) and do not capture the complex interaction of the situation (including other people and other activities) in which the task takes place. In applying these theories to educational settings and academic tasks, care must be taken to carefully consider how changes in the duration of the situation, the context, and the importance of the activity to the participant may alter the way in which affect relates to cognitive processing. As is clear from our review, recent attempts to apply these theories to academic contexts is difficult, even when there are similarities in terms of the context and duration of the task. Therefore, we urge researchers to carefully manipulate these various components so that we can better understand when and how the theories reviewed can be applied to educational settings.

Third, in our own work (Linnenbrink & Pintrich, 2002b, 2003), we have assessed effort regulation and cognitive regulation in addition to performance or learning. The findings for these outcomes are consistent, suggesting that positive affect enhances engagement in terms of effort and higher order strategy use. This idea is also supported by Pekrun et al.'s (2002) research linking positive academic emotions such as enjoyment and hope to greater effort, deeper cognitive engagement, more self-regulated learning in academic settings. The relation between affect and engagement as well as cognitive processing suggests that there may be a complex interplay among affect, cognition, and motivation that needs to be further investigated. Indeed, we are working on developing an asymmetrical bidirectional model linking achievement motivation to affect (Linnenbrink & Pintrich, 2002a). However, given the lack of research on affect and cognitive processing in academic contexts, it is rather difficulty to speculate on the interaction of all three variables on students' learning (see Linnenbrink & Pintrich, 2003, for a recent attempt to consider all three outcomes). It is well beyond the scope of the current chapter to attempt to integrate our asymmetrical bidirectional model linking achievement goals to affect with the current review of affect and cognitive processing. As we more carefully refine these models of affect and cognitive processing and affect and motivation, it will be easier to integrate the three components.

Fourth, the current state of the field makes it difficult to make suggestions to educators, particularly to classroom teachers. As we are yet unsure exactly how moods and emotions relate to cognitive processing in a broad variety of tasks, it is difficult to make recommendations for educators regarding the types of affect that may be beneficial for processing. Furthermore, even if we do determine that certain types of affect are more beneficial for certain types of tasks, we must seriously question whether we would want teachers to induce negative affect before students began working on a task requiring detail-oriented processing. Rather, when applying this research to school settings, we may want to focus more on the instances in which positive affect is particularly beneficial and encourage educators to focus on fostering positive affect in those contexts. In addition, in instances were negative affect is beneficial, we may instead want to encourage teachers to work with their students in regulating their affect, so that they are not overwhelmed by positive affect. That is, rather than attempting to enhance negative affect, students might be encouraged to diminish their positive affect. Obviously this research raises some difficult questions when applying it directly to educational settings. However, more information is needed about the basic processes involved in linking affect to cognitive processing before we make any specific recommendations to teachers.

Finally, in terms of future research, much work needs to be done in applying these social psychological theories to education. As is apparent from our review, there are very few empirical studies that directly examine how affect influences cognitive processing in academic contexts. Therefore, we urge other researchers to consider how mood and emotions relate to cognitive processing on a variety of educational tasks. In doing so, it may be important to first conduct research on simple academic tasks that can be clearly classified as involving heuristic versus detailed processing. Then, we need to consider larger, more complex tasks to gain a better understanding of how affect influences tasks that require both types of processing. In addition to the type of task, it is also important to consider how the duration of the task and the focus on current affect versus affect over the course of a section or unit differentially influence students' learning. While this research is in its infancy and will require much work to refine these models, the integration of affect into our models of cognitive processing should help us develop a more comprehensive and accurate picture of student learning in academic settings. Once this integration is better understood based on empirical evidence, we suggest that future research tackle the complex issue of integrating affect, cognitive processing, and motivation into one model for learning in school. The integration and expansion of these models not only will better reflect the reality of student learning, but also may have important implications for the improvement of instruction.

REFERENCES

Ashby, F. G., Isen, A. M., & Turken, A. U. (1999). A neuropsychological theory of positive affect and its influence on cognition. *Psychological Review, 106*, 529–550.

Batson, C. D., Shaw, L. L., & Oleson, K. C. (1992). Differentiating affect, mood, and emotion: Toward functionally based conceptual distinctions. In M. S. Clark (Ed.), *Review of personality and social psychology: Vol. 13. Emotion* (pp. 294–326). Newbury Park, CA: Sage.

Bless, H. (2000). The interplay of affect and cognition: The mediating role of general knowledge structures. In J. P. Forgas (Ed.), *Feeling and thinking: The role of affect in social cognition* (pp. 201–222). New York: Cambridge University Press.

Bless, H., Clore, G., Schwarz, N., Golisano, V., Rabe, C., & Wolk, M. (1996). Mood and use of scripts: Does a happy mood really lead to mindlessness? *Journal of Personality and Social Psychology, 71*, 665–679.

Bodenhausen, G. V., Kramer, G. P., & Susser, K. (1994). Happiness and stereotypic thinking in social judgment. *Journal of Personality and Social Psychology, 66*, 621–632.

Boekaerts, M. (1993). Being concerned with well-being and with learning. *Educational Psychologist, 28*, 149–167.

Bower, G. H. (1981). Mood and memory. *American Psychologist, 36*, 129–148.

Bower, G. H., & Mayer, J. D. (1991). In search of mood-dependent retrieval. In D. Kuiken (Ed.), *Mood and memory: Theory, research, and applications* (pp. 169–184). Newbury Park, CA: Sage.

Bryan, T., & Bryan, J. (1991). Positive mood and math performance. *Journal of Learning Disabilities, 24*, 490–494.

Cacioppo, J. T., Gardner, W. L., & Berntson, G. G. (1999). The affect system has parallel and integrative processing components: Form follows function. *Journal of Personality and Social Psychology, 76*(5), 839–855.

Dalgleish, T., & Power, M. J. (1999). Cognition and emotion: Future directions. In T. Dalgleish & M. Power (Eds.), *Handbook of cognition and emotion* (pp. 799–805). Chichester, England: Wiley.

Duncker, K. (1945). On problem solving. *Psychological Monographs, 58*(5, Whole No. 270).

Ellis, H. C., & Ashbrook, T. W. (1988). Resource allocation model of the effects of depressed mood state on memory. In K. Fiedler & J. Forgas (Eds.), *Affect, cognition, and social behavior* (pp. 25–43). Toronto, Canada: Hogrefe.

Ellis, H., Seibert, P., & Varner, L. (1995). Emotion and memory: Effects of mood states on immediate and unexpected delayed recall. *Journal of Social Behavior and Personality, 10*, 349–362.

Fiedler, K. (2000). Toward an integrative account of affect and cognition phenomena using the BIAS computer algorithm. In J. P. Forgas (Ed.), *Feeling and thinking: The role of affect in social cognition* (pp. 223–252). New York: Cambridge University Press.

Forgas, J. P. (1995). Mood and judgment: The affect infusion model (AIM). *Psychological Bulletin, 117*, 39–66.

Forgas, J. P. (2000a). Affect and information processing strategies: An interactive relationship. In J. P. Forgas (Ed.), *Feeling and thinking: The role of affect in social cognition* (pp. 253–280). New York: Cambridge University Press.

Forgas, J. P. (2000b). Feeling and thinking: Summary and integration. In J. P. Forgas (Ed.), *Feeling and thinking: The role of affect in social cognition* (pp. 387–406). New York: Cambridge University Press.

Forgas, J. P. (2000c). *Feeling and thinking: The role of affect in social cognition.* New York: Cambridge University Press.

Fredrickson, B. L. (1998). What good are positive emotions? *Review of General Psychology, 2,* 300–219.

Fredrickson, B. L. (2001). The role of positive emotions in positive psychology: The broaden-and-build theory of positive emotions. *American Psychologist, 56,* 218–226.

Hill, K. T., & Wigfield, A. (1984). Test anxiety: A major educational problem and what can be done about it. *Elementary School Journal, 85,* 105–126.

Isen, A. (1984). Toward understanding the role of affect in cognition. In R. Wyer & T. Srull (Eds.), *Handbook of social cognition* (pp. 174–236). Hillsdale, NJ: Lawrence Erlbaum Associates.

Isen, A., Daubman, K., & Nowicki, G. (1987). Positive affect facilitates creative problem solving. *Journal of Personality and Social Psychology, 52,* 1122–1131.

Linnenbrink, E. A., & Pintrich, P. R. (2002a). Achievement goal theory and affect: An asymmetrical bidirectional model. *Educational Psychologist, 37,* 69–78.

Linnenbrink, E. A., & Pintrich, P. R. (2002b). The role of motivational beliefs in conceptual change. In M. Limon & L. Mason (Eds.), *Reconsidering conceptual change: Issues in theory and practice* (pp. 115–135). Dordrecht, The Netherlands: Kluwer Academic Publishers.

Linnenbrink, E. A., & Pintrich, P. R. (2003, April). *Motivation, affect, and cognitive processing: What role does affect play?* Paper presented at the annual meeting of the American Educational Research Association, Chicago, IL.

Linnenbrink, E. A., Ryan, A. M., & Pintrich, P. R. (1999). The role of goals and affect in working memory functioning. *Learning and Individual Differences, 11,* 213–230.

Mackie, D. M., & Worth, L. T. (1989). Processing deficits and the mediation of positive affect in persuasion. *Journal of Personality & Social Psychology, 57,* 27–40.

Masters, J., Barden, C., & Ford, M. (1979). Affective states, expressive behavior, and learning in children. *Journal of Personality and Social Psychology, 37,* 380–390.

Miyake, A., & Shah, P. (1999). *Models of working memory: Mechanisms of active maintenance and executive control.* New York: Cambridge University Press.

Morris, W. N. (1992). A functional analysis of the role of mood in affective systems. In M. S. Clark (Ed.), *Review of personality and social psychology: Vol. 13. Emotion* (pp. 256–293). Newbury Park, CA: Sage.

Pekrun, R. (1992). The impact of emotion on learning and achievement: Towards a theory of cognitive/motivational mediators. *Applied Psychology: An International Review, 41,* 359–376.

Pekrun, R., Goetz, T., Titz, W., & Perry, R. P. (2002). Academic emotions in students' self-regulated learning and achievement: A program of qualitative and quantitative research. *Educational Psychologist, 37,* 91–106.

Pintrich, P. R. (2000). The role of goal orientation in self-regulated learning. In M. Boekarts, P. R. Pintrich, & M. Zeidner (Eds.), *Handbook of self-regulation: Theory, research and applications* (pp. 451–502). San Diego, CA: Academic Press.

Prawat, R. S., & Anderson, A. L. H. (1994). The affective experiences of children during mathematics. *Journal of Mathematical Behavior, 13,* 201–222.

Revelle, W., & Loftus, D. (1990). Individual differences and arousal: Implications for study of mood and memory. *Cognition and Emotion, 4,* 209–237.

Rosenberg, E. L. (1998). Levels of analysis and the organization of affect. *Review of General Psychology, 2,* 247–270.

Russell, J. A., & Feldman Barrett, L. (1999). Core affect, prototypical emotional episodes, and other things called emotion: Dissecting the elephant. *Journal of Personality and Social Psychology, 76*(5), 805–819.

Scherer, K. R. (1999). Appraisal theory. In T. Dalgleish & M. J. Power (Eds.), *Handbook of cognition and emotion* (pp. 637–663). Chichester, England: Wiley.

Schwarz, N. (1990). Feelings as information: Informational and motivational functions of affective states. In E. T. Higgins & R. M. Sorrentino (Eds.). *Handbook of motivation and cognition: Foundations of social behavior: Vol. 2* (pp. 528–561). New York: Guilford.

Schwarz, N., & Clore, G. L. (1996). Feelings and phenomenal experiences. In E. T. Higgins & A. Kruglanski (Eds.), *Social psychology: Handbook of basic principles* (pp. 433–465). New York: Guilford.

Smith, C. A., & Lazarus, R. S. (1990). Emotion and adaptation. In L. A. Pervin (Ed.), *Handbook of personality: Theory and research* (pp. 609–637). New York: Guilford.

Sternberg, R. J. (1985). *Beyond IQ: A triarchic theory of human intelligence.* New York: Cambridge University Press.

Tellegen, A., Watson, D., & Clark, L. A. (1999). On the dimensional and hierarchical structure of affect. *Psychological Science, 10,* 297–309.

Thayer, R. E. (1986). Activation-deactivation adjective checklist: Current overview and structural analysis. *Psychological Reports, 58,* 607–614.

Watson, D., Wiese, D., Vaidya, J., & Tellegen, A. (1999). The two general activation systems of affect: Structural findings, evolutionary considerations, and psychobiological evidence. *Journal of Personality and Social Psychology, 76*(5), 820–838.

Winne, P. H., & Perry, N. E. (2000). Measuring self-regulated learning. In M. Boekarts, P. R. Pintrich, & M. Zeidner (Eds.), *Handbook of self-regulation* (pp. 531–566). San Diego, CA: Academic Press.

Yasutake, D., & Bryan, T. (1995). The influence of induced positive affect on middle school children with and without learning disabilities. *Learning Disabilities Research & Practice, 10,* 38–45.

4

▼▼▼▼▼▼▼

Interest, a Motivational Variable
That Combines Affective
and Cognitive Functioning

Suzanne Hidi
Ontario Institute for Studies in Education of the University of Toronto

K. Ann Renninger
Swarthmore College

Andreas Krapp
University of the Federal Armed Forces—Munich

Theories and empirical research about the interrelation of motivation, emotion and cognition have a long tradition in education and educational–psychology (e.g., Claparède, 1905; Dewey, 1913; James, 1890; Leontjew, 1977). In comparison to most research approaches and theoretical traditions in other fields of psychology, educational-psychological approaches to these concepts have been related more closely to practice in a wide variety of educational settings in and out of schools. For example, topics of research in the areas of motivation and cognition have been concerned with learning and achievement, and the language used has tended to be familiar to educators and teachers.

Educational psychologists integrated new concepts and methods from other fields of psychology into their research as a way to more fully address issues of practice. Thus, when psychometric approaches relying on quantitative measures became dominant in the area of intelligence research, many investigators in the field of educational psychology began to conceptualize and measure variables using psychometric approaches. Statistical tools were adopted to measure talent (giftedness), as well as cognitive factors based on traditional intelligence tests. As a consequence, research efforts focused on interindividual differences. This line of research however, did not address intraindividual development, nor information about the relations between the variables under consideration (Krapp, 1999; Medved, Hidi, & Ainley, 2002; Murphy & Alexander, 2000).

When in the 1970s, mainstream psychology began to shift from a behavioral to a cognitive paradigm, a similar shift occurred in educational psychology, particularly in the field of motivation research. In fact, most theories of learning motivation have been based on a cognitive framework focusing on learners' thoughts and beliefs (Meyer & Turner, 2002). For example, achievement goal theory (Ames, 1992; Dweck & Leggett, 1988; Dweck, Mangels, & Good, chap. 2) focuses on how students' goals are related to academic performance. According to this theory, individual achievement goals provide a framework to establish learning purposes and a general approach to academic activities and achievement tasks. In addition, achievement goals have also been presumed to influence affective reactions to engagements. Task value theory, another basically cognitively driven approach (Eccles et al., 1983; Wigfield & Eccles, 1992, 2002) describes motivation as resulting from students' expectations of task value. Such expectations reflect students' beliefs as to how desirable a given activity is. Incentive value, utility value, intrinsic value and cost are components of the total value students establish cognitively for future activities. Yet another motivational theory based on a cognitive framework is self-efficacy theory (Bandura, 1977, 1982, 1997; Zimmerman, 1989, 2000). Self-efficacy theory postulates that individuals' beliefs about their ability to produce successful outcomes and attain designated goals are critical to their achievement motivation. Students' goals, task value and self-efficacy have been found to positively affect students' effort, the quality of their academic performance and their willingness to participate in challenging academic tasks (Ames, 1992; Bandura, 1997; Bandura & Schunk, 1981; Heckhausen, 1991; Pajares, 1996; Pintrich & De Groot, 1990; Wigfield & Eccles, 2002; Zimmerman, 2000).

As a consequence of the shift to a cognitive paradigm in motivational research, emotions and affective variables were pushed into the background and studied in only a few areas (Hidi & Baird, 1986; Pekrun, 2000). Eventually, it was recognized that emotional and motivational processes of learning also needed to be explored. In particular, researchers considered it necessary to examine the conditions of intraindividual differences and development. They noted that cognitive theories do not tend to take into account motivational factors that have an influence on a subconscious level and that are related to situation-specific emotional experiences (Hidi, 1990; Krapp, 2002b, 2003). For instance, goal theories have been concerned with general issues of goal-fulfillment, such as mastering a topic or task or achieving certain learning goals, etc. Yet for education, questions arise as to why individuals are interested in one area or topic but not in another.

In fact, from both a psychological and an educational point of view, it is essential to explain why and how students can become interested in new content and subject areas (H. Schiefele, 1978). Results from investigations of this type, furthermore, can provide a basis for understanding the functional relations between motivation, learning and achievement (Heckhausen, 1991; Krapp, 2003). Such explanations can address how school curriculum could best provide opportunities for interest development and increased motivation of students. Thus, for example, Hoffmann (2002) described the implications of interest for curriculum development and classroom composition; Renninger and Wozniak (1985) pointed to the power of interest as a facilitator of student attention and memory; and Sansone, Weir, Harpster, and Morgan (1992) suggested that older students can be supported to regulate their attention and at least a maintained situational interest for boring tasks.

EDUCATIONAL PSYCHOLOGY RESEARCH RELATED TO INTEREST, MOTIVATION, AFFECT, AND COGNITION

Interest Research: A Historical Review

Traditionally, the concept of interest held a central position in educators' thinking about learning. Educational laypersons (e.g., parents), as well as professional educators (e.g., teachers, trainers) often refer to interest when they consider the motivational prerequisites for teaching and learning, or think about students' more or less successful developmental processes. In fact, most educators agree that an important goal of education is the differentiation and stabilization of interests relevant to learning (Dewey, 1913; H. Schiefele, 1978, 1981). In view of the significance attributed to interest within the educational context, it would not be surprising that interest-related research be an important field of educational psychology. Accordingly, at the turn of the 20th century, prominent psychologists advocated that interests were the most important motivational factors in learning and development (e.g., Arnold, 1906; Claparède, 1905; Dewey, 1913; James, 1890; Thorndike, 1935).

Subsequently, however, the interest concept was pushed into the background as first behaviorism and later the shift towards cognitive approaches in psychology spawned numerous other motivational concepts related to learning and development (cf. Ames & Ames, 1984; Heckhausen, 1991; Weiner, 1972). Research on motivation and learning that began to emerge focused on seemingly immediate problems that could be easily studied empirically (e.g., the explanation and prediction of academic achievement). During this period, only diagnostic approaches to vocational interests continued to use interest as a psychological construct (e.g., Fryer, 1931; Strong, 1943; Walsh & Osipow, 1986). In this line of research, interest was conceptualized as a kind of motivational trait, rooted in a stable person and environment relationship (e.g., a person was considered to be social or artistic, see Holland, 1973).

In the last two decades of the 20th century, interest research reemerged in educational psychology due to recognition that aspects of learning motivation central to discussions of interest could not be adequately reconstructed given the theoretical concepts most popular in modern cognitively oriented motivation research. For example, in the area of text-based learning it was demonstrated that the type and the extent of learning from text depended on psychological factors that were related to the content or the topic of the text, as well as cognitive and motivational variables (Hidi, 1990). Thus, one area in which the rejuvenation of interest research took place was in investigations of text-based learning (e.g., Anderson, 1982; Asher, 1980; Hidi & Baird, 1986, 1988; Hidi, Baird, & Hildyard, 1982; Kintsch, 1980; Schank, 1979). Subsequently, a relatively large number of empirical studies concerned with the influence of interest on learning and with the development of interests were conducted (cf. Hidi & Anderson, 1992; Krapp, 1989; Prenzel, 1988; Renninger & Lecrone, 1991; Renninger & Wozniak, 1985). This work primarily built on research traditions in psychology and educational psychology (see Hoffmann, Krapp, Renninger, & Baumert, 1998; Lehrke, Hoffmann, & Gardner, 1985; Renninger, Hidi, & Krapp, 1992).

Recent interest research has focused on studying the relationships between interest, learning and achievement at different levels of education (Baumert & Köller, 1998; Krapp, Hidi, & Renninger, 1992; Prenzel, 1988; Renninger, Ewan, & Lasher, 2002; Renninger & Hidi, 2002; Sansone et. al., 1992; Schiefele, 1999, 2001; Schiefele, Krapp, & Winteler, 1992). Findings from this work suggest that an interest-based motivation to learn positively influences both how learners realize and organize a given learning task (e.g., the kind of learning strategies used) and the quantity and quality of learning outcomes.

Developmental studies have also been undertaken in order to address the development of interests. These investigations tended to be undertaken with younger students in pre-schools and in elementary schools (Fink, 1991; Fölling-Albers & Hartinger, 1998; Krapp & Fink, 1992; Renninger, 1989, 1990; Renninger & Leckrone, 1991). Such studies have focused on interest held over time, changes in interests, and the relation between cognitive and affective processing during engagement. Unfortunately, empirical studies using cross-sectional as well as longitudinal studies suggest a decline in student interest for school subjects as students' level of schooling increases (e.g.,

Gardner, 1998). In fact, decline in school subject interests have been found as early as the first year of elementary school when classrooms constrain children's abilities to explore new contents and engage interests (Fölling-Albers & Hartinger, 1998; Helmke, 1993), and have also been widely reported for secondary school students. Declines in interest for these students have been most evident in the fields of physics, chemistry, and mathematics, and it appears to be more pronounced for girls than for boys in these subjects (Gardner, 1985; Hoffmann et al., 1998). It also appears likely that such declines are partially due to a lack of environmental support for engaging student interest rather than a developmental shift in the capacity to have interest, suggesting that school culture could make a significant contribution to the likelihood that interest for particular content continues to develop and can be sustained (Eccles, Wigfield, & Schiefele, 1998; Hoffmann, 2002; Renninger, Ewen, & Lasher, 2002; Renninger & Hidi, 2002; Renninger, Sansone, & Smith, 2004; Schraw & Dennison, 1994).

Another question that has received considerable attention concerns how individuals' patterns of interests change over time. For example, with the beginning of puberty dramatic changes in individuals' personal interests can be observed (Gardner, 1985, 1998; Krapp, 2000). In part, these shifts are the result of the general tendency of adolescents to adapt the contents and pattern of their interest to gender role stereotypes (Hannover, 1998; Todt, 1985). Among studies that attempt to explore gender-related developmental processes over a longer period of the life span are those of Gisbert (1998, 2001) who showed that the development of an individual interest in academic subjects is highly influenced by adolescent developmental processes, especially by the quality of occupational and university enrollment decisions. Young people, who carefully explore their future aspirations and commit themselves to their decisions, show long term interests in their chosen subject, even in the case of a gender atypical major (e.g., women in mathematics). In the long run, interests become important components of a person's identity (Hannover, 1998; Hidi & Ainley, 2002).

Several research programs have analyzed in detail the relations between cognitive and affective processing during interest-based learning activities (e.g., Harackiewicz & Durik, 2003; Renninger & Hidi, 2002). Empirical studies in the field of physics education have examined the continuous relations between students' situation-specific individual experiences, cognitive processes and the occurrence and stabilization of content-specific interests (Fischer & Horstendahl, 1997; Krapp & Lewalter, 2001; Lewalter, Krapp, Schreyer, & Wild, 1998; von Aufschnaiter, Schoster, & von Aufschnaiter, 1999). Results from these studies demonstrated a marked influence of the continuous experiential feedback during tasks on subsequent motivation for learning.

The Construct of Interest

The term interest has been used in a variety of different ways. In everyday usage, interest almost always refers to positive feelings and is equally likely to refer to an attraction, a preference, or a passion (Valsiner, 1992). Among educational researchers, interest has had almost as many different meanings. For example, links between interest and more trait-like conceptualizations such as general curiosity (Ainley, 1987, 1993) or love of learning (Renninger et al., 2004) can be made. Interest has been studied as a habitual preference (or attitude), a motivational belief, and as a characteristic of the developing self (or personality) (Krapp, Renninger, & Hoffmann, 1998).

In the present chapter, we focus on interest-based motivation, that is, a motivational state that results either from a situational interest or an individual interest. Briefly, situational interest is conceptualized as being generated by particular aspects of the environment that focus attention, and it represents an affective reaction that may or may not last (see Hidi, 2001, for a review). Whereas, individual interest is conceptualized as being both a relatively enduring predisposition to attend to objects and events and to reengage in certain activities over time (Krapp, 1993, 2000; Renninger & Wozniak, 1985; see Renninger, 2000, for a review) and a motivational state. In this conceptualization, a motivational state during engagement can be fueled by processes, dispositions, or both that are related to some type of interest, thus interests can be examined and reconstructed theoretically at two levels of analyses. First, interest research can focus on the psychological processes and states that occur during concrete interactions between a person and his or her object of interest. In this case the analysis focuses on the description and explanation of interest-triggered actions. Second, interest research can focus on interest as a relatively enduring disposition. In summary, interest is both a motivational process or state and a relatively enduring disposition to reengage with particular content.

Hidi and Renninger (2003) noted that the dual meaning of interest as a psychological state and as a predisposition to reengage with objects, events and ideas over time has frequently not been acknowledged in the literature. Hidi and Renninger (2003) further suggested that there is a developmental thread that links the repeated experiences of interested engagements to produce the psychological state of interest and its development as a disposition (Hidi & Anderson, 1992; Krapp, 2002b; Renninger, 2000; Silvia, 2001).

Independent of whether interest is examined at the level of the ongoing processes and resulting states or at the level of the dispositional structures of the individual, three features of the interest construct distinguish it from other motivational variables. First, a general characteristic of interest is its content or object specificity. As Hidi and Renninger (2003) pointed out, interest refers to focused attention, engagement, or both with the affordances of particular content and it is this content that can be said to suggest possibilities for activity. As such, the content of interest does not share the type of universality that characterizes other motivational variables.

Second, the conceptualization of interest exists in a particular relation between a person and content, and does not simply reside either in the person or in the content of interest. In accordance with the ideas of Hidi and Baird (1986), Lewin (1936), Nuttin (1984), H. Schiefele (1978), and many others, it is postulated that the individual, as a potential source of action, and the environment as the object of action, constitute a bipolar unit. This relation has been recognized to be central to both situational interest (Hidi, 1990) and individual interest (Renninger, 1990; Renninger & Wozniak, 1985), and among researchers in the German research community, it has been referred to as person-object theory (Krapp, 2002a, 2003). The relation is dynamic rather than static and has particular relevance to educational practice because educators can have an influence on environmental aspects (see discussions in Hidi & Anderson, 1992; Mitchell, 1993; Renninger, 2000; Schraw & Dennison, 1994). Thus, according to this theoretical approach, interest-related learning and development is conceptualized to be the result of an interaction between a person and his or her social and physical environment.

Third, interest has both cognitive and affective components (Hidi, 1990; Renninger, 1992). As Hidi and Renninger (2003) pointed out, the relative amount of cognitive evaluation and affect generated may vary depending on the particular phase of interest development. Thus, a triggered situational interest may involve only minimal cognitive evaluation and positive affect; whereas, a well-developed individual interest for particular content would include both stored knowledge and stored value, as well as positive affect.

The close relation between cognitive and affective components of interest-informed activity have been described as accounting for why no contradiction is experienced between the cognitive-rational assessment of personally experienced importance and positive emotional evaluations of an activity itself (Dewey, 1913; Krapp, 2000, 2002a; Rathunde, 1993; Schiefele, 1999). The affect associated with interested engagement tends to be positive. Possible exceptions are triggered situational interest which may be negative (Bergin, 1999; Hidi, 2001; Hidi & Anderson, 1992; Hidi & Harackiewicz, 2000; Hidi & Renninger, 2003; Iran-Nejad, 1987) and experiences of temporary frustration by persons who have well-developed interest for particular content (Krapp & Fink, 1992; Prenzel, 1992; Renninger, 2000; Renninger & Leckrone, 1991).

It is positive emotion that is likely to fuel the development of interest and learning behaviors that have been characterized as focused, generative, and deep. In fact, as Dewey (1913) postulated, when conditions to support interest are in place, effort will follow (see discussion in Renninger, 2003). This is one of the reasons why an interest-based action (e.g., knowledge acquisition of content that is an identified interest) seems to have the quality of intrinsic motivation (Deci, 1998).

In their recent paper, Meyer and Turner (2002) noted that psychologists have tended to study the processes of cognition, motivation, and emotion separately. They further note that current cognitive theories of motivation focus on cognition and motivation, and emotions have not been central features of influential motivational theories such as goal theory, expectancy-value theory and self-efficacy theory. In these theories, affect has been considered as an outcome variable (Hidi, 2003a, 2003b; Meyer & Turner, 2002), and it has been assumed that desirable thoughts and beliefs such as mastery goals, high task-value and increased levels of self-efficacy produce positive affect and/or reduce negative affect. However, as Meyer's and Turner's (2002) students' surveys indicate, emotions are central to an understanding of students' goals, strategies and self-efficacy. Emotions are not necessarily outcomes of cognitive processes.

The assumption that affect is an inherent component of interest is a critical feature of the interest construct and sets interest apart from other motivational constructs (Hidi, 2003a, 2003b; Hidi & Renninger, 2003). Experiencing interest involves affect from the outset of experience and can be assumed to be combined or integrated with cognition (Krapp, 2003; Renninger, 2000). An important aspect of this view is that it allows the integration of psychological and neuroscientific approaches with motivation which has not previously been an easy association (Boekaerts, in press; Kuhl, 2000). Future work needs to address the distinctive neural correlates of interest-based information processing that involves both emotional and cognitive systems.

Neuroscientists studying affect have started to identify the neural circuits involved in emotional processing. Some researchers have proposed two basic systems of approach and avoidance (see Davidson, 2000, for a detailed neurophysiological discussion of these systems). The approach system has been associated with appetitive behavior and with generating certain types of approach-related positive affect. Parts of this system appear to be involved in the expression and movement toward abstract goals in action plans and in the anticipation of rewards. Although the association between interest and the approach system, to the best of our knowledge, has not yet been fully explored, recent research has established the neural basis of negative emotions such as fear and its relation to learning and motivation (LeDoux, 2000). Hidi (2003b) and Hidi and Renninger (2003) have suggested that the "seeking system"—one of the evolutionary and genetically ingrained emotional brain systems specified by Panksepp (1998, 2003)—is one of the major biological foundations of the psychological state of interest. Research examining further this relation may lead to the integration of psychological and neuroscientific components of interest.

Situational and Individual Interest
From a Developmental Perspective

Although the authors of this chapter have previously described two or three phases of interest development (e.g., Hidi & Anderson, 1992; Krapp, 2002b; Krapp et al., 1992), Hidi and Renninger (2003) recently proposed a Four-Phase Model of Interest Development. According to this model, in the first phase, situational interest for a particular subject content is triggered. If this triggered situational interest is sustained, the second phase, referred to as maintained situational interest, evolves. The shift from maintained situational interest to an emerging individual interest is fueled by a person's curiosity questions about the content of interest (Renninger, 2000). These questions are accompanied by efforts to self-regulate and identify with the content of interest (Hannover, 1998; Krapp, 2000, 2003; Todt & Shreiber, 1998). With increased ability to self-regulate and identify with particular content, a student moves into the final phase of development that is referred to as well-developed individual interest.

In the following section of this chapter, research related to each of the four phases of interest is overviewed. Research on triggered and maintained situational interest is presented first, followed by research on emerging (or less-developed) and well-developed individual interest.

Research Related to Phases of Situational Interest

Because by definition, situational interest is triggered by environmental factors, objects, individuals, or both, research has focused on identifying the conditions that contribute to the triggering of this type of interest. In two early studies, Schank (1979) and Kintsch (1980) distinguished between interest that is related to feelings (emotional interest) and interest that they saw as an outcome of cognitive processing. Although researchers at that time did not acknowledge the distinction between situational and individual interest, in retrospect we can conclude that both Schank and Kintsch were describing situational interest. Recently, Harp and Mayer (1997) revisited the notion that emotional and cognitive sources of situational interest may result in different types of processing and set out to demonstrate empirically this assumption. In their study, they compared the effect of coherent text that according to their theory would elicit cognitive interest, with the effects of seductive text segments and illustrations, presumed to elicit emotional interest. The results indicated that texts aimed at increasing emotional interest failed to improve understanding of scientific explanations, whereas coherent texts contributed to increased comprehension and increased learning. The authors maintained that these results indicate a qualitative difference in the two types of interest and that, in the case of cognitive interest, processing of coherent texts promoted a sense of positive affect about the passage that led to increased learning.

Whereas it is possible to set up research paradigms that separate emotional and cognitive interests, we believe that such separations may be artificial, as emotional and cognitive functioning appear to continuously interact in interest development. In addition, we have no neurophysiological indications of unique neural processes underlying exclusively emotional and cognitive processes, and it is more likely that both systems are involved to varying degrees.

Focusing more specifically on discourse, several research groups worked on identifying text characteristics that contribute to triggering readers'/listeners' situational interest. In early studies of text features, novelty, unexpected surprising information, intensity, concreteness and visual imagery were found to contribute to situational interest (Anderson, Shirey, Wilson, & Fielding, 1987; Hidi & Baird, 1986, 1988). Following this work, Schraw, Brunning, and Svoboda (1995) identified six sources of text-based (situational) interest: (a) ease of comprehension (Mitchell, 1993; Wade, Buxton, & Kelly, 1999); (b) prior knowledge (Alexander, 1997; Alexander, Jetton, & Kulikowich, 1995); (c) text cohesion (Kintsch, 1980; Wade, 1992); (d) vividness (Sadoski, Goetz, & Fritz, 1993); (e) reader engagement (Mitchell, 1993); and (f) evocative emotional reactions (Krapp et al., 1992). The experimental findings of Schraw et al. (1995) further indicated that only some of these sources of interest were related significantly to subjects' actual feeling of interest (referred to as perceived interest by the authors). Furthermore, a lack of interactions between the six sources of interest suggested that a number of individual factors rather than complex interactive relationships between factors were responsible for the elicited situational interest. Finally, the finding that prior knowledge ratings were only marginally related to perceived interest, and they were unrelated to recall, suggested that knowledge alone is not a sufficient factor to increase text-based (situational) interest and learning.

In an investigation that also focused on sources of interest, Wade et al. (1999) studied the characteristics associated with self-reported interest of informational (science) texts. Their findings overlap with those of Schraw et al. (1995) in some areas such as comprehension and imagery. Other text characteristics that Wade et al. (1999) found to be associated with higher interest were novelty and importance/value.

Social aspects of the environment have also been found to influence the development of situational interest. For example, Isaac, Sansone, and Smith (1999) reported that working with others increased some individuals' situational interest. Häussler and Hoffmann (1998) found that girls' situational interest was mediated by the gender of those who were present in the learning situation. More specifically, girls' interest in physic lessons was supported by mono-educational classes. Hidi, Weiss, Berndorff, and Nolan's (1998) research that focused on learning in a science museum setting, indicated that the social structuring of the learning experience through a cooperative learning technique called a jigsaw (Aronson, Blaney, Stephen, Sikes, & Snapp, 1978; Slavin, 1991) can contribute to the elicitation of situational interest (Hidi & Harackiewicz, 2000). Similarly, provision of scaffolds in the organization of classroom instruction can provide students with opportunities to make connections to learning, and to maintain situational interest (Renninger & Hidi, 2002; Renninger, Sansone, & Smith, 2003). In addition, an individual's ability to self-regulate activity can increase his or her situational interest. For example, Sansone and Smith (2000) and Wolters (1998) demonstrated in separate studies that individuals can devise and use interest-enhancing strategies to overcome boredom.

In many of the previously mentioned studies, the distinction between the two phases of situational interest (triggered and maintained) have not been acknowledged. However, this distinction has special educational relevance, since research indicates that environmental factors that trigger situational interest may be different from those that help maintain it (Hidi & Baird, 1986). Mitchell (1993) empirically demonstrated that whereas group work, puzzles and computers sparked adolescents' interest in math, only meaningfulness of tasks and personal involvement held and sustained (maintained) students' interest over time. Harackiewicz, Barron, Tauer, Carter, and Elliot (2000) extended these findings by showing that factors that maintained college students' interest were better predictors of their continuing interest in psychology than factors that only triggered their interest. These findings suggest that the outcomes associated with triggered situational interest only involve short-term changes in affective and cognitive processing, such as sudden changes in affect and increased automatically allocated attention, whereas maintained situational interest is more likely to have relatively longer term affective and cognitive outcomes. For example, early studies demonstrated that interest narrows the range of inferences people need to consider, and facilitates the integration of information with prior knowledge (Schank, 1979). Hidi and Berndorff (1998) and Schraw and Lehman (2001) summarized the most frequently found learning outcomes associated with situational interest.

Attention as a Mediator Between Interest and Learning

In general, the literature indicates that the psychological state of interest is a positive influence on learning, and that the relation between interest and learning is mediated by attention (e.g., Berlyne, 1960; Dewey, 1913; Hidi, 1995; James, 1890; Renninger, 1990; and Thorndike, 1935). Early on, Roe and Siegelman (1964) defined interest as any activity (action, thought, observation) to which one gives effortless and automatic attention. Subsequent research also supported the mediating role of attention between interest and learning (e.g., Izard, 1977; Larson, 1988; Renninger & Wozniak, 1985). Miller and colleagues (Miller & Weiss, 1982; Miller & Zalenski, 1982) demonstrated that even children in kindergarten are aware that interest influences their attention and subsequent learning.

The relation between interest and attention is complex however, and its importance has been the subject of recent discussion. Like those who first contemplated the relation of interest, attention, and learning, Hidi and colleagues (Hidi, 1990, 1995, 2001; Hidi & Anderson, 1992; Hidi & Berndorff, 1998) maintained that attention is a critical mediating variable. Anderson and colleagues (Anderson, 1982; Anderson, Mason & Shirey, 1984; Shirey & Reynolds, 1988; etc.) and Schiefele (1998), however, claimed that attention is an epiphenomenon that occurs simultaneously with learning, but is not causally related to increased learning of interesting information. Their conclusions were based on the results of a number of studies in which it was assumed that interesting information is processed the same way as important information. That is, they assumed that as readers process text segments, they rate them for interest and importance and then consciously allocate attention to selected text segments. Importantly, attention in these investigations was measured through reading and secondary task reaction times and the following predictions were made: (a) interest would result in escalated learning; (b) interest would result in increased attention which could be measured by slower reading and secondary task reaction times; and (c) the increased time spent on the tasks could be shown to be causally related to learning.

Anderson and colleagues found that whereas the first prediction pertaining to interest resulting in increased learning was substantiated, the other predictions were not. Adult readers, contrary to expectations, read interesting information faster than less interesting information. Children, as predicted, read interesting information slower than other information, however a complex statistical analysis suggested that the relationship between attention and learning was not causal. Based on these findings, the researchers had concluded that attention was not on the causal path between interest and learning.

In response to the Anderson (1982), Anderson et al. (1984) studies, Hidi (1995, 2001) argued that some of the results may have been inappropriately interpreted. They questioned the prediction that increased attention due to interest would necessarily result in slower reading and secondary task reaction times. Such predictions have been based on the paradigm that has been used to explain the processing and superior recall of important information. However, different cognitive and affective functioning may be involved in processing interesting versus important information. More specifically, to determine importance, readers have to evaluate information relative either to previously processed information or to some self-generated standard, and they have to keep continuously updating their evaluations. These operations may significantly add to the cognitive load of the readers and the time they spend on the task of reading important sentences. However, to recognize that a sentence is interesting does not require the same kind of cognitive evaluation and decision making process. With the help of affective reactions, readers may recognize interesting information instantaneously, without having to compare it to previously presented information, and therefore more efficient processing that results in faster reading and secondary task reaction times could be predicted.

Recently, McDaniel, Waddill, Finstad, and Bourg (2000) examined whether interest fosters greater selective allocation of attention that results in slower text processing (Anderson, 1982), or does interest result in automatic allocation of attention, freeing up cognitive resources in the process, and allowing for more rapid processing of information (Hidi, 1990, 1995). Mc-Daniel et al. (2000) developed stories that differed globally in how much interest they generated, rather than adopting the more common procedure of varying the interest value of individual sentences (e.g., Wade, Schraw, Buxton, & Hayes, 1993). Secondary task reaction times were used to evaluate the time needed for processing the texts. Since the beginning of stories tend to have similar levels of interest and only as stories develop, could one expect differences in the interest levels that they generate, the authors presented secondary task probes at various points in the stories. This procedure allowed them to obtain and compare reaction times during the first and second halves of the stories. The results showed that, whereas the reaction times for the early portion of the texts did not differ across high and low interest stories, reaction time for the second half of the narratives showed significant differences. More specifically, readers of less interesting narratives took significantly longer time responding to the probes placed in the second half of the texts than those reading more interesting texts.

In addition, for low interest stories, subjects' reaction times were significantly lower during their reading of the later parts than the earlier parts of the text. No such differences were found for the more interesting stories. The authors concluded that the readers allocated more selective attention to the later half of the low interest stories than to the first half, while they maintained a fairly consistent level of selective attention allocation in the case of high-interest stories. McDaniel et al. (2000) concluded that their findings supported Hidi's hypothesis that interest generates spontaneous (automatic) attention resulting in more efficient and faster processing of information.

In none of the previously reviewed investigations did researchers specify the type of interest that was studied. Considered in light of Hidi and Renninger's (2003) proposed Four-Phase Model of Interest Development, it appears that these studies focused on readers' psychological state in the triggered and maintained phases of situational interest, elicited by the stories that they were reading. In stories, readers do not have problems with organization and unimportant details, nor with the evaluation of what is important versus what is interesting and they read faster what is more interesting. However, reading speed and secondary task reaction times may be less appropriate measures of the attentional processes involved in reading texts that are not stories. For example, in the case of expository texts, not only do readers have to process text, but they also have to deal with the evaluation of the importance of text segments and such evaluations may require allocation of selective attention that slows down the reading process. Reading times and secondary task reaction times also may not be appropriate or serve as the best way to measure attention related to individual interest.

Research Related to Phases of Individual Interest

While individual interest can refer to forms of only more skilled (expert) performance, especially among older students and adults (Alexander, 1997, this volume), here individual interest is used to describe the motivated engagement of people of all ages and all levels of skills, and it refers to a person's relatively enduring predisposition to reengage particular content(s) over time and his or her psychological state during this engagement. Research on individual interest addresses both the process and progress of student learning over time. A close relation between the changing structure of a person's longer lasting individual interest for content and the course of individual personality development begins at a very early age (Krapp, 1999). Children appear to develop relatively stable preferences for particular objects and these are related to their cognitive engagement (Kasten & Krapp, 1986). Furthermore, findings from studies of young children's free play indicate that girls and boys will explore operations such as balance or sequencing, and will use more strategies in their play with play objects of well-developed rather than less-developed individual interest (Fink, 1991; Krapp & Fink, 1992; Renninger, 1989, 1990, 1992, 1998; Renninger & Leckrone, 1991).

Individual interest has been found to support school-age students' abilities to work with difficult texts, mathematical word problems, and school projects (Renninger et al., 2002; Renninger & Hidi, 2002) and to enhance the contexts within which they learn (Fölling-Albers & Hartinger, 1998; Goldman et al., 1998; Hoffmann, 2002; Hoffmann & Häussler, 1998; Renninger & Hidi, 2002). Although the presence of an identified individual interest will not in itself teach students skills (Renninger, 1992), it does appear to provide a forum for learning skills when instruction, television or computer programming, museum education, etc. is adjusted to include such individual interests as problem solving contexts (Fay, 1998; Hoffmann & Häussler, 1998; Renninger et al., 2002).

Schiefele and Krapp (1996) reported that among university students, individual interest was positively related to comprehension of meaning, or propositional recall and negatively related to word, or verbatim, recall. Findings from this study further confirm the impact of individual interest on cognitive functioning. Alexander and Murphy's (1998) and Alexander, Murphy, Woods, Duhon, and Parker's (1997) studies of differences in the learning profiles of college-age students also support the importance of individual interest to the generation of strategies for learning.

Studies of individual interest have considered the role of interest at different developmental stages, with respect to different school subjects, across varying educational settings including preschool and elementary school (Renninger, 1998), secondary school (Baumert & Köller, 1998), colleges and universities (Alexander et al., 1997; Alexander & Murphy, 1998; Krapp, 1997), and vocational education and training (Krapp & Wild, 1998; Prenzel, 1998; Wild, Krapp, Schreyer, & Lewalter, 1998). Briefly, findings from these studies suggest that individual interest has an effect on students' course selection (Bargel, Framheim-Peisert, & Sandberger, 1989; Drottz-Sjoeberg, 1989), as well as their choice of occupation (Gottfredson, 1981; Krapp, 2000). Furthermore, social relationships appear to influence both the maintenance and continuity of individual interest (Gisbert, 1998, 2001; Pressick-Kilborn & Walker, 2003; Renninger, 1989, 2000; Renninger & Hidi, 2002).

Studies of individual interest have also focused on mediating variables that may explain the positive effects of interest-based learning at the level of functional processes (Ainley, Hidi, & Berndorff, 2002; Schiefele & Rheinberg, 1997). Attention, as discussed previously, is one of the few variables that have been analyzed in detail. Others include learning strategies (Alexander et al., 1997; Alexander & Murphy, 1998; Wild, 2000) and emotional experiences (Krapp & Lewalter, 2001; Lewalter et al., 1998; Schiefele, 1996; Schiefele & Csikszentmihalyi, 1994). Importantly, study of the conditions and processes that lead people to learn and continue to work with content over time, consistently refer to the significant role of emotional experiences associated with genuine interest (Drottz-Sjoeberg, 1989) or "undivided interest" (Rathunde, 1993, 1998).

From a developmental point of view, the usefulness of acknowledging the existence of two phases of individual interest has been suggested (Renninger, 2000). These two phases of interest include: emerging (or less-well developed) individual interest and well-developed individual interest. An emerging individual interest is conceptualized as a particular relation of a person to content that is characterized by strong positive feelings for and knowledge—although there are some conceptual and methodological differences about the prominence of the role of knowledge for emerging individual interest.[1]

---

[1] Older students' and adults' knowledge about content has been assumed in some studies and measures focus only on the affective state of individual interest, whereas other studies account for the valuing, including feelings, and prior knowledge a person brings to engagement with particular content relative to his or her other activity.

In contrast, a well-developed individual interest describes a relation to a particular content for which a person has significant levels of both stored value and stored knowledge relative to the other content with which he or she may be engaged. The two phases of individual interest are temporally related. An emerging individual interest is a phase of interest development that emerges from a maintained situational interest, and may or may not transition into being a well-developed individual interest over time (Hidi & Renninger, 2003; Krapp, 2002b; Renninger, 2000).

The emergence of individual interest has been attributed to the ability to begin seeking answers to curiosity questions—the kind of questions that enable an individual to begin to organize information for him or herself (Renninger, 2000). This type of information builds on a person's positive feelings about content and his or her metacognitive awareness of what is known and what still needs to be figured out (Prenzel, 1988). Thus, an individual with a maintained situational interest for playing cards with family members, may begin to notice patterns in the play that need to be factored into the probabilities associated with people's bidding and may wish more information about probability in order to better his or her performance. This type of information seeking characterizes both types of individual interest. The person has ascertained particular information and has a sense of what needs to be figured out. In working with a content of individual interest, an individual is positioned to begin self-regulating behaviors (to seek additional information), experience feelings of self-efficacy, and have an understanding of the usefulness or importance of activity.

The two phases of individual interest are similar in that they can influence a person's attention and memory for tasks (Renninger, 1990; Renninger & Wozniak, 1985), the strategies they bring to learning (Alexander & Murphy, 1998; Alexander et al., 1997; Renninger, 1990; Renninger et al., 2002; Renninger & Hidi, 2002; Schiefele, 1996; Wild, 2000), and the likelihood that in these phases of interest, a person comes to identify with the content of individual interest (Hannover, 1998; Krapp, 1999, 2000, 2002a; Renninger, 2000).

These two phases of individual interest also differ. It is more likely that the person with a well-developed, rather than an emerging individual interest for particular content will persevere to work with content-related tasks despite the extent of the challenge and/or the temporary experiences of frustration such work represents (Ainley et al., 2002; Renninger, 2000; Renninger & Hidi, 2002; Renninger & Leckrone, 1991). This ability to work through frustration may indicate that the person with a well-developed interest for content is more resourceful in working with content than a person with a less-developed interest (Renninger & Shumar, 2002). It also suggests that a person is better positioned to anticipate next steps in the process of working with content of well-developed rather than emerging, or less-developed, individual interest.

Further, the support that a person in each phase of individual interest needs can also be expected to differ (Hidi & Renninger, 2003). A person with an emerging individual interest is likely to need external support to persevere in work with, develop resourcefulness for working with, and anticipate possible next steps or strategies to work with contents of interest. Whereas, a person working with a well-developed individual interest would not need such help. Instead, the person working with content of well-developed individual interest might instead need support in the form of models or others that allow his or her present understanding to be stretched (Renninger, 2000; Renninger & Hidi, 2002). Identification with well-developed interest enables a person to be both motivated and able to self-regulate his or her activity to make continued learning about content possible (Krapp, 2002b; Krapp & Lewalter, 2001; Renninger, 2000; Renninger & Hidi, 2002; Renninger et al., 2003).

CHALLENGES AND FUTURE DIRECTIONS

In this chapter, it has been argued that research on interest is positioned to make a significant contribution to understanding the functional relations among motivation, learning and emotions. Three features of interest based motivation set it apart from cognitively based motivational theories and call for the integration of the psychological aspects of interested engagement with findings of neuropsychological research. Specifically, (a) interest is content specific; (b) it evolves in the interaction of the person and his or her environment; and (c) it is both a cognitive and an affective variable.

Prior research has addressed the role of interest in text learning (Hidi, 2001; Schiefele, 1996, 1999), the interrelation between interest, personal goals, and self-concept (Hannover, 1998), and the effects of interest on learning at different developmental stages and across a variety of educational contexts, including preschool and elementary school (Renninger, 1992; Renninger et al., 2002; Renninger & Hidi, 2002), secondary school (Baumert & Köller, 1998; Renninger et al., 2003), college and university (Alexander et al., 1997; Harackiewicz et al., 2000; Krapp, 1997; Schiefele, 1999), and vocational education and training (Krapp & Lewalter, 2001; Krapp & Wild, 1998; Prenzel et al., 1998). A related line of research is focused on identifying mediating variables that can explain the (positive) effects of interest-based learning in terms of functional processes (Schiefele & Rheinberg, 1997). Mediating variables that have been analyzed in some detail include: attention (Ainley et al., 2002; Hidi, 1995; Renninger & Wozniak, 1985), learning strategies (Alexander & Murphy, 1998; Renninger et al., 2002; Renninger & Hidi, 2002; Wild, 2000), and emotional experiences (Ainley et al., 2002; Krapp & Lewalter, 2001; Lewalter et al., 1998; Renninger & Leckrone, 1991; Renninger et al., 2004; Schiefele, 1996; Schiefele & Csikszentmihalyi, 1994).

Recently, it has been suggested that the particular phase of interest under discussion influences the nature of the relation among motivation, learning, and emotions (Hidi & Renninger, 2003). For example, attention may be equated with the triggering of situational interest, but depending on the phase of interest being discussed, it may also be considered to be a mediator of the relation between individual interest and learning.

Missing in discussions of interest research have been detailed and well-founded analyses of the functional principles of interest-based learning. Why is it the case that students who have an interest for the content to be learned are more likely to reengage and learn that content more intensively and acquire a more interrelated knowledge structure for that content? What is the interrelation between interest as a content-specific motivational disposition and development from an ontogenetic perspective (see Heckhausen, 2000; Krapp, 2003). Answers to questions such as these appear to be within reach.

Interest research allows for the investigation of specific processes through which interest may influence learning and student achievement. For example, Ainley and colleagues (Ainley et al., 2002; Ainley, Hillman, & Hidi, 2002) investigated students' interests, affective reactions, persistence, and related learning outcomes. In these investigations, traditional self-report measures were combined with dynamic online recordings of students' affective and cognitive reactions while they were reading scientific and popular texts. The results showed that students' interest for the topics of the texts and their individual interest for the domain were related to their affective responses. Their affective responses were also associated with persistence and persistence was related to learning. Students who reported feeling interested were more likely to continue reading than students who were bored. Furthermore, online recordings of the affective reactions permitted identification of points in the text where (and when) student made decisions about whether to continue reading. Together with findings suggesting that interest impacts students' attention and memory for tasks (Renninger & Wozniak, 1985) and their depth of processing (Schiefele, 1999, 2001), it appears that interest makes a significant impact on intellectual functioning. Furthermore, the ability to sustain and develop new interest has also been associated with lifelong learning (Krapp & Lewalter, 2001; Renninger & Shumar, 2002; Snowden, 2001) and suggest that interest should have a central role in pedagogical practice.

As Berninger and Richards (2002) noted, academic tasks, emotions, and motivation are intricately linked with cognitive and executive functions in the neural circuitry that spans subcortical and cortical regions of the brain. There is, however, little in the way of information about ways to support the development of positive affect and motivation so that students who do not have interest for particular content can become academically motivated individuals (for exceptions, see Sansone & Smith, 2000; Sansone et al., 1992; Sansone, Wiebe, & Morgan, 1999). Work to support pedagogical use of situational interest as a scaffold to engagement is a step in this direction (e.g., Hidi & Harackiewicz, 2002; Schraw & Lehman, 2001). As Renninger and Hidi's (2002) case study illustrated, however, students need to be supported over time in multiple ways if deliberate interventions with situational interest are to really have an impact on student learning. Case analyses of students' interest for learning in Latin and history classes further suggests that teachers have a pivotal role as supporters of students' developing abilities to develop an interest for content, and a love of learning more generally (Renninger et al., 2003). In particular, teachers are in a position to adjust their instruction to meet students' strengths, needs, and interests, and to structure the classroom environment so that students can learn (see related discussion in Turner et al., 2002).

Interestingly, however, it appears that interventions to support the development of interest, or love of learning, have primarily targeted older students and adults who because of metacognitive abilities, are also able to learn to self-regulate their learning if they have reason to do the tasks to be learned and take steps themselves to make these tasks more interesting (Renninger et al., 2003). It appears that next steps for interest research might address ways in which interest, as a locus of the integration of psychological and neuroscientific functioning, might inform and support conditions for learning that would both position and enable younger students to become more focused, motivated, and successful learners.

ACKNOWLEDGMENTS

The authors gratefully acknowledge the Humbolt Foundation for support of their collaboration on this chapter; and a Social Science and Humanities Research Council of Canada grant to Suzanne Hidi. The authors would also like to thank Jeremy Schiefeling and Hofan Chau for their research assistance on portions of this chapter. They were supported through the Swarthmore College Faculty Research Fund. Finally, our thanks go to Dagmar Berndorff and André Tremblay for their support in preparing the manuscript.

REFERENCES

Ainley, M. D. (1987). The factor structure of curiosity measures. Breadth and depth of interest curiosity styles. *Australian Journal of Psychology, 39*, 53–59.

Ainley, M. D. (1993). Styles of engagement with learning: A multidimensional assessment of the relationship between student goals and strategy use and school achievement. *Journal of Educational Psychology, 85*, 395–405.

Ainley, M. D., Hidi, S., & Berndorff, D. (2002). Interest, learning, and the psychological processes that mediate their relationship. *Journal of Educational Psychology, 94*, 1–17.

Ainley, M., Hillman, K., & Hidi, S. (2002). Individual and situational interest: Gender and interest in prescribed English texts. *Learning and Instruction, 12*, 411–428.

Alexander, P. A. (1997). Mapping the multidimensional nature of domain learning: The interplay of cognitive, motivational, and strategic forces. In M. L. Maehr & P. R. Pintrich (Eds.), *Advances in motivation and achievement, Vol. 10* (pp. 213–250). Greenwich, CT: JAI.

Alexander, P. A., Jetton, T. L., & Kulikowich, J. M. (1995). Interrelationship of knowledge, interest, and recall: Assessing a model of domain learning. *Journal of Educational Psychology, 87*, 559–575.

Alexander, P. A., & Murphy, P. K. (1998). Profiling the differences in students' knowledge, interest, and strategic processing. *Journal of Educational Psychology, 90*, 435–447.

Alexander, P. A., Murphy, P. K., Woods, B. S., Duhon, K. E., & Parker, D. (1997). College instruction and concomitant changes in students' knowledge, interest, and strategy use: A study of domain learning. *Contemporary Educational Psychology, 22*, 125–146.

Ames, C. (1992). Classrooms: Goals, structures, and student motivation. *Journal of Educational Psychology, 84*, 261–271.

Ames, R., & Ames, C. (Eds.). (1984). *Research on motivation in education. Vol. 1: Student motivation.* London: Academic Press.

Anderson, R. C. (1982). Allocation of attention during reading. In A. Flammer & W. Kintsch (Eds.), *Discourse processing* (pp. 287–299). New York: North-Holland Publishing.

Anderson, R. C., Mason, J., & Shirey, L. (1984). The reading group: An experimental investigation of a labyrinth. *Reading Research Quarterly, 20*, 6–37.

Anderson, R. C., Shirey, L. L., Wilson, P. T., & Fielding, L. G. (1987). Interestingness of children's reading material. In R. E. Snow & M. J. Farr (Eds.), *Aptitude, learning and instruction: Vol. 3, Cognitive and affective process analyses* (pp. 287–299). Hillsdale, NJ: Lawrence Erlbaum Associates.

Arnold, F. (1906). The psychology of interest. I/II. *Psychological Review, 13*, 221–238/291–315.

Aronson, E., Blaney, N., Stephen, C., Sikes, J., & Snapp, M. (1978). *The jigsaw classroom.* Beverly Hills, CA: Sage.

Asher, S. R. (1980). Topic interest and children's reading comprehension. In R. J. Spiro, B. C. Bruce, & W. F. Brewer (Eds.), *Theoretical issues in reading comprehension* (pp. 525–534). Hillsdale, NJ: Lawrence Erlbaum Associates.

Bandura, A. (1977). Self-efficacy: Toward a unifying theory of behavior change. *Psychological Review, 84*, 191–215.

Bandura, A. (1982). Self-efficacy mechanism in human agency. *American Psychologist, 37*, 122–147.

Bandura, A. (1997). *Self-efficacy: The exercise of control.* New York: Freeman.

Bandura, A., & Schunk, D. H. (1981). Cultivating competence, self-efficacy, and intrinsic interest through proximal self-motivation. *Journal of Personality and Social Psychology, 41*, 586–598.

Bargel, T., Framheim-Peisert, G., & Sandberger, J. U. (1989). *Studienerfahrungen und studentische Orientierungen in den 80er Jahren. Trends und Stabiltaten* [Studies experience and studies orientation in the 80s: Trends and stabilities]. Bonn, Germany: Bock.

Baumert, J., & Köller, O. (1998). Interest research in secondary level 1: An overview. In L. Hoffmann, A. Krapp, K. A. Renninger, & J. Baumert (Eds.), *Interest and learning: Proceedings of the Seeon Conference on Interest and Gender* (pp. 241–256). Kiel, Germany: IPN.

Bergin, D. A. (1999). Influences on classroom interest. *Educational Psychologist, 34*, 87–98.

Berlyne, D. E. (1960). *Conflict, arousal, and curiosity.* New York: McGraw-Hill.

Berninger, V., & Richards, T. L. (2002). *Brain literacy for educators and psychologists.* New York: Academic Press.

Boekaerts, M. (in press). Towards a model that integrates motivation, affect and learning. *British Journal of Educational Psychology.*

Claparède, E. (1905). *Psychologie de l'enfant et pedagogie expérimentale* [Child psychology and experimental pedagogies]. Genève, Switzerland: Kundig.

Davidson, R. J. (2000). The neuroscience of affective style. In M. Gazzaniga (Ed.), *The new cognitive neurosciences* (2nd ed., pp. 1149–1162). Cambridge, MA: MIT Press.

Deci, E. L. (1998). The relation of interest to motivation and human needs: The self-determination theory viewpoint. In L. Hoffmann, A. Krapp, K. A. Renninger, & J. Baumert (Eds.), *Interest and learning: Proceedings of the Seeon Conference on Interest and Gender* (pp. 146–163). Kiel, Germany: IPN.

Dewey, J. (1913). *Interest and effort in education.* Boston: Riverside Press.

Drottz-Sjöberg, B. M. (1989). Interest in science education and research: A study of graduate students. *Göteborg Psychological Reports, 19*(14), 1–33.

Dweck, C. S., & Leggett, E. L. (1988). A social-cognitive approach to motivation and personality. *Psychological Review, 95,* 256–273.

Eccles, J. S., Adler, T. F., Futterman, R., Goff, S. B., Kaczala, C. M., Meece, J. L., & Midgley, C. (1983). Expectancies, values, and academic behaviors. In J. T. Spence (Ed.), *Achievement and achievement motivation* (pp. 75–146). San Francisco: Freeman.

Eccles (Parsons), J., Wigfield, A., & Schiefele, U. (1998). Motivation to succeed. In N. Eisenberg (Ed.), *Handbook of child psychology* (5th ed., pp. 1017–1095). New York: Wiley.

Fay, A. (1998). The impact of CRO on children's interest in and comprehension of science and technology. In L. Hoffmann, A. Krapp, K. A. Renninger, & J. Baumert (Eds.), *Interest and learning: Proceedings of the Seeon Conference on Interest and Gender* (pp. 205–214). Kiel, Germany: IPN.

Fink, B. (1991). Interest development as structural change in person-object relationships. In L. Oppenheimer & J. Valsiner (Eds.), *The origins of action: Interdisciplinary and international perspectives* (pp. 175–204). New York: Springer.

Fischer, H. E., & Horstendahl, M. (1997). Motivation and learning physics. *Research and Science Education, 27,* 411–424.

Fölling-Albers, M., & Hartinger, A. (1998). Interest of girls and boys in elementary school. In L. Hoffmann, A. Krapp, K. A. Renninger, & J. Baumert (Eds.), *Interest and learning: Proceedings of the Seeon Conference on Interest and Gender* (pp. 175–183). Kiel, Germany: IPN.

Fryer, D. (1931). *The measurement of interest.* New York: Holt.

Gardner, P. L. (1985). Students' interest in science and technology: An international overview. In M. Lehrke, L. Hoffmann, & P. L. Gardner (Eds.), *Interests in science and technology education* (pp. 15–34). Kiel, Germany: IPN.

Gardner, P. L. (1998). The development of males' and females' interests in science and technology. In L. Hoffmann, A. Krapp, K. A. Renninger, & J. Baumert (Eds.), *Interest and learning: Proceedings of the Seeon Conference on Interest and Gender* (pp. 41–57). Kiel, Germany: IPN.

Gisbert, K. (1998). Individual interest in mathematics and femal gender identity: Biographical case studies. In L. Hoffmann, A. Krapp, K. A. Renninger, & J. Baumert (Eds.), *Interest and learning: Proceedings of the Seeon Conference on Interest and Gender* (pp. 387–401). Kiel, Germany: IPN.

Gisbert, K. (2001). *Geschlecht und Studienwahl. Biographische Analysen geschlechtstypischer und -untypischer Bildungswege* [Gender and studies choice: Biographical analyses gender typical and atypical educational channels]. Münster, Germany: Waxmann.

Goldman, S. R., Mayfield-Stewart, C., Bateman, H. V., Pellegrino, J. W., & The Technology Group at Vanderbilt. (1998). Environments that support meaningful learning. In L. Hoffmann, A. Krapp, K. A. Renninger, & J. Baumert (Eds.), *Interest and learning: Proceedings of the Seeon Conference on Interest and Gender* (pp. 184–197). Kiel, Germany: IPN.

Gottfredson, L. S. (1981). Circumscription and compromise: A developmental theory of occupational aspirations. *Journal of Counselling Psychology* [Monograph], *Nr. 6, 28,* 545–579.

Hannover, B. (1998). The development of self-concept and interests. In L. Hoffmann, A. Krapp, K. A. Renninger, & J. Baumert (Eds.), *Interest and learning: Proceedings of the Seeon Conference on Interest and Gender* (pp. 105–125). Kiel, Germany: IPN.

Harackiewicz, J. M., Barron, K. E., Tauer, J. M., Carter, S. M., & Elliot, A. J. (2000). Short-term and long-term consequences of achievement: Predicting continued interest and performance over time. *Journal of Educational Psychology, 92*(2), 316–330.

Harackiewicz, J. M., & Durik, A. M. (2003). *Task value in the college classroom: Predicting goals, interest and performance*. Paper presented at the biannual meeting of the European Association for Learning and Instruction, Padua, Italy.

Harp, S. F., & Mayer, R. E. (1997). The role of interest in learning from scientific text and illustrations: On the distinction between emotional interest and cognitive interest. *Journal of Educational Psychology, 89*, 92–102.

Häussler, P., & Hoffmann, L. (1998). Qualitative differences in students' interest in physics and the dependence on gender and age. In L. Hoffmann, A. Krapp, K. A. Renninger, & J. Baumert (Eds.), *Interest and learning: Proceedings of the Seeon Conference on Interest and Gender* (pp. 280–289). Kiel, Germany: IPN.

Heckhausen, H. (1991). *Motivation and action*. Berlin, Germany: Springer.

Heckhausen, J. (2000). *Motivational psychology of human development*. London: Elsevier.

Helmke, A. (1993). Die Entwicklung der Lernfreude vom Kindergarten bis zur 5. Klassenstufe [Development of affective attitudes toward learning from kindergarten to grade five]. *Zeitschrift für Pädagogische Psychologie, 7*, 77–86.

Hidi, S. (1990). Interest and its contribution as a mental resource for learning. *Review of Educational Research, 60*, 549–571.

Hidi, S. (1995). A re-examination of the role of attention in learning from text. *Educational Psychology Review, 7*, 323–350.

Hidi, S. (2001). Interest, reading, and learning: Theoretical and practical considerations. *Educational Psychology Review, 13*, 191–208.

Hidi, S. (2003a). *Interest and emotions*. Paper presented at the annual meeting of the American Educational Research Association, Chicago.

Hidi, S. (2003b). *Interest: A motivational variable with a difference*. Paper presented at the biannual meeting of the European Association for Learning and Instruction, Padua, Italy.

Hidi, S., & Ainley, M. (2002). Interest and adolescence. In F. Pajares & T. Urdan (Eds.), *Academic motivation of adolescents* (pp. 247–275). Greenwich, CT: IAP.

Hidi, S., & Anderson, V. (1992). Situational interest and its impact on reading and expository writing. In K. A. Renninger, S. Hidi, & A. Krapp (Eds.), *The role of interest in learning and development* (pp. 215–238). Hillsdale, NJ: Lawrence Erlbaum Associates.

Hidi, S., & Baird, W. (1986). Interestingness—A neglected variable in discourse processing. *Cognitive Science, 10*, 179–194.

Hidi, S., & Baird, W. (1988). Strategies for increasing text-based interest and students' recall of expository texts. *Reading Research Quarterly, 23*, 465–483.

Hidi, S., Baird, W., & Hildyard, A. (1982). That's important but is it interesting? Two factors in text processing. In A. Flammer & W. Kintsch (Eds.), *Discourse processing* (pp. 63–75). New York: North-Holland Publishing.

Hidi, S., & Berndorff, D. (1998). Situational interest and learning. In L. Hoffmann, A. Krapp, K. A. Renninger, & J. Baumert (Eds.), *Interest and learning: Proceedings of the Seeon Conference on Interest and Gender* (pp. 74–90). Kiel, Germany: IPN.

Hidi, S., & Harackiewicz, J. M. (2000). Motivating the academically unmotivated: A critical issue for the 21st century. *Review of Educational Research, 70*(2), 151–179.

Hidi, S., & Renninger, K. A. (2003). *The four-phase model of interest development*. Manuscript submitted for publication.

Hidi, S., Weiss, J., Berndorff, D., & Nolan, J. (1998). The role of gender, instruction and a cooperative learning technique in science education across formal and informal settings. In L. Hoffmann, A. Krapp, K. A. Renninger, & J. Baumert (Eds.), *Interest and learning: Proceedings of the Seeon Conference on Interest and Gender* (pp. 215–227). Kiel, Germany: IPN.

Hoffmann, L. (2002). Promoting girls' interest and achievement in physics classes for beginners. *Learning and Instruction, 12*(4), 447–466.

Hoffmann, L., & Häussler, P. (1998). An intervention project promoting girls' and boys' interest in physics. In L. Hoffmann, A. Krapp, K. A. Renninger, & J. Baumert (Eds.), *Interest and* learning: Proceedings of the Seeon Conference on Interest and Gender (pp. 301–316). Kiel, Germany: IPN.

Hoffmann, L., Krapp, A., Renninger, K. A., & Baumert, J. (Eds.). (1998). Interest and learning: Proceedings of the Seeon Conference on Interest and Gender. Kiel, Germany: IPN.

Holland, J. L. (1973). Making vocational choices: A theory of careers. Englewood Cliffs, NJ: Prentice-Hall.

Iran-Nejad, A. (1987). Cognitive and affective causes of interest and liking. Journal of Educational Psychology, 7, 120–130.

Isaac, J., Sansone, C., & Smith, J. L. (1999). Other people as a source of interest in an activity. Journal of Experimental Social Psychology, 35, 239–265.

Izard, C. E. (1977). Human emotions. New York: Plenum.

James, W. (1890). Talks to teachers on psychology. London: Longmans, Green and Comp.

Kasten, H., & Krapp, A. (1986). Das Interessengenese-Projekt—eine Pilotstudie [The interest-genesis study—a pilot project]. Zeitschrift für Pädagogik, 32, 175–188.

Kintsch, W. (1980). Learning from texts, levels of comprehension, or: Why anyone would read a story anyway? Poetics, 9, 87–98.

Krapp, A. (1989, September). Interest, learning and academic achievement. In P. Nenninger (Chair), Task motivation by interest. Paper presented at Third European Conference of Learning and Instruction (EARLI), Madrid, Spain.

Krapp, A. (1993). Die Psychologie Lernmotivation [The psychology of learning motivation]. Perspektiven der Forschung und Probleme ihrer Paedagogischen Rezeption, 39, 187–206.

Krapp, A. (1997). Interesse und Studium [Interest and higher education]. In H. Gruber & A. Renkl (Eds.), Wege zum Können. Determinanten des Kompetenzerwerbs (pp. 45–58). Bern, Switzerland: Huber.

Krapp, A. (1999). Interest, motivation and learning: An educational-psychological perspective. European Journal of Psychology of Education, 14, 23–40.

Krapp, A. (2000). Interest and human development during adolescence: An educational-psychological approach. In J. Heckhausen (Ed.), Motivational psychology of human development (pp. 109–128). London: Elsevier.

Krapp, A. (2002a). An educational-psychological theory of interest and its relation to self-determination theory. In E. L. Deci & R. Ryan (Eds.), The handbook of self-determination research (pp. 405–427). Rochester, NY: University of Rochester Press.

Krapp, A. (2002b). Structural and dynamic aspects of interest development. Theoretical considerations from an ontogenetic perspective. Learning and Instruction, 12, 383–409.

Krapp, A. (2003). Interest and human development: An educational psychology perspective. British Journal of Educational Psychology. Monograph Series II, 57–84.

Krapp, A., & Fink, B. (1992). The development and function of interests during the critical transition from home to preschool. In K. A. Renninger, S. Hidi, & A. Krapp (Eds.), The role of interest in learning and development (pp. 397–429). Hillsdale, NJ: Lawrence Erlbaum Associates.

Krapp, A., Hidi, S., & Renninger, K. A. (1992). Interest, learning and development. In K. A. Renninger, S. Hidi, & A. Krapp (Eds.), The role of interest in learning and development (pp. 3–25). Hillsdale, NJ: Lawrence Erlbaum Associates.

Krapp, A., & Lewalter, D. (2001). Development of interests and interest-based motivational orientations: A longitudinal study in school and work settings. In S. Volet & S. Järvelä (Eds.), Motivation in learning contexts: Theoretical advances and methodological implications (pp. 201–232). London: Elsevier.

Krapp, A., Renninger, K. A., & Hoffmann, L. (1998). Some thoughts about the development of a unifying framework for the study of individual interest. In L. Hoffmann, A. Krapp, K. A. Renninger, & J. Baumert (Eds.), Interest and learning: Proceedings of the Seeon Conference on Interest and Gender (pp. 455–468). Kiel, Germany: IPN.

Krapp, A. & Wild, K. P. (1998, August 9–14). *The development of interest in school and work settings: A longitudinal study based on experience-sampling data.* Paper presented at the 24th International Congress of Applied Psychology, San Francisco.

Kuhl, J. (2000). A functional-design approach to motivation and self-regulation. The dynamics of personality systems interactions. In M. Boekaerts, P. R. Pintrich, & M. Zeidner (Eds.), *Handbook of self-regulation: Theory, research and applications* (pp. 451–502). San Diego, CA: Academic Press.

Larson, R. (1988). Flow and writing. In M. Csikszentmihalyi & I. S. Csikszentmihalyi (Eds.), *Optimal experience* (pp. 151–171). New York: Cambridge University Press.

LeDoux, J. E. (2000). Emotion circuits in the brain. *Annual Review of Neurosciences, 23,* 155–184.

Lehrke, M., Hoffmann, L., & Gardner, P. L. (Eds.). (1985). *Interests in science and technology education.* Kiel, Germany: IPN.

Leontjew, A. N. (1977). *Tätigkeit, Bewußtsein, Persönlichkeit* [Activity, consciousness, personality]. Stuttgart, Germany: Klett.

Lewalter, D., Krapp, A., Schreyer, I., & Wild, K.-P. (1998). Die Bedeutsamkeit des Erlebens von Kompetenz, Autonomie und sozialer Eingebundenheit für die Entwicklung berufsspezifischer Interessen [The relevance of experiencing competence, autonomy and social relatedness for the development of job-related interests]. *Zeitschrift für Berufs- und Wirtschaftspädagogik,* Beiheft Nr. 14., 143–168.

Lewin, K. (1936). *A dynamic theory of personality.* New York: McGraw-Hill.

McDaniel, M. A., Waddill, P. J., Finstad, K., & Bourg, T. (2000). The effects of text-based interest on attention and recall. *Journal of Educational Psychology, 92,* 492–502.

Medved, M., Hidi, S., & Ainley, M. (2002). *How interest relates to other motivational variables: A multidimensional investigation of students' motivation to study science.* Manuscript submitted for publication.

Meyer, D. K., & Turner, J. C. (2002). Discovering emotion in classroom motivation research. *Educational Psychologist, 37,* 107–114.

Miller, P. H., & Weiss, M. G. (1982). Children's and adults' knowledge about variables affect selective attention. *Child Development, 53,* 543–549.

Miller, P. H., & Zalenski, R. (1982). Preschoolers knowledge about attention. *Developmental Psychology, 8,* 871–875.

Mitchell, M. (1993). Situational interest: Its multifaceted structure in the secondary school mathematics classroom. *Journal of Educational Psychology, 85,* 424–436.

Murphy, P. K., & Alexander, P. A. (2000). A motivated exploration of motivation terminology. *Contemporary Educational Psychology, 25,* 3–53.

Nuttin, J. (1984). *Motivation, planning, and action.* Leuven/Louvain, Belgium: Leuven University Press.

Pajares, F. (1996). Self-efficacy beliefs in academic settings. *Review of Educational Research, 66,* 543–578.

Panksepp, J. (1998). *Affective neuroscience: The foundations of human and animal emotion.* New York: Oxford University Press.

Panksepp, J. (2003). At the interface of the affective, behavioral and cognitive neurosciences: Decoding the emotional feelings of the brain. *Brain and Cognition, 52,* 4–14.

Pekrun, R. (2000). A social-cognitive, control-value theory of achievement emotions. In J. Heckhausen (Ed.), *Motivational psychology of human development* (pp. 143–164). London: Elsevier.

Pintrich, P. R., & De Groot, E. V. (1990). Motivational and self-regulated learning components of classroom academic performance. *Journal of Educational Psychology, 82,* 33–40.

Prenzel, M. (1988). *Die Wirkungsweise von Interesse* [The impact of interest]. Opladen: Westdeutscher Verlag.

Prenzel, M. (1992). The selective persistence of interest. In K. A. Renninger, S. Hidi, & A. Krapp (Eds.), *The role of interest in learning and development* (pp. 71–98). Hillsdale, NJ: Lawrence Erlbaum Associates.

Prenzel, M. (1998). Interest research concerning the upper secondary level, college, and vocational education: An overview. In L. Hoffmann, A. Krapp, K. A. Renninger, & J. Baumert (Eds.), *Interest and learning: Proceedings of the Seeon Conference on Interest and Gender* (pp. 355–366). Kiel, Germany: IPN.

Prenzel, M., Kramer, K., & Drechsel, B. (1998). Changes in learning, motivation, and interest in vocational education: Halfway through the study. In L. Hoffmann, A. Krapp, K. A. Renninger, & J. Baumert (Eds.), *Interest and learning: Proceedings of the Seeon Conference on Interest and Gender* (pp. 441–454). Kiel, Germany: IPN.

Pressick-Kilbourn, K., & Walker, R. (2002). The social construction of interest in a learning community. In D. M. McInerney & S. Van Etten (Eds.), *Research on socio-cultural influences on motivation and learning: Vol. 2* (pp. 153–182). Greenwich, CT: Information Age Publishing.

Rathunde, K. (1993). The experience of interest: A theoretical and empirical look at its role in adolescent talent development. In P. Pintrich & M. Maehr (Eds.), *Advances in motivation and achievement, Vol. 8* (pp. 59–98). Greenwich, CT: JAI.

Rathunde, K. (1998). Undivided and abiding interest: Comparisons across studies of talented adolescents and creative adults. In L. Hoffmann, A. Krapp, K. A. Renninger, & J. Baumert (Eds.), *Interest and learning: Proceedings of the Seeon Conference on Interest and Gender* (pp. 367–376). Kiel, Germany: IPN.

Renninger, K. A. (1989). Individual patterns in children's play interests. In L. T. Winegar (Ed.), *Social interaction and the development of children's understanding* (pp. 147–172). Norwood, NJ: Ablex.

Renninger, K. A. (1990). Children's play interests, representation, and activity. In R. Fivush & J. A. Hudson (Eds.), *Knowing and remembering in young children.* Emory Cognition Series (Vol. III) (pp. 127–165). Cambridge, MA: Cambridge University Press.

Renninger, K. A. (1992). Individual interest and development: Implications for theory and practice. In K. A. Renninger, S. Hidi, & A. Krapp (Eds.), *The role of interest in learning and development* (pp. 361–376). Hillsdale, NJ: Lawrence Erlbaum Associates.

Renninger, K. A. (1998). The roles of individual interest(s) and gender in learning: An overview of research on preschool and elementary school-aged children/students. In L. Hoffmann, A. Krapp, K. A. Renninger, & J. Baumert (Eds.), *Interest and learning: Proceedings of the Seeon Conference on Interest and Gender* (pp. 165–175). Kiel, Germany: IPN.

Renninger, K. A. (2000). Individual interest and its implications for understanding intrinsic motivation. In C. Sansone & J. M. Harackiewicz (Eds.), *Intrinsic motivation: Controversies and new directions* (pp. 373–404). New York: Academic Press.

Renninger, K. A. (2003). Effort and interest. In J. Gutherie (Gen. Ed.), *The Encyclopedia of Education, 2nd ed.* (pp. 704–709). New York: Macmillan.

Renninger, K. A., Ewen, L., & Lasher, A. K. (2002). Individual interest as context in expository text and mathematical word problems. *Learning and Instruction, 12*, 467–491.

Renninger, K. A., & Hidi, S. (2002). Student interest and achievement: Developmental issues raised by a case study. In A. Wigfield & J. S. Eccles (Eds.), *The development of achievement motivation* (pp. 173–195). New York: Academic Press.

Renninger, K. A., Hidi, S., & Krapp, A. (Eds.). (1992). *The role of interest in learning and development.* Hillsdale, NJ: Lawrence Erlbaum Associates.

Renninger, K. A., & Leckrone, T. (1991). Continuity in young children's actions: A consideration of interest and temperament. In L. Oppenheimer & J. Valsiner (Eds.), *The origins of action: Interdisciplinary and international perspectives* (pp. 205–238). New York: Springer-Verlag.

Renninger, K. A., Sansone, C., & Smith, J. (2004). Love of learning. In C. Peterson & M. E. P. Seligman (Eds.), *Character strengths and virtues: A classification and handbook.* New York: Oxford University Press.

Renninger, K. A., & Shumar, W. (2002). Community building with and for teachers: The Math Forum as a resource for teacher professional development. In K. A. Renninger & W. Shumar (Eds.), *Building virtual communities: Learning and change in cyberspace* (pp. 60–95). New York: Cambridge University Press.

Renninger, K. A., & Wozniak, R. H. (1985). Effect of interest on attentional shift, recognition, and recall in young children. *Developmental Psychology, 21*, 624–632.

Roe, A., & Siegelman, M. (1964). The origin of interests. *APGA Inquiry Studies, 1*, 98–110.

Sadoski, M., Goetz, T., & Fritz, J. B. (1993). A causal model of sentence recall: Effects of familiarity, concreteness, comprehensibility, and interestingness. *Journal of Reading Behavior, 25*(1), 5–16.

Sansone, C., & Smith, J. L. (2000). Self-regulating interest: When, why and how. In C. Sansone & J. M. Harackiewicz (Eds.), *Intrinsic motivation: Controversies and new directions* (pp. 343–372). New York: Academic Press.

Sansone, C., Weir, C., Harpster, L., & Morgan, C. (1992). Once a boring task always a boring task? Interest as a self-regulatory mechanism. *Journal of Personality and Social Psychology, 63*, 379–390.

Sansone, C., Wiebe, D. J., & Morgan, C. (1999). Self-regulating interest: The moderating role of hardiness and conscientiousness. *Journal of Personality, 67*, 701–733.

Schank, R. C. (1979). Interestingness: Controlling inferences. *Artificial Intelligence, 12*, 273–297.

Schiefele, H. (1978). *Lernmotivation und Motivlernen* [Learning motivation and learning of motives] (2nd ed.). München, Germany: Ehrenwirth.

Schiefele, H. (1981). Handeln aus Interesse: Versuch einer erziehungswissenschaftlichen Konzeption [Behavior from interest: Test of an education scientific conception]. In H. Kasten & W. Einsiedler (Hrsg.), *Aspekte einer pädagogisch-psychologischen Interessentheorie* (pp. 30–49). München, Germany: HSBw (Gelbe Reihe Nr.1).

Schiefele, U. (1996). Topic interest, text representation, and quality of experience. *Contemporary Educational Psychology, 12*, 3–18.

Schiefele, U. (1998). Individual interest and learning, what we know and what we don't know. In L. Hoffmann, A. Krapp, K. A. Renninger, & J. Baumert (Eds.), *Interest and learning: Proceedings of the Seeon Conference on Interest and Gender* (pp. 91–104). Kiel, Germany: IPN.

Schiefele, U. (1999). Interest and learning from text. *Scientific Studies of Reading, 3*(3), 257–279.

Schiefele, U. (2001). The role of interest in motivation and learning. In J. M. Collis & S. Messick (Ed.), *Intelligence and personality* (pp. 163–194). Mahwah, NJ: Lawrence Erlbaum Associates.

Schiefele, U., & Csikszentmihalyi, M. (1994). Interest and the quality of experience in classrooms. *European Journal of Psychology of Education, IX*(3), 251–270.

Schiefele, U., & Krapp, A. (1996). Topic interest and free recall of expository test. *Learning and Individual Differences, 8*, 141–160.

Schiefele, U., Krapp, A., & Winteler, A. (1992). Interest as a predictor of academic achievement: A meta-analysis of research. In K. A. Renninger, S. Hidi, & A. Krapp (Eds.), *The role of interest in learning and development* (pp. 183–212). Hillsdale, NJ: Lawrence Erlbaum Associates.

Schiefele, U., & Rheinberg, F. (1997). Motivation and knowledge acquisition: Searching for mediating processes. In M. L. Maehr & P. R. Pintrich (Eds.), *Advances in motivation and achievement, Vol. 10* (pp. 251–301). London: JAI.

Schraw, G., Bruning, R., & Svoboda, C. (1995). Sources of situational interest. *Journal of Reading Behavior, 27*, 1–17.

Schraw, G., & Dennison, R. S. (1994). The effect of reader purpose on interest and recall. *Journal of Reading Behavior, 26*, 1–18.

Schraw, G., & Lehman, S. (2001). Situational interest: A review of the literature and directions for future research. *Educational Psychology Review, 13*, 23–52.

Shirey, L. L., & Reynolds, R. E. (1988). Effect of interest on attention and learning. *Journal of Educational Psychology, 80*, 159–166.

Silvia, P. J. (2001). Interest and interests: The psychology of constructive capriciousness. *Review of General Psychology, 5*, 270–290.

Slavin, R. E. (1991). *Student team learning: A practical guide to cooperative learning.* 3rd edition. Washington, DC: National Education Association.

Snowden, D. (2001). *Aging with grace.* New York: Bantam.

Strong, E. K. (1943). *Vocational interests of men and women.* Palo Alto, CA: Stanford University Press.

Thorndike, E. L. (1935). *The psychology of wants, interests, and attitudes.* New York: Appleton-Century.

Todt, E. (1985). Elements of a theory of science interests. In M. Lehrke, L. Hoffmann, & P. L. Gardner (Eds.), *Interests in science and technology* (pp. 59–69). Kiel, Germany: IPN.

Todt, E., & Schreiber, S. (1998). Development of interests. In L. Hoffmann, A. Krapp, K. A. Renninger, & J. Baumert (Eds.), *Interest and learning: Proceedings of the Seeon Conference on Interest and Gender* (pp. 25–40). Kiel, Germany: IPN.

Turner, J. C., Midgley, C., Meyer, D. K., Ghenn, M., Anderman, E. M., & Kang, Y. (2002). The classroom environment and students' reports of avoidance strategies in mathematics: A multi method study. *Journal of Educational Psychology, 94*, 88-106.

Valsiner, J. (1992). Interest: A meta-theoretical perspective. In K. A. Renninger, S. Hidi, & A. Krapp (Eds.), *The role of interest in learning and development* (pp. 27–41). Hillsdale, NJ: Lawrence Erlbaum Associates.

von Aufschnaiter, C., Schoster, A., & von Aufschnaiter, S. (1999). The influence of students' individual experiences of physics learning environments on cognitive processes. In J. Leach & A. C. Paulsen (Eds.), *Practical work in science education—recent research studies* (pp. 281–296). Dordrecht, Germany: Kluwer.

Wade, S. E. (1992). How interest affects learning from text. In K. A. Renninger, S. Hidi, & A. Krapp (Eds.), *The role of interest in learning and development* (pp. 27–41). Hillsdale, NJ: Lawrence Erlbaum Associates.

Wade, S. E., Buxton, W. M., & Kelly, M. (1999). Using think-alouds to examine reader-text interest. *Reading Research Quarterly, 34*, 194–216.

Wade, S. E., Schraw, G., Buxton, W. M., & Hayes, M. T. (1993). Seduction of the strategic reader: Effects of interest on strategies and recall. *Reading Research Quarterly, 28*, 93–114.

Walsh, W. B., & Osipow, S. H. (Eds.). (1986). *Advances in vocational psychology. Volume 1: The assessment of interests.* Hillsdale, NJ: Lawrence Erlbaum Associates.

Weiner, B. (1972). *Theories of motivation.* Chicago: Markham.

Wigfield, A., & Eccles, J. S. (1992). The development of achievement task values: A theoretical analysis. *Developmental Review, 12*, 265–310.

Wigfield, A., & Eccles, J. S. (2002). The development of competence beliefs, expectancies for success, and achievement values from childhood through adolescence. In A. Wigfield & J. S. Eccles (Eds.), *Development of achievement motivation* (pp. 91–120). San Diego, CA: Academic Press.

Wild, K. P. (2000). *Lernstrategien im Studium* [Learning strategies during the studies]. Münster, Germany: Waxmann.

Wild, K.-P., Krapp, A., Schreyer, I., & Lewalter, D. (1998). The development of interest and motivational orientations: Gender differences in vocational education. In L. Hoffmann, A. Krapp, K. A. Renninger, & J. Baumert (Eds.), *Interest and learning: Proceedings of the Seeon Conference on Interest and Gender* (pp. 441–454). Kiel, Germany: IPN.

Wolters, C. A. (1998). Self-regulated learning and college students' regulation of motivation. *Journal of Educational Psychology, 90*, 224–235.

Zimmerman, B. J. (1989). A social cognitive view of self-regulated academic learning. *Journal of Educational Psychology, 81*, 329–339.

Zimmerman, B. J. (2000). Self-efficacy: An essential motive to learn. *Contemporary Educational Psychology, 25*, 82–91.

III

INTELLIGENCE AND PERSONALITY:
FROM PSYCHOMETRICS
TO PERSONAL DYNAMICS

III

5

▼▼▼▼▼▼▼

Cognitive, Affective, and Conative Aspects of Adult Intellect Within a Typical and Maximal Performance Framework

Phillip L. Ackerman
Ruth Kanfer
Georgia Institute of Technology

CHOICES: TYPICAL BEHAVIOR OR MAXIMAL PERFORMANCE

When modern psychology first became established in the academy by Wundt and his students, the study of human behavior became both standardized and often artificial. For example, the procedures of early introspection experiments on sensation and perception required that observers mentally decompose an image into its components and not simply say that "I perceive a chair." When intellectual assessments were introduced (to some degree first by Galton, and then later by Binet), standardization was a key ingredient to the methodology. Although one may argue whether Binet's assessments of intellectual abilities were more or less artificial, it is clear that Binet was interested in obtaining the child's maximal performance. That is, Binet instructed examinees to do whatever was appropriate (whether encouragement for one child, or admonishment for another) in order to obtain the child's best performance on the test (e.g., see Binet & Simon, 1916; see also Ackerman, 1996, for a review). This paradigm for assessing intellectual abilities has been passed down through succeeding generations of assessment instruments, under the heading of 'establishing rapport with the examinee.' In the developed world, testing is so ubiquitous, and the consequences of poor performance so well entrenched, that by the time a high school student attempts the SAT, or a college student attempts the Graduate Record Examination, it is almost certainly superfluous to verbally encourage the examinee to attempt to perform well on the test.

In contrast to ability assessment, measures of affect or personality are almost always concerned with assessment of typical behaviors (e.g., see Butler & Fiske, 1955; Cronbach, 1949; Fiske & Butler, 1963). In both structured and projective techniques of personality assessment, the client or examinee is told to 'respond as you would typically behave.' Structured personality assessments thus ask the individual what he or she likes to do, or how he or she usually behaves in particular situations. The individual is told that 'there are no right or wrong answers' on personality measures, though the individual may not actually feel that way when the purpose of the assessment is not counseling or self-discovery, but organizational selection or placement. Note that our consideration of affect in this chapter is on the relatively stable aspects— that is, personality traits, rather than moods or other transient states. (For a discussion of other approaches to affect in this context, see Linnenbrink & Pintrich, chap. 3.)

As we discuss in the following, this traditional distinction between maximal performance and typical behaviors for intelligence and personality is in some sense an accident of history. These respective approaches may be suboptimal for the comprehensive study of intelligence and affect, and it is most certainly suboptimal for considering how intelligence and affect might interact with one another. In the criterion domain, however, this distinction is a useful one. That is, an investigator must understand the nature of the criterion from this perspective. Is the investigator interested in an individual's maximal performance (whether in terms of intellectual activities or even in terms of personality), or is the interest more in the domain of typical behaviors? One could reasonably argue that the larger domain of school or job performance is much more appropriately considered to be typical behavior—as the criterion is best conceptualized as what the individual achieves over an extended period of time, rather than in a brief slice of time. Or, one might be more interested in what the individual is capable of, when the conditions are optimized for maximal effort. For example, an individual's preference for introverted activities may in fact be largely irrelevant in determining whether the individual is capable of giving an effective lecture to a large audience.

We review the constructs of cognition, affect, and conation, in terms of both typical behaviors and maximal performance. An integrative theory is presented that focuses on typical intellectual functioning and the interactions between various trait families in determining intellectual development and intellectual functioning. Results from empirical studies are also reviewed, and an agenda for future research is presented.

INTELLECTUAL ABILITIES AND TYPICAL–MAXIMAL PERFORMANCE

Although not a precise match, Hebb's (1942) distinction of Intelligence A and Intelligence B and Cattell's (1943) distinction of fluid intelligence (Gf) and crystallized intelligence (Gc) provided a reasonably close categorization of abilities that are associated with maximal performance and typical perform-ance, respectively. Intelligence A and Gf are most associated with relatively decontextualized information processing, reasoning, and memory. The pro-totypical measures of Gf, such as the Raven Progressive Matrices Test (Pen-rose & Raven, 1936; Raven, Court, & Raven, 1977) or the so-called Culture Fair Intelligence Test (CFIT; Cattell & Cattell, 1957) present the examinee with test items that allow for minimal transfer of learning or knowledge in solving the problems. Instead, they rely on the examinee's ability to use mem-ory resources and reasoning skills to derive the correct answers to the items. The Raven test is unspeeded, but the CFIT has relatively strong time limits on performance. In both cases, the examinee must devote a maximal level of attentional effort to obtain the highest possible score.

Tests of general information (such as are found on the WAIS–III, Wechs-ler, 1997 or the Stanford–Binet IV, Thorndike, Hagen, & Sattler, 1986) are good prototypes for Intelligence B and Gc—that is, knowledge that the examinee has acquired and maintained over a long period of time. What makes these measures particularly appropriate for assessing typical intellec-tual performance, is that the examinee must know the information prior to testing—it cannot be derived in the testing situation. If an examinee is asked to name his or her state's elected politicians, a search of long-term memory is needed, but this activity generally requires far less intellectual effort than solving an abstract spatial reasoning test item.

Many scales of intellectual abilities assess a mixture of typical behaviors and maximal performance. A test of reading comprehension, for example, draws substantially on previously learned skills and knowledge (such as reading skills, vocabulary knowledge, and even sometimes factual knowl-edge), and new learning (which involves allocation of working memory re-sources to understanding a new text passage). For this reason, it is not un-usual to find that such tests correlate substantially with both Gf and Gc factors. Although Gc type tests can provide the best single estimate of intel-ligence (e.g., the information test on the WAIS is the most highly correlated subscale with overall IQ, see Wechsler, 1944, and the Ebbinghaus comple-tion test has the highest correlation with an estimate of Spearman's general ability factor (*g*), see Spearman [1927]), the traditional approach to omni-bus intelligence assessment includes a wide sampling of both Gf and Gc-associated items.

In criterion-related validity studies, the framework of Brunswik Symmetry (Wittmann & Suß, 1999) is useful for considering the roles of Gf and Gc, or maximal performance and typical behaviors. This framework states that maximal validity is obtained when there is both a direct correspondence between the predictor space and the criterion space, and the breadth of the predictors and the breadth of the criterion are matched. That is, broad predictors are most appropriate for broad criteria, and narrow predictors are most appropriate for narrow criteria, as long as the correspondence is matched. If the wrong narrow predictor is used to predict a narrow criterion, it will perform more poorly than a broad predictor. Thus, when it comes to validating intelligence measures, a high level of Brunswik Symmetry is obtained when the intelligence measure has ample representation of both maximal performance and typical behavior, because primary school success is predicated on both maximal performance (e.g., aptitude tests) and typical behaviors (e.g., cumulative grades on homework, in-class assignments, and end of term achievement assessments).

Such omnibus intelligence tests, however, are less well suited for predicting post-secondary academic performance (e.g., the Stanford–Binet or Wechsler tests have poorer predictive validities for college and university performance, compared to primary school performance, even after taking into account the restriction-of-range of talent and explicit prior selection at post-secondary institutions), because the criteria for academic success are dominated by typical behavior measures (e.g., term papers and final examinations) and less dependent on maximal performance. Performance in graduate school and beyond is better predicted by measures of domain knowledge (which falls under the wide category of Gc and typical behavior) than it is predicted by abstract reasoning or other general aptitude measures (e.g., see Willingham, 1974). One of the popular criticisms of the traditional IQ-type tests is that they do not well predict occupational performance (Anastasi, 1982). From the perspective provided above, it seems clear that one reason for such findings is that there is a lack of Brunswik Symmetry, stemming from the inclusion of maximal performance measures when they have relatively less impact on occupational performance than measures of typical intellectual behaviors.

AFFECT AND TYPICAL–MAXIMAL PERFORMANCE

Where modern intelligence assessments have increasingly focused on maximal performance (especially in terms of those who advocate using only Raven-type tests for assessing intellect), measures of affect (personality) have focused on typical behaviors. Indeed, one could argue that the underlying theme of the trait–situation controversy—where researchers argued about whether traits or situations had dominant influences on behavior (Mischel, 1968; Rushton, Brainerd, & Pressley, 1983) was largely predicted on a form of contrasting typical behaviors and maximal behaviors. That is, one theme that emerged as a potential resolution of this controversy was the concept of aggregation. Personality theorists argued that when behaviors are aggregated across many situations, trait measures predict behavioral tendencies relatively well. Such aggregation essentially involves an estimate of an individual's typical behaviors. In contrast, situations can be designed to elicit behaviors that individuals are capable of, but would not necessarily engage in under unconstrained circumstances.

Only a few trait researchers have attempted to assess personality specifically in the context of maximal performance (e.g., see Willerman, Turner, & Peterson, 1976). The data are too sparse to derive any substantive conclusions, but the general theme of this research is consistent with the notion that the behavior of many individuals can be responsive to such circumstances. Moreover, other research has suggested that personality traits may not be all that consistent in different contexts. We can speak of traits like conscientiousness, in the context of work, home, and with friends—where individuals may have different tendencies in these different contexts (see Murtha, Kanfer, & Ackerman, 1996).

It is quite reasonable to speculate that not all personality traits are affected to equal degrees under typical behavior and maximal performance conditions. Although there are literally dozens of different posited personality traits (e.g., see French, 1953), in recent decades many researchers have converged on a five-factor model of personality, which includes the most general and highly replicated traits of Neuroticism, Agreeableness, Openness–Culture, Extroversion, and Conscientiousness (Costa & McCrae, 1992; Digman, 1990; Goldberg, 1971; though see Block, 1995, for a contrasting view). Extroversion, for example, seems to be more variable in typical–maximal situations—with certain limitations (see Humphreys & Revelle, 1984). That is, level of extroversion may interact with underlying information processing capabilities, so that cognitive performance of extroverts and introverts may have a relatively low level of malleability. Moreover, responsivity may be asymmetric, such that all but the most extreme introverts may be able to function quite well for brief periods in highly extroverted situations (such as at a party, or giving a public lecture). Extroverts may do reasonably well in introverted activities when required (such as studying), but can be expected to be much more susceptible to intrusive interpersonal stimuli (such as when a roommate walks into the dormitory room while the extrovert is trying to study).

It is an open question how reactive individuals are to maximal performance situations, in terms of Agreeableness, Openness–Culture, and Conscientiousness. Part of the question will have to do with the strength of the situation under these circumstances (e.g., see the review by Epstein & O'Brien, 1985). Least responsive, at least on the low side, is likely to be Neuroticism. Because there are substantial autonomic responses to perceived threats of external stimuli associated with high levels of Neuroticism (Matthews & Deary, 1998), it seems likely that such individuals will have a limited ability to ignore such stimuli, and thus respond relatively poorly in a context where low Neuroticism is encouraged. In fact, high levels of Neuroticism and Anxiety (which is strongly correlated with Neuroticism) do appear to be substantially associated with performance under maximal situations—most likely because there is a strong performance evaluation apprehension that is often triggered under maximal performance situations, which in turn, is substantially disruptive to highly anxious individuals (for a more extensive discussion of this issue, see Matthews & Zeidner, chap. 6). In contrast, it should be much easier for an individual with low Neuroticism to react as if he or she had high levels of Neuroticism, especially if given instruction on how such an individual would respond to the environment.

When it comes to intellectual functioning and intellectual development, typical orientation towards learning, thinking, and problem solving are clearly related to particular abilities. In a direct investigation of this proposition, Goff and Ackerman (1992; see also Ackerman, 1994) developed a scale of Typical Intellectual Engagement (TIE), which asked respondents about their preferences and typical behaviors for intellectual activities. The investigators hypothesized that scores on the TIE scale would be more highly related to measures of Gc than it would be related to Gf, based on the hypothesis that this personality characteristic would be associated with level of intellectual investment over an extended period of time. Because measures of Gf are relatively less influenced by intellectual investment, and more influenced by maximal effort in the testing conditions, they were expected to have relatively low correlations with this personality trait. This hypothesis was supported in several separate studies of adults. A meta-analytic computation of estimated correlations between TIE and Gf–Gc (Ackerman & Heggestad, 1997), found positive correlations between TIE scores and Gc (mean $r = .35$), while TIE scores were largely uncorrelated with Gf (mean $r = -.07$). Similar results have been found in more recent studies of adults between age 18 and 65 (e.g., $r = .29$ and $r = .08$ for Gc and Gf, respectively; Ackerman, 2000; and $r = .49$ and $r = .02$ for Gc and Gf, respectively; Ackerman & Rolfhus, 1999).

CONATION AND TYPICAL–MAXIMAL PERFORMANCE

The construct of conation or will, is usually construed to include aspects of motivation and interests—two related, but distinct domains of psychological research. The concept of graded levels of effort is inherent in the construct of conation. When considering interests, the inherent assumption is that an individual will be most likely to typically devote effort when the task domain matches the individual's underlying interests (such as the assignment of an art project to individuals who are high or low on artistic interests). Clearly, as with affective traits, the imposed situation may have a substantial overriding effect on behaviors. A strong environmental press (such as monetary rewards) can be effective in reducing the variance in behavior attributable to interests, at least in the short term. In the long term, extant data suggest that a mismatch between a pattern of underlying interests and occupation or educational activities may lead to dissatisfaction or withdrawal (e.g., see Super, 1940), which in turn, would be expected to lead to lower levels of typical performance.

According to Holland's (1959) theory of vocational interests, there were two components to consider—the individual's dominant interest theme (such as intellectual or enterprising) and the occupational level, which is tied to the intellectual demands of the particular job. Self-concept (what the individual thinks he or she is capable of doing) and objective intellectual abilities combine to yield an orientation toward higher or lower occupational level. Although the occupational level aspect of the theory has not received as much empirical research as vocational themes have, the issue may be complicated by an underlying asymmetry. That is, individuals with high self-concept and high abilities may not actually aspire to high occupational levels, but instead may be quite content with a lower occupational level that may have fewer work demands, and greater opportunities for avocational interests (such as family, community, or hobbies). Individuals with low self-concept and low abilities obviously would not realistically have the kinds of choices in occupational level that are available to high ability persons.

For distal motivational traits (such as need for achievement—*n*Ach), individuals are hypothesized to differ in terms of their ad hoc orientation toward accomplishing tasks, which in turn, would be associated with their desire to allocate effort on a task. Ceteris paribus (everything else being equal), individuals with low *n*Ach will typically allocate less effort to an assigned task with some anticipation of evaluation, while individuals with higher *n*Ach will allocate more effort. Unlike TIE, we would hypothesize that *n*Ach would be positively related to both Gf and Gc. The reason for this is that high levels of *n*Ach would be associated with both short term levels of maximum effort (i.e., during performance of a Gf test) and longer term typical effort expenditures (i.e., for acquisition of Gc knowledge and skills). A meta-analysis of the literature supports this general assertion (Ackerman & Heggestad, 1997). Narrower motivational traits such as a learning orientation, which is conceptually closer in content to the TIE personality construct, tend to show positive correlations with Gc and negligible correlations with Gf (Kanfer & Ackerman, 2000).

TRAIT COMPLEXES

The concept that particular constellations of traits may be more or less effective for learning was first introduced by Snow (1963). Snow called such constellations of traits aptitude complexes—a concept that was central to his investigation of various sources of aptitude–treatment interactions in learning contexts. Ackerman and Heggestad (1997) adapted and expanded this concept into trait complexes—which are considered to be constellations of traits across cognitive, affective, and conative trait families. The conceptualization of trait complexes does not imply the existence of interactions with learning treatments, but instead does suggest that there is a value added (over and above consideration of single traits or single trait families) in predicting and understanding adult intellectual development and express. In a meta-analysis and review of the personality, ability, and interest literature, Ackerman and Heggestad (1997) determined the existence of four broad trait complexes, called Social, Clerical/Conventional, Science/Math, and Intellectual/Cultural.

The Clerical/Conventional and Intellectual/Cultural trait complexes have components of all three trait families. The Social trait complex has only interest and personality traits, probably because there is little extant literature on valid social or interpersonal intelligence measures. The Science/Math trait complex has only ability and interest components, perhaps because there is an insufficient literature on the specific personality characteristics that are uniquely associated with spatial and math abilities, along with realistic vocational interests. The literature, however, supports that notion that the Intellectual/Cultural trait complex will be positively associated with adult intellect along the lines of Gc, the Science/Math trait complex will be associated with Gf, and the Clerical/Conventional trait complex might only be associated with perceptual speed and psychomotor abilities. The Social trait complex is not associated with traditional measures of intellectual abilities—suggesting that individuals with high levels of this complex, might not be oriented toward academically oriented intellectual activities.

It should be noted that the Ackerman and Heggestad (1997) meta-analysis and review found significant, but not large associations among many of these variables. This finding was not particularly surprising, given the divergence between typical behavior assessments (for personality and interests) and maximal performance assessments (for abilities). As such, these findings provide an important starting point for evaluating the overlap among different trait families under similar conditions (either typical or maximal), but obviously do not yield a final answer to the question of the degree of overlap among the underlying traits.

AN INVESTMENT THEORY OF ADULT INTELLECTUAL DEVELOPMENT

A theory that integrates the concepts of typical behavior and maximal performance, trait complexes, and domain knowledge has been offered by Ackerman (1996). The four component theoretical framework has been referred to as

PPIK, for intelligence-as-Process, Personality, Interests, and intelligence as Knowledge. Some basic attributes of the theory are similar to those offered by Cattell (1957), in that there is much shared conceptualization regarding process-type abilities (e.g., Gf) and the development of knowledge (e.g., Gc). In Cattell's investment hypothesis, Gc grows out of the investments of Gf. Other influences, such as personality, interests, and so on affect both intellectual development and other domains (such as scholastic achievement)—for details see Cattell (1971/1987). There are also salient differences between Cattell's approach and the PPIK approach. Domain knowledge is contained within Cattell's original depiction of Gc, but as noted by Cattell, was seen as impractical for assessment, because one might need a test for every identifiable area of knowledge. Instead, most Gc assessments focus on knowledge that is common to a dominant culture, or they focus on verbal knowledge and skills (such as reading comprehension and general vocabulary). In contrast, the criteria of interest for the PPIK approach are the breadth and depth of content, or domain knowledge, for two important reasons: The first reason is that there is extant justification that for most intents and purposes, adult intellectual effectiveness, in terms of what tasks an individual can perform, is determined more by what the individual knows and less by the individual's ability to perform context-independent working memory or abstract reasoning tasks. The second reason is that, rather than approaching the question of commonality among cognition, affect, and conation by only looking at laboratory tasks that have little in the way of real-world relevance, the question of commonality might best be approached by looking for communalities where they are most likely to be found—that is, in terms of what the individual brings with him or her to the assessment situation.

The PPIK approach gains a substantial degree of Brunswik Symmetry between predictors and criteria, and at the same time, it takes the investigation of adult intellectual development beyond analysis of obscure laboratory tasks that only tend to show that middle-aged and older adults are less able learners of trivial tasks, when compared to younger adults. One key hypothesis for the PPIK approach is that, when one considers that middle-aged and older adults are likely to have much higher levels of investment in acquisition and maintenance of domain knowledge than do younger adults, it is likely that the average middle-aged adult is quite a bit more knowledgeable than the average 18-year-old. Given the notion that knowledge is a more important determinant of intellectual performance (e.g., see Hunter, 1983), the PPIK approach suggests that inclusion of domain knowledge, along with intelligence-as-process and traditional measures of Gc, might yield an evaluation that shows that, on average, middle-aged adults have higher overall intelligence than younger adults. Such an orientation is consistent with the speculations of many investigators over the past 70 or so years (e.g., see Miles, 1934), but is inconsistent with the traditional IQ or g-centered approach that suggests peak levels of intelligence are found in the 18–25-year-old population (e.g., see Raven, Court, & Raven, 1977; Wechsler, 1944, 1997).

From a trait-complex perspective, the PPIK approach views particular complexes as supportive or impeding of the development of domain knowledge, or as supportive of one domain over another; to the degree that the complexes are associated with both the intensity and the direction of intellectual investment over long time periods. Integrating the PPIK perspective and the trait complexes found by Ackerman and Heggestad (1997), predictions can be made for the patterns of influence and development of adult domain knowledge. Figure 5.1 illustrates the framework and a set of predicted relations among traditional Gf and Gc ability measures, trait complexes, and knowledge across domains of physical sciences–technology, civics, humanities, current events, and business. Consistent with Cattell's theory, traditional

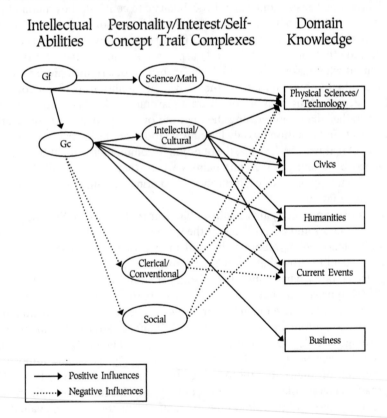

FIG. 5.1. A conceptual representation of the PPIK theory, including traditional measures of fluid intelligence (Gf), crystallized intelligence (Gc), four selected trait complexes, and five knowledge domains. Dotted arrows indicate negative or impeding influences, and solid arrows indicate positive or supportive influences.

measures of Gc are viewed as resulting from early investments of Gf. Subsequent domain knowledge acquisition and maintenance is a function of Gf and Gc abilities, both as direct influences and indirectly through positive influences of Science/Math and Intellectual/Cultural trait complexes, and through negative influences of Clerical/Conventional and Social trait complexes. Not shown is an important developmental component, which is that increments in domain knowledge will result in small, but significant increments in traditional measures of Gc (because such measures sample broadly from many of the areas of domain knowledge—especially those that are general to the wider cultural milieu). It is important to note that one key difference between the traditional Gc approach and the current approach is that domain knowledge is envisioned to include many different areas that individuals in a culture do not share, such as occupational knowledge and avocational knowledge. Thus, acquisition of domain knowledge in most areas (such as technical jargon, or specific job-relevant information) will probably have a very limited effect on traditional Gc measures.

EMPIRICAL DATA: TRAIT COMPLEXES AND DOMAIN KNOWLEDGE

Although longitudinal data are necessary to test the developmental elements of the PPIK theory, the cross-sectional data collected to date have provided broad support for several aspects of the approach. Below we provide a few illustrations of the results from these studies, in the context of basic age-related patterns, and trait complex associations.

Age and Domain Knowledge

In a study of 228 adults between age 21 and 62, all of whom had achieved at least a baccalaureate level of education, Ackerman (2000) administered a large battery of traditional Gf and Gc ability tests, along with measures of personality, interests, and self concept, to obtain trait complex measures. In addition, 18 separate domain-knowledge scales were administered to the participants. The domains included physical sciences and technology (e.g., chemistry, physics, biology, technology), civics (e.g., U.S. history, U.S. government, economics), humanities (e.g., art, literature, music), and business (e.g., management, law). As would be expected from the extant abilities literature (e.g., Horn, 1989), middle-aged adults performed on average, more poorly than younger adults on Gf tests ($r_{GF,age} = -.39$) and performed slightly better on Gc tests ($r_{GC,age} = +.14$). Scatterplots for these abilities and age are shown in Fig. 5.2. A single composite of Gf and Gc that ignored domain knowledge

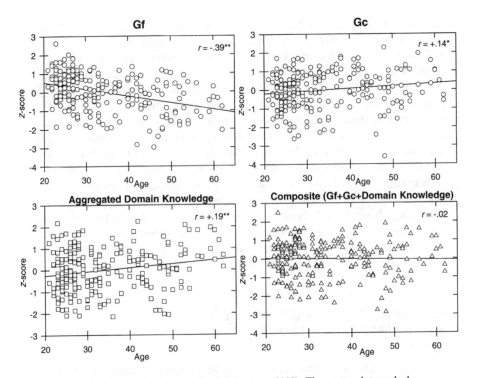

FIG. 5.2. Scatterplots of data from Ackerman (2000). The scatterplots each show age (the abscissa) and z-score (ordinate) for fluid intelligence (Gf), crystallized intelligence (Gc), an aggregated score across all of knowledge domains, and an equally weighted composite of Gf, Gc, and the aggregated knowledge score. Symbols represent each participant. $N = 228$.

yields a significant negative correlation with age ($r_{g,age} = -.14$), consistent with the existing literature on age and intelligence.

For the most part, the knowledge domains were well represented in the academic world, and thus could be considered to give an advantage to younger adults, in comparison with middle-aged adults, who would be further removed from the academic environment. Nonetheless, scores on only three knowledge domains were significantly negatively related to age—they were all in the sciences domain (physics, chemistry, and biology). Ten of the remaining domain knowledge tests were significantly positively related to age, meaning that middle-aged adults performed, on average, better than the younger adults. If we average across all of the 18 knowledge domains, there remained a significant positive correlation between age and performance ($r_{aggregated\ domain\ knowledge,age} = +.19$). To be consistent with the notion that typical performance (reflected by Gc and domain knowledge scores) is a more important component of adult intelligence than Gf (or intelligence-as-process), we might obtain an estimate of overall adult intellect that more heavily weights Gc and domain knowledge in comparison to Gf. Such a weighting would certainly indicate that, according to this definition, middle-aged adults are more intelligent than younger adults. With an equal weighting of Gf, Gc, and overall domain knowledge, the correlation between age and overall intellect is essentially zero ($r_{composite,age} = -.02$), which indicates that middle-aged adults are, on average, equally intelligent, compared to younger adults.

In this study, three of the four trait complexes identified by Ackerman and Heggestad (1997)—Science/Math, Intellectual/Cultural, and Social were assessed. The complexes were derived from a joint factor analysis of ability, personality, interest, and self-concept measures. A simple structure solution was obtained with an orthogonal rotation—which means that the trait complex scores were essentially uncorrelated with one another. That is, individuals can have widely different patterns of trait complex profiles (e.g., high on one, low on others, high on all, low on all, etc.). Thus, an individual could have high Intellectual/Cultural trait complex and would be just as likely to have high, medium, or low scores on the Social trait complex. Correlations between derived trait complex scores (after the ability components of the trait complexes were removed) and composite domain knowledge scores are shown in Fig. 5.3. As the figure indicates, individuals with high

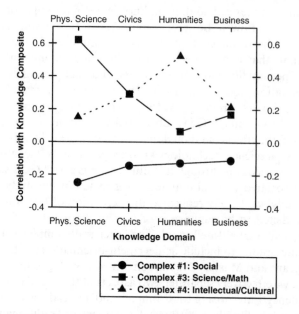

FIG. 5.3. Correlations between trait complex scores (after ability measures were removed) and domain knowledge for Physical Sciences, Civics, Humanities, and Business composites. Shown are correlations with Social, Science/Math, and Intellectual/Cultural trait complexes. Data from Ackerman (2000).

levels of the Science/Math trait complex were likely to have much higher-than-average scores on physical sciences domain knowledge, and somewhat higher scores on civics and business knowledge. Individuals with high Intellectual/Cultural trait complex scores were most likely to have high humanities domain knowledge levels, but also had greater than average scores on the other knowledge domains. Those individuals who had high Social trait complex scores, however, were likely to be less knowledgeable about all of the knowledge domains assessed. Overall, these results are consistent with two predictions: (a) Science/Math and Intellectual/Cultural trait complexes that are supportive of domain knowledge and that the Social trait complex was impeding of domain knowledge; and (b) for the two supportive trait complexes, they differed in their respective correlations with the kinds of domain knowledge. The results, then, support the idea that these trait complexes are associated with the direction and intensity of domain knowledge for adults across a substantial age range.

Trait Complexes, Domain Knowledge, and Gender in a College Sample

Another study of the PPIK approach focused on individual differences in abilities, trait complexes, and domain knowledge in a sample of college students (Ackerman, Bowen, Beier, & Kanfer, 2001). In this study, a sample of 320 first-year college–university students was administered a battery of measures similar to that of the Ackerman (2000) study, along with additional measures of personality, motivational traits, and background experiences. A structural equation model of the ability determinants of domain knowledge is shown in Fig. 5.4. The model provides a useful demonstration that for these young adults, even though Gc is substantially determined by individual differences in Gf, the effects of Gf on domain knowledge are largely indirect (except for physical sciences/technology knowledge). That is, the influence of Gf on domain knowledge is through its influence on Gc, and Gc is substantially positively associated with all domains investigated in the study.

In this study, we largely replicated the derivation of two trait complexes that are predicted to be supportive of domain knowledge—Science/Math/Technology and Verbal/Intellectual. The latter trait complex was expanded from previous studies to include achievement-oriented motivational traits of Desire to Learn and Mastery orientation (Kanfer & Heggestad, 1997, 2000). In addition, we effectively separated two aspects of the Social trait complex—a Social Potency/Enterprising trait complex and a Social Closeness/Femininity trait complex. Finally, a fifth trait complex of Traditionalism/Worry/Emotionality was derived—it included personality measures, but also avoidance-related motivational traits (the Worry and Emotionality scales refer specifically to performance contexts—Kanfer & Heggestad, 2000). Consis-

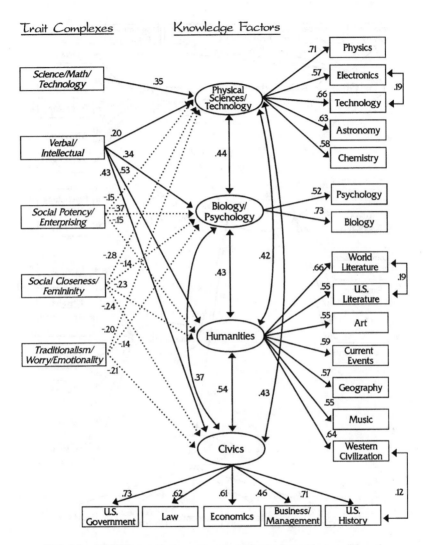

FIG. 5.5.   LISREL structural equation model for trait complexes and knowledge factors. Lines indicate significant path coefficients. Negative paths shown
in dotted lines. Reprinted from Ackerman et al. (2001). Copyright American
Psychological Association. Reprinted by permission.

end of academic orientation, the other three trait complexes showed clearly
negative associations with the measured knowledge domains.

Of some importance to those studying gender differences, men had significantly higher scores on the Science/Math/Technology trait complex, and
women had significantly higher scores on Social Closeness/Femininity and
Traditionalism/Worry/Emotionality trait complexes. These trait complex dif-

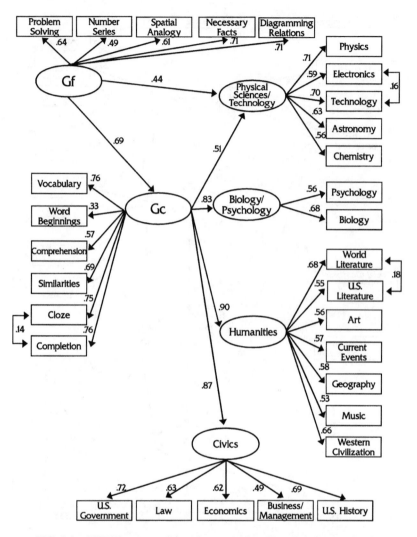

FIG. 5.4. LISREL structural equation model for ability factors and knowledge factors. Lines indicate significant path coefficients. Gf = fluid intelligence; Gc = Crystallized intelligence. Reprinted from Ackerman et al. (2001). Copyright American Psychological Association. Reprinted by permission.

tent with the PPIK theory, and with the earlier results, Science/Math/Technology trait complex was supportive of knowledge in the Physical Sciences/Technology domain, and the Verbal/Intellectual trait complex was supportive of knowledge in all of the measured domains. A structural equation model of the trait complexes and domain knowledge is shown in Fig. 5.5. Even though this sample was undoubtedly restricted in range at the higher

h as math or writing) can be expected to result in an increase in
erform such tasks in the future. If the interests are followed-
main knowledge will increase in that area, which in turn will both
increment in self-concept and interests, in a virtuous circle. In
rly failures at a task may be expected to decrement interests, and
n both lower self-concept and avoidance of future opportunities
lomain knowledge—a vicious circle. Although these hypotheses
e appeal, experimental confirmation awaits the expense and time
construct and evaluate longitudinal studies. We have found the
approach to determining development and change to be a quite
On the one hand, it is important to note that although this ap-
tures a substantial portion of the variance in behavioral predic-
dual lives are undoubtedly more complicated than can be captured
a perspective. On the other hand, the trait complex perspective al-
profile approach to describing individuals. An adequate profile
de an array of trait complex scores, traditional ability measures,
res of the breadth and depth of knowledge. While this does not
h an ideographic level of description for an individual, it goes far
aditional approaches, and it allows for an integration that usually
trained psychometrist to qualitatively assemble different, but re-
nains of assessments to provide vocational or academic advice.

NCES

P. L. (1984). Multivariate evaluation of workload, resources, and performance in
sk data. *Proceedings of the 28th annual meeting of the Human Factors Society, 28,*
4.
P. L. (1994). Intelligence, attention, and learning: Maximal and typical performance.
. Detterman (Ed.), *Current topics in human intelligence: Theories of intelligence* (Vol.
1–27). Norwood, NJ: Ablex.
P. L. (1996). A theory of adult intellectual development: Process, personality, inter-
d knowledge. *Intelligence, 22,* 229–259.
P. L. (2000). Domain-specific knowledge as the "dark matter" of adult intelligence:
personality and interest correlates. *Journal of Gerontology: Psychological Sciences,*
P69–P84.
, P. L. (2002). Gender differences in intelligence and knowledge: How should we look
ievement score differences? *Issues in Education: Contributions from Educational Psy-*
y, 8(1), 21–29.
, P. L., Bowen, K. R., Beier, M. B., & Kanfer, R. (2001). Determinants of individual
nces and gender differences in knowledge. *Journal of Educational Psychology, 93,*
25.
, P. L., & Heggestad, E. D. (1997). Intelligence, personality, and interests: Evidence
verlapping traits. *Psychological Bulletin, 121,* 219–245.
, P. L., & Rolfhus, E. L. (1999). The locus of adult intelligence: Knowledge, abilities,
non-ability traits. *Psychology and Aging, 14,* 314–330.
, A. (1982). *Psychological testing* (5th ed.). New York: Macmillan.

ferences accounted for some, but not all, of the gender differences in domain
knowledge—where women tend to perform more poorly overall (for an extensive discussion of this issue, see Ackerman, 2002; Ackerman et al., 2001).
Results from other studies have been consistent with these findings (e.g., see
Rolfhus & Ackerman, 1999), and have extended the investigation to include
domain knowledge in current events (Beier & Ackerman, 2001) and health
and nutrition (Beier & Ackerman, 2003). However, in the current events domain knowledge, few gender differences were noted, and in the health and
nutrition knowledge domains, women outperformed men on average. Together, these results show the efficacy of the PPIK approach for the trait
complex determinants of individual differences in domain knowledge—
which represent an important component of typical performance on intellectual tasks.

CHALLENGES AND FUTURE RESEARCH

The chapter has focused mainly on typical behavior and maximal performance, but it should be clear that these are extreme endpoints of a single continuum. Many different variables are certain to influence the level of effort
put forth, both across individuals, but also within-individuals. In some ways
this issue is similar to the underlying trait versus situation debate that confronted personality theorists in the 1960s and 1970s (e.g., see Mischel, 1968).
Mischel initially argued that personality traits were largely unpredictive of
behaviors, whereas behavior was largely determined by situations instead.
The major source of resolution to the controversy was the notion of aggregation of behavior—that is, when multiple behaviors are observed across many
situations, the influence of personality traits in predicting behavior was much
greater.

Environmental Press or Situations

The aggregation issue is not only central to the trait versus situation controversy, it is an integral aspect of the typical behavior perspective described
here. Thus, an appreciation of the situation, or more precisely, the level of environmental press, will be an important component of future progress in this
area. Numerous investigations of motivational interventions, such as the extensive literature on goal setting (e.g., see Kanfer, 1991, for a review), provide
some insight into the determinants of effort allocations. Nonetheless, there is
not a taxonomy of situations that can predict how much effort will be ex-
pended under a particular environmental press. Ironically, the elicitation of
effort under aptitude and intelligence testing conditions is probably one of
the few situations that psychologists and educators use (or even could use)

that maximizes individual effort. Aside from valued sports competitions, the availability of substantial monetary awards that are characteristic of televised game shows, or a few isolated educational situations (such as a final oral examination), and few other interventions are similarly effective in obtaining maximal levels of effort for all or most individuals. Past research has suggested that less severe situations often don't have a great influence on specific behaviors (see Funder & Ozer, 1983, for a discussion of this issue).

The effectiveness of miscellaneous extrinsic motivational interventions, such as competition in the classroom, personalized goal setting, small monetary rewards, and the like, almost certainly interact with interindividual differences in motivational and personality traits. Individual differences in *n*Ach, in competitive excellence, in social potency, susceptibility to demand characteristics, and a variety of other needs (e.g., see Murray, 1938) will affect the utility of performance differentially (see Kanfer, 1987), and thus affect the level of effort allocated by different individuals to the task at hand. In addition, individuals differ in their own personal effort-utility function (Kanfer, 1987). That is, some individuals seek a low level of typical effort to most tasks, while others seek a higher level of effort, even under the same degree of situational press. There are probably underlying personality and physiological bases to this variable (e.g., Guilford's notion of activity—see Guilford & Zimmerman, 1957). Just being able to assess what proportion of the individual's total effort available is actually allocated to a task would be an important contribution to the field.

It is unknown to what degree long-term environmental presses have on typical behaviors. The concept of a long-term environmental press may be implicit, but it is central to innumerable educational interventions (such as enrolling a child in a challenging private school environment or taking an extensive scholastic aptitude test preparation course). In some sense, school in general, or job training programs can be thought of as long-term environmental press interventions. In many cases, the long-term goals of the individual are instrumental determinants of an increase in typical intellectual effort. An intention to make partner in an accounting firm or a law office, or to become a board-certified physician, can be expected to change an individual's typical intellectual effort, at least until such time as the goal is reached (or failure occurs). We would speculate that this is a fundamental issue in the process of acquiring tenure in academic settings. That is, some individuals choose to devote extraordinary levels of intellectual effort through the seven or so years it takes to achieve tenure. We cannot remember how many tenure meetings we have attended where the central question on the minds of many discussants is 'Does the individual's scholarly output represent his or her baseline level, or could one expect that output level will drop precipitously once tenure is granted?' This question is a fundamental one about inferring typical intellectual engagement from observation of what may be either typi-

---

cal, maximal, or some in-between level the academy appear to agree, there is grea prediction of typical behavior from obse mal effort conditions.

Effort Demanded Versus Effort Allocat

The literature on attention and performanc & Bobrow, 1975) has an excellent set of m to task performance. However, validating difficult (e.g., see Navon, 1984), partly bec get participants to provide finely graded lev than trivially easy (e.g., see Wood, Mento, gies of secondary-task, dual-task, or time adopted in an attempt to examine the relatic ance, to mixed success (e.g., see Ackerman, 1 for the difficulty in obtaining graded levels laboratory, and in the field, is due to an under lationship between the effort demanded by th sired level of effort. That is, as we have seen tasks (as long as they are not impossibly difficu attention from the participants, and as such, i end up allocating more attention to the task th prior to engaging the task. In some sense, the much in the way that inclement weather or traf dividual to have a substantial increase in latenc a cell-phone conversation. The long-term effect they are higher or lower than the individual's unknown. It may be that, consistent with a gene adaptation level theory, the individual may shif better adjust to the demands of the ongoing t scheme actually operates, it may be that typical in necessarily stable over the adult life-span, but it ways in conjunction with task–job demands.

Longitudinal Study and Developmental Hypo

The PPIK theory is essentially a developmental a absence of longitudinal data, it is not possible to as actions among cognitive, affective, and conative d lectual development. It is likely that, as proposed b terests, personality, self-concept, and ultimately develop in an interactive fashion. Initial success at a

---

of tasks (su
interest to
through, do
result in an
contrast, ea
thus result
to acquire
have intuiti
necessary t
nomothetic
useful one
proach cap
tion, indivi
from such
lows for a
might incl
and meas
quite reac
beyond tr
requires
lated, do

REFERE

Ackerman,
  dual ta
  210–21
Ackerman
  In D.
  4, pp.
Ackerma
  ests, a
Ackerma
  Gf/gc
  55*B*(2
Ackerma
  at ac
  cholo
Ackerma
  diffe
  797–
Ackerma
  for
Ackerm
  and
Anasta

Beier, M. E., & Ackerman, P. L. (2001). Current events knowledge in adults: An investigation of age, intelligence and non-ability determinants. *Psychology and Aging, 16,* 615–628.

Beier, M. E., & Ackerman, P. L. (2003). Determinants of health knowledge: An investigation of age, gender, abilities, personality, and interests. *Journal of Personality and Social Psychology, 84,* 439–448.

Binet, A., & Simon, T. (1916). *The development of intelligence in children* (E. S. Kite, Trans.). Baltimore: Williams & Wilkins.

Block, J. (1995). A contrarian view of the five-factor approach to personality description. *Psychological Bulletin, 117,* 187–215.

Butler, J. M., & Fiske, D. W. (1955). Theory and techniques of assessment. In C. P. Stone & Q. McNemar (Eds.), *Annual review of psychology* (pp. 327–356). Stanford, CA: Annual Reviews Inc.

Cattell, R. B. (1943). The measurement of adult intelligence. *Psychological Bulletin, 40,* 153–193.

Cattell, R. B. (1957). Fluid and crystallized intelligence. In R. B. Cattell, *Personality and motivation* (pp. 871–880). New York: Harcourt Brace.

Cattell, R. B. (1987). *Intelligence: Its structure, growth, and action.* (Revised and reprinted from *Abilities: Their structure, growth and action,* 1971). Amsterdam: North-Holland.

Cattell, R. B., & Cattell, A. K. S. (1957). *The IPAT Culture Fair Intelligence Scales.* Champaign, IL: Institute for Personality and Ability Testing.

Costa, P. T., Jr., & McCrae, R. R. (1992). *Revised NEO Personality Inventory and Five-Factor Inventory professional manual.* Odessa, FL: Psychological Assessment Resources.

Cronbach, L. J. (1949). *Essentials of psychological testing.* New York: Harper.

Digman, J. M. (1990). Personality structure: Emergence of the five-factor model. *Annual Review of Psychology, 41,* 417–440.

Epstein, S., & O'Brien, E. J. (1985). The person-situation debate in historical and current perspective. *Psychological Bulletin, 98,* 513–537.

Fiske, D. W., & Butler, J. M. (1963). The experimental conditions for measuring individual differences. *Educational and Psychological Measurement, 23,* 249–266.

French, J. W. (1953). *The description of personality traits in terms of rotated factors.* Princeton, NJ: Educational Testing Service.

Funder, D. C., & Ozer, D. J. (1983). Behavior as a function of the situation. *Journal of Personality and Social Psychology, 44,* 107–112.

Goff, M., & Ackerman, P. L. (1992). Personality-intelligence relations: Assessing typical intellectual engagement. *Journal of Educational Psychology, 84,* 537–552.

Goldberg, L. R. (1971). A historical survey of personality scales and inventories. In P. Reynolds (Ed.), *Advances in psychological assessment* (Vol. 2, pp. 293–336). Palo Alto, CA: Science and Behavior Books, Inc.

Guilford, J. P., & Zimmerman, W. S. (1957). Fourteen dimensions of personality. *Psychological Monographs, 70*(10), 1–26.

Hebb, D. O. (1942). The effect of early and late brain injury upon test scores, and the nature of normal adult intelligence. *Proceedings of the American Philosophical Society, 85,* 275–292.

Helson, H. (1948). Adaptation-level as a basis for a quantitative theory of frames of reference. *Psychological Review, 55,* 297–313.

Holland, J. L. (1959). A theory of vocational choice. *Journal of Counseling Psychology, 6*(1), 35–45.

Horn, J. L. (1989). Cognitive diversity: A framework of learning. In P. L. Ackerman, R. J. Sternberg, & R. Glaser (Eds.), *Learning and individual differences. Advances in theory and research* (pp. 61–116). New York: Freeman.

Humphreys, M. S., & Revelle, W. (1984). Personality, motivation, and performance: A theory of the relationship between individual differences and information processing. *Psychological Review,* 153–184.

Hunter, J. E. (1983). A causal analysis of cognitive ability, job knowledge, job performance, and supervisor ratings. In F. Landy, S. Zedeck, & J. Cleveland (Eds.), *Performance measurement and theory* (pp. 257–266). Hillsdale, NJ: Lawrence Erlbaum Associates.

Kahneman, D. (1973). *Attention and effort.* Englewood Cliffs, NJ: Prentice-Hall.

Kanfer, R. (1987). Task-specific motivation: An integrative approach to issues of measurement, mechanisms, processes, and determinants. *Journal of Social and Clinical Psychology, 5,* 251–278.

Kanfer, R. (1991). Motivation theory and industrial and organizational psychology. In M. D. Dunnette & L. M. Hough (Eds.), *Handbook of industrial and organizational psychology* (2nd ed., Vol. 1, pp. 75–170). Palo Alto, CA: Consulting Psychologists Press

Kanfer, R., & Ackerman, P. L. (2000). Individual differences in work motivation: Further explorations of a trait framework. *Applied Psychology: An International Review, 49*(3), 469–481.

Kanfer, R., & Heggestad, E. (1997). Motivational traits and skills: A person-centered approach to work motivation. In L. L. Cummings & B. M. Staw (Eds.), *Research in organizational behavior* (Vol. 19, pp. 1–57). Greenwich, CT: JAI.

Kanfer, R., & Heggestad, E. (2000). Individual differences in trait motivation: Development of the Motivational Trait Questionnaire (MTQ). *International Journal of Educational Research, 33,* 751–776.

Matthews, G., & Deary, I. J. (1998). *Personality traits.* New York: Cambridge University Press.

Miles, C. C. (1934). Influence of speed and age on intelligence scores of adults. *Journal of General Psychology, 10,* 208–210.

Mischel, W. (1968). *Personality and assessment.* New York: Wiley.

Murray, H. A. (1938). *Explorations in personality.* New York: Oxford University Press.

Murtha, T. C., Kanfer, R., & Ackerman, P. L. (1996). Towards an interactionist taxonomy of personality and situations: An integrative situational-dispositional representation of personality traits. *Journal of Personality and Social Psychology, 71,* 193–207.

Navon, D. (1984). Resources—a theoretical soup stone? *Psychological Review, 91,* 216–234.

Norman, D. A., & Bobrow, D. G. (1975). On data-limited and resource-limited processes. *Cognitive Psychology, 7,* 44–64.

Penrose, L. S., & Raven, J. C. (1936). A new series of perceptual tests: Preliminary communication. *British Journal of Medical Psychology, 16,* 97–104.

Raven, J. C., Court, J. H., & Raven, J. (1977). *Raven's progressive matrices and vocabulary scales.* New York: Psychological Corporation.

Rolfhus, E. L., & Ackerman, P. L. (1999). Assessing individual differences in knowledge: Knowledge structures and traits. *Journal of Educational Psychology, 91,* 511–526.

Rushton, J. P., Brainerd, C. J., & Pressley, M. (1983). Behavioral development and construct validity: The principle of aggregation. *Psychological Bulletin, 94,* 18–38.

Snow, R. E. (1963). *Effects of learner characteristics in learning from instructional films.* Unpublished doctoral thesis. Purdue University, University Microfilms #6404928, West Lafayette, IN.

Spearman, C. (1927). *The nature of "Intelligence" and the principles of cognition.* New York: Macmillan.

Super, D. (1940). *Avocational interest patterns.* Stanford, CA: Stanford University Press.

Thorndike, R. L., Hagen, E., & Sattler, J. (1986). *Stanford–Binet Intelligence Scale* (4th ed.). Chicago: Riverside.

Wechsler, D. (1944). *The measurement of adult intelligence.* Baltimore: Williams & Wilkins.

Wechsler, D. (1997). *Wechsler Adult Intelligence Scale* (3rd ed.). San Antonio, TX: The Psychological Corporation.

Willerman, L., Turner, R. G., & Peterson, M. (1976). A comparison of the predictive validity of typical and maximal personality measures. *Journal of Research in Personality, 10,* 482–492.

Willingham, W. W. (1974). Predicting success in graduate education. *Science, 183,* 273–278.

Wittmann, W. W., & Süß, H. M. (1999). Investigating the paths between working memory, intelligence, knowledge, and complex problem-solving performances via Brunswik Symmetry. In P. L. Ackerman, P. C. Kyllonen, & R. D. Roberts (Eds.), *Learning and individual differences: Process, trait, and content determinants* (pp. 77–108). Washington, DC: American Psychological Association.

Wood, R. E., Mento, A. J., & Locke, E. A. (1987). Task complexity as a moderator of goal effects: A meta-analysis. *Journal of Applied Psychology, 72,* 416–425.

6

▼▼▼▼▼▼▼

Traits, States, and the Trilogy of Mind: An Adaptive Perspective on Intellectual Functioning

Gerald Matthews
University of Cincinnati

Moshe Zeidner
University of Haifa

Real-world intellectual problem-solving operates in concert with motivational and emotional processes, sometimes harmoniously and sometimes discordantly. Our aim in this chapter is to explore the nature of systematic individual differences in the process of solving problems posed by adaptation to life challenges. We focus on personality as a systematic influence on cognition, motivation and affect, in line with Kihlstrom and Cantor's (2000) suggestion that personality represents social intelligence. That is, personality reflects the cognitive structures that guide the individual's interpersonal behavior in solving the problems of everyday social life. As Kihlstrom and Cantor (2000) stated, social behavior is intelligent: cognitive processes of perception, memory, and reasoning support progress toward personal goals.

This chapter focuses on nomothetic constructs, by contrast with Kihlstrom and Cantor's (2000) ideographic perspective on personality. We link stable personality traits to characteristic modes or styles of adaptive social problem-solving, expressed in cognitive, emotional, and motivational processes. We also describe how more transient state factors relate to short-term adaptive choices. Our thesis is that traits and states are supported by a plethora of separate self-regulative processes, which may be categorized via two dimensions. These are: (a) their degree of abstraction from brain functioning (low-level vs. high-level processes), and (b) the domain of psychological function to which they belong (cognition, motivation, or emotion). Traditionally, intellectual functioning is seen as a set of high-level cognitive processes. Individual differences in these processes are captured by conventional ability tests, that are only weakly related to measures of personality traits, implying that intelligence and personality represent two largely separate spheres of inquiry (see Ackerman & Heggestad, 1997; Zeidner & Matthews, 2000).

We adopt a broad view of intellectual functioning. Social problem solving requires more than just the abstract processes of analysis and reasoning that are at the core of conventional intelligence. Studies of practical intelligence (e.g., Sternberg & Grigorenko, 2000) emphasize that much real-world expertise is supported by acquired skills tailored to a particular problem or context. We argue that individual differences in such expertise are shaped by basic biological and cognitive processes, as well as situational exposure. In addition, reasoning processes are biased by other, parallel cognitive processes such as selective attention and retrieval from memory, and by emotional and motivational influences. For example, in real life, decision making may be biased due to selective processing of data, excessive emotional commitment to a course of action, and impulsive action motivated by external pressures (Mann, 1992). Thus, our approach is to see intellectual functioning as one aspect of a wider self-regulative process that is not captured well by standard ability tests.

It is a considerable challenge to relate the multiplicity of processes supporting self-regulation to personality factors. The traditional trilogy of mind represents domains of cognition, emotion, and motivation (or conation) as distinct, though interacting, mental systems (Hilgard, 1980). Mayer, Frasier Chabot, and Carlsmith (1997) set out the case for treating the domains as three separate systems, each with its own function, developmental onset, temporal characteristics, and brain localizations (consciousness may reflect a further domain). At the same time, there is considerable conceptual and empirical overlap between the different systems. Theories of basic emotions link each emotion to characteristic cognitions and action tendencies (Lazarus, 1993). Anger, for example, relates to attributions of hostility to others, and motivations to strike out at others. Personality traits are increasingly defined in terms of the trilogy. Extraversion and neuroticism have been related to positive and negative affect, conscientiousness to achievement striving, agreeableness to social beliefs and motivations, and openness to intellectual interests. An exceedingly rich empirical literature shows that traits predict many criteria relating to emotion, cognition and motivation (Matthews, Deary, & Whiteman, in press).

The picture is similar for transient states. The state construct is best known from studies of affect, that is, basic moods and more differentiated emotions. However, it is difficult to disentangle affective from cognitive and motivational states. Stress may be experienced not just as affects such as tension and unhappiness, but also through disturbances in cognition (e.g., worry) and loss of motivation, as in the burnout syndrome (Matthews et al., 2002). Thus, transient impairments of intellectual functioning induced by stressors such as evaluation anxiety (Zeidner, 1998) are typically part of a more far-reaching change in mental state.

In this chapter, we outline a cognitive-adaptive perspective on the overlaps between emotion, cognition and motivation found in differential psychology. It explains trait and state effects on intellectual functioning as one aspect of self-regulation, the set of processes and behaviors that support pursuit of personal goals within a changing external environment (Matthews, Schwean, et al., 2000). Processes associated with separate domains are linked adaptively, in supporting common self-regulative goals. Effective adaptation to environmental demands requires some coherent integration of processes within the three domains in support of common self-regulative goals, including but not limited to intellectual processes. This functional organization generates consistencies at the level of both states and traits. We will also argue that cognition is the most fundamental of the trilogy for understanding individual differences.

It is convenient to conceptualize adaptation and self-regulation as operating over longer and shorter time spans. Over the long term, self-regulation acts to fulfill important personal goals, as expressed in constructs such as life tasks and personal strivings (e.g., Emmons, 1997). In differential psychology, long-term self-regulation has been explored most often through studies of basic needs (e.g., achievement motivation) and, more recently, motives toward self-determination, such as autonomy (Ryan & Deci, 2000). Over the short-term, self-regulation is directed toward the demands of the immediate situation, including stressful situations that the person might prefer to avoid. Exposure to challenging situations in part reflects the person's long-term aims, but also reflects environmental factors outside of personal control. Changes in state, such as increased anxiety, have been explained by models of self-regulation that focus on coping with some immediate discrepancy between preferred and actual status (e.g., Carver & Scheier, 1988; Matthews, 2001). Often too, there is an element of conflict between long-term and short-term regulative activities. For example, students are motivated to take examinations to work towards long-term motives of achievement and security, but, at the same time, often find exposure to the test environment distressing.

We do not suggest any fundamental difference between long- and short-term adaptation. For example, both may be controlled by goals at different levels within a goal hierarchy (Powers, 1973). However, we can separate them as fuzzy concepts as shown in Table 6.1. Specifically, long-term goals are more related to the stable needs, values, and beliefs of the self. In addition, they are less constrained by noncontrollable attributes of the environment, and they promote self-directed action. Over the longer term, changes in behavior reflect acquisition of competencies and skills, whereas short-term behavioral variance reflects how effectively those competencies are expressed in performance. We emphasize this is a rough and ready distinction, in that

TABLE 6.1
Typical Properties of Long-Term and Short-Term Adaptive Processes

Timescale	Long-Term	Short-Term
Determinants of action	Self-directed	Reactive to circumstances
Temporal constraints	Low	High
Choice of environments	High	Low
Behavior change reflects:	Competence	Performance
Individual difference constructs	Stable traits	Transient states

long-term adaptation may be disrupted by unexpected events, and short-term adaptation may be eased by prior planning and familiarity.

We seek to relate long-term goals to personality and short-term goal to states. Hence, we first present a cognitive-adaptive perspective on traits. We focus especially on extraversion and neuroticism, the traits for which the behavioral data base is richest. We relate each trait to specialized adaptive goals, and to biases in cognition and self-regulation that support attainment of those goals. We discuss how these biases influence the course of intellectual functioning and social problem solving. Next, we present an analysis of states, focusing on recent work that discriminates integrated complexes of emotional, cognitive, and motivational states. We argue that state responses in performance settings reflect the person's short-term adaptive goals, and modulate the dynamic transaction between person and situation. States are influenced by the person's appraisal of the personal relevance of the task, and themselves affect information processing, coping strategy, and task performance. Implications of this bidirectional process for intellectual functioning are discussed. This chapter is concerned primarily with conceptual issues: what traits and states mean as psychological constructs spanning the trilogy of mind, and their implications for intellectual functioning. Thus, we do not present detailed reviews of empirical studies (see Matthews, 1997, 1999; Matthews, Schwean, et al., 2000; Zeidner, 1998; Zeidner & Matthews, 2000).

PERSONALITY TRAITS: A COGNITIVE-ADAPTIVE FRAMEWORK

Traditionally, personality traits have been linked to individual differences in brain function, consistent with evidence for the heritability of traits. For example, interactive effects of personality and environmental stressors on intelligence test performance have been attributed to overarousal of the cerebral cortex (see Revelle, 1993). We do not deny the biological substrate for personality. However, biological models have proved to be of limited use in explaining the behavioral correlates of traits (Matthews & Gilliland, 1999). Effects of traits on objective performance are moderated by cognitive factors that are difficult to conceptualize in biological terms. Thus, the way is open for a psychological account of traits, within which the neurological characteristics of traits may be seen as partial or indirect influences on behavior, rather than the sole basis for theory.

An Example: Extraversion–Introversion

We outline our cognitive-adaptive model initially with regard to extraversion–introversion. A key observation is that traits are expressed behaviorally through many qualitatively different kinds of criterion measure, representing all three domains of the trilogy of mind. Furthermore, traits relate to criteria abstracted to different degrees from the neural substrate, ranging from low-level responses such as the startle reflex to high-level self-beliefs, cognitions, and metacognitions with greater intellectual content (Matthews, Schwean, et al., 2000). Figure 6.1 summarizes some illustrative correlates of extraversion-introversion from this perspective: higher-level constructs are placed further out in the pie. Thus, intellectual functions are located toward the periphery of

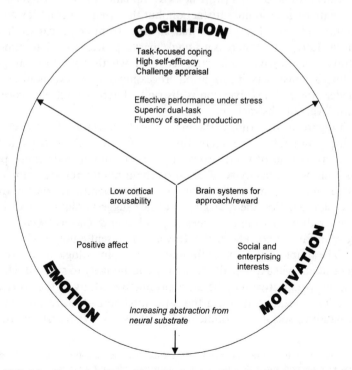

FIG. 6.1.   Examples of cognitive, emotional, and motivational correlates of extraversion.

the cognitive segment. Some data explicitly link extraversion–introversion to intellectual performance. Several studies show that extraverts perform better than introverts on intelligence tests under conditions of high stress or arousal, although the extraversion–arousal interaction reverses in the evening (Revelle, 1993). These results are paralleled by similar interactive effects on information-processing tasks requiring semantic processing (Matthews & Harley, 1993). There are also stylistic differences between extraverts and introverts,[1] in that extraverts are poorer at reflective problem solving, because they exit from the problem prematurely (Matthews, 1997).

A second observation is that the magnitude of correlations between extraversion and behavioral criteria is typically quite small (e.g., 0.2–0.3). The paradox of personality is that constructs such as those of the Big Five (Goldberg, 1993) emerge very strongly in psychometric studies, and yet the role of personality is often elusive when we look at physiological and cognitive functioning in controlled experiments (Matthews & Gilliland, 1999). We note briefly that we reject the view that extraversion is essentially dispositional positive affect (Watson, 2000). Studies of mood in controlled environments show that correlations between extraversion and affective states are typically around 0.1–0.4 (Matthews & Gilliland, 1999). Extraversion may indeed relate to general life satisfaction, but this itself is a complex construct with multiple facets. The picture that emerges from empirical studies (e.g., Matthews, 1997) is that there is no single master process that determines level of extraversion–introversion, irrespective of whether we look at psychophysiological constructs, information processing or high-level goals, and self-knowledge. Instead, extraversion is distributed across multiple processes at different levels of abstraction.

With regard to the trilogy, the higher level correlates of extraversion include dispositional happiness (emotion), self-efficacy beliefs (cognition), and social interests (motivation). Lower-level correlates include more positive moods (emotion), sensitivity of brain mechanisms for reward (motivation), and biases in attentional and memory processes (cognition). Even at the level of molecular genetics, the emerging evidence suggests that extraversion will relate in small ways to many genes (e.g., Plomin & Caspi, 1998).

The multifarious correlates of extraversion present a unique challenge for theory. The simple approach, of finding one key physiological or psychological process that will explain all the data, seems unlikely to succeed. However, an adaptive perspective may be more productive. Many of the correlates of extraversion appear to point in the same direction—toward an adaptation for demanding social environments (Matthews, 1997; Matthews & Dorn,

---

[1]It is convenient to contrast behavioral differences between 'extraverts' and 'introverts', but note that extraversion–introversion is a continuous variable, not a typology.

1995). Extraverts excel at behavioral tasks which mirror the cognitive demands of social encounters, such as speech production, verbal short-term memory, retrieval of verbal material from memory, resistance to distraction, and rapid response. The extravert seems to be designed to be an effective conversationalist: speaking quickly and fluently, keeping track of the conversation, and retrieving topics to speak about. Indeed, these skills might be seen as an emotional intelligence for handling demanding social encounters (Matthews, Zeidner, & Roberts, 2003). Furthermore, social encounters with strangers are prone to be stressful and arousing, so that extraverts' superior intellectual abilities in arousing environments (Revelle, 1993) may also support the higher-level adaptation.[2] Motivational and emotional attributes of extraversion may support similar functional roles, including, of course, the social interests of extraverts. Positive affect has also been linked to sociability (Argyle & Lu, 1990).

By contrast, the cognitive strengths of introversion, including good sustained attention and reflective problem solving, are supportive of more solitary, reflective activities. In terms of intellectual functioning, introverts are well-equipped to persist in efforts at problem solving that may eventually lead to problem solution (Matthews, 1997). Introverts' capacity to resist boredom and sustain attention in monotonous environments supports this adaptation. These cognitive and motivational qualities of introversion may be advantageous in higher education. Several studies (see Furnham & Heaven, 1999) concur that introverts tend to attain higher academic grades than do extraverts, perhaps because college requires solitary study. Extraverted children may do better in school, because of the greater emphasis on classroom participation. Consistent with these hypotheses, introverted students do well at essay writing, but extraverts are more likely to participate in oral seminar activities (Furnham & Medhurst, 1995). Thus, extraversion–introversion influences the academic strengths and weaknesses of the student.

So far, we have just the general observation that the various correlates of extraversion seem like they should help the extraverted individual to adapt to socially demanding environments. How can we take this idea further, by understanding how self-regulation relates to personality dynamically? Matthews (1999) pointed out that, for the most part, adaptation to real-life pressures and demands depends on acquired skills rather than fundamental components of information processing. Furthermore, skills are linked to specific contexts: Verbal skills for making friends and influencing people at a party may not generalize to other social settings, such as seeking a loan from one's bank manager.

---

[2]Matthews and Harley (1993) suggest that circadian variation in extraversion effects reflects an adaptive mechanism that maintains cognitive efficiency in the evening hours during which much social interaction takes place.

The cognitive-adaptive framework for personality identifies individual differences in skills for real-world adaptation as a central issue for personality research. Figure 6.2 shows what Zeidner and Matthews (2000) called the adaptive triangle. Personality traits entail a set of intrinsic biases in neural and cognitive functioning that are shaped by genetics and early learning, although each individual bias may be quite small in magnitude. The package of biases facilitates or impairs the learning of contextualized skills, which in turn support adaptation to the context concerned. However, adaptation is not solely dependent on cognitive skills. The person's motivations to learn, deploy, and refine skills are also important, as are the emotional factors that may impinge on skill execution. In broad terms, these factors can be grouped together as self-knowledge: the stable goals, beliefs, and emotional dispositions that support or interfere with skilled behavior. Thus, we can see the adaptive process as an interplay between cold cognitive skills, hot self-knowledge, and action in significant real-world settings.

Figure 6.3 illustrates in more detail how this framework applies to extraversion. Basic component processes such as low cortical arousability, sensitivity to reward, and the various information-processing correlates of extraversion provide a platform for acquiring skills such as effective conversation, and handling cognitive overload. Two types of positive feedback operate. Going clockwise around the adaptive triangle, effective skills build positive self-appraisals, leading to increased self-efficacy, and other aspects of self-knowledge, that in turn encourages the extravert to participate in social encounters, further enhancing skill. Going counter-clockwise, expertise leads to more effective behaviors and successful outcomes, leading to positive appraisals of outcomes, that build self-confidence for demanding social settings, and coping strategies (e.g., task-focus) that allow skills to be deployed to maximum effect. Although we cannot review empirical studies in any detail here, there is evidence from studies of self-regulation, coping, and activity preference that links extraversion to each of the six feedback arrows

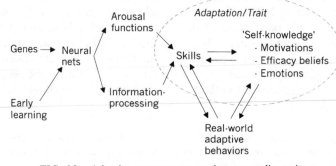

FIG. 6.2.   Adaptive processes supporting personality traits.

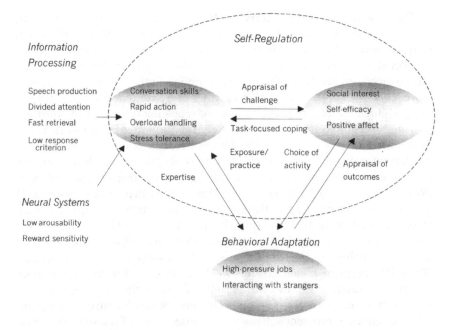

FIG. 6.3.   Styles of adaptive self-regulation supporting extraversion.

within the adaptive triangle, shown in Fig. 6.3 (Matthews, 1999; Matthews et al., in press).

The cognitive-adaptive model integrates the various correlates of extraversion illustrated in Fig. 6.2. The lower level components at the center of the pie provide the initial predisposition, with emotional, cognitive, and motivational aspects. Being preequipped to acquire social skills entails emotional attributes that confer stress-resistance: interacting with strangers is prone to induce anxiety. The predisposition includes cognitive components that facilitate the process of compiling new, procedural skills from existing competencies, as described by Anderson's (1996) skill theory. It also entails motivational tendencies linked to reward sensitivity, such as curiosity about people, that encourage social interaction and opportunities to learn. Likewise, following skill acquisition, all three domains of the trilogy of mind are implicated in maintaining and refining skills linked to the demanding social context. We can break down high-level self-knowledge into social interests, emotional dispositions, and various cognitions including self-efficacy, confidence, and coping strategies geared to the social environment. Although these processes are distinct from one another, they are functionally interrelated, so that the extraversion trait relates to multiple, independent biases in emotion, cognition and motivation.

Thus, whether one's personality is extraverted or introverted represents an adaptive choice (though probably not a conscious choice). One option (extraversion) is to benefit from seeking out and influencing other people, supported by appropriate social skills, including social problem solving (cf. Sternberg & Grigorenko, 2000). A second option (introversion) is to follow a more self-sufficient path, requiring a greater degree of reflection and sustaining goal-directed activity in the absence of social reinforcement. A third option (ambiversion) is to follow a middle course, supported by moderate proficiency at both types of skill. The effects of extraversion–introversion on intellectual performance may be seen as concomitants of these adaptive choices. Extraverts perform better on intelligence tests in arousing conditions (Revelle, 1993) as a by-product of adaptation to demanding, potentially stressful social encounters. Extraversion may also relate to the quality of intellectual functioning directed explicitly toward social problem solving, as evidenced by data relating the trait to social skills and related components of emotional intelligence (Matthews et al., 2003; Saklofske, Austin, & Minski, 2003). However, the reliance of this work on self-report means that a more definite conclusion must await the results of studies that link the cognitive skills of extraverts to objective social behaviors. Similarly, introverts' advantages in reflective problem solving are a consequence of a more self-reliant adaptive orientation, that supports the systematic intellectual study required by college students (Furnham & Heaven, 1999).

Neuroticism and Trait Anxiety

The cognitive-adaptive framework also gives us a new perspective on the closely related traits of neuroticism and trait anxiety. The literature on these traits often gives the impression that they represent deficits in functioning, linked to excessive negative affect. For example, there is extensive evidence showing that negative affect is linked to poorer performance on ability tests, although correlation magnitudes are modest (Zeidner, 1998; Zeidner & Matthews, 2000). Negative affectivity (in the form of both anxiety and depression) is also associated with impairments in social problem solving (Belzer, D'Zurilla, & Maydeu-Olivares, 2002), which may contribute to clinical disorder. The deficit view may be true for extreme levels of neuroticism, but, in non-clinical populations, the evidence points toward a more subtle view of the adaptive significance of neuroticism (Matthews, Derryberry, & Siegle, 2000). In particular, there may be adaptive advantages to maintaining awareness of subtle, disguised, or delayed threats, that allows the person to avoid or prepare for danger.

A cognitive-adaptive account of trait anxiety can be sketched as for extraversion–introversion. Figure 6.4 shows correlates of trait anxiety and neuroticism at: (a) different levels of abstraction, and (b) within each of the

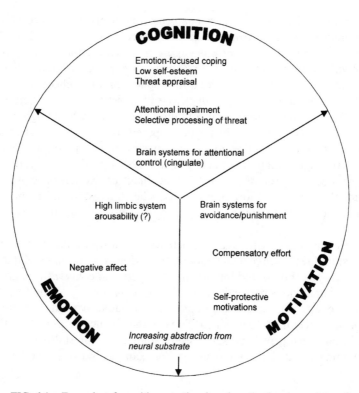

FIG. 6.4.   Examples of cognitive, emotional, and motivational correlates of neuroticism–trait anxiety.

domains of cognition, emotion, and motivation. The emotional (e.g., state anxiety) and cognitive (e.g., intellectual impairment) correlates of trait anxiety are well known, but some of the potential benefits are not. For example, there is a substantial literature on decision making that suggests that negative mood (correlated with trait anxiety) may sometimes lead to more considered, substantive reasoning (Forgas, 1995). Motivational factors are also important. Trait anxiety may sometimes relate to increased effort that compensates for cognitive deficits (Eysenck & Calvo, 1992), especially in structured environments that offer a clear course of action for compensatory coping (Matthews, 1999). In other settings, trait anxiety is characterized by avoidance and escape motives (Geen, 1987).

Again, we have a diverse set of empirical correlates of the trait that cannot easily be reduced to a single mechanism. Matthews (1999) suggested that trait anxiety relates to individual differences in strategies for dealing with threat. Broadly, there are two adaptive options. First, the person may be geared to anticipating and avoiding threat. Such a strategy requires a heightened awareness of threat, readiness to reflect on whether events are potentially threatening, and readiness to use compensatory effort in advance of anticipated danger. Evidence from studies of metacognition (reviewed by Wells, 2000) shows that anxious persons engage in much high-level thought over their own disturbing thoughts, in reflecting on their meaning and import. Excessive metacognition may reflect a misapplication of intellectual functioning. We link this anticipatory strategy to trait anxiety. It should operate most successfully in environments that contain subtle threats which might be overlooked. Second, the person might be prepared to confront threat more directly. This strategy requires low responsiveness to threat stimuli, readiness to cope through taking direct action, and physiological and cognitive resilience in stressful circumstances. We link direct confrontation of threat to emotional stability and low trait anxiety. The strategy should be most successful when the environment regularly imposes threats that cannot be avoided.

Figure 6.5 presents the dynamic perspective on trait anxiety. Again, it is assumed that skills are central to adaptation. However, in this case, it is skills for recognizing threats and relating them to personal concerns that are critical. The trait anxious person is alert to being denigrated by others, even if the insult is covert. Of course, these skills can be maladaptive and generate clinical social anxiety if overdeveloped. Thus, in the absence of immediate threat, the anxious person may be successfully adapted to forestalling threat and maintaining social status and security. For example, in two studies, Mughal,

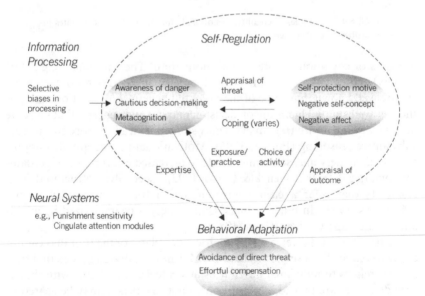

FIG. 6.5.   Styles of adaptive self-regulation supporting neuroticism and anxiety.

Walsh, and Wilding (1996) found that neurotic insurance salespersons worked longer hours and closed more sales. Perhaps, dispositional anxiety sometimes acts as a spur to achievement. The negative moods typical of the neurotic disposition may also serve to support more systematic, substantive decision making, depending on various moderator factors (Forgas, 1995).

Again, there is a dynamic interplay between skills, real-world behaviors, and self-knowledge that includes motives toward self-protection, various negative self-beliefs, and negative affect. Acquisition and execution of skills for threat detection build a self-concept characterized by personal vulnerability and needs for self-protection. This negative self-knowledge in turn leads to avoidance of feared situations coupled with compensatory effort, reinforcing these skills—but also blocking direct exposure to feared situations. Thus, at best, the adaptation helps the anxious person to negotiate the minefield of relations with people who may not be supportive or friendly. However, it also carries risks of excessive suspicion, personal sensitivity, and hostility, which tend to lead to interpersonal difficulties (Matthews et al., in press).

By contrast, an emotionally stable adaptation confers resilience to stress and the capacity to profit from threatening situations. The downside of such an adaptation may be vulnerability to complacency, and lack of preparedness for stress. However, emotional stability typically seems to ease social adaptation, perhaps because most people manage to surround themselves with more friends than enemies. It may also support intellectual function in stressful environments, due to lack of interference from disturbing cognitions.

Contextualized Anxiety Traits

Thus far, we have focused exclusively on broad traits, such as those of the Five Factor Model. However, dispositional vulnerability to threats is often represented by contextualized traits that relate to a specific category of potential threat. We make a brief argument here that these traits resemble neuroticism functionally, but represent more narrowly targeted adaptations toward specific threats. We briefly outline and compare three traits: test anxiety, social anxiety, and driving anxiety. We describe their multiple expressions, their impact on cognitive-adaptive skills, their relationships with self-knowledge, and their overall adaptive functions.

Test and social anxiety are closely related constructs subsumed under the social-evaluation anxiety domain. As such, they show a number of structural similarities. Both test and social anxiety are associated with cognitive (i.e., self-preoccupation, worry, irrelevant thoughts, negative self-evaluations, low self-esteem, and feelings of inferiority), affective (i.e., arousal, tension, discomfort, somatic arousal) and behavioral components (i.e., avoidance, attempts at escape) in the face of social-evaluation stress (Sarason, Sarason, & Pierce, 1995). Indeed, research by Zeidner (1989) suggested that social anxiety may have the same factor structure as test anxiety (cf. Sarason & Sarason, 1990), being comprised of the following facets: worry, task irrelevant thinking, somatic arousal, and tension. Driving anxiety is a less well-known construct, but also seems to comprise both negative affect and cognitive components, such as disturbing thoughts about driving (Matthews, 2002). As with neuroticism, it is likely that the various expressions of the anxiety traits reflect multiple levels of abstraction. Social anxiety relates both to sympathetic arousal in social settings (Beck, 1989), and to high level self-regulative cognitions that generate pessimistic outcome expectancies in social situations (Carver & Scheier, 1988).

All three types of anxiety are known to have detrimental effects on cognitive skills. The adverse impact of test anxiety on intellectual functioning and examination performance is well-known, although the effect is fairly modest. Meta-analyses suggest a correlation of about −.2 between test anxiety and indices of academic performance such as grade point average (Zeidner, 1998). Several studies suggest that social anxiety is related to deficits in social skills, such as lack of fluency in conversational speech and delivering and decoding nonverbal signals (Bruch, 2001). Studies of driving anxiety using a driving simulator show that this trait relates to impairments in vehicle control and attention to secondary task stimuli, especially when the driver is exposed to a stressful experience of losing control of the vehicle (Matthews, 2002). There may be various mechanisms that mediate the behavioral effects of the anxiety traits, but there are at least two common features. First, detrimental effects are most reliable in stressful settings; indeed, test anxiety may even be positively correlated with performance in reassuring situations (Zeidner, 1998). Second, a major mediating mechanism in each case is cognitive interference; worry-related thoughts divert attention from task-related processing and interfere with execution of skills. For example, social situations (public speaking, dating, meeting new persons, talking with a supervisor) provoke disruptive thinking for many people (Sarason et al., 1995). Common themes in these disruptive cognitions involve inadequacy in meeting demands of the situation and expectations of others. Thus, many socially anxious persons worry, often quite unrealistically, about what they see as unappealing features of their personality, social skills, behavior, or physical appearance, producing errors and uncertainties in performance, discomfort in social situations, and degraded interpersonal behavior.

There are also commonalities in the bases for the different types of anxiety in self-knowledge. Both social and test anxiety can be couched within self-regulative models, that attribute both types of anxiety to concerns about being negatively evaluated, socially or academically (Carver & Scheier, 1988; Sarason et al., 1995). In both social and test situations, people periodically interrupt their task efforts to assess the degree to which they are attaining their desired goals, and, in the anxious person, these self-evaluations are typically negative, leading to cycles of self-preoccupation and worry. Thus both constructs have been shown to relate to various biases in self-concept that leave the person prone to negative affect. Social anxiety, for example, relates to various negative self-beliefs, low self-esteem, and low self-efficacy in social settings, biases that may be related to an underlying 'relational schema' that represents beliefs that one will be rejected by other people (Leary, 2001). Again, the smaller literature on driving anxiety supports a similar conclusion. Anxiety-prone drivers see themselves as less competent and more accident-prone, in comparison to those low in dispositional anxiety (Matthews, 2002).

Thus, all three forms of contextualized anxiety are potentially maladaptive, in that the anxious person is ill equipped to handle the potentially threatening situations congruent with the trait, whether these are talking to strangers, taking a difficult test or driving in adverse road conditions. Test anxiety may lead to poorer career outcomes, and social anxiety may hinder the development of personal friendships and sexual relationships (e.g., Endler, 1983). However, there is an upside to all three traits. Test anxiety may be motivating in the absence of immediate pressures to perform. Zeidner (1998) reviewed various studies suggesting that high test anxious subjects may outperform low test anxious subjects in reassuring environments for performance, in line with the principle that anxiety generates compensatory effort (Eysenck & Calvo, 1992). Social anxiety may also have an adaptive function in that a realistic and proportionate concern about others' opinions and evaluations can inhibit behavior that is socially unacceptable (Leitenberg, 1990). Indeed, when placed in evaluative situations, high socially anxious subjects may demonstrate enhanced processing of information concerning potential evaluations (Smith, Ingram, & Brehm, 1983). Thus, high and low social anxiety may represent adaptations toward different goals. The socially anxious person is concerned with avoiding disapproval, leading to self-protective behavioral strategies (Meleshko & Alden, 1993). By contrast, the person low in social anxiety may be motivated to gain approval and social dominance through acquisitive strategies that are designed to lead to rewarding social outcomes (Arkin, 1987).

Finally, driving anxiety provides an interesting example of how the adaptive perspective adds to the deficit account of anxiety traits. Although anxiety is linked to objective performance decrements on the driving simulator, and to self-reported errors while driving, anxiety does not predict overall accident likelihood (see Matthews, 2002, for a review of the evidence). It turns out that anxiety is also related to more cautious behaviors, including, on the simulator, slower speed and reluctance to pass in heavy traffic, effects that may be mediated by judgment and decision making. In real life, anxiety correlates with fewer speeding tickets. Thus, the dangers of worry and cognitive interference are balanced by the benefits of lower risk taking. All the various contextualized anxiety traits may represent an adaptation characterized by evading rather than confronting danger. The strategy may work well in terms of preempting and avoiding threats, but poorly when the context requires that the threat be confronted directly, as in the case of taking a test or managing a necessary social encounter.

Personality Traits as Self-Regulative Constructs

To summarize, personality traits have a coherence that derives from their status as adaptations. The multiple emotional, cognitive, and motivational correlates of traits in one sense represent quite different psychological attributes and processes. However, they are interrelated because they subserve common adaptive goals. To function effectively in stressful environments takes more than just a calm disposition, for example. Adaptation requires the capacity to cope through taking direct action, despite the potential risks. It also requires motivations that support such active engagement, such as seeking challenges. Hence, traits represent a set of biases in emotion, cognition, and motivation that work together to prepare the person to acquire and execute the skills needed for specific environments. These biases may also be expressed, modestly, via intellectual functions, such as the deficits on ability tests shown by individuals high in neuroticism, trait anxiety, and test anxiety (Zeidner & Matthews, 2000). The anxious person allocates attention to self-evaluative processing that interferes with intellectual functioning, especially in stressful environments.

The structure of personality traits tell us something about the main adaptive challenges of human life are organized. As we have already described, extraversion–introversion is associated with social relationships. Should one be a pack animal, seeking success by climbing the social hierarchy, or a lone wolf, with less social support but free from the distractions of social competition? Neuroticism and emotional stability similarly relate to the choice between avoidance and confrontation of threat and danger, as do the contextualized anxiety traits. Other traits of the Five Factor Model may also refer to adaptive tradeoffs (Matthews, Zeidner, & Roberts, 2003). Conscientiousness refers to the adaptive choice between sustained work for long-term benefit and capitalization on short-term opportunities. Agreeableness may refer to choosing between cooperation and competition (note that extraversion entails more of both types of interaction). Openness may describe choosing self-directed intellectual analysis of one's environment, over reliance on traditional wisdom and authority.

This perspective also contributes to understanding traits as a product of both genetics and the social environment (see Zeidner, Matthews, Roberts, & McCann, 2003, for a more detailed developmental account). The human species is unique in the varied nature of the physical and social environments within which people may thrive. There are more degrees of freedom to being human than to being other animals. We are forced to choose between different types and levels of social engagement, beginning in infancy. Personality reflects these choices—whether to specialize for one or more environments, or whether to be moderately well-equipped to handle a variety of challenges. The intellect, in the sense of use of reason and judgment, is one of several tools that can be employed in meeting these challenges. The success with which intellectual capabilities can be directed toward specialized contextual challenges, such as influencing the opinions of others in a meeting at work, or evaluating the benefits and risks of driving in icy conditions, depends on the overall self-regulative process, including its emotional and motivational aspects. In turn, the goals and functions of self-regulation relate to personality traits.

The heritability of traits reflects the fact that adaptive choices are part of the human condition, that cut across different cultures (although culture has a moderating effect). People, of course, have common adaptations that are characteristic of the species. However, personality is perhaps also shaped by adaptations to more marginal environments with which engagement may or not be profitable, such as some threatening or stressful situations. The emotionally stable person can survive and reproduce in such situations, passing on a package of genes that allows his or her offspring to also thrive under stress.

At the same time, the diversity of the environment requires a learned element to personality. Children are typically exposed to a variety of different types of situation, with opportunities to learn through conditioning, modeling and insightful understanding (Zeidner et al., 2003). The outcomes of these learning will bias personality. For example, even a child with an emotionally stable temperament may be traumatized by adverse events, leading to a bias toward a more neurotic personality. More typically, the child's constitutional temperament will steer it toward congruent learning experiences. For example, emotionally stable children appear to handle stressful encounters more effectively (Kochanska & Coy, 2002). Goldberg (1993) referred to the Big Five as corresponding to the main themes of human life: power, emotion, work, love, and intellect. Inherited traits and social learning work together to shape the individual's adaptation to these challenges, an adaptation that includes specialized intellectual competencies.

TRANSIENT STATES AND SITUATIONAL ADAPTATION

By comparison with studies of traits, the development of validated measures of transient states has been uneven. Most work has focused on affective states. Studies support either a two-dimensional model of basic affect or mood, or a three-dimensional model discriminating energy, tension and pleasantness of mood (Schimmack & Grob, 2000). Most investigations of cognitive states have been inspired by anxiety research, which suggests that tense emotion and worry are distinct elements of anxiety states, with differing behavioral correlates (Zeidner, 1998). The Cognitive Interference Questionnaire (see Sarason et al., 1995) is one of the best known cognitive state measures. It indexes levels of intrusive thoughts related to task performance and to task-irrelevant personal concerns. Many other general qualities of cognition such as self-focus of attention and confidence may be operationalized similarly. The assessment of motivational states has been neglected, but the literature on motivation suggests various constructs that might be operationalized as states, including achievement motivation, and intrinsic and extrinsic motivation. Unlike trait research, there have been few attempts to map state constructs systematically across all three domains of the trilogy.

Recent research has explored overlaps between emotional, cognitive and motivational constructs, focusing on task performance environments. Matthews, Joyner, et al. (1999) sampled items from each of the domains that represented the principal state constructs relevant to human performance. Item factor analyses identified 10 robust primary state factors, included in a new questionnaire, the Dundee Stress State Questionnaire (DSSQ). A further factor-analytic study (Matthews, Campbell, & Falconer, 2001) differentiated an additional motivational state factor. Thus, as shown in Table 6.2, subjective state can be described by multiple factors, each of which relates exclusively to emotion, cognition or motivation, supporting a differentiated view of states.

The primary state factors are themselves correlated. Second-order factor analyses have extracted three higher-level factors that define broader syndromes of subjective experience, summarized in Table 6.3 (Matthews et al.,

TABLE 6.2
A Summary of the Scales of the DDSQ
(data from Matthews et al., 1999; Matthews, Campbell, & Falconer, 2001)

Domain	Scale	Items	Example Item	α
Emotion–mood	Energetic arousal	8	I feel . . . Vigorous	80
	Tension	8	I feel . . . Nervous	82
	Hedonic Tone	8	I feel . . . Contented	86
Motivation	Task Interest	7	The content of the task is interesting	75
	Success Motivation	7	I want to perform better than most people do	87
Cognition	Self-focus	8	I am reflecting about myself	85
	Self-esteem	7	I am worrying about looking foolish (-ve)	87
	Concentration	7	My mind is wandering a great deal (-ve)	85
	Confidence-control	6	I feel confident about my abilities	80
	CI-TR	8	I have thoughts of . . . How much time I have left	78
	CI-TI	8	I have thoughts of . . . Personal worries	86

Note. CI-TR = Task-Relevant Cognitive Interference, CI-TI = Task-Irrelevant Cognitive Interference.

TABLE 6.3
Three Fundamental Stress State Syndromes

	Task Engagement	Distress	Worry
Scales	Energetic arousal	Tense arousal	Self-consciousness
	Motivation (interest)	Low hedonic tone	Low self-esteem
	Motivation (success)	Low confidence-control	Cog. Interference (task-related)
	Concentration		Cog. Interference (personal concerns)

2002). Two of these factors integrate aspects of emotion, cognition and motivation. Task engagement relates to energy (affect), concentration (cognition), and two aspects of task motivation, and may represent a broad approach tendency. Distress relates to tension, low hedonic tone (affect), confidence, and perceived control (cognition). It may also relate to avoidance motivation, but this element of state has yet to be operationalized. The third factor, worry, relates exclusively to cognitive states of self-focus, low self-esteem, and interfering thoughts. These factors explained approximately 80% of the reliable variance in the primary factors.

Processes Supporting Adaptation

The psychometric evidence suggests that emotional and motivational states are closely intertwined with cognition. However, the factor analyses are not informative about the self-regulative processes assumed to generate these states. Figure 6.6 shows how we conceptualize self-regulation in performance environments. In line with transactional theories of stress and emotion (Lazarus, 1993), we assume a dynamic interplay between the person and situational demands (see Fig. 6.6). First, the person acts on the environment

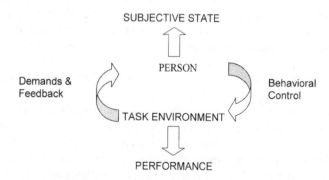

FIG. 6.6.   Dynamic interaction between person and environment during task performance.

through their attempts at competent task performance. The person's subjective state may influence the efficiency and style of performance, including performance on intellectual tasks. For example, high levels of distress and worry are prone to be disruptive. However, the environment also influences the person. Stress factors such as ambient temperature and noise, high workload, and feedback indicating success or failure change the person's physiological and subjective state.

Thus, the self-regulative process is dynamic. The person seeks to fulfill personal goals, such as maintaining a sense of self-competence, within the context of an environment that changes as a result of the person's own efforts at coping, and (in real-life) due to other, extraneous factors. This framework for stress and performance differs from more traditional work in this area (see Matthews, Davies, Westerman, & Stammers, 2000, for a review) that focuses primarily on stress as an influence on performance, neglecting the reverse influence. Consequently there are large experimental literatures on effects of stressors on performance such as noise, heat, vibration, etc., but relatively few studies of effects of performance on stress. One exception is provided by the test anxiety literature that describes both the effects of being evaluated on anxiety and worry states, and the process by which the anxious state interferes with attention and intellectual performance (Sarason & Sarason, 1990; Sarason et al., 1995; Zeidner, 1998).

Research in the first author's laboratory has demonstrated how changes in motivation, emotion and cognition are integrated via the self-regulative process. Figure 6.7 shows subjective state responses to performing three tasks requiring sustained attention: two laboratory vigilance tasks and a simulation of driving in fatiguing conditions ($Ns = 50, 99, 80$). Figure 6.7a shows change in state from pre-task to post-task, expressed in standardized units. Fatiguing tasks of this kind consistently elicit decreased task engagement (e.g., Matthews, Campbell, et al., 2002; Matthews & Desmond, 2002). Each task exhibits a coherent change in primary states relating to different domains of the trilogy. Thus, decreased energy is accompanied by loss of concentration and motivation. High workload tasks typically provoke increases in distress (Matthews et al., 2002). Figure 6.7b shows data from three tasks that provoke such responses, including two laboratory tasks, and a simulation that required agents to reply to typical customer inquiries, by phone ($Ns = 137, 50, 91$). Changes in mood toward greater tension and more unpleasant mood were accompanied by cognitions expressing loss of confidence and perceived control.

The concept of coping is critical to the self-regulative process. The transactional model of stress and coping (Lazarus, 1993) construes coping as a process of transaction between a person and event that plays out across time and changing circumstances. Accordingly, coping effectiveness must be examined in the context in which stress occurs: "without information about the social context we would have half the story" (Lazarus & Folkman, 1984,

(a) The task disengagement response: Task-induced decreases in state variables

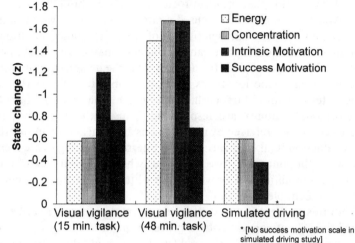

(b) The distress response: Task-induced increases in state variables

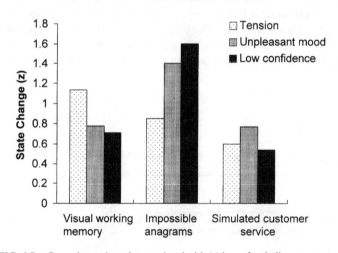

FIG. 6.7.   State change in tasks associated with (a) loss of task disengagement, and (b) distress.

p. 299). Adaptive coping requires a good fit between the person–environment transaction, the person's appraisal of the transaction, and the consequent coping behavior (Lazarus, 1993; Lazarus & Folkman, 1984). Thus, coping strategies should not be prejudged as adaptive or maladaptive on an a priori basis. As research demonstrates, coping specific coping strategies are more or less effective depending on the nature of the stressor, the time-course of the transaction and the skill with which coping is applied (Pearlin & Schooler,

1978; Zeidner & Saklofske, 1996). In performance contexts, we might have a general expectation that problem-focused strategies should be more adaptive than avoidance or emotion-focused strategies. However, we must also take into account the personal significance of the performance situation. If performing well has no adaptive value, avoidance may be the most appropriate strategy. Why expend effort for no reward? If the person cannot hope to succeed at the task, emotion–focus may be adaptive if it allows the person to come to terms with failure, perhaps recognizing that external factors rather than personal inability are responsible. Thus, although active, problem-focused coping is preferred by most persons and is generally more effective in stress reduction (Gal & Lazarus, 1975), alternative strategies are increasingly used when the source of stress is unclear, when there is a lack of knowledge about stress modification, or when there is little one can do to eliminate stress (Pearlin & Schooler, 1978).

With this background to coping and adaptation, further studies have explored the role of cognitive-stress processes in state changes induced by the task environment (see Matthews, Derryberry, et al., 2000, for a summary). These studies measured situational appraisal and coping immediately following task performance using scales for standard constructs in the stress literature (e.g., Endler & Parker, 1990). With baseline, pre-task state held constant, appraisal and coping explain substantial variance in state change. Figure 6.8 gives representative regression statistics from a study in which pre-task state,

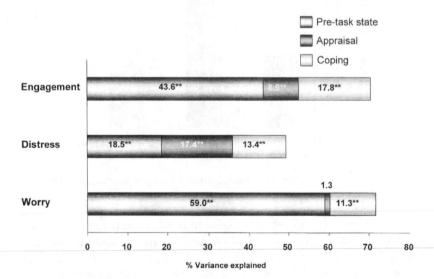

FIG. 6.8. Percentages of variance explained by three types of predictors of post-task state—pre-task state, appraisal, and coping—in a study of 108 participants performing a rapid information-processing task (Matthews, Derryberry, & Siegle, 2000). *Note.* **Significance of predictor set at entry: $p < .01$.

appraisal variables, and coping variables were entered in successive steps (Matthews, Derryberry, et al., 2000). Substantial variance in post-task scores carries over from pre-task state, but appraisal and coping together add a further 13–31% of the variance, depending on the state factor criterion. Across studies a fairly consistent picture emerges, such that changes in task engagement tend to relate to challenge appraisal and use of task-focused coping, changes in distress relate to threat appraisal, high perceived workload, failure to attain performance standards, and emotion-focused coping, and worry relates to both avoidance and emotion-focused coping. Thus, the cognitive processes of appraisal and coping provide the primary support for self-regulation, and concurrently generate changes in cognitive, emotional and motivational states. State change tells us something about the person's self-regulative goals within the constrained performance environment. However, in line with the ambiguity of the adaptive significance of coping (Zeidner & Saklofske, 1996), state change does not tell us directly whether those goals elicit adaptive or maladaptive coping behaviors.

Effects of Stress State on Performance

As previously stated, changes in stress state feed back into changes in information processing and performance. Various studies have explored how state variables relate to objective indices of performance. The majority of studies have focused on energy and task engagement. These states appear to be markers for availability of attentional resources. High energy facilitates performance of demanding attentional tasks, but not other types of task (Matthews, Davies, et al., 2000). Other studies have related distress to impairments of dual-task performance and executive function (e.g., Matthews, Joyner, et al., 1999). There is a large literature on worry in the context of test anxiety that suggests high worry impairs high-level verbal processing of the kind required for performance of academic tests (Sarason & Sarason, 1990; Zeidner, 1998).

What can we say about effects of stress states on performance from a self-regulative perspective? Matthews (2001) distinguished two kinds of mechanisms. First, stressors, especially those of a biological nature such as drugs and infections, may change the basic functioning of neural and cognitive processes, in some cases (e.g., some toxic agents) without the person being aware of these changes. A second level of state effects refers to voluntary coping, driven by attempts to reduce discrepancy between performance goals and appraisals that one is failing to attain those goals. Figure 6.9 shows how different kinds of control activity may generate differing coping strategies that may impact on performance (Matthews & Desmond, 2002). One option is to increase effort that compensates for task and environmental demands, or to change strategy qualitatively (task-focused coping). A second option is

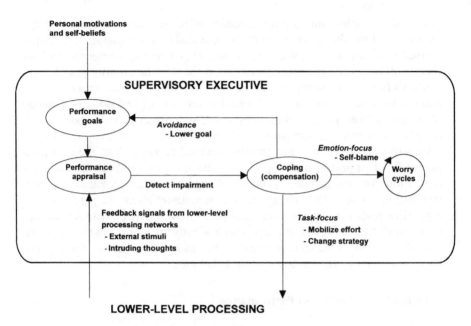

FIG. 6.9.   A self-regulative model of coping.

to reduce discrepancy by lowering one's personal goals, so that suboptimal performance is reappraised as acceptable (avoidance). A third option is to adopt self-critical and ruminative strategies that are liable to perpetuate worry about personal difficulties and interfere with task-relevant cognition (emotion–focus). Empirical studies, for example, are beginning to show that use of these coping strategies does indeed correlate with performance on certain tasks, and may mediate some effects of subjective state. Test anxiety relates to maladaptive patterns of coping (Matthews, Hillyard, & Campbell, 1999), that may influence intellectual functioning. In sum, the same appraisal and coping processes that control subjective state response to stressors may also influence how stress response impacts on performance, and consequently, changes in the external environment.

The Role of Traits

There is an extensive literature on states as correlates of traits. A simple equation is often made between extraversion and positive affect, and neuroticism and negative affect (e.g., Watson, 2000). Elsewhere, we have rejected this view as simplistic (Matthews & Gilliland, 1999). It does not adequately explain the situational moderation of trait–state correlations, or the modest magnitudes of trait–state correlations observed in controlled settings. Traits do not affect only emotions. We have found that neuroticism affects most of the cognitive components of the distress and worry states, including low confidence and control, low self-esteem and high levels of cognitive interference, although it has proved to difficult to find reliable correlates of task motivation using standard trait measures (Matthews, Joyner, et al., 1999).

We conceptualize traits as one of several factors that bias short-term adaptation. As previously indicated, traits bias in-situation processing at various levels, including appraisal and coping. For example, extraversion relates to challenge appraisal and task-focused coping, and neuroticism to threat appraisal and emotion-focused coping (Matthews et al., in press). Thus, traits operate to reframe the situation toward personal concerns. For example, the processing attributes of neuroticism work so as to interpret ambiguous situations as threatening, engaging the self-protective motives characteristic of the trait. The state correlates of traits reflect, in macro terms, the different subjective worlds that people of differing trait characteristics inhabit, and in micro terms, the differing sets of biases that support adaptations.

For example, in performance settings, there is typically a correlation of .3–.4 between neuroticism and the distress state. Broadly, neurotic individuals interpret task situations, including those involving intellectual tasks, differently to more emotionally stable persons: the situation affords opportunities for personal failure and inadequacy. At the micro level, the relationship between trait and state is statistically mediated by effects of neuroticism on intervening variables such as heightened threat appraisal and use of emotion-focused coping (Matthews, Derryberry, et al., 2000).

States as Self-Regulative Constructs

As in the transactional theory of stress and emotions (Lazarus, 1993), transient states tell us something about how the person stands in relation to the surrounding environment. The three higher-order factors of state may correspond to the three predominant adaptive choices of the performance environment (Matthews et al., 2002; see Table 6.4). The first is how much effort to commit to the task, corresponding to task engagement. The second is whether the situation is recognized as imposing uncontrollable demands and inevitable failure to attain performance goals (distress). The third is whether the situation calls for pulling back mentally from the task and reevaluating its personal relevance and significance (worry). These transactional themes represent an abstraction of the status of self-regulation. At a descriptive level, we give equal status to emotion, motivation and cognition as expressions of the different modes of self-regulation that govern the person's management of performance situations. At a process level, we emphasize cognitive processes as the main drivers of all three aspects of state, consistent with self-regulative

TABLE 6.4
Cognitive-Adaptive Perspective on Three Fundamental States

	Task Engagement	Distress	Worry
Appraisals	High demands Challenge	High workload Threat Failure to attain goals	
Coping	Task-focus Low Avoidance	Emotion-focus	Emotion-focus Avoidance
Performance	Enhances attentional resources	Impairs multitasking, executive control	Impairs high-level ver- bal tasks
Adaptation	Maintaining effort and focused attention	Mitigating overload	Reevaluating personal relevance of task

models of emotion (Carver & Scheier, 1998; Wells & Matthews, 1994), and cognitive models of motivation (Weiner, 2000).

Each state is associated with multiple processes, including appraisals, choice of coping strategy, and changes in the processing of task stimuli. However, states are nonisomorphic with the various processes that support self-regulation. Multiple regressions show that state change relates to several different predictors independently (Matthews, Derryberry, et al., 2000). The subjective state is an outcome of the various cues to the status of self-regulation provided by appraisals and coping (and, probably, unconscious processes also). Thus, the higher-order structuring of awareness binds together functionally related aspects of emotion, motivation and subjective cognition.

Further exploration of the behavioral consequences of states requires a more detailed account of the cognitive architecture of self-regulation, which is beyond the scope of this article (see Matthews & Desmond, 2002; Wells & Matthews, 1994). Table 6.4 outlines in brief some consequences of states for performance. Broadly, engagement tends to benefit performance, whereas distress and worry are detrimental, but whether performance is actually affected by state depends on the information-processing demands of the task. Whether performance changes induced by states are beneficial or not to the person is a separate issue that is often hard to determine (Zeidner & Saklofske, 1996). Thus, in many real-world situations, task-directed effort will pay off for the performer, so that task engagement, along with concomitant task-focused coping, is adaptive. However, task engagement may also be associated with misdirected effort, for example, in investing substantial time in playing a video game. In general, the three states prepare the person for handling different types of situational demand, but whether state change is tied to genuine adaptive exigencies will vary from person to person, and from context to context.

Thus, we arrive at a transactional perspective on the significance of transient states for intellectual functioning, within a bidirectional model of interaction between the person and the task environment. One key issue is how the task environment, in conjunction with personality factors, influences the adaptive significance of task performance. The person performing an intellectual task must, in effect, decide whether it is worthwhile to commit effort, whether the task is beyond their capabilities, and whether there is a need for personal reflection. These issues have been explored, in part, in the test anxiety literature, but this research has tended to focus on distress and worry, neglecting the role of task engagement. The second key issue is how the state changes driven by self-regulation may feed back into objective performance. While the effects of state factors on intellectual performance are often modest, task and contextual factors appear to moderate correlations between states and performance. Some effects of states on information processing seem to generalize across contexts, but are moderated by task demands. These include the detrimental effect of cognitive interference, whose effects on performance depend on the processing demands of the task. It appears that tasks that require elaborated encoding, that require extensive use of working memory, and that require retrieval of relatively inaccessible memories are maximally sensitive to worry, anxiety, or both (Zeidner, 1998). Likewise, intellectual tasks that require sustaining attention under high workload conditions may be most sensitive to the variations in resource availability associated with task engagement. Other effects of state, that are mediated by changes in coping, depend more on personal and contextual factors. For example, the influence of task focus on performance is likely to depend on the person's ability to formulate and implement a workable strategy for performance enhancement: task-focused coping does not automatically confer improved intellectual functioning (Zeidner, 1998). Furthermore, task strategy varies qualitatively with adaptive goals congruent with state. For example, in fatigued, disengaged states, people prefer to use decision-making strategies that minimize effort, and are reactive rather than proactive (Matthews, Davies, et al., 2000). Thus, it is not very informative to pose traditional questions, such as "what is the magnitude of the relationship between intelligence and anxiety?" Instead, research should emphasize how states facilitate or impair the ability to perform at the person's level of competence within specific social contexts, on tasks making specified demands on processing. That is, states may signal the extent to which typical performance within a given context approaches maximal performance (see Ackerman & Kanfer, chap. 5).

CONCLUSIONS

In this chapter, we have approached intellectual functioning, in the sense of reasoning and problem-solving, as one of several, interrelated classes of process that support adaptation. Coping and appraisal may be seen as intellectual in that they operate in the service of social-problem solving. We might link appraisal to the apprehension of experience and coping to practical intelligence (cf. Zeidner & Matthews, 2000). However, especially in challenging and stressful circumstances, adaptation is multilayered, requiring not just higher-level cognitive skills but also lower level, often implicit processes, such as threat evaluation, and neural processes controlling arousal and stress responses. Lower-level processes may influence both skill acquisition (competence), and the extent to which skills can be successfully executed within a given context (performance).

In general, adaptation involves a multitude of independent processes, at different levels of abstraction. However, despite the distributed nature of adaptive processing, individual differences are given coherence by self-regulation. Over the long term, self-regulation supports personal goals and aspirations. Understanding the individual's long-term goals is necessarily ideographic (Kihlstrom & Cantor, 2000), but we can identify some consistencies associated with personality traits. We have argued that traits represent adaptations to the major challenges of human life that constrain long-term self-regulation, shaped by both heredity and social learning. For example, if extraversion represents adaptation to cognitively demanding social environments, we expect that, typically, extraverts' long-term goals will involve what are, in the occupational field, termed social and enterprising interests (e.g., Ackerman & Heggestad, 1997).

The stable adaptations described as traits are supported by a set of often small biases in cognition, emotion and motivation. Biases include both low-level biases in biocognitive components, and high-level biases in assigning personal meaning to situations. Thus, we have an explanation for the personality paradox. Traits are not controlled by some single master-process, such as arousability. Instead, we see the trait most clearly through its gross, adaptive features. Even the lay observer can see that extraverts are more sociable than introverts, but the roots of individual differences in sociability are a complex set of small influences, that feed into social skill acquisition over time. Effects of personality traits on intellectual functioning may reflect several of these separate biases, depending on the context. In this chapter, we discussed how traits may influence: (a) social skills and problem-solving abilities, (b) effects of arousal and stress on basic information-processing functions, (c) the priority given to self-evaluative thinking that may interfere with intellectual functioning, and (d) the priority given to applying the intellect to detecting and evaluating personal risk.

In the short term, the task for self-regulation is to solve some immediate adaptive problem, whose terms are often outside of personal control. Again, we emphasize that within-situation adaptation is supported by multiple levels and domains of process. Studies of transient states suggest how emotions, cognitions and motivations may cohere around self-regulative goals. For example, we defined the state of task engagement in terms of increased concentration, task motivation and energetic arousal. The task engagement response may reflect a variety of mechanisms (including direct influence of neural systems), but evidence especially highlights the role of high-level cognitions; appraising the situation as challenging, and initiating task-focused coping. The state concomitants of these processes jointly function to support the adaptive goal of commitment of effort to the task. These may be differentiated to some extent as resisting distractions (concentration), mobilizing and directing effort (task motivation), and increasing resource availability (energetic arousal). However, the close linkages between the different state responses suggest that they typically operate as an integrated system. The exquisite sensitivity of states to feedback from the situation functions to keep self-regulation attuned to changing environmental contingencies. Again, multiple mechanisms may contribute to effects of state on intellectual functioning, depending on task demands and contextual factors. These mechanisms include generalized changes in information processing, such as loss of functional resources, and the person's appraisal of how application of the intellect may help solve the adaptive problems of a particular social context.

Thus, intellectual functioning should be seen as one aspect of self-regulative processes. Indeed, the clearest picture of the role of intellectual functioning may come from analyzing its adaptive relevance, over the life course and in specific situations. Like practical intelligence (Sternberg & Grigorenko, 2000), intellectual functioning is adaptive through its specialization to deal with specific situational challenges and tasks, that is, as a set of contextualized skills. The functional analysis here provides a broad conceptual framework for understanding the relationship between traits, states and intellectual performance. However, more detailed predictive models require a more complete account of the cognitive architecture and acquired skills supporting performance of specific tasks, an issue beyond the scope of this chapter.

REFERENCES

Ackerman, P. L., & Heggestad, E. D. (1997). Intelligence, personality and interests: Evidence for overlapping traits. *Psychological Bulletin, 121*, 219–245.

Anderson, J. R. (1996). ACT: A simple theory of complex cognition. *American Psychologist, 51*, 355–365.

Argyle, M., & Lu, L. (1990). The happiness of extraverts. *Personality and Individual Differences, 11*, 1011–1018.

Arkin, R. M. (1987). Shyness and self-presentation. In K. Yardley & T. Honess (Eds.), *Self and identity: Psychosocial perspectives* (pp. 187–195). New York: Routledge & Kegan Paul.

Beck, A. (1989). Evaluation anxieties. In C. Lindemann (Ed.), *Handbook of phobia therapy: Rapid symptom relief in anxiety disorders* (pp. 89–112). Northvale, NJ: J. Aronson.

Belzer, K. D., D'Zurilla, T. J., & Maydeu-Olivares, A. (2002). Social problem solving and trait anxiety as predictors of worry in a college student population. *Personality & Individual Differences, 33*, 573–585.

Bruch, M. A. (2001). Shyness and social interaction. In W. R. Crozier & L. E. Alden (Eds.), *International handbook of social anxiety: Concepts, research and interventions relating to the self and shyness* (pp. 195–215). New York: Wiley.

Carver, C. S., & Scheier, M. F. (1988). A control-process perspective on anxiety. *Anxiety Research, 1*, 17–22.

Emmons, R. A. (1997). Motives and goals. In R. Hogan & J. A. Johnson (Eds.), *Handbook of personality psychology* (pp. 485–512). San Diego, CA: Academic Press.

Endler, N. S. (1983). Generality of the interaction model of anxiety with respect to two social evaluation field studies. *Canadian Journal of the Behavioral Sciences, 15*, 60–69.

Endler, N., & Parker, J. (1990). Multi dimensional assessment of coping: A critical review. *Journal of Personality and Social Psychology, 58*, 844–854.

Eysenck, M. W., & Calvo, M. G. (1992). Anxiety and performance: The processing efficiency theory. *Cognition & Emotion, 6*, 409–434.

Forgas, J. P. (1995). The Affect Infusion Model (AIM): Review and an integrative theory of mood effects on judgment. *Psychological Bulletin, 117*, 39–66.

Furnham, A., & Heaven, P. (1999). *Personality and social behaviour*. London: Arnold.

Furnham, A., & Medhurst, S. (1995). Personality correlates of academic seminar behavior: A study of four instruments. *Personality & Individual Differences, 19*, 197–208.

Gal, R., & Lazarus, R. (1975). The role of activity in anticipation and confronting stressful situations. *Journal of Human Stress, 1*, 4–20.

Geen, R. G. (1987). Test anxiety and behavioral avoidance. *Journal of Research in Personality, 21*, 481–488.

Goldberg, L. R. (1993). The structure of phenotypic personality traits. *American Psychologist, 48*, 26–34.

Hilgard, E. R. (1980). The trilogy of mind: Cognition, affection, and conation. *Journal of the History of the Behavioral Sciences, 16*, 107–117.

Kihlstrom, J. F., & Cantor, N. (2000). Social intelligence. In R. J. Sternberg (Ed.), *Handbook of human intelligence* (pp. 359–379). New York: Cambridge University Press.

Kochanska, G., & Coy, K. C. (2002). Child emotionality and maternal responsiveness as predictors of reunion behaviors in the strange situation: Links mediated and unmediated by separation distress. *Child Development, 73*, 228–240.

Lazarus, R. (1993). Why we should think of stress as a subset of emotion. In L. Goldberger & S. Breznitz (Eds.), *Stress: Theoretical and clinical aspects* (pp. 21–39). New York: Free Press.

Lazarus, R. S., & Folkman, S. (1984). *Stress, appraisal, and coping*. New York: Springer.

Leary, M. R. (2001). Shyness and the self: Attentional, motivational, and cognitive self-processes in social anxiety and inhibition. In W. R. Crozier & L. E. Alden (Eds.), *International handbook of social anxiety: Concepts, research and interventions relating to the self and shyness* (pp. 217–234). New York: Wiley.

Leitenberg, H. (1990). Introduction. In H. Leitenberg (Ed.), *Handbook of social and evaluative anxiety* (pp. 1–6). New York: Plenum.

Mann, L. (1992). Stress, affect and risk-taking. In J. F. Yates (Ed.), *Risk-taking behavior* (pp. 201–230). New York: Wiley.

Matthews, G. (1997). Extraversion, emotion and performance: A cognitive-adaptive model. In G. Matthews (Ed.), *Cognitive science perspectives on personality and emotion* (pp. 339–442). Amsterdam: Elsevier.

Matthews, G. (1999). Personality and skill: A cognitive-adaptive framework. In P. L. Ackerman, P. C. Kyllonen, & R. D. Roberts (Eds.), *The future of learning and individual differences research: Processes, traits, and content* (pp. 251–270). Washington, DC: American Psychological Association.

Matthews, G. (2001). Levels of transaction: A cognitive science framework for operator stress. In P. A. Hancock & P. A. Desmond (Eds.), *Stress, workload and fatigue* (pp. 5–33). Mahwah, NJ: Lawrence Erlbaum Associates.

Matthews, G. (2002). Towards a transactional ergonomics for driver stress and fatigue. *Theoretical Issues in Ergonomics Science, 3,* 195–211.

Matthews, G., Campbell, S., & Falconer, S. (2001). Assessment of motivational states in performance environments. In *Proceedings of the Human Factors and Ergonomics Society 45th Annual Meeting* (pp. 906–910). Santa Monica, CA: HFES.

Matthews, G., Campbell, S. E., Falconer, S., Joyner, L., Huggins, J., Gilliland, K., Grier, R., & Warm, J. S. (2002). Fundamental dimensions of subjective state in performance settings: Task engagement, distress and worry. *Emotion, 2,* 315–340.

Matthews, G., Davies, D. R., Westerman, S. J., & Stammers, R. B. (2000). *Human performance: Cognition, stress and individual differences.* London: Psychology Press.

Matthews, G., Deary, I. J., & Whiteman, M. (in press). *Personality traits* (2nd ed.). Cambridge, England: Cambridge University Press.

Matthews, G., Derryberry, D., & Siegle, G. J. (2000). Personality and emotion: Cognitive science perspectives. In S. E. Hampson (Ed.), *Advances in personality psychology* (Vol. 1, pp. 199–237). London: Routledge.

Matthews, G., & Desmond, P. A. (2002). Task-induced fatigue states and simulated driving performance. *Quarterly Journal of Experimental Psychology, 55A,* 659–686.

Matthews, G., & Dorn, L. (1995). Personality and intelligence: Cognitive and attentional processes. In D. Saklofske & M. Zeidner (Eds.), *International handbook of personality and intelligence* (pp. 367–396). New York: Plenum.

Matthews, G., & Gilliland, K. (1999). The personality theories of H. J. Eysenck and J. A. Gray: A comparative review. *Personality and Individual Differences, 26,* 583–626.

Matthews, G., & Harley, T. A. (1993). Effects of extraversion and self-report arousal on semantic priming: A connectionist approach. *Journal of Personality and Social Psychology, 65,* 735–756.

Matthews, G., Hillyard, E. J., & Campbell, S. E. (1999). Metacognition and maladaptive coping as components of test anxiety. *Clinical Psychology and Psychotherapy, 6,* 111–125.

Matthews, G., Joyner, L., Gilliland, K., Campbell, S. E., Huggins, J., & Falconer, S. (1999). Validation of a comprehensive stress state questionnaire: Towards a state 'Big Three'? In I. Mervielde, I. J. Deary, F. De Fruyt, & F. Ostendorf (Eds.), *Personality psychology in Europe* (Vol. 7, pp. 335–350). Tilburg, Netherlands: Tilburg University Press.

Matthews, G., Schwean, V. L., Campbell, S. E., Saklofske, D. H., & Mohamed, A. A. R. (2000). Personality, self-regulation and adaptation: A cognitive-social framework. In M. Boekarts, P. R. Pintrich, & M. Zeidner (Eds.), *Handbook of self-regulation* (pp. 171–207). New York: Academic Press.

Matthews, G., Zeidner, M., & Roberts, R. (2003). *Emotional intelligence: Science and myth.* Cambridge, MA: MIT Press.

Mayer, J. D., Frasier Chabot, H., & Carlsmith, K. M. (1997). Conation, affect, and cognition in personality. In G. Matthews (Ed.), *Cognitive science perspectives on personality and emotion* (pp. 31–63). Amsterdam: Elsevier Science.

Meleshko, K.G., & Alden, L. E. (1993). Anxiety and self-disclosure: Toward a motivational model. *Journal of Personality & Social Psychology, 64,* 1000–1009.

Mughal, S., Walsh, J., & Wilding, J. (1996). Stress and work performance: The role of trait anxiety. *Personality & Individual Differences, 20,* 685–691.

Pearlin, L. I., & Schooler, C. (1978). The structure of coping. *Journal of Health and Social Behavior, 19,* 2–21.

Plomin, R., & Caspi, A. (1998). DNA and personality. *European Journal of Personality, 12,* 387–407.

Powers, W. T. (1973). *Behavior: The control of perception.* Chicago: Aldine.

Revelle, W. (1993). Individual differences in personality and motivation: 'Non-cognitive' determinants of cognitive performance. In A. D. Baddeley & L. Weiskrantz (Eds.), *Attention: Selection, awareness, and control* (pp. 346–373). Oxford, England: Oxford University Press.

Ryan, R. M., & Deci, E. L. (2000). The darker and brighter sides of human existence: Basic psychological needs as a unifying concept. *Psychological Inquiry, 11*, 319–338.

Saklofske, D. H., Austin, E. J., & Minski, P. S. (2003). Factor structure and validity of a trait emotional intelligence measure. *Personality and Individual Differences, 34*, 707–721.

Sarason, I. G., & Sarason, B. R. (1990). Test anxiety. In H. Leitenberg (Ed.), *Handbook of social and evaluative anxiety* (pp. 475–496). New York: Plenum.

Sarason, I. G., Sarason, B. R., & Pierce, G. R. (1995). Cognitive interference: At the intelligence-personality crossroads. In D. Saklofske & M. Zeidner (Eds.), *International handbook of personality and intelligence* (pp. 285–296). New York: Plenum.

Schimmack, U., & Grob, A. (2000). Dimensional models of core affect: A quantitative comparison by means of structural equation modeling. *European Journal of Personality, 14*, 325–345.

Smith, T. W., Ingram, R. E., & Brehm, S. S. (1983). Social anxiety, anxious preoccupation and recall of self-relevant information. *Journal of Personality and Social Psychology, 44*, 1276–1283.

Sternberg, R. J., & Grigorenko, E. L. (2000). Practical intelligence and its development. In R. Bar-On & J. D. A. Parker (Eds.), *The handbook of emotional intelligence* (pp. 215–243). San Francisco: Jossey-Bass.

Watson, D. (2000). *Mood and temperament.* New York: Guilford Press.

Weiner, B. (2000). Intrapersonal and interpersonal theories of motivation from an attributional perspective. *Educational Psychology Review, 12*, 1–14.

Wells, A. (2000). *Emotional disorders and metacognition: Innovative cognitive therapy.* Chichester, England: Wiley.

Wells, A., & Matthews, G. (1994). *Attention and emotion: A clinical perspective.* Hillsdale, NJ: Lawrence Erlbaum Associates.

Zeidner, M. (1989). Social anxiety among Jewish and Arab students in Israel. *Journal of Social Psychology, 129*, 415–417.

Zeidner, M. (1998). *Test anxiety: The state of the art.* New York: Plenum.

Zeidner, M., & Matthews, G. (2000). Personality and intelligence. In R. J. Sternberg (Ed.), *Handbook of human intelligence* (2nd ed., pp. 581–610). Cambridge: Cambridge University Press.

Zeidner, M., Matthews, G., Roberts, R. D., & McCann, C. (2003). Development of emotional intelligence: Towards a multi-level investment model. *Human Development, 46*, 69–96.

Zeidner, M., & Saklofske, D. (1996). Adaptive and maladaptive coping. In M. Zeidner & N. S. Endler (Eds.), *Handbook of coping: Theory, research, applications* (pp. 505–531). New York: Wiley.

7

▼▼▼▼▼▼▼

Integrating Emotion and Cognition: The Role of Emotional Intelligence

Marc A. Brackett
Paulo N. Lopes
Yale University

Zorana Ivcevic
John D. Mayer
University of New Hampshire

Peter Salovey
Yale University

The Stoic philosophers of ancient Greece argued that emotions were unreliable and idiosyncratic sources of information (Lloyd, 1978). They emphasized the superiority of reason, cognition, and intelligence (Kerferd, 1978). The presence of an emotional intelligence (EI) would likely have seemed inconceivable to them—an oxymoron. Two millennia later psychologists and philosophers still debate whether emotions are disorganized interruptions of mental activity or whether they contribute to logical thought and intelligent behavior (De Sousa, 1987). For example, Woodworth (1940) viewed emotions as disorganizing interruptions of mental activity, whereas Leeper (1948, p. 17) suggested that emotions "arouse, sustain, and direct activity" and contribute to logical thought and adaptive behavior. It is no wonder that the identification of an EI occurred rather late relative to other sorts of intelligence.

EI is one way to reconceptualize the relation between reason and emotion. It can be viewed as an outgrowth of two areas of psychological research that emerged in the 1970s and 1980s. The first area, termed cognition and affect, examined how emotions interacted with thought (Bower, 1981; Clark & Fiske, 1982; Isen, Shalker, Clark, & Karp, 1978; Zajonc, 1980). Isen et al. (1978), for example, proposed the idea of a cognitive loop that connected mood to judgment. Bower (1981) also introduced a spreading activation model of memory demonstrating that happy moods activated happy thoughts and sad moods activated sad thoughts. Furthermore, a large body of research showed that thought processes could be affected by mood inductions (e.g., Forgas & Moylan, 1987; Mayer & Bremer, 1985; Salovey & Birnbaum, 1989; Singer & Salovey, 1988). By 1987, the field had become prominent enough to warrant the founding of an eponymously named journal, *Cognition and Emotion*.

The second influence on EI pertained to the loosening of the concept of intelligence to include a broad array of mental abilities rather than a monolithic "g" (e.g., Cantor & Kihlstrom, 1987; Gardner, 1983; Sternberg, 1985). Gardner (1983), for example, urged educators and scientists to place a greater emphasis on the search for multiple intelligences. He was primarily interested in helping educators to appreciate students with different learning styles and potentials. Gardner (1983) wrote of an intrapersonal intelligence, which involves, among many other things, a capacity to notice one's own moods and the ability to draw conclusions about one's feelings as a means of understanding and guiding behavior.

EI includes the processes involved in the recognition, use, understanding, and management of one's own and others' emotional states to solve emotion-laden problems and regulate behavior (Mayer & Salovey, 1997; Salovey & Mayer, 1990). The term was introduced to psychology in 1990 through two articles. The first formally defined EI as "the ability to monitor one's own and others' feelings and emotions, to discriminate among them and to use this information to guide one's thinking and actions" (Salovey & Mayer, 1990, p. 189). The second presented a demonstration of how the construct could be tested as a mental ability (Mayer, DiPaolo, & Salovey, 1990). Findings from the empirical study provided a first hint that that emotion and cognition can be combined to perform sophisticated information processing.

EI, however, was mostly unknown to laypeople and academicians alike until Goleman (1995) popularized the term. Goleman's book, *Emotional Intelligence*, quickly captured the interest of the media, general public, and investigators. It saw violence as a serious problem plaguing both the nation and the nation's schools; it claimed that scientists had discovered a connection between EI and prosocial behavior; and it claimed that EI was "as powerful and at times more powerful than IQ" in predicting success in life (Goleman, 1995, p. 34). Goleman (1995, 1998) described EI as an array of positive personality attributes, including political awareness, self-confidence, conscientiousness, and achievement motive (pp. 26–28). Goleman's views on EI often went far beyond the evidence available (Davies, Stankov, & Roberts, 1998; Epstein, 1998; Hedlund & Sternberg, 2000; Mayer & Cobb, 2000; Mayer, Salovey, & Caruso, 2000).

In the following years, numerous tests were packaged purportedly measuring EI, and educators and human resource professionals began to consult on EI—mostly defining the construct as a set of personality variables related to character and important to achieving success in life. Mayer and Salovey

(1997) clarified their definition of EI as one that is strictly ability-based or competency-based as distinguished from one rooted in a broad array of personality traits (see also Mayer et al., 2000; Salovey, Mayer, & Caruso, 2002). More specifically, they defined EI as the ability to accurately perceive and express emotion, to use emotion to facilitate thought, to understand emotions, and to manage emotions for both emotional and personal growth (Mayer & Salovey, 1997).

Today, the field is filled with both empirical articles and popular books on the topic. As a result, the definitions, claims, and measures of EI have become extremely diverse, making it difficult for the researcher or layperson that encounters the field to decipher what EI actually is. In this chapter, our goal is to introduce researchers to the theory, measurement, and research associated with Mayer and Salovey's (1997) ability model of EI. In the first section, we define EI and describe a new performance-based test for its measurement, the Mayer-Salovey-Caruso Emotional Intelligence Test (MSCEIT; Mayer, Salovey, & Caruso, 2002a). We also briefly distinguish ability and popular models of EI. In the second section, we place EI in the context of major areas of psychological functioning and social behavior. We then present recent empirical research on EI, concentrating on its relation to these areas. In the final section, we draw some conclusions and discuss future directions for research on EI.

EMOTIONAL INTELLIGENCE: THEORY AND MEASUREMENT

Competing Models of Emotional Intelligence

There are two general approaches to EI in the literature. They can be characterized as ability models and mixed models (Mayer et al., 2000). Ability models view EI as a standard intelligence and argue that EI meets traditional criteria for an intelligence. Mixed models, which arose mostly after initial popularization of the construct, are so-called because they combine the ability conception of EI with numerous self-reported attributes including optimism, self-awareness, self-esteem, and self-actualization (e.g., Bar-On, 1997; Boyatzis, Goleman, & Rhee, 2000; Goleman, 1995, 1998).

Because mixed-model measures of EI do not directly assess a person's ability to solve problems pertaining to emotions or intelligence, as psychologists define them, they are unlikely to be highly correlated with ability tests. In fact, a recent study showed that the most popular mixed model and ability measures of EI are only related at $r < .22$ (Brackett & Mayer, 2003). Furthermore, because mixed models pertain to a broad constellation of personality variables, such measures are likely to lack discriminant validity. Indeed, mixed-model measures are highly correlated (positively) with well-being and positive mood, and highly correlated (negatively) with neuroticism and depression (r's $= \pm.50$ to $.75$; Bar-On, 1997, 2000; Brackett & Mayer, 2003). In contrast, ability measures only weakly correlate with Big Five personality factors such as openness (or intellect) and agreeableness (r's $< .35$; Brackett & Mayer, 2003; Brackett, Mayer, & Warner, in press; Lopes, Salovey, & Straus, 2003). Therefore, the ability model of EI makes it possible to analyze the degree to which EI is a distinct mental ability and whether it specifically contributes to healthy behavior.

Measuring Emotional Intelligence With the MSCEIT

Mayer and Salovey's (1997) analysis of emotion-related abilities led them to divide their ability model of EI into four areas or branches of abilities. Elsewhere the theory is explained in more detail (Mayer, Caruso, & Salovey, 1999; Salovey, Bedell, Detweiler, & Mayer, 2000; Salovey, Woolery, & Mayer, 2000). Here, we review its major components. As earlier noted, the four branches of EI concern the ability to: (a) perceive emotions, (b) use emotions to facilitate thought, (c) understand emotions, and (d) manage emotions to foster personal growth and healthy social relations. Whereas the perception, understanding, and management of emotions (Branches 1, 3, and 4) involve reasoning about emotions, and Branch 2 (use of emotions to facilitate thought) involves using emotions to enhance reasoning. The four branches of EI are viewed as forming a hierarchy, increasing in complexity from emotion perception to management. According to the theory, one's overall EI is the combination of the four abilities.

Branch 1, Perception of Emotion, concerns the capacity to perceive and identify correctly the emotional content in faces and pictures. Branch 2 concerns the use of emotion information to facilitate thought. This branch specifically deals with the ability to generate, use, and feel emotions as necessary to communicate feelings, or to employ them in other mental processes. Branch 3 involves understanding emotional information, how emotions combine and progress, and how to reason about emotional meanings. Branch 4 concerns the management of emotions. It specifically pertains to a person's ability to manage and regulate feelings in oneself and others so as to promote personal understanding, growth, and the attainment of personal goals.

The four EI abilities were first measured with a test called the Multifactor Emotional Intelligence Test (MEIS; Mayer et al., 1999). This instrument has been improved upon, leading to a shorter and more reliable test, the MSCEIT (Mayer et al., 2002a). The MSCEIT assesses the four-branch model of EI (i.e., perceiving, using, understanding, and regulating emotions) with 141 items that are divided among 8 tasks (see Table 7.1 for a description of the Tasks). The MSCEIT yields seven scores: one for each of the four

TABLE 7.1

A Hierarchical View of Emotional Intelligence Abilities as Measured by the MSCEIT

Emotional Intelligence

Area 1: Experiential EI		Area 2: Strategic EI	
Branch 1: (Perception of emotion)	Branch 2: (Use of emotion)	Branch 3: (Understanding of emotion)	Branch 4: (Regulation of emotion)
Task 1: Faces Participants view photographs of faces and identify the emotions in them.	Task 3: Sensation Which tactile, taste, and color sensations are reminiscent of a specific emotion?	Task 5: Blends Which emotions might blend together to form a more complex feeling?	Task 7: Emotion Management How effective alternative actions would be in achieving a certain outcome, in emotion-laden situations where individuals must regulate their feelings.
Task 2: Pictures Participants view photographs of faces and artistic representations and identify the emotions in them.	Task 4: Facilitation How moods enhance thinking, reasoning, and other cognitive processes.	Task 6: Changes How emotions progress and change from one state to another.	Task 8: Relationship Management Test-takers evaluate how effective different actions would be in achieving an emotion-laden outcome involving other people.

branches, 2 areas scores, and a total score. The two area scores are termed: Experiential EI, which combines branches 1 and 2, and Strategic EI, which combines branches 3 and 4.

The MSCEIT is an objective test because there are better and worse answers on it, as determined by consensus or expert scoring. Consensus scores reflect the proportion of people in the normative sample (over 5,000 people from various countries) who endorsed each MSCEIT test item. Expert norms were obtained from a sample of 21 members of the International Society Research on Emotions (ISRE) who provided their expert judgment on each of the test's items. Emotional intelligence scores based on the two methods are closely related $r > .90$; Mayer, Salovey, Caruso, & Sitarenios, 2003).

Mayer et al. (1999) and Mayer, Salovey, Caruso, and Sitarenios, (2001, 2003) assert that the emotional abilities measured by the MSCEIT meet the criteria for an intelligence because: (a) the MSCEIT has a factor structure congruent with the four branches of the theoretical model; (b) the four abilities show unique variance, but are meaningfully related to other mental abilities such as verbal intelligence; (c) EI develops with age and experience, and finally (d) the abilities can be objectively measured.

Concerns about the psychometric properties of earlier EI tests such as the MEIS were raised by Davies et al. (1998) and recently repeated by Roberts, Zeidner, and Matthews (2001). The revised MSCEIT V 2.0, however, is reliable at the full-scale level (r's = .90 to .96), the area level (r's = .84 to .91), and the branch level (r's = .74 to .91; Mayer et al., 2003).

EMOTIONAL INTELLIGENCE FROM A SYSTEMS PERSPECTIVE

EI is best understood in the broader context of an individual's functioning. This means looking at the interaction between EI and other cognitive abilities, emotional and motivational traits, and behavioral criteria. The importance of investigating a mental ability in relation to other areas of psychological functioning is not new (Eysenck, 1979; Sternberg & Ruzgis, 1994; Wechsler, 1958). For example, Eysenck (1979) asserted that nonintellectual attributes (e.g., impulsivity) might interfere with aspects of intelligence such as checking for errors. Thus, viewing a mental ability such as EI within a complete personality system can elucidate how it contributes to diverse psychological processes and behavior.

A number of psychologists have emphasized the need to adopt a systems perspective to organize and understand psychological variables (e.g., Bronfenbrenner, 1979; Csikszentmihalyi, 1999; Lewin, 1936; Magnusson & Stattin, 1998). It is useful to divide the personality system into its major functional elements, and a variety of divisions have been employed to do this. One recently proposed functional division organizes personality into four broad areas: (a) a knowledge works, which includes mental models and cognitive capacities that operate on them, (b) an energy lattice, which combines motives and emotions, (c) a role player, that executes social acts, and (d) an executive consciousness (Mayer, 1998, 2001a, 2001b).

The knowledge works pertains to cognitive or intellectual functions that enable understanding of both the self and the world. Components of knowledge works include mental models (e.g., explanatory style), intellectual abilities (e.g., general intelligence), and cognitive styles (e.g., field-dependence). The energy lattice pertains to motivational and emotional attributes that energize and direct behavior. Components of the energy lattice are motives (e.g., achievement), emotions (e.g., happiness), and emotional styles (e.g., neuroticism vs. emotional stability). The role player pertains to the social functions of personality and is responsible for planning and executing social behavior through social roles (e.g., leadership), social skills (e.g., acting skill), or physical-motor expression (e.g., gracefulness). Finally, the executive consciousness pertains to conscious awareness and self-regulatory functions. It also controls behavior by overseeing other areas of personality functioning. Functions of the executive consciousness include awareness (e.g., absorption), coping strategies (e.g., problem-solving coping), and self-awareness (e.g., self-consciousness).

Mayer and Salovey's (1997) model of EI described an intelligence that draws on functions from the emotion system (in the energy lattice) and the cognitive knowledge and capacity of the knowledge works. Furthermore, the self-regulatory aspects of the EI model may draw on the executive consciousness portion of personality.

The fact that the EI model draws on features from a number of areas of personality has several implications. For example, cognitive abilities share some common variance. Because both cognitive IQ and EI draw on cognitive abilities, EI is expected to share some variance with general intelligence, while remaining distinct from it (Mayer et al., 2000). Furthermore, EI should be related to other cognitive abilities such as creative and practical intelligence (Sternberg, 1999).

With regard to the energy lattice, components of EI such as emotional regulation may be related to a person's experience of more positive and less negative emotions. EI could also inform the motivation system by helping people to choose tasks in which they are likely to succeed. The ability to use emotions to facilitate thinking might also help a person to invest time and effort in actions that are most appropriate for current mood states. For example, an emotionally intelligent person could be expected to work on inductive reasoning and creative tasks when in happy moods, and tasks requiring deductive reasoning when in sad moods (Isen, Daubman, & Nowicki, 1987; Palfai & Salovey, 1993).

EI may also be important for social interactions (i.e., role player functions) because it involves the ability to decode nonverbal and emotional signals and to manage one's own and others' emotions. Therefore, an emotionally intelligent person is predicted to have more harmonious social relationships that include mutual care and understanding and less conflict (see Ciarrochi, Forgas, & Mayer, 2001; Lopes et al., 2003).

Finally, EI should be related to aspects of the executive consciousness. In particular, the regulation of emotion branch could be expected to correlate negatively with impulsive behavior and positively with healthier life decisions. Therefore, it is expected that EI would negatively correlate with physical fighting, and excessive drug and alcohol consumption.

EMOTIONAL INTELLIGENCE RELATED TO COMPONENTS OF THE PERSONALITY SYSTEMS SET

The framework previously described suggests that EI should be associated with a number of mental abilities, motivational and emotional qualities, and social behavior. In this section, we discuss how EI is both conceptually and empirically related to the four components of the systems set: knowledge works (e.g., verbal intelligence), energy lattice (e.g., well-being), role player (e.g., social relationships), and executive consciousness (e.g., maladaptive behaviors). Note that we do not expect EI to be highly correlated to many areas of psychological functioning, or to explain large amounts of variance in specific behaviors, but to contribute to important predictions above and beyond other abilities and traits. Even moderate associations are considered important when they signal theoretically important links between psychological processes and entail far-reaching consequences for applied purposes (Abelson, 1985; Prentice & Miller, 1992).

KNOWLEDGE WORKS

Traditional Intelligence

Because most IQ tests rely on vocabulary and basic reading comprehension skills there should be a relation between EI, in particular, understanding of emotions, with traditional intelligence. Furthermore, because IQ partly reflects self-regulatory and executive function capacities such as the ability to sustain attention (Lynam, Moffitt, & Southamer-Loeber, 1993), we expect the management of emotion branch to correlate with traditional measures of intelligence. For example, unregulated anxiety can undermine focus and concentration, inhibiting smooth performance in challenging intellectual or physical activities (Baumeister & Tice, 1990; Csikszentmihalyi, 1992), including performance on IQ tests.

Recent empirical work suggests that EI is modestly associated with traditional intelligence and academic achievement. In two large-sample studies with students at the University of New Hampshire, Brackett and colleagues found low but significant associations between MSCEIT scores and measures of academic ability and achievement, as assessed by verbal SAT scores, high school rank, and college grades (r's < .35; Brackett & Mayer, 2003; Brackett et al., in press). In another study, the understanding emotions subscale of the MSCEIT, which taps into knowledge of emotional vocabulary, correlated the highest with both verbal ability—as measured through the WAIS-III (Wechsler, 1997) vocabulary subtest and verbal SAT scores (Lopes et al., 2003). Finally, David (2002) found significant correlations between all four branches of the MSCEIT and the Wonderlic Personnel Test (WPT; Wonderlic, 1998). The highest correlation was with the understanding of emotions branch. Additional findings between the MSCEIT and measures of general intelligence can be found in the test manual (Mayer et al., 2002b). Note that correlations between EI and intelligence measures based on college student samples may be somewhat attenuated due to restriction of range on IQ.

Practical Intelligence

Practical intelligence (Sternberg, 1999) helps one to implement solutions effectively, drawing on previous experience and tacit knowledge. Sternberg's view of practical intelligence encompasses social and emotional skills, and emphasizes the notion of common sense. Common sense embodies all the tacit knowledge or procedural know-how that is often not explicitly taught, nor easily verbalized (Sternberg et al., 2000). To assess practical intelligence, Sternberg and colleagues have developed tests that ask people to rate the effectiveness of different strategies for dealing with situations likely to arise in everyday life. There is evidence that measures of practical intelligence predict academic achievement and supervisor ratings of work performance over and above traditional measures of intelligence (Grigorenko & Sternberg, 2001; Sternberg et al., 2000).

We expect emotional and practical abilities to be somewhat associated, in so far as emotional abilities reflect attunement to social norms and expectations, and thus reflect common sense, as well. However, we have only just started to investigate the relationship between emotional and practical intelligence. In a preliminary study with 70 college students, modest correlations (r's = .25) were found between the understanding and managing of emotions branches on the MSCEIT and the College Students' Tacit Knowledge Inventory (CSTKI; Grigorenko, Gil, Jarvin, & Sternberg, 2002). Further research is needed to replicate these findings and better understand the relationship between the two realms of ability.

Creativity

Although no investigator has directly correlated ability measures of EI with measures of creativity, emotions are intimately involved in the creative process, and research on creativity and affect suggests that EI abilities should be related to creativity (Csikszentmihalyi, 1996; Domino, 1989; Shaw & Runco, 1994). Perception of emotion in colors, for instance, has been linked to creativity in studies by Dailey, Martindale, and Borkum (1997). People with high scores on the Remote Associates Test, an index of creative ability, were better able to discriminate emotions in colors than less creative individuals.

Another way EI may influence creativity is that creative individuals appear to plan and direct their behavior in ways that optimize their performance (Csikszentmihalyi, 1996). Two EI abilities, the use of emotion to facilitate thinking and management of emotions, may aid in directing behavior to enhance creativity. For example, people who are aware of the influence of mood on their thinking may capitalize on emotional ups and downs so as to enhance their creativity. Positive moods were found to facilitate inductive and creative thinking, while negative moods may facilitate attention to detail and deductive reasoning (Isen et al., 1987; Palfai & Salovey, 1993).

The ability to experience synesthesia, which involves associating feelings and other sensations (one task on the MSCEIT's use of emotions branch), has also been linked to creativity (e.g., Dailey et al., 1997; Domino, 1989). For example, Domino (1989) showed that people who report frequent experiences of synesthesia score higher on personality traits (i.e., Adjective Checklist for Creativity; Domino, 1970), attributes of perceptual style (i.e., preference for complexity; Barron, 1953), and divergent thinking. Finally, the ability to access one's emotions and use them in thinking has been described as the basis of metaphor generation (Lubart & Getz, 1998). The ability to generate metaphors may facilitate the creative process by suggesting analogies or unique ways to redefine problems (Lubart & Getz, 1998).

Following a different line of research, Averill (Averill, 1999; Averill & Thomas-Knowles, 1991) wrote about emotional creativity as the ability to experience emotions that are novel, authentic to self, and adaptive. Emotional intelligence is likely to be related to emotional creativity as cognitive intelligence is related to cognitive creativity. These two constructs are thought to be related because both EI and emotional creativity are defined as abilities, reflect individual differences, and rely on the understanding and regulation of emotional experience.

ENERGY LATTICE

Psychological Well-Being

Several studies have linked EI to psychological well-being as measured by Ryff's (1989) scales. The scales tap into autonomy, mastery, personal growth, positive relations with others, purpose in life, and self-acceptance. Brackett and Mayer (2003) reported significant correlations between MSCEIT total scores and five out of the six dimensions (all but autonomy). The highest correlations were found with personal growth and positive relations with others (r's = .36, .27, respectively). In another study, Brackett (2001) reported a small, but significant correlation between EI and Diener's (1984) satisfaction with life scale (r = .12).

Depression and Anxiety

EI also appears to be related to less depressive symptoms and anxiety. Head (2002), for instance, found significant correlations between the managing emotions subscale of the MSCEIT and measures of depression ($r = -.33$), assessed with the Beck Depression Inventory, and trait anxiety ($r = -.29$), measured by the State-Trait Anxiety Inventory (Spielberger, Gorsuch, & Lushene, 1970). There is also a rich literature, which suggests individual differences in emotional regulation among children are associated with adaptation in all domains of life (Caspi, 1998, 2000; Eisenberg, Fabes, Guthrie, & Reiser, 2000; Kagan, 1998).

ROLE PLAYER

Evidence has accumulated on the importance of EI abilities for prosocial behavior. Studies with children, using a variety of assessment tools, have linked many EI abilities (e.g., reading emotions in faces, understanding emotional vocabulary, and regulation of emotions) to social competence and adaptation using peer, parent, and teacher ratings (for reviews see Eisenberg et al., 2000; Halberstadt, Denham, & Dunsmore, 2001; Saarni, 1999). In a preliminary study, schoolchildren scoring higher on the MEIS were rated by their peers as less aggressive, and by their teachers as more prosocial, than students scoring lower on EI (Rubin, 1999).

There is also evidence that EI is associated with adults' quality of social relationships. In several studies with college students, EI was associated with various indicators of positive social relations (r's in the .40 range), even after personality and traditional intelligence were statistically controlled. For example, Lopes et al. (2003) reported a correlation between the managing emotions subscale of the MSCEIT and global self-perceived quality of interpersonal relationships (Ryff, 1989). The MSCEIT was also associated with more supportive relationships with parents and less antagonistic and conflictive relationships with a close friend, as assessed by Furman and Buhrmester's (1985) Network of Relationships Inventory. Another study looked at college students' interactions on a 10-week group project at the University of Toronto. Students with high scores on the managing emotions subscale of the MSCEIT were more satisfied with other group members, with the quality of the communication within the group, and with the social support they received from their peers (Côté, Lopes, & Salovey, 2002). Students with higher EI were also exhibited high visionary leadership as rated by their peers (r's in the .30 range).

A study with German college students examined the relationship between EI and the self-perceived quality of daily social interactions. Participants reported all social interactions that lasted 10 minutes or longer, every day, for 2 weeks (Lopes, Brackett, Schütz, Sellin, Nezlek, & Salovey, in press). Results showed that individuals with high scores on the managing emotions subscale of the MSCEIT tended to be more satisfied with their daily interactions with people of the opposite sex (r's in the .3 to .4 range). They also perceived themselves to be more successful at impression management in daily social interactions.

There is also evidence that EI is related to peer perceptions of social and emotional competencies. Lopes et al. (in press) asked college students to rate themselves and nominate up to eight peers living in their residential college on a questionnaire pertaining to social and emotional competencies. Students who scored higher on the managing emotions branch of the MSCEIT not only reported higher self-perceived social competence, but were also more favorably viewed by their residential college classmates.

It is worth mentioning that the relations between EI and the various criteria in the previous four studies remained significant after controlling for the Big Five personality traits (and traditional analytic intelligence as well, in two of the studies). It is also noteworthy that the managing emotions branch was more strongly associated with the criteria than the other branches of EI. This may be due, in part, to the fact that managing emotions is a higher-order ability that draws upon the other three EI abilities. Managing emotions may also influence social interactions by facilitating other social skills and through emotional contagion.

Finally, Brackett et al. (in press) measured the quality of interpersonal relationships by asking people to report the number of times that they engaged in both positive and negative behaviors with best friends, significant others, and parents. Positive relations were assessed with factor-based life space scales (self-reported behaviors) that had questions pertaining to having long conversations with friends and displaying affection with a significant other.

Negative interactions were assessed with scales that had questions pertaining to behaviors such as getting screamed at by a parent or drinking alcohol heavily with a friend. Results of the study showed that EI was associated with more positive interactions and fewer negative interactions, although the latter effect was only significant for men.

EXECUTIVE CONSCIOUSNESS

Flow Experiences

Flow entails a state of balance in consciousness between psychological resources and task demands, enjoyment of the activity at hand, lack of self-preoccupation, and a sense of personal growth. EI may contribute to flow experiences because of the crucial role of emotional regulation and attention in flow (Csikszentmihalyi, 1992). Entering the flow state entails a delicate emotional equilibrium: avoiding both anxiety, usually associated with excessive challenge for one's level of skill, and boredom, associated with insufficient challenge.

Maladaptive Behaviors

The ability to manage emotions and their expression is vital for coping with life's challenges. The excessive use of recreational drugs and alcohol, as well as the involvement in high risk and violent behavior are likely to reflect deficits in EI. EI theory posits that a person's ability to accurately perceive, use, understand, and regulate emotions may help to prevent involvement in potentially harmful behaviors.

In an initial study, Formica (1998) reported a negative correlation ($r = -.37$) between a measure of destructive behavior (e.g., drug and alcohol use, selling drugs, engaging in acts of mischief–destruction) and the MEIS, an earlier measure of EI. Brackett et al. (in press) extended Formica's findings using the new MSCEIT and more extensive behavioral criteria. College students' self-reported use of illegal drugs (e.g., number of times smoked marijuana, used cocaine, or both), alcohol consumption (e.g., most amount of beer drank in one evening, number of times fallen asleep because of intoxication), and violent–mischievous behavior (number of fights in the last month, number of times arrested in the last year) all correlated negatively with the MSCEIT (r's $= -.28$ to $-.45$). The previous findings remained significant after controlling for the Big Five and verbal SAT scores. The correlations in Brackett et al.'s study were only significant for males, however.

This may be due, in part, to restricted ranges in scores on some of the outcome variables for females.

FUTURE DIRECTIONS AND SUMMARY

In this chapter, we discussed how emotional, motivational, and cognitive processes are related to intelligent behavior from the perspective of EI theory and research. We provided evidence that EI can be reliably measured, that it shows discriminant validity in relation to other cognitive abilities and personality traits, and that it has incremental validity in predicting outcomes that are important for the individual and for society. Evidence thus far suggests that individual differences in EI are associated (positively) with the quality of social interactions, healthy behavior, and psychological well-being in late adolescence and early adulthood. EI is also associated (negatively) with depressive symptoms and maladaptive behavior such as drug use and violence. These findings lend support to a broader view of intelligence—one that goes beyond verbal IQ and looks at other abilities that have important implications for people's lives.

Research on EI is still in its early stage and many questions have yet to be investigated. Now that important concerns about the reliability and factor structure of ability measures have been addressed (Mayer et al., 2003), it is time for researchers to seek a deeper understanding of EI. In particular, it is important to examine how EI develops, its covariance with other mental abilities and traits, and its criterion and predictive validity with respect to important life outcomes at home, school, and work.

In the area cognitive functioning, it is possible that IQ is the single best predictor of work performance when we look at people of all levels of intelligence (Herrnstein & Murray, 1994; Schmidt & Hunter, 1998). However, if we look at a pool of candidates of fairly high IQ, it may well be that EI abilities, rather than IQ, make the difference between a top professional and a mediocre one. The relationship between EI and creative abilities still has to be investigated. Several hypotheses regarding the relation between creativity and intelligence (Sternberg, 1999) may also be applied to EI and emotional creativity. For example, is emotional creativity just a correlate of EI or is it an additional factor of EI?

There is reason to believe that EI will correlate with motivation. Specifically, a person's ability to use emotions to facilitate thought might help trigger behaviors in which the person has the highest likelihood of success. For example, experimental research employing mood induction would be necessary to assess whether individuals higher on EI are better able to direct their behavior into productive tasks. If this were the case, EI may be related to higher frequencies of flow experiences and in turn contribute to a person's happiness (Csikszentmihalyi, 1990). Given the preliminary evidence of the negative relation between EI and depression, we might also wonder whether lower EI is a risk factor for mental illness.

Now that we know that EI correlates with positive social relationships (e.g., Brackett et al., in press; Lopes et al., 2003, in press), it would be important to understand the processes through which EI operates in interpersonal relationships, and the social contexts or situations in which specific emotional abilities are likely to play an important role. For example, how does EI relate to marital satisfaction? Future research might assess the congruence between the kinds of abilities involved in EI and the abilities required to successfully negotiate marital ups and downs (Fitness, 2001).

Emotionally intelligent people can manage their emotions more effectively and, consequently, they should be able to cope better with life's challenges. Thus, research is needed to understand whether emotionally intelligent people select the most appropriate coping strategies for different types of situations. For example, when faced with a negative life event that cannot be changed (e.g., loss of a loved one), will emotionally intelligent people recognize the importance of using emotion-oriented coping strategies and successfully regulate their emotions?

Finally, research on how EI develops and the extent to which it is biologically based or learned is in urgent need of investigation. To the extent that EI is learned, Gottman, Katz, and Hooven (1997) suggested that EI may be influenced by parental behaviors that he calls emotion coaching and emotion dismissing. Indeed, recent research suggests an association between young adults retrospective self-reports of parental emotion dismissing and lower EI (Kroell, 2002).

To what extent can EI be taught? The authors of this chapter differ in their beliefs regarding the extent to which intelligence in general, and EI in particular, is relatively fixed or malleable. It is unlikely that superficial training programs can boost EI substantially because emotional skills reflect a lifetime of learning. However, if traditional schooling increases cognitive abilities (Gustafsson, 2001), it is possible that educational programs focusing on social and emotional abilities might stimulate EI. In fact, there is evidence that school-based programs of social and emotional learning produce beneficial outcomes in terms of adaptation to school and school learning (e.g., Hawkins, Catalano, Kosterman, Abbott, & Hill, 1999; Kusché & Greenberg, 2001). It is worth mentioning, however, that a recent review of EI intervention programs cautions that most programs to date are not specifically designed to improve components of ability EI and lack both internal and external validity (Zeidner, Roberts, & Matthews, 2002). One possible reason for this is that most existing programs were not originally designed as EI intervention programs, but as preventative tools against the problems of drug abuse and delinquency facing many schools.

CONCLUSION

In spite of the claims of popular authors, we do not believe that EI will prove to be twice as important as cognitive intelligence in predicting "success" in life (Goleman, 1998, p. 31). We do, however, expect EI to be an important predictor of significant outcomes. The research presented here suggests that EI, defined and measured as a mental ability, is likely to take its place alongside other salient psychological variables as an important correlate of adaptation and performance at school, home, and the workplace.

ACKNOWLEDGMENT

This work was supported in part by funding from Portugal's *Fundação para a Ciência e a Tecnologia* and the European Social Fund to Paulo Lopes.

REFERENCES

Abelson, R. P. (1985). A variance explanation paradox: When a little is a lot. *Psychological Bulletin, 97,* 129–133.

Averill, J. R. (1999). Individual differences in emotional creativity: Structure and correlates. *Journal of Personality, 67,* 331–371.

Averill, J. R., & Thomas-Knowles, C. (1991). Emotional creativity. In K. T. Strongman (Ed.), *International review of studies on emotion* (Vol. 1, pp. 269–299). London: Wiley.

Bar-On, R. (1997). *Bar-On Emotional Quotient Inventory (EQ-i): Technical manual.* Toronto, Canada: Multi-Health Systems.

Barron, F. (1953). Complexity-simplicity as a personality dimension. *Journal of Abnormal and Social Psychology, 48,* 163–172.

Baumeister, R. F., & Tice, D. M. (1990). Anxiety and social exclusion. *Journal of Social and Clinical Psychology, 9,* 165–195.

Bower, G. H. (1981). Mood and memory. *American Psychologist, 36,* 129–148.

Boyatzsis, R. E., Goleman, D., & Rhee, K. S. (2000). Clustering competence in emotional intelligence. In R. Bar-On & J. D. A. Parker (Eds.), *The handbook of emotional intelligence* (pp. 343–362). San Francisco: Jossey-Bass.

Brackett, M. A. (2001). *Emotional intelligence and its expression in the life space.* Unpublished master's thesis, University of New Hampshire, Durham, NH.

Brackett, M. A., & Mayer, J. D. (2003). Convergent, discriminant, and incremental validity of competing measures of emotional intelligence. *Personality and Social Psychology Bulletin, 29,* 1147–1158.

Brackett, M. A., Mayer, J. D., & Warner, R. M. (in press). Emotional intelligence and its expression in everyday behavior. *Personality and Individual Differences.*

Bronfenbrenner, U. (1979). Contexts of child rearing: Problems and prospects. *American Psychologist, 34,* 844–850.

Cantor, N., & Kihlstrom, J. F. (1987). *Personality and social intelligence.* Englewood Cliffs, NJ: New Jersey: Prentice-Hall.

Caspi, A. (1998). Personality development across the life course. In W. Damon (Series Ed.) & N. Eisenberg (Vol. Ed.), *Social, emotional, and personality development: Vol. 3. Handbook of child psychology* (pp. 311–388). New York: Wiley.

Caspi, A. (2000). The child is father to the man: Personality continuities from childhood to adulthood. *Journal of Personality and Social Psychology, 78*, 158–172.

Ciarrochi, J., Forgas, J. P., & Mayer, J. D. (2001). *Emotional intelligence in everyday life.* Philadelphia: Psychology Press.

Clark, M. S., & Fiske, S. T. (1982). *Affect and cognition: The 17th annual Carnegie Symposium on Cognition.* Hillsdale, NJ: Lawrence Erlbaum Associates.

Côté, S., Lopes, P. N., & Salovey, P. (2002). *The divergent and predictive validity of emotional intelligence in a group context.* Manuscript submitted for publication.

Csikszentmihalyi, M. (1990). *Flow: The psychology of optimal experience.* New York: Harper Collins.

Csikszentmihalyi, M. (1992). *Flow: The psychology of happiness.* New York: Harper & Row.

Csikszentmihalyi, M. (1996). *Creativity: Flow and the psychology of discovery and invention.* New York: Harper Collins.

Csikszentmihalyi, M. (1999). Implications of a systems perspective for the study of creativity. In R. J. Sternberg (Ed.), *Handbook of creativity* (pp. 313–338). New York: Cambridge University Press.

Dailey, A., Martindale, C., & Borkum, J. (1997). Creativity, synesthesia and physiognomic perception. *Creativity Research Journal, 10*, 1–8.

David, S. A. (2002). *Emotional intelligence: Developmental antecedents, psychological and social outcomes.* Unpublished doctoral dissertation, The University of Melbourne, Melbourne, Australia.

Davies, M., Stankov, L., & Roberts, R. D. (1998). Emotional intelligence: In search of an elusive construct. *Journal of Personality and Social Psychology, 75*, 989–1015.

De Sousa, R. (1987). *The rationality of emotion.* Cambridge, MA: MIT Press.

Diener, E. (1984). Subjective well-being. *Psychological Bulletin, 95*, 542–575.

Domino, G. (1970). Identification of potentially creative persons from the adjective check list. *Journal of Consulting and Clinical Psychology, 35*, 48–51.

Domino, G. (1989). Synesthesia and creativity in fine arts students: An empirical look. *Research Journal, 2*, 17–29.

Eisenberg, N., Fabes, R. A., Guthrie, I. K., & Reiser, M. (2000). Dispositional emotionality and regulation: Their role in predicting quality of social functioning. *Journal of Personality and Social Psychology, 78*, 136–157.

Epstein, S. (1998). *Constructive thinking: The key to emotional intelligence.* Westport, CT: Praeger.

Eysenck, H. J. (1979). *The structure and measurement of intelligence.* New York: Springer-Verlag.

Fitness, J. (2001). Emotional intelligence an intimate relationships. In J. Ciarrochi, J. P. Forgas, & J. D. Mayer (Eds.), *Emotional intelligence in everyday life* (pp. 98–112). Philadelphia: Psychology Press.

Forgas, J. P., & Moylan, S. J. (1987). After the movies: Transient mood and social judgments. *Personality and Social Psychology Bulletin, 13*, 467–477.

Formica, S. (1998). *Describing the socio-emotional life space.* Unpublished senior's honor thesis, University of New Hampshire, Durham, NH.

Furman, W., & Buhrmester, D. (1985). Children's perceptions of the personal relationships in their social networks. *Developmental Psychology, 21*, 1016–1024.

Gardner, H. (1983). *Frames of mind: The theory of multiple intelligences.* New York: Basic Books.

Goleman, D. (1995). *Emotional intelligence.* New York: Bantam.

Goleman, D. (1998). *Working with emotional intelligence.* New York: Bantam.

Gottman, J. M., Katz, L. F., & Hooven, C. (1997). *Meta-emotions: How families communicate emotionally.* Mahwah, NJ: Lawrence Erlbaum Associates.

Grigorenko, E. L., Gil, G., Jarvin, L., & Sternberg, R. J. (2002). *Toward a validation of aspects of the theory of successful intelligence.* Manuscript submitted for publication.

Grigorenko, E. L., & Sternberg, R. J. (2001). Analytical, creative, and practical intelligence as predictors of self-reported adaptive functioning: A case study in Russia. *Intelligence, 29,* 57–73.

Gustafsson, J. E. (2001). *Schooling and intelligence: Effects of track of study on level and profile of cognitive abilities.* Paper presented to the 3rd Annual Spearman Conference, Sydney, Australia.

Halberstadt, A. G., Denham, S. A., & Dunsmore, J. C. (2001). Affective social competence. *Social Development, 10,* 79–119.

Hawkins, J. D., Catalano, R. F., Kosterman, R., Abbott, R., & Hill, K. G. (1999). Preventing adolescent health-risk behaviors by strengthening protection during childhood. *Archives of Pediatric & Adolescent Medicine, 153,* 226–334.

Head, C. (2002). *Revealing moods: A diary study of everyday events, personality, and mood.* Unpublished senior thesis, Yale University, New Haven, CT.

Hedlund, J., & Sternberg, R. J. (2000). Too many intelligences? Integrating social, emotional, and practical intelligence. In R. Bar-On & J. D. A. Parker (Eds.), *The handbook of emotional intelligence* (pp. 136–167). San Francisco: Jossey-Bass.

Herrnstein, R. J., & Murray, C. (1994). *The bell curve.* New York: Free Press.

Isen, A. M., Daubman, K. A., & Nowicki, G. P. (1987). Positive affect facilitates creative problem solving. *Journal of Personality and Social Psychology, 52,* 1122–1131.

Isen, A. M., Shalker, T. E., Clark, M., & Karp, L. (1978). Affect, accessibility of material in memory, and behavior: A cognitive loop? *Journal of Personality and Social Psychology, 36,* 1–12.

Kagan, J. (1998). *Galen's prophecy.* Boulder, CO: Westview Press.

Kerferd, G. B. (1978). What does the wise man know? In J. M. Rist (Ed), *The stoics* (pp. 125–135). Los Angeles: University of California Press.

Kroell, I. S. (2002). *Fostering emotional intelligence: Can emotional intelligence be predicted from parental emotion coaching and emotion dismissing?* Unpublished master's thesis, University of New Hampshire, Durham, NH.

Kusché, C. A., & Greenberg, M. T. (2001). PATHS in your classroom: Promoting emotional literacy and alleviating emotional distress. In J. Cohen (Ed.), *Social emotional learning and the elementary school child: A guide for educators* (pp. 140–161). New York: Teachers College Press.

Leeper, R. W. (1948). A motivational theory of emotions to replace "emotions as disorganized response." *Psychological Review, 55,* 5–21.

Lewin, K. (1936). *A dynamic theory of personality.* New York: McGraw-Hill.

Lloyd, A. C. (1978). Emotion and decision in stoic psychology. In J. M. Rist (Ed.), *The stoics* (pp. 233–246). Los Angeles: University of California Press.

Lopes, P. N., Brackett, M. A., Schütz, A., Sellin, I., Nezlek, J., & Salovey, P. (in press). Emotional intelligence and daily social interactions. *Personality and Social Psychology Bulletin.*

Lopes, P. N., Salovey, P., Jarvin, L., Sternberg, R. J., & Beers, M. (2002). *Emotional and practical intelligence and social networks.* Unpublished data, Yale University, New Haven, CT.

Lopes, P. N., Salovey, P., & Straus, R. (2003). Emotional intelligence, personality, and the perceived quality of social relationships. *Personality and Individual Differences, 35,* 641–658.

Lubart, T. I., & Getz, I. (1997). Emotion, metaphor, and the creative process. *Creativity Research Journal, 10,* 285–301.

Lynam, D., Moffitt, T., & Southamer-Loeber, M. (1993). Explaining the relation between IQ and delinquency: Class, race, test motivation, school failure, or self-control? *Journal of Abnormal Psychology, 102,* 187–197.

Magnusson, D., & Stattin, H. (1998). Person-context interaction theories. In W. Damon (Series Ed.) & R. M. Lerner (Vol. Ed.), *Handbook of child psychology: Vol. 1. Theoretical models of human development* (5th ed., pp. 685–760). New York: Wiley.

Mayer, J. D. (1998). A systems framework for the field of personality. *Psychological Inquiry, 9,* 118–144.

Mayer, J. D. (2001a). A field guide to emotional intelligence. In J. Ciarrochi, J. P. Forgas, & J. D. Mayer (Eds.), *Emotional intelligence in everyday life* (pp. 3–24). Philadelphia: Psychology Press.

Mayer, J. D. (2001b). Primary divisions of personality and their scientific contributions: From the trilogy-of-mind to the systems set. *Journal for the Theory of Social Behaviour, 31,* 449–477.

Mayer, J. D., & Bremer, D. (1985). Assessing mood with affect-sensitive tasks. *Journal of Personality Assessment, 49,* 95–99.

Mayer, J. D., Caruso, D., & Salovey, P. (1999). Emotional intelligence meets traditional standards for an intelligence. *Intelligence, 27,* 267–298.

Mayer, J. D., & Cobb, C. D. (2000). Educational policy and emotional intelligence: Does it make sense? *Educational Psychology Review, 12,* 163–183.

Mayer, J. D., DiPaolo, M., & Salovey, P. (1990). Perceiving affective content in ambiguous visual stimuli: A component of emotional intelligence. *Journal of Personality Assessment, 54,* 772–781.

Mayer, J. D., & Salovey, P. (1997). What is emotional intelligence? In P. Salovey & D. Sluyter (Eds.), *Emotional development and emotional intelligence: Educational implications* (pp. 3–31). New York: Basic Books.

Mayer, J. D., Salovey, P., & Caruso, D. (2000). Models of emotional intelligence. In R. J. Sternberg (Ed.), *Handbook of human intelligence* (pp. 396–420). New York: Cambridge.

Mayer, J. D., Salovey, P., & Caruso, D. (2002a). *Mayer-Salovey-Caruso Emotional Intelligence Test (MSCEIT), Version 2.0.* Toronto, Canada: Multi-Health Systems.

Mayer, J. D., Salovey, P., & Caruso, D. (2002b). *Mayer-Salovey-Caruso Emotional Intelligence Test User's Manual.* Toronto, Canada: Multi-Health Systems.

Mayer, J. D., Salovey, P., Caruso, D., & Sitarenios, G. (2001). Emotional intelligence does meet traditional standards for an intelligence. *Emotion, 1,* 232–242.

Mayer, J. D., Salovey, P., Caruso, D., & Sitarenios, G. (2003). Measuring emotional intelligence with the MSCEIT V2.0. *Emotion, 3,* 97–105.

Palfai, T. P., & Salovey, P. (1993). The influence of depressed and elated mood on deductive and inductive reasoning. *Imagination, Cognition, and Personality, 13,* 57–71.

Prentice, D. A., & Miller, D. T. (1992). When small effects are impressive. *Psychological Bulletin, 112,* 160–164.

Roberts, R. D., Zeidner, M., & Matthews, G. (2001). Does emotional intelligence meet traditional standards for an intelligence? Some new data and conclusions. *Emotions, 1,* 196–231.

Rubin, M. M. (1999). *Emotional intelligence and its role in mitigating aggression: A correlational study of the relationship between emotional intelligence and aggression in urban adolescents.* Unpublished dissertation, Immaculata College, Immaculata, PA.

Ryff, C. D. (1989). Happiness is everything, or is it? Explorations on the meaning of psychological well-being. *Journal of Personality and Social Psychology, 57,* 1069–1081.

Saarni, C. (1999). *The development of emotional competence.* New York: Guilford.

Salovey, P., Bedell, B. T., Detweiler, J. B., & Mayer, J. D. (2000). Current directions in emotional intelligence research. In M. Lewis & J. M. Haviland-Jones (Eds.), *Handbook of emotions* (2nd edition, pp. 504–520). New York: Guilford.

Salovey, P., & Birnbaum, D. (1989). Influence of mood on health-relevant cognitions. *Journal of Personality and Social Psychology, 57,* 539–551.

Salovey, P., & Mayer, J. D. (1990). Emotional intelligence. *Imagination, Cognition, and Personality, 9,* 185–211.

Salovey, P., Mayer, J. D., & Caruso, D. (2002). The positive psychology of emotional intelligence. In C. R. Synder & S. Lopez (Eds.), *Handbook of positive psychology* (pp. 159–171). New York: Oxford University Press.

Salovey, P., Woolery, A., & Mayer, J. D. (2000). Emotional intelligence: Conceptualization and measurement. In G. Fletcher & M. Clark (Eds.), *The Blackwell handbook of social psychology: Interpersonal processes* (pp. 279–307). London: Blackwell.

Schmidt, F. L., & Hunter, J. E. (1998). The validity and utility of selection methods in personnel psychology: Practical and theoretical implications of 85 years of research findings. *Psychological Bulletin, 124,* 262–274.

Shaw, M. P., & Runco, M. A. (1994). *Creativity and affect.* Westport, CT: Ablex.

Singer, J. A., & Salovey, P. (1988). Mood and memory: Evaluating the network theory of affect. *Clinical Psychology Review, 8,* 211–251.

Spielberger, C. D., Gorsuch, R. L., & Lushene, R. E. (1970). *Manual for the State-Trait Anxiety Inventory (Self-Evaluation Questionnaire).* Palo Alto, CA: Consulting Psychologists Press.

Sternberg, R. J. (1985). *Beyond IQ: A triarchic theory of human intelligence.* New York: Cambridge University Press.

Sternberg, R. J. (1999). The theory of successful intelligence. *Review of General Psychology, 3,* 292–316.

Sternberg, R. J., Forsythe, G. B., Hedlund, J., Horvath, J. A., Wagner, R. K., Williams, W. M., Snook, S. A., & Grigorenko, E. L. (2000). *Practical intelligence in everyday life.* New York: Cambridge University Press.

Sternberg, R. J., & Ruzgis, P. (1994). *Personality and intelligence.* New York: Cambridge University Press.

Wechsler, D. (1958). *The measurement of adult intelligence.* Baltimore: Williams & Wilkins.

Wechsler, D. (1997). *WAIS-III: Wechsler Adult Intelligence Scale* (3rd ed.). San Antonio, TX: The Psychological Corporation.

Wonderlic, E. F. (1998). *Wonderlic Personnel Test and Scholastic Level Exam user's manual.* Libertyville, IL: Wonderlic Personnel Test.

Woodworth, R. S. (1940). *Psychology* (4th ed.). New York: Henry Holt.

Zajonc, R. B. (1980). Feeling and thinking: Preferences need no inferences. *American Psychologist, 35,* 151–175.

Zeidner, M., Roberts, R. D., & Matthews, G. (2002). Can emotional intelligence be schooled? A critical review. *Educational Psychologist, 37,* 215–231.

IV

DEVELOPMENT OF INTELLECTUAL COMPETENCIES

8
▼▼▼▼▼▼▼

Affect, Self-Motivation, and Cognitive Development: A Dialectical Constructivist View

Juan Pascual-Leone
Janice Johnson
York University

> *However, a person who has just cut his finger on a knife and watches the blood ooze over his palm has no uncertainty about the existence of objects that can cause blood to flow, and is certain that he feels different than he did moments earlier.*
>
> —Kagan (2002, p. 72)

> *The energy for initiating an intended action can come from the situation encountered . . . or it can be self-generated through a volitional process called* self-motivation.
>
> —Kuhl (2000, p. 191)

The field of motivation addresses the issue of what determines–induces a person to act or behave in a particular way. A dialectical-constructivist approach to motivation should add to this a causal account of how–why the organism synthesizes performances vis-à-vis situations. This integrative perspective has not always been there. Research in the 1940s, 1950s, 1960s, and even 1970s often construed motivation as the cognitive–behavioral manifestation of instinctual–innate drives such as hunger, sex, fear, attachment, and other positive or negative affects. Research in the 1970s, 1980s, and 1990s was dominated by an emphasis on social-learning determinants of motivation; and by a growing awareness that human motivation results from complex structural learning processes that synthesize and adapt organismic functional structures to constitute people's plans–projects for action within situations. Although the current literature on human motivation offers extensive discussions of relevant issues and constructs, it lacks an adequate, explicit, dynamic, and unified organismic theory or framework that can explain the ontogenetic evolution of motivation. By the term *organismic* we mean compatible with and interpretable into what is now known about brain and biological processes of the human organism. Our aim is to contribute new clear ideas and some tentative unifying models that might be useful to the theory-building enterprise.

In this chapter, we sketch our idea of an organismic general model (or framework) that can serve to address the analysis of human motivation from a developmental organismic perspective. To this end, we describe some plausible organismic processes and resources, we define with their help basic concepts such as motive and specific interests, and use analytical methods that can serve to clarify developmental timetables of many motivational constructs, as well as sources of individual differences. We illustrate some of these ideas with our own and others' data.

THE CAUSAL TEXTURE OF THE ENVIRONMENT: ORGANISMIC SCHEMES

We focus first on epistemological problems relevant to motivational theory, such as the nature of reality and of human activity (understood as goal-directed interaction with situations, aimed to control or understand the objects, persons, or both therein; Leontiev, 1981). The question of motivation concerns mechanisms and processes that can bridge the gap between a person's makeup (his or her *psychological organism*) and the actual situation out there, in order to explain the person's agency and his or her implicit construal of tasks and obligations. Kant (1965; Pascual-Leone, 1998) saw the schema as the organism's way of bridging the gap between the organism and its situational context as such, that is, the constraints–resistances of the actual situation. However schemas or schemes of Kant or Piaget are neither organismic (i.e., embodied) nor situated (i.e., contextualized) enough to serve as tools in motivational process analysis.

Motivation attempts to explain the "what," "why," and "where" of a person's more or less conscious praxis and practice. By *praxis* we mean cognitive or motor goal-directed actions addressed to the environment, to satisfy central and intrinsic personal needs (i.e., affective goals). *Practice* is similar to a conscious or unconscious praxis that often uses automatized operations, and is enacted to satisfy marginal and predominantly extrinsic needs or affective goals. In these definitions, *intrinsic* (or endogenous) means stemming from processes initiated by the organism itself; *extrinsic* (or exogenous) refers to processes originally induced by others or by the situation. We call *motivationally central* those needs or affective goals that subjects address for their own sake, in a self-fulfilling manner. We call *motivationally marginal* those needs or affective goals that subjects address only as means for attaining something else. *Affective goals* correspond to organismic processes that cause the well-recognized concept of needs and stem from the activity-directing function of affects (or instincts). Spinoza called these organismic causal processes conation (conatus—Deleuze, 1990; Spinoza, 1995); and today they are called conative effects of affect (Fredrickson, 2001; Greenberg, 2002; Pascual-Leone, 1991). These distinctions are important, because praxis is often more motivating than practice, and central motives are often more motivating than marginal ones. In contrast, extrinsic versus intrinsic motivation is subject to individual and developmental differences (Eccles, Wigfield, & Schiefele, 1998; Koller, 2000). We shall use this terminology to emphasize that actual goals always involve an affective–emotive component that is expression of the organism's infrastructure (essential internal constraints) and dynamism.

Motivation interfaces or intertwines the organism's affects–emotions and knowing functions with the nature (constraints or resistances) of external–internal reality and the person's activities in this environment. We think of the reality-out-there as a universe of species-specific *resistances* (i.e., kinds of relational perceptual patterning or of experiential outcomes) that emerge in the individual's activity, both praxis and practice, within a given context–situation. These resistances often are found to have dependency relations among themselves. Thus reality is populated with packages of interdependent resistances that are relative to each species. These packages can be interpreted, without falling into empiricist excesses, as indexing *real invariants* (cf. Gibson, 1979; Nakayama, 1994; Nozick, 2001; Ullmo, 1967); that is, relational aspects of reality that the individual can cognize and, in a nonempiricist but constructivist way, learn to re-present to himself or herself (as alluded by Kagan in the epigraph). Furthermore, these packages maintain with each other fairly invariant interdependencies, which are exhibited by human activity (praxis–practice) and are experienced as reality supports for activity (these are Gibson's affordances), or as hindrances that reality opposes to us (obstacles or proper resistances). Motivation (which functionally intertwines affect–emotion, cognition, and reality) leads the person to *internalize* (learn) these packages and their interdependencies, thus acquiring some, schematic and actively modeled, re-presentation of what Tolman and Brunswik (1966) called the *causal texture of the environment*.

From this bio–psychological causal perspective, it is appropriate to recognize that internalization (learning) of these reality packages, and the learning of how they change conditional to our activity, necessarily implies three distinct categories of invariant, packaged resistances: (a) those that stand for the targets of the person's praxis or practice, which we shall call *obs*, to emphasize that they are not objects but are dialectical-constructivist substrata for the empiricist objects of experience; (b) those packages that stand for patterns of action or operation (praxis or practice) that are causally instrumental for changing obs, or the relations among obs, in expectable ways—these are packages that we call *pros*, that is, the constructivist substrata for the empiricist procedures and operative processes; and (c) those packages of resistances, simple or complex, that functionally serve to provide adjunct information about obs, pros, and the situations in which they usefully can be applied. These packages, which we call *ads*, can describe properties or relations pertaining to obs or situations, and can also describe conditions or parameters that pros needs to satisfy in order to be applicable to obs and situations. *Ad*jectives, *ad*verbs, the meaning of relative clauses, and *ad*vertisements all have this category of *adjunct-information* as their reality foundation.

For instance, in the quote of Kagan we give in the epigraph, the finger, the knife, the blood, and the palm are each represented in the person's brain as *ob* schemes. The category description "objects that can cause blood to flow" is an *ad* scheme that causally relates *obs* such as knives to parts of the body (e.g., fingers) and to blood. The brain representation of the knife's action, which actually caused the blood to flow, is a *pro* scheme. Notice that at a finer, less molar level, each of these scheme units can be decomposed as constituted by finer, lower level, *ads* (releasing conditions), *obs* (intended distal–cognitive objects), *pros* (intended action, e.g., the procedure of cutting), or all of the above.

Although pros are correlates of people's blueprints for actions or transformations, that is, of what Piaget and neo-Piagetians would call *operative processes* (essentially the procedural knowledge of cognitive science), both obs and ads are correlates of people's descriptions of states, which Piaget and neo-Piagetians call *figurative processes* (related to declarative knowledge of cognitive science, but which could be either explicit or implicit). One main difference between obs and ads seems to be motivational: obs, but not ads, serve as possible targets for the person's praxis. Notice further that abstraction and internalization (i.e., learning) of obs, ads, and pros cannot be made in a piecemeal manner. The three sorts of functional category constitute a dialectical trio. They dynamically emerge together, in the context of activity within situations, as the functional structure of this activity becomes internalized; that is, the three functional categories are abstracted together in coordinated packages, thus producing *organismic schemes* (i.e., collections of neurons distributed over the brain that are cofunctional and often coactivated).

These organismic schemes are *situated* semantic-pragmatic functional systems that carry some coherent knowledge or know-how about relevant activities. *Schemes* are dynamic systems, abstracted across situations for a given sort of praxis, coordinating internalized models of obs, ads, and pros in their interaction. From a structural perspective, a scheme can be understood as expressing the well-learned coordination of three components: (a) a functional system that embodies the gist (the pros or obs, and activity) of the scheme's semantic-pragmatic organization; (b) a set of conditions (ads, obs, or pros) that release the scheme; and (c) a set of effects (pros, obs, or ads) that follow from the scheme's application to experienced reality. Schemes must be internally consistent to be formed, and they are recursive. Conditions, effects of schemes, or both can in turn be constituted by (copies of) other schemes. These complex schemes, often called *structures*, could be interpreted as semantic networks (Fuster, 1995; Kagan, 2002).

Notice that schemes are self-propelling (i.e., they tend to actively assimilate or structure experience); and they are natural units of functional information processing, because the person's intercourse with experienced reality (with praxis or practice resulting from application of schemes) is in turn internalized into schemes (i.e., repeatable semantic-pragmatic invariances) that embody components of the (external or mental) performance that satisfy the person's affective (positive or negative) goals.

AFFECTS, EMOTIONS, AND OTHER SCHEMES OR STRUCTURES THAT INFLUENCE DEVELOPMENT OF MOTIVATION

It is well recognized that affects–emotions (see Greenberg & Pascual-Leone, 1995, 2001; Pascual-Leone, 1990, 1991; for our detailed formulation of their developmental emergence) are a set of qualitatively distinct, epigenetically evolved, functional systems (Ekman & Davidson, 1994; Fredrickson, 2001), whose function is to evaluate by way of feelings. As Damasio (2001) put it, *feelings* are the complex mental states that result from emotional states (i.e., from the activation–application within the organism of the person's own affective–emotion schemes—and feelings are ads, related to experiences, brought about by these schemes as their effects). Or to say it as Merleau-Ponty (1968) preferred: Feelings are subjective–biological feedback that we receive from our "flesh." Affects evaluate ongoing (or about to happen) experiences and the organism's current states, as good or bad, appealing or aversive, positive or negative, etc., and then inform the psychological organization (in humans the self "hidden" in the brain) about these evaluations. This automatically sets in motion modes of processing and functioning that prepare body reactions and bias mental and behavioral functioning, in directions congruent with tacit anticipations of results. These specific action tendencies are caused by affects, as they apply within the organism. For instance, fear biases the organism toward escape, anger toward fighting, love toward tender physical contact, etc. (Beck, 1996; Edelman & Tonioni, 2001; Ekman & Davidson, 1994; Fredrickson, 2001; Frijda, 1987; Frijda, Kuipers, & Schure, 1989; Greenberg, 2002). These conative modes of processing are what we call *affective goals.* We interpret affects and their often-tacit goals to be *affective schemes* (Pascual-Leone, 1991). The affective goals are effects produced by affective schemes when they are released within and expressed–manifested in the organism. Part of this expression is the occurring physiological changes suitable for the affective tendency in question.

Purely affective processes, as we define them, seem to be initiated in brain activities of the limbic system, of which the amygdala plays an important role in preattentive processing of situations and in recognition of affectively salient stimuli, at least for negative affective reactions (Anderson & Phelps, 2001; Damasio, 2001; Habib, 2000; LeDoux, 1995; Rolls, 1995; Schaefer et al., 2002). In contrast, the medial orbitofrontal cortex (ventromedial prefrontal region) and the anterior cingulate cortex are important in re-presenting to consciousness pleasant or unpleasant affective values of experiences (Allman, Hakeem, Erwin, Nimchinsky, & Hop, 2001; Bechara, Damasio, Damasio, & Lee, 1999; Davidson, 2001; Ochsner, Bunge, Gross, & Gabrieli, 2002). Cognitive expression of affective goals may be related to the orbitofrontal cortex and the anterior cingulate cortex, at least for the high cognitive functions (Albright, Jessell, Kandel, & Posner, 2001; Davidson, 2001). For low-cognitive or automatized cognition other brain structures, such as the Broca language center, the insula, or the entorhinal cortex, may play a similar role (Albright et al., 2001; Barraquer Bordas, 1995). The effortful control of affects and emotions seems to be related to the dorsal part of anterior cingulate gyrus,[1] the lateral and medial prefrontal regions, and perhaps also the basal ganglia, together with the prefrontal cortex (Albright et al., 2001; Allman et al., 2001; Ochsner et al., 2002). Interestingly, the left prefrontal hemisphere seems to be concerned with the control of positive affects–emotions, whereas the right prefrontal hemisphere deals with negative affects–emotions (Davidson, 2001; Fox, Henderson, & Marshall, 2001). We shall elaborate on this in the following.

Application–implementation of affective goals necessarily involves activation and application of cognitive schemes. In contrast to affective schemes, which only evaluate organismic states, cognitive schemes tell organisms about packages of resistances encountered outside or inside (bodily) reality; they carry factual information and not evaluation. When the affective goals are aroused and perhaps implemented, cognitive schemes must be part of it, however; and thus affective and cognitive schemes soon become coordinated within many different affective–emotion systems (Pascual-Leone, 1991). The resulting hybrid schemes (i.e., affective and cognitive) are main causal deter-

---

[1]The anterior cingulate gyrus has two parts, ventral and dorsal, which seem to be mutually inhibitory (Albright et al., 2001) and are concerned, respectively, with emotions and cognition; "cognitive conflict tasks tend to reduce activity in the more ventral area of the cingulate" (Albright et al., 2001, p. 34).

minants of emotions and of personal–personality processes, and so we call them *personal or emotion schemes* (Greenberg, 2002; Greenberg & Pascual-Leone, 2001; Greenberg, Rice, & Elliot, 1993; Pascual-Leone, 1991). As the child develops, the initial innate affects (affective schemes), released by the circumstances, come to be more or less coordinated with their corresponding cognitive schemes, producing emotion schemes (causal substratum of emotions) and personal structures. Affect in consciousness is always carried by emotions, and this is possibly why many authors (e.g., Ekman & Davidson, 1994) treat affect and emotion as synonymous. In our opinion, this is an error. Primary affects (e.g., Pascual-Leone, 1991) are clearly innate, but cognitive components of emotions cannot be innate because they are situated (i.e., context specific). This error obscures the development of emotions and motivational processes.

Most of the schemes that make up the conscious or preconscious processes (the person's ego), whether they refer to one's own person–organism (*self-schemes*), to the outer world or the others (*interpersonal* and intersubjective schemes), are hybrids. That is, they are personal or emotion schemes, even when emotional *defense mechanisms* (special sorts of executive self-schemes) may keep the emotional component out of consciousness. *Executive schemes* are operative schemes that embody plans of action and control and allocate brain resources to schemes congruently with the current task demands (Pascual-Leone, 1995, 1996, 1998; Pascual-Leone & Goodman, 1979; Pascual-Leone, Goodman, Ammon, & Subelman, 1978; Pascual-Leone & Irwin, 1998; Pascual-Leone & Johnson, 1991; Pascual-Leone, Johnson, Baskind, Dworsky, & Severtson, 2000). We do not discuss executive processes, because they are well recognized in the current literature. We should emphasize, however, that in our view there is no single central executive system. Rather, there is a multiplicity of executive schemes that are more or less situation-specific and context bound and are learned locally in a situated manner (Pascual-Leone, 2000a).

Affective schemes, and their aptitude to coordinate with cognitive schemes with the help of mental attentional capacity monitored by executive schemes (Pascual-Leone, 1991), serve to explain the difference between motives and *specific* interests,[2] and among interest, utility, and personal importance (e.g., Eccles et al., 1998). The distinction between motives and interests, not altogether clear in the literature, is important from the perspective of developmental motivation theory. *Motives,* from an organismic perspective, express affective goals (i.e., specific action tendencies) that are strong enough to in-

---

[2]Some emotion researchers, such as Izard (1977) and ourselves (Pascual-Leone, 1991), refer to interest as a general disposition elicited by novelty and curiosity. This is not the sense of interest we are referring to in this paper. Here we refer to specific–substantive interests, as described in the educational–developmental literature (Renninger, Hidi, & Krapp, 1992).

fluence the choice of activity. They constitute, as Oerter (2000) would say, the basic frame of a person's here-and-now motivation. Motives may be strong and yet unclear about the objects (obs) that can satisfy them. For instance, in inexperienced or naïve people, sex or even hunger (but only with children from well-fed families) may be strong and yet leave the person confused about a suitable object of desire. Experience is needed to discover that pangs in the stomach and lack of mental focus are expression of hunger, or that restlessness and the eyes' attraction to the bodies of others are caused by the sex motive. These discoveries (i.e., the learning or differentiation of motive schemes) do bring interest to the objects in question. *Specific interests*, in contrast, are constructs–schemes ontogenetically derived from motives; they constitute the manifestation in human activity (and in the person's object representation, i.e., in the internalized obs) of more or less enduring affective goals.

MOTIVATIONAL PROCESSES ARE NOT JUST DUE TO SCHEMES: BRAIN RESOURCES, OVERDETERMINATION, AND CONSTRUCTIVE LEVELS OF PROCESSING

Information-carrying processes (i.e., schemes—knowledge, affects, or other learned or innate substantive dispositions) are not sufficient to explain the emergence of suitable intrinsic motivations. Our theoretical model must be enriched with a consideration of brain resources and their control mechanisms. Perhaps the least understood brain resources for the process analysis of motivation are those that in their dialectical coordination lead to emergence of what, after William James, we call *mental attention* (Pascual-Leone & Baillargeon, 1994; Pascual-Leone et al., 2000). Mental attention appears as a complex content-free (i.e., general-purpose) brain organization of capacities, a dialectical system constituted by four different sorts of resources, which we consider main determinants of consciousness and its causal power. One of these resources is M-capacity (one of the causal determinants of working memory—Pascual-Leone, 2000a). When mobilized (which gives the feeling of mental effort) and applied–focused on chosen schemes, M-capacity can hyperactivate them (i.e., maximally activate schemes, inducing synchronized firing in their neuronal circuits—Singer, 1994, 2001). Another of these resources is mental-attentional *interruption*, which actively inhibits (to a controllable degree, we think) the schemes on which it applies (Case, 1992, 1998; Fuster, 1989; Pascual-Leone, 1987, 1989; Posner & DiGirolamo, 1998; Stuss, 1992). Human consciousness can change its current contents because of these two mechanisms that modulate mental attention and produce the stream of consciousness (James, 1892/1961).

We model this mental attention (MA) mechanism in terms of a dialectical system of four functional resources, which we discuss in four MA points :

MA1. The first constituent of mental attention is the currently dominant cluster of executive schemes that carry cognitive goals and are activated initially by affective goals. Notice that our model does not contain the construct of a single central executive. Rather, we propose a repertoire of context-bound (more or less situation specific) executive schemes that rally in clusters of compatible schemes (this is a competition model based on overdetermination), with the result that the currently dominant cluster of compatible executive schemes runs the show. These executive schemes can mobilize and allocate the resources (MA2) and (MA3). In Fig. 8.1 these compatible and dominant executive schemes are symbolized by the letter *E*. Although the concept of executive processes is not altogether clear in the literature, it is generally agreed that these processes (which in our construal are executive

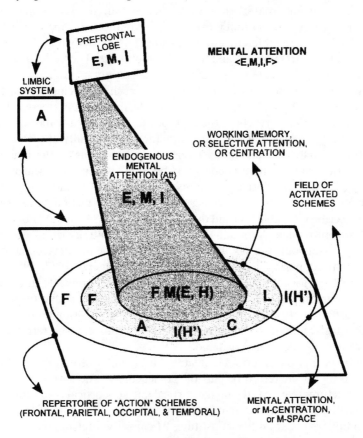

FIG. 8.1. Model of endogenous mental attention.

schemes) seem to be located in (or at least controlled by) the lateral prefrontal areas of the brain (Brodmann Areas—BA 9, 46, 45, 44, 47; e.g., Goldman-Rakic, 1995; Muller, Machado, & Knight, 2002). However "the precise functioning and neural implementation of these executive functions is still unresolved" (Szameitat, Schubert, Muller, & von Cramon, 2002, p. 1184).

MA2. The second constituent is a mental energy or scheme-booster capacity, which we call the *M*-operator—a limited resource that grows in power (i.e., in the number of schemes that it can boost simultaneously) throughout childhood until adolescence. The hyperactivation of schemes by this resource helps to produce what James (1892/1961) and others (e.g., Crick, 1994) have called the beam of mental attention. Figure 8.1 denotes by *H* the schemes upon which *M*-capacity is applied at the moment; and it denotes by *H'* other schemes in the subject's repertoire that currently are not attended to. *M*-capacity increases endogenously from the first month of age up to adolescence, according to an idealized schedule that, when measured behaviorally in terms of the number of schemes that it can boost simultaneously, appears in Tables 8.1 and 8.2. In these tables, the total measure of *M*-capacity (i.e., *M*-power) is divided in two parts: the "e" and the "k" components. The "e" component is the *M*-capacity that emerges during the sensorimotor period, and which at the end of this period is equal to 6 (sensorimotor schemes being *M*-boosted simultaneously). The "k" component is the *M*-capacity that emerges from 3 years of age onward, reaching the asymptotic value of 7 mental schemes at 15–16 years. Notice that we are estimating behaviorally the amount of attentional capacity available at a certain age, in terms of the number of schemes that can be simultaneously *M*-boosted. Because the sensorimotor schemes and their network connections are much simpler (and so would need less mental energy) than the schemes from subsequent mental stages, the "e" scale (described in Table 8.1) and the "k" scale (Table 8.2) should not be combined or confounded. Although this model for estimating mental attentional capacity is still controversial, there is much experimental-developmental research that supports it (see Case, 1998; Pascual-Leone, 1987, 1989, 1995, 1997, 2000a; Pascual-Leone & Johnson, 2001). To appreciate and use the present chapter, however, the reader need not accept our quantification of mental attention. It will suffice to accept that mental attention grows with age and that task analytical methods can be used to rank tasks in terms of their relative mental-attentional demand.

We think that the anterior cingulate gyrus, a limbic structure that Allman et al. (2001) considered to be part of the neocortex, and several subcortical brain structures (e.g., basal ganglia, cortical and subcortical connections with reticular formation, and thalamic reticular complex) are part of the still unclear brain organization that constitutes *M*-capacity. Prefrontal areas related to *M*-capacity control are those of the lateral prefrontal cortex: ventrolateral

TABLE 8.1
The Sensorimotor Period (Six Substages)

Expected M-Capacity	Landmark Performances
1. Me = 0	The use of reflexes (0–1 mo)
2. Me = 1	Acquired adaptations & primary circular reaction (1–4 mos)
3. Me = 2	Beginning of secondary circular reactions & procedures for making interesting sights last (4–8 mos)
4. Me = 3	Coordination of secondary schemes & application of schemes to new situations (8–12 mos)
5. Me = 4	Beginning of tertiary circular reactions & discovery of new means by active experimentation (12–18 mos)
6. Me = 5	Invention of new means through mental combinations (18–26 mos). Executive performance representation is not possible until this stage. Five or four units are needed to spontaneously construct an executive.
7. Me = 6	Transition to mental processing (26–34 mos)
8. Me = 7	Early preoperational period (34–59 mos). The child is able to mobilize an executive and relate one symbolic scheme to another. The child has an M-capacity of Me = 7, or Mk = e + 1.

TABLE 8.2
M-Levels in the Mental Period: Ideal Maximal M-Power Values
as a Function of Age (Years) and Correspondence
to the Piagetian Substage Sequence

M-Capacity ($e + k$)	Piagetian Substage	Normative Chronological Age
e + 1	Low preoperations	3, 4
e + 2	High preoperations	5, 6
e + 3	Low concrete operations	7, 8
e + 4	High concrete operations	9, 10
e + 5	Substage introductory to formal operations	11, 12
e + 6	Low formal operations	13, 14
e + 7	High formal operations	15–adult

(BA 44, 45, 47) and, in more effortful tasks, dorsolateral (BA 9, 46, 9/46) regions (Goldman-Rakic, 1995; Jonides et al., 1997; Klingberg, Forssberg, & Westerberg, 2002; Rypma, Berger, & D'Esposito, 2002; Szameitat et al., 2002). Klingberg et al. (2002) showed positive correlations between age (from 9 to 18 years) and amount of activity specific to a visuospatial working memory task, in the superior frontal sulcus (possibly BA 8, 9 and 46). We believe that M-capacity is the functional brain organization that underlies what Posner (Posner & DiGirolamo, 1998; Rothbart & Posner, 2001) called executive attention. However, neuroscience cannot today clearly distinguish between executive processes (such as executive schemes) and the general-purpose hidden resources (such as M-capacity or I-capacity) used by them to change performance. Yet executive processes and hidden resources must be distinguished, because substantive executive processes are mostly acquired, whereas the hidden general resources (mental attentional capacities, content-learning and structural-learning capabilities, etc.) have to be innate.

MA3. The third mental-attention resource is a capacity (which we call I-operator) for central attentional inhibition of schemes, or mental-attentional interruption. This is used by the dominant cluster of compatible executive schemes to inhibit schemes that are irrelevant or misleading for the goals being pursued. The searchlight analogy for mental attention (Crick, 1994) is made possible by mental-attentional automatic interruption of the schemes that at each moment are not being boosted with M-capacity, that is, not selected for attention at this moment (call these schemes H'). Automatic interruption (by the I-operator) is symbolized in Fig. 8.1 by the expression $I(H')$. The developmental growth of I-capacity occurs, we believe, concurrently with the growth of M-capacity. The control of mental-attentional inhibition may take place in the ventrolateral (e.g., BA 44, 45, 47) and dorsolateral (BA 9, 46) prefrontal cortex (Durston et al., 2002; Mitchell, Macrae, & Gilchrist, 2002; Szameitat et al., 2002) in coordination with the M-capacity control. The dorsal anterior cingulate and the ventromedial PFC, which Luria (1973) emphasized, may intervene in mobilizing both M-capacity and interruption I-capacity, by bringing in the appropriate affective goals and converting them into cognitive goals (Albright et al., 2001).

MA4. The fourth and last constituent of mental attention serves to create the closure of the beam of attention. This is an endogenous capacity of the organism that (jointly with the principle of schemes' overdetermination discussed below) dynamically integrates, into a single minimally complex performance totality, the whole cluster of dominant compatible schemes at the point when performance takes place (this often is called the binding problem). This performance-closure dynamism (possibly caused in the cortex by automatic lateral inhibitory processes) is what neo-Gestalt psychologists and others (e.g., Piaget) called internal or autochthonous field processes (e.g., the Minimum Principle of perception, the S-R Compatibility principle of performance, etc.). We call F-operator this performance-closure dynamism that causes perception, imagery, thinking, language, motor activity, etc., to be integrated and minimally complex in an adaptive way. In this dynamic endeavor the F-operator works in tandem with a psychological and neural principle that we call principle of schematic overdetermination of performance (SOP; Pascual-Leone, 1995, 1997). This construct (derivable from Piaget's principle of schemes' assimilation and also from the summation principle for neuronal firing) can be formulated for schemes in the following manner. Performance, at any time, is synthesized by the dominant (most activated) cluster of compatible schemes available in the brain's field of activation at the time of responding (Pascual-Leone, 1997). In this process the schemes that are incompatible with the dominant cluster, even after accommodation (i.e., relaxation) of their constraints, are locally or centrally (this is interruption) inhibited. In this way, mental attention focuses on the schemes of the dominant cluster, and incompatible schemes, left out of M-space, are inhibited by an automatic interruption mechanism.

Figure 8.1 symbolizes this dynamic model of mental attention. The three key constituents of mental attention—the M-operator (mental energy M), the I-operator (central inhibition or interrupt I), and the currently dominant cluster of executive schemes E, are symbolized by a rectangular flashlight controlled, at least in part, from the prefrontal lobes. This flashlight of mental attention illuminates (boosts the activation of) a region (the inner ellipse in Fig. 8.1) of the repertoire of action schemes. This region is the M-space (i.e., M-centration) or focus of endogenous attention. Mental energy is exerted on E and on the chosen action schemes H, to empower them to produce performance. Figure 8.1 assumes that the task the subject is dealing with is a *misleading* one, that is, a situation that provides cues for and activates schemes that are inadequate/misleading for the task at hand. Consequently, schemes that are not relevant (and outside the M-space) must be interrupted to reduce interference. Notice that, as Fig. 8.1 indicates (middle ellipse), *working memory* in our model is a set of simultaneously hyperactivated (and synchronized) schemes in the brain's *field of activation* (the outer ellipse). Working memory includes the M-space, but is larger than it within *facilitating* situations (i.e., situations that cue only task-relevant schemes and thus do not require I-interruption). Notice that in misleading situations, working memory will be restricted to the M-space, because the schemes outside it will have been inhibited by the I-operator. In contrast, in facilitating situations working memory will be larger than M-space, because of the schemes that are being hyperactivated by affects–emotions (A in Fig. 8.1), by content learning (C), or by logical-structural learning (L). Thus working memory could be much larger than M-space in facilitating situations. Pascual-Leone and Baillargeon (1994) discussed this model of mental attention in more detail and used it to model probabilistic performance patterns exhibited in an M-capacity task.

This model of mental attention often has been ignored, due to failure to see the processual differences imposed by facilitating versus misleading situations. In *misleading situations*, a processing conflict (dialectical contradictions or strategy competition) usually emerges between two or more different, implicit or explicit, strategies. One strategy, Y, is unsuitable, but is facilitated by well learned or automatized schemes (often congruent with the field factor—our F-operator). The other strategy, X, is suitable, but needs to be effortfully boosted by the mental-attentional mechanisms, such as executive schemes and M- and I-capacities (Pascual-Leone, 1989, 1995; Pascual-Leone & Baillargeon, 1994). Because in misleading situations the unsuitable strategy Y is more or less automatized or overlearned, this is the first strategy to be mobilized and activated. Consequently, in order for the suitable strategy X to determine performance, application of the Y strategy must be averted by using active–central inhibition (i.e., mental-attentional interruption); and strategy X must be boosted by efficiently mobilizing mental-attention. Misleading situations are common in problem solving, cognitive development, and emotional–interpersonal development, and they exhibit individual cognitive-style differences indexed by the ability to cope well with them. For instance, Witkin's field-independent persons cope well; and despite having good developmental intelligence, field-dependent persons often cope badly (Pascual-Leone, 1989; Wapner & Demick, 1991; Witkin & Goodenough, 1981).

Misleading situations also typically exhibit discontinuous or stage-wise trajectories in their cross-sectional developmental traces of performance. Stable stages of development exist (contrary to Piaget's claims) only in misleading situations. The reason for this restriction is that in misleading situations misleading schemes must be interrupted (actively inhibited) and task-activated schemes not currently boosted by M-capacity (i.e., not in active working memory) will tend to be interrupted with them; consequently the schemes needed to solve the task will have to be activated (directly or indirectly) by M-capacity. In contrast, within facilitating situations task-relevant schemes are not interrupted and remain active throughout, enabling solution of the task without much need of M-capacity use; thus facilitating situations provide poor criteria for true developmental stages (caused by the maturational growth of M-capacity).[3]

A common example of a misleading situation, in the affective–motivational domain, is the case of a child–student–scholar who in the midst of working under a close deadline for an important and difficult assignment–exam–paper, receives a visit from a dear friend offering a very tempting opportunity to do something together. Strategy Y will then become doing the appealing thing, and X will be to continue working on the exam–paper. To

---

[3]In the neo-Piagetian Theory of Constructive Operators (Pascual-Leone, 1987, 1989, 1995, 1997; Pascual-Leone & Baillargeon, 1994) *misleading situations* are those that strongly elicit schemes that are inconvenient for the task at hand for two important reasons: (a) the result of their application is detrimental to the required task performance; (b) these schemes are released by features of the situation shared by other task-relevant schemes, thus when misleading schemes apply and interpret–incorporate the features in question, the subsequent probability of activation of these other task-relevant schemes will tend to be lowered. Notice that a *distracting situation* is one that elicits schemes satisfying condition (a) but not condition (b). A *facilitating situation* is one in which the schemes elicited are relevant to the task, so that they do not satisfy either of the above conditions.

avoid falling prey to strategy Y, the person must mobilize and apply both *I*-interruption and *M*-capacity in the context of exerting his or her will. From our perspective (Pascual-Leone, 1990; Pascual-Leone & Irwin, 1998), the Will is an X strategy, driven by personal–emotive executive schemes, that, mindful of other self-priorities (e.g., an urgent life project), interrupts the schemes of Y and boosts with *M*-capacity the schemes of X. James (1892/1961) was already defining the Will along these lines: *"effort of attention is thus the essential phenomenon of the Will"* (p. 317, emphasis in the original).

Because mental-attention (*M* and *I* in coordination) usually grows in power with chronological age up to adolescence (see Tables 8.1 and 8.2), the X-boosting (and Y-interrupting) power of the Will grows (other things equal) with the growth of *developmental intelligence* (i.e., the maturational growth of mental attentional capacity and of learning potential). However, this maturation of the Will is a small factor in the emergence of *emotional intelligence*, which is influenced more by the development of affective control variables, life experiences, family context, mentoring, etc. (Pascual-Leone, 1990, 2000b).

The progressive developmental growth of mental attention (i.e., *E*, *M*, *I*, *F*) causes the emergence of epistemological levels of processing that are indexed by the mental-processing complexity (estimated in terms of *M*-capacity demand) of *novel* (not already learned or automatized) misleading situations, which subjects of a certain age can solve by themselves. This is what we retain of the controversial concept of developmental stages.

IMPACT OF AFFECT AND MOTIVATION ON INTELLECTUAL DEVELOPMENT

Contrary to the brilliant recent school of developmental neo-nativists (e.g., Baillargeon, 2002) and consistently with most neo-Piagetians, we believe that children are not born with a large repertoire of complex, content-specific and situation-specific cognitive schemes, whether concepts, percepts, or procedures. Instead we think that only a more modest repertoire of simpler innate (cognitive or affective) schemes might actually exist, which includes a variety of primary affect–emotion schemes and also a few more-complex schemes that carry specific emotions (such as schemes for emotional attachment, i.e., the need for "mother love"; or positive emotions such as mastery–control, curiosity, etc.; or innate negative–aversive emotions such as fear, etc.). Other substantive schemes would be acquired from experience with the support of a rich collection of innate general-purpose functional mechanisms; mechanisms that we call *hidden* organismic operators and principles.

Examples of these hidden operators are the operators of endogenous mental attention previously described, that is, *E*, *M*, *I*, and *F*. Other examples are content learning (e.g., basic, conditioning or perceptual learning) and logical–structural learning mechanisms (Case, 1998; Pascual-Leone, 1995; Pascual-Leone & Goodman, 1979), which we call respectively C learning and L learning. There are also innate general-purpose mechanisms (hidden operators) that aid in the situated effortless here-and-now integration of *spatial relations* (relations of coexistence among schemes, that is, the cortical brain processes related to the "where" question) and of *time relations* (sequential relations among schemes; these are cortical processes that by collating current sequential dependency relations among activated schemes help to construct the *distal objects* of experience, with their pragmatic or conceptual meaning, enabling construction of objects' identity that clarifies "what" is the object at hand). These are processes that we respectively call S operator and T operator (Pascual-Leone, 1995, 2000a).

This collection of general-purpose brain mechanisms, together with a modest repertoire of innate schemes (which include innate affects and emotions generating affective goals), enables currently activated affective–emotion schemes within the person to initiate activities that are prompted by the situation or the current internal state. These activities are caused jointly (i.e., overdetermined) by the *dominant* (most activated) set of compatible schemes currently active in the person's repertoire (long-term memory). Schemes may be dominant because they are activated by the situational context, or because they satisfy affective goals, and thus receive activation from corresponding affects–emotions (whether implicit or explicitly experienced). Alternatively, schemes may be dominant because the current set of executive schemes (i.e., E) directs mental-attentional *effort* to them (i.e., M–capacity) causing their hyperactivation. Likewise, contextually activated schemes that are incongruous with the dominant set of affective goals will tend to be actively inhibited (by mental-attentional *interruption* or I-operator monitored by E). In this manner, performances that are relevant to the currently dominant set of affective–emotion schemes (which in turn result from affective–personal processing and its affective choice) emerge by way of an effortful executive-driven action processing and an effortful but implicit action choice. Even truly-novel performances emerge this way, overdetermined by sets of goal-relevant compatible schemes that are together applied to the situation. This sort of *effortful processing strategy* at the service of affective goals, which relevant executive schemes formulate into cognitive goals, constitutes what in the previous section we called an X strategy.

There is also an alternative *automatic* (automatized) *form of strategies* that results from automatic action processing driven by overlearned perceptual cues of cognitive goals (often from automatized schemes) suitable to strong affective goals. This is what we called Y strategies, which fast-track performance implementation from automatic action or perceptual processing during initial moments of the situation, to unreflected production of the performance. Figure 8.2 provides a flow chart that illustrates schematically different

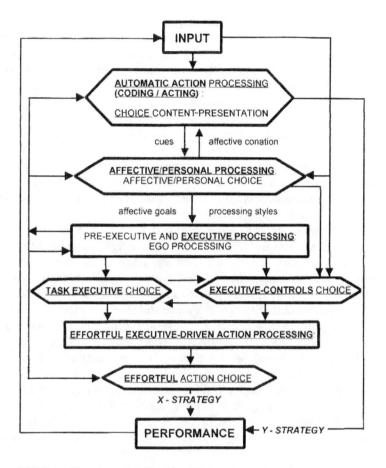

FIG. 8.2.   Flow chart of the fundamental steps involved in high-cognitive (X-strategy) and low-cognitive (Y-strategy) processing. Misleading situations are ones in which X-strategies and Y-strategies are in conflict.

steps of these two important sorts of strategies. It is worth noticing, as Fig. 8.2 shows, that in every case both processing strategies (Y and X) are initiated by, and serve, past or present affective goals (directly, or indirectly via the executive–cognitive goals they generate). Thus internalization of cognitive schemes and structures, which often is mediated by X strategies, initially is primed by, and at the service of, affective goals. Without affective goals, the organismic choice of suitable cognitive schemes would be hard to achieve.

Further, whenever a subject enters a situation where a strategy X and one (or more) strategy Y are simultaneously elicited and in conflict, because the more peremptory strategy Y leads to unwelcome results, the situation in question will qualify as a *misleading situation,* because the more-or-less automatic Y strategies are liable to cause errors unless controlled. In misleading situations, two competing affective or cognitive goals (pertinent respectively to X and Y) can be found; and to solve these misleading situations subjects must first learn to control their affects–emotions, to delay response and critically contrast–evaluate the two strategies, directing effort of mental attention to inhibit Y strategies and hyperactivate X. The appraisal of this state of affairs is done by executive schemes that with experience, via cognitive (L) learning, develop situated *criteria of relevance* driven by preeminent affective goals active in the concrete situation(s). Via these criteria of relevance, affective–emotion schemes ultimately determine the direction that children's coping-with-situations, and subsequent cognitive learning, will take. In this way, they determine knowledge children acquire, and the personality that emerges from these experiences and learning.

Although the innate or acquired cognitive–constructive mechanisms of a child or adult, such as hidden operators and current repertoire of habitual (i.e., learned) schemes, serve to interpret and construe the actual experience causing cognitive learning, the direction taken by this interpretive and constructive process is due, at every turn, to activated affective–emotion schemes, because they determine criteria of relevance and choice of executives to be applied. All cognitive goals have one or several preeminent affective goals as their driving force, although consolidated (i.e., habitual) cognitive goals, because they are self-propelling, also have an intrinsic motivational value and tend to apply by themselves,[4] at times leading to unwanted strategies Y.

To illustrate in an intuitive fashion, this interaction between affective–emotion schemes and cognitive schemes during development, consider the well-established psychodynamic processes that in infants lead to *fear of strangers* at about 7–8 months and *separation anxiety* at around 9–12 months, both often lasting into the second year. We believe that these forms of anxiety result from dialectical interaction among developmentally evolving affect–emotion schemes and cognitive schemes. Interpreting ideas and findings of developmentalists such as Bowlby, Spitz, and others (Saarni, Mumme, & Campos, 1998; Thomson, 1998), we think that infants construct early a scheme of their mothers as specific companions and protectors. They are born "looking for mother." Attachment is a complex innate emotional scheme, and this scheme "looks for mother." Across interactions with mother, this mother-attachment scheme differentiates, and because at first mother typically is only rewarding for the baby, this scheme comes to express–expect a *good mother*. As baby grows older, however, mother is forced (perhaps to protect the child from harm) to introduce interdictions, obstacles to his or her actions, etc., repeatedly leading the baby to frustration and an-

---

[4]This is Piaget's concept of assimilation that causes the principle of scheme's overdetermination of performance.

ger. From 4 months on, babies express anger to being restrained, and after 8 months, when baby moves around more easily, mothers appear more willing to convey negative emotions.

> [L]ocomotion changes mothers' attributions, resulting in sharp increase in their targeting of both anger and fear expressions towards their children as they recognize the dangers to them inherent in some objects, such as house plants, vases and electrical appliances . . . For the child such heightened signals can lead to apprehension and frustration (Campos et al., 1992). (Saarni et al., 1998, pp. 245–246)

From a dialectical constructivist perspective, because the *good mother* attachment scheme is contradictory with punishments and negative feelings that mother brings to the infant under these circumstances, and because schemes must be internally consistent, a separate but complementary scheme of mother gets formed. This is the *bad mother* attachment scheme, which embodies these negative expectations of a punishing mother. Because the *bad mother* is a scheme that has split away from the usually dominant *good mother* scheme, its onset will never be expected, and should evoke in the baby unpleasant surprise, frustration, and confusion. Consequently, when strangers appear in the baby's proximity and he or she can discriminate them from the familiar persons, because *familiar person* schemes attempt to assimilate the appearance of strangers (and anomalies, mismatches confusing essential discrepancies, ensue), the resulting state of confusion and uncertainty should cue and elicit activation of the *bad mother* scheme.

Thus when the baby's mental attentional capacity (M-operator) is capable of focusing and coordinating (this is scheme #1) simultaneously on the features of the familiar person (scheme #2), and also the unfamiliar discrepant features of the stranger (scheme #3; i.e., when the baby can coordinate simultaneously 2 or 3 schemes), the fear of strangers should and does appear as expression of the *bad mother* scheme. As Table 8.1 shows this M-capacity is certainly available at about 8 months (sensorimotor stage #4). Separation anxiety appears in the same manner when the child can simultaneously coordinate (scheme #1) three or four schemes: the mother's presence (scheme #2), the actions of the mother that indicate her imminent departure (scheme #3), the meaning of #2 plus #3 as signifying that *good mother* will no longer be on call as a protector–companion and *bad mother* (confusion, anxiety) might appear instead (scheme #4). When the baby can coordinate these 4 schemes, at about 12 months (see Table 8.1) if not earlier, separation anxiety appears.

It is known that fear of strangers and separation anxiety vary considerably both with biogenetic characteristics of the child (innate emotionality) and with a variety of parenting and interpersonal variables. It is also known that when these forms of anxiety (i.e., strangers and separation) are strong, patterns of interpersonal relations and exploratory initiatives might become dysfunctional—children behaving as overly shy or lacking agency (as in Ainsworth's insecurely attached children–see the following). Because this lack of interpersonal openness and agency affects later experiences, the cognitive and executive repertoires of children will become progressively more affected as time proceeds. Affective goals and emotions influence considerably life choices and opportunities adopted or rejected by children, thus codetermining children's cognition and life course.

THE ROLE OF MENTAL ATTENTION IN MOTIVATIONAL PROCESSES

The Emergence of Motives

In this section, we examine the role of mental attention in the emergence of motives. Motives appear very early in a human's life; securely attached babies always are motivated. A clear expression of distinct motives that condition cognitive goals comes to full flower only in the second year, however, when at about 18 months the baby can represent its own object of experience and its own subject of experience (i.e., when his or her consciousness can first experience self as distinct from the object–situation). This is a primitive self, which we call *self1* (Pascual-Leone, 2000b), the level of self-consciousness that others call by terms such as primary consciousness (Edelman & Tononi, 2000) or core consciousness (Damasio, 1999). At this time, clearly distinct motives, such as attachment appear (Ainsworth, Blehar, Waters, & Wall, 1978). As Oerter (2000, p. 65) emphasized: "*attachment behavior seems to emerge in every society around the age of one to one-and-a-half years* (Waters, Vaughn, Posada, & Kondo-Ikemura, 1995)."

This is due, we claim, to the mental attention needed to boost (i.e., hyperactivate) schemes that constitute the infrastructure of the motive in question, so as to allow it to be internalized–learned as a relational structural invariant (i.e., a distinct motivational scheme). Indeed, to cognitively construct the motive of attachment as an invariant (and thus potentially become conscious of it), the baby must be able to coordinate simultaneously four or five sensorimotor schemes (see Table 8.1). These are:

Scheme #1: mother*OB*:   The *personal* (i.e., affective and cognitive) *ob scheme* of the mother: This is the representational structure (complex scheme) of the mother as a personal object of desire, a protector, caring company, etc. We postfix *OB* to the name of this complex scheme to signify that it functions as a predicative operative scheme, which *applies to* (i.e., assimilates, in

Piaget's sense of this term) scheme #2 to cognitively and emotionally categorize it as expressing presence of the person in question.

Scheme #2: *mother*per*:   The mother-ob scheme #1 usually is released by a proximal perceptual object, that is, the perceptual scheme motherper, which gives a perceptual representation of the mother's perceivable characteristics (her face, movements, hand, voice, etc.), marking the mother's actual presence here-and-now available. We name this scheme motherper, with a star prefixed to it to index it as a figurative scheme. We use elementary operator–predicate logic to indicate, in Formula #1 following, that scheme #1 applies to (i.e., assimilates, which variously means categorizes, interprets, or transforms) scheme #2 to yield its significance ("Mother is here!"). Here the operator applies on the objects (schemes) located to its immediate right and enclosed by parentheses, so as to demarcate them. Thus we shall write "mother*OB*(*mother*per*)" to indicate that #1 applies on #2 to endow the latter with the meaning of #1.

Scheme #3: *self1*:   The baby's own primary self-consciousness personal (affective and cognitive) scheme, previously discussed.

Scheme #4: *context: A global, low-cognitive (perceptual) and affective, representation of the *context* or situation in which the baby finds himself or herself; together with the possible negative emotions elicited by it.

Scheme #5: BE-WITH: This is an emotion scheme, the NEED to BE WITH, or be protected by, a personal protector–companion (i.e., the mother). The scheme is written in capitals to signify that it is an *operative scheme* (a *pro*). In this case, it is an emotion operative: an affective-and-cognitive impulse or *conation*.

With these five schemes, and the notational conventions explained, we can model within a single mental-modeling formula, the mental operation (*M-operation*) that allows the baby to achieve the *motive scheme of attachment*:

$$\text{BE-WITH } (*\text{context}, \textit{self1}, \text{motherOB}(*\text{mother}\textit{per})) \qquad (\text{F\#1})$$

The expressions in F#1 summarize a model of the sort of mental operation that the baby might undertake to construct a motive scheme of attachment—and thus understand with basic (sensorimotor) executive consciousness that he or she needs to be with (close to) mom in emotionally stressing (*context) situations. Notice that for many children, the scheme motherOB will have previously applied to the perceptual scheme *mother*per* often enough to already have structured the two schemes into a single scheme complex or chunk. If this is so, the coordination of four distinct schemes will suffice to achieve this practical (self1-conscious) scheme of attachment. Further, notice that all schemes in F#1 are being boosted directly by affect—the conative effects of the innate (primary-affect) attachment scheme (Pascual-Leone,

1991), which is the affective precursor of the attachment motive; and all the schemes are directly anchored and released by the here-and-now, immediate situation. For these reasons the *M-operation* indicated in F#1 can be said to be *affectively immediate*, being boosted directly by affect, which here plays the role of executive schemes not yet available. Because executive schemes are not used or needed in this *M*-operation, this is a purely sensorimotor operation that uses the *M*e scale of measurement stipulated in Table 8.1.

Four (or at most five) schemes have to be boosted by *M*-capacity in order to internalize F#1 into a motive scheme of attachment. Therefore, children between 12 and 18 months of age (Piaget's fifth sensorimotor stage), but not younger, will be likely to construct–internalize this explicit motive of attachment—an internal working model (Oerter, 2000) that explains attachment behavior. This predicted timetable is consistent with empirical findings reviewed by Oerter (2000). Notice, however, that scheme *self1* (#3) might in some children already be structured–chunked with scheme BE-WITH (#5), due to special family–milieu experiences. In such cases, the attachment scheme could emerge earlier, when the child's mental-attentional capacity (*M*-capacity) can handle and coordinate three schemes (i.e., in 8–12-month-olds according to Table 8.1).

Developmental timing of acquisition of the attachment motive is constrained by the attachment affect, by the mental demand (*M*-demand) of the scheme to be acquired, and by the intersubjective–empathic learning opportunities available in the family environment. The particular emotional and cognitive content of this scheme is distinct, however, from its mental demand; and it depends solely on the child's own innate affective dispositions vis-à-vis others, and his or her particular bonding with mother–father–caretakers. Thus, as Oerter (2000) pointed out, the particular emerging motive (or frame motivation) will differ accordingly. The securely attached child (type B of Ainsworth) will feel free to explore the new context, secure in the mother's potential availability; the insecurely attached child (type A) will explore objects and avoid persons; and the insecure ambivalently attached child (type C) will require mother's close presence in order to feel secure in the new context.

A more complex, although still affectively elicited, motive scheme is that of *independence*. It demands greater mental processes, because its construction requires schemes that make reference to past–future cognitive experiences that are not cued by the present context. As discussed by Oerter (2000, p. 66): "In the second and third year of life a child shows the need to achieve self-reliance." This is the time when the child's *M*-capacity can cope with as many as six or seven sensorimotor schemes simultaneously (see Table 8.1). From our theoretical perspective, the motive of independence (i.e., explicit–conscious need to achieve self-reliance) demands no fewer than six schemes to be coordinated with the help of *M*-capacity boosting. Using the notational conventions previously explained, the requisite schemes are as follows:

Scheme #1: *task*ob*:   This is a figurative scheme of the tasks–objects that the subject regards as worth *mastering* (the mastery affect is possibly innate— Pascual-Leone, 1991).

Scheme #2: *self1*:   The self's primary consciousness representation.

Scheme #3: *context: As previously described, a representation of the context or situation.

Scheme #4: AGENCY: A practical operative scheme of Agency, that is, a disposition to actively and personally solve tasks or object problems. The mastery primary affect helps to develop agency, or at least the desire for it, across experiences.

Scheme #5: #successful*ad*:   This is a practical concept–predicate (an ad scheme) that functions as a parameter (i.e., a condition, this is the meaning of the prefix #) to the operative AGENCY. Children whose life experience has given occasion for many successful acts of agency, already have structured–chunked together schemes #4 and #5. Children whose experiences of agency have been predominantly unsuccessful, might have to activate the two schemes separately in order to reach the idea–motive of independence.

Scheme #6: *self2*:   This is the child's self-conscious self, which we call *self2*.[5]

Scheme #7: BE-INDEPENDENT: Operative scheme, supported by the innate *mastery affect,* expressing the affective need for independence (i.e., doing things without help).

Using these schemes the mental operation for constructing the *independence* motive might be as follows:

$$\text{BE-INDEPENDENT(AGENCY(\#successful}ad,$$
$$\text{*context, }self1\text{, *task}ob\text{) }self2) \qquad \text{(F\#2)}$$

In English this expression might be paraphrased as follows: "When a child's unreflective consciousness (*self1*) has sufficiently experienced across tasks (*task*ob*) and in various contexts (*context) his or her own powers of agency (AGENCY), his or her reflective self (*self2*) develops the desire–motive of being independent (BE-INDEPENDENT)."

Consider children who have had few experiences of self-produced success. For these children, schemes #4 and #5 will still be separated. To achieve the motive of independence, they must first internalize the idea of their own successful agency. This is attained (look in F#2 at the schemes inside the AGENCY-parentheses) when *self1* has repeatedly achieved successful Agency. This primary-consciousness experience involves coordination of five

---

[5]Others might perhaps consider this to be a higher order consciousness or autobiographical consciousness of a very low level (Damasio, 1999; Edelman & Tononi, 2000).

schemes (only four would be needed for the usually successful children). In our model, this sets the timetable for acquisition of the idea of having achieved successful agency between 12 and 26 months (see Table 8.1). The practical concept of successful agency is different, however, from the motive of independence. To reach the latter, the child must still reflectively (*self2*) consider that she herself can always (most often) exert successful agency and thus be independent (self-reliant). This affectively-immediate mental operation is expressed by the full formula F#2, and requires coordinating (boosting with sensorimotor *M*-capacity) a total of six or seven schemes. As Table 8.1 shows, this corresponds to the ages of 2 to 3 years, which Oerter (2000) gave as proper data estimates. The result of this mental operation, when suitably internalized, is a "quasi-need" (as Lewin, 1951, would have called it) that constitutes the motive of independence.

The Emergence of Specific Interests

Finally, consider the emergence of *specific interests*, which derive from motives and are the manifestation of more of less enduring affective goals. Specific interests emerge when relevant object-schemes become connected to their affective goals. This sets the *obs* in question as suitable targets (i.e., *cognitive goals*) when the affective goals in question are dominant in the organism. Considerable neuroscientific research (e.g., Albright et al., 2001; Allman et al., 2001; Damasio, 1994, 2001; Davidson, 2001; Habib, 2000; Ochsner et al., 2002) points to the idea that the cingulate gyrus is a main determinant in the dynamic conversion of motives (i.e., affective goals) into cognitive goals to be pursued by high cognition, in particular within misleading (cognitive conflict) situations (van Veen & Carter, 2002), and possibly also in the subsequent development of specific interests as enduring cognitive expressions of affective or cognitive goals. Thus interests (Ainley, Hidi, & Berndorff, 2002; Krapp, 2000; Renninger, Hidi, & Krapp, 1992), when interpreted as personal–emotion schemes, express the conative importance (for stipulated activities) of the object in question, making it a potential target in cognitive-goal-seeking praxis. Motives (affective-goal motivations) and interests (specific object-indexed motivations) are the kernel that educators, parents and psychologists attempt first to change, whenever a suitable *intrinsic motivation* (or *self-motivation,* we discuss the difference later) is found to be lacking.

Because interest, in a general (nonspecific) sense, is an innate primary affect (Pascual-Leone, 1991), often related to curiosity and novelty (*orienting reactions* and so forth), the expectable mental (*M*-) demand of specific interest will vary widely with the support (human mediation, mentoring) provided by family, teachers, and friends. If much suitable support for a given specific interest (e.g., music, acting) is provided, the specific interest in question will develop much earlier than described below. This is the case of what we call *hot interests*, obtained by way of putting children into a "hot house" life dedicated to cultivate that interest (cf. Walmsley & Margolis, 1987). We reckon that 5–6-year-olds, if not earlier, could develop hot interests. The other specific interests are *cool interests,* because they do not benefit for their development from any hot mediation and mentoring. They develop much later, and it is to these cool specific interests that our current task analysis refers.

Eccles et al. (1998) reviewed developmental work (including their own), which showed that the conscious distinction between the concepts of (cool) specific interest and utility–importance appears for the first time in the elementary school years. Why it should not occur earlier becomes clear if we deconstruct this kind of complex, personal scheme (an internalized and self-reflective volitional plan) and consider the set of essential constituent schemes that it has to coordinate in an act of mental judgment (*M-operation*) in order to be internalized–learned. The essential schemes involved—paraphrased and coordinated by means of a suitable English phrase—can be formulated as follows: "*I* need to PURSUE *persistently*, within the appropriate *context* of use, the LEARNING of (and/or the high performance in) the task–activity that I LIKE so much."

This generalized English formula captures what we believe are the six essential dimensional constraints of any enduring (but cool) specific interest. We wrote in capitals the constraints that are embodied by operative schemes and in italics those embodied by figurative schemes. As the English formula indicates, this construction requires the coordination of six schemes, which generally are self-reflective, symbolic, and conceptually complex (i.e., are generic, standing for categories or kinds of schemes). Thus a mental processing mediated by executives is needed to carry out this volitional judgment and learn it. As a consequence, Table 8.2 (and not Table 8.1) should be used to estimate the *M*-capacity demand of this sort of mental construction–operation. Table 8.2 indicates that with a maximal *M*-demand of six mental schemes, (cool) specific interests may not emerge until the early teen years. This is consistent with the empirical data (Eccles et al., 1998). In what follows, we give a more detailed account of the same analysis. Readers not interested in this detail may proceed, without loss of continuity, to the final paragraph of this section.

There are a total of seven essential schemes involved in the constructive abstraction of specific interests:

Scheme #1: AGENCY*task:i: This is the chunked structure of constituent schemes that in formula F#2 produce an instance *i* of Agency (as formula F#2 shows, these schemes are #successful, *context, *self1*, and *task*ob*). With repeated life experiences that induce acts of Agency in one or another specific task i, these constituent schemes become coordinated (even in the preschool and early school years) into multiple complex schemes of Agency; we shall denote these Agency schemes collectively as AGENCY*task:i. These complex Agency schemes, driven by motives (or general affective goals), serve as the core around which task or object preferences, and then *specific interests,* are built. In the present task analysis this scheme #1 intervenes in the emergence of scheme # 3, used in formula F#3 to model construction of specific interests.

Scheme #2: *self2:*   This is the child's reflectively conscious self previously mentioned, and linguistically expressed by "I" or "me."

Scheme #3: LIKE*task:i: This is a more or less automatized "I-LIKE-it" (affective preference) judgment; a scheme that expresses a consciously explicit preference of the child for activities of a certain kind *i* that he or she pursues using scheme #1, that is, AGENCY*task:i.

Scheme #4: NEED-PURSUING: This is a specific volitional judgment and expression of Will, which crystallizes a complex cognitive goal (brought into consciousness by the cumulative effect of affective goals evoked by multiple experiences related to scheme #3, i.e., LIKE*task:i).

Scheme #5: #persistently: This is a parameter of #4, the NEED-PURSUING operative scheme. It stipulates, as a condition of #4, that the activity be continued or repeated in the future.

Scheme #6: *context: Stands for the overall construal of the situation and task at hand.

Scheme #7: LEARNING–PERFORMANCE: This is the *goal orientation* (Dweck, 1998; Koller, 2000) that guides activity in specific interests: whether a *learning–mastery goal* (i.e., an intrinsic motive towards achieving mastery in the task) or a *performance goal* (an ego orientation in which the intention is to satisfy high expectations of others by performing well). In the latter case, the focus of attention is extrinsic, not on the task itself but on the expected results. Considerable evidence shows that these are the two alternative orientations of children and adults; the former leads to better results in both achievement and self-satisfaction. Nonetheless, the orientation tacitly chosen is much influenced by personal values–expectations of mentors and human milieu.

Using this notation and definitions, the sort of mental operation that can constructively abstract (cool) specific interests can be summarized as follows:

The repeated self-conscious experiences of successful or satisfying Agency in task:i (this is scheme #1), lead the child eventually to internalize a complex scheme (structure) expressing this recurrent preference for task:i. This is scheme #3: LIKE*task:i, which stands for a stable conscious preference. Repeated reexperiencing of this self-preference generates a new motive (affective goal) toward seeking it, and the self-conscious planning based on this motive engenders the *specific interest.* The latter is symbolized in F#3:

$$\text{NEED-PURSUING}(\#\text{persistently},*\text{context}, self2,$$
$$\text{LEARNING–PERFORMANCE}(\text{LIKE}*\text{task:i})) \qquad (\text{F\#3})$$

Once the child–person has acquired his or her stable self-preference LIKE*task:i, adopting the goal orientation characteristic of his or her personality (a LEARNING goal or a PERFORMANCE goal), he or she begins to practice the chosen activity. The practice eventually leads to a reflectively conscious need or decision to pursue the activity in question. Enduring praxis along these lines creates the specific interest. This construction must be mediated by executives (which we omitted in the formula) because the six schemes to be coordinated are generally symbolic and conceptually complex (i.e., are generic, standing for categories or kinds of schemes). Thus Table 8.2 (and not Table 8.1) has to be used in estimating the M-capacity demand of this mental operation. With a maximal M-demand of six (six schemes to be coordinated), specific interests might not emerge until 13 or 14 years of age. However, there are learning shortcuts: The schemes #persistently and *context (see formula F#3) are in practice closely connected with NEED-PURSUING, at least within facilitating situations; so they could be chunked–structured with NEED-PURSUING when life circumstances give the opportunity. In this case, M-demand of formula F#3 reduces from six to four, that is, the mental capacity of 9–10-year-olds. Other similarly acquired schemes can be described that reflect judgments of utility or personal importance instead of specific interests. When all these schemes have been attained, the child should be able to self-consciously differentiate between–among them (e.g., interest versus utility schemes–situations). The age estimates that our analyses yield are consistent with Eccles et al.'s (1998, p. 1040) conclusion that "children in Grades 5 through 12 differentiate task value" and reach the distinction between interest, utility, and personal importance.

These theoretical results offer partial explanation of developmental ages of acquisition found in the motivation literature; and suggest that subjects' failure to activate sufficient mental-attentional capacity could cause inadequate motivational arousal and induce underdevelopment of motivational schemes in children and adults' cognitive repertoire. We currently are investigating this idea by comparing performance under conditions that might increase or decrease the person's normal state of mental arousal. Our dependent variable is the subject's performance on a well-studied visuospatial measure of M-capacity, the Figural Intersections Task (FIT; Pascual-Leone & Baillargeon, 1994; Pascual-Leone & Johnson, 2001; Pascual-Leone et al., 2000). In a between-subjects experimental study (Aro, 2002) adults were tested individually with the FIT under two conditions: (a) wearing earphones that produced no sound, or (b) wearing earphones that allowed subjects to hear an intermittent low (60 Hertz) tone that lasted about 2 seconds each time with silent intervals of about 4 seconds. Based on pilot work and current ideas about arousal and binding mechanisms of consciousness (e.g., Singer, 2001), we predicted that the tone would induce a higher state of attentional arousal in subjects, thus increasing their mobilization of M-capacity during the FIT solution process and improving their performance level. Results showed the predicted statistically significant difference, which took place against the subjects' own claim (made in a final questionnaire) that the 60 Hertz tone was annoying–distracting them.

OTHER DYNAMIC ORGANISMIC INTERACTIONS RELATED TO WILL AND SELF-MOTIVATION

There are interesting dynamic interactions between affective–emotive processes and modes of cognitive processing (cf. Beck, 1996; Damasio, 1994, 2001; Greenberg, 2002; Kuhl, 2000), possibly related to constraints already built into the brain's processes (Fox et al., 2001; Kagan, 1998, 2002). Particularly central for motivation are the constraints and dynamic interactions that relate the right-hemisphere versus left-hemisphere modes of cognitive processing to various dialectically complementary dimensions of processual description: negative versus positive affects; the two sorts of situations, facilitating versus misleading, previously mentioned; and the two sorts of volition, implicit or unconscious (i.e., primary *conation*) versus the explicitly conscious *Will* (these are the main functional utilities for intrinsic motivation and self-motivation respectively).[6]

In the field of motivational psychology, Kuhl and associates (Kuhl, 2000; Kuhl & Fuhrmann, 1998) proposed that positive affects versus negative affects, on the one hand, and intuitive–holistic processing versus analytic–serial processing, on the other, are interdependent; and we wish to add: They form part of a perhaps prewired *affective-cognitive regulatory* (dialectical) *system*. This interdependence shows in that positive affects and emotions do bias the organism towards the use of intuitive–holistic (right hemisphere—RH) mental strategies, whereas negative affects and emotions promote the use of analytic–serial (left hemisphere—LH) mental strategies. Kuhl called this dialectical system of built-in biases the "affect-cognition modulation hypothesis," and attempted to use it as first foundation for a theory of volitional processes. Related views were put forward by Fredrickson (2001) from a different perspective, that of the adaptive value of positive emotions and positive psychology. She emphasizes, and illustrates with experiments, that positive emotions "including joy, interest, contentment, pride, and love—although phe-

---

[6]Notice that in the recent psychological literature (e.g., Corno et al., 2002) the term conation has been used as an umbrella term to encompass the organismic determinants of any sort of motivation, whether unconscious or volitional. Thus we must distinguish between *primary* conation (i.e., unconscious impulses of the organismic flesh) and *secondary* or willful conation (i.e., the Will in the sense of organismic mechanisms causing volitional processes). The contrast we make between primary conation and Will should be understood in this manner.

nomenologically distinct, all share the ability to broaden people's momentary thought-action repertoires and build their enduring personal resources, ranging from physical and intellectual resources to social and psychological resources" (Fredrickson, 2001, p. 219). In contrast, she looks at negative affects–emotions as promoting narrow, specific action tendencies (i.e., narrow specific schemes) for coping with unwanted (and often misleading, we wish to emphasize) situations. This is consistent with our theory. Negative–withdrawal emotions are likely to produce cognitive–emotional conflicts that would induce the use of mental-attentional interruption, as a cognitive defense strategy; and this automatic or effortful interruption would cause the narrow mental focus of attention and action tendencies. Fredrickson (2001) says as much descriptively: These action tendencies of negative affects–emotions are the "outcome of a psychological process that narrows a person's momentary thought-action repertoire by calling to mind an urge to act in a particular way (e.g., escape, attack, expel)" (p. 220). She concludes that: "Specific action tendencies called forth by negative emotions represent the sort of actions that likely worked best to save human ancestors' lives and limbs in similar situations" (Fredrickson, 2001, p. 220).

Thus conceived, these affective biases built into brain-wired *affect-cognition regulations* are different but consistent with current tenets of cognitive neuroscience (Fox et al., 2001). It is now well established that the left prefrontal cortex (PFC) serves to control–regulate–potentiate positive emotions, which induce affective goals (leading to cognitive goals) of approach and exploration. In contrast, the right PFC regulates–potentiates negative emotions leading to affective–cognitive goals of withdrawal, flight, or aversive reactions (Davidson, 2001; Fox et al., 2001). These findings of Davidson and Fox can be related to the just mentioned work on motivation and affects of Kuhl and of Fredrickson, by means of the model of mental attention discussed in the previous two sections. Indeed we have long upheld the view, for which there is some empirical support (Pascual-Leone, 1987), that left PFC is specialized in *effortful mental processes* (which engage M-capacity and mental attentional interruption or I-operator, both under the control of the dominant executive schemes or E-operator); and these processes often are needed to handle novel and misleading situations. In contrast, we believe that right PFC specializes in *familiar*, already learned and more or less automatized, *mental processes*, which do not demand as much effort (minimizing the need of M, I, and E). We also believe that the right-PFC strategy is suitable in facilitating situations, in which the rich content (C-) learning of the right hemisphere, the principle of schemes' overdetermination of performance (i.e., SOP), and the lack of need for interrupting (I-operator) misleading schemes, provide open and broad experiential learning opportunities.

We have synthesized this *dialectical system of affective-cognitive regulations* in Fig. 8.3. Because this model goes beyond what is well established in

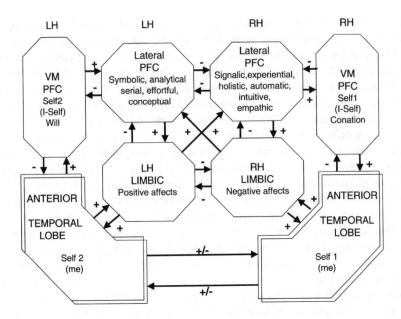

FIG. 8.3.   Speculative idealized model of affective-cognitive interregulations.

neuroscience, it should be considered to be tentative and idealized. As this figure shows, we propose that the right (RH) limbic system is the focal site of negative–avoidance affects, whereas the left (LH) limbic system is the main site of positive–approach affects. Each limbic system, in turn, potentiates activity in the prefrontal cortex of the opposite side (limbic RH to left PFC, and limbic LH to right PFC). At the same time, the PFC of each side controls–potentiates activity of the limbic system of its own side (left PFC to limbic LH; right PFC to limbic RH). In addition, structures (PFC and limbic system) of each hemisphere dialectically compete and tend to reduce–inhibit the activity of the corresponding structures in the other hemisphere. Finally, we believe, as discussed in the following, that self-conscious *self2* is situated predominantly in the ventromedial left PFC and anterior temporal LH, whereas the purely experiential *self1* is predominantly in the right PFC and anterior temporal RH. These two self-organizations, in turn, are part of the dialectical system of affective-cognitive regulatory checks and balances as indicated in Fig. 8.3.

If we interpret this model using the views of Kuhl, Fredickson, Davidson, and Fox, it becomes plausible to think that the affective bias of negative emotions towards activating left PFC is part of Evolution's way to prepare us for specific effortful problem-solving activities (praxis!), which negative affects–emotions (and their usually accompanying misleading situations) often necessitate. Because the mental and behavioral work needed to succeed in this praxis could be taxing, it is fitting that left PFC be prewired to regulate–potentiate the positive affects–emotions, so that left PFC can boost them and consequently gain positive expectations and persistency for coping with the tasks at hand. This is of course a winner's formula that evolution might have given us and experience might refine (Kagan, 2001, 2002). Likewise, when the organism is taken by positive emotions and facilitating situations, it is fitting that right PFC be called on first, so that the first view and exploration of the situation and circumstances (Kagan, 2002; Pascual-Leone, 1990; Pascual-Leone & Irwin, 1998) be as open and broad as possible (before the left PFC intervenes, activated by the right PFC priming of negative affects elicited by surprising–displeasing aspects of this unrestrained exploratory approach). This is why Fredrickson (2001) aptly calls her theory of positive emotions the Broaden-and-Build Theory.

We can sketch a better picture of the motivational controls if we add to this regulation model a concept of where the *self-schemes* (i.e., the child's self-referential representations) might be centered in the brain (see Fig. 8.3). We share the views of those who believe that self-schemes exist both in LH and in RH (Eccles, 1980; Gazzaniga, 1995; Levy, 1990; Sperry, 1990). We have discussed above and elsewhere (Pascual-Leone, 2000b) the two different organizations of self-schemes. Namely: *Self1* (which appears earlier but consolidates at about 18 months of age, when the child becomes aware of both object and self as subject of experience, but is not symbolically self-conscious); and *self2* (which begins in the second year but consolidates at about 3 years of age, when children, in a self-conscious and symbolic manner, begin to have explicit views about self and others and so can for the first time draw a man or woman). Self1 is purely experiential, and we speculate that it might be the sort of self-consciousness that is created predominately by RH processes. Self2 is symbolic and explicitly (i.e., self-consciously) interpersonal and dialogical. We speculate that self2 is situated predominantly in LH. It is tempting to think that self1 and self2 are connected closely both with the ventromedial prefrontal cortex and the anterior temporal lobe. The ventromedial cortex (Bechara et al., 1999; Davidson, 2001; Kelley et al., 2002) might be a site for the operative (or acting) self, that is, the *I* or *I-self* of the person (Pascual-Leone, 1990, 2000b; Pascual-Leone & Irwin, 1998). The anterior part of the temporal lobes may be related to the figurative (or representational) self, better known as the *me* or *me-self*. In this manner, the self would be in contact with the operative (agency) side of mental attention, and (via the anterior temporal pole, BA38) it would also be in contact with the limbic system.

We speculate that the LH limbic system is more closely connected with positive–approach affects, whereas the RH limbic lobe is more related to negative–withdrawal affects. This idea seems consistent with Davidson's theory of affective styles (Davidson, 2001). This affective-style limbic assumption

helps to explain why each prefrontal lobe can control and selectively potentiate the homologous limbic system, and in the process, control one category of
affects (positive or negative). The model we have outlined also serves to clarify the two different kinds of *will* (or I-will) *schemes* (Pascual-Leone, 1990):
the complex self-conscious *Will* schemes (Pascual-Leone, 1990; Pascual-
Leone & Irwin, 1998), located predominantly in LH; and the much simpler
and often unconscious *will* that we call *primary conation*, constituted by
strong, well-learned or automatized schemes (affective or cognitive) with
their self-propelling (Piaget's assimilation) disposition to express themselves
in performance. Conation (by this term we always mean primary conation)
creates impulses to act in ways stipulated by the strong, self-propelled
schemes predominantly found in RH.

From this perspective, *intrinsic motivation* (i.e., an interest-based action
prompted by self-own affective–cognitive goals—Krapp, 2000) can be distinguished clearly from *self-motivation* (i.e., a self-conscious willful motivation—Kuhl, 2000). We think that self-motivation is an executive–operative
function of self2. This executive function stems predominantly from LH and,
via the Will (i.e., conscious volition), uses the effortful power of mental attention. Intrinsic motivation, in contrast, tends not to need mental effort, may
be unconscious, and may stem predominantly from RH. As has long been
recognized (Piaget claimed that his teacher Claparede was the first to raise
this issue—Pascual-Leone, 1990), the practice of the Will leads to automati-
zation of it. For us Will-automatization is a new sort of (complex) intrinsic
motivation that is spontaneous, easy to follow, and stems predominantly
from RH.

We have conducted an experiment that illustrates this transition. Four
samples of 9- to 12-year-old children, two cognitively gifted and two mainstream (i.e., nongifted), were tested with a visuospatial *M*-capacity task, the
Compound Stimuli Visual Information (CSVI) task (Pascual-Leone, 1970).
The samples were tested under one of two task-instruction conditions. In one
condition, children were told that the task was hard and was designed for
children older than they were. In the other condition, children were told that
the task was easy and designed for younger children. The instructions and
task administration differed only in the brief *hard* versus *easy* instruction re-
marks. We expected that gifted, but not perhaps mainstream children, would
have a superior executive repertoire and a well practiced Will, which might
have become in part automatized, producing intrinsically-motivated performances. We thus predicted that our instructional manipulation would
have a greater effect with the mainstream students. Consistent with predictions, the two gifted samples did not differ in their superior performance
level. In mainstream children, however, performance of the hard-task sample
was statistically higher than that of the easy-task sample, although gifted
children performed better. Further, among mainstream children, those in the

hard-task condition rated the task as more difficult than did those in the easy-task condition. In contrast, ratings did not vary by condition for the gifted children; both gifted samples tended to rate the task as difficult.

FINAL REMARKS

In this chapter, we have attempted to convey, in a manner detailed enough to be theoretically useful, how processes of affect–motivation intertwine with those of cognitive development. The chapter is unusual in a number of ways, and it may be appropriate to review its basic metatheoretical claims, in order to highlight the chapter's overall purpose. First we have provided a novel definition and explication of the construct of scheme (or schema) that shows its functionalist character rooted in evolution. Scheme is, we believe, the missing unit of processing needed to exhibit how performance (whether affect–emotional or cognitive) is dynamically constructed–synthesized by semantic-pragmatically organized information processes of the organism. These dynamic syntheses of schemes are made possible by deeper general purpose mechanisms (which we call hidden operators) that express in psychological terms organismic hardware constraints that can dynamically change schemes, integrate them, or both into actual performances. Central to this integration, and to the developmental emergence of progressively more complex motivational and cognitive schemes, are the mental attentional mechanisms that grow in capacity with chronological age up to adolescence, and also the principle of schemes' overdetermination of performance. Descriptive performance is thus deconstructed into dynamically interacting constructs for which we provided some plausible neuroscientific interpretations.

The substantive theory based on these ideas serves as rational basis for the method of process–task analysis (metasubjective analysis) that we use. With these methods we formulate here qualitative models of the emergence, during affective-and-cognitive development, of two infancy landmarks (fear of strangers, separation anxiety) and of some key motives and specific interests of older children. These analyses show what we take to be the mental demand (i.e., organismic complexity) of the affective-and-cognitive, or motivational, developmental landmarks discussed, which illustrates how affect–emotions and cognitive processes dialectically codetermine developmental growth.

To appreciate our proposal on affective-and-cognitive developmental dialectics, readers need not, however, accept our precise complexity counting. It suffices to accept the concept of a developmentally growing M-capacity (working memory if you will), which our method demarcates in task analysis with the power of at least an ordinal scale (we think the underlying scale is in fact an interval one—e.g., Pascual-Leone & Baillargeon, 1994). With these assumptions we still make a case for our main idea: There are innate primary affects–emotions (innate schemes) and powerful general-purpose innate resources (hidden operators, such as those that constitute mental attention). There are also a few simple (largely sensorial–perceptual) innate cognitive schemes. With this equipment, development proceeds via the interaction between affective goals and cognitive appraisals of experience, made possible by both the organismic hidden operators and the reality constraints. These cognitive appraisals become embodied in the form of new schemes. Affects–emotions set the direction development might take by valuing or rejecting action possibilities opened by actual situations. Cognition unfolds developmentally to mediate between the affective–emotion directions (conation) and the constraints of external reality.

ACKNOWLEDGMENTS

Preparation of this chapter was supported by a grant awarded to the authors by the Social Sciences and Humanities Research Council of Canada. We thank Drs. L. S. Greenberg and P. Roosen-Runge for comments on the chapter, and A. Calvo and C. Pascual-Leone for help in preparing figures.

REFERENCES

Ainley, M., Hidi, S., & Berndorff, D. (2002). Interest, learning, and psychological processes that mediate their relationship. *Journal of Educational Psychology, 95,* 545–561.

Ainsworth, M. D. S., Blehar, M. C., Waters, E., & Wall, S. (1978). *Patterns of attachment: A psychological study of the strange situation.* Hillsdale, NJ: Lawrence Erlbaum Associates.

Albright, T. D., Jessell, T. M., Kandel, E. R., & Posner, M. J. (2001). Progress in the neural sciences in the century after Cajal (and the mysteries that remain). In P. Marijuan (Ed.), *Cajal and consciousness* (pp. 11–40). New York: New York Academy of Sciences.

Allman, J. M., Hakeem, A., Erwin, J. M., Nimchinsky, E., & Hop, P. (2001). The anterior cingulate cortex: The evolution of an interface between emotion and cognition. In A. R. Damasio, A. Harrington, J. Kagan, B. S. McEwen, H. Moss, & R. Shaikh (Eds.), *Unity of knowledge: The convergence of natural and human science* (pp. 107–117). New York: New York Academy of Sciences.

Anderson, A. K., & Phelps, E. A. (2001). Lesions of the human amygdala impair enhanced perception of emotionally salient events. *Nature, 411,* 305–309.

Aro, C. (2002). *Does cognitive arousal enhance problem solving capabilities?* Unpublished Honours BSc thesis, York University, Toronto, Ontario, Canada.

Baillargeon, R. (2002). The acquisition of physical knowledge in infancy: A summary in eight lessons. In U. Goswami (Ed.), *Blackwell handbook of childhood cognitive development* (pp. 47–83). Malden, MA: Blackwell.

Barraque Bordas, L. (1995). *El sistema nervioso como un todo* [The central nervous system as a totality]. Barcelona, Spain: Edicion Paidos.

Bechara, A., Damasio, H., Damasio, A. R., & Lee, G. P. (1999). Different contributions of the human amygdala and ventromedial prefrontal cortex to decision making. *Journal of Neuroscience, 19,* 5473–5481.

Beck, A. T. (1996). Beyond belief: A theory of modes, personality, and psychopathology. In P. M. Salkovskis (Ed.), *Frontiers of cognitive therapy* (pp.1–25). New York: Guilford.

Case, R. (1992). The role of the frontal lobes in the regulation of cognitive development. *Brain and Cognition, 20*, 51–72.

Case, R. (1998). The development of conceptual structures. In D. Kuhn & R. S. Siegler (Eds.), *Handbook of child psychology: Vol. 2. Cognition, perception, and language* (pp. 745–800). New York: Wiley.

Corno, L., Cronbach, L. J., Kupermintz, H., Lohman, D. F., Mandinach, E. B., Porteus, A. W., & Talbert, J. E. (2002). *Remaking the concept of aptitude: Extending the legacy of Richard E. Snow.* Mahwah, NJ: Lawrence Erlbaum Associates.

Crick, F. (1994). *The astonishing hypothesis.* London: Touchtone Books.

Damasio, A. R. (1994). *Descartes' error.* New York: Putnam.

Damasio, A. R. (1999). *The feeling of what happens.* San Diego: Harcourt.

Damasio, A. R. (2001). Emotion and the human brain. In A. R. Damasio, A. Harrington, J. Kagan, B. S. McEwen, H. Moss, & R. Shaikh (Eds.), *Unity of knowledge: The convergence of natural and human science* (pp. 101–106). New York: New York Academy of Sciences.

Davidson, R. J. (2001). Towards a biology of personality and emotion. In A. R. Damasio, A. Harrington, J. Kagan, B. S. McEwen, H. Moss, & R. Shaikh (Eds.), *Unity of knowledge: The convergence of natural and human science* (pp. 191–207). New York: New York Academy of Sciences.

Deleuze, G. (1990). *Expressionism in philosophy: Spinoza.* New York: Zone Books.

Durston, S., Thomas, K., Yang, Y., Ulug, A., Zimmerman, R., & Casey, B. (2002). A neural basis for the development of inhibitory control. *Developmental Science, 5*, F9–F16.

Dweck, C. S. (1998). The development of early self-conceptions: Their relevance for motivational processes. In J. Heckhausen & C. S. Dweck (Eds.), *Life span perspectives in motivation and control* (pp. 257–280). Mahwah, NJ: Lawrence Erlbaum Associates.

Eccles, J. C. (1980). *The human psyche.* Berlin, Germany: Springer-Verlag.

Eccles, J. S., Wigfield, A., & Schiefele, U. (1998). Motivation to succeed. In N. Eisenberg (Ed.), *Handbook of child psychology: Vol. 3. Social, emotional, and personality development* (pp. 1017–1095). New York: Wiley.

Edelman, G. M., & Tononi, G. (2000). *A universe of consciousness.* New York: Basic Books.

Ekman, P., & Davidson, R. J. (Eds.). (1994). *The nature of emotion.* New York: Oxford University Press.

Fox, N. A., Henderson, H. A., & Marshall, P. J. (2001). The biology of temperament: An integrative view. In C. A. Nelson & M. Luciana (Eds.), *Handbook of developmental cognitive neuroscience* (pp. 631–645). Cambridge, MA: MIT Press.

Fredrickson, B. L. (2001). The role of positive emotions in positive psychology. *American Psychologist, 56*, 218–226.

Frijda, N. H. (1987). Emotions, cognitive structure, and action tendency. *Cognition and Emotion, 1*, 115–144.

Frijda, N. H., Kuipers, P., & Schure, E. (1989). Relations among emotions, appraisal, and emotional action readiness. *Journal of Personality and Social Psychology, 57*, 212–228.

Fuster, J. M. (1989). *The prefrontal cortex* (2nd ed.). New York: Raven.

Fuster, J. M. (1995). *Memory in the cerebral cortex.* Cambridge, MA: MIT Press.

Gazzaniga, M. S. (1995). Consciousness and the cerebral hemispheres. In M. S. Gazzaniga (Ed.), *The cognitive neurosciences* (pp. 1391–1400). Cambridge, MA: MIT Press.

Gibson, J. J. (1979). *The ecological approach to visual perception.* Boston: Houghton Mifflin.

Goldman-Rakic, P. S. (1995). Architecture of the prefrontal cortex and the central executive. In J. Grafman, K. J. Holyoak, & F. Boller (Eds.), *Structure and function of the human prefrontal cortex* (pp. 71–83). New York: New York Academy of Science.

Greenberg, L. S. (2002). Integrating an emotion-focused approach to treatment into psychotherapy integration. *Journal of Psychotherapy Integration, 12*, 154–189.

Greenberg, L. S., & Pascual-Leone, J. (1995). A dialectical constructivist approach to experiential change. In R. Neimeyer & M. Mahoney (Eds.), *Constructivism in psychotherapy* (pp. 169–191). Washington, DC: American Psychological Association Press.

Greenberg, L. S., & Pascual-Leone, J. (2001). A dialectical constructivist view of the creation of personal meaning. *Journal of Constructivist Psychology, 14,* 165–186.

Greenberg, L. S., Rice, L. N., & Elliott, R. (1993). *Facilitating emotional change: The moment-by-moment process.* New York: Guilford.

Habib, M. (2000). Disorders of motivation. In J. Bogousslavsky & J. L. Cummings (Eds.), *Behavior and mood disorders in focal brain lesions* (pp. 261–284). Cambridge, England: Cambridge University Press.

Izard, G. E. (1977). *Human emotions.* New York: Plenum.

James, W. (1961). *Psychology: The briefer course* (G. Allport, Ed.). New York: Harper & Row. (Original work published 1892)

Jonides, J., Schumacher, E. H., Smith, E. E., Lauber, E. J., Awh, E., Minoshima, S., & Koeppe, R. A. (1997). Verbal working memory load affects brain activation as measured by PET. *Journal of Cognitive Neuroscience, 9,* 462–475.

Kagan, J. (1998). *Galen's prophecy.* Boulder, CO: Westview.

Kagan, J. (2001). Future directions for social sciences. In A. R. Damasio, A. Harrington, J. Kagan, B. S. McEwen, H. Moss, & R. Shaikh (Eds.), *Unity of knowledge: The convergence of natural and human science* (pp. 177–190). New York: New York Academy of Sciences.

Kagan, J. (2002). *Surprise, uncertainty, and mental structures.* Cambridge, MA: Harvard University Press.

Kant, I. (1965). *Critique of pure reason.* New York: St. Martin's Press.

Kelley, W. M., Macrae, C. N., Wyland., C. L., Caglar, S., Inati, S., & Heatherton, T. F. (2002). Finding the self? An even-related fMRI study. *Journal of Cognitive Neuroscience, 14,* 785–794.

Klingberg, T., Forssberg, H., & Westerberg, H. (2002). Increased brain activity in frontal parietal cortex underlies the development of the visuospatial working memory capacity during childhood. *Journal of Cognitive Neuroscience, 14,* 1–10.

Koller, O. (2000). Goal orientations: Their impact on academic learning and their development during early adolescence. In J. Heckhausen (Ed.), *Motivational psychology of human development* (pp. 129–142). Amsterdam: Elsevier.

Krapp, A. (2000). Interests and human development during adolescence: An educational-psychological approach. In J. Heckhausen (Ed.), *Motivational psychology of human development* (pp. 109–128). Amsterdam: Elsevier.

Kuhl, J. (2000). A theory of self-development: Affective fixation and the STAR model of personality disorders and related styles. In J. Heckhausen (Ed.), *Motivational psychology of human development* (pp. 187–211). Amsterdam: Elsevier.

Kuhl, J., & Fuhrmann, A. (1998). Decomposing self-regulation and self-control: The volitional components inventory. In J. Heckhausen & C. S. Deweck (Eds.), *Life span perspectives in motivation and control* (pp. 15–49). Mahwah, NJ: Lawrence Erlbaum Associates.

LeDoux, J. E. (1995). In search of an emotional system in the brain: Leaping from fear to emotion and consciousness. In M. S. Gazzaniga (Ed.), *The cognitive neurosciences* (pp. 1047–1061). Cambridge, MA: MIT Press.

Leontiev, A. N. (1981). The problem of activity in psychology. In J. V. Wertsch (Ed.), *The concept of activity in Soviet psychology* (pp. 37–71). Armonk, NY: Sharpe.

Levy, J. (1990). Regulation and generation of perception in the asymmetric brain. In C. Trevarthen (Ed.), *Brain circuits and functions of the mind* (pp. 331–348). New York: Cambridge University Press.

Lewin, K. (1951). *Field theory in social science.* New York: Harper and Row.

Luria, A. R. (1973). *The working brain.* Middlesex, England: Penguin Books.

Merleau-Ponty, M. (1968). *The visible and the invisible.* Evanston, IL: Northwestern University Press.

Mitchel, J. P., Macrae, C. N., & Gilchrist, I. D. (2002). Working memory and the suppression of reflexive saccades. *Journal of Cognitive Neuroscience, 14,* 95–103.

Muller, N. G., Machado, L., & Knight, R. T. (2002). Contribution of subregions of the prefrontal cortex to working memory: Evidence from brain lesions in humans. *Journal of Cognitive Neuroscience, 14,* 673–686.

Nakayama, K. (1994). James J. Gibson: An appreciation. *Psychological Review, 10,* 329–335.

Nozick, R. (2001). *Invariances: The structure of the objective world.* Cambridge, MA: Belknap.

Ochsner, K. N., Bunge, S. A., Gross, J. J., & Gabrieli, J. D. E. (2002). Rethinking feeling: An fMRI study of the cognitive regulation of emotion. *Journal of Cognitive Neuroscience, 14,* 1215–1229.

Oerter, R. (2000). Activity and motivation: A plea for a human frame motivation. In J. Heckhausen (Ed.), *Motivational psychology of human development* (pp. 57–78). Amsterdam: Elsevier.

Pascual-Leone, J. (1970). A mathematical model for the transition rule in Piaget's developmental stages. *Acta Psychologica, 32,* 301–345.

Pascual-Leone, J. (1987). Organismic processes for neo-Piagetian theories: A dialectical causal account of cognitive development. *International Journal of Psychology, 22,* 531–570.

Pascual-Leone, J. (1989). An organismic process model of Witkin's field-dependence-independence. In T. Globerson & T. Zelnikar (Eds.), *Cognitive style and cognitive development* (pp. 36–70). Norwood, NJ: Ablex.

Pascual-Leone, J. (1990). An essay on wisdom: Towards organismic processes that make it possible. In R. J. Sternberg (Ed.), *Wisdom: Its nature, origin and development* (pp. 244–278). New York: Cambridge University Press.

Pascual-Leone, J. (1991). Emotions, development, and psychotherapy: A dialectical constructivist perspective. In J. Safran & L. Greenberg (Eds.), *Emotion, psychotherapy, and change* (pp. 302–335). New York: Guilford.

Pascual-Leone, J. (1995). Learning and development as dialectical factors in cognitive growth. *Human Development, 38,* 338–348.

Pascual-Leone, J. (1996). Vygotsky, Piaget, and the problems of Plato. *Swiss Journal of Psychology, 55,* 84–92.

Pascual-Leone, J. (1997). Metasubjective processes: The missing *lingua franca* of cognitive science. In D. M. Johnson & C. E. Erneling (Eds.), *The future of the cognitive revolution* (pp. 75–101). New York: Oxford University Press.

Pascual-Leone, J. (1998). SSSs or functionalist modes of processing? A commentary on Kargopoulos and Demetriou's paper. *New Ideas in Psychology, 16,* 89–95.

Pascual-Leone, J. (2000a). Reflections on working memory: Are the two models complementary? *Journal of Experimental Child Psychology, 77,* 138–154.

Pascual-Leone, J. (2000b). Mental attention, consciousness, and the progressive emergence of wisdom. *Journal of Adult Development, 7,* 141–254.

Pascual-Leone, J., & Baillargeon, R. (1994). Developmental measurement of mental attention. *International Journal of Behavioral Development, 17,* 161–200.

Pascual-Leone, J., & Goodman, D. (1979). Intelligence and experience: A neoPiagetian approach. *Instructional Science, 8,* 301–367.

Pascual-Leone, J., Goodman, D., Ammon, P., & Subelman, I. (1978). Piagetian theory and neo-Piagetian analysis as psychological guides in education. In J. McCarthy Gallagher & J. A. Easley (Eds.), *Knowledge and development: Vol. 2: Piaget and education* (pp. 243–289). New York: Plenum.

Pascual-Leone, J., & Irwin, R. (1998). Abstraction, the will, the self, and models of learning in adulthood. In M. C. Smith & T. Pourchot (Eds.), *Adult learning and development: Perspectives from educational psychology* (pp. 35–66). Mahwah, NJ: Lawrence Erlbaum Associates.

Pascual-Leone, J., & Johnson, J. (1991). The psychological unit and its role in task analysis: A reinterpretation of object permanence. In M. Candler & M. Chapman (Eds.), *Criteria for competence* (pp. 155–187). Hillsdale, NJ: Lawrence Erlbaum Associates.

Pascual-Leone, J., & Johnson, J. (2001). *Manual for FIT: Figural Intersections Task.* Developmental Processes Laboratory, Department of Psychology, York University, Toronto, Ontario, Canada.

Pascual-Leone, J., Johnson, J., Baskind, S., Dworsky, S., & Severtson, E. (2000). Culture-fair assessment and the processes of mental attention. In A. Kozulin & Y. Rand (Eds.), *Experience of mediated learning: An impact of Feuerstein's theory in education and psychology* (pp. 191–214). New York: Pergamon.

Posner, M. I., & DiGirolamo, G. J. (1998). Executive attention: Conflict, target detection, and cognitive control. In R. Parasuraman (Ed.), *The attentive brain* (pp. 401–423). Cambridge, MA: MIT Press.

Renninger, K. A., Hidi, S., & Krapp, A. (Eds.). (1992). *The role of interest in learning and development.* Hillsdale, NJ: Lawrence Erlbaum Associates.

Rolls, E. T. (1995). A theory of emotion and consciousness, and its application to understanding the natural basis of emotion. In M. S. Gazzaniga (Ed.), *The cognitive neurosciences* (pp. 1091–1106). Cambridge, MA: MIT Press.

Rothbart, M. K., & Posner, M. I. (2001). Mechanism and variation in the development of attentional networks. In C. A. Nelson & M. Luciana (Eds.), *Handbook of developmental cognitive neuroscience* (pp. 353–363). Cambridge, MA: MIT Press.

Rypma, B., Berger, J. S., & D'Esposito, M. (2002). The influence of working memory demand and subject performance on prefrontal cortical activity. *Journal of Cognitive Neuroscience, 14,* 721–731.

Saarni, C., Mumme, D. L., & Campos, J. J. (1998). Emotional development: Action, communication, and understanding. In N. Eisenberg (Ed.), *Handbook of child psychology: Vol. 3. Social, emotional, and personality development* (pp. 237–309). New York: Wiley.

Schaefer, S. M., Jackson, D. C., Davidson, R. J., Aguirre, G. K., Kimberg, D. Y., & Thompson-Schill, S. L. (2002). Modulation of amigdalar activity by the conscious regulation of negative emotion. *Journal of Cognitive Neuroscience, 14,* 913–921.

Singer, W. (1994). Putative functions of temporal correlations in neocortical processing. In C. Koch & J. L. Davis (Eds.), *Large-scale neuronal theories of the brain* (pp. 201–237). Cambridge, MA: MIT Press.

Singer, W. (2001). Consciousness and the binding process. In P. Marijuan (Ed.), *Cajal and consciousness* (pp. 123–146). New York: New York Academy of Sciences.

Sperry, R. W. (1990). Forebrain commissurotomy and conscious awareness. In C. Trevarthen (Ed.), *Brain circuits and functions of the mind* (pp. 371–388). New York: Cambridge University Press.

Spinoza, B. (1995). *On the improvement of understanding. The ethics. Correspondence.* New York: Dover Publications.

Stuss, D. T. (1992). Biological and psychological development of executive functions. *Brain and Cognition, 20,* 8–23.

Szameitat, A. J., Schubert, T., Muller, K., & von Cramon, D. Y. (2002). Localization of executive functions in dual-task performance with fMRI. *Journal of Cognitive Neuroscience, 14,* 1184–1199.

Thompson, R. A. (1998). Early sociopersonality development. In N. Eisenberg (Ed.), *Handbook of child psychology: Vol. 3. Social, emotional, and personality development* (pp. 25–104). New York: Wiley.

Tolman, E. C., & Brunswik, E. (1966). The organism and the causal texture of the environment. In K. R. Hammond (Ed.), *The psychology of Egon Brunswik* (pp. 457–486). New York: Rinehart & Winston.

Ullmo, J. (1967). Les concepts physiques [The physical concepts]. In J. Piaget (Ed.), *Logique et connaissance scientifique* (pp. 623–705). Paris: Gallimard.

van Veen, V., & Carter, C. S. (2002). The timing of action monitoring processes in the anterior cingulate cortex. *Journal of Cognitive Neuroscience, 14*, 593–609.

Wapner, S., & Demick, J. (Eds.). (1991). *Field dependence-independence.* Hillsdale, NJ: Lawrence Erlbaum Associates.

Waters, E., Vaughn, B. E., Posada, G., & Kondo-Ikemura, K. (Eds.). (1995). Caregiving, cultural and cognitive perspectives on secure-based behavior and working models. *Monographs of the Society for Research in Child Development, 60*(2–3, Serial No. 244).

Walmsley, J., & Margolis, J. (1987). *Hot house people.* London: Pan Books.

Witkin, H. A., & Goodenough, D. E. (1981). *Cognitive styles: Essence and origin.* New York: International Universities Press.

9

▼▼▼▼▼▼▼

Dynamic Integration: Affect Optimization and Differentiation in Development

Gisela Labouvie-Vief
Wayne State University

María Márquez González
Universidad Autónoma de Madrid

A core problem of self- and emotion-regulation is how to strike a proper balance between two sometimes competing goals and strategies. On one hand, good self-regulation requires that individuals optimize affect. To do so ensures a sufficiently positive balance of affect and the ability to resiliently recover from negative affect. On the other hand, good self-regulation often requires that individuals forgo the personal need for affect optimization as they accept tension and delay of positive affect and endure prolonged negative affect in the interest of adapting to the external demands of reality.

The tension between these two goals is reflected in the fact that theories of affect and self-regulation often emphasize either one or the other of those strategies. Some researchers point out that regulating emotions through the maintenance of relatively high levels of positive and low levels of negative affect has been consistently related to better psychological outcomes and adjustment (Fredrickson, 1998; Isen, 1987; Salovey, Rothman, Detweiler, & Steward, 2000; Taylor, Kemeny, Reed, Bower, & Gruenewald, 2000; Watson & Pennebaker, 1989). Nevertheless, a growing body of research suggests that the processing of negative affect also is an important aspect of psychological health, and that exclusive focus on positive aspects of experience can be related to undesirable outcomes (Baumeister & Cairns, 1992; Norem, 1998; Showers & Kevlyn, 1999; Showers & Kling, 1996; Taylor & Brown, 1988; Weinberger, 1990).

Since maintaining positive affective balance, though one important adaptive outcome, is not the only criterion of well-being, there has been a growing emphasis on how individuals organize positive and negative affect in terms of differentiated cognitive-affective structures. Anticipated by Loevinger's (1976) work on ego development, this orientation recently has led to several proposals that focus on individuals' understanding and organization of affect terms across time, context, and emotion category or valence. Variously referred to by such terms as cognitive-affective complexity or differentiation (Labouvie-Vief, DeVoe, & Bulka, 1989; Labouvie-Vief & Medler, 2002), emotional awareness (Lane, 2000; Lane & Schwartz, 1987), or emotional intelligence (Mayer & Salovey, 1995), some authors (e.g., Labouvie-Vief, 1999; Labouvie-Vief & Medler, 2002; Ryan & Deci, 2001) have suggested that these terms refer to a second criterion of adaptive emotion regulation that is somewhat independent of valence-based ones, per se.

In this chapter, we suggest that ideally in development, individuals coordinate these modes into integrated cognitive-affective structures. Each of those modes implies a different criterion of what constitutes optimal functioning, however. The first mode, affect optimization, emphasizes hedonic quality through an emphasis on maximizing positive and minimizing negative affect. In contrast, the second mode, affect differentiation, emphasizes conceptual and emotional complexity, individuation and personal growth, and the ability to maintain open, elaborated and objective representations of reality even in the face of negative though vital information. We further suggest that these apparently different patterns of self and emotion development in adulthood can be reconciled by the assumption that ideally, the two modes of affect regulation cooperate in an integrated fashion, assuring well being through an emphasis on both hedonic tone and open, complex representations. In many cases, however, individuals may come to favor one mode over the other, creating less balanced and well-integrated regulation as they sacrifice a complex, objective representation of reality for positive affect, or else sacrifice positive affect for complexity. Such a lack of integration has important implications for describing individual differences in patterns of successful aging, and those individual differences, in turn, may have profound implications for physical and psychological health. Below, we summarize the general theoretical model of integration and its implications for examining adult age differences and age changes.

AFFECT AND COGNITION IN DEVELOPMENT: CONSTRUCTIVIST-DEVELOPMENTAL PERSPECTIVES

The paradox that positive affect may not be a sufficient criterion of well-being and adaptation has a long historical tradition. Since Freud's (1925/1963) suggestion that the demands of the Id's pleasure principle must be balanced by the objective and veridical function of the Ego's reality principle, many theoreticians have stressed that affective adaptation implies that we are constituted as dual human beings. On one hand, our inborn reflexes, affects, and proclivities appear to make us into machine-like automatons that react to the environment and in so doing maximize personal pleasure and minimize personal pain. On the other hand, we are able to endure and even embrace negative affect in the pursuit of growth and the creation of meaning. Thus, we are not merely reactive creatures but also able to proactively and consciously direct our growth, to act with self-determination and to strive for self-realization.

A Duality of Regulatory Strategies

While the more reactive aspect of affect is being emphasized by modern emotion theorists, its proactive and self-constructive aspect has been the focus of attention of cognitive-developmental approaches to self and affect. Spearheaded by Piaget's (1980) writings on affect, this approach has animated a body of writings suggesting that with advancing development, individuals consciously strive to transform their emotions and identity into systems that expand on original hereditary organizations and create more complex cognitive-affective structures (e.g., Fischer, Kenny, & Pipp, 1990; Kegan, 1982; Kohlberg, 1969; Labouvie-Vief, 1982; Loevinger, 1976; Selman, 1980). One aspect of that complexity concerns the ability to drive away from the comfort of the accustomed-to and to endure unfamiliar and affectively negative experience in an effort to eventually construct integrated cognitive-affective representations. How such integration can be achieved, however, often has remained a source of some disagreement, and theoreticians have tended either to point to the primacy of affect in directing cognition, or to else the capacity of cognitive representations to modulate affect and even alter its very nature.

The view basic to the integration offered in this chapter has been stimulated by Piaget's theory of cognitive-affective development. This may appear a paradoxical choice at first since, although Piaget has occasionally written on affect (e.g., Piaget, 1980), his theory of affect remains limited since it tends to make the affective dimension secondary rather than affording it the same powerful status that cognitive operations occupy. Even so, one reading of his theory is quite compatible with that of an emerging view of many modern emotion theorists who suggest that complex cognitive-affective structures emerge out of systems that are primarily instinct-based, reflex-like, and sensorimotor at the outset, but that in the course of development become increasingly integrated into higher-order cognitive control mechanisms (e.g., Fonagy, Gergely, Jurist, & Target, 2002; Labouvie-Vief, 1982, 1994; Metcalfe & Mischel, 1999; Schore, 1994; Sroufe, 1996). Before offering a more modern view of how such integration is accomplished, we focus in this section a relatively brief summary of the core processes that appear to drive this integration as it has been developed over the years by one of us (Labouvie-Vief, 1981, 1982, 1994).

A unique aspect of Piaget's view of affect is that it rejects any dualism between affect and cognition but claims that the two are like different sides of the same coin—that is, Piaget (1980) viewed affect as the dynamic aspect of cognition, or conversely, cognition as the structural aspect of emotions. That is, cognition structures the dynamics of emotional experience. As a consequence, as the cognitive system develops, so does the affective system. At the beginning are hereditary organizations and instinctual drives that provide the affective base at birth and tie affect to the survival function of the first adaptive mechanisms. This view is quite compatible with that of modern emotion theorists such as Ekman (1984), Izard (1997), or Tomkins (1980) who, following Darwin's lead, proposed that there are a limited number of basic, hard-wired, primary emotion systems. According to Piaget (for a summary, see Labouvie-Vief & DeVoe, 1991), however, these original affect systems like other sensorimotor schemas become reorganized so as to conserve and stabilize affect over larger segments of time and space and coordinate it with other affects. In this way, at the preoperational stage, representation and language allow emotions to be manipulated in an internal and imaginary way, as in symbolic play, when the child can rehearse aspects of experience that seem frightening. During concrete operations, Piaget (1980) suggested that children learn common rules about the socially appropriate display of affect and show the beginning of feelings concerning morality. The focus on a world of should is even more pronounced in adolescence when individuals are able to relate to interpersonal systems of regulation. Individuals invest emotions in abstract and collective ideals and guide their behavior according to complex plans that involve wide extension across time and space.

How do relatively simple cognitive-affective structures transform into complex ones related to complex goals and issues of self and identity? In his later work, Piaget (1980) extensively outlined such transformations in the cognitive realm, expanding on his earlier suggestions that transformations evolve as a result of an interplay of relatively reactive, equilibrium-maintaining and relatively proactive, equilibrium expanding (or disequilibrating) strategies. Each of those strategies involves a distinct way of relating to the world and processing information abstracted from it.

The interplay between equilibration and disequilibration is similar to the familiar interplay of strategies of assimilation and accommodation. When the individual functions in an "as usual" modality he or she is at equilibrium—reality is structured, from both cognitive and affective perspectives, in a way that is familiar and self-evident. This self-evidence, to be sure, is not necessarily a reflective one but can be rather automatic and reactive, inherent in accustomed-to ways of responding that are integrated into the self. The individual then functions in an assimilative mode that affirms a reality that is

already familiar and within one's conceptual reach—that is, already has been schematized into a well-integrated cognitive-affective structure. At the same time, this integrative function implies that knowledge that has not yet been schematized is negated—that is, gated out by being excluded from attention, or by being considered irrelevant or even faulty. This basic mode of functioning, then, is oriented towards keeping the self in a stable and inertial mode, maintaining associations that are familiar and close to the self. A control system of the kind just described is similar to a homeostatic system such as a thermostat that minimizes deviations from a set point. Such a system is called a feedback dampening or negative feedback system (e.g., Brent, 1978; Carver & Scheier, 1995; Powers, 1973; Pribram & Gill, 1976). This name derives from the fact that it acts to negate or reduce discrepancy, while affirming a particular set point or image of achievement (Miller, Galanter, & Pribram, 1960) through acting in such a way that the image of achievement is kept constant within a sufficiently small range of deviations.

An example is offered by the preoperational child who fails to conserve in the familiar beaker problem. The child focuses on a single perspective—say, width—of the beaker but in so doing gates out information relating to the second relevant dimension, height. Alternatively, she attends to the other perspective while gating out the former, without being able to consider the simultaneous transformations in both dimensions. However, at certain junctures of their development (and we will return to this issue immediately) individuals acknowledge the resulting errors in their own conceptual constructions. That is, they realize gaps in their knowledge, implying that familiar ways of organizing reality are being disequilibrated. Such disequilibration is not merely a passive process; rather, having grasped the implications of their gaps for possible expansion of their knowledge, individuals begin to actively drive away from equilibrium.

The active process of driving away from equilibrium implies that the individual shifts from a feedback-dampening mode to one that is aimed at amplification of affect and cognitive-affective information. The basic mode now is no longer affirmative and stability-maintaining, but an open one as the self actively turns to an exploration of novel information and associations. Such active disequilibration happens as individuals inhibit automated thoughts and behaviors and instead, begin a process of questioning, directed search, experimentation, and consequent revision of old schemas. This process of differentiation involves examining existing schemas and relating them to one's actions, to other schemas, and to new information in the external world. As a result of this process, individuals gradually create cognitive-affective schemas that are more differentiated, yet that involve many interconnections among the newly differentiated components.

Amplification can imply a degree of discomfort, conflict, or even crisis as the self ventures out into unexplored and unfamiliar territory—congruent with the frequent notion that developmental transitions can be related to a degree of distress, instability, and discontinuity. Yet eventually, a new level of relative stability is reached—as a result of the process of differentiating and interrelating, knowledge becomes reequilibrated or reintegrated at a new level. That new level again functions in an affirmative mode—that is, it is activated as a totality or integrated unit. However, that new level is more complex than the starting point, since the individual now both can affirm and negate former knowledge by relating it to a higher-order structure—that is, they can affirm not only the sameness of volume, but can relate that sameness to the changes in the separate dimensions. In that way, for example, the concrete operational child in the beaker conservation task immediately sees (or affirms) a constant volume even though its dimensions change; yet, when asked about the apparent contradiction with perception, the child can resolve that contradiction by pointing to the compensatory nature of increases–decreases in the two dimensions, stating something like "yes, it has become higher, but at the same time, it has become more narrow." Such a knowledge structure, then, is able to create a new organized system of inhibition and facilitation with the realization that each dimension (e.g., height and width) places constraints on the other, and the superordinate structure, the volume, only can be interpreted in the context of their interplay.

The resulting cognitive-affective schemas can be of extraordinary complexity. A good example of such complex cognitive-affective schemas is given by Kuhn's (1962) discussion of scientific paradigms, that serve not only a cognitive function of interpreting available knowledge, but also a social-emotional function. Thus Kuhn argued that when a paradigm prevails, it also serves the function of social-affective regulation. Those who adhere to the paradigm are considered competent or acceptable, while those who reject it are considered incompetent or even heretic. Less controversially than Kuhn's analysis, perhaps, are examples of such cultural symbol and knowledge systems as religions which bind together not only cognitive insight but also powerful affects (Pyszczynski, Greenberg, & Solomon, 2000).

Limits to Integration

The previous analysis has emphasized the potential for cognitive-affective integration. However, it is necessary here to add that such integration remains somewhat of an ideal; in reality, many factors can impede integration. Piaget (1955, 1962) himself noted this possibility when suggesting that development sometimes produces an overbalance of one or the other strategies. In the case of assimilation, this can result in a somewhat egocentric tendency to remain stuck in a private world, to represent and act so as to suit the self, and to distort reality to one's own needs. On the other hand, if there is an overbalance relying on the reinstatement of familiar (previously learned) conditions. Since such reinstatement involves highly automated networks, a total pattern can be activated *pars pro toto* even from fragments of the input to which the network was trained (Tucker, 1992; see also Clore & Ortony, 2000; Epstein & Pacini, 1999). In contrast, affect differentiation involves explicit appraisal as individuals differentiate schemas into their components that are processed in an individuating fashion—weighing and comparing different goals and outcomes in terms of whether they promote or thwart one's goals and desires; thus, attention is consciously directed to a systematic treatment of different dimensions of emotion-relevant information. As different goals are weighted, individuals' emotions themselves can change (Clore & Ortony, 2000). Hence this mode typically involves the unfolding of compact emotional information into blends of differentiated emotions, including different valences (e.g., Harter, 1999; Labouvie-Vief, Hakim-Larson, DeVoe, & Schoeberlein, 1989; Lane & Schwartz, 1987).

Another aspect that differentiates the modes is the way in which they create meaning (Bruner, 1986; Piaget, 1955; Werner, 1955). Affect optimization is inherently tied to personal experience or inner states of the individual. It appears to be especially closely related to the activation of emotions in settings that involve subjective and intersubjective experience that is relatively implicit—such as affective communication through facial gestures or prosodic features (Gianotti, 1999; Tucker, 1992; Vingerhoets, Berckmoes, & Stroobant, 2003). Hence meanings are inherently ineffable—experiential and nondeclarative, personal, and connotative. Affect differentiation, in contrast, is based on denotative, precise meanings. These meanings, moreover, are relatively formal and decontextualized through semantic structures and propositions. They refer less to intimate personal or interpersonal experience but rather represent experience in terms of relatively impersonal and conventional structures of meaning.

Related to the relatively personal–interpersonal versus relatively formal nature of meaning is a further difference of how the two modes are affected by learning and experience. Although optimization often applies to amygdala-based biological triggers (Metcalfe & Jacobs, 1998; Metcalfe & Mischel, 1999), these triggers can be conditioned to new ones through implicit learning processes that bypass consciousness. LeDoux (1996; LeDoux & Phelps, 2000) suggested that this implies a low road route, exemplified in the conditioning of fear reactions to tone. In this case, direct pathways from sensory cortex to amygdala provide subcortical circuits for learning, providing a quick and dirty processing road of high survival value in certain emergency situation. Such implicit learning also permits priming of the amygdala to evaluate subsequent information received along cortical pathways.

This low road contrasts with the high road cortical pathway in which prefrontal cortical mechanisms participate in behavior change through proc-

of accommodation, individuals may become excessively dependent on others to define aspects of reality for the self.

Even though Piaget addressed such limits to genuine integration, yet his theory has not fully explored the depth of affect and its possible role not only in facilitating such integration, but also in impeding it (Labouvie-Vief, 1994). Perhaps most significant is the fact that cognitive-developmental models tend to adopt a notion of integration that is primarily oriented by criteria of cognitive or formal fit. That integration in development is not primarily a cognitive achievement is a tenet basic to more psychodynamic approaches to development. These approaches emphasize that integration arises out of strengths of the self—a sense of basic self-worth and goodness of self, a core faith in the benevolence of others and reality in general—that are more directly emotional in nature—in particular emotions that arise out of the interpersonal world. Erikson (e.g., 1984) has referred to those mechanisms as ones that encourage a sense of basic trust and the resilience in emotion-regulation and self-regulation that emerges from this dimension, and modern attachment theory (e.g., Bowlby, 1978, 1989) has elaborated those mechanisms as they evolve out of the early relationship between parents and children. The basic sense of trust that hopefully emerges out of this core relationship in turn supports a positive self core that is able to integrate experience and afford resilience.

Considerations such as those previously mentioned suggest that the ability to integrate hinges not only on emerging cognitive capacities in a narrower and formal sense. Rather, cognitive capacities and accomplishments are embedded in an interpersonal and intersubjective frame that gives those skills validation and meaning (Labouvie-Vief, 1994). Does the self find a social environment that mirrors, affirms, and enhances emerging cognitive constructions, or one that opposes and undermines them? In the former case, integration of feeling and thinking will be enhanced but in the latter, individuals will need to search for defensive solutions that reflect a compromise between feeling and thinking. Thus, even though cognitive theories often describe cognition as a relatively isolated act in which the self interacts with inanimate objects, a more complete description of cognitive-affective development also needs to include how objects are related to an interpersonal and subjective world in which they acquire definition and meaning (see also Werner & Kaplan, 1962).

A related limitation of cognitive-developmental approaches rests in their assumption of what drives the tendency toward disequilibration, differentiation, and amplification. Piaget (1981), for example, assumed that the primary motives are purely information-related ones, such as surprise and interest that result from the realization that accustomed-to knowledge no longer works. In some sense, to be sure, this assumption is a unique strength, since it points to mechanisms of development that reside in positive motives toward openness, growth, and change. However, much literature suggests that differ-

entiation and amplification can be the result of emotions that are more negative, as well as more violent—emotions such as anger and rage, or fear and
terror that drive the individual toward differentiation in the pursuit of more
defensive goals of self-preservation. What is the difference in the processes of
differentiation that are more truly growth-oriented and ones that are aimed
at more defensive goals (see Baumeister, 1989; Fredrickson, 2001; Magai &
Haviland-Jones, 2002; Pyszczynski et al., 2000; White, 1969)?

Turning back to the analysis of the limitations of the cognitivist bias in
Piaget's theory, an important one is the fact that although in some contexts
Piaget (1980) discussed how cognitive development alters the very nature of
emotions, yet in others he devaluated the sensorimotor and figurative aspects
that are part and parcel of emotional experience. Thus his model retained
many hierarchical features according to which emotions are subordinated to
cognitions. A result is that whole domains of important emotional development are not considered; rather, they tend to be discounted as less developed,
more primitive ways of relating to reality. This is especially true of the nature
of symbolism that plays such a pervasive role in art, literature, myth, and re-
ligion. A result of this discounting is that the theory does not permit us to differentiate between relatively evolved and mature forms of these activities as
compared to relatively primitive and even pathological ones. Yet many recent
developments suggest that emotion-related domains themselves develop even
if they do not become representational in the same way that relatively formal
cognitions do (Labouvie-Vief, 1994; Schore, 1994). All of these factors require a model of cognitive-affective integration that is more explicit in highlighting dynamic features of cognition–affect relations.

GROWTH AS DYNAMIC INTEGRATION
OF OPTIMIZATION AND DIFFERENTIATION

In the previous section we suggested that the evolving cognitive system alters
the dynamics of emotional functioning, widening and broadening it, but also
altering it qualitatively. Of core importance in that process is the interplay between two core strategies, one aimed at deviation dampening, maintaining
equilibrium, and stability, the other at deviation amplification, disequilibrium, and change—two core processes we have referred to as optimization
and differentiation. In the current section, we draw on recent theories of self-
regulation and affect regulation to spell out how cognitive-affective schemas
coordinate the demands of strong affective activation on one hand with those
of careful, ego-oriented, and objective cognitive analysis. When are they able
to secure well-integrated functioning of the two systems and when, in contrast, do they fail to achieve an effective integration? In the current section,
we first discuss the general mechanism underlying this dynamic process of in-

tegration while in the following section, we apply this mechanisms t[
cussion of patterns of development and aging.

Two Modes of Processing

The notion that two modes of processing are orchestrated in affect regul
is congruent with much recent theorizing about the processing of social i[
mation (e.g., Chaiken & Trope, 1999; Clore & Ortony, 2000; Damasio, 1
Epstein & Pacini, 1999; LeDoux, 1996; Schore, 1994; Tucker, 1992) an[
flects the dual-process framework in cognitive science (Epstein, 1994; Sta
vich, 1999), which suggests the existence of two different cognitive archi[
tures with different functions and processing characteristics. According
that theorizing, information is processed in one of two modes. In one of th[
modes—the one we refer to as optimization—processing is essentially scl
matic. Relatively holistic and undifferentiated structures of knowledge a[
activated in an all-or-none, highly automatic way that requires relatively l[
resources. Processing is tightly integrated into heuristics and inherently tie
to personal meanings and the activation of emotional processes. In contrast,
second mode—the one we refer to as affect differentiation here—is based o[
systematic, effortful processing in which components of a knowledge structur[
can be accessed separately through processes of selective facilitation and inhibition, imparting on behavior a higher degree of choice and flexibility. This
mode involves more formal meanings that are elaborated through processes
of differentiation of already existing knowledge through selective facilitation
and inhibition.

The two modes are widely thought to constitute two general ways in which
information can be processed, and this is true of how emotional information
is processed, as well. Because of these general implications, Metcalfe and
Mischel (1999) referred to them as hot and cool systems. In the hot system,
affect optimization, information is tied intimately to personal inner states
such as affect. When this system is activated, information of high survival
value to the self is given priority, ensuring quick action in high emergency situations. Hence information is, in essence, organized hedonically—that is, pri-
oritized according to a good–bad, pleasure–pain polarity. In contrast, the
cool system involves a process of differentiation by which the automatic activation of inner states is interrupted and information is processed in terms of
semantic structures, problem solving, systematic appraisal, and deliberation—the evaluation of emotional information at a relatively conceptual and
representational level.

The two modes involve different ways of being activated. Affect optimization involves information that already is tightly integrated—whether as a result of biological predispositions or of experience. Thus it is relatively low in
differentiation. Appraisal of information is relatively implicit and automatic,

esses of inhibition and executive control. As already noted, this route to change has been of special interest to cognitive accounts of emotion (Lazarus, 1966, 1982, 1991; Lazarus, Averill, & Opton, 1970). It also has received a great deal of attention by many developmental psychologists who point out that emotion regulation changes as individuals acquire complex structures of emotion knowledge that involve differentiated logical relations that are explicitly and systematically structured. In the case of logical learning (Pascual-Leone, 1991), change is based on explicit principles whose mastery depends on the availability of cognitive resources.

Dynamic Integration Versus Degradation

Although the two modes appear to be based on different processing systems and may often function in parallel, in actuality they interact in many performances. It is widely assumed that the principle that constrains this interaction is the fact that the two modes of processing share a common processing mechanism with limited resources. At least, this appears to be true in tasks that require some kind of emotion or self-regulatory effort (Baumeister, 1989). Hence, a compensatory process comes into play that downregulates one process as another becomes more resource demanding.

The resulting interaction is captured by a generalization of the Yerkes-Dodson (1908) law as recently elaborated by Metcalfe and Mischel (1999). This law postulates a compensatory and curvilinear relationship between level of activation–arousal on one hand, and the degree to which complex, integrated behavior is possible (Labouvie-Vief, 2003). The resulting relationship is depicted in Fig. 9.1. Accordingly, when levels of emotional activation–arousal are low, complex and well-integrated thinking, planning, and remembering are possible. That is, reality can be described in terms of rela-

Activation and Complexity

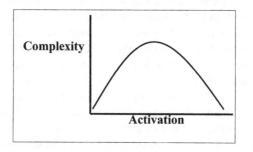

FIG. 9.1. Cognitive and behavioral organization and efficiency decrease as arousal increases beyond an optimal point (Duffy, 1957; Yerkes & Dodson, 1908).

tively cool cognitions. Thus the individual is able to think in a well-ordered way about aspects of experience and reality that are emotionally salient, including emotions themselves. However, in contrast to the facilitative effect of slight levels of arousal, when arousal rises to extremely high levels, it tends to render complex, cool cognitions and behavior dysfunctional and poorly integrated. Instead, automated, non-conscious schemas take over—presumably, because they are less susceptible to disruption by high levels of arousal (Norman, 1976). Thus, automatic mechanisms assert themselves that aim to maintain affect balance in a sufficiently positive range.

The principle of dynamic integration is one of the reasons that development ideally proceeds in a context of relatively low and well-regulated arousal or activation. Thus, experience needs to be assimilable if the individual is to explore and tolerate the disequilibrium such exploration implies. Yet, if the individual is able to accept a degree of disequilibration and engage in the kinds of exploratory, deviation amplifying strategies Piaget (1980) described, then new schemas can develop as the individual achieves a new level of equilibrium. These more complex schemas, in turn, expand the range of what is familiar and allow the individual to maintain relatively cool cognitions in contexts that would be extremely disruptive for the individual that does not have available similarly highly developed cognitive-affective schemas.

The principle of dynamic integration assumes, then, that an individual's ability to integrate new experience is constrained by a particular currently realized level of integrative ability or cognitive resources. As this level increases, activation previously experienced as disruptive no longer is experienced as disruptive. The effect of such increases in cognitive-affective complexity can be depicted by expanding the simple law described in Fig. 9.1. Figure 9.2 adds to Fig. 9.1 the assumption that individuals, over the course of their development or as a result of some other variable, may differ in such resources as the cognitive-affective structures they have available. This figure shows the degree to which cognition becomes disorganized or degraded for individuals low, medium, and high in resources. Thus at an equal level of emotional activation, this figure suggests that high resource individuals not only are overall more integrated, but also degrade their behavior–cognitions more gradually than those of medium and low resources. We turn to a discussion of the effects of degradation in the next section of this chapter, but before we do so, we first discuss what constitutes progression in cognitive-affective development.

Since the principle of dynamic integration suggests that a critical demand in the gradual expansion of cognitive-affective schemas is that arousal be regulated within levels that are not disruptive, it is critical that the development of these schemas be embedded in systems that provide appropriate levels of emotion modulation that the growing individual himself or herself cannot provide. This critical regulatory function of containment is provided, on one hand, by the graduation of experience typical of educational settings. How-

Dynamic Integration of Activation, Complexity, and Resources

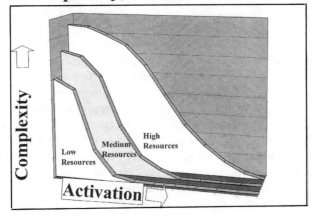

FIG. 9.2.   Resources moderate the degree to which integration is degraded.

ever, it also involves less formal ways in which affect is regulated—those that are provided by social networks such as parents and peers. Thus the availability or unavailability of such social-emotional resources is one important factor influencing the process of dynamic integration, along with purely cognitive resources.

Growth as Increasing Integration

How do the principles outlined above apply to development? In the first section of this chapter, we presented a general overview of Piaget's (e.g., 1955, 1962, 1965, 1967, 1980, 1981) notions of cognitive-affective development. Subsequent research in general has extended and elaborated Piaget's early notions of the relationship between cognitive and affective development. Thus relatively primary emotions are present early in development, but even so, they appear to emerge in concert with evolving cognitive capacities (see Labouvie-Vief & DeVoe, 1991; Lewis, 2000). For example, at birth emotions are mainly bipolar and concerned with distress or pleasure. As soon as 3 months of age, however, joy and excitement emerge as infants recognize familiar faces–events, or sadness when positive events stop. Surprise emerges a little later and is associated to the violation of an expected event or the appearance of an unexpected one. Fearfulness emerges a little later; it is thought to be a somewhat more complex emotion since it requires the comparison of one image with another one (Lewis, 2000).

The emergence of language is accompanied by yet more complex cognitive-affective systems. Harris (2000) noted that already at the age of 2, emotion utterances are not related to the immediate situation only, but about half of them are concerned with past, future, and recurrent feelings. This emergence of more complex cognitive-affective structures extending through time and space is supported by the development of several specific but interrelated competencies. One of those is the development of the self as a reflective agent—that is, somebody who has inner resources such as intentions, desires, and thoughts—in other words, an agent who possesses a mind that affords regulatory capacities. Second order feelings emerge that reflect the progressive emergence of a theory of mind (Baron-Cohen, Leslie, & Frith, 1985; Dennett, 1987; Leslie, 1987; Premack & Woodruff, 1978), which enables the child to understand others' minds in terms of concepts of intentional states such as beliefs and desires, and thus, to understand others as separate beings that can evaluate the self—self-conscious forms of regulation. Lewis (2000) suggested that in the second half of the second year of life the cognitive capacity of objective self-awareness emerges, with emotions such as embarrassment, empathy, and envy. Between 2 and 3 years of age, a somewhat more complex ability emerges—that of evaluating one's behavior according to a standard (external or internal). This marks the beginning of self-conscious evaluative emotions such as pride, shame, or guilt.

Lewis (2000) noted that the emergence of self-conscious evaluative emotions marks the beginning of new emotions that are different from so-called primary emotions, such as happiness or sadness. For example, if we fail at something, we might feel sad, but if we thought it was our fault, we might feel shame or guilt—emotions that already require a higher degree of reflective awareness and control. This capacity for reflective awareness and self-control becomes further differentiated and reintegrated as throughout childhood and into adolescence, individuals elaborate an inner world of mental and subjective processes such as thinking, wishing, goal-setting, and decision making.

A second dimension, self–other differentiation, is interwoven with the reflective one. This dimension indicates an increasing ability to experience others as individuals distinct from the self (see Kegan, 1982; Kohlberg, 1969; Selman, 1980). Yet this distinctness must be coordinated with the experience of intersubjective bonds that provide an important basis of security, meaning and self-validation. The experience of such intersubjective support hinges on the understanding of a reciprocity of intentions, thoughts, and values that is able to incorporate increasing diversity and differences. At first, the child is able to understand that others' feelings and judgments imply an evaluation of one's self, an understanding that matures into the realization that self and others share a world of emotions and inner perspectives that can differ yet

provide a basis for conflict free interchanges. For example, the adoption of standards for one's behavior, reflected in such emotions as shame and guilt, assumes the presence of an other, such as a parent, who expresses approval or disapproval, pleasure or displeasure, with the behavior and emotions of the self. Feeling such emotions, then involves the ability to take on the perspective of an other with an inner world of reflections and mental states somewhat independent of the self. At somewhat more advanced levels, that other becomes even more abstract. For example, the other of the adolescent is no longer the parent, but a larger social group whose shared system of values becomes the reference norm for one's own behavior. This third person perspective involves the ability to guide one's behavior by the standards of an abstract other such as a rule applicable to all, or a system of conventions that regulates the behavior of all possible members of the group.

Yet a third dimension implies increasing affective differentiation, or the degree to which the individual is able to differentiate and organize different, and often opposite emotions. At a low level, it involves global and polarized, static emotions. With advancing development, however, emotions are differentiated in terms of fine shadings and gradations as well as extensions across time and context. A particularly important aspect of such emotion differentiation is the ability to coordinate positive and negative affect is self and others. As the work of Fischer (e.g., Fischer & Ayoub, 1994) and Harter (1999) discovered, children's ability to coordinate positive and negative feelings in self and other demonstrates, is not mastered until adolescence.

By far the most active research on these three aspects of increasing cognitive-affective integration has been on the period from childhood to adolescence, but research on adults indicates that important developments continue well into adulthood (Labouvie-Vief, Chiodo, Goguen, Diehl, & Orwoll, 1995; Labouvie-Vief, Diehl, Chiodo, & Coyle, 1995). For example, the ability of adolescents to effectively regulate their emotions is limited by a tendency toward dualistic thinking in which a world of rational reflection is juxtaposed to a domain of emotions. Similarly, youth often assume that the third person perspective has universal status rather than being an empirical generalization or abstraction dependent, in many ways, on one's own personal experience with its particular cultural and historical situatedness. In a related fashion, in the domain of affective differentiation, they can confer polarized affective meanings to abstract systems such as ideologies. The resulting dualisms between mind and body, self and other, and good and bad are increasingly integrated as adults move beyond young adulthood and into midlife. Thus individuals attempt to search for a new notion of standards by relativizing their own autobiography and emotions in a system that takes on more pancultural and pan-historical dimensions. This evolving interpersonal perspective allows individuals to assume a shared and normative reality which changes during development from first dyadic exchanges, to the immediate social group, to a more abstract system or third person perspective, to set of relations and values defining all human beings. The ability to handle such complex understandings of emotion and to apply them toward continued examination and reconstruction of the self appears to increase well into middle adulthood. However, as discussed in the following, later life may bring a simplification of these high levels of affect complexity as intellectual and social resources become restricted.

Processes of Degradation in Development

Thus far we have assumed that development proceeds in a context of well-regulated emotions in such a way that the individual is protected from too extreme levels of activation, levels that would result in disruption and even disorganization of behavior. This is an idealized assumption, of course, that is not always realistic. Even so, it provides a useful framework for discussing less ideal forms of development and behavior, since these can be described as deviations from more well-integrated forms. In the remainder of this chapter, we outline general features of such well-integrated or degraded forms of integration and development. We then apply these features to a description of two major cases: less-than-optimal paths that result from regulatory failures that may be acquired early in development, and adaptive restrictions that appear to be related to resource restrictions related to aging.

Features of Degradation. The dynamic integration principle implies that if activation is at extreme levels, behavior and cognition can become thoroughly disorganized and dysfunctional. But what if activation is at a more intermediate level, neither sufficiently slight to support good integration nor extremely disruptive? A number of authors suggest that in this case the individual, while responding to a situation of some salience and even emergency, still is able to engage in fairly coherent action and to construct moderately adaptive representations. Nevertheless, that coherence is less than in well-integrated cases, as thinking and behavior become restricted to aspects that are most relevant to the individual's survival. Tucker (1992) has referred to this aspect of selective simplification as graceful degradation. Such forms of degradation of cognitive-affective responses remain adaptive in the sense that they enhance the individual's chances of survival and optimize his or her positive affect.

Since integration is the result of the collaboration of the two processes, optimization and differentiation, it is possible to distinguish two different ways of maintaining relatively graceful degradation. First, the individual can err on the side of optimization, sacrificing differentiation and complexity in an attempt to assert positive affect balance. Second, an individual can err on the side of differentiation, placing less emphasis on positive affect balance than on efforts at differentiation, analysis, and understanding. These forms of dynamic interplay and their more or less integrative solutions can best be conveyed by referring to Werner's (1957) developmental theory. In Werner's theory, integration presumes the presence of differentiated substructures; hence, positive affect in the absence of affect differentiation would not be described as integration, but rather as globality or underdifferentiation. In turn, an overemphasis on differentiation similarly would not be an integrative solution. Yet both underdifferentiation and overdifferentiation can be relatively organized and coherent patterns, in contrast to genuine disorganization (see Labouvie-Vief & Medler, 2002). What, specifically, are the features related to both of these solutions?

Processes of Degradation. The dynamic integration principle suggests that in the case of underdifferentiation, forms of representation reappear that maintain positive affect for the self, yet that also display some of the features of developmentally less complex behaviors. On a most general level, such degradation of complexity implies, as noted by Metcalfe and Mischel (1999), that strong emotional activation (especially fear about one's security) results in a higher level of automaticity of responses. Eysenck (1982) already proposed that high arousal biases retrieval processes toward high probability responses, while debilitating lower probability responses. Individuals' ability to engage in differentiated and analytical processing is constrained and instead they engage in simple, relatively undemanding processing that is based on relatively few available categories, schemas, and heuristics (e.g., Forgas, 2001; Kruglanski & Freund, 1983). As Metcalfe and Mischel (1999) put it, the hot system gets activated as the cool system is suspended.

The suspension of reflective control is accompanied by a reduction in the complexity of responses that can be discerned by several aspects. First, attention is restricted to features that are less abstract, and to a narrower range of features and as well as a narrower range of contexts. Specifically, attention is focused on those features and contexts that are most personally significant—following the dictum that even in decline there often is a marvelously adaptive restriction to what is most vital and essential in securing survival. Easterbrook's (1959) classic theory also suggested that overarousal narrows the range of information an organism processes (from peripheral toward central information)—central here can refer to information that is more critical to the self's survival. Hence, there is an overall narrowing of the attentional field to what is most self-relevant.

A second and related feature of complexity degradation is a reduction in the complexity of affect. Paulhus and Lim (1994), for example, suggested that as arousal increases, the extremity of evaluative judgments increases, and the dimensionality of judgments decreases. Often, this increase in extremity results in greater polarization of affect. For example Paulhus and Levitt (1987) showed that presentation of emotionally charged distractor words leads to higher endorsement of positive trait descriptors, but decreases in the endorsement of negative ones.

One aspect closely related to increasing affect extremity is a polarization of the interpersonal world, or a decrease in the ability to represent the self and others in terms of reciprocal relationships among individuals who have different though similarly valuable perspectives. Thus decreases in reflective control have been linked to a higher likelihood to engage in stereotypic thinking—a form of thinking that denies reciprocity of perspectives. Similarly, a large number of studies suggest that threats to one's sense of security, such as reminders of one's mortality, often are related to a number of distortions in the interpersonal realm such as ingroup–outgroup polarization, stereotyping of members of other ideological, ethnic, and religious groups (see Pyszczynki et al., 2000). In a similar fashion, threats to individuals' attachment security (see Mikulincer & Horesh, 1999; Mikulincer & Shaver, 2001) are likely to engage in stereotypes and disruption of emphathic responses. Such aspects of the degradation of cognitive complexity have been termed pseudospeciation by Erikson (1984), suggesting that they deny that different ideological, religious, cultural, or racial groups share in the same common human heritage.

From a more modern emotion-theoretical perspective, such narrowing makes good adaptive sense, since strong arousal usually is the result of situations that pose a threat to the well-being or even survival of the self. As Selye pointed out long ago (e.g., Selye, 1978), such situations stimulate defensive emergency responses in which the individual's resources are focused on the immediate and self-relevant task of restoring equilibrium and securing survival. In that precise sense, all of the previous constitute defensive responses—that is, responses that, even though they are locally adaptive, nevertheless involve a restricted range of cognition–emotion integrations.

Yet note that another solution is possible. Rather than opting for optimization, the individual may become concerned with understanding and figuring out or maintaining a differentiated and fairly objective picture of reality. For example, he or she may turn to a careful analysis of the different possible causes that may be related to activation in an attempt to reduce its level to more bearable levels. In that case, the individual may not be able to reduce levels of activation to relatively comfortable levels. In other words, he or she may fail to achieve integration by remaining stuck in a cycle of ruminative attempts to reduce activation. Such emphasis on objective and veridical representation of reality is often related to higher levels of negative affect and depression (Taylor & Brown, 1988). They also can represent a form of degradation since it hinders positive integration.

INTEGRATION AND DEGRADATION
IN DEVELOPMENT AND AGING

Styles of Regulation

We have thus far assumed that the dynamic integration principle operates according to a dynamic process by which the degree of complexity and integration of cognitive-affective representations are not fixed, but respond to moment-to-moment fluctuations. In this way, the tradeoff between affect optimization and affect differentiation describes a dynamic interplay that usually functions in a resilient way, shifting from temporary arousal to resilient recovery (Selye, 1978). We assume that such fluctuation is a normal and adaptive response to the ups and downs of affective activation, and characterizes psychologically healthy individuals, as well as ones less healthy. This state-like dynamic character usually takes place outside of the consciousness of the individual and provides a highly automatic and nonconscious but flexible and vital means by which the organism can adjust to changing demands.

Even though this interplay overall is an adaptive one, it does mimic certain regressive features of growth and development. This regression-like aspect reflects, however, fairly naïve forms of fragmentation that are a natural part of early development. Such regressive features can take on a more motivated and stable, and hence defensive, form—namely, in cases where continued anxiety and overactivation become habitual. In such cases, one should observe systematic deviations from a pattern of integration.

We recently turned to an examination of such stylistic deviations (Labouvie-Vief & Medler, 2002). To do so, we defined, in the context of an ongoing longitudinal-sequential study, two regulation components, affect optimization and cognitive-affective complexity (affect complexity, in short) through a factor analysis of coping and defense variables from the California Psychological Inventory (CPI; Gough & Bradley, 1996). Briefly, high optimizers are individuals characterized by minimizing feelings. They do not engage in inappropriate behavior and fantasy, do not attend to feelings and nonrational process in a rich and flexible way, and tend to ignore unpleasant facts. However, they also are low in doubt and find it easy to make decisions. Individuals high on complexity–differentiation are able to bring intellectual analysis to emotions, both in ways that are integrative and adaptive and in ones that reflect retreats from affect through rationalization and intellectualization. At the same time, they are high in tolerance of ambiguity and low in repression. Crossing these two dimensions yielded four distinct regulation styles reflecting the way in which individuals can coordinate these dimensions. Through factor analytic and cluster analytic methods, we (Labouvie-Vief & Medler, 2002) have identified four such styles or groups.

The first, or integrated (high complexity, high optimization) group, presents a style in which individuals combine affective differentiation with an emphasis on affect optimization. These individuals maintain high levels of positive affect and well-being and are socially well adjusted. At the same time, they combine this with an attitude of openness and give cognitive-affective representations that are complex and that integrate positive and negative information.

The integrated group contrasts with two groups that are less well integrated. The complex (high complexity, low optimization) are tolerant, open, and complex, yet show signs of less positive adjustment such as lower positive affect and social relationships. These individuals appear to marshal all their cognitive resources to cope with a core sense of social inadequacy and isolation. The self-protective (low complexity, high optimization) on the other hand, have high levels of positive affect and judge their relationships as positive, yet they show low levels of complexity as indicated by low tolerance and high denial and repression. The fourth or dysregulated (low complexity, low optimization) group, finally, is overall most poorly adapted, showing both low complexity and low social-emotional adjustment.

In a subsequent study (Labouvie-Vief, Zhang, & Jain, 2003), we validated these four groups in terms of an additional set of variables and both European and African Americans. Significant group comparisons indicated that the integrated subgroup scored high in positive affect but low in negative affect, had high well-being, high scores on good impression and empathy, and high self-rated health. In contrast, the dysregulated scored lowest on all of these variables, except on negative affect, on which they score highest. However, the self-protective and the complex displayed more mixed patterns that nevertheless are fairly coherent. While the complex and the self-protective differed in negative affect, they did not differ in positive affect nor in self-rated health. However, compared to the complex, the defended placed less emphasis on personal growth but more on environmental mastery. They also obtain higher scores on good impression, but lower scores on empathy, compared to the complex. Both groups are also less likely to have secure attachment than the integrated, but score higher than the dysregulated.

These data lend support to our contention that a complex style is one that is open and involves less distortions of intersubjective balance. In addition, they indicate that one of the major aspects differentiating the groups is how they deal with negative affect, even though they do not significantly differ in terms of positive affect. The self-protective tend to dampen negative affect, while the complex amplify it. This difference is further demonstrated by examining the relationship of the cognitive-affective complexity and optimization dimensions to life history variables that indicate how individuals construct their autobiography. Results indicated that optimizers report that their life is not characterized by major negative life events and turning points, such as emotional problems, loss of friends, experience with severe punishment or discrimination, and identity crises. In contrast, those high in cognitive-affective complexity describe their lives as containing major negative experiences such as severe punishment and discrimination and by major turning points such as changes in self-concept, spiritual belief, or social status. These data confirm those of others who report that individuals of high conceptual complexity (as assessed by ego level) are more likely to give constructions of their lives as complex and as involving difficult and life changing events (Helson & Roberts, 1994; McAdams, 2001). At this time, we do not know if the difference reflects the fact that complex individuals construct more differentiated representations of their life course as a result of their rich intellectual resources, or if their experience of negative events leads them to marshal these resources in an attempt to cognitively master a difficult life history.

The four groups in many ways resemble similar subgroups identified in Helson's research (Helson & Srivastava, 2001; Helson & Wink, 1987). In Helson and Wink's (1987) work, these subgroups were identified as a combination of two dimensions. One of those represents smooth adaptation to the social world, the other intrapsychic development and independence from normative values. More recently, Helson and Srivastava (2001) described these types as four identity styles: achievers who value both openness and growth and environmental mastery (tradition, security, and conformity); conservers who value environmental mastery but not personal growth; seekers who value personal growth over environmental mastery; and the depleted who score low on either of these two dimensions. Like the styles identified in our research, these groups also display characteristic differences in how they organize positive and negative affect, the seekers aimed at amplifying affect and the conservers at dampening negative affect.

In general, the regulation styles we have identified in our research appear to represent systematic individual differences in how individuals structure their lives and how they cope with a multitude of emotional experiences. Our results indicate that to rely on positive affect as a primary criterion of well-being and positive development may not be sufficient, but that individuals may organize the valence of emotions in different characteristic ways. Beyond emotional experience per se, these ways of organizing positive and negative emotions may form the basis of characteristic ways of constructing self and identity. Our results show that these style differences are more important than chronological age, and also that group membership remains fairly constant over a 6-year period. However, the causes associated with change–constancy over time remain to be explored in future research.

The notion that individual differences related to affect regulation reflect systematic differences in identity and personality is congruent with much existing literature. Individual differences in affect complexity may run in parallel with other differences in more classic personality variables. Emotional complexity of the self has been found to be associated with higher levels of education and intelligence, openness to experience and more reflective and less avoidant coping strategies (Lyster, 2001). Kang (2002) found that well-differentiated emotional experience, one of the features defining affect complexity, was associated with private self-consciousness, openness to experience, empathic tendencies, cognitive complexity, range of emotions experienced in everyday life, and interpersonal adaptability. Bacelar (1999) found openness to experience and meaning-making to be related to adult cognitive complexity. His finding that life events and person characteristics were better predictors than age of adult cognitive complexity led him to the conclusion that more attention should be paid to the increasing differences within age groups rather than between age groups.

Affect complexity may also be related to sensation-seeking. Cognitive complexity, a concept related to that of affect complexity, and preference for complexity have been found to be highly associated with sensation-seeking tendencies and nonconformity (Coren & Suedfeld, 1995; Zuckerman, Neary, & Brustman, 1970). Very relatedly, individual differences in need for cognition (Cacioppo & Petty, 1982) may contribute to explain differences in affect complexity. In its modern conceptualization, need for cognition refers to an individual's tendency to seek, engage in and enjoy effortful cognitive endeavors (Cacioppo, Petty, Feinstein, & Jarvis, 1996). In their extensive review of the literature on the construct, Cacioppo et al. (1996) described different empirical findings regarding the association of need for cognition with other variables. In this sense, people high in need for cognition have been found to be curious and sensation-seekers and to have active and exploring minds (Olson, Camp, & Fuller, 1984), to formulate complex attributions (Petty & Jarvis, 1996), to have intrinsic motivation to engage in effortful cognitive endeavors (Amabile, Hill, Hennessey, & Tighe, 1994), to be open to actions, ideas, feelings, and values (Berzonsky & Sullivan, 1992), and to desire new experiences that stimulate thinking (Venkatraman, Marlino, Kardes, & Sklar, 1990). Although there is still a lack of studies analyzing the relationships between emotional variables and need for cognition, initial findings from studies on alexithymia suggest that need for cognition is associated with a higher capacity to identify and communicate feelings and to discriminate these feelings from bodily sensations (Taylor, Bagby, & Parker, 1992). Other studies have found negative associations between need for cognition and social anxiety, especially in elderly people (Mueller & Grove, 1991; Mueller & Johnson, 1990) and neuroticism (Dornic, Ekehammar, & Laaksonen, 1991). Self-esteem seems to be positively related to need for cognition (Kernis, Grannemann, & Barclay, 1992; Mueller & Grove, 1991).

Creativity and originality or number of divergent thinking responses have also been found to be related to preference for complexity in the artistic–aesthetic field (Rawlings, Twomey, Burns, & Morris, 1998). Analyzing creative problem solving in high school students, Pufal-Struzik (1996) found demand for varied stimulation (adventure, novelty, risk) to be associated with cognitive flexibility and complexity, nonconformism and spontaneity, as well as tolerance for cognitive incompatibilities.

Optimization, Complexity, and Aging

Although in the research on regulation styles, the role of group membership seemed to outweigh that of age, our results also showed that age did matter. When comparing young, middle aged, and old adults, our results indicate that among the older age group, a significantly smaller number of individuals falls into the complex group, while a disproportionately high number falls into the self-protective group. Our interpretation of this finding is that, as individuals grow older and experience declines in cognitive-affective complexity, they tend to rely more strongly on optimization strategies. Indeed, our longitudinal data indicate that among the old, 6-year declines in cognitive-affective complexity predict increases in optimization, lending support to such a compensatory interpretation (Labouvie-Vief et al., 2003).

The notion that changes in cognitive resources associated with normal aging produce lower integration and more degradation is in line with the dynamic integration principle. A paradigm case of such a change in resources is that of normal aging. In the Labouvie-Vief (Labouvie-Vief, Chiodo, et al., 1995; Labouvie-Vief, Diehl, et al., 1995) research on life span changes in cognitive-affective complexity, the initial expectation was that the kinds of positive developments apparent in the young to middle adulthood range would continue into later life. However, the data clearly suggested that this was not the case. From about age 60 onward, affect complexity appeared to decline, a pattern we recently confirmed with longitudinal data (Labouvie-Vief, Zhang, & Jain, 2003). In retrospect, however, this growth-then-decline pattern makes good theoretical sense given the cognitive-developmental cast of this work, since a plethora of data suggests that older individuals suffer from deficits in working memory (Hasher & Zacks, 1988; Mitchell, Johnson, Raye, Mather, & D'Esposito, 2000; Salthouse, 1994; Shimamura, 1995), and inhibitory (Hasher, Stoltzfus, Zacks, & Rypma, 1991; McDowd, Oseas-Kreger, & Filion, 1995) and executive control (Rabbitt & Lowe, 2000; West, 1996), as well as evidencing decline in the neurobiological structures (Cabeza, 2002; Raz, 2000) that support these functions. Indeed, as we discuss later in this section, patterns of growth-then-decline in cognitive-affective differentiation–complexity are in line with a wide body of emerging data on the role of cognition in emotion regulation. Nevertheless, a significant body of evidence shows that even though cognitive-affective complexity decreases in later life, increasing age is related to linear increases in well-being (Carstensen, 1991; Davis & Smith, 1995; Diehl, Coyle, & Labouvie-Vief, 1996; Lucas & Diener, 2000; Mroczek & Kolarz, 1998; Ryff, 1989; Staudinger, Marsiske, & Baltes, 1995). Such data suggest that the ability to dampen negative and maximize positive affect may be quite independent of cognitive-affective complexity, again providing support to the notion that affect differentiation and optimization refer to rather distinct processes that can remain dissociated. To examine the nature and cause of such dissociations thus remains an important aspect of developmental theory.

The tradeoff between optimization and differentiation can offer an integration of the dual pattern (linear increase, curvilinear rise-and-drop) of aging and affect regulation discussed previously. Thus it is possible that the widely documented limitation of complex cognitive resources in later life plays a critical factor in regulating arousal if older individuals cannot rely on relatively overlearned or crystallized cognitive-affective schemas. In accordance with the hot–cool system distinction and the principle of dynamic integration, some lifespan researchers emphasizing the optimization criterion propose that improvements in affect balance in later life reflect older individuals' tendency to have a wealth of well-integrated schemas. Relying on these schemas allows them to maintain lowered arousal levels through more effective antecedent rather than less effective and more disruptive consequent control (Gross, 1998; Gross et al., 1997).

Research on social cognition and aging has indeed shown that older adults rely more heavily on scripts in the encoding of events (Hess, Donley, & Vandermaas, 1989), but show poorer memory performance than young people with information that cannot easily be integrated in preexisting knowledge structures (Hess & Tate, 1992). In the same line, older adults are more likely than younger ones to falsely recognize words semantically associated with sets of studied words (Norman & Schachter, 1997) and pictures categorically related to previously presented pictures (Koutstaal & Schachter, 1997) as studied or presented, respectively. Johnson, Hashtroudi, and Lindsay (1993) explained these findings by means of an age-related decline in the capacity to engage in effortful, resource-consuming evaluation processes that can help identify the origins of memories (source memory). Waddell and Rogoff (1981) found that age differences in memory were lower if test stimuli are more meaningfully organized, what, once again, suggests that older adults are able to rely on general knowledge, maybe as a mean to potentiate their recall.

Reliance on the familiar also can serve an affect-regulating function by protecting the aging individual from exposure to unfamiliar and unstructured situations that may arouse difficult to manage affect. Such a tradeoff function was suggested in 1973 by Lawton (Lawton & Nahemow, 1973): individuals, as they experience restrictions in inner resources (competence) can maintain positive affect by simplifying their environments. In a similar fashion, as individuals experience reductions in affect differentiation, they can maintain a strategy of affect optimization, as long as they reduce the demands made on them by their external environment (Labouvie-Vief, 1999; Schaie, 1998). Further, older individuals appear to maximize positive affect by simplifying and optimizing their social networks (Carstensen, 1993; Carstensen, Gross, & Fung, 1998). More generally, as Baltes and Baltes (1990) suggested, aging individuals can adjust to increasing resource restrictions by restricting their goals and activities or becoming more and more selective; at the same time, they can compensate for some losses by adopting simplifying strategies. Thus, researchers emphasizing the affect complexity–differentiation criterion suggest that after a rise in affect complexity from young to middle adulthood, older individuals' general cognitive restrictions can lead to a degradation and simplification of cognitive-affective structures as suggested by Blanchard-Fields (1999), Hess (1994, 1999), and Labouvie-Vief (2003; Labouvie-Vief & Medler, 2002).

Taken conjointly, the combined pattern of increases in affect optimization and decreases in affect differentiation suggests that later life involves a compensatory relationship between the arousal regulating function of optimization and the cognitive resources that can be brought to bear on regulation. Overall, such compensation allows individuals to maintain positive affect, yet with reduced flexibility—in other words, by degrading their representations of reality.

What evidence suggests that possible deficits of regulation may play a role in older individuals? In a recent study, we (Wurm, Labouvie-Vief, Rebucal, & Koch, 2003) examined the hypothesis inherent in the dynamic integration principle that in less familiar situations older individuals' lowered complexity may make it more difficult to process highly arousing–activating information. To test this hypothesis we (Wurm et al., 2003) used Bradley and Lang's (1999) library of emotion words rated for arousal and valence to create an emotional Stroop task. Specifically, younger and older individuals were presented with the words printed in different colors and instructed to read the color of the word. Findings showed an age by arousal interaction. There were no arousal level differences for the young whose mean was 676 msec/word. In contrast, the older showed a significant rise of reading times for the high arousal condition (923 msec for high arousal, 891 for low, 887 for medium). These results indicate that older individuals may have a problem inhibiting arousal in novel situations, especially if those involve relatively high levels of activation. As Eisdorfer (1968) showed, older individuals seem to experience more disruption from arousal than do younger ones.

It might be objected that our emotional Stroop data reflect the relatively low structure of the task we used, but difficulty with arousal in the older individual can also occur in tasks that involve good structure but using a sample with more highly arousing stimuli than ones often used in research on emotion and aging. An example is a recent study by Kunzmann (Kunzmann & Grün, 2003) in which young and old adults watched a brief movie about a woman confronted with a diagnosis of early signs of Alzheimer's and the need to make provisions for her expected decline. This quite dramatic stimulus produced significantly more sadness in the older than the young adults, suggesting that conclusions about the generalized ability to maintain positive and ward off negative emotions in later life may not be warranted; rather, affect regulation will depend to a great degree on how emotion is elicited.

If resource restrictions resulting in decreased inhibitory and reflective control play a role in such regulatory deficits, then degraded cognitive-affective representations should widely occur in older populations. One consequence of such simplification is a tendency to become more polarized affectively, neglecting negative information while favoring positive information (Carstensen et al., 1998; Carstensen, Isaacowitz, & Charles, 1999). Such positive distortion was shown in a study by Mather, Shafir, and Johnson (2000), who found that older people retrospectively distorted memories, recalling options they had actually chosen over ones they had discarded. Thus the emotion-regulation function of selectively attending to positive information is traded off for an increasing distortion of memory. That such an emphasis on affect optimization contains a compensatory component was also shown in our own research indicating that over a 6-year span, decreases in affect complexity predicted increases in optimization (Labouvie-Vief et al., 2003; see also Labouvie-Vief & Medler, 2002).

One specific way in which lowered reflective control is evidenced is in older individuals' increased reliance on stereotypes. In a recent study, Mather, Johnson, and De Leonardis (1999) showed that aging individuals' poor source monitoring leads to greater stereotype reliance in the elderly. In a similar fashion, Von Hippel, Silver, and Lynch (2000) found that elderly individuals relied more heavily on stereotypes even when instructed not to do so. The Von Hippel et al. (2000) study further showed, as would be expected from the principle of dynamic integration, that this process is entirely automatic and may occur despite the consciously held values individuals adhere to. Indeed, many older individuals were bothered by their automatically activated stereotypes.

Older adults' tendency to give relatively stereotypic and less-differentiated snap judgments about others has also been emphasized in Blanchard-Fields' (1999) research on attributional style across the adult life span. In a series of studies, Blanchard-Fields and colleagues observed that older adults (and adolescents) made less differentiated or dialectical attributional explanations than young and middle-aged adults (see also Follett & Hess, 2002). This was especially true in negative relationship outcomes, where the elderly tended to attribute the cause of the negative outcome more to internal characteristics of the primary agent than young adults did (Blanchard-Fields, 1994; Blanchard-Fields, Baldi, & Stein, 1999; Blanchard-Fields & Norris, 1994). Blanchard-Fields and Norris (1994) suggested that this finding reflects older individuals' strong reliance on salient sociocultural schemas, leading them to focus more on violations of the social rules (dispositional judgments). This finding is consistent with a recent study by Rahhal, May, and Hasher (2002) indicating that older individuals selectively attend to information that highlights moral values such as truth and character. Such reliance on standards, norms, and rules may reflect the fact that dispositional attributions require less effort and consume less cognitive resources than more complex dialectical ones that integrate more contextual and causal information (Gilbert, Palham, & Krull, 1988).

The hypothesis that an age-related reduction in processing efficiency underlies a host of affective processing data is congruent, then, with much available research. Even so, according to Hess (2001), it may not be the age-related reduction in processing efficiency per se that is explaining some of these data, but rather the motivational shift this reduction brings with it: a heightened motivation for preserving available resources and engaging in activities and tasks that minimize effort. Hess (2001) proposed the construct personal need for structure (PNS) to account for this dispositional preference or "desire for simplicity in both cognitive activities and structures" (p. 482). The PNS has been found to be related to less complex ways of organizing information (Neuberg & Newsom, 1993) and spend less time processing schema-inconsistent information (Hess, Follett, & McGee, 1998), among other findings. The documented age-related increment in the selectivity of cognitive activities (Baltes, 1997), situations (Gross et al., 1997), or relationships and social partners (Carstensen, 1991) may also be consequences of such an age-related motivational shift that may be only partially accounted for by cognitive resource declines (see Hess, Rosenberg, & Waters, 2001).

CONCLUSIONS

In the present chapter, we have suggested that well-being and positive self-regulation require the coordination of two strategies of regulation. One, affect optimization, is aimed at dampening negative while maximizing positive affect. The second, cognitive-affective differentiation, has as its primary aim the formation of objective representations of reality. We proposed that the ability to coordinate these two strategies yields integration. The capacity for integration is fostered at low to intermediate levels of emotional activation but impeded at extreme levels of activation, when integration yields to systematic forms of degradation, involving distortions of intersubjectivity such as ingroup–outgroup and stereotype formation. This dynamic mechanism of compensation can be altered by the availability of cognitive resources, such as age-related shifts in processing capacity or habitual mechanisms of less-than-optimal regulation.

The principle of dynamic integration is, as its core, a normal principle of affect regulation and equilibrium maintenance by which organisms can respond flexibly to variations in affect and engage in proper emergency responses. However, as a result of normative cognitive development or individual differences in self-regulatory capacity, individuals can come to habitually adopt more or less integrated forms of regulation. To demonstrate relatively permanent movements to higher integration, we discuss cognitive-affective growth from childhood to adulthood, while a relatively permanent movement to degradation may occur in later life when individual's resources decline. However, these general patterns are likely to be modified by relatively enduring individual differences patterns or regulation styles.

The proposed theory offers a coherent process-oriented view of integrated and defensive forms of affect regulation. While being process oriented and applicable to relatively microlevel experimental interactions of affect and cognitive resources, it also can be extended to more macroanalytical processes of self, personality, and development. Thus, it implies a plethora of rich suggestions for the study of integrated development across the life span, as well as mechanisms and causes for more degraded and defensive forms of development. To explore these implications for a process-oriented analysis of cognition-affect relations across the life span forms the focus of our current research.

ACKNOWLEDGMENT

Preparation of this chapter and the research reported in it was supported by a NIA grant (RO1 AG009203) to the first author.

REFERENCES

Amabile, T. M., Hill, K., Hennessey, B. A., & Tighe, E. (1994). The work preference inventory: Assessing intrinsic and extrinsic motivational orientations. *Journal of Personality and Social Psychology, 66*, 950–967.

Bacelar, W. (1999). Age differences in adult cognitive complexity: The role of life experiences and personality. *Dissertation Abstracts International, Section B: The Sciences & Engineering, 59*, 4505.

Baltes, P. B. (1997). On the incomplete architecture of human ontogeny: Selection, optimization, and compensation as foundation of developmental theory. *American Psychologist, 52*, 366–380.

Baltes, P. B., & Baltes, M. M. (1990). Psychological perspectives on successful aging: The model of selective optimization with compensation. In P. B. Baltes & M. M. Baltes (Eds.), *Successful aging: Perspectives from the behavioral sciences* (pp. 1–34). New York: Cambridge University Press.

Baron-Cohen, S., Leslie, A. M., & Frith, U. (1985). Does the autistic child have a theory of mind? *Cognition, 21*, 37–46.

Baumeister, R. F. (1989). The optimal margin of illusion. *Journal of Social and Clinical Psychology, 8*, 176–189.

Baumeister, R. F., & Cairns, K. J. (1992). Repression and self-presentation: When audiences interfere with self-deceptive strategies. *Journal of Personality and Social Psychology, 62,* 851–862.

Berzonsky, M. D., & Sullivan, C. (1992). Social-cognitive aspects of identity style: Need for cognition, experiential openness, and introspection. *Journal of Adolescent Research, 7,* 140–155.

Blanchard-Fields, F. (1994). Age differences in causal attributions from an adult developmental perspective. *Journals of Gerontology, Series B: Psychological Sciences & Social Sciences, 49,* P43–P51.

Blanchard-Fields, F. (1999). Social schemacity and causal attributions. In T. M. Hess & F. Blanchard-Fields (Eds.), *Social cognition and aging* (pp. 219–236). San Diego, CA: Academic Press.

Blanchard-Fields, F., Baldi, R., & Stein, R. (1999). Age relevance and context effects on attributions across the adult life span. *International Journal of Behavioral Development, 23,* 665–683.

Blanchard-Fields, F., & Norris, L. (1994). Causal attributions from adolescence through adulthood: Age differences, ego level, and generalized response style. *Aging, Neuropsychology, and Cognition, 1,* 67–86.

Bowlby, J. (1978). Attachment theory and its therapeutic implications. *Adolescent Psychiatry, 6,* 5–33.

Bowlby, J. (1989). The role of attachment in personality development and psychopathology. In S. I. Greenspan & G. H. Pollock (Eds.), *The course of life, Vol. 1: Infancy* (pp. 229–270). Madison, CT: International Universities Press.

Bradley, M. M., & Lang, P. J. (1999). Affective norms for English words (ANEW). Gainesville, FL: The NIMH Center for the Study of Emotions and Attention, University of Florida.

Brent, S. B. (1978). Motivation, steady-state, and structural development: A general model of psychological homeostasis. *Motivation and Emotion, 2,* 299–332.

Bruner, J. (1986). *Actual minds, possible worlds.* Cambridge, MA: Harvard University Press.

Cabeza, R. (2002). Hemispheric asymmetry reduction in older adults: The HAROLD model. *Psychology and Aging, 17,* 85–100.

Cacioppo, J. T., & Petty, R. E. (1982). The need of cognition. *Journal of Personality and Social Psychology, 42,* 116–131.

Cacioppo, J. T., Petty, R. E., Feinstein, J., & Jarvis, W. (1996). Dispositional differences in cognitive motivation: The life and times of individuals varying in need for cognition. *Psychological Bulletin, 119,* 197–253.

Carstensen, L. L. (1991). Socioemotional selectivity theory: Social activity in life-span context. *Annual Review of Gerontology and Geriatrics, 11,* 195–217.

Carstensen, L. L. (1993). Motivation for social contact across the life span: A theory of socioemotional selectivity. In J. E. Jacobs (Ed.), *Nebraska symposium on motivation, 1992: Developmental perspectives on motivation* (pp. 209–254). Lincoln, NE: University of Nebraska Press.

Carstensen, L. L., Gross, J. J., & Fung, H. H. (1998). The social context of emotional experience. In K. W. Schaie & M. P. Lawton (Eds.), *Annual review of gerontology and geriatrics, Vol. 17: Focus on emotion and adult development* (pp. 325–352). New York: Springer.

Carstensen, L. L., Isaacowitz, D. M., & Charles, S. T. (1999). Taking time seriously: A theory of socioemotional selectivity. *American Psychologist, 54,* 165–181.

Carver, C. S., & Scheier, M. F. (1995). The role of optimism versus pessimism in the experience of the self. In A. Oosterwegel & R. A. Wicklund (Eds.), *The self in European and North American culture: Development and processes* (pp. 193–204). New York: Plenum.

Chaiken, S., & Trope, Y. (Eds.). (1999). *Dual-process theories in social psychology.* New York: Guilford.

Clore, G. L., & Ortony, A. (2000). Cognition in emotion: Always, sometimes, or never? In R. D. Lane & L. Nadel (Eds.), *Cognitive neuroscience of emotion* (pp. 24–61). New York: Oxford University Press.

Coren, S., & Suedfeld, P. (1995). Personality correlates of conceptual complexity. *Journal of Social Behavior and Personality, 10,* 229–242.
Damasio, A. R. (1995). *Descartes' error: Emotion, reason, and the human brain.* New York: Avon Books.
Davis, J. A., & Smith, T. W. (1995). *General social surveys, 1972–1994: Cumulative file (ICPSR 6217)* [Electronic database]. Ann Arbor, MI: International Consortium of Political and Social Research [Producer and Distributor].
Dennet, D. C. (1987). *The intentional stance.* Cambridge, MA: MIT Press.
Diehl, M., Coyle, N., & Labouvie-Vief, G. (1996). Age and sex differences in strategies of coping and defense across the life span. *Psychology and Aging, 11,* 127–139.
Dornic, S., Ekehammar, B., & Laaksonen, T. (1991). Tolerance for mental effort: Self-ratings related to perception, performance, and personality. *Personality & Individual Differences, 12,* 313–319.
Duffy, E. (1957). The psychological significance of the concept of "arousal" or "activation." *Psychological Review, 64,* 265–275.
Easterbrook, J. A. (1959). The effect of emotion on cue utilization and the organization of behavior. *Psychological Review, 66,* 183–201.
Eisdorfer, C. (1968). Arousal and performance: Experiments in verbal learning and a tentative theory. In G. A. Talland (Ed.), *Human aging and behavior: Recent advances in research and theory* (pp. 189–216). New York: Academic Press.
Ekman, P. (1984). Expression and the nature of emotion. In K. R. Scherer & P. Ekman (Eds.), *Approaches to emotion* (pp. 319–343). Hillsdale, NJ: Lawrence Erlbaum Associates.
Epstein, S. (1994). Integration of the cognitive and psychodynamic unconscious. *American Psychologist, 49,* 709–724.
Epstein, S., & Pacini, R. (1999). Some basic issues regarding dual-process theories from the perspective of cognitive-experiential self theory. In S. Chaiken & Y. Trope (Eds.), *Dual-process theories in social psychology* (pp. 462–482). New York: Guilford.
Erikson, E. H. (1984). *The life cycle completed: A review.* New York: Norton.
Eysenck, M. W. (1982). *Attention and arousal: Cognition and performance.* New York: Springer-Verlag.
Fischer, K. W., & Ayoub, C. (1994). Affective splitting and dissociation in normal and maltreated children: Developmental pathways for self in relationships. In D. Cicchetti & S. L. Toth (Eds.), *Disorders and dysfunctions of the self* (pp. 147–222). Rochester, NY: University of Rochester Press.
Fischer, K. W., Kenny, S., & Pipp, S. (1990). How cognitive processes and environmental conditions organize discontinuities in the development of abstractions. In C. N. Alexander & E. J. Langer (Eds.), *Higher stages of human development: Perspectives on adult growth* (pp. 162–187). New York: Oxford University Press.
Follett, K., & Hess, T. M. (2002). Aging, cognitive complexity, and the fundamental attribution error. *Journals of Gerontology, Series B: Psychological Sciences and Social Sciences, 57B,* P312–P323.
Fonagy, P., Gergely, G., Jurist, E. L., & Target, M. (2002). *Affect regulation, mentalization, and the development of the self.* New York: Other Press.
Forgas, J. P. (2001). The affect infusion model (AIM): An integrative theory of mood effects on cognition and judgements. In L. L. Martin & G. L. Clore (Eds.), *Theories of mood and cognition: A user's guidebook* (pp. 99–134). Mahwah, NJ: Lawrence Erlbaum Associates.
Fredrickson, B. L. (1998). What good are positive emotions? *Review of General Psychology, 2,* 300–319.
Fredrickson, B. L. (2001). The role of positive emotions in positive psychology: The broaden-and-build theory of positive emotions. *American Psychologist, 56,* 218–226.
Freud, S. (1963). Some psychological consequences of the anatomical differences between the sexes. In P. Rieff (Ed.), *Sexuality and the psychology of love* (pp. 183–193). New York: Macmillan. (Original work published 1925)

Gianotti, G. (1999). Emotions as a biologically adapative system: An introduction. In G. Gianotti (Ed.), *Handbook of neuropsychology (2nd ed.), Vol .5: Emotional behavior and its disorders* (pp. 1–15). London: Elsevier.

Gilbert, D. T., Palham, B. W., & Krull, D. S. (1988). On cognitive busyness: When person perceivers meet person perceived. *Journal of Personality and Social Psychology, 54,* 733–740.

Gough, H. G., & Bradley, P. (1996). *CPI manual: California psychological inventory (3rd ed.).* Palo Alto, CA: Consulting Psychologists Press.

Gross, J. J. (1998). Antecedent- and response-focused emotion regulation: Divergent consequences for experience, expression, and physiology. *Journal of Personality and Social Psychology, 74,* 224–237.

Gross, J. J., Carstensen, L. L., Pasupathi, M., Tsai, J., Skorpen, C. G., & Hsu, A. Y. C. (1997). Emotion and aging: Experience, expression, and control. *Psychology and Aging, 12,* 590–599.

Harris, P. L. (2000). Understanding emotion. In M. Lewis & J. Haviland-Jones (Eds.), *Handbook of emotions (2nd ed.)* (pp. 281–292). New York: Guilford.

Harter, S. (1999). *The construction of the self: A developmental perspective.* New York: Guilford.

Hasher, L., Stoltzfus, E. R., Zacks, R. T., & Rypma, B. (1991). Age and inhibition. *Journal of Experimental Psychology: Learning, Memory and Cognition, 17,* 163–169.

Hasher, L., & Zacks, R. T. (1988). Working memory, comprehension, and aging: A review and a new view. In G. H. Bower (Ed.), *The psychology of learning and motivation: Advances in research and theory, Vol. 22* (pp. 193–225). San Diego, CA: Academic Press.

Helson, R., & Roberts, B. W. (1994). Ego development and personality change in adulthood. *Journal of Personality and Social Psychology, 66,* 911–920.

Helson, R., & Srivastava, S. (2001). Three paths of adult development: Conservers, seekers, and achievers. *Journal of Personality and Social Psychology, 80,* 995–1010.

Helson, R., & Wink, P. (1987). Two conceptions of maturity examined in the findings of a longitudinal study. *Journal of Personality and Social Psychology, 53,* 531–541.

Hess, T. M. (1994). Social cognition in adulthood: Aging-related changes in knowledge and processing mechanisms. *Developmental Review, 14,* 373–412.

Hess, T. M. (1999). Cognitive and knowledge-based influences on social representations. In T. M. Hess & F. Blanchard-Fields (Eds.), *Social cognition and aging* (pp. 237–263). San Diego, CA: Academic Press.

Hess, T. M. (2001). Ageing-related influences on personal need for structure. *International Journal of Behavioral Development, 25,* 482–490.

Hess, T. M., Donley, J., & Vandermaas, M. O. (1989). Aging-related changes in the processing and retention of script information. *Experimental Aging Research, 15,* 89–96.

Hess, T. M., Follet, K. J., & McGee, K. A. (1998). Aging and impression formation: The impact of processing skills and goals. *Journal of Gerontology, Series B: Psychological Sciences and Social Sciences, 53B,* P175–P187.

Hess, T. M., Rosenberg, D. C., & Waters, S. J. (2001). Motivation and representational processes in adulthood: The effects of social accountability and information relevance. *Psychology & Aging, 16*(4), 629–642.

Hess, T. M., & Tate, C. S. (1992). Direct and indirect assessments of memory for script-based narratives in young and older adults. *Cognitive Development, 7,* 467–484.

Isen, A. M. (1987). Positive affect, cognitive processes, and social behavior. In L. Berkowitz (Ed.), *Advances in experimental social psychology, Vol. 20* (pp. 203–253). San Diego, CA: Academic Press.

Izard, C. E. (1997). *Human emotions.* New York: Plenum.

Johnson, M. K., Hashtroudi, S., & Lindsay, D. S. (1993). Source monitoring. *Psychological Bulletin, 114,* 3–28.

Kang, S. (2002). Individual differences in well-differentiated emotional experience: Their psychological implications. *Dissertation Abstracts International, Section B: The Sciences & Engineering, 62,* 4262.

Kegan, J. (1982). *The evolving self.* Cambridge, MA: Harvard University Press.

Kernis, M. H., Grannemann, B. D., & Barclay, L. C. (1992). Stability of self-esteem: Assessment, correlates, and excuse making. *Journal of Personality, 60,* 621–643.

Kohlberg, L. (1969). Stage and sequence: The cognitive-developmental approach to socialization. In D. A. Goslin (Ed.), *Handbook of socialization theory and research* (pp. 347–380). Chicago: Rand McNally.

Koutstaal, W., & Schachter, D. L. (1997). Gist-based false recognition of pictures in older and younger adults. *Journal of Memory and Language, 37,* 555–583.

Kruglanski, A. W., & Freund, T. (1983). The freezing and unfreezing of lay-inferences: Effects of impressional primacy, ethnic stereotyping and numerical anchoring. *Journal of Experimental Social Psychology, 19,* 448–468.

Kuhn, T. S. (1962). *The structure of scientific revolutions.* Chicago: University of Chicago Press.

Kunzmann, U., & Grün, D. (2003, August). *Emotional reactions to sad film clips: Evidence for greater reactivity in old age.* Paper presented at the annual meeting of the American Psychological Association, Toronto.

Labouvie-Vief, G. (1981). Re-active and pro-active aspects of constructivism: Growth and aging in life span perspective. In R. M. Lerner & N. A. Busch-Rossnagel (Eds.), *Individuals as products of their development: A life-span perspective* (pp. 197–320). New York: Academic Press.

Labouvie-Vief, G. (1982). Dynamic development and mature autonomy: A theoretical prologue. *Human Development, 25,* 161–191.

Labouvie-Vief, G. (1994). *Psyche and Eros: Mind and gender in the life course.* New York: Cambridge University Press.

Labouvie-Vief, G. (1999). Emotions in adulthood. In V. L. Bengtson & K. W. Schaie (Eds.), *Handbook of theories of aging* (pp. 253–267). New York: Springer.

Labouvie-Vief, G. (2003). Dynamic integration: Affect, cognition, and the self in adulthood. *Current Directions in Psychological Science, 12,* 201–206.

Labouvie-Vief, G., Chiodo, L. M., Goguen, L. A., Diehl, M., & Orwoll, L. (1995). Representations of self across the life span. *Psychology and Aging, 10,* 404–415. (a)

Labouvie-Vief, G., & DeVoe, M. (1991). Emotional regulation in adulthood and later life: A developmental view. In K. W. Schaie (Ed.), *Annual review of gerontology and geriatrics* (Vol. II, pp. 172–194). New York: Springer.

Labouvie-Vief, G., DeVoe, M., & Bulka, D. (1989). Speaking about feelings: Conceptions of emotion across the life span. *Psychology and Aging, 4,* 425–437.

Labouvie-Vief, G., Diehl, M., Chiodo, L. M., & Coyle, N. (1995). Representations of self and parents across the life span. *Journal of Adult Development, 2,* 207–222.

Labouvie-Vief, G., Hakim-Larson, J., DeVoe, M., & Schoeberlein, S. (1989). Emotions and self-regulation: A life-span view. *Human Development, 32,* 279–299.

Labouvie-Vief, G., & Medler, M. (2002). Affect optimization and affect complexity: Modes and styles of regulation in adulthood. *Psychology and Aging, 17,* 571–587.

Labouvie-Vief, G., Zhang, F., & Jain, E. (2003). *Affect complexity and affect optimization: Cross-sectional validation and longitudinal examination.* Unpublished manuscript, Wayne State University, Michigan.

Lane, R. D. (2000). Levels of emotional awareness: Neurological, psychological, and social perspectives. In R. Bar-On & J. D. A. Parker (Eds.), *The handbook of emotional intelligence: Theory, development, assessment, and application at home, school, and in the workplace* (pp. 171–191). San Francisco: Jossey-Bass.

Lane, R. D., & Schwartz, G. E. (1987). Levels of emotional awareness: A cognitive-developmental theory and its application to psychopathology. *American Journal of Psychiatry, 144,* 133–143.

Lawton, M. P., & Nahemow, L. (1973). Ecology and the aging process. In C. Eisdorfer & M. P. Lawton (Eds.), *The psychology of adult development and aging* (pp. 619–674). Washington, DC: American Psychological Association.

Lazarus, R. S. (1966). *Psychological stress and the coping process.* New York: McGraw-Hill.

Lazarus, R. S. (1982). Thoughts on the relations between emotion and cognition. *American Psychologist, 37,* 1019–1024.

Lazarus, R. S. (1991). Cognition and motivation in emotion. *American Psychologist, 46,* 352–367.

Lazarus, R. S., Averill, J. R., & Opton, E. M. Jr. (1970). Toward a cognitive theory of emotion. In M. B. Arnold (Ed.), *Feelings and emotion* (pp. 207–232). New York: Academic Press.

LeDoux, J. E. (1996). *The emotional brain: The mysterious underpinnings of emotional life.* New York: Simon & Schuster.

LeDoux, J. E., & Phelps, E. A. (2000). Emotional networks in the brain. In M. Lewis & J. M. Haviland-Jones (Eds.), *Handbook of emotions (2nd ed.)* (pp. 157–172). New York: Guilford.

Leslie, A. M. (1987). Pretence and representation: The origins of 'theory of mind'. *Psychological Review, 94,* 412–426.

Lewis, M. D. (2000). Emotional self-organization at three time scales. In M. D. Lewis & I. Granic (Eds.), *Emotion, development, and self-organization: Dynamic systems approaches to emotional development* (pp. 37–69). New York: Cambridge University Press.

Loevinger, J. (1976). *Ego development.* San Francisco: Jossey-Bass.

Lucas, R. E., & Diener, E. (2000). Personality and subjective well-being across the life span. In V. J. Molfese & D. L. Molfese (Eds.), *Temperament and personality development across the life span* (pp. 211–234). Mahwah, NJ: Lawrence Erlbaum Associates.

Lyster, T. L. (2001). A nomination approach to the study of wisdom in old age. *Dissertation Abstracts International, Section B: The Sciences & Engineering, 61,* 6737.

Magai, C., & Haviland-Jones, J. M. (2002). *The hidden genius of emotion: Lifespan transformations of personality.* New York: Cambridge University Press.

Mather, M. J., & Johnson, M. K. (2000). Choice-supportive source monitoring: Do our decisions seem better to us as we age? *Psychology and Aging, 15,* 596–606.

Mather, M., Johnson, M. K., & DeLeonardis, D. M. (1999). Stereotype reliance in source monitoring: Age differences and neuropsychological test correlates. *Cognitive Neuropsychology, 16,* 437–458.

Mather, M., Shafir, E., & Johnson, M. K. (2000). Misremembrance of options past: Source monitoring and choice. *Psychological Science, 11*(2), 132–138.

Mayer, J. D., & Salovey, P. (1995). Emotional intelligence and the construction and regulation of feelings. *Applied and Preventive Psychology, 4,* 197–208.

McAdams, D. P. (2001). *The person: An integrated introduction to personality psychology (3rd ed.).* Fort Worth, TX: Harcourt College Publishing.

McDowd, J. M., Oseas-Kreger, D. M., & Filion, D. L. (1995). Inhibitory processes in cognition and aging. In F. N. Dempster & C. J. Brainerd (Eds.), *Interference and inhibition in cognition* (pp. 363–400). San Diego: Academic Press.

Metcalfe, J., & Jacobs, W. J. (1998). Emotional memory: The effects of stress on "cool" and "hot" memory systems. In D. L. Medin (Ed.), *The psychology of learning and motivation: Advances in research and theory, Vol. 38* (pp. 187–222). San Diego: Academic Press.

Metcalfe, J., & Mischel, W. (1999). A hot/cool-system analysis of delay of gratification: Dynamics of willpower. *Psychological Review, 106,* 3–19.

Mikulincer, M., & Horesh, N. (1999). Adult attachment style and the perception of others: The role of projective mechanisms. *Journal of Personality & Social Psychology, 76,* 1022–1034.

Mikulincer, M., & Shaver, P. R. (2001). Attachment theory and intergroup bias: Evidence that priming the secure base schema attenuates negative reactions to out-groups. *Journal of Personality & Social Psychology, 81,* 97–115.

Miller, G. A., Galanter, E., & Pribram, K. H. (1960). *Plans and the structure of behavior.* New York: Holt.

Mitchell, K. J., Johnson, M. K., Raye, C. L., Mather, M., & D'Esposito, M. (2000). Aging and reflective processes of working memory: Binding and test load deficits. *Psychology & Aging, 15,* 527–541.

Mroczek, D. K., & Kolarz, C. M. (1998). The effect of age on positive and negative affect: A developmental perspective on happiness. *Journal of Personality and Social Psychology, 75*, 1333–1349.

Mueller, J. H., & Grove, T. R. (1991). Trait actualization and self-reference effects. *Bulletin of the Psychonomic Society, 29*, 13–16.

Mueller, J. H., & Johnson, W. C. (1990). Trait distinctiveness and age specificity in self-referent information processing. *Bulletin of the Psychonomic Society, 28*, 119–122.

Neuberg, S. L., & Newsom, J. T. (1993). Personal need for structure: Individual differences in the desire for simpler structure. *Journal of Personality and Social Psychology, 65*, 113–131.

Norem, J. K. (1998). Cognitive strategies as personality: Effectiveness, specificity, flexibility and change. In D. M. Buss & N. Cantor (Eds.), *Personality psychology: Recent trends and emerging issues* (pp. 45–60). New York: Springer-Verlag.

Norman, D. A.(1976). *Memory and attention (2nd ed.)*. New York: Wiley.

Norman, K. A., & Schachter, D. L. (1997). False recognition in younger and older adults: Exploring the characteristics of illusory memories. *Memory and Cognition, 25*, 838–848.

Olson, K. R., Camp, C. J., & Fuller, D. (1984). Curiosity and need for cognition. *Psychological Reports, 54*, 71–74.

Pascual-Leone, J. (1991). Emotions, development, and psychotherapy: A dialectical-constructivist perspective. In J. D. Safran & L. S. Greenberg (Eds.), *Emotion, psychotherapy, and change* (pp. 302–335). New York: Guilford.

Paulhus, D. L., & Levitt, K. (1987). Desirable responding triggered by affect: Automatic egotism? *Journal of Personality and Social Psychology, 52*, 245–259.

Paulhus, D. L., & Lim, D. T. K. (1994). Arousal and evaluative extremity in social judgments: A dynamic complexity model. *European Journal of Social Psychology, 24*, 89–99.

Petty, R. E., & Jarvis, B. G. (1996). An individual differences perspective on assessing cognitive processes. In N. Schwarz & S. Sudman (Eds.), *Answering questions: Methodology for determining cognitive and communicative processes in survey research* (pp. 221–257). San Francisco: Jossey-Bass.

Piaget, J. (1955). *The language and thought of the child*. New York: New American Library.

Piaget, J. (1962). *Play, dreams, and imitation in childhood*. New York: Norton.

Piaget, J. (1965). *The moral judgment of the child*. New York: Free Press.

Piaget, J. (1967). *Six psychological studies*. New York: Random House.

Piaget, J. (1980). *Experiments in contradiction* (D. Coleman, Trans.). Chicago: University of Chicago Press.

Piaget, J. (1981). *Intelligence and affectivity: Their relationship during child development*. Palo Alto, CA: Annual Reviews.

Powers, W. T. (1973). *Behavior: The control of perception*. Chicago: Aldine.

Premack, D., & Woodruff, G. (1978). Does a chimpanzee have a theory of mind? *Brain and Behavioural Sciences, 4*, 515–526.

Pribram, K. H., & Gill, M. M. (1976). *Freud's "project" reassessed*. New York: Basic Books.

Pufal-Struzik, I. (1996). Demand for stimulation in young people with different levels of creativity. *High Ability Studies, 7*, 145–150.

Pyszczynski, T., Greenberg, J., & Solomon, S. (2000). Toward a dialectical analysis of growth and defensive motives. *Psychological Inquiry, 11*, 301–305.

Rabbitt, P., & Lowe, C. (2000). Patterns of cognitive ageing. *Psychological Research, 63*, 308–316.

Rahhal, T. A., May, C. P., & Hasher, L. (2002). Truth and character: Sources that older adults can remember. *Psychological Science, 13*, 101–105.

Rawlings, D., Twomey, F., Burns, E., & Morris, S. (1998). Personality, creativity and aesthetic preference: Comparing psychoticism, sensation seeking, schizotypy and openness to experience. *Empirical Studies of the Arts, 16*, 153–178.

Raz, N. (2000). Aging of the brain and its impact on cognitive performance: Integration of structural and functional findings. In F. I. M. Craik & T. A. Salthouse (Eds.), *The handbook of aging and cognition (2nd ed.)* (pp. 1–90). Mahwah, NJ: Lawrence Erlbaum Associates.

Ryan, R. M., & Deci, E. L. (2001). On happiness and human potentials: A review of research on hedonic and eudaimonic well-being. *Annual Review of Psychology, 52,* 141–166.

Ryff, C. D. (1989). Happiness is everything, or is it? Explorations on the meaning of psychological well-being. *Journal of Personality and Social Psychology, 57,* 1069–1081.

Salovey, P., Rothman, A. J., Detweiler, J. B., & Steward, W. T. (2000). Emotional states and physical health. *American Psychologist, 55,* 110–121.

Salthouse, T. A. (1994). The aging of working memory. *Neuropsychology, 8,* 535–543.

Schaie, K. W. (1998). The Seattle longitudinal studies of adult intelligence. In M. P. Lawton & T. A. Salthouse (Eds.), *Essential papers on the psychology of aging* (pp. 263–271). New York: New York University Press.

Schore, A. N. (1994). *Affect regulation and the origin of the self: The neurobiology of emotional development.* Hillsdale, NJ: Lawrence Erlbaum Associates.

Selman, R. L. (1980). *The growth of interpersonal understanding: Developmental and clinical analyses.* New York: Academic Press.

Selye, H. (1978). *The stress of life (2nd ed.).* New York: McGraw-Hill.

Shimamura, A. P. (1995). Memory and frontal lobe function. In M. S. Gazzaniga (Ed.), *The cognitive neurosciences* (pp. 803–813). Cambridge, MA: MIT Press.

Showers, C. J., & Kevlyn, S. B. (1999). Organization of knowledge about a relationship partner: Implications for liking and loving. *Journal of Personality and Social Psychology, 76,* 958–971.

Showers, C. J., & Kling, K. C. (1996). Organization of self-knowledge: Implications for recovery from sad mood. *Journal of Personality and Social Psychology, 70,* 578–590.

Sloman, S. A. (1996). The empirical case for two systems of reasoning. *Psychological Bulletin, 119,* 3–22.

Sroufe, L. A. (1996). *Emotional development: The organization of emotional life in the first years.* New York: Cambridge University Press.

Stanovich, K. E. (1999). *Who is rational? Studies of individual differences in reasoning.* Mahwah, NJ: Lawrence Erlbaum Associates.

Staudinger, U. M., Marsiske, M., & Baltes, P. B. (1995). Resilience and reserve capacity in later adulthood: Potentials and limits of development across the life span. In D. Chicchetti & D. J. Cohen (Eds.), *Developmental psychopathology, Vol. 2: Risk, disorder and adaptation* (pp. 801–847). New York: Wiley.

Taylor, G. J., Bagby, R. M., & Parker, J. D. A. (1992). The revised Toronto scale: Some reliability, validity, and normative data. *Psychotherapy and Psychosomatics, 57,* 34–41.

Taylor, S. E., & Brown, J. D. (1988). Illusion and well-being: A social psychological perspective on mental health. *Psychological Bulletin, 103,* 193–210.

Taylor, S. E., Kemeny, M. E., Reed, G., Bower, J. E., & Gruenewald, T. L. (2000). Psychological resources, positive illusions, and health. *American Psychologist, 55,* 99–109.

Tomkins, S. S. (1980). Affect as amplification: Some modifications in theory. In R. Plutchik & H. Kellerman (Eds.), *Emotion: Theory, research, and experience, Vol. 1: Theories of emotion* (pp. 141–164). New York: Academic Press.

Tucker, D. M. (1992). Developing emotions and cortical networks. In M. R. Gunnar, C. A. Nelson, et al., (Eds.), *Developmental behavioral neuroscience* (pp. 75–128). Hillsdale, NJ: Lawrence Erlbaum Associates.

Venkatraman, M. P., Marlino, D., Kardes, F. R., & Sklar, K. B. (1990). Effects of individual difference variables on responses to factual and evaluative ads. *Advances in Consumer Research, 17,* 761–765.

Vingerhoets, G., Berckmoes, C., & Stroobant, N. (2003). Cerebral hemodynamics during discrimination of prosodic and semantic emotion in speech studied by transcranial Doppler ultrasonography. *Neuropsychology, 17,* 93–99.

Von Hippel, W., Silver, L. A., & Lynch, M. E. (2000). Stereotyping against your will: The role of inhibitory ability in stereotyping and prejudice among the elderly. *Personality and Social Psychology Bulletin, 26,* 523–532.

Waddell, K. J., & Rogoff, B. (1981). Effect of contextual organization on spatial memory of middle-aged and older women. *Developmental Psychology, 17,* 878–885.

Watson, D., & Pennebaker, J. W. (1989). Health complaints, stress, and disease: Exploring the central role of negative affectivity. *Psychological Review, 96,* 234–254.

Weinberger, D. A. (1990). The construct validity of the repressive coping style. In J. L. Singer (Ed.), *Repression and dissociation* (pp. 337–386). Chicago: University of Chicago Press.

Werner, H. (1955). *On expressive language.* Worcester, MA: Clark Univerity Press.

Werner, H. (1957). *Comparative psychology of mental development.* New York: International Universities Press.

Werner, H., & Kaplan, B. (1962). *Symbol formation.* New York: Wiley.

West, R. L. (1996). An application of prefrontal cortex function theory to cognitive aging. *Psychological Bulletin, 120,* 272–292.

White, R. (1969). Motivation reconsidered: The concept of competence. *Psychological Review, 66,* 297–333.

Wurm, L. H., Labouvie-Vief, G., Rebucal, K. A., & Koch, H. E. (2003). *Age and inhibition in an emotional Stroop task: A comparison of older and younger adults.* Unpublished paper, Wayne State University, Michigan.

Yerkes, R. M., & Dodson, J. D. (1908). The relation of stress of stimulus to rapidity of habit-formation. *Journal of Comparative and Neurological Psychology, 18,* 459–482.

Zuckerman, M., Neary, R. S., & Brustman, B. A. (1970). Sensation-seeking scale correlates in experience (smoking, drugs, alcohol, "hallucinations," and sex) and preferences for complexity (designs). *Proceedings of the Annual Convention of the American Psychological Association, 5,* 317–318.

10

▼▼▼▼▼▼▼

A Model of Domain Learning: Reinterpreting Expertise as a Multidimensional, Multistage Process

Patricia A. Alexander
University of Maryland

Jason is a bright, energetic second grader. When asked how he would explain history to a student living in a faraway place, Jason says it is a book that he has in his classroom. When he is asked to show the adult interviewer how to do history, he takes a toy clock from among the props in the room and shows the interviewer how to tell time. He is not able to explain what telling time has to do with history, however. When asked if he likes history, Jason simply shrugs his shoulders, as if to say, "I don't know."

Evie describes herself as a "history buff." It was probably inevitable that she would become a high-school history teacher. As long as she can remember, historical writings, fiction, and documentaries have been among her favorite entertainments. No matter how busy life gets, she enjoys volunteering as a docent at the city museum. She recently decided to pursue her master's degree in history education. As she explains it, she wants to be a better teacher for her students. She also wants the chance to improve her knowledge of African and Asian history, which she feels are neglected areas in the school curriculum and in her own understanding.

Bruce has devoted most of his adult life to the study of American history. In fact, he is considered one of the leading authorities on the early Colonial Period. According to Bruce, there is much to understand about this formative period in American society and the intricate relations that existed between the social, political, religious, and economic systems of the time. Bruce says that he could easily spend another 20 years immersed in this research. As he puts it: "People think they know so much about this time and place. But, there are so many mis-

conceptions out there, so many unresolved issues, and so much conflicting evidence. And every day there are new discoveries, new artifacts, and new interpretations that bring accepted lore into question."

Jason, Evie, and Bruce are three individuals with varied understandings and personal associations with the domain of history. Their differences are even apparent to the untrained eye. For Jason, history is little more than a label attached to a book in the classroom. There appears to be little breadth and depth to his base of history knowledge, and his feelings about history are unformed. In Evie, we find an individual for whom history has a personal relevance. She is a knowledge-seeker and apparently enjoys sharing her knowledge with others, both in and out of the classroom. Bruce is someone that we might readily identify as an expert—a recognized authority who has devoted himself to the study of history. That devotion and Bruce's labors in the field have not only brought about a change in him over the years, but have also contributed to the field itself.

What I see in Jason, Evie, and Bruce are three people at very different points in a life-long journey toward expertise in an academic domain. For individuals like Evie and Bruce, that journey has been on-going for some time and has brought them to places that are personally rewarding and professionally enriching. Jason, by comparison, is an individual who has just begun this challenging journey. We do not know how the years ahead will alter Jason's knowledge of history or transform his current attitudes toward that domain. For all the obvious contrasts between Jason, Evie, and Bruce, it is precisely this transformational process that captivates me the most, both as a teacher and as a researcher. It is also this transformational process that is understudied and underrepresented in the literature on expert–novice differences.

When I became a teacher decades ago, it was to help students like Jason grow in their knowledge and skills in academic domains, like history, reading, mathematics, or science. As with Dewey (1916/1944), I retain the belief that one of the fundamental missions of formal education is to help the citizenry become more knowledgeable and thoughtful in a range of subject-matter domains. In effect, I believe strongly in the academic development of students (Alexander, 2000). To achieve that end, however, educators must understand the nature of the process that can potentially transform a true neophyte, like Jason, into a recognized authority, like Bruce. What systematic cognitive and motivational developments should we expect in individuals if we, as educators, are contributing to their continued growth in academic domains, the foundations of the formal educational system?

In this chapter, I offer the Model of Domain Learning (MDL) as a means of conceptualizing the critical journey toward academic competence. There are many literatures that underlie the MDL, including theory and research on human development, domain-specific learning, motivation, and strategic processing. One of the most important is the literature on expertise or expert–novice differences. Still, as the MDL has taken shape and been repeatedly tested in various academic domains, some of the basic attributes of the extant literature on expertise have been brought into question.

TRADITIONAL EXPERT–NOVICE STUDIES

During the 1970s and 1980s, under the theoretical umbrellas of artificial intelligence (AI) and information-processing theory (IPT), programs of research formed around the problem-solving performance of experts. There were at least two goals for this inquiry. For one, the intention was to capture the characteristics of expert performance and to validate them over a variety of problem-solving tasks so that those characteristics could be programmed into nonhuman systems (Alexander, 2003; Ericsson & Smith, 1991). The result would be smart machines that approximated effective human behavior. Another goal was to determine what cognitive attributes distinguished experts from novices so that those attributes could be trained in nonexpert human populations (Chi, Glaser, & Farr, 1988).

First Generation: Expertise as Generic Problem Solving

According to Holyoak (1991), at least two prior generations of theory and research have shaped current understandings about expertise. The first generation, represented by research in AI, conceptualized expertise as the efficient and effective solution of generic problems. Researchers of this generation, such as Newell and Simon (1972), set out to isolate the search strategies that experts employ to identify and then solve problems for which content knowledge presumably would play an insignificant role. The classic cannibal–missionary problem that follows is representative of the knowledge-lean problems that served as the experimental stimuli for studying expert performance and for documenting search heuristics (e.g., means–end analysis) in this initial generation. Those tasks are called knowledge-lean because it is assumed that all the information needed to answer them is given in the problem statement:

There are three missionaries and three cannibals on a river bank. The missionaries and cannibals need to cross over to the other side of the river. For this purpose, they have a small rowboat that holds just two people. There is one problem, however. If the number of cannibals on either river bank exceeds the number of missionaries, the cannibals will eat the missionaries. How can all six get across to the other side of the river in a way that guarantees that they all arrive alive and uneaten? (Sternberg, 1986, p. 57)

If we asked members of that pioneering generation of expert–novice re-searchers to judge Jason, Evie, and Bruce's expertise, they would not be inter-ested in any of the history-specific information provided in the opening sce-nario. Such descriptions (e.g., Jason's understanding of history or Evie's volunteering as a docent) would merely distract from critical determinations. Rather, these first-generation expertise researchers would assess Jason, Evie, and Bruce's ability to tackle demanding but generic problems with speed, ac-curacy, and efficiency.

Second Generation: Expertise as Knowledge-Rich Problem Solving

Soon there followed a second generation of expertise researchers who dem-onstrated that general problem-solving strategies did not adequately distin-guish experts from nonexperts (Holyoak, 1991). This second generation, like the first, continued to focus on problem solving as the mechanism for opera-tionalizing expertise. However, the second-generation researchers were not interested in general search strategies applied to knowledge-lean problems. Instead, they targeted tasks within particular problem-solving contexts, such as playing chess, typewriting, waiting tables, or solving physics problems, for which certain knowledge was expected to matter (Anderson, 1983; Chi, 1978; Chi, Feltovich, & Glaser, 1981). Careful task selection allowed the research-ers to document that domain-specific knowledge and associated problem per-ceptions were significant determiners in expert performance (Ericsson & Smith, 1991).

Take the pioneering research of de Groot (1946/1978) and Chase and Si-mon (1973; Simon & Chase, 1973) as a case in point. Because these research-ers wanted to discern the nature and defining attributes of expertise, they chose to study chess. Chess was ideal as a task domain for this research be-cause the game has a limited number of performance rules. However, there is great diversity in the execution of those rules between very inexperienced and highly skilled players. Further, problem-solving moves are externalized in chess. Thus, researchers could record and analyze the perceptions and rea-soning that instigated various moves by prompting players to verbalize their actions. Finally, the procedural nature of chess and other selected problem domains allowed researchers to create simulations or laboratory versions of real-life tasks that could be studied without the contextual influences present in everyday performance (Ericsson & Smith, 1991).

Second-generation expertise researchers would likely judge the expertise of Jason, Evie, and Bruce by examining their performance of a carefully crafted history task. They would select or construct a task that would rely on solution procedures that could be represented as a series of production rules or solution steps (Anderson, 1987). It is likely that our three individuals would also be required to explain their reasoning and their solution steps as they worked through the given problem. For example, Evie and Bruce might be presented with a problem like the following and asked to share their analysis aloud:

> Assume you are the head of the Soviet Ministry of Agriculture and assume that crop productivity has been low over the past several years. You now have the responsibility of increasing crop production. How would you go about doing this? (Voss, Tyler, & Yengo, 1983, p. 211)

Their responses could then be evaluated against those of experts in the Soviet political system in terms of how they represent the problem, consider the historical background, formulate possible solutions, and assess the adequacy of those potential solutions (Voss et al., 1983).

Contributions of the First and Second Generations

It has been common practice in the past generations of expertise research to contrast the performance of acknowledged experts (e.g., chess Grandmasters or Soviet Union experts) with individuals who are unfamiliar or less proficient at the task. The sharp distinctions arising between novices and experts helped to establish the reasons for superior task performance. This approach also pointed to the abilities or features that novices must eventually acquire if they are to operate as experts.

Certainly, the research community has garnered a great deal from the preceding decades of expert–novice research. For example, these programs of inquiry have provided us with evidence that experts:

- Have devoted time and effort to improved performance;
- Possess a base of domain-specific knowledge that is rich and very well integrated;
- Perceive a domain-specific problem in a complex and integrated manner;
- Engage in planning and self-analysis;
- Select and execute strategies well matched to the problem at hand (e.g., Bransford, Brown, & Cocking, 1999; Byrnes, 2001; Chi et al., 1988; Ericsson & Smith, 1991).

These indicators of expertise would seem to have direct relevance to learning within the context of formal schooling. Indeed, there have been efforts to translate such consistent and significant findings into instructional metaphors, models, and programs intent on facilitating academic development

(Bereiter & Scardamalia, 1993; Brown, Collins, & Duguid, 1989). However, this translation has not been particularly easy nor readily apparent (Sternberg, 2003). Unquestionably, many of the barriers to this translation have little to do with the expertise research itself, but can be attributed to other social–political and educational circumstances beyond the scope of this chapter (Alexander, Murphy, & Woods, 1996; Berliner & Biddle, 1995). Still, we must look to the goals, premises, and methodologies of traditional expert–novice research for plausible reasons for this research-into-practice conundrum.

Limitations of Traditional Expert–Novice Studies

Given its long and productive history, one might question the need for continued exploration of expertise or wonder about the value of pursuing alternative conceptualizations. Despite the rich legacy of prior generations of expertise research, limitations to those studies must be acknowledged, particularly if the goal is to improve student learning and development in academic domains (Ackerman, 2003). Five of those limitations are as follows:

• *Highly selective problem-solving tasks and domains.* The expertise research has historically targeted a range of performance tasks and domains that do not necessarily translate into learning in complex academic domains (Alexander, 2003; Ericsson & Smith, 1991). Beyond the classic studies of chess, there are investigations dealing with typewriting, table waiting, dancing, as well as physics and medical diagnosis (Allard & Starkes, 1991; Ericsson & Polson, 1988; Gentner, 1988; Patel & Groen, 1986). Within these problem-solving domains, experimental tasks have been very carefully selected for their perceptual demands or their procedural characteristics (Holyoak, 1991).

Nonetheless, the correspondence that exists between expert waiters or typists and students learning history, mathematics, or other academic domain is tenuous at best. Even when the problem-solving domains were more academic in nature, as with physics or mathematics, first-generation and second-generation researchers did not look broadly at expertise within those domains, but remained focused on how experts tackled particular kinds of problems associated with those domains (e.g., Anzai & Yokoyama, 1984). Thus, it remains questionable whether the highly consistent findings for expertise research derived from very purposefully chosen tasks, frequently performed under more laboratory than real-life conditions, transfer to student learning in the dynamic and messy context of the classroom.

• *Lack of developmental focus.* Another limitation of past research on expertise has been its focus on extremes. In essence, traditional expertise research has been a study in contrasts. Not only were the profiles of experts built on their performance of very carefully selected problems, but also on the performance of individuals at the other end of the expertise spectrum. The absence of certain cognitive abilities or processes in novices validated their significance for experts. For example, it was not just that experts perceived the problem space in a particular manner that was critical, but also that novices perceived the problem in quite a different, seemingly less sophisticated way.

Such a methodological approach has been helpful in grounding the research on expertise. However, this orientation fails to illuminate the process by which one progresses from true novice to documented expert. It certainly would be informative to juxtapose Jason and Bruce's problem-solving behaviors or those of Evie and Bruce as they perform a selected history task. But this informative analysis could not explain what specifically would be required to set Jason on the right course toward competence or prompt Evie to take the next step toward proficiency in the domain of history.

• *Concentration on "coldly cognitive" attributes.* One of the most evident limitations of past research on expertise was its concentration on strictly cognitive dimensions of outstanding performance. Concentration on search strategies and the structure of domain knowledge is a worthwhile pursuit. Such a focus would help us distinguish between Jason, Evie, and Bruce as history experts. But this approach remains "coldly cognitive" (Pintrich, Marx, & Boyle, 1993). It does not address the personality, social, or motivational factors that are tied to cognitive processing (i.e., "hot cognition") and that have a great deal to do with whether someone like Jason or Evie devotes the time and energy needed to build the knowledge structures or domain strategies consistently associated with expert performance.

These "hot" factors would also be important to ascertaining why Evie finds her museum activities motivating or why someone like Bruce retains his fascination with history even after decades of concerted effort. That is to say, Evie's growing competence or Bruce's established expertise in such a complex and evolving domain as history cannot be fully captured by assessing their knowledge structures, memory, perception, or domain strategies. Their persistence, interests, curiosities, and other such forces matter as well and may underlie the emergence of defining cognitive attributes, such as an integrated body of domain knowledge (Ainley, 1998; Reio & Wiswell, 2000).

• *Disregard of learner goals and intentions.* In the prior generations of expertise research, the conation (will) and intentionality of the learner did not enter into the equation (Sinatra & Pintrich, 2002; Snow, Corno, & Jackson, 1996). Experts were defined as those with superior problem-solving skills fueled by certain cognitive advantages (Ackerman, 2003). Novices were simply those who had yet to acquire those distinguishing attributes.

Yet, there are willful or goal-directed aspects to the transformation from novice to expert that are acknowledged in the literature (Ackerman, Kyllonen, & Roberts, 1999), but not necessarily incorporated into research designs or empirical measures. Perhaps because students in K–12 are a captive audience, educators forget that those students are active participants in their own learning and can choose to engage strategically in a domain task or not (Snow et al., 1996). Further, students' goals for engagement can range from learning the content to getting a grade or avoiding embarrassment (Meece, Blumenfeld, & Hoyle, 1988; Pintrich, 2000). If students do not manifest the knowledge and processes associated with expertise, is it a case of ability or a lack of personal investment in the task or the domain?

Educators also cannot operate under the assumption that the myriad of novices moving through the educational system have the goal of becoming experts in any academic domain, or any intention of committing the requisite time and energy to achieve expertise, even in those cases where the requisite cognitive abilities exist (Bransford et al., 1993; Meece et al., 1988).

- *Limited consideration of the school context.* Anyone who has spent time in classrooms recently knows that schools are unique places. Educational communities operate under their own set of accepted practices, routine tasks, and value systems (Senge, 1990). Thus, there is always a risk when educators seek to build instructional models around research conducted largely outside of the educational context. This is true for the research on expertise.

Traditional expertise research requires us to overlay the findings from non-academic domains or laboratory settings onto the educational system. However, if there is truly a desire to transfer the wisdom of expert–novice studies to schooling, then it would be wise to work within the system more directly. Study expertise *in situ*, for instance, or at least with an array of measures that draw directly on the tasks, procedures, and conditions aligned with educational practice (Sternberg, 2003).

In light of the aforementioned limitations, the search for alternative conceptions of expertise that circumvent the theoretical and methodological shortcomings of past generations of expert–novice research seems worthwhile.

PRECURSOR STUDIES TO THE MDL

Unlike researchers in AI and IPT, I did not set out to study expertise when I began my program of inquiry. My interests in past decades were centered on text-based learning (e.g., Garner & Alexander, 1981; Judy, Alexander, Kulikowich, & Willson, 1988). How do students make sense of the linguistic materials they encounter? What factors contribute to students' successes or difficulties at that endeavor, and what can be done to facilitate their learning *through* and *with* text? Despite the differences in goals, my past explorations of text-based learning went through some of the same generational shifts as I previously ascribed to the expert–novice research.

Knowledge-Lean Studies

In the early 1980s, my colleagues and I wanted to identify the generic strategies used by effective readers as they process written text (e.g., Alexander, Hare, & Garner, 1984; Garner, Hare, Alexander, Haynes, & Winograd, 1984). As with the first generation of expert–novice researchers, we sought out those strategies that made a difference in learning without regard to the topic or domain knowledge of the reader. That approach was somewhat successful in that we and others identified general strategies that were potent factors in separating good readers from poor readers (Paris, Lipson, & Wixson, 1983; Pressley, Goodchild, Fleet, Zajchowski, & Evans, 1989). We also worked diligently to convert those general strategies into procedures that could be effectively taught to students, and did so with some degree of success (e.g., Alexander, White, Haensly, & Crimmins-Jeanes, 1987; Judy et al., 1988). However, the transformation from poor reader to good reader was elusive and the picture of reading development remained blurry and fragmented.

Knowledge-Rich Studies

When the emphasis on general strategic processing did not sufficiently explain students' success (or lack thereof) at text-based learning, my colleagues and I became more interested in the relationship between topic or domain knowledge and strategy use (Alexander & Judy, 1988). Specifically, Judith Judy and I (1988) reviewed the literature to ascertain the potential relations between knowledge and strategy use. Based on that review, we posited that those with less knowledge were more dependent on general cognitive strategies, but that some level of relevant knowledge was required for the efficient and effective use of those strategies. Further, we hypothesized that both general and domain-specific strategies were critical to learning, albeit in different ways.

Later, my colleagues and I (e.g., Alexander & Kulikowich, 1991; Alexander, Pate, Kulikowich, Farrell, & Wright, 1989) put some of those emerging hypotheses to the test in an extensive study of knowledge and strategic processing in history and human biology. Those knowledge–strategy studies were important catalysts for the formulation of the MDL for several reasons. First, those investigations, which were often cross-age, cross-topic, and cross-domain, highlighted the strong but shifting relation between individuals' knowledge and their successful use of strategies. A simple linear path could not adequately capture this knowledge–strategy relation. Whereas too much relevant knowledge meant that certain strategies were of limited value, too little relevant knowledge meant that strategies were often poorly executed.

Second, while differences in topic or domain resulted in varied patterns within individuals, performance patterns were quite consistent for topics and domains across individuals. For instance, an undergraduate student reading about Hawking and Grand Unification Theory or about quarks might well perform differently on those two passages. However, when the data for all the undergraduates were averaged and results correlated, predictable associations between knowledge, strategy use, and text learning emerged (Alexander & Kulikowich, 1994). Those with demonstrated knowledge of the subject matter reported more strategy use during reading and remembered more from the passages than those with little relevant knowledge (e.g., Alexander, Kulikowich, & Schulze, 1994).

Third, understanding the relation between knowledge and strategic processing was highly dependent on our ability to craft measures that are not only statistically reliable and valid but also relevant to educational practice. Our experience at creating reliable and valid subject-matter tests was duly informed by the extant assessment literature (e.g., Linn & Gronlund, 2000). However, the improvements we made in our knowledge measures over the past 15 years have contributed to our modeling of domain expertise. For example, when we devised multiple-choice tests of domain knowledge, we identified a response-option model appropriate for the target population and we followed that model consistently in item generation. In Alexander et al. (1989), for instance, the human biology model for sixth grade was as follows: human biology (HB) correct, HB incorrect, science not HB incorrect, and nonscience incorrect. Such hierarchical options permitted more sophisticated analyses of students' knowledge than is typical for multiple-choice measures.

Knowledge and Interest Studies

As studies of knowledge and strategies were continuing, I was drawn into questions about the relation between knowledge and interest. At the time, there was debate in the literature as to whether students' reported interests reflected their knowledge (Tobias, 1994). On one side was the argument that these two constructs were not well-linked (Schiefele, 1991), a position supported by studies in which student knowledge was controlled or in which readers processed texts on an unfamiliar topic. On the other side was the argument that knowledge and interest appear highly linked, especially for those more competent in a subject (Renninger, 1992). Ultimately, our studies of knowledge and interest helped clarify the knowledge–interest relation, and simultaneously taught my colleagues and me a few critical lessons about the role in interest in developing expertise (e.g., Alexander & Jetton, 1996; Garner, Alexander, Gillingham, Kulikowich, & Brown, 1991).

First, it was evident that clarifying the relation between interest and knowledge required a level of specificity to the constructs not common in the research. In particular, whether knowledge and interest were related depended on the type of knowledge and the form of interest being measured. When researchers examined domain or topic knowledge in relation to individuals' abiding interest in that domain or topic, the positive association between knowledge and interest emerged. Moreover, the strength of that association became stronger as knowledge in the domain rose.

Second, motivational and affective variables, not often studied in the reading literature, could be potent forces in students' text-based learning (Hidi, 1990; Wigfield & Guthrie, 1997). Students who reported higher interest in a particular topic (e.g., frogs) or in reading performed better on text-based learning tasks than their less interested classmates. Third, there were often no pre-reading measures of knowledge or interest that allowed post-reading data to be more adequately judged (Alexander, Kulikowich, & Jetton, 1994). Consequently, individual or group differences that might preexist an intervention or experiment could not be eliminated as factors in outcome effects.

In hindsight, it seems evident that the more researchers knew about participants prior to any reading activity or experimental intervention, the better they could determine the degree to which knowledge or interest interacted as consequence of that activity or intervention.

As the picture of text-based learning became more complicated, I found that a model that captured the interplay among critical forces over time was needed. Once the MDL was initially formulated and predictions forwarded, studies were undertaken to test the hypothesized relations within-individuals over time and across domains, as well as between individuals for the same domain.

THE MDL: EXPERTISE AS ACADEMIC DEVELOPMENT

While I refer to the MDL (Fig. 10.1) as a model of developing expertise in academic domains, there have been evolving versions of the model. Since 1993 research has resulted in a multidimensional and multistage representation of domain learning. The earliest prototype for the MDL, which appeared in Alexander, Kulikowich, and Schulze (1994), was quite stark by comparison, offering simple linear contrasts between subject-matter knowledge and two forms of interest. Before discussing the findings and implications of MDL studies, I want to overview the central dimensions and stages of the model.

Multiple Dimensions of the MDL

Three dimensions frame the MDL—knowledge, interest, and strategic processing—with subcomponents to each (Alexander, 1997). As the traditional expert–novice research strongly established, knowledge and strategic processing

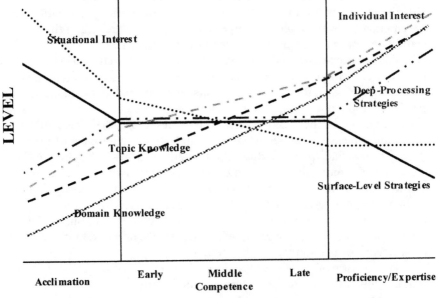

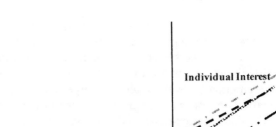

STAGES

FIG. 10.1.   The components and stages of the Model of Domain Learning, as modified from Alexander, P. A., Jetton, T. L., & Kulikowich, J. M. (1995). Interrelationship of knowledge, interest, and recall: Assessing a model of domain learning. *Journal of Educational Psychology, 87*, p. 560.

are defining dimensions of expertise. However, knowledge and strategies, as previously discussed, do not function independently but in concert. As indispensable as knowledge and strategies to unraveling the mystery of expertise is the dimension of interest. Not only is interest tied to domain-specific knowledge, but it is also linked to strategies. Because general strategies are procedures willfully or intentionally invoked, interest would serve as a catalyst for their implementation. Thus, knowledge, strategies, and interest operating in association represent essential keys to unlocking expertise. Of course, this does not mean that knowledge, strategies, and interest are the sole factors that explain expertise development. Yet they remain indispensable dimensions nonetheless.

Knowledge.   Subject-matter knowledge refers to an individual's breadth and depth of knowledge about a given academic domain, such as biology, history, or physics (Alexander, Schallert, & Hare, 1991). From the outset, my colleagues and I have drawn distinctions between two forms of subject-matter knowledge—domain and topic knowledge (e.g., Alexander & Kulikowich, 1994). Domain knowledge represents the breadth of one's knowledge, whereas topic knowledge deals with understanding of a particular topic or concept within that field.

Thus, in Alexander, Kulikowich, and Schulze (1994), we tested undergraduates' knowledge of astrophysics by means of a multiple-choice test covering a range of astrophysics content, and also focused on students' depth of understanding about certain topics from that field, such as black holes, quarks, or Stephen Hawking. We considered it important to examine both forms, given that those relatively new to an academic domain may not know a great deal about the domain of astrophysics but they may know something about select topics in that domain. In fact, in Alexander et al. (1989), we found that elementary students could demonstrate knowledge of certain biological concepts (e.g., heart) without understanding how those concepts related to biological systems (e.g., circulatory) or to the domain itself.

Strategies. The second dimension examined in the MDL is strategic processing, which relates to both general cognitive procedures used in task performance (e.g., summarization) and metacognitive strategies (e.g., self-testing or self-evaluation) pertaining to the monitoring or regulation of one's learning (e.g., Garner & Alexander, 1989; Weinstein & Mayer, 1986). Domain-specific strategies, which are similarly critical to expert performance, are incorporated in the MDL as part of domain knowledge. Initially, I hypothesized a single curvilinear trajectory for strategic processing across the stages of domain learning, disregarding the possibility of quality shifts in strategy use (Alexander, 1997). My colleagues and I later determined that such an approach masked important developmental differences and did not allow the shifting relations between strategy use and knowledge to manifest (Alexander & Murphy, 1998).

Thus, in more recent investigations, my fellow researchers and I have sorted strategies into two classes—surface level and deep processing (Alexander, Sperl, Buehl, Fives, & Chiu, 2002; Murphy & Alexander, 2002; VanSledright & Alexander, 2001). This classification has resulted in a clearer distinction between novices and more competent or more proficient learners. Surface-level reading strategies, such as rereading or omitting unfamiliar words, facilitate the initial comprehension of the domain text. In effect, these strategies give readers access to the message. By comparison, deep-level processing strategies, such as relating text to prior knowledge or questioning the author, involve the personalization or transformation of the message.

We have also included what we call interactive measures in recent studies (Alexander et al., 2002; Murphy & Alexander, 2002). These measures permit

us to examine the shared influence of domain knowledge and general strate-
gic knowledge in problem-solving performance (Alexander, Murphy, &
Kulikowich, 1998; Alexander, Murphy, Woods, Duhon, & Parker, 1997).
Specifically, we used domain-specific analogies:

knowing what : declarative knowledge :: knowing how : _?_ (procedural knowledge)

one limb : monoplegia :: side of body : _?_ (hemiplegia)

and domain-specific commonalities (Murphy & Alexander, 2002):

nominal   ordinal   interval   ratio

levels of measurement
_____

These interactive items have proven useful in cluster-analytic studies as external criterion measures that help establish the statistical differences between emerging expertise profiles.

Interest.   Interest, the third dimension of the MDL, can be interpreted as
the energizing of learners' underlying needs or desires (Ames, 1992; Dweck &
Leggett, 1988). As we did with the knowledge factor, we disentangled two potentially competing forms of interest in the MDL, situational and individual
interest. Situational interest pertains to the temporary arousal or attention
triggered by conditions within the immediate environment. Individual interest signifies a long-term investment or deep-seated involvement in the target
field (Hidi, 1990; Schiefele, 1991). Based on the emerging literature, I expected situational interest to play a stronger role in the early periods of domain learning than individual interest, which I presumed would be relatively
nonexistent at this point in development (Alexander, 1997).

Multiple Stages of Expertise Development

The MDL hypothesizes three stages in the development of domain-specific
expertise: acclimation, competence, and proficiency–expertise. As seen in
Fig. 10.1, each of these stages is distinguished by varied interrelations between knowledge, strategic processing, and interest. What follows are profiles of those three stages. Those profiles have been supported by various
cross-sectional and longitudinal studies summarized in Table 10.1.

Acclimation.   I refer to the initial stage of expertise development as acclimation. I have chosen this term over the common label of novice for several
reasons. First, I wanted to establish that this perspective on expertise deviates
from traditional views in nontrivial ways. The choice of a new, process-

TABLE 10.1
Overview of Prior MDL Studies

	Alexander, Kulikowich, & Schulze (1994)	Alexander, Jetton, & Kulikowich (1995)	Alexander, Murphy, Woods, Duhon, & Parker (1997)	Alexander & Murphy (1998)	Murphy & Alexander (2002)	Alexander, Sperl, Buehl, Fives, & Chiu (2002)
Participants	209 college students	Exp. 1: 30 premed and 17 ed. psy graduate students Exp. 2: 78 undergraduates	329 undergraduates enrolled in intro. educational psychology course	329 educational psychology undergraduates	77 undergraduates in educational psychology	111 general ed. undergraduates; 56 special education undergraduates; 21 special education graduate students, and 20 special education faculty
Domain: Texts	Physics: Two popular-press articles on Hawking and Grand Unification Theory and on quarks	Human immunology: Viral nucleic acids and bacteriophages	Educational psychology: Two segments of scholarly chapters on knowledge and motivation	Educational psychology: Passages on knowledge and motivation	Educational psychology: Passages on knowledge and motivation	Special education: Segment of scholarly chapter on effectiveness of special education
Measures	Topic and domain knowledge tests; passage interest ratings; recall measures	Domain knowledge test; interest ratings; recall measure	Domain knowledge test; personal interest ratings; recall measure	Domain knowledge test; interest scale; strategic processing inventory; domain-specific analogy measure	Subject-matter knowledge test; interactive (knowledge & strategies) test; interest measure; strategy inventory	Procedural and declarative knowledge test; activity-based interest measure; strategy use inventory; recall measure; domain-specific analogy measure

(Continued)

TABLE 10.1
(Continued)

	Alexander, Kulikowich, & Schulze (1994)	Alexander, Jetton, & Kulikowich (1995)	Alexander, Murphy, Woods, Duhon, & Parker (1997)	Alexander & Murphy (1998)	Murphy & Alexander (2002)	Alexander, Sperl, Buehl, Fives, & Chiu (2002)
Analyses	MANOVA; Regression	MANOVA; Cluster analysis	MANOVA; SEM	Cluster analysis	MANOVA; Path analyses	MANOVA; Cluster analysis
Findings	Domain knowledge predicted students' recall and interest; Relations between domain knowledge, interest, and recall grew stronger across performance groups	Exp. 1: Three distinct clusters varying by knowledge, interest, and recall Exp. 2: Four clusters ranging from high knowledge, interest, and recall to low on all variables	Significant increases in knowledge and interest over time and decreased use of text-based (surface-level) strategies; expected relations between and among model factors	Three distinct clusters formed at pretest and four clusters were identified at posttest. Characteristics of clusters confirmed strongly to model predictions.	Path analyses showed that posttest subject-matter knowledge was directly and indirectly predicted by pretest knowledge, surface- and deep-level strategies, interactive knowledge, and pretest interest	Four clusters emerged with the characteristics of acclimation, mid-competence, high-competence, and proficiency.

288

oriented term served that end. Second, the focus of the MDL is on academic domains and I wanted to capture the sense that students new to an academic domain must become oriented (i.e., acclimated) to that unfamiliar terrain, a process that demands their time and energy. Further, unlike certain problem-solving arenas, such as chess, students in the educational system are not free to explore academic domains or not. This is a requirement of the formal educational system. Therefore, each student in postindustrial societies will experience this period of acclimation for multiple academic domains.

Jason, the second grader introduced in the opening scenario, exemplifies many of the characteristics of learners acclimating to an academic domain. His overall perception of history as a domain is understandably underdeveloped. History, as a domain, has little meaning to Jason beyond this class text. If we were to test Jason, as we have in other studies, we would expect to find his domain and topic knowledge to be limited and fragmented. Like Jason, learners in the throes of acclimation lack principled knowledge (Gelman & Greeno, 1989)—a conceptually integrated body of domain-specific knowledge. Jason's limited and unprincipled knowledge means that he will likely experience difficulty distinguishing between information that is relevant versus tangential or accurate versus inaccurate (Alexander, Kulikowich, & Schulze, 1994; Jetton & Alexander, 1997).

Also, Jason's unfamiliarity with the domain and its typical problems means that he would have to rely on surface-level strategies to make sense of his history tests and to begin the process of building a foundation of subject-matter knowledge. Finally, we would expect to find that Jason relies on situational interest to maintain his attention and stimulate his engagement in history learning. Jason's reliance on situational interest makes sense since any seed of individual interest planted by stimulating instruction, would have had limited opportunity to take root and grow (Mitchell, 1993).

Competence. The MDL builds on the presumption that most learners should be able to make the journey from acclimation to competence with the benefits of meaningful formal instruction. Specifically, I hypothesized that the boundary between acclimation and competence can be crossed if learners achieve either a sufficient base of subject-matter knowledge, an effective repertoire of surface-level and deep-processing strategies, or a growing personal association with the domain. The base of knowledge provides the learner with a foothold in the domain—a sense of its structure and lexicon. The repertoire of strategies permits the individual management of problems representative of the domain, whereas the rising interest sparks further exploration or maintains learner investment when subsequent difficulties are encountered.

Of course, the journey toward competence is much easier for those students with profiles that reveal a positive trend in all three of these model dimensions (Alexander, Jetton, & Kulikowich, 1995; Alexander & Murphy,

1998). Likewise, the students who demonstrate low knowledge, little interest, and limited strategic processing must struggle greatly to make any significant progress toward competence in a given domain. In all our cluster analytic studies, my colleagues and I have identified just such disabling profiles (Alexander et al., 1995; Alexander et al., 2002; Murphy & Alexander, 2002).

Thankfully, most individuals who embark on the journey toward expertise in an academic domain will progress into the stage of competence—the most encompassing stage of academic development (see Fig. 10.1). I refer to it as the most encompassing because most students will manage to cross into competence in foundational academic domains. Yet, few will ever achieve proficiency or expertise in any one domain. Moreover, as I (2000) and others (e.g., Bereiter & Scardamalia, 1993; Bransford et al., 1999) have argued, the K–12 educational experience is not equipped to prepare experts in any complex, academic domains. Nor is it likely that the vast majority of students enrolled in schools have any desire to become domain experts. Nonetheless, it is fair to expect that formal education can: (a) help learners develop a foundation of subject-matter knowledge, (b) contribute to learners' strategic processing abilities, and (c) create learning environments that plant the seeds of individual interest. In effect, the fostering of learner competence can and should be a laudable goal for the K–12 educational system.

Fundamentally, there are several characteristics of competent learners that distinguish them from those in acclimation or proficiency. For one, the MDL predicts a quantitative and qualitative shift in the subject-matter knowledge of competent learners. It is not just that these individuals have acquired more domain and topic knowledge, which they have. That body of knowledge is much more conceptually principled and the linkages between topic and domain knowledge far more integrated. Unlike the elementary students my colleagues and I tested (Alexander et al., 1989), the undergraduate and graduate students could provide much more information about human biological concepts and they also understood how these concepts interrelated. We have seen evidence of this qualitative and quantitative shift repeatedly in our research (Alexander et al., 1995). This principled base of subject-matter knowledge has also been well documented in the more traditional research on expert–novice differences (Chi et al., 1981).

Second, studies of the MDL have shown that competence is related to an increasing personal identification with the domain. This characteristic of competence became more apparent in the research when my colleagues and I improved our measures for ascertaining participants' interest in the target domain (Alexander et al., 2002; VanSledright & Alexander, 2002). Specifically, in several of the earlier MDL studies, my colleagues and I simply asked respondents to rate their level of interest in the domain or in topics related to that domain (Alexander, Kulikowich, & Schulze, 1994; Alexander et al., 1997). The procedure did not help us distinguish clearly between fleeting curiosity and ingrained interest. In recent studies, we have been more effective at overcoming those methodological concerns by taking an activity-based approach to gauging individual interest (Schiefele & Csikszentmihalyi, 1994). In this approach, we ask respondents to document how often they engage in a range of domain-related activities during the past year. Those frequencies serve as indicators of their personal and professional investment in the target domain.

The rise in individual interest during competence emerged more clearly when we used this alternative assessment. Individual interest apparently becomes a particularly important dimension during competence. Perhaps that is because individuals' level of personal and professional involvement at this juncture must exceed whatever engagement is required of students in the K–12 system (Alexander, 2000). In our recent study of special education, for example, we found just such a high level of personal engagement in the competence cluster dominated by graduate students from that field. We see a similar level of interest in our history buff Evie, whose activities reflect personal choices not required from any external source.

In the MDL, I (1997) also predicted that the period of competence would be fertile ground for strategic processing. The quantitative and qualitative shifts in learners' knowledge, combined with their growing familiarity with problems typical of the domain, allow competent learners to delve into domain tasks with an orchestration of surface-level and deep-processing strategies. Competent learners' individual interest adds to this strategic performance since these individuals often have reason to ponder and persist at demanding domain tasks. Such predictions have been supported by several of our cluster analytic studies (e.g., Alexander et al., 1995; Alexander & Murphy, 1998).

The recent study of expertise in the domain of special education afforded us new insights into the stage of competence (Alexander et al., 2002). The four educational communities we studied in that investigation (i.e., undergraduate nonspecial education majors, and undergraduates, graduate students, and faculty in special education) pointed to some important differences between individuals in the early period of competence and those progressing deeper into that stage. Specifically, the Early Competence cluster we identified, which consisted primarily of undergraduate special education majors, performed better on the domain knowledge test and the interactive analogy task, and they reported greater individual interest in special education, general and professional, than those in the Acclimation cluster. Those in the Mid-Competence cluster, by comparison, used significantly fewer text-based strategies and descriptively more deep-processing strategies than individuals in the Early Competence cluster. The Mid-Competence cluster also reported a higher level of professional interest than members of either the Acclimation or Early Competence cluster. Thus, it would appear that the relatively different positions of knowledge, interest, and strategic processing at the early, middle, and later periods of competence (see Fig. 10.1) were upheld.

Proficiency–Expertise. It is predicted that the force of any one of the MDL dimensions could catapult students from acclimation into competence. In contrast, a synergy of forces is presumably required for movement from competence into expertise (Alexander, 1997, 2003). To achieve expertise and to maintain that position even in the face of dramatic advancements in a domain requires high levels of domain and topic knowledge, deep-strategic processing, and individual interest. As we see in Bruce, our history scholar, the knowledge base of experts is both broad and deep. What is particularly significant is that these experts, like Bruce, are also contributing new knowledge to their domain. This knowledge creation means that experts must be well versed in prototypic domain problems and methodologies.

Domain experts must also be actively engaged in problem finding. What I mean by problem finding is that these experts are posing questions and conducting studies that push the domain envelope. Bruce's research into Colonial America is a case in point. This problem finding translates into a high level of strategy use among experts, although it is assumed that those strategies are almost exclusively of a deep-processing nature (see Fig. 10.1). This was precisely the strategy use pattern my colleagues and I uncovered in our study in special education. Individuals in the Proficiency cluster, composed of faculty and several advanced doctoral students, were markedly different in their strategic processing than all other clusters, and their documented strategies were exclusively deep processing in form. These individuals were also significantly more knowledgeable than members of the Acclimation and Early Competence groups, as predicted.

Moreover, the individual interest of experts is expected to be higher than the interest of those in the other stages of expertise development. It is also hypothesized that the strength of situational interest evidenced in earlier stages would level off in the proficiency stage. These predictions about interest have been upheld in prior MDL studies. For example, Alexander et al. (2002) demonstrated that those in the Proficiency cluster reported higher engagement in professionally related activities than in all other clusters, including the Mid-Competence group. Interestingly, these experts' reported activities in more personal forms of individual interest were statistically lower than those reported by the Mid-Competence cluster. The predicted relations between interest and subject-matter knowledge for clusters have also been confirmed by this and other cluster analytic studies (e.g., Alexander et al., 1995; Murphy & Alexander, 2002). We would expect Bruce to reflect similar engagement in his chosen profession. Unlike Evie, whose avenues tended toward personal and professional activities, Bruce's involvement would predictably illustrate a more professional focus, including conference presentations, document analyses, and the like.

IMPLICATIONS OF EXPERTISE RECONCEPTUALIZATION

To bring this look at the MDL to a close, I revisit its deviations from traditional expert–novice research, and consider the model's educational implications. Of course, this discussion must be weighed in light of the limitations to this program of research. For example, while longitudinal examinations of MDL dimensions have been undertaken (e.g., Alexander et al., 1997; Lawless & Kulikowich, 1998), more such examinations conducted over longer time spans are required to capture the transformational processes within and across stages of expertise development richly and effectively.

Focus on Academic Domains

The MDL deals with the development of expertise in domains that are core to the educational experience. The goal of this research is to capture academic development by studying the domains that are at the heart of formal schooling, rather than areas somewhat related to or far removed from that unique context. My colleagues and I are not alone in our belief that academic domains can be fertile terrain for understanding how and why expertise develops (Leinhardt, 1989; Wineburg, 1991a, 1991b). Certainly, we can learn about academic development by studying expertise in many forms and in many contexts. However, we can complement and extend traditional experiments into expert–novice differences by taking a more direct path to exploration.

Consideration of the Transformation Process

Central to the MDL are not just the documented differences between those in acclimation and those in expertise. It is the gradual transformation in students' knowledge, interests, and strategic processing that brings about such documented differences. In effect, the trajectories plotted in the MDL offer a process versus product look at expertise. By understanding the process of expertise development, educators can better conceptualize and carry out their roles as guides for learners at different points in this journey.

Teachers in the K–12 system cannot expect to see the characteristics of expertise emerge in their students, regardless of the quality of instruction. These educators can expect to witness the gradual improvement in their students' subject-matter knowledge, individual interest, and deep strategic processing, even as they observe a decreased reliance on students' situational interest and their need for surface-level strategies. Rather than hope for expertise, these teachers can work for competence in their students, attending to both the cognitive and noncognitive dimensions that propel these learners forward in an academic domain.

Multidimensional, Multistage Perspective

The inclusion of motivational and strategic processing variables, along with a knowledge component, brings an added dimension to the MDL not evident in traditional models or theories. The argument is that expertise cannot be understood solely as mental enrichment disconnected from human goals, interests, curiosities, and personality traits (Ackerman, 2003). Granted, the MDL tracks only two forms of interest across three stages. Yet those interest factors have illuminated critical differences between those like Jason, acclimating to an academic domain, those like Evie who are experienced travelers in an academic territory, and those like Bruce who have successfully made the trek from novice to expert. It is hoped that others will contribute to this emerging portrait of expertise my colleagues and I have sketched by exploring other motivational and cognitive forces at work in this developing process.

Intraindividual and Interindividual Analyses

Finally, the perspective on expertise stimulated by the MDL reminds us that expertise is not only a difference observed between individuals but it is also a difference that exists within individuals. While no human can be at more than one place in the physical world, we are all at varied locations when it comes to the world of expertise. For instance, I would classify myself in acclimation in astrophysics, early competence in human biology immunology, mid-competence in special education, and proficiency in educational psychology—four domains targeted in studies of the MDL. Such a diverse pattern is by no means unique, and serves to remind educators that each learner manifests different profiles that need to be identified, appreciated, and instructionally addressed. I believe this attention to individual variability across domains within the educational context will go a long way toward helping learners reach their full academic potential.

REFERENCES

Ackerman, P. L. (2003). Cognitive ability and non-ability trait determinants of expertise. *Educational Researcher, 32*(8), 15–20.

Ackerman, P. L., Kyllonen, P. C., & Roberts, R. D. (1999). *Learning and individual differences: Process, trait, and content determinants.* Washington, DC: American Psychological Association.

Ainley, M. D. (1998). Interest in learning in the disposition of curiosity in secondary students: Investigating process and context. In L. Hoffman, A. Krapp, K. Renninger, & J. Baumert (Eds.), *Interest and learning: Proceedings of the Seeon Conference on interest and gender* (pp. 257–266). Kiel, Germany: IPN.

Alexander, P. A. (1997). Mapping the multidimensional nature of domain learning: The interplay of cognitive, motivational, and strategic forces. In M. L. Maehr & P. R. Pintrich (Eds.), *Advances in motivation and achievement* (Vol. 10, pp. 213–250). Greenwich, CT: JAI.

Alexander, P. A. (2000). Toward a model of academic development: Schooling and the acquisition of knowledge: The sequel. *Educational Researcher, 29*(2), 28–33, 44.

Alexander, P. A. (2003). The development of expertise: The journey from acclimation to proficiency. *Educational Researcher, 32*(8), 10–14.

Alexander, P. A., Hare, V. C., & Garner, R. (1984). Effects of time, access and question type on the response accuracy and frequency of lookbacks in older, proficient readers. *Journal of Reading Behavior, XVI,* 119–130.

Alexander, P. A., & Jetton, T. L. (1996). The role of importance and interest in the processing of text. *Educational Psychology Review, 8*(1), 89–122.

Alexander, P. A., Jetton, T. L., & Kulikowich, J. M. (1995). Interrelationship of knowledge, interest, and recall: Assessing a model of domain learning. *Journal of Educational Psychology, 87,* 559–575.

Alexander, P. A., & Judy, J. E. (1988). The interaction of domain-specific and strategic knowledge in academic performance. *Review of Educational Research, 58,* 375–404.

Alexander, P. A., & Kulikowich, J. M. (1991). Domain-specific and strategic knowledge as predictors of expository text comprehension. *Journal of Reading Behavior, 23,* 165–190.

Alexander, P. A., & Kulikowich, J. M. (1994). Learning from physics text: A synthesis of recent research. *Journal of Research in Science Teaching* [Special Issue on Print Based Language Arts and Science Learning], *31,* 895–911.

Alexander, P. A., Kulikowich, J. M., & Jetton, T. L. (1994). The role of subject-matter knowledge and interest in the processing of linear and nonlinear texts. *Review of Educational Research, 64,* 201–252.

Alexander, P. A., Kulikowich, J. M., & Schulze, S. K. (1994). How subject-matter knowledge affects recall and interest. *American Educational Research Journal, 31,* 313–337.

Alexander, P. A., & Murphy, P. K. (1998). Profiling the differences in students' knowledge, interest, and strategic processing. *Journal of Educational Psychology, 90,* 435–447.

Alexander, P. A., Murphy, P. K., & Kulikowich, J. M. (1998). What responses to domain-specific analogy problems reveal about emerging competence: A new perspective on an old acquaintance. *Journal of Educational Psychology, 90,* 397–406.

Alexander, P. A., Murphy, P. K., & Woods, B. S. (1996). Of squalls and fathoms: Navigating the seas of educational innovation. *Educational Researcher, 25*(3), 31–36, 39.

Alexander, P. A., Murphy, P. K., Woods, B. S., Duhon, K. E., & Parker, D. (1997). College instruction and concomitant changes in students' knowledge, interest, and strategy use: A study of domain learning. *Contemporary Educational Psychology, 22,* 125–146.

Alexander, P. A., Pate, P. E., Kulikowich, J. M., Farrell, D. M., & Wright, N. L. (1989). Domain-specific and strategic knowledge: Effects of training on students of differing ages or competence levels. *Learning and Individual Differences, 1,* 283–325.

Alexander, P. A., Schallert, D. L., & Hare, V. C. (1991). Coming to terms: How researchers in learning and literacy talk about knowledge. *Review of Educational Research, 61,* 315–343.

Alexander, P. A., Sperl, C. T., Buehl, M. M., Fives, H., & Chiu, S. (2002, June). *Modeling domain learning: Profiles from the field of special education.* Manuscript submitted for publication.

Alexander, P. A., White, C. S., Haensly, P. A., & Crimmins-Jeanes, M. (1987). Training in analogical reasoning. *American Educational Research Journal, 24,* 387–404.

Allard, F., & Starkes, J. L. (1991). Motor-skill experts in sports, dance, and other domains. In
K. A. Ericcson & J. Smith (Eds.), *Toward a general theory of expertise: Prospects and limits*
(pp. 126–152). New York: Cambridge University Press.

Ames, C. (1992). Classrooms: Goals, structures, and student motivation. *Journal of Educational
Psychology, 84,* 261–271.

Anderson, J. R. (1983). *The architecture of cognition.* Cambridge, MA: Harvard University
Press.

Anderson, J. R. (1987). Skill acquisition: Compilation of weak-method problem solutions. *Psychological Review, 94,* 192–210.

Anzai, Y., & Yokoyama, T. (1984). Internal models in physics problem solving. *Cognition and
Instruction, 1,* 397–450.

Bereiter, C., & Scardamalia, M. (1993). *Surpassing ourselves: An inquiry into the nature and implications of expertise.* Chicago: Open Court.

Berliner, D. C., & Biddle, B. J. (1995). *The manufactured crisis: Myths, fraud, and the attack on
American's public schools.* Reading, MA: Addison-Wesley.

Bransford, J. D., Brown, A. L., & Cocking, R. R. (1999). *How people learn: Brain, mind, experience, and school.* Washington, DC: National Academy Press.

Brown, J. S., Collins, A., & Duguid, P. (1989). Situated cognition and the culture of learning. *Educational Researcher, 18*(1), 32–42.

Byrnes, J. P. (2001). *Cognitive development and learning* (2nd ed.). Boston: Allyn & Bacon.

Chase, W. G., & Simon, H. A. (1973). Perception in chess. *Cognitive Psychology, 4,* 55–81.

Chi, M. T. H. (1978). Knowledge structures and memory development. In R. Siegler (Ed.),
Children's thinking: What develops? (pp. 73–96). Hillsdale, NJ: Lawrence Erlbaum Associates.

Chi, M. T. H., Feltovich, P. J., & Glaser, R. (1981). Categorization and representation of physics
problems by experts and novices. *Cognitive Science, 5,* 121–152.

Chi, M. T. H., Glaser, R., & Farr, M. (1988). *The nature of expertise.* Hillsdale, NJ: Lawrence
Erlbaum Associates.

de Groot, A. D. (1978). *Thought and choice in chess.* The Hague, Netherlands: Mouton. (Original
work published 1946)

Dewey, J. (1944). *Democracy and education.* New York: Macmillan. (Original work published
1916)

Dweck, C., & Leggett, E. (1988). A social-cognitive approach to motivation and personality.
Psychological Review, 95(2), 56–273.

Ericsson, K. A., & Polson, P. G. (1988). A cognitive analysis of exceptional memory for restau-
rant orders. In M. T. H. Chi, R. Glaser, & M. J. Farr (Eds.), *The nature of expertise* (pp.
23–70). Hillsdale, NJ: Lawrence Erlbaum Associates.

Ericsson, K. A., & Smith, J. (1991). *Toward a general theory of expertise: Prospects and limits.*
New York: Cambridge University Press.

Garner, R., & Alexander, P. A. (1981). Use of passage cues in answering of questions: Investigation of the effects of an explicit external criterion on adults' studying behavior. *Journal of
Reading Behavior, 13,* 335–346.

Garner, R., & Alexander, P. A. (1989). Metacognition: Answered and unanswered questions.
Educational Psychologist, 24, 143–148.

Garner, R., Alexander, P. A., Gillingham, M. G., Kulikowich, J. M., & Brown, R. (1991). Interest and learning from text. *American Educational Research Journal, 28,* 643–659.

Garner, R., Hare, V. C., Alexander, P. A., Haynes, J., & Winograd, P. (1984). Inducing use of a
text lookback strategy among unsuccessful readers. *American Educational Research Journal,
21,* 780–798.

Gelman, R., & Greeno, J. G. (1989). On the nature of competence: Principles for understanding in a domain. In L. B. Resnick (Ed.), *Knowing, learning, and instruction: Essays in honor of Robert Glaser* (pp. 125–186). Hillsdale, NJ: Lawrence Erlbaum Associates.

Gentner, D. R. (1988). Expertise in typewriting. In M. T. H. Chi, R. Glaser, & M. J. Farr (Eds.), *The nature of expertise* (pp. 1–21). Hillsdale, NJ: Lawrence Erlbaum Associates.

Hidi, S. (1990). Interest and its contribution as a mental resource for learning. *Review of Educational Research, 60*, 549–571.

Holyoak, K. J. (1991). Symbolic connectionism: Toward third-generation theories of expertise. In K. A. Ericcson & J. Smith (Eds.), *Toward a general theory of expertise: Prospects and limits* (pp. 301–335). New York: Cambridge University Press.

Jetton, T. L., & Alexander, P. A. (1997). Instructional importance: What teachers value and what students learn. *Reading Research Quarterly, 32*, 290–308.

Judy, J. E., Alexander, P. A., Kulikowich, J. M., & Willson, V. L. (1988). Effects of two instructional approaches and peer tutoring on gifted and nongifted sixth graders' analogy performance. *Reading Research Quarterly, 23*, 236–256.

Lawless, K. A., & Kulikowich, J. M. (1998). Domain knowledge, interest, and hypertext navigation: A study of individual differences. *Journal of Educational Multimedia and Hypermedia, 7*, 51–69.

Leinhardt, G. (1989). Math lessons: A contrast of novice and expert competence. *Journal for Research in Mathematics Education, 20*, 52–75.

Linn, R. L., & Gronlund, N. E. (2000). *Measurement and assessment in teaching* (8th ed.). Upper Saddle River, NJ: Merrill/Prentice Hall.

Meece, J. L., Blumenfeld, P. C., & Hoyle, R. (1988). Students' goal orientations and cognitive engagement in classroom activities. *Journal of Educational Psychology, 80*, 514–523.

Mitchell, M. (1993). Situational interest: Its multifaceted structure in the secondary school mathematics classroom. *Journal of Educational Psychology, 85*, 424–436.

Murphy, P. K., & Alexander, P. A. (2002). What counts?: The predictive power of subject-matter knowledge, strategic processing, and interest in domain-specific performance. *Journal of Experimental Education, 70*, 197–214.

Newell, A., & Simon, H. A. (1972). *Human problem solving*. Englewood Cliffs, NJ: Prentice-Hall.

Paris, S. G., Lipson, M. Y., & Wixson, K. K. (1983). Becoming a strategic reader. *Contemporary Educational Psychology, 8*, 293–316.

Patel, V. L., & Groen, G. J. (1986). Knowledge-based solution strategies in medical reasoning. *Cognitive Science, 10*, 91–116.

Pintrich, P. R. (2000). An achievement goal theory perspective on issues in motivation terminology, theory, and research. *Contemporary Educational Psychology, 25*, 92–104.

Pintrich, P. R., Marx, R. W., & Boyle, R. A. (1993). Beyond cold conceptual change: The role of motivational beliefs and classroom contextual factors in the process of conceptual change. *Review of Educational Research, 63*, 167–199.

Pressley, M., Goodchild, F., Fleet, J., Zajchowski, R., & Evans, E. D. (1989). The challenges of classroom strategy instruction. *Elementary School Journal, 89*, 301–342.

Reio, T. G., Jr., & Wiswell, A. (2000). Field investigation of the relationship between adult curiosity, workplace learning and job performance. *Human Resource Development Quarterly, 11*(1), 1–36.

Renninger, K. A. (1992). Individual interest and development: Implications for theory and practice. In K. A. Renninger, S. Hidi, & A. Krapp (Eds.), *The role of interest in learning and development* (pp. 361–395). Hillsdale, NJ: Lawrence Erlbaum Associates.

Schiefele, U. (1991). Interest, learning, and motivation. *Educational Psychologist, 26*, 229–323.

Schiefele, U., & Csikszentmihalyi, M. (1994). Interest and the quality of experience in classrooms. *European Journal of Psychology in Education, 9*, 251–270.

Senge, P. A. (1990). *The fifth discipline: The art and practice of the learning organization*. New York: Doubleday.

Simon, H. A., & Chase, W. G. (1973). Skill in chess. *American Scientist, 61*, 394–403.

Sinatra, G., & Pintrich, P. R. (2002). *Intentional conceptual change.* Mahwah, NJ: Lawrence Erlbaum Associates.

Snow, R. E., Corno, L., & Jackson, D. (1996). Individual differences in affective and conative functions. In D. C. Berliner & R. C. Calfee (Eds.), *Handbook of educational psychology* (pp. 242–310). New York: Macmillan.

Sternberg, R. J. (1986). *Intelligence applied: Understanding and increasing your intellectual skills.* San Diego, CA: Harcourt Brace.

Sternberg, R. J. (2003). Who is an expert student? *Educational Researcher, 32*(8), 5–9.

Tobias, S. (1994). Interest, prior knowledge, and learning. *Review of Educational Research, 64*, 37–54.

VanSledright, B., & Alexander, P. A. (2002). *Historical knowledge, thinking, and beliefs: Evaluation component of the Corps of Historical Discovery Project* (#S215X010242). United States Department of Education.

Voss, J. F., Tyler, S. W., & Yengo, L. A. (1983). Individual differences in the solving of social science problems. In R. F. Dillon & R. R. Schmeck (Eds.), *Individual differences in cognition* (pp. 205–232). New York: Academic Press.

Weinstein, C. E., & Mayer, R. E. (1986). The teaching of learning strategies. In M. C. Wittrock (Ed.), *Handbook of research on teaching* (3rd ed., pp. 315–327). New York: Macmillan.

Wigfield, A., & Guthrie, J. T. (Eds.). (1997). Motivation for reading: Individual, home, textual, and classroom perspectives [Special Issue]. *Educational Psychologist, 32*(2).

Wineburg, S. S. (1991a). Historical problem solving: A study of the cognitive processes used in the evaluation of documentary and pictorial evidence. *Journal of Educational Psychology, 83*, 73–87.

Wineburg, S. S. (1991b). On the reading of historical texts: Notes on the breach between school and academy. *American Educational Research Journal, 28*, 495–519.

11

▼▼▼▼▼▼▼

Motivation, Emotion,
and Expert Skill Acquisition

Neil Charness
Michael Tuffiash
Tiffany Jastrzembski
Florida State University

Why do some people attain high levels of skill while others, who may appear to put in equal amounts of time at the activity, do not? Attempts to address this question often revolve around the existence and definition of innate talent (Howe, Davidson, & Sloboda, 1998; Simonton, 1999). However, careful consideration of the available scientific evidence leads to a more complex scenario. Regardless of any innate biological advantages that some individuals may possess, all people must engage in significant amounts of what has been called deliberate practice, that is, practice aimed at improving performance with appropriate subgoals (Ericsson & Charness, 1994; Ericsson, Krampe, & Tesch-Romer, 1993) in order to reach and sustain elite levels of skill. In fact, established experts in a variety of domains report thousands of hours of deliberate practice prior to reaching professional levels of performance (e.g., chess: Charness, Krampe, & Mayr, 1996; music: Ericsson et al., 1993; sports: Starkes, Deakin, Allard, Hodges, & Hayes, 1996), and even the most precocious individuals in these domains show evidence of extended periods of intense preparation prior to their greatest achievements (Charness et al., 1996; Ericsson et al., 1993; Howe et al., 1998).

However, the concept of high-quality goal-directed practice usually implies difficult and repetitive activities that are undertaken during extended periods of isolation, and thus it is not surprising to find that deliberate practice is rated as particularly effortful and unpleasant compared with other domain-relevant activities (Ericsson et al., 1993; Starkes et al., 1996). Thus, an important subquestion arises: Why would anyone take on an inherently disagreeable task for hours, years, or in the case of experts, decades of time? This leads to issues of motivation and personality, as well as to consideration of the environment surrounding training opportunities. A useful framework for considering these factors in chess is offered in Charness et al. (1996) shown in Fig. 11.1.

As cognitive psychologists, we have generally been concerned with drawing out the relationships on the right side of the figure and the links between practice, the cognitive and physical system, and performance are reasonably well understood. In contrast, relatively little attention has been paid to the relationships between intrapersonal and interpersonal factors and their impact on practice. However, these relationships encompass a considerable range of topics, some of which have already been addressed elsewhere (Charness et al., 1996; Sloboda, Davidson, Howe, & Moore, 1996). In this chapter, we are concerned primarily with issues related to motivation, personality, and other intrapersonal constructs as they relate to the development and maintenance of skilled performance. In addition, we focus our attention primarily on the domains of chess and music. Aside from being the subject of the most entrenched views related to talent and training, these two domains also allow one to make interesting comparisons regarding motivational and emotional constructs in two intellectual skill domains that are notably different in terms of their task demands (e.g., psychomotor coordination and creative expression in music vs. mental search–recall, analytical problem solving in chess) and goals (collaboration vs. competition). We turn our attention first to chess.

A Taxonomy of Skill Factors

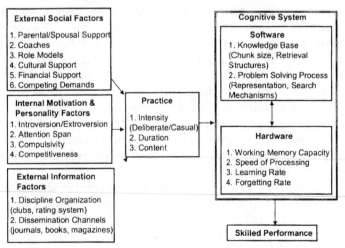

FIG. 11.1.   Framework for understanding factors mediating expert performance.

MOTIVATION IN CHESS

Task Value

People can be motivated to engage in an activity for intrinsic and extrinsic reasons. In both cases, there must be some reward mechanism linked to the activity. One prominent theory of intrinsic motivation suggests that people derive pleasure from pursuing an activity when they reach a flow state.

Csikszentmihalyi's (1975) theory of flow was formulated to define features related to intrinsic motivation and intrinsic rewards. He proposed that when individuals experience flow, they are acting with total involvement in the situation, maintain an internal locus of control, and sustain focused mental concentration on a task; such that even distracter variables like environment and personal concerns are ignored. Individuals who experience flow are rewarded by the thrill of competition and the challenge it presents, rather than by external rewards. As one outstanding chess player noted: "I get a tyrannical sense of power . . . as though I have the fate of another human in my grasp . . . Although I am not aware of specific things, I have a general feeling of well-being, and that I am in complete control of my world" (Csikszentmihalyi, 1975, p. 51). It is also necessary for individuals in the flow state to perceive opportunities for action as being evenly matched by their capabilities, so that boredom or anxiety do not enter the equation. These characteristics allow the individual to feel in control of the situation, desire a mental or physical challenge, enjoy the activity for its sake, and crave the thrill enough to seek out future opportunities—the critical indicators of intrinsic motivation.

Although flow theory may describe practice in some domains, it seems somewhat implausible for expert chess players to experience all the qualities of flow for any sustained amount of time, as defined by Csikszentmihalyi. Since chess skill is measured by a well validated interval-level rating system (Elo, 1986), serious players typically know exactly how proficient they are, and exactly how proficient their opponents are. One quality related to flow, namely the perception of the task matched to level of capability, becomes nearly irrelevant since rated players know the exact skill of their opponent.

Another example of why skilled chess players may not experience flow stems from physiological research. During tournament chess alone, physiological parameters vary greatly, suggesting that the individual is very cognizant of external factors and may waver in feelings of control and confidence (Leedy & Dubeck, 1971). Maximum changes often occur immediately after the opponent makes a move, and are associated with feelings of surprise, anger, and fear, depending on the quality of the move and whether or not it was foreseen. Leedy and Dubeck's (1971) research also showed a correlation between the score of a player on a motivation test and the degree of physiological changes over the course of the game, such that those who put forth the most effort had the greatest physiological changes. These data clearly suggest that individuals with higher intrinsic motivation are actually more prone to factors that would be out of the flow experience. In fact, old homilies in chess such as "sit on your hands" (do not make an impulsive move) and "when considering making a move, think of a better move" are aimed at getting players to control potential negative emotional influences on cognitive processes supporting the goal of choosing the best move.

We turn next to consider the role of external motivators on internal motivation, a topic that has engendered some debate (e.g., Eisenberger & Cameron, 1996). Deci, Cascio, and Krussel (1975) defined intrinsic motivation as behavior that allows a person to feel competent and self-determined. They theorized that when contingent extrinsic rewards are introduced into situations, an individual's locus of causality shifts from the self to the environment, feelings of competence decrease, and intrinsic motivation suffers. Pritchard, Campbell, and Campbell (1977) tested this hypothesis to determine the relationship between intrinsic and extrinsic motivation. They utilized a set of chess problems that asked experienced chess players to check the Black King with the White pieces in two moves, taking into account the possible countermoves made by a hypothetical player. They split subjects into two groups and tested individuals over two sessions, 1 week apart. For the first session, one group was simply asked to complete as many problems as possible within 30 minutes. The second group was told that the individual who solved the largest number of chess problems in the allotted time would receive $5.00, and that the reward was a one-time offer not to be proffered at the follow-up session. Thus, when subjects returned for the second session, both groups were given the same instructions to complete as many problems as possible within 30 minutes. Results revealed that subjects in the paid group showed a much larger decrease in the time spent working on problems from the first to second session than the unpaid group. Task satisfaction suffered for the paid group as well, with a difference that approached significance.

Pritchard et al. (1977) interpreted these results to mean that in the case of extrinsic rewards, intermediate factors related to intrinsic motivation, like feelings of self-determination, may decrease, but the link between extrinsic and intrinsic motivation is not necessarily direct. It is plausible that intrinsic motivation would increase in the face of an extrinsic reward if, for example, increased feedback (to enhance feelings of accomplishment) was also incorporated. By extrapolating these results and conclusions to elite chess players, it seems evident that the most highly skilled players probably operate on more than external motivation, because rewards do not provide the incentive to excel and gain skills, nor do they directly promote a desire to persist with practice. In fact, in the history of chess, very few professional chess players have been able to support themselves solely by winning monetary prizes in chess tournaments. Most have had to hold other jobs, and teach or write about chess to supplement tournament winnings.

Self-Regulation and Goal Setting

Our review thus far focuses on internal and external reward effects on motivation. Given the long preparation period necessary to reach high levels of performance, it is clear that people must set goals and monitor progress toward those goals. Personal initiative, diligence, self-efficacy, and self-regulation are some key characteristics of individuals who succeed in planning and meeting goals (Bandura, 1997; Schunk & Zimmerman, 1994; Zimmerman & Schunk, chap. 12). These characteristics are highly correlated with participating in and sustaining deliberate practice over extended periods of time, a known predictor of expert performance (Ericsson et al., 1993). The question of interest then becomes: why are some individuals so strongly driven to excel in a given domain, while others lose interest and fall by the wayside?

Schunk and Zimmerman (1997) argued that specific task competencies are learned and developed in a series of four stages (observation, emulation, self-control, and self-regulation). These competencies lay the groundwork for intrinsic motivation to develop and promote a desire to advance to higher levels within a domain. In the earliest stages of skill development, learners rely on advanced students and experts to teach and show them pertinent concepts related to the skill and to emulate and hone their own abilities through feedback and guidance from those mentors. Learners hear the motivational orientation, self-expressed beliefs, and performance standards of role models and ultimately adopt some or all of them as their own (Zimmerman & Ringle, 1981). Research has shown that the higher the perseverance of a model, the higher the perseverance of the observer; and the greater the observer's perceived similarity to the model, the greater the motivation to continue practice (Zimmerman & Rosenthal, 1974).

Later stages of development shift the locus of learning from social to internal sources (Schunk & Zimmerman, 1997). The competent learner focuses on the process rather than the outcome to master components of the skill, and chooses to deliberately practice weak (and often unpleasant) areas in order to achieve mastery. The learner possesses the ability to self-direct practice sessions and monitors the distance between the current state and goal without relying on guidance from social support. With increased perception of self-efficacy, the learner has the ability to sustain motivation and adaptively implement skills in dynamic situations. In sum, this model theorizes that intrinsic motivation and self-regulation emerge from initially extensive social guidance that diminish over time as motivational qualities and monitoring abilities of mentors are internalized by the learner. Horgan's (1992) research with chess-playing children fits this theory quite well, in that children expected to be in the advanced stages of this motivation model are highly accurate calibrators of what they know, what needs to be worked on, and how practice time should be allotted to strengthen weaknesses.

Goal setting is another important factor related to motivation and self-regulation. Classic research by Locke (1968) demonstrated that individuals with difficult goals perform better than those with easy or unspecified goals. He suggested that when an individual sets a clear goal, he is motivated to achieve that goal and must exert more effort when the bar is set high. Campbell and Ilgen (1976) refined Locke's explanation by theorizing that setting higher goals early on in skill acquisition may reflect more than an effect of intrinsic motivation. They argued that performance may improve more because task skills themselves are enhanced. Thus, better performance could just as likely result from learning as from internalized motivation. They substantiated their hypothesis by manipulating task difficulty (three levels) and goal setting (three levels) in a set of chess problems for undergraduate chess players. Results revealed that individuals who worked on more complex problems from the beginning gained skills to deal with harder situations later on, and individuals who worked toward higher goals put forth more effort to achieve higher levels of intended performance. This research shows that elite chess players may perform better not only because of an inherent intrinsic motivation to achieve, but because they attained task skills early on to deal with more difficult situations by setting goals higher.

Horgan (1992) studied skill attributions of child chess players (ages 6.5–16) covering a wide range of skill, from beginner to advanced levels. Using hypothetical situations, players were asked to predict future wins in nonchess tasks after a series of wins and losses. Results revealed that higher skilled players became less overconfident after wins, but maintained overconfidence after losses, suggesting a mindset that is excellent for maintaining motivation. This implies that chess not only improves problem solving, but competition in chess may help form this highly functional motivational pattern. Future studies will need to assess whether this pattern of motivation carries over into other real-life domains and try to tease apart the directionality of causation between motivation and competition in chess.

Personality and Chess

Much literature exists regarding the hypothesis that personality plays a central role in guiding choices in vocation and leisure, due to the reasoning that people are drawn to and become involved in activities that allow for natural personal expression (e.g., Holland, 1966). Thus, the degree of pleasure and enjoyment an individual experiences is theorized to be a function of the fit between personality traits and the nature of the domain (Avni, Kipper, & Fox, 1987). In chess, research has suggested that players of different skill levels are differentiated from each other and from the general population in terms of personality characteristics. Kelly (1985) administered the Myers–Briggs Type Indicator to a large sample of chess players varying in skill. On the temperament dimension, chess players had much higher scores for introversion, intuition, and thinking than the general population, and master-level players were even more likely to be introverted and intuitive than average players. To the extent that we can link introversion to willingness to spend more time with things (e.g., chess books) than with people, and intuition to pattern recognition versus calculation, these results are consistent with other research on expert performance.

Avni et al. (1987) recruited players ranked from the intermediate to grandmaster level, and divided them into competitive and moderately competitive groups based on the number of tournaments they competed in per year and the most current rating they possessed. These groups were compared against a control group of participants who did not play chess or other strategic games. All participants were administered subscales from the Minnesota Multiphasic Personality Inventory (MMPI) to measure unconventional thinking (Infrequency [F] scale), neuroticism (Ne scale), hostility (Hos scale), and suspicion (Paranoia [Pa] scale). The Lie (L) and Correction (C) scales were utilized as validity indices for the aforementioned elements.

Results indicated that different trait profiles distinguished the groups from one another. Highly competitive players exuded more suspicion, distrust, guardedness, and intense concentration than both nonplayers and moderately competitive players. These qualities are highly compatible with the nature of the game of chess, as they are likely to assist in formulating sound strategy and predicting moves made by the other player. It is reasonable to argue that because the fit between these traits and the domain of chess is quite compatible, competitive players are able to express their personality tendencies and enjoy the game for the challenge it offers and the desire to win. It is also possible that playing chess a great deal (constantly defending against threats to your army's well-being) elevates such traits, (the classic case of even a paranoid is right sometimes) though the well-known stability of personality traits across the life span would tend to argue against this interpretation. It is also possible that there are reciprocal relationships between personality and environment in the same sense that has been shown for work environments and intellectual ability (see Schooler, Mulatu, & Oates, 1999). That is, personality traits may initially lead to selecting particular environmental niches that in turn continue to modify and shape personality.

Highly competitive and moderately competitive chess players were also differentiated from the control group of nonplayers by unconventional mode of thinking and inordinate attention to detail, characteristics that are critical to playing a strategic game of chess, but perhaps also reflect a different goal the player wishes to achieve. These results could be taken in line with Csikszentmihalyi's (1982) research, revealing that the best players were motivated to meet challenges in a competitive fashion and enhance status, whereas intermediate players generally played for the problem-solving element of the game and the experience it offered. Clearly, the personality profiles associated with each group seem to assist in achieving intended goals, and are closely tied to how motivated one would be to advance task skills.

Joireman, Fick, and Anderson (2002) hypothesized that sensation seeking is a personality characteristic correlated with participation, persistence, and skill in chess due to the fact that the game requires intense concentration, offers opportunity to demonstrate dominance, and includes an element of risk which adds thrill and excitement. Taking measurements from the previously validated Sensation Seeking Scale (SSS; Zuckerman, 1979), this study utilized undergraduate chess players of varying self-reported skill. Results supported the hypotheses that sensation seekers (high scorers on Total SSS) were more likely to have tried chess and to have had more experience with the game than those who were not (low scorers on Total SSS). This finding was primarily determined by the degree to which the individual sought out exciting and perhaps risky activities, providing support to the claim that chess is an engaging and thrilling activity, and therefore attracts people whose personalities complement those feelings. It would be a fruitful endeavor to replicate this study with rated chess players to see whether this dimension of personality is associated with elite levels of performance.

MOTIVATION IN MUSIC

Drives, Traits, and the Musical Temperament

As noted in the introduction, while there is a strong relationship between the quantity of high-quality training and the level of attained skill in music, chess, and other domains, those activities that are known to be most relevant to improvements in performance are also generally viewed as the most aversive. In spite of this conflict, a small number of individuals seem willing and able to persist on the path to excellence. One historically significant interpretation of the previous scenario, put forth by Galton (1869/1978), is that the motivation to pursue and persist in challenging activities is part of a cluster of innate qualities or capacities that allow for the emergence of exceptional ability. Though much of the research that followed did not specifically focus on the motivational component of talent, this area has recently been revived. Based on evidence from prodigies and savants, Winner (1996, 2000) argued that the characteristic drive or rage to master among gifted and precocious individuals stems from innate sources. The application of this argument to music has focused on historical accounts of famous prodigies who appeared to be obsessed with sound during infancy, as well as interview studies with the parents of contemporary musical prodigies who report stories of children who began to sing spontaneously or played with musical toys for hours at a time without prompting (Feldman, 1986; Winner & Martino, 1993).

Some have dismissed these anecdotes as unreliable on the grounds that retrospective accounts of childhood events or second-hand reports of skilled performance and its antecedents are particularly vulnerable to confirmation bias and other measurement distortions (Ericsson & Faivre, 1988; Howe, 1990). In some cases, it appears that some accounts of the precocious behaviors of musical and other artistic prodigies may be outright fabrications (see Ericsson & Charness, 1994). However, even if this type of data were admitted as a reliable source of evidence, one would also need to account for the results of other interview studies in which high-achieving music students and elite adult musicians did not show evidence of exceptional promise at early ages and were not exceptionally motivated to practice at the start of training (Sloboda & Howe, 1991; Sosniak, 1985). Skeptics may counter that perhaps the right environmental triggers or catalysts were simply not presented to the participants of these studies in order to allow their exceptional abilities and internal motivation to emerge earlier in development (Gagne, 1993). Thus, long-lasting motivational drives in musically precocious or talented children may need to be set in motion by some kind of early crystallizing experience (Freeman, 1999; Walters & Gardner, 1986) in which his or her attention becomes transfixed on music due to some salient quality or feature of a specific event and its connection with biological dispositions related to high musical intelligence (Gardner, 1983). In fact, Walters and Gardner (1986) went so far as to suggest that talent actually causes motivation, such that an individual who already possesses extraordinary intellectual powers in a particular domain is more likely to be interested in and curious about domain-relevant problems and challenges.

We have several reasons for being skeptical of this claim. First, several studies of musical precocity, giftedness, or talent make reference to the exceptionally supportive parents and the exceptional opportunities for learning that they begin to provide prior to the emergence of exceptional performance (Sloboda & Howe, 1991; see also Howe et al., 1998). This raises the question regarding whether or not some form of behavioral reinforcement, either intentional or unintentional, might account for at least some of the precocious musical behaviors that are frequently attributed to innate biological sources. Thus, we might imagine a situation in which a child accidentally makes a rhythmic noise in the presence of a parent, who subsequently gives a verbal prompt or perhaps a material reward for child's behavior, thus encouraging the child to repeat it. This kind of scenario may be very difficult to capture in a laboratory setting, and even longitudinal observations may fail to catch it. However, there is some evidence to suggest that strong behavioral contingencies operate during formal musical learning at very early stages of development. For example, the Suzuki method, which promotes high levels of teacher approval, parental involvement, and concentrated rehearsal, may provide the necessary prerequisites for the acquisition of musical skill and motivation to practice through optimal behavioral shaping (Colprit, 2000; Duke, 1999; Scott, 1992). One might even interpret this sort of experience as an example of a broader behavioral phenomenon known as learned industriousness, whereby early extrinsic reinforcers can help shape behavior into patterns that are consistent with indices of intrinsic motivation (Eisenberger, 1992). Nevertheless, even if the evidence in favor of innate motivational dispositions can be accounted for by behavioral mechanisms or other explanations, this does not preclude the possibility that biologically determined factors have other indirect effects. As discussed in our review of the personality of chess players, we may also want to consider whether broader emotional and social dispositions are important precursors of musical ability, or whether such traits or temperaments might predispose certain individuals to engage in the activities of a particular domain.

Taking into consideration the necessity of solitary practice, as well as the expectations of expressive performance among critics and audiences, one might expect to find a high degree of introversion and emotionality among musicians (at least those in the classical genre; Kemp, 1996). The empirical literature is somewhat consistent with this argument, in that professional classical musicians as a group do generally score higher than the norm on various trait measures of introversion and emotionality (Hamilton, Kella, & Hamilton, 1995; Kemp, 1981a; Marchant-Haycox & Wilson, 1992; Steptoe & Fidler, 1987). However, most of the sample means from these studies rest well inside the normal range, and the degree of variability within the samples often spans both ends of the trait poles. In addition, the predicted profile is even less clear when one examines the same personality traits in college music students. For instance, some researchers have found music majors to be more introverted relative to normative samples (Bell & Cresswell, 1984; Kemp, 1981a), but others have observed a tendency toward extraversion (Cooley, 1961; Kemp, 1982; Shuter-Dyson, 2000; Wubbenhorst, 1994). Similarly, while some researchers (Kemp, 1981a; Shuter-Dyson, 2000) report above average scores for music students on measures of emotionality, others have observed the opposite trend (Bell & Cresswell, 1984; Cooley, 1961). One might explain the previous inconsistencies by arguing that college students preparing for a career in musical performance fit a different personality profile than those pursuing an educational track. Kemp (1982) highlighted this point directly, and it should be noted that in studies where extraversion was the predominant profile (Cooley, 1961; Shuter-Dyson, 2000), the samples were largely comprised of music education majors. One possible exception is the study by Wubbenhorst (1994), who found roughly equal proportions of introverts and extraverts among education majors and performance majors based on scores from the Myers–Briggs Type Indicator (MBTI; Myers & McCauley, 1985). However, Kemp (1996), using the same measure, reported a ratio of nearly two introverts for every one extravert in a sample of 210 performance majors.

As suggested in the discussion of personality and chess, one must also consider the possibility that the experience of the musical skill acquisition process shapes a musician's personality as much as his or her personality shapes the experience. In the case of introversion, Kemp (1981a) was careful to point out that years of exposure to solitary activity may evoke a tendency to withdrawal from social situations, and other researchers have suggested that solitary practice may serve a protective function among children subjected to adverse domestic conditions or other social stresses (Ericsson & Faivre, 1988; Howe, 1990). Likewise, high levels of emotional sensitivity or instability among professional musicians are a predictable outcome of the intense pressures and anxieties of a career in public performance (Cooper & Wills, 1989; Hamilton et al., 1995). Similar explanations may also account for the tendency to find the least consistency in personality profiles of novice music students (Cutietta & McAllister, 1997; Freeman, 1974; Sample & Hotchkiss, 1971; Schleuter, 1972; Shuter-Dyson, 1977; Thayer, 1972; Wragg, 1974), and increasingly distinctive profiles among samples engaged in advanced stages of training and professional activity (see earlier studies).

Proponents of the innate talent perspective may counter that those who possess the proper character prior to training are still more likely to make it to the top of the heap and that the exaggerated personality profiles of adult professional musicians relative to amateurs or young beginners reflect psychological selection mechanisms that weed out individuals with incongruent profiles. However, we can say with some degree of certainty that this is unlikely for two reasons. First, the correlations between traditional personality traits and tests or ratings of musical talent during childhood, adolescence, and adulthood are either too small in magnitude or too unreliable in terms of their direction or consistency across studies to be worthy of serious discussion (Cooley, 1961; Freeman, 1974; Lehmann, 1951; Schleuter, 1972; Shuter-Dyson, 1977; Thayer, 1972; Tunstall, 1982; Wragg, 1974). Second, a close examination of the data from those studies where selected personality traits among musically trained or talented samples appear to be significantly different from established norms reveals that the degree of variability within the musical group is much more striking than the deviations of musicians from the general population. Such variability further calls into question the validity of using personality measures to predict future participation or achievement in music.

It should be noted that while our perspective on innate musical disposi- tions is somewhat negative, we do not mean to imply that personality and similar constructs are completely irrelevant to musical skill acquisition. For instance, individual differences in emotional temperaments might account for significant variability in musical tastes or choice of instrument (Kemp, 1996), though again, the influence of early upbringing and other subtle social forces (e.g., gender stereotypes, see O'Neill, 1997) should not be discounted. However, it is also likely that any significant influences of dispositional vari- ables on musical behavior are mediated by some set of intervening motiva- tional constructs. It is to the latter that we now turn our attention.

Expectations, Values, and Goal Orientations

In contrast to earlier motivational theories and their emphasis on uncon- scious, innate drives, proponents of contemporary motivational frameworks tend to emphasize the role of conscious, explicit attitudes, such as the subjec- tive value of different tasks or goals and the expectations that individuals set for their potential performance. Proponents of this perspective argue that an individual's willingness to engage and persist in effortful activities is a func- tion of the importance or enjoyment that they ascribe to achieving a goal and their beliefs regarding the relevance or usefulness of particular activities in reaching those goals (Eccles & Wigfield, 2002).

Expectancy-value theory and related concepts have also been somewhat successful in accounting for participation and success in musical endeavors. For instance, Hallam (1998) reported that students' attitudes regarding the value of practice were significant predictors of performance on a standard- ized test of instrumental musical skill after accounting for the influence of time spent in training. In addition, a follow-up study revealed that those stu- dents who dropped out of musical instruction during the subsequent year tended to feel less strongly about the value of practice during the initial sur- vey. Although the author did not report the correlation between practice- related values and actual practice time, other studies have addressed this issue in detail. For instance, O'Neill (1999) reported a small but statistically signifi- cant positive relationship between the subjective value (i.e., perceived impor- tance) and the quantity of current practice among 60 adolescent instrumental music students, but did not elaborate on the contents of that practice. In a more detailed investigation, McPherson and McCormick (1999) found that the degree of self-reported intrinsic value, described as both the importance of doing well and the enjoyment of playing the instrument, was a modest but statistically significant predictor of the frequency of formal practice (techni- cal exercises and repertoire) and informal practice (improvising or playing for fun) among 190 piano students. Further studies with the same sample revealed that while expectations of success were the strongest predictors of performance on a standardized test of piano skill, intrinsic value accounted for additional variability among those piano students classified as beginners or intermediate-level performers (McPherson & McCormick, 2000).

Though the effects of intrinsic value on practice in the above studies were fairly small, the expectancy-value perspective may provide a potentially useful framework for describing the discrepancy between low levels of enjoyment and high levels of engagement in serious practice among full-time music students. That is, while they may view the daily grind of the practice room as unpleasant or boring, they are willing to stick with it because they have firsthand knowledge regarding its relevance to performance. The data from conservatory violin students in Ericsson et al. (1993) was consistent with this explanation, but further investigation is warranted in order to clarify the strength and nature of these relationships.

Another contemporary perspective on achievement motivation is concerned with the manner in which individuals orient themselves to learning situations and the reasons that they cite for their success or failure in achieving a particular goal. The empirical foundation for this perspective is based on observations of students who are exposed to experimentally induced failure (i.e., attempting extremely difficult tasks or being told that their responses are incorrect regardless of their actual performance; Diener & Dweck, 1978). Under these conditions, many children give up and are resigned to the attitude that they simply lack the ability to succeed at the task. This attitude is labeled as a performance or ego orientation, with the implication that the child is forming a theory of competence based on the lack of a stable ability that appears to be present among their relatively successful peers. Some children, however, take a more adaptive approach to failure, focusing on self-development and learning relative to internal standards and goals. This category of responses is labeled as the task or mastery goal orientation.

Dweck and colleagues (e.g., see chap. 2) argued that through time and repeated experiences of success or failure, these beliefs begin to crystallize into trait-like tendencies or orientations, and that such orientations may predict responses to challenging tasks in the future. The implication of this theory for expert skill acquisition is that mastery-oriented children are more likely to persist at activities such as deliberate practice that are inherently challenging and require extended durations of effort before real progress becomes evident. Conversely, performance or ego-oriented children are more likely give up or simply to avoid such challenges.

In the case of music, there is some preliminary evidence to suggest that goal orientations may influence the quantity and possibly the quality of instrumental practice. Yoon (1997) asked grade-school music students to rank eight different reasons for practicing or playing a musical instrument and to indicate their frequency of musical practice. The author reported a positive correlation between the rank of a mastery goal statement (wanting to learn or practice new skills or repertoire) and the frequency of current practice, as well as a negative correlation between practice and the rank of a performance–ego-oriented goal statement (wanting to be better at playing music than other students). It should be noted that while the sizes of the correlations were fairly small, the conditions of the study were perhaps not ideal for detecting these effects—neither practice time nor goal orientations were measured directly. However, one study that rectified these problems produced contradictory results. O'Neill (1999) found a negative relationship between mastery goal orientations and quantity of practice: students who exhibited mastery-oriented responses to experimentally induced failure tended to practice less during the subsequent year than those who exhibited performance-oriented responses. In order to explain this unusual finding, O'Neill suggested that the mastery-oriented music students may have made more effective use of their practice time than the performance-oriented students and were thus able to accomplish similar goals in shorter durations. Smith (2003) provided data that are somewhat consistent with this explanation. Smith asked a large sample of college music majors to complete measures of goal orientation and an index of practice strategies. Smith found significant relationships between mastery– task orientation scores and self-reported frequencies of effective practice strategies, though the magnitudes of the correlations were fairly small and the predicted negative relationships with the performance–ego goal-orientations were not observed.

Given the discrepancies between the goal orientation studies previously discussed, and the generally small effects in each study, it is it is probably the case that like personality traits, goal orientations may have only a secondary influence on practice and other skill-related behaviors. Yet again, whether or not their influence is mediated by the more explicit motivational constructs outlined earlier remains to be explored.

The Power and Problems of Attributed Talent

While our present review has focused primarily on intrapersonal variables, we would also like to highlight the potential significance of the relationship between those factors we have identified as intrapersonal and interpersonal influences on skill acquisition. Of particular concern is the potential role of attributions of talent (or lack thereof) by meaningful others. There is evidence from recent research to suggest that in spite of substantial weaknesses in the empirical evidence, the concept of innate talents or giftedness, particularly in domains like music, continues to exert a powerful influence on the attributional beliefs of parents, teachers, and students (Davis, 1994; Evans, Bickel, & Pendarvis, 2000; Tremblay & Gagne, 2001). These trends may be due in part to a broader heuristic in human judgment known as the fundamental attribution error, a tendency to attribute the behaviors of others to internal, stable causes (Ross, 1977), and it has been suggested that such tendencies may be further exaggerated during attributions of skill in domains like chess where most domain-relevant practice is unlikely to be observed (Charness et al., 1996).

Some researchers have speculated on the potential social and psychological consequences of falsely attributed talent. One radical but plausible suggestion is that successful talent selection and development is essentially a self-fulfilling prophecy rather than a calculated response to genuinely innate gifts (Bloom, 1982; Howe et al., 1998). That is, if parents, teachers, or other influential people believe strongly enough that a given child is gifted or talented and capable of exceptional achievements, and they consequently provide the emotional, motivational, and pedagogical support that they feel is warranted by the perceived talent, then perhaps it matters little whether or not the gift actually existed, because the resulting boost to the child's confidence will encourage the kind of persistence that is critical to the attainment of success. On the other hand, if a parent says to a child that he or she does not have talent, either because a teacher does not see it or a test does not show it, then that child may be deprived of the opportunity to engage in an educational regimen that might very well lead to exceptional levels of performance.

Critics may respond that misattributions of ability are relatively benign, and that the negative social implications of disregarding talent or giftedness in the educational process far outweigh the ramifications of inaccurate rejections. However, there is growing empirical evidence that false talent attributions may have immediate and potentially chronic negative psychological consequences for their recipients. First, the giftedness or talent label is not always received in a positive manner. For example, many accomplished musicians do not like being called prodigies or naturally talented because these labels imply skill without effort (Bastian, 1992). Having spent thousands of hours in the practice room, they are all too familiar with the immense quantity of hard work required to prepare for a public performance. Consequently, they may feel slighted by the notion that they had it easy simply because they were born into the right family. Moreover, merely being labeled as gifted or precocious may result in parents or teachers imposing expectations far beyond what is reasonable for a given age, thus causing long-term emotional problems that may overshadow the attainment of meaningful goals later in life (Freeman, 2001; Holahan & Holahan, 1999). In some cases, the individual who is the predominant source of the talent attribution (usually a parent) may form such extremely irrational expectations and beliefs about a child's abilities as to constitute a clinically significant psychological condition known as achievement by proxy, characterized by extreme financial or psychological sacrifice, objectification of the target child, and increased potential for emotional or physical abuse (Tofler, Knapp, & Drell, 1999). Perhaps only a few children are subjected to these kinds of situations, but such a concession is not a sufficient justification to disregard the larger hazards of false talent attributions. It is worth considering the heavy dependence of domains like classical music or chess on the continuation of amateur participants, general social approval from nonparticipants, and their associated financial contributions (grants, sponsorships, endowments, donations, subscriptions, ticket sales, etc.). When one couples the need for participation by the vast number of potentially untalented individuals with the admission by Winner and other talent researchers (Feldman, 1986; Winner & Martino, 1993) that most intellectual and creative prodigies (i.e., the individuals who are often given the most attention and resources) do not usually make outstanding contributions to their fields as adults, it seems fairly obvious that the dominant philosophies and procedures for the identification and development of talent need to be closely reexamined. In short, if existing policies and attitudes regarding the nature of exceptional abilities are contributing to inappropriate levels and forms of social and educational selection, we may be inadvertently alienating large segments of the population that are critical to the very survival of these domains.

SUMMARY

We have reviewed relevant literature on motivation, personality, and emotion in the domains of chess and music performance. The literature shows that there are significant bivariate relationships in directions consistent with the view that motivational factors are important determinants of practice. Nonetheless, it is worth noting that such variables typically play weak roles (r values < .3, meaning less than 10% of the variance) in predicting either the extent of practice or its end state: current skill level. Such relations are quite modest compared to those found in Charness et al. (1996), where 60% of the variance in current level of chess expertise could be accounted for by factors such as cumulative deliberate practice, age (negatively, for older adults), and size of chess library. However, the latter variables lie somewhat closer to the mechanisms that are hypothesized to be directly responsible for skilled performance in the framework depicted in Fig. 11.1.

It is also worth noting that the two domains highlighted by our review probably played little or no role in our species' early evolutionary history. Rather than postulate domain-specific abilities, motivations, and personalities that were honed by millennia of evolutionary pressures, a more modest view might be that evolutionary pressures molded humans into general learning machines that can often be directed (via our social nature) into the many highly specialized roles that both ancient societies required and that modern societies demand. We have reviewed some of the general internal and external influences that may guide such processes. However, we also need to take a more integrated perspective on skill development, and the evidence would seem to indicate that motivational and affective forces may act as important filters that stream people toward one domain or another, and perhaps make it more or less likely that they will experience and respond to internal and external reward mechanisms in a manner that fosters the development of exceptional performance.

Like many psychological inquiries, our exploration of the motivational factors involved in expert performance has led to more questions than it has resolved. Hence, in closing we wish to stress the need for further systematic explorations of the relevant variables related to motivation and expert skill acquisition. Although we have focused on chess and music performance, there may be particular advantages to using other domains. A promising one is sports, in that skill levels as measured by win–loss ratios or other measures of the probability of success (i.e., batting averages in baseball, handicap in golf) are undoubtedly more objective and easier to obtain than judgments of skill in music and other artistic or intellectual disciplines. We certainly favor longitudinal studies as the best, though most expensive method to trace the development of expertise.

As one example, for a longitudinal study of chess skill acquisition, participants could be tested initially to ascertain individual differences in the kinds of intrapersonal variables reviewed earlier (expectations and values, self-efficacy and skill attributions, personality traits and goal orientations) along with interpersonal variables (parental, peer, and teacher influences, organizational and material resources) as well as some type of psychometric battery of perceptual and cognitive tasks to examine the predictive value of traditional intelligence-related constructs (mental speed, working memory, deductive reasoning). The sample could then be reinterviewed and retested over a long enough interval, perhaps 10 years, on the previous variables, along with representative tasks from the domain of interest, over the subsequent decade. In addition to providing a fairly strong empirical test of the oft-cited 10-year rule for the attainment of expertise (e.g., Simon & Chase, 1973), such a study would significantly advance our understanding of the interrelations of the factors outlined in our framework, and in particular, changes in the roles of personality and motivation in skill acquisition over extended periods of time.

ACKNOWLEDGMENT

This research was supported by a grant from the National Institute of Aging (5R01 AG13969) to Neil Charness.

REFERENCES

Avni, A., Kipper, D. A., & Fox, S. (1987). Personality and leisure activities: An illustration with chess players. *Personality and Individual Differences, 8*(5), 715–719.

Bandura, A. (1997). *Self-efficacy: The exercise of control.* New York: Freeman.

Bastian, H. G. (1992). From the every-day world and the musical way of life of highly talented young instrumentalists. In K. A. Heller & E. A. Hany (Eds.), *Proceedings of the Third European Conference of The European Council for High Ability* (pp. 153–163). Seattle, WA: Hogrefe & Huber Publishers.

Bell, C. R., & Cresswell, A. (1984). Personality differences among musical instrumentalists. *Psychology of Music, 12*(2), 83–93.

Bloom, B. S. (1982). The role of gifts and markers in the development of talent. *Exceptional Children, 48*(6), 510–522.

Campbell, D. J., & Ilgen, D. R. (1976). Additive effects of task difficulty and goal setting on subsequent task performance. *Journal of Applied Psychology, 61,* 319–324.

Charness, N., Krampe, R., & Mayr, U. (1996). The role of practice and coaching in entrepreneurial skill domains: An international comparison of life-span chess skill acquisition. In K. A. Ericsson (Ed.), *The road to excellence: The acquisition of expert performance in the arts and sciences, sports and games* (pp. 51–80). Mahwah, NJ: Lawrence Erlbaum Associates.

Colprit, E. J. (2000). Observation and analysis of Suzuki string teaching. *Journal of Research in Music Education, 48*(3), 206–221.

Cooley, J. C. (1961). A study of the relation between certain mental and personality traits and ratings of musical abilities. *Journal of Research in Music Education, 9*(2), 108–117.

Cooper, C. L., & Wills, G. I. D. (1989). Popular musicians under pressure. *Psychology of Music, 17*(1), 22–36.

Csikszentmihalyi, M. (1975). Play and intrinsic rewards. *Journal of Humanistic Psychology, 15*(3), 41–63.

Csikszentmihalyi, M. (1982). *Beyond boredom and anxiety.* San Francisco: Jossey-Bass.

Cutietta, R. A., & McAllister, P. A. (1997). Student personality and instrumental participation, continuation, and choice. *Journal of Research in Music Education, 45*(2), 282–294.

Davis, M. (1994). Folk music psychology. *Psychologist, 7*(12), 537.

Deci, E. L., Cascio, W. F., & Krussell, J. (1975). Cognitive evaluation theory. *Journal of Personality and Social Psychology, 31,* 81–85.

Diener, C. I., & Dweck, C. S. (1978). An analysis of learned helplessness: Continuous changes in performance, strategy, and achievement cognitions following failure. *Journal of Personality and Social Psychology, 36*(5), 451–462.

Duke, R. A. (1999). Teacher and student behavior in Suzuki string lessons: Results from the International Research Symposium on Talent Education. *Journal of Research in Music Education, 47*(4), 293–307.

Eccles, J. S., & Wigfield, A. (2002). Motivational beliefs, values, and goals. *Annual Review of Psychology, 53,* 109–132.

Eisenberger, R. (1992). Learned industriousness. *Psychological Review, 99*(2), 248–267.

Eisenberger, R., & Cameron, J. (1996). Detrimental effects of reward: Reality or myth? *American Psychologist, 51*(11), 1153–1166.

Elo, A. E. (1986). *The rating of chessplayers, past and present* (2nd ed.). New York: Arco.

Ericsson, K. A., & Charness, N. (1994). Expert performance: Its structure and acquisition. *American Psychologist, 49*(8), 725–747.

Ericsson, K. A., & Faivre, I. A. (1988). What's exceptional about exceptional abilities? In L. K. Obler & D. Fein (Eds.), *The exceptional brain: Neuropsychology of talent and special abilities* (pp. 436–473). New York: Guilford.

Ericsson, K. A., Krampe, R. T., & Tesch-Romer, C. (1993). The role of deliberate practice in the acquisition of expert performance. *Psychological Review, 100*(3), 363–406.

Evans, R. J., Bickel, R., & Pendarvis, E. D. (2000). Musical talent: Innate or acquired? Perception of students, parents, and teachers. *Gifted Child Quarterly, 44*(2), 80–90.

Feldman, D. H. (1986). *Nature's gambit: Child prodigies and the development of human potential.* New York: Basic Books.

Freeman, C. (1999). The crystallizing experience: A study in musical precocity. *Gifted Child Quarterly, 43*(2), 75–85.

Freeman, J. (1974). Musical and artistic talent in children. *Psychology of Music, 2*(1), 5–12.

Freeman, J. (2001). *Gifted children grown up.* London: David Fulton.

Gagne, F. (1993). Constructs and models pertaining to exceptional human abilities. In K. A. Heller, F. J. Monks, & A. H. Passow (Eds.), *International handbook of research and development of giftedness and talent* (pp. 69–87). Oxford, England: Pergamon Press.

Galton, F. (1978). *Hereditary genius: An inquiry into its laws and consequences.* London: J. Friedman. (Originally published in 1869)

Gardner, H. (1983). *Frames of mind: The theory of multiple intelligences.* New York: Basic Books.

Hallam, S. (1998). The predictors of achievement and dropout in instrumental tuition. *Psychology of Music, 26*(2), 116–132.

Hamilton, L. H., Kella, J. J., & Hamilton, W. G. (1995). Personality and occupational stress in elite performers. *Medical Problems of Performing Artists, 10*(3), 86–89.

Holahan, C. K., & Holahan, C. J. (1999). Being labeled as gifted, self-appraisal, and psychological well-being: A life span developmental perspective. *International Journal of Aging and Human Development, 48*(3), 161–173.

Holland, J. L. (1966). *The psychology of vocational choice.* Waltham, MA: Blaisdell.

Horgan, D. D. (1992). Children and chess expertise: The role of calibration. *Psychological Research, 54*(1), 44–50.

Howe, M. J. A. (1990). *The origins of exceptional abilities.* Oxford, England: Blackwell.

Howe, M. J. A., Davidson, J. W., & Sloboda, J. A. (1998). Innate gifts and talents: Reality or myth? *Behavioral and Brain Sciences, 21*(3), 399–442.

Joireman, J. A., Fick, C. S., & Anderson, J. W. (2002). Sensation seeking and involvement in chess. *Personality and Individual Differences, 32*(3), 509–515.

Kelly, E. J. (1985). The personality of chess players. *Journal of Personality Assessment, 49*(3), 282–284.

Kemp, A. E. (1981a). The personality structure of the musician: I. Identifying a profile of traits for the performer. *Psychology of Music, 9*(1), 3–14.

Kemp, A. E. (1981b). Personality differences between the players or string, woodwind, brass and keyboard instruments, and singers. *Council for Research in Music Education Bulletin, 66–67,* 33–38.

Kemp, A. E. (1982). Personality traits of successful music teachers [Special Issue]. *Psychology of Music,* 72–75.

Kemp, A. E. (1996). *The musical temperament: Psychology and personality of musicians.* Oxford, England: Oxford University Press.

Leedy, C., & Dubeck, L. (1971). The effects of tournament chess playing on selected physiological responses of individuals varying in level of aspiration and skill. *Chess Life and Review, 26*(12), 708–712.

Lehmann, C. F. (1951). A comparative study of instrumental musicians on the basis of the Otis Intelligence Test, the Kwalwasser-Dykema music test and the Minnesota Multiphasic Personality Inventory. *Journal of Educational Research, 44*(1), 57–61.

Locke, E. (1968). Toward a theory of task motivation and incentives. *Organizational Behavior and Human Performance, 3*(2), 157–189.

Marchant-Haycox, S. E., & Wilson, G. D. (1982). Personality and stress in performing artists. *Personality and Individual Differences, 13*(10), 1061–1068.

McPherson, G., & McCormick, J. (1999). Motivational and self-regulated learning components of musical practice. *Bulletin of the Council for Research in Music Education, 141,* 98–102.

McPherson, G., & McCormick, J. (2000). The contribution of motivational factors to instrumental performance in a music examination. *Research Studies in Music Education, 15,* 31–39.

Myers, I. B., & McCauley, M. H. (1985). *Manual: A guide to the development and use of the Myers–Briggs Type Indicator* (2nd ed.). Palo Alto, CA: Consulting Psychologists Press.

O'Neill, S. (1997). Gender and music. In D. J. Hargreaves & A. C. North (Eds.), *The social psychology of music* (pp. 46–63). Oxford, England: Oxford University Press.

O'Neill, S. (1999). The role of motivation in the practice and achievement of young musicians. In S. W. Yi (Ed.), *Music, mind, and science* (pp. 420–433). Seoul, Korea: Seoul National University Press.

Pritchard, R. D., Campbell, K. M., & Campbell, D. J. (1977). Effects of extrinsic financial rewards on intrinsic motivation. *Journal of Applied Psychology, 62*(1), 9–15.

Ross, L. (1977). The intuitive psychologist and his shortcomings: Distortions in the attribution process. In L. Berkowitz (Ed.), *Advances in experimental social psychology* (Vol. 10, pp. 173–220). New York: Academic Press.

Sample, D., & Hotchkiss, S. M. (1971). An investigation of relationships between personality characteristics and success in instrumental study. *Journal of Research in Music Education, 19*(3), 307–313.

Schleuter, S. L. (1972). An investigation of the interrelation of personality traits, musical aptitude, and musical achievement. *Studies in the Psychology of Music, 8,* 90–102.

Schooler, C., Mulatu, M. S., & Oates, G. (1999). The continuing effects of substantively complex work on the intellectual functioning of older workers. *Psychology and Aging, 14,* 483–506.

Schunk, D. H., & Zimmerman, B. J. (1994). *Self-regulation of learning and performance: Issues and educational applications.* Hillsdale, NJ: Lawrence Erlbaum Associates.

Schunk, D. H., & Zimmerman, B. J. (1997). Social origins of self-regulatory competence. *Educational Psychologist, 32,* 195–208.

Scott, L. (1992). Attention and perseverance behaviors of preschool children enrolled in Suzuki violin lessons and other activities. *Journal of Research in Music Education, 40*(3), 225–235.

Shuter-Dyson, R. (1977). The relationship between musical abilities and certain personality characteristics in secondary schoolchildren: A pilot study. *Council for Research in Music Education Bulletin, 50,* 11–13.

Shuter-Dyson, R. (2000). Profiling music students: Personality and religiosity. *Psychology of Music, 28*(2), 190–196.

Simon, H. A., & Chase, W. G. (1973). Skill in chess. *American Scientist, 61,* 394–403.

Simonton, D. K. (1999). Talent and its development: An emergenic and epigenetic model. *Psychological Review, 106*(3), 435–457.

Sloboda, J. A., Davidson, J. W., Howe, M. J. A., & Moore, D. G. (1996). The role of practice in the development of performing musicians. *British Journal of Psychology, 87*(2), 287–309.

Sloboda, J. A., & Howe, M. J. A. (1991). Biographical precursors of musical excellence: An interview study. *Psychology of Music, 19*(1), 3–21.

Smith, B. P. (2003). *Goal orientation, implicit theory of ability, and collegiate instrumental music practice.* Manuscript submitted for publication.

Sosniak, L. A. (1985). Learning to be a concert pianist. In B. S. Bloom (Ed.), *Developing talent in young people* (pp. 19–67). New York: Ballantine.

Starkes, J. L., Deakin, J. M., Allard, F., Hodges, N. J., & Hayes, A. (1996). Deliberate practice in sports: What is it anyway? In K. A. Ericsson (Ed.), *The road to excellence: The acquisition of expert performance in the arts and sciences, sports and games* (pp. 81–106). Mahwah, NJ: Lawrence Erlbaum Associates.

Steptoe, A., & Fidler, H. (1987). Stage fright in orchestral musicians: A study of cognitive and behavioral strategies in performance anxiety. *British Journal of Psychology, 78*(2), 241–249.

Thayer, R. W. (1972). The interrelation of personality traits, musical achievement, and different measures of musical aptitude. *Studies in the Psychology of Music, 8,* 103–118.

Tofler, I. R., Knapp, P. K., & Drell, M. J. (1999). The "achievement by proxy" spectrum: Recognition and clinical response to pressured and high-achieving children and adolescence. *Journal of the Academy of Child and Adolescent Psychiatry, 38*(2), 213–216.

Tremblay, T., & Gagne, F. (2001). Beliefs of students talented in academics, music, and dance concerning the heritability of human abilities in these fields. *Roeper Review, 23*(3), 173–177.

Tunstall, W. W. (1982). Personality correlates of musical talent. *Journal of Musicological Research, 4*(1–2), 159–173.

Walters, J. W., & Gardner, H. (1986). The crystallizing experience: Discovering an intellectual gift. In R. J. Sternberg & J. E. Davidson (Eds.), *Conceptions of giftedness* (pp. 306–331). Cambridge: Cambridge University Press.

Winner, E. (1996). *Gifted children: Myths and realities.* New York: Basic Books.

Winner, E. (2000). The origins and ends of giftedness. *American Psychologist, 55*(1), 159–169.

Winner, E., & Martino, G. (1993). Giftedness in the visual arts and music. In K. A. Heller, F. J. Monks, & A. H. Passow (Eds.), *International handbook of research and development of giftedness and talent* (pp. 253–281). Oxford, England: Pergamon Press.

Wragg, D. (1974). An investigation into some factors affecting the carry-over of music interest and involvement during the transition period between primary and secondary education. *Psychology of Music, 2*(1), 13–23.

Wubbenhorst, T. M. (1994). Personality characteristics of music educators and performers. *Psychology of Music, 22*(1), 63–74.

Yoon, K. S. (1997, April). *Exploring children's motivation for instrumental music.* Paper presented at the biennial meeting of the Society for Research in Child Development, Washington, DC.

Zimmerman, B. J., & Ringle, J. (1981). Effects of model persistence and statements of confidence on children's self-efficacy and problem solving. *Journal of Educational Psychology, 73*(4), 485–493.

Zimmerman, B. J., & Rosenthal, T. L. (1974). Observational learning of rule-governed behavior by children. *Psychological Bulletin, 81*(1), 29–42.

Zuckerman, M. (1979). *Sensation seeking: Beyond the optimal level of arousal.* Hillsdale, NJ: Lawrence Erlbaum Associates.

INTELLECTUAL FUNCTIONING AND DEVELOPMENT IN SOCIAL AND CULTURAL CONTEXTS

V

INTELLECTUAL FUNCTIONING AND DEVELOPMENT IN SOCIAL AND CULTURAL CONTEXTS

12
▼▼▼▼▼▼▼

Self-Regulating Intellectual Processes and Outcomes: A Social Cognitive Perspective

Barry J. Zimmerman
Graduate School and University Center
City University of New York

Dale H. Schunk
University of North Carolina at Greensboro

At the dawn of the 21st century, many educational and psychological researchers are seeking to move beyond scientific understanding of human intellectual functioning based on correlations between motivational constructs and academic outcomes to a deeper understanding based on analyses of the causal interdependence of specific learning experiences, motivational beliefs, and academic outcomes. As research on strategy training has shown (Pressley, Borkowski, & Schneider, 1987), instructional efforts that lead to positive learning outcomes do not always produce sustained motivation, and conversely, instructional efforts to boost motivation of students without simultaneously improving their learning processes or competencies do not always produce sustained achievement (Schunk, 1991). Solving the reciprocity issue between learning and motivation is thus crucial to the advancement of educational practice.

The need to explain the interdependence of learning and motivational processes within an encompassing model of intellectual functioning has been a particular interest of social cognitive researchers studying students' academic self-regulation. Self-regulation has been defined formally as self-generated thoughts, feelings, and actions for attaining academic goals (Schunk & Zimmerman, 1994). A social cognitive perspective envisions learning and motivation from a triadic model wherein personal cognitive and affective processes are reciprocally influenced by behavioral and environmental events. According to this triadic formulation (which will be described in detail below), learning and motivation are linked by a sense of personal agency about possessing the requisite cognitive and behavioral processes (or means) to achieve desired environmental outcomes (or ends). A primary index of personal agency is a belief in one's self-efficacy to learn or perform at certain designated levels (Bandura, 1986; Pajares, 1996). Self-efficacy beliefs are distinctive because they refer to the process of learning rather than outcomes of it. The distinction between process and outcome beliefs is central to a social cognitive perspective on learning and motivation, a topic we address next. Subsequently, we consider students' intellectual self-regulation from a triadic perspective, key self-regulatory processes and self-motivational beliefs, a developmental perspective on how process goals become linked to outcome goals, and how proactive process learners differ from reactive outcome learners in their cycles of self-regulation and their sense of personal agency. Finally, we consider challenges to students' use of self-regulatory processes, such as counterproductive outcomes.

SELF-EFFICACY AND THE MEANS–END DISTINCTION

Unlike information processing and metacognitive theories that view intellectual functioning in terms of acquiring and applying systems of knowledge, social cognitive researchers see it in broader triadic terms—namely, personal, behavioral, and environmental interacting influences (Zimmerman, 1995). To optimally self-regulate their intellectual functioning, students must not only select cognitive strategies and metacognitively monitor their use, these students need to feel self-efficacious about succeeding, set effective goals for themselves, choose or create advantageous environments, optimize covert affective states, and systematically self-evaluate their behavioral effectiveness. A triadic formulation also seeks to explain the academic failures of metacognitively capable students based on underestimates of personal efficacy, setting ineffective goals, choice of adverse social environments, uncontrolled emotions, and unsystematic self-evaluation. As we discuss in the following, the highest level of intellectual functioning is achieved when students can self-regulate all triadic sources of influence.

Historically, social cognitive researchers (Bandura, 1969) emphasized the importance of personal expectations regarding performance outcomes, such as receiving monetary or occupational rewards following successful task completion, as a major source of motivation. In 1977, Bandura hypothesized the presence of a second related motive, which he termed self-efficacy. Unlike outcome expectations, which refer to personal beliefs about the effectiveness of a behavior in achieving an outcome, self-efficacy expectations refer to personal beliefs about one's capability or competence to perform a particular behavior. For example, a student's beliefs about being able to solve a math problem would be an efficacy expectation whereas a student's beliefs about the consequences of doing well in a math course, such as future employment as an engineer, would be an outcome expectation. The sequential linkage of these two human motives is depicted in Fig. 12.1.

Bandura (1986) suggested that self-efficacy and outcome judgments are distinguished cognitively because people can believe that a particular course of action will produce certain outcomes, but they do not act on that outcome belief because they doubt whether they can actually execute the necessary actions. Because of this sequential dependence, Bandura suggested that self-efficacy judgments would prove more predictive of personal effectiveness than outcome beliefs. For example, a student may believe that graduation from prestigious law school might lead to a high income, but he or she may not enter a pre-law program because of doubts about mastering the underlying requirements.

There is empirical support for Bandura's (1986) hypothesis that self-efficacy expectations are more predictive of outcomes than outcome expectations. Shell, Murphy, and Bruning (1989) assessed self-efficacy and outcome beliefs regarding reading and writing in school. These researchers measured self-efficacy in terms of perceived capability to perform various reading and writing skills, such as finding main ideas and correcting grammatical errors. Outcome expectations were assessed by ratings of the importance of reading and writing in producing such outcomes as employment, social pursuits, family life, education, and citizenship. Regarding reading achievement, self-efficacy and outcome beliefs jointly predicted 32% of the variance, with self-efficacy predicting 28% of the variance and outcome expectations predicting 4% of the variance. Regarding writing achievement, only self-efficacy was a significant predictor. Lent, Lopez, and Bieschke (1991) also found that self-efficacy was a better predictor of academic outcomes than outcome expectations. Clearly the distinction between self-efficacy and outcome expectations is important in predicting students' academic functioning.

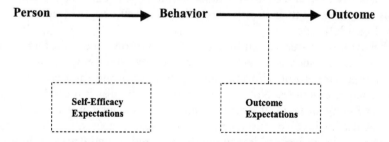

FIG. 12.1.   Diagrammatic representation of the difference between efficacy expectations and outcome expectations. From "Self-efficacy: Toward a unifying theory of behavioral change" by A. Bandura, 1977, *Psychological Review, 84*, p. 193. Copyright © 1977 by the American Psychological Association. Reprinted with permission.

This distinction reflects the difference between means and ends:

> Means are not results. An efficacious technique is a means for producing out-
> comes, but it is not itself an outcome expectation. For example, an effective
> cognitive skill for solving problems can be put to diverse uses to gain all kinds
> of outcomes. Useful means serve as the vehicles for exercising personal efficacy.
> (Bandura, 1986, p. 392)

Yet how does the means–ends distinction between behavioral processes and
environmental outcomes become linked to personal sources of control?

Triadic Forms of Self-Regulation

Social cognitive researchers hypothesize bidirectional relationships between
personal (cognitive and emotional), behavioral, and environmental sources
of influence (Bandura, 1986). Changes in behavior lead to changes in environments and personal beliefs, such as when an illiterate person becomes able
to read. This new literary capability leads that person to form new social relationships as well as to experience an enhanced sense of personal efficacy and
satisfaction, such as personal pride in discussing a newspaper article with fellow passenger on a bus. Triadic efforts to self-regulate can be described in
terms of a person's proactive use of strategies and their resulting feedback
(Zimmerman, 1989). Mastery of any skill usually requires repeated attempts
to learn (i.e., practice) because it involves coordinating personal, behavioral,
and environmental components, each of which changes during the course of
learning. For example, the strategy needed by a novice writer to plan an essay
is very different from the strategy needed to correct the grammar of a draft.
Because the effectiveness of a learning strategy depends on changing personal, behavioral, and environmental conditions, self-regulated learners must
constantly reassess their effectiveness using three self-oriented feedback loops
(see Fig. 12.2).

Behavioral self-regulation involves self-monitoring and adjusting behavioral processes, such as a method of learning, whereas environmental self-
regulation refers to monitoring and adjusting environmental conditions or
performance outcomes. Note that this model distinguishes formally between
self-regulating behavioral processes and environmental outcomes. Covert
self-regulation involves monitoring and adjusting cognitive and affective
strategies, such as writers' imagining the personal consequences of failure to
motivate them to work harder. These three cyclical feedback and adaptation
loops operate jointly to produce changes in learners' self-beliefs, overt behavior, and environment. The accuracy and constancy of learners' self-monitoring of these triadic sources of self-control directly influence the effective-

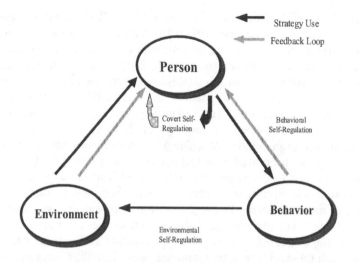

FIG. 12.2. Triadic forms of self-regulation. From "A social cognitive view of self-regulated academic learning" by B. J. Zimmerman, 1989, *Journal of Educational Psychology, 81*, p. 11. Copyright © 1989 by the American Psychological Association. Adapted with permission.

ness of their strategic adjustments and the nature of their self-efficacy beliefs (Zimmerman, 1989).

Affective states, such as elation, arousal, anxiety, or depression, play an important role in human functioning and often need to be self-regulated through specific strategies, such as thought-stopping, self-instruction, and relaxation (Bandura, 1986). There is evidence of a bidirectional relation between personal affective states, such as depression, and self-regulatory beliefs, such as self-efficacy. For example, depression has been traced to low self-efficacy beliefs (Holahan & Holahan, 1987), such as the depression that high school star athlete feels when he or she lacks a sense of self-efficacy about remaining academically eligible to participate in his or her sport. Conversely, students experiencing emotional symptoms of anxiety, such as muscle tension, shallow breathing, and a racing pulse, interpret these signs as ominous and feel less self-efficacious about performing optimally (Bandura, 1997). Interestingly, when self-efficacy has been included in path analyses along with a measure of anxiety, self-efficacy has emerged as the primary mediator of students' functioning (Siegel, Galassi, & Ware, 1985). Thus, the influence of personal affective states on academic performance was mediated through their self-efficacy beliefs. From a triadic perspective, personal emotional reactions are linked to behavioral performance in specific environmental settings via motivational beliefs, such as self-efficacy, task interest, or valuing.

A wide variety of self-regulatory processes have been identified and studied inside and outside the field of academic functioning, and there is extensive anecdotal, as well as experimental evidence of the effectiveness of these techniques (Schunk & Zimmerman, 1994). The biographies and autobiographies of successful writers, musicians, and athletes often reveal use of these self-regulatory techniques (Zimmerman, 1998, 2001). For example, among the common personal self-regulation strategies, writers and athletes use goal setting to help them perform or practice more effectively. Another personal process, imagery, is used by writers to create vivid scenes, by pianists to prepare for concert performances, and by golfers to visualize difficult shots. Among the common behavioral self-regulation strategies, self-instruction or verbalization has been used by tennis players to stay focused after bad shots and by musicians to count out the timing of difficult passages. Professional writers often behaviorally self-record and chart their daily literary outputs to guide and motivate them. Two common forms of environmental self-regulatory strategies are environmental structuring, such as locating a quiet place to study, and social help-seeking, such as soliciting advice from a teacher.

Although these self-regulation strategies were described according to their primary source of triadic influence (personal, behavioral, environmental), each technique affects the other two sources of influence indirectly because of their triadic interdependence. To optimize learning and motivation, students should use all three strategic sources in synchrony, such as setting specific goals, self-monitoring and self-rewarding their attainment. Later we discuss how these and other self-regulatory processes interact within three cyclical phases.

Learning Strategies, Self-Monitoring, and Strategy Attributions

Social cognitive researchers are not alone in making means–ends distinctions or in hypothesizing that self-beliefs about possessing the behavioral process means (i.e., competence) to attain important environmental ends (i.e., performance outcomes) are key to solving the reciprocity issue between learning and motivation. Metacognitive theories (Flavell, 1979) have also stressed the importance of strategies as a means for achieving personal outcomes or ends. Strategies are conscious methods for learning in a systematic and parsimonious way, such as a mnemonic grouping strategy for memorizing a social security number. Educators have developed a wide assortment of task-specific strategies to assist students to learn, such as analyzing complex academic tasks into components for sequential solving (Wood, Woloshyn, & Willoughby, 1995). To think strategically is: (a) to envision one's methods of learning as a personally controllable process that can produce differential outcomes, and (b) to appreciate that successful outcomes depend on constructing or adapting strategies to specific personal settings. Viewing oneself metacognitively as an effective strategy user is assumed to be a major source of motivation to learn (Pressley, Borkowski, & Schneider, 1987), but which self-regulatory processes influence a user's self-perceptions of strategic effectiveness?

The self-regulatory process of self-monitoring is a metacognitive form of self-observation, and it refers to online mental tracking of strategic processes and their outcomes (Schunk, 1983). There is evidence that self-monitoring is neither an easy nor a straightforward process. For example, researchers have found that many students fail to monitor their test preparation accurately and tend to overestimate their learning (e.g., Ghatala, Levin, Foorman, & Pressley, 1989), which leads students to study insufficiently and perform poorly on tests. Yet there is evidence that training students to attribute their learning outcomes to strategy use results in more accurate self-monitoring of strategic outcomes (Ghatala, Levin, Pressley, & Goodwin, 1986). Anderson and Jennings (1980) found that students who were taught to attribute failure to ineffective strategies displayed higher expectations for success than students who were taught to attribute failure to ability. These researchers also discovered that participants who attributed task outcomes to their strategies monitored the effectiveness of their strategy outcomes more closely and modified their strategies more frequently than participants who attributed outcomes to personal talent or ability. The latter participants failed to attend to strategic outcomes and did not believe they could improve their performance.

There is also evidence that attributing adverse outcomes to strategy use sustains student motivation more effectively than attributing outcomes to effort. Clifford (1986) hypothesized that strategy attributions will sustain student motivation in the face of negative results better than effort attributions because strategies enable changes in the direction of learning attempts whereas effort attributions produce only changes in the intensity of learning attempts. Clifford gave a self-rating form wherein hypothetical students attributed course outcomes to ability, effort, and strategy use, and she asked the respondents to rate their expectancy regarding future course outcomes. The data revealed that strategy attributions for academic failures were associated with more positive student judgments and greater expectations for future success than effort or ability attributions. Clearly, attributions of failure to a specific strategic method (or means that the students used to learn) were more effective in preserving expectations about eventually attaining successful outcomes. Zimmerman and Kitsantas (1999) found that self-monitoring the strategic quality of one's writing processes not only leads to more frequent strategy attributions and higher achievement but also to increased perceptions of self-efficacy and valuing of the intrinsic properties of the task.

Intrinsic Motivation Beliefs

Research on intrinsic motivation is also based on a means–ends distinction (Lepper & Greene, 1978). Intrinsic motivation describes self-initiated task engagement with no apparent extrinsic rewards beyond the activity itself (Deci,

1972). Intrinsic motivation, such as the pleasure that actors experience when they practice a role on their own, is assumed to stem from the inherently rewarding properties of the task rather than from positive environmental outcomes of task performance, such as the reactions of an audience. However, which rewards are perceived as apparent and beyond an activity ultimately reflect a personal judgment by each learner, and as a result, extrinsic motivation can be difficult to study and interpret (Bandura, 1986).

Deci (1972) found that extrinsic outcome rewards, such as money or food, reduced students' intrinsic motivation on a task when these rewards were no longer present. Lepper and Greene (1978) suggested that these adverse means–ends effects were due to cognitive attributions of causation. Extrinsic outcomes led students to attribute causation to these overt rewards, and this led to decrements in engagement in the task when the rewards were no longer present. Research by Lepper, Greene, and Nisbett (1973) indicated that declines in motivation were the result of a means–end cognitive representation rather than a reinforcement event. Participants who expected rewards for engaging in an activity (i.e., the end) displayed decreased task engagement when the rewards were withdrawn whereas participants who received extrinsic rewards unexpectedly did not show declines in task engagement when the rewards were withdrawn.

Although intrinsic motivation theorists often emphasize the adverse effects of extrinsic outcomes on intrinsically motivated individuals, these negative means–ends effects are contextually limited in several important ways (Lepper & Greene, 1978). First, they occurred with participants having high but not low initial motivation on a task, and second, these studies dealt with performance rather than learning situations in which the participants already possessed the requisite skills to engage in the activities and experience the satisfying qualities. Participants without competencies in a task area, such as children initially learning to read, do not show adverse effects when extrinsic rewards are given (Zimmerman, 1985). In fact, extrinsic rewards can convey knowledge of high competence at an activity, and these performance-contingent rewards have been found to sustain intrinsic motivation whereas rewards for mere task-engagement (i.e., task-contingent) have been found to undermine it (Karniol & Ross, 1977). Thus, information about the ends of a task in the form of external rewards does not detract from people's valuing of the intrinsic properties of a task (or means) if those rewards imply high competence in controlling the means. Attributing outcomes to one's underlying competence may also influence the key social cognitive motivational variable of self-efficacy beliefs.

There is evidence that extrinsic rewards for increasing competence enhance not only children's task choice but also their self-efficacy beliefs and task interest ratings (Zimmerman, 1985). Elementary school students receiving performance-contingent (i.e., process) rewards played significantly longer with interesting puzzles than students receiving task-contingent (i.e., outcome) rewards or students in an unrewarded control group. Parallel findings were found regarding the two measures designed to uncover reasons for the students' task choices: self-efficacy beliefs and task interest ratings. These data imply that when task outcomes (the perceived ends) indicated more effective learning processes (the perceived means), the students' beliefs in their self-efficacy as a puzzle solver grew as did their interest in and play with the puzzles. There is other evidence that motivating power of outcome rewards (i.e., the ends of learning) depends on whether or not they convey information about personal competence (i.e., having the means to learn). Schunk (1983) compared the effectiveness of performance-contingent (i.e., learning) rewards with task-contingent (i.e., outcomes) rewards in teaching elementary school students arithmetic division. Children received division strategy instruction and then engaged in self-directed practice over a number of separate sessions. Performance-contingent rewards led to the greatest problem solving, division self-efficacy, and achievement. Offering rewards for participation led to no benefits compared to a no-reward control condition. These two studies indicate that when rewards for performance outcomes (or ends) are linked to the quality of students' processes (or means), their self-efficacy beliefs and motivation to learn in a self-motivated fashion are greatly enhanced.

Goal Beliefs and Orientations

Goal orientation theories make a means–ends distinction between learning and performance personal goal perspectives (Ames, 1992; Dweck & Leggett, 1988; Maehr & Midgely, 1991; Nicholls, 1984; Pintrich, 2000). Learning goals refer to acquiring strategic knowledge and skill (i.e., the means of learning) whereas performance goals refer to task completion, positive social comparisons, and ego-enhancement (i.e., the ends of learning). Learning goals (also labeled as task or mastery goals) seek to enhance competency beliefs whereas performance goals (also called ego goals) seek to enhance social and personal outcomes. A learning goal implies that a skill is potentially acquirable whereas a performance goal implies that a skill is a consequence of an inherent ability (Dweck & Leggett, 1988), and these beliefs greatly affect how learners interpret errors. For example, students with a learning goal see errors as sources of information regarding adaptive solutions whereas students with a performance goal see errors as indications of an inherent lack of ability.

Wood and Bandura (1989) studied the impact of students' goal setting with management training students using a complex computer simulation human management task. Students given a learning goal were told that managerial competence on the simulation task is an acquirable skill whereas students given a performance goal were told that managerial competence on the managerial task is indicative of inherent competence. It was discovered that managers who were given a learning goal displayed greater self-efficacy and managerial effectiveness than managers given performance goal. What was remarkable about this study was that the two groups of managers were identical in actual talent and in the feedback they received; what differed were the types of goals or ability conception they held. Students who focused on the process of learning outperformed students who focused on performance outcomes.

Goal orientation theories have historically viewed students' goal orientation as a stable personality trait, which is measured in a transsituational fashion, rather than as a cognitive process, which is measured in a context-specific way. The addition of the word orientation to goals was meant to convey the dispositional quality of this construct. Goal orientation measures do not focus on attaining a particular goal within a particular time frame but rather on a general valuing of learning competence (i.e., the means) or performance outcomes (i.e., the ends). Locke and Latham (2002) asked whether cognitive measures of goal orientations are better predictors of academic outcomes than personality measures. Recently, Seijts and Latham (2001) found that individuals with a high performance goal orientation achieved as well as students with a high learning goal orientation when the former were given a specific learning goals to attain. It appears that assigned learning goals can neutralize students' initial goal orientation. There is also evidence that adoption of task-specific learning goals can change students' goal orientations. Schunk (1996) studied changes in the students' goal orientation as function of specific goal learning experiences in mathematics. Schunk found that students given task (i.e., learning) goal instructions displayed higher posttest learning goal orientations than students given performance goal instructions. Conversely, students given performance goal instructions displayed higher posttest ego (i.e., performance) goal orientations than students given learning goal instructions. This evidence of change in students' goal orientation conflicts with dispositional assumptions and has led social cognitive theorists to emphasize instead students' cognitive goals and the processes used to evaluate progress.

A recent review of the goal orientation literature with college students (Harackiewicz, Barron, Pintrich, Elliot, & Thrash, 2002) uncovered widespread evidence of three major goal orientation factors—a performance goal orientation for attaining positive outcomes (i.e., approach), a performance goal orientation for avoiding negative outcomes (i.e., avoidance), and a learning goal orientation (i.e., mastery). Interestingly, a mastery goal orientation consistently predicted task interest but not academic performance outcomes (e.g., college grades) whereas an approach performance goal orientation consistently predicted academic performance outcomes but not task interest. Performance avoidance goals were linked to maladaptive outcomes. These findings conflict with the traditional theoretical assumption that all performance goal orientations detract from academic attainment and suggest instead that different types of goal orientations may be effective in various situations. A mastery orientation appears to be effective in sustaining interest in learning (as a process) whereas an approach goal orientation may be effective in motivating the attainment of academic outcomes. These findings are consistent with evidence that successful college students report striving for positive performance outcomes, such as academic grades, as well as high quality learning processes (Van Etten, Freebern, & Pressley, 1997). Later we discuss evidence that students who shift from learning processes to performance outcomes display superior learning and motivation than students who rigidly adhere to either learning or performance goals (Zimmerman & Kitsantas, 1999).

Goals With Progress Feedback and Self-Evaluation

Whether learners pursue learning or performance goals, it is important that they perceive themselves as making progress toward goal attainment (Locke & Latham, 2002). However, it is difficult to ascertain progress in achieving one's goals when standards of progress are unclear and when signs of progress are subtle (e.g., during reading comprehension or composing textual material). In these circumstances, social feedback from a teacher indicating learning progress can strengthen learners' self-efficacy beliefs and motivation.

Schunk and Swartz (1993a, 1993b) hypothesized that providing learners with goals and progress feedback would positively affect writing achievement outcomes and self-regulation beyond the learning setting. An adult modeled a five-step writing strategy (e.g., choose a topic to write about, pick the main idea, etc.). After watching a model use the strategy, the children received guided practice in applying the strategy to writing, and the children had a series of opportunities to practice applying the strategy by themselves. Process-goal children received instructions at the start of each session that emphasized learning to use the writing strategy whereas product-goal students received instructions emphasizing completing the assigned paragraphs; general goal children were merely asked to do their best. A subgroup of children in the process goal condition received verbal progress feedback from the model periodically that linked strategy use causally with improved performance (e.g., "You're doing well because you applied the steps in order"). Process-goal plus feedback students outperformed product-goal and general-goal students in self-efficacy, writing achievement, and strategy use when writing paragraphs and displayed greater transfer to new writing tasks after 6 weeks.

Schunk (1996) subsequently investigated how goals and self-evaluation affect mathematical learning and achievement outcomes. After instruction and during self-directed practice, students were asked to set either a learning goal (how to solve problems) or a performance goal (merely completing the problems). In a first experiment, half of the students in each goal condition evaluated their problem-solving capabilities after each session. The learning goal with or without self-evaluation and the performance goal with self-evaluation led to higher self-efficacy, math skill, and motivation (i.e., problem completion during the practice sessions) than did the performance goal without self-evaluation. The frequency of the self-evaluation experiences appear to have led to a ceiling effect and masked the effects of goal setting. This was corrected in the second experiment, in which the students in each goal condition evaluated their progress in skill acquisition only once. As found in prior research, the learning goal led to higher motivation and achievement outcomes than did the performance goal. These results suggested that self-evaluation and goal setting were reciprocally dependent.

Schunk and Ertmer (1999) extended this research on goal setting to learning of computer skills by college students. These researchers found that when self-evaluation experiences were limited, process goals led to higher perceptions of self-efficacy, self-evaluations of learning progress, strategy use, and achievement. However, frequent opportunities for self-evaluation produced comparable outcomes regardless of process or outcome goals. These findings point to the need for an encompassing theory of self-regulation that can explain the interdependence of goal setting with other self-regulatory processes, such as self-monitoring and self-evaluation. Such a model is presented later in this chapter.

Process and Outcome Goals in Development of Self-Regulatory Skill

Paralleling the distinction between self-efficacy and outcome expectations, social cognitive researchers have also made a means–ends distinction between process and outcome goals in the acquisition of self-regulatory competence. This issue is discussed as part of a social cognitive model (Schunk & Zimmerman, 1997; Zimmerman, 2000) that envisions self-regulation of a particular skill as initially having social origins, but as ultimately involving students' development of personal control processes to adaptively manage social and physical environmental outcomes on their own.

There are four markers on a social cognitive path to self-regulatory skill. At the first marker or observational level, a novice must learn to discriminate the correct form of the skill from a model's performance and verbal descriptions, such as when a novice journalist discerns a difference between a seasoned editor's description of a routine news event and cub reporter's (see Table 12.1 first row). An observational level of skill is seldom induced from a

TABLE 12.1
Multi-Level Features of Self-Regulation

	Features of Regulation			
Levels of Regulation	Sources of Regulation	Sources of Motivation	Task Conditions	Performance Indices
1. Observation	Modeling	Vicarious reinforcement	Presence of models	Discrimination
2. Emulation	Performance and social feedback	Direct–social reinforcement	Correspond to model's	Stylistic duplication
3. Self-control	Representation of process standards	Self-reinforcement	Structured	Automaticity
4. Self-regulation	Performance outcomes	Self-efficacy beliefs	Dynamic	Adaptation

Note. From Table 1.1 in "Achieving self-regulation: The trial and triumph of adolescence" by B. J. Zimmerman, 2003, in F. Pajares & T. Urdan (Eds.), *Academic motivation of adolescents* (Vol. 2, p. 5). Greenwich, CT: Information Age. Copyright by Information Age.

single exposure to a model's performance but instead generally requires repeated observation, especially across variations in task such as seeing a series of articles by the editor (Rosenthal & Zimmerman, 1976). A novice's motivation to learn at an observational level is greatly enhanced by positive vicarious consequences to the model, such as news awards given to the editor. Although vicarious consequences can motivate without necessarily producing affect, there is evidence that they can also lead to emotional conditioning (Bandura & Rosenthal, 1966). Observers' perception of similarity to a skilled model and perception of positive consequences to a model will increase their motivation to develop the skill further (Brown & Inouye, 1978). There is evidence (Bandura, 1997; Zimmerman, 2000; Zimmerman & Rosenthal, 1974) of observational learning of a wide variety of academic, sport, and work skills from both live and symbolic (recorded or described) models. In addition to task skills, observers typically acquire self-regulatory processes, such as adherence to performance standards, motivational orientations, and task values. For example, journalist models who edit their articles extensively for errors in grammar or accuracy helps observers to discriminate and rectify common errors in their own work. Motivationally, this coping model also conveys the high value placed on journalistic quality (Zimmerman & Koussa, 1979) and the need to persistently revise in order to improve the quality of one's own work (Zimmerman & Ringle, 1981).

At the second social cognitive marker or emulation level of self-regulation, a novice learns to duplicate a model's response on a corresponding task, which typically involves emulating a model's general pattern or style of functioning rather than specific responses (Rosenthal, Zimmerman, & Durning, 1970). For example, an aspiring journalist might emulate the succinct prose style rather than the actual words of a senior editor. Learners will increase their accuracy and motivation during efforts to emulate, if a model provides them with guidance, feedback, and social reinforcement (see Table 12.1 second row). Reception of social rewards is negatively associated with detrimental academic emotions, such as school anxiety (Zimmerman, 1970). In order to emulate a skill, novice learners need to incorporate modeled features of a complex skill into their behavioral repertoires. By emulating using a model's task, novice learners can master basic response elements in a setting where corrective feedback, social modeling and assistance are available. Once an advanced level of mastery is attained, a model's support is reduced usually. Some critics have decried teaching to promote emulation because of fears that such teaching may produce nothing more than response mimicry, but these fears are largely unwarranted because mimicry constitutes only a small part of emulative learning (Zimmerman & Rosenthal, 1974).

At a third marker or a self-controlled level of self-regulation, learners should practice outside the presence of models in structured settings, such as when aspiring journalists practice writing articles on their own (see Table 12.1 third row). To optimize this form of learning, novices should self-monitor and control their practice using cognitive and behavioral process standards gleaned from an expert model's performance (Bandura & Jeffery, 1973). Learners' success in matching a covert process standard during practice will determine their amount of self-reinforcement (Bandura & Kupers, 1964). Regarding the importance of self-reinforcement, Bandura (1986) commented, "by making self-satisfaction conditional on a selected level of performance, individuals create their own incentives to persist in their efforts until their performances match internal standards" (p. 467). Persistent failures to reach one's standards can lead to severe emotional reactions, such as depression (Bandura, 1986). Use of a skill can be self-controlled better when learners engage in self-instruction (Schunk & Rice, 1984, 1985). At level three, learners who set learning process or technique goals rather than performance outcome goals will achieve automaticity more readily (Zimmerman & Kitsantas, 1997, 1999). Automaticity refers to the execution of learning processes without specific attention to their form and represents the completion of level three functioning. By focusing their practice goals on the strategic processes of proven models, level three learners can circumvent the frustrations of trial-and-error outcome learning and experience self-reinforcement for personal mastery of a model's technique.

To achieve the fourth developmental marker or self-regulated level functioning, learners should practice a skill in dynamic personal settings (see Table 12.1 fourth row). To become fully self-regulated, novices must learn to make adjustments in their skill based on the outcomes of practice or performance. By definition, outcome goals, such as readers' reactions to a journalist's article, provide the ultimate criterion by which process attainments can be measured, and, as such, outcome goals can motivate moderately successful learners to continue the quest toward higher levels of mastery (Locke & Latham, 2002). At level four, learners can practice a skill with minimal process monitoring because of automaticity, and their attention can be shifted to performance outcomes without detrimental consequences, such as when student journalists can shift their attention from their writing techniques to desired audience reactions regarding an article for the school newspaper. However, like level three self-controllers, level four self-regulators will attribute unsuccessful performance outcomes to ineffective processes or techniques because level three learning focused on the importance of the quality of these processes (or means) to an expert model's success (or ends). As a result of their process attributions, level four students will display higher self-efficacy for positive outcomes and minimal reversals in self-efficacy for setbacks, which can greatly reduce pernicious swings in emotions.

A self-regulated level of skill is reached when learners can adapt their performance successfully to changing personal conditions and outcomes. Thus, a multilevel analysis of the development of self-regulatory competence begins with most extensive social guidance at the first level, and this social support is reduced systematically as learners acquire underlying self-regulatory skill. This systematic reduction in social assistance to enhance students' development of self-regulation is similar to apprenticeship formulations advocated by Vygotskian researchers (Rogoff, 1990). However, learners' level four functioning continues to depend on social resources on a self-initiated basis, such as when a journalist seeks advice from a colleague about whether a draft of an article is compelling. Because the effectiveness of one's task skills depends on variations in contexts, new performance tasks can uncover limitations in existing processes and can require additional social learning experiences. This multilevel formulation does not assume that learners must advance through the four levels in an invariant sequence as developmental stage models assume, or that once the highest level is attained, it will be used universally. Instead, this multilevel model assumes that students who master each skill level in sequence will learn more easily and effectively. Although level four learners have the competence to perform self-regulatively, they may not choose to do so because of low levels of self-motivation (Bandura, 1997).

Evidence of Levels in Self-Regulatory Development of Skill

There is a growing body of evidence indicating that the speed and quality of learners' self-regulatory development and self-motivation are enhanced significantly if learners proceed according to a multilevel developmental hierarchy. To test the sequential validity of the first and second of levels in the hierarchy, Zimmerman and colleagues compared the two primary sources of regulation for each level (i.e., modeling for the observation level, performance and social feedback for the emulation level) in several studies (see column two in Table 12.1). Zimmerman and Kitsantas (2002) studied acquisition of writing revision skill with college students. The students learned a three-step strategy for revising these multisentence problems from a coping model, a mastery model, or verbal description. The mastery model performed flawlessly from the outset of the training, whereas the coping model initially made errors but gradually corrected them. Coping models were viewed as a qualitatively superior exemplar for observational learning because they convey self-regulatory actions, such as self-monitoring and self-correction, as well as writing revision skill. Students in the two modeling groups significantly surpassed the revision skill of students who attempted to learn from only verbal description and performance outcomes. As expected, students who observed the higher quality coping model outperformed students who observed the lower quality mastery model. Social feedback was insufficient for students in the no modeling group to make up for their absence of vicarious experience. These academic writing results confirmed the sequential advantages of engaging in observational learning before attempting enactive learning experiences. There is other evidence that coping models are more effective than mastery models on both academic (Schunk & Hanson, 1985; Schunk, Hanson, & Cox, 1987) and athletic tasks (Kitsantas, Zimmerman, & Cleary, 2000) especially with students who struggle to achieve mastery.

To test the sequentiality of the third and fourth levels (i.e., self-control and self-regulation) of skill, Zimmerman and Kitsantas (1999) studied writing acquisition by high school girls. After initial strategy training through observation and emulation (regulatory levels one and two), the girls set one of three types of goals. Process goals focused on strategic steps for revising each writing task whereas outcome goals focused on decreasing the number of words in the revised passage (i.e., a succinct but comprehensive description). Shifting goal subjects changed from process to outcomes when automaticity was achieved. A subgroup of girls in each goal setting group were asked to self-record their goal attainments. The results were consistent with a multilevel view of goal setting. Girls who shifted goals from processes to outcomes after reaching level four (i.e., having achieved automaticity) surpassed the writing revision skill of girls who adhered exclusively to process goals or to outcome goals. Girls who focused on outcomes exclusively displayed the least writing skill, and self-recording enhanced writing acquisition for all goal-setting groups. In addition to their superior writing skill outcomes, girls who shifted their goals displayed advantageous forms of self-motivation, such as enhanced self-efficacy beliefs, self-reactions, intrinsic interest, and strategy attributions. As expected, students who shifted goals from learning to outcomes attributed their unsuccessful responses to strategy use indicating that the means–end relationship was clearly understood. Students who set process goals also made strategy attributions unlike students setting outcome goals. Similar sequential goal setting effects were found in a study conducted with a motor learning task with high school girls (Zimmerman & Kitsantas, 1997).

These studies indicate the importance of the various sources of self-regulatory development at each level in the hierarchy (see column 2 of Table 12.1), such as the quality of modeling, social feedback, process goals, and performance outcomes. Regarding the means–end issue, these studies reveal that although learning process goals were more effective than performance outcome goals in enhancing motivation and achievement, the latter were very effective when they were linked sequentially to effective prior learning experiences. But how are goal setting, self-efficacy, as well as other self-regulatory processes and self-motivational beliefs, interrelated, and how do they lead to self-sustaining learning?

A Cyclic Phase Model of Academic Self-Regulation

Zimmerman (2000) hypothesized that self-regulatory beliefs and processes are linked in a cycle involving three major phases: forethought, performance control, and self-reflection (see Fig. 12.3). Forethought refers to influential learning processes and motivational beliefs that precede efforts to learn and set the stage for such learning. The performance phase involves processes that occur during learning and affect concentration and performance, and the self-reflection phase involves processes that occur after learning and influence a learner's reactions to that experience. These self-reflections, in turn, influence forethought regarding subsequent learning, which completes the self-regulatory cycle. Although all students attempt to self-regulate their personal functioning in some way, those who are most successful in academics, sport, as well as other fields, focus proactively on learning processes (i.e., as a means to an end) during the forethought and performance control phases rather than merely focusing reactively on outcomes (i.e., ends) during self-reflection.

Forethought Phase. Two major categories of forethought are task analysis and self-motivational beliefs. To analyze the tasks effectively, students need to set effective goals for themselves and plan an effective strategy for attaining those goals. As we have already discussed, setting learning goals, especially if they are specific, proximal, and challenging, are associated with greater learning and motivation than outcome goals, which are not linked intentionally to learning processes. The goal systems of the most effective self-regulators are proactively organized in a hierarchy, with proximal process goals linked to distal outcome goals (Bandura, 1986; Carver & Scheier, 2000). Hierarchical goal systems enable these learners to guide their learning over

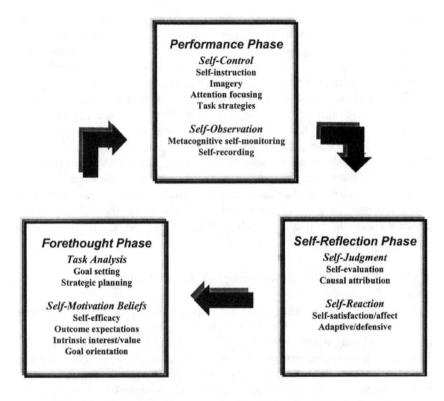

FIG. 12.3. Phases and subprocesses of self-regulation. From "Motivating self-regulated problem solvers" by B. J. Zimmerman & M. Campillo, 2003, in J. E. Davidson & R. J. Sternberg (Eds.), *The nature of problem solving* (p. 239). New York: Cambridge University Press. Copyright by Cambridge University Press.

longer time intervals without outside support because as one goal is accomplished, the learner shifts to the next goal in a hierarchy, such as the next item in a priority list of homework assignments. Proactive learners engage in strategic planning because strategies represent an effective means to learn (Pressley et al., 1987), such as using a graphic organizer to write an essay. In contrast, reactive self-regulators seldom engage in systematic task analyses during forethought.

Proactive learners' willingness to engage in optimal forms of goal setting and strategy use depends on high levels of self-motivation. As we noted earlier, goal setting and strategic planning are linked in both theory and research to such self-motivational beliefs as self-efficacy, outcome expectations, intrinsic interest or task valuing, and goal orientation. Students who focus proactively on learning processes are more self-efficacious (Schunk & Swartz, 1993a, 1993b), and these positive self-beliefs let them set higher learning goals for themselves (Zimmerman & Bandura, 1994) and be more committed to those goals (Locke & Latham, 2002). Because proactive learners view learning processes as effective means to an end, they are motivated more by the attraction of positive outcomes of learning than by the fear of adverse outcomes (Pintrich, 2000). Outcomes that reflect underlying learning competence have been found to increase the intrinsic value of a task and not diminish it as task-contingent outcomes do (Karniol & Ross, 1977; Zimmerman, 1985). Because of their valuing of the intrinsic properties of a task, proactive learners are more motivated to continue learning in the absence of external rewards (Lepper & Greene, 1978) and yet experience positive emotions, such as elation. As a result of their advantageous learning goals, proactive learners are apt to form a broader learning goal orientation (Schunk, 1996), and this motivational disposition has been linked to a wide variety of subsequent self-regulatory phase processes, such as strategy use (Pintrich & DeGroot, 1990) and adaptive self-reactions (Dweck & Leggett, 1988).

Performance Phase. There are two major classes of performance phase processes: self-control and self-observation. As noted earlier, self-control refers to students' use of powerful methods, such as self-instructions, use of imagery, attention focusing, and task strategies, to optimize functioning. The process goals of proactive self-controllers, such as steps in a writing revision strategy, prepare and motivate them to use self-control processes to enhance their attention, encode information visually, guide action, and control their feelings (Zimmerman & Kitsantas, 1999). Proactive self-controllers also observe the execution of their control processes and outcomes more systematically than reactive self-controllers. Proactive learners who set hierarchical process-outcome goals during forethought are especially well oriented to track the effectiveness of these process means. In contrast, reactive self-regulators are preoccupied with outcomes, and as a result, they seldom monitor any particular process systematically and must rely on reactive methods of learning, such as subjective impressions or trial-and-error.

Although the benefits of self-observation may seem obvious, most reactive learners engage in this process in only a cursory way. Metacognitive self-monitoring is difficult for reactive students because the amount of information involved in complex performances can easily overwhelm and can lead to inconsistent or superficial tracking, such as when a novice writer tries to focus on content accuracy, grammar, and originality of expression simultaneously. Furthermore, reactive learners are unaware of the benefits of self-recording, such as daily records of progress in finishing a 20-page essay. In contrast, proactive self-regulators can be selective in their cognitive self-monitoring because of the specificity of their learning goals, and they will self-record when they need to capture personal information as it occurs, preserve its accuracy, and provide a longer database for discerning change. As a result of their selective process-outcome monitoring, proactive self-regulators know how far they have progressed in their learning without waiting for delayed outcomes.

Self-Reflection Phase. There are two major classes of self-reflection processes. One type of self-judgment, self-evaluation, refers to comparing self-monitored information with a standard or goal, such as when an aspiring spelling contestant compares daily practice outcomes to her best previous effort (i.e., a self-improvement criterion), to the efforts of local competitors (i.e., a social comparison criterion), or to national spelling bee records (e.g., a mastery criterion). Self-evaluations are not automatic outcomes of performance but rather depend on learners' motivation to improve and on their selection and interpretation of an appropriate criterion. Proactive self-regulators prefer to self-evaluate using a self-improvement or mastery criteria because of their learning process goals. The self-improvement criterion involves comparing current learning efforts with earlier ones, and the resulting self-evaluations are likely to reveal improvement with time. A mastery criterion involves comparing daily improvements against a stable standard, and these self-evaluations are also likely to show improvement with practice. In contrast, reactive self-regulators tend to self-evaluate using a comparative criterion because of their focus on outcomes and lack of forethought (Zimmerman & Kitsantas, 1997, 1999). They turn to social comparison criteria, such as the performance of competitors, because they lack an alternative criterion for self-judgment, such as self-improvement or mastery goals (Festinger, 1954). The resulting self-evaluations are often unfavorable because one's competitors may start ahead or progress faster. In addition, adverse social comparisons can be publicly stigmatizing (i.e., being perceived as a loser) and lead to the debilitating ego goal orientation described by Nicholls (1984).

A second self-judgment also plays a pivotal role in self-reflection because causal attributions of errors to uncontrollable sources, such as a fixed method or fixed ability, prompt learners to react negatively and discourage further efforts to improve (Weiner, 1979). By contrast, attributions of error to personally controllable sources, such as strategies for writing an essay, have been shown to sustain motivation during periods of deficient performance (Zimmerman & Kitsantas, 1997, 1999). According to Weiner (1986), personal perceptions of high controllability over adverse outcomes lead to a sense of guilt whereas perceptions of low controllability lead to a sense of shame. Fortunately, attributions are not automatic products of favorable or unfavorable self-evaluations, but rather, they depend also on preceding self-regulatory processes and beliefs, such as task analysis, goal setting, and perceptions of self-efficacy (Bandura, 1991). Reactive self-regulators are prone to attributing causation for errors to uncontrollable sources, such as ability, task difficulty, or luck because they lack process goals and strategy process methods of learning (Cleary & Zimmerman, 2001; Kitsantas & Zimmerman, 2002). Attributions of failure to insufficient effort can have a positive effect on achievement when learners are already using an effective learning strategy. However, as was noted earlier, when a strategy needs to be changed or adapted, effort attributions can adversely affect subsequent learning (Anderson & Jennings, 1980; Clifford, 1986; Zimmerman & Kitsantas, 1997). In contrast, proactive self-regulators are primed by their process goals and their use of strategies to attribute negative outcomes to ineffective strategy use. Because strategies can be self-controlled, these attributions will sustain motivation to adapt the strategies further.

Self-evaluation and attribution self-judgments are closely linked to two key self-reactions: self-satisfaction and adaptive inferences. The former refers to perceptions of self-satisfaction or dissatisfaction and associated emotional affect, such as elation or depression, regarding one's performance, which influences the courses of action that people pursue (Bandura, 1991). Like other self-reflective processes, self-satisfaction is not an automatic outcome of performance but rather depends on learners' self-judgmental criteria, as well as forethought goals and performance phase strategies. Adaptive or defensive inferences refer to self-reactions by students about how to alter their self-regulatory approach during subsequent efforts to learn or perform, such as shifting from a text creation writing strategy to a text revision strategy. Adaptive inferences are important because they guide students to new and potentially more effective forms of performance self-regulation whereas defensive inferences serve primarily to protect the person from future dissatisfaction and aversive affect. Defensive self-reactions, such as helplessness, procrastination, task avoidance, cognitive disengagement, and apathy, are self-handicapping because they ultimately limit personal growth (Garcia & Pintrich, 1994).

As we previously noted, proactive learners' attributions of errors to learning processes, such as strategies, sustains their self-satisfaction and fosters variations in strategy use until learners discover an improved version (Cleary & Zimmerman, 2001). Attributions of unfavorable results to uncontrollable factors by reactive self-regulators lead to dissatisfaction and undermines further adaptive efforts. Because of their preoccupation with outcomes, reactive self-regulators will often engage in self-protection and may actively avoid future learning efforts or create barriers that diminish their perceived responsibility for future adverse outcomes. By contrast, proactive self-regulators systematically adapt their performance on the basis of their process goals, learning strategy, process self-monitoring, and self-evaluation judgments. In this way, the strategic process goals of proactive self-regulators lead to greater self-satisfaction and more effective forms of adaptation. These outcomes cyclically influence forethought self-motivational beliefs, goals and strategy choices for further self-regulatory efforts to learn (Cleary & Zimmerman, 2001; Kitsantas & Zimmerman, 2002).

Challenges to Self-Regulation

Can purposeful efforts to self-regulate prove unproductive or even counterproductive in some circumstances? As we previously discussed, reactive self-regulators are often unsuccessful despite their best intentions. For example, an adolescent girl who wants to lose weight may choose the counterproductive strategy of vomiting after eating a meal, and she becomes bulimic. Furthermore, strategies that are initially effective must be adjusted to frequently changing personal and environmental conditions, and poor self-monitoring can lead to faulty strategy adjustments, such as when golfers allow bad habits to slip into their game. Several researchers have argued that conscious efforts to self-regulate one's learning can interfere with adaptive performance in dynamic settings (Kanfer & Ackerman, 1989; Singer, Lidor, & Cauraugh, 1993) or with the flow of spontaneous creative ideas (Csikszentmihalyi, 1996). These two interpretations of self-regulation are based on differing assumptions about the value of unconsciousness in intellectual functioning, namely as a source of automaticity (Singer, Lidor, & Cauraugh, 1993) or spontaneity (Csikszentmihalyi, 1996). According to the intellectual automaticity view, unconscious learning is the highest form of self-regulation, but according to the intellectual spontaneity view, unconscious learning is the antithesis of intentional self-regulation.

In contrast, social cognitive researchers have avoided dualistic conscious–unconscious views of human intellectual functioning and instead have embraced hierarchical goal formulations in which learners can shift their attention from one level of functioning to another, such as between process and outcome goals (Zimmerman & Schunk, 2001). As we discussed earlier, automaticity in performance is viewed as an outgrowth of the intentional use of self-regulatory processes, and this high level of performance proficiency enables learners to shift their attention to self-regulatory outcome goals without dysfunction. Both before automaticity is attained and after, learners are conscious of their intellectual functioning. What has changed is the target of their attention (i.e., their goals). As we previously noted, research on the development of writing proficiency has revealed that shifting goals hierarchically from process to outcomes at the point of automaticity produces significantly more learning than no (conscious) goals, process goals alone, or outcome goals alone (Zimmerman & Kitsantas, 1999). Furthermore, when unexpected outcomes are experienced, hierarchical learners shift cyclically from outcome goals to process goals, demonstrating the cognitive flexibility predicted by a hierarchical view of intellectual functioning.

Flow experiences, which reflect students' lack of awareness of the passage of time due to their cognitive immersion in an academic task, can be interpreted as a shift in attention from temporal outcomes to task processes rather than as a loss of consciousness because students remain conscious of atemporal aspects their intellectual functioning. Although an awareness of time can be interpreted as a sign of overregulation and may inhibit some forms of learning (Morgan, 1985), that perspective ignores the importance of time management to the success of students' in school and to a wide range of experts who plan their time and place of learning to enhance their creativity (Zimmerman, 1998). Concerns that self-regulatory efforts might stifle creativity must be reconciled with evidence that professional writers use a wide variety of self-regulatory processes to optimize their creative endeavors rather than awaiting an unconscious visit by the muse (Zimmerman & Risemberg, 1997). Thus, although efforts to self-regulate one's intellectual functioning are often initially ineffective, students are better advised to focus on adapting their goals and choice of methods rather than relying on the fortuity of unconscious methods (Kitsantas & Zimmerman, 1998).

CONCLUSION

How students conceive of achievement tasks—whether as opportunities to improve key processes as the means for increasing their competence or to improve their outcomes as ends in themselves—greatly affects the cyclical self-regulatory path they take and the sources of self-motivation they will experience. Because of their process orientation to learning and performance, proactive self-regulators engage in more effective forethought, performance, and self-reflection phase processes than reactive learners. By understanding this cycle of phases, especially the way that advantageous forethought processes set the stage for superior forms of performance and self-reflection, teachers can help students to pursue a proactive path. Students who become proactive self-regulators will experience a heightened sense of personal agency because their process orientation not only changes their approach to learning but also their perspective on its ultimate end.

ACKNOWLEDGMENTS

We would like to thank David Y. Dai and Robert J. Sternberg for their helpful comments on an earlier draft of this chapter.

REFERENCES

Ames, C. (1992). Achievement goals and the classroom motivational climate. In D. H. Schunk & J. L. Meece (Eds.), *Student perceptions in the classroom* (pp. 327–348). Hillsdale, NJ: Lawrence Erlbaum Associates.

Anderson, C. A., & Jennings, D. L. (1980). When experiences of failure promote expectations of success: The impact of attributing failure to ineffective strategies. *Journal of Personality, 48*, 393–405.

Bandura, A. (1969). *Principles of behavior modification.* New York: Holt, Rinehart & Winston.

Bandura, A. (1977). Self-efficacy: Toward a unifying theory of behavioral change. *Psychological Review, 84*, 191–215.

Bandura, A. (1986). *Social foundations of thought and action: A social cognitive theory.* Englewood Cliffs, NJ: Prentice Hall.

Bandura, A. (1991). Self-regulation of motivation through anticipatory and self-reactive mechanisms. In R. A. Dienstbier (Ed.), *Perspectives on motivation: Nebraska symposium on motivation* (Vol. 38, pp. 69–164). Lincoln, NE: University of Nebraska Press.

Bandura, A. (1997). *Self-efficacy: The exercise of control.* New York: Freeman.

Bandura, A., & Jeffery, R. W. (1973). Role of symbolic coding and rehearsal processes in observational learning. *Journal of Personality and Social Psychology, 26*, 122–130.

Bandura, A., & Kupers, C. (1964). Transmission of patterns of self-reinforcement through modeling. *Journal of Abnormal and Social Psychology, 69*, 1–9.

Bandura, A., & Rosenthal, T. L. (1966). Vicarious classical conditioning as a function of arousal level. *Journal of Personality and Social Psychology, 3*, 54–66.

Brown, I., Jr., & Inouye, D. K. (1978). Learned helplessness through modeling: The role of perceived similarity in competence. *Journal of Personality and Social Psychology, 36*, 900–908.

Carver, C., & Scheier, M. (2000). On the structure of behavioral self-regulation. In M. Boekaerts, P. R. Pintrich, & M. Zeidner (Eds.), *Handbook of self-regulation* (pp. 42–84). San Diego, CA: Academic Press.

Cleary, T., & Zimmerman, B. J. (2001). Self-regulation differences during athletic practice by experts, non-experts, and novices. *Journal of Applied Sport Psychology, 13*, 61–82.

Clifford, M. (1986). Comparative effects of strategy and effort attributions. *British Journal of Educational Psychology, 56*, 75–83.

Csikszentmihalyi, M. (1996). *Creativity: Flow and the psychology of discovery and invention.* New York: HarperCollins.

Deci, E. L. (1972). The effects of contingent and noncontingent rewards and controls on intrinsic motivation. *Organizational Behavior and Human Performance, 8*, 217–229.

Dweck, C. S., & Leggett, E. L. (1988). A social cognitive approach to motivation and personality. *Psychological Review, 95*, 256–273.

Festinger, L. (1954). A theory of social comparison processes. *Human Relations, 7*, 117–140.

Flavell, J. H. (1979). Metacognition and cognitive monitoring: A new era of cognitive developmental inquiry. *American Psychologist, 34*, 906–911.

Garcia, T., & Pintrich, P. R. (1994). Regulating motivation and cognition in the classroom: The role of self-schemas and self-regulatory strategies. In D. H. Schunk & B. J. Zimmerman (Eds.), *Self-regulation of learning and performance: Issues and educational applications* (pp. 127–53). Hillsdale, NJ: Lawrence Erlbaum Associates.

Ghatala, E. S., Levin, J. R., Foorsman, B. R., & Pressley, M. (1989). Improving children's regulation of their reading PREP time. *Contemporary Educational Psychology, 14*, 49–66.

Ghatala, E. S., Levin, J. R., Pressley, M., & Goodwin, D. (1986). A componential analysis of the effects of derived and supplied strategy-utility information on children's strategy selections. *Journal of Experimental Child Psychology, 41*, 76–92.

Harackiewicz, J. M., Barron, K. E., Pintrich, P. R., Elliot, A. J., & Thrash, T. M. (2002). Revision of achievement goal theory: Necessary and illuminating. *Journal of Educational Psychology, 94*, 638–645.

Holahan, C. K., & Holahan, C. J. (1987). Self-efficacy, social support, and depression in aging: A longitudinal analysis. *Journal of Gerontology, 42*, 65–68.

Kanfer, R., & Ackerman, P. L. (1989). Motivation and cognitive abilities: An integrative/aptitude-treatment approach to skill acquisition. *Journal of Applied Psychology, 74*, 657–690.

Karniol, R., & Ross, M. (1977). The effects of performance-relevant and performance-irrelevant rewards on motivation. *Child Development, 48*, 482–487.

Kitsantas, A., & Zimmerman, B. J. (1998). Self-regulation of motoric learning: A strategic cycle view. *Journal of Applied Sport Psychology, 10*, 220–239.

Kitsantas, A., & Zimmerman, B. J. (2002). Comparing self-regulatory processes among novice, non-expert, and expert volleyball players: A microanalytic study. *Journal of Applied Sport Psychology, 14*, 91–105.

Kitsantas, A., Zimmerman, B. J., & Cleary, T. (2000). The role of observation and emulation in the development of athletic self-regulation. *Journal of Educational Psychology, 91*, 241–250.

Lent, R. W., Lopez, F. G., & Bieschke, K. J. (1991). Mathematics self-efficacy: Sources and relation to science-based career choice. *Journal of Counseling Psychology, 38*, 424–430.

Lepper, M. R., & Greene, D. (1978). Overjustification research and beyond: Toward a means-ends analysis of intrinsic and extrinsic motivation. In M. R. Lepper & D. Greene (Eds.), *The hidden costs of reward: New perspectives on the psychology of human motivation* (pp. 109–148). Hillsdale, NJ: Lawrence Erlbaum Associates.

Lepper, M. R., Greene, D., & Nesbett, R. E. (1973). Undermining children's intrinsic interest with extrinsic rewards: A test of the over-justification hypothesis. *Journal of Personality and Social Psychology, 28*, 129–137.

Locke, E. A., & Latham, G. P. (2002). Building a practically useful theory of goal setting and task motivation: A 35-year odyssey. *American Psychologist, 57*, 705–717.

Maehr, M. L., & Midgely, C. (1991). Enhancing student motivation: A schoolwide approach. *Educational Psychologist, 26*, 399–427.

Morgan, M. (1985). Self-monitoring of attained subgoals in a private study. *Journal of Educational Psychology, 77*, 623–630.

Nicholls, J. (1984). Achievement motivation: Conceptions of ability, subjective experience, task choice, and performance. *Psychological Review, 91*, 328–346.

Pajares, F. (1996). Self-efficacy beliefs in achievement settings. *Review of Educational Research, 66*, 543–578.

Pintrich, P. R. (2000). Multiple goals, multiple pathways: The role of goal orientation in learning and achievement. *Journal of Educational Psychology, 92*, 544–555.

Pintrich, P. R., & De Groot, E. V. (1990). Motivational and self-regulated learning components of classroom academic performance. *Journal of Educational Psychology, 82*, 33–40.

Pressley, M., Borkowski, J. G., & Schneider, W. (1987). Cognitive strategies: Good strategy users coordinate metacognition and knowledge. In R. Vasta & G. Whitehurst (Eds.), *Annals of child development, Vol. 5* (pp. 89–129). Greenwich, CT: JAI.

Rogoff, B. (1990). *Apprenticeship in thinking: Cognitive development in social context.* New York: Oxford University Press.

Rosenthal, T. L., & Zimmerman, B. J. (1976). Organization and stability of transfer in vicarious concept attainment. *Child Development, 44*, 606–613.

Rosenthal, T. L., Zimmerman, B. J., & Durning, K. (1970). Observational induced changes in children's interrogative classes. *Journal of Personality and Social Psychology, 16*, 681–688.

Schunk, D. H. (1983). Progress self-monitoring: Effects on children's self-efficacy and achievement. *Journal of Experimental Education, 51*, 89–93.

Schunk, D. H. (1991). Self-efficacy and academic motivation. *Educational Psychologist, 26*, 207–231.

Schunk, D. H. (1996). Goal and self-evaluative influences during children's cognitive skill learning. *American Educational Research Journal, 33*, 359–382.

Schunk, D. H., & Ertmer, P. A. (1999). Self-regulatory processes during computer skill acquisition: Goal and self-evaluative influences. *Journal of Educational Psychology, 91*, 251–260.

Schunk, D. H., & Hanson, A. R. (1985). Peer models: Influence on children's self-efficacy and achievement. *Journal of Educational Psychology, 77*, 313–322.

Schunk, D. H., Hanson, A. R., & Cox, P. D. (1987). Peer model attributes and children's achievement behaviors. *Journal of Educational Psychology, 79*, 54–61.

Schunk, D. H., & Rice, J. M. (1984). Strategy self-verbalization during remedial listening comprehension instruction. *Journal of Experimental Education, 53*, 49–54.

Schunk, D. H., & Rice, J. M. (1985). Verbalization of comprehension strategies: Effects on children's achievement outcomes. *Human Learning, 4,* 1–10.

Schunk, D. H., & Swartz, C. W. (1993a). Goals and progress feedback: Effects on self-efficacy and writing achievement. *Contemporary Educational Psychology, 18,* 337–354.

Schunk, D. H., & Swartz, C. W. (1993b). Writing strategy instruction with gifted students: Effects of goals and feedback on self-efficacy and skills. *Roeper Review, 15,* 125–137.

Schunk, D. H., & Zimmerman, B. J. (1994). *Self-regulation of learning and performance: Issues and educational applications.* Mahwah, NJ: Lawrence Erlbaum Associates.

Schunk, D. H., & Zimmerman, B. J. (1997). Social origins of self-regulatory competence. *Educational Psychologist, 32,* 195–208.

Seijts, G. H., & Latham, B. W. (2001, June). *Can goal orientation be induced? Further exploration of the state versus trait debate.* Paper presented at the annual meeting of the Canadian Psychological Association, St. Foy, Quebec, Canada.

Shell, D. F., Murphy, C. C., & Bruning, R. H. (1989). Self-efficacy and outcome expectancy mechanisms in reading and writing achievement. *Journal of Educational Psychology, 81,* 91–100.

Siegel, R. G., Galassi, J. P., & Ware, W. B. (1985). A comparison of two models for predicting mathematics performance: Social learning versus math aptitude-anxiety. *Journal of Counseling Psychology, 32,* 531–538.

Singer, R. M., Lidor, R., & Cauraugh, J. H. (1993). To be aware or not aware? What to think about while learning and performing a motor skill. *The Sport Psychologist, 7,* 19–30.

Van Etten, S., Freebern, G., & Pressley, M. (1997). An interview study of college freshmen's beliefs about their academic motivation. *Contemporary Educational Psychology, 13,* 105–130.

Weiner, B. (1979). A theory of motivation for some classroom experiences. *Journal of Educational Psychology, 71,* 3–25.

Weiner, B. (1986). *An attributional theory of motivation and emotion.* New York: Springer-Verlag.

Wood, E., Woloshyn, V. E., & Willoughby, T. (1995). *Cognitive strategy instruction for middle and high schools.* Cambridge, MA: Bookline Books.

Wood, R. E., & Bandura, A. (1989). Impact of conceptions of ability on self-regulatory mechanisms and complex decision making. *Journal of Personality and Social Psychology, 56,* 407–415.

Zimmerman, B. J. (1970). The relationship between teacher classroom behavior and student school anxiety levels. *Psychology in the Schools, 7,* 89–93.

Zimmerman, B. J. (1985). The development of intrinsic motivation: a social learning analysis. In G. Whiteurst & R. Vasta (Eds.), *Annals of child development* (Vol. 2, pp. 117–160). Greenwich, CT: JAI.

Zimmerman, B. J. (1989). A social cognitive view of self-regulated academic learning. *Journal of Educational Psychology, 81,* 329–339.

Zimmerman, B. J. (1995). Self-regulation involves more than metacognition: A social cognitive perspective. *Educational Psychologist, 30,* 217–221.

Zimmerman, B. J. (1998). Academic studying and the development of personal skill: A self-regulatory perspective. *Educational Psychologist, 33,* 73–86.

Zimmerman, B. J. (2000). Attaining self-regulation: A social cognitive perspective. In M. Boekaerts, P. R. Pintrich, & M. Zeidner (Eds.), *Handbook of self-regulation* (pp. 13–39). San Diego, CA: Academic Press.

Zimmerman B. J. (2001). Achieving academic excellence: A self-regulatory perspective. In M. Ferrari (Ed.), *Pursuit of excellence* (pp. 85–109). Mahwah, NJ: Lawrence Erlbaum Associates.

Zimmerman, B. J., & Bandura, A. (1994). Impact of self-regulatory influences on writing course attainment. *American Educational Research Journal, 31,* 845–862.

Zimmerman, B. J., & Campillo, M. (2003). Motivating self-regulated problem solvers. In J. E. Davidson & R. J. Sternberg (Eds.), *The nature of problem solving* (pp. 233–262). New York: Cambridge University Press.

Zimmerman, B. J., & Kitsantas, A. (1997). Developmental phases in self-regulation: Shifting from process to outcome goals. *Journal of Educational Psychology, 89,* 29–36.

Zimmerman, B. J., & Kitsantas, A. (1999). Acquiring writing revision skill: Shifting from process to outcome self-regulatory goals. *Journal of Educational Psychology, 91,* 1–10.

Zimmerman, B. J., & Kitsantas, A. (2002). Acquiring writing revision and self-regulatory skill through observation and emulation. *Journal of Educational Psychology, 94,* 660–668.

Zimmerman, B. J., & Koussa, R. (1979). Social influences on children's toy preferences: Effects of model rewardingness and affect. *Contemporary Educational Psychology, 4,* 55–66.

Zimmerman, B. J., & Ringle, J. (1981). Effects of model persistence and statements of confidence on children's self-efficacy and problem solving. *Journal of Educational Psychology, 73,* 485–493.

Zimmerman, B. J., & Risemberg, R. (1997). Becoming a self-regulated writer: A social cognitive perspective. *Contemporary Educational Psychology, 22,* 73–101.

Zimmerman, B. J., & Rosenthal, T. L. (1974). Observational learning of rule governed behavior by children. *Psychological Bulletin, 81,* 29–42.

Zimmerman, B. J., & Schunk, D. H. (2001). Reflections on theories of self-regulated learning and academic achievement. In B. J. Zimmerman & D. H. Schunk (Eds.), *Self-regulated learning and academic achievement: Theoretical perspectives* (2nd ed., pp. 289–307). Mahwah, NJ: Lawrence Erlbaum Associates.

13

▼▼▼▼▼▼▼

When Is Good Thinking?

David Perkins
Ron Ritchhart
Project Zero, Harvard Graduate School of Education

What is good thinking? To ask this is to pose one of the most venerable questions of scholarship. Aristotle's (350 B. C. E.) analysis of syllogisms, Bacon's (1620/1878) account of scientific inquiry, Kant's (1785/1994) categorical imperative, Von Neumann and Morgenstern's (1944) exposition of game theory, Inhelder and Piaget's (1958) notion of formal operational thinking, Wertheimer's (1945) formulation of productive thinking all set forth normative conceptions of various kinds of thinking. Contemporary work expands, ramifies, and refines the analysis into many particular kinds of thinking (e.g. Baron, 1985; Basseches, 1984; Case, 1992; Elgin, 1996; Langer, 1989; Paul, 1990; Toulmin, 1958).

Not only is the normative question important in itself, but it informs another central question of psychology: "How good a thinker are you?" This is a question about individual traits. Psychologists typically try to measure such traits by posing tasks that sample some range of thinking and then looking for consistent levels of performance within individuals, across tasks. When the tasks are unfamiliar and varied, this usually leads to indices like IQ that supposedly gauge a general capacity for handling complex cognitive challenges (e.g. Brody, 1992; Herrnstein & Murray, 1994; Jensen, 1980, 1998). When the tasks range across practical problems in a particular domain, the results may gauge practical intelligence in that domain (Sternberg & Wagner, 1986; Wagner & Sternberg, 1985, 1990).

However, the marriage between the normative question "What is good thinking?" and the trait question "How good a thinker are you" may not be as close as it looks. The argument here is that persistent good thinking in realistic situations has at least as much to do with another question: "When is good thinking?" This question draws attention to another important dimension of thinking, broadly, good timing—attempting the right kind of thinking at the right moment. It asks how thinking gets activated or mobilized when needed.

Both psychological and lay views of thinking tend to treat this matter as secondary. It is assumed that people usually think about as well as they can whenever they need to. When they do not, it is mostly because they cannot. To compare with rowing across a rushing river, it is not that people miss the boat or decline to take it. It is that they simply cannot row well enough. Suppose just the opposite: It is not that people cannot row well enough, but that they often miss the boat or decline to take it. Occasions that call for thinking pass them by or they choose not to engage those occasions. This would yield a very different account of how thinking works in the world and what it is to be a good thinker, an account more situated in the flow of everyday events and human motives.

Such an account lies at the heart of what is commonly called a dispositional view of thinking. A dispositional view looks not only to what kinds of thinking people are able to do well, but what kinds of thinking they are disposed to undertake. The question "How good a thinker are you?" must be answered as much in terms of people's attitudes, motivations, commitments, and habits of mind as in terms of their cognitive abilities. Although this is hardly the dominant view, several scholars have developed dispositional perspectives, for instance Baron (1985), Dewey (1922), Ennis (1986), Facione, Sanchez, Facione, & Gainen (1995), Perkins, Jay, & Tishman (1993), Ritchhart (2002), and Stanovich (1999).

A plausibility argument supports a dispositional view of thinking. We tend to associate thinking with its more blatant occasions—the test item, the crossword puzzle, the choice of colleges, the investment decision—situations where there is a problem conspicuously on the table and a strong clear reason (including enjoyment) to pursue it. We tend to take as paradigmatic those situations that call for thinking with a loud voice.

However, many situations call for thinking with a softer voice and there are many reasons why one might not engage them thoughtfully: blinding confidence in one's own view, obliviousness to the possibility that others might see things differently, aversion to the complexities and ambiguities of some kinds of thinking ("thinking makes my head hurt"), avoidance of sensitive topics that one would rather not think about, reliance on quick judgment rather than analytic exploration (which may serve well, but only if the judgment reflects a rich base of relevant experience), force of habit overriding a deliberative pause, and so on. The ready presence of such thinking shortfalls is why, for example, Dewey (1922) emphasized the importance of good habits of mind, which can carry people past moments of distraction and reluctance. This is why Scheffler (1991) underscored the role of cognitive emotions in guiding thought, emotions such as curiosity, surprise, and the love of truth.

Further encouragement for a dispositional perspective comes from common discourse. The everyday language of thinking includes terms for a range of positive and negative dispositional traits considered important. A person may be open-minded or closed-minded, curious or indifferent, judicious or impulsive, systematic or careless, rational or irrational, gullible or skeptical. Such contrasts, at least in their intent, have more to do with how well people actually use their minds than how well their minds work. Terms like these capture the essence of what has been called intellectual character (Ritchhart, 2002; Tishman, 1994, 1995).

Of course, such plausibility arguments do not make a full case for a dispositional view. Although good habits of mind, refined cognitive emotions, and other dispositional characteristics are different sorts of constructs than cognitive abilities as usually conceived, it still might turn out that they have a negligible influence compared to abilities on thinking about what matters in one's life. Accordingly, the actual contribution of the dispositional side of thinking becomes a central issue.

We and our colleagues have pursued a line of empirical research and theory building in this area since 1993 (Perkins et al., 1993; Perkins & Tishman, 2001; Perkins, Tishman, Ritchhart, Donis, & Andrade, 2000; Ritchhart, 2002; Tishman, Jay, & Perkins, 1993; Tishman & Perkins, 1997; Tishman, Perkins, & Jay, 1995). Our findings, to be reviewed along with others in the following, support the importance of a dispositional perspective. Moreover, they challenge a presupposition of most dispositional accounts: being disposed to engage situations thoughtfully is essentially a motivational matter of attitudes, commitments, incentives, and so on. We argue that thinking often falters through missing the moment altogether rather than declining to seize it. Obliviousness contributes at least as much as reluctance.

The pages to follow review dispositional accounts of thinking in the literature, outline our own triadic analysis of thinking dispositions, summarize our research on the contribution of dispositions to thinking performance, examine the case for dispositions as traits, analyze children's knowledge of conditions when thinking is called for, and explore how settings can cultivate thinking dispositions. The article concludes with a summary argument advocating dispositional accounts of thinking over abilities-centric accounts.

DISPOSITIONAL VIEWS OF THINKING

The Philosophical Roots of the Concept of Dispositions

The term thinking dispositions has its roots in philosophy. However, the general notion that good thinking involves detecting and acting on occasions is found in many accounts of complex cognitive activity. Models of self–regulation emphasize volitional aspects of thinking and individuals' motivation to engage thoughtfully (Schunk & Zimmerman, 1994). Research on mindfulness, which Langer (1989, p. 44) defined as "an open, creative, and probabilistic state of mind," attends to the situational factors that provoke increased awareness of possibilities and to the underlying beliefs that encourage one to look for options. Beliefs and preferences such as the need for cognitive closure (Kruglanski, 1990) and the need for cognition (Cacioppo & Petty, 1982) have been shown to influence when and to what extent individuals engage in thinking. Constructs such as habits of mind honor the importance of sustained thinking behavior across multiple contexts. A brief examination of such perspectives not only elaborates a dispositional view of thinking but also clarifies some of the confusions about the term itself.

Philosophy has traditionally defined a disposition as a capacity, tendency, potentiality, or power to act or be acted on in a certain way (Honderich, 1995). Dispositions are latent tendencies that foretell predictable outcomes under certain conditions. Imagine an inanimate object—glass is a common example (Ryle, 1949)—and ponder the characteristics it is likely to display under certain conditions. When suddenly chilled, glass often will crack; when struck with a hard object, it will shatter; if one tries to force it into a different shape through bending, it breaks. Thus, glass is said to have a brittle disposition. Even if no one is chilling, striking, or bending the glass at the moment, the disposition is still there. The way the glass would behave is predictably determined by an internal set of conditions. Ryle (1949) stated that to possess a dispositional property "is not to be in a particular state, or to undergo a particular change; it is to be bound or liable to be in a particular state, or undergo a particular change, when a particular condition is realized" (p. 43). Although some might refer to this as just another trait like transparency or density, analytic philosophers such as Ennis (1986), Ryle (1949), and Siegel (1997) called it a disposition.

Psychological dispositions, whether about thinking or other behaviors, can be viewed as loosely analogous to such dispositional properties. Just as glass is disposed to break when struck, a good thinker is disposed to look at both sides of the case upon encountering a broad generalization and disposed to look for hidden assumptions when a problem as initially framed proves troublesome. However, such a descriptive approach to defining dispositions only goes so far. Just as scientists and engineers trying to understand and improve the strength of glass would have to look to its inner structure, so too do psychologists and educators concerned with thinking need to look underneath the basic philosophical idea of thinking dispositions for mechanisms of internal control, motivation, and acquisition.

Psychological Perspectives on Dispositions

In this spirit, Dewey (1922) approached this terrain in a more flexible manner. While recognizing the general problem of terminology, he chose to emphasize the importance of clarifying the construct through its underlying mechanisms:

> We need a word to express the kind of human activity which is influenced by prior activity and in that sense acquired; which contains within itself a certain ordering or systematization of minor elements of action; which is projective, dynamic in quality, ready for overt manifestation; and which is operative in some subdued subordinate form even when not obviously dominating activity. (p. 41)

Dewey chose habit, stating: "Habit even in its ordinary usage comes nearer to denoting these facts than any other word. If the facts are recognized we may also use the words attitude and disposition" (p. 41). Dewey (1922) goes on to state that if the term disposition is to be used, it must be understood as a "readiness to act overtly in a specific fashion whenever opportunity is presented" (p. 41), as a predisposition, and not as a latent potential. In this stipulated definition of habit and disposition, Dewey (1922) emphasized the importance of acquisition and development, thus separating habits and dispositions from innate qualities such as capacities, traits, or temperament. Furthermore, Dewey (1922) asserted that habits have their roots in knowledge, motivation, and attitudes, thus indicating their complex nature and situatedness.

Like Dewey, other philosophers have recognized the limits of a purely descriptive view of dispositions and dug deeper into the mechanisms at work. Specifically: When does good thinking happen? And what triggers and motivates it in the moment?

For example, Norris (2002) included a volitional component in his definition of dispositions, stating, "Individuals must either have formed habits to use certain abilities, or overtly think and choose to use the abilities they possess" (p. 317), underscoring the importance of noticing when to think and choosing to follow through. Working from this definition, Norris (2002) constructed a simple assessment of the extent to which noticing when to use one's abilities affected thinking performance. Using the Ennis-Weir Critical Thinking Essay Test, Norris (2002) produced a new version of the test with hints, such as "think of other explanations for the results" (p. 322), after each paragraph.

The hints were designed to "provide suggestions (surrogate dispositions), but for an examinee who does not know how to do what is suggested, they will be useless" (Norris, 2002, p. 322). Norris found that thinking performance is not synonymous with thinking ability; the group receiving the hints scored over 60% higher on average than those taking the traditional test.

Facione et al. (1995) offered another view of dispositions as related to but separable from ability. They characterize dispositions as consisting of both behavior and beliefs. Using a small sample of college students and college-bound high school students and later a sample of nursing students, Facione and Facione (1992) compared students' dispositions scores, based on a self-report measure that evaluated both frequency of behavior and strength of belief in certain types of thinking, with performance on a critical thinking skills test. They found a significant correlation of .67 between the two measures. Although this does not of course establish causation, it shows that 45% of the variation in skills test performance can be explained statistically by variation in dispositions. While Norris (1995) showed that increasing awareness boosted performance, the Facione et al. (1995) results suggest that inclination and habit also enhance performance. Combined, these experiments call into question the validity of any pure tests of ability apart from dispositions.

Other Disposition-Like Constructs

As these examples show, viewing dispositions as initiators and motivators of abilities rather than abilities themselves allows exploring what dispositions contribute to thinking performance and how. Many philosophers concerned with educational issues and the promotion of good thinking proceed in similar spirit but with different nomenclature. Instead of discussing dispositions or habits, they refer to beliefs, virtues, passions, character, attitudes, and traits as important mobilizers of thinking (Paul, 1993; Scheffler, 1991; Schrag, 1988). Many address the roles of affect and the environment in shaping intellectual behavior. Scheffler (1991) and Paul (1986, 1993) both discussed rational passions and emotions as shapers of thinking. "Emotions, feelings, and passions of some kind or other underlie all human behavior" (Paul, 1993, p. 348). Scheffler (1991) stated: "emotion without cognition is blind, and . . . cognition without emotion is vacuous" (p. 4). Paul and Elder (1997) took the stance that the "mind is a function of three interrelated factors: how we think, how we feel, and what we seek" (p. 3). Only the first of these factors is purely cognitive, the other two relying on affect. These constructs connect to the general dispositional view advocated here because they focus on bridging the gap between one's abilities, the what of good thinking, and one's actions, the when of good thinking.

Similarly, several psychologists address how thinking gets mobilized through dispositions and related constructs. Baron (1985) in his search-inference theory of thinking considered cognitive capacities roughly as a matter of what we can do in principle. Within the latitude allowed by capacities, dispositions such as open-mindedness, curiosity, impulsiveness, and dogmatism influence what we actually do. Investigators in the field of personality and social psychology have identified several constructions that bridge between cognitive ability and thoughtful engagement. These include curiosity (Maw & Magoon, 1971), the need for cognitive closure (Kruglanski, 1990) and the need for cognition (Cacioppo & Petty, 1982).

Kruglanski identified the need for cognitive closure specifically as "a dispositional construct . . . manifested through several different aspects, namely, desire for predictability, preference for order and structure, discomfort with ambiguity, decisiveness, and closed-mindedness" that can influence one's thinking performance in the moment (Webster & Kruglanski, 1994, p. 1049). Kruglanski demonstrated that the need for closure is both a trait that remains fairly stable over time in an individual and a manipulable state that can be induced by circumstances (Kruglanski & Freund, 1983), thus showing that ability alone does not account for performance.

Similarly, Cacioppo and Petty advanced (1982) the need for cognition as a dispositional construct describing an individual's tendency to seek, engage in, and enjoy cognitively effortful activity. Their efforts build on the earlier conceptual work of Murray (1938), who developed the notion of a need for understanding, and Fiske (1949), who examined the idea of an inquiring intellect. According to Cacioppo and colleagues (Cacioppo, Petty, Feinstein, & Jarvis, 1996), individuals with a high need for cognition do not so much seek closure and structure as they do understanding. These individuals focus on the process of making sense of events and stimuli rather than on quickly producing tidy theories or explanations. Measures of an individual's need for cognition developed by Cacioppo and colleagues have shown that it is a construct distinguishable from ability but highly predictive of performance in many situations (Cacioppo, et al., 1996).

Drawing on information-processing models of cognition, Stanovich and West (1997) claimed that cognitive capacities and thinking dispositions "map onto different levels of analysis in cognitive theory. Variation in cognitive ability refers to individual difference in the efficiency of processing at the algorithmic level. In contrast, thinking dispositions index individual difference at the rational level" (p. 9). Their research provides additional evidence that dispositions are distinguishable from abilities. Using self-report measures of dogmatism, categorical thinking, openness, counterfactual thinking, superstitious thinking, and actively open-minded thinking, Stanovich and West (1997) found these measures useful in predicting performance on tests of argument evaluation even after controlling for cognitive capacities.

Dweck and colleagues have investigated another dispositional construct for a number of years—the contrast between entity learners and incremental learners (Dweck, 1975, 1999). This work argued that degree of persistence in the face of intellectual challenge reflects underlying belief systems. Entity learners, who see intelligence as fixed, want to look as good as they can and tend to quit when problems prove difficult because they conclude the problems are beyond them. In contrast, incremental learners, who see intelligence as learnable, prove stubborn in the face of intellectual challenge and labor through problems to improve themselves, with less concern for looking good in the short term. An extended program of research has shown that these traits are independent of cognitive abilities, but often influence cognitive performance greatly. Also teaching style and classroom culture can influence considerably the extent to which students adopt entity versus incremental mindsets.

As this brief review demonstrates, dispositional views of thinking abound in both philosophy and psychology. Even though the term disposition is not always used, may scholars have examined what mobilizes the thinking abilities people have. The next section examines these causal mechanisms further, proposing a specific model of how dispositions operate.

THE TRIADIC ANALYSIS OF THINKING DISPOSITIONS

You read a newspaper article reporting studies showing that less sleep correlates with greater health. You wonder whether you should cut back on your sleep and live longer. Yet wait, isn't this identifying correlation with causation? You are curious and also it matters to you, so you ask yourself: Are there other reasons why studies might show such a correlation? In a few moments, you assemble several. For example, ill people might need more sleep. You decide to leave your sleeping habits alone.

In the spirit of Dewey, Norris, Stanovich, and others mentioned earlier who have emphasized the dispositional side of thinking, this anecdote illustrates the importance of "When is good thinking?" alongside "What is good thinking?" As to the what, it is good thinking to be cautious about inferring causation from correlation and to identify alternative plausible reasons for a correlation. As to when, one has to register the situation in the first place as a possibly hasty causal inference, and care enough to think it through. These are dispositional aspects of thinking.

The anecdote introduces a three-way analysis of thinking behavior that has guided our research for several years. The three aspects of thinking are called sensitivity, inclination, and ability. Sensitivity concerns whether a person notices occasions in the ongoing flow of events that might call for thinking, as in noticing a possibly hasty causal inference, a sweeping generalization, a limiting assumption to be challenged, or a provocative problem to be solved. Inclination concerns whether a person is inclined to invest effort in thinking the matter through, because of curiosity, personal relevance (as in the health case), habits of mind, and so on. Ability concerns the capability to think effectively about the matter in a sustained way, for instance, to generate alternative explanations for the supposed causal relationship. (Sensitivity could be called an ability of a sort—the ability to notice—but in our nomenclature ability refers to thinking capabilities once the person is engaged in an effort to think something through.) Sensitivity and inclination are the dispositional aspects of this triad, speaking to "When is good thinking?"

The three reflect a logic inherent not only in thinking but also other kinds of behavior. Recall from the introduction the challenge of crossing the turbulent river. To do so by rowboat, you have to notice conditions that recommend a boat, including the boat itself, the state of the weather and such (sensitivity), decide to try the boat, rather than say walking three miles to the bridge (inclination), and be able to row the boat well enough to make it (ability). The same pattern plays out in many contexts. Sensitivity, inclination, and ability are individually necessary and collectively sufficient to enable a behavior.

Here this pattern gets applied to thinking. Its distinctive contribution is the separation of sensitivity and inclination. Characteristically, dispositional analyses of thinking either treat dispositions as a matter of motivation broadly speaking—interests, commitments, values—or simply lump sensitivity and inclination together. However, the two need to be distinguished, since one might notice an occasion that invites thinking but not care, or fail to notice a situation about which one would care. Empirical research reported later demonstrates that indeed these are separable aspects of thinking.

Although it is useful to examine thinking behavior with sensitivity, inclination, and ability in mind, they are not monolithic traits nor do they operate in an acontextual way. Sensitivity, for example, may reflect a general alertness or mindfulness (Langer, 1989), but also particular repertoire, such as knowing the risks of inferring causation from correlation. Moreover, such knowledge needs not to be inert (cf. Bransford, Franks, Vye, & Sherwood, 1989; Whitehead 1929), but active enough to get triggered on the fly while reading a newspaper article.

Likewise, inclination on a particular occasion might reflect broad cognitive traits like need for cognition (Cacioppo & Petty, 1982), good *habits of mind* (Dewey, 1922), and attitudes such as curiosity and love of truth (Scheffler, 1991). However, it will also reflect the pulls and pushes of the moment—whether for instance the relationship between sleep and health seems personally important and whether you have the time to think about it right then.

Inclination also speaks to persistence. Whether you think something all the way through will reflect broad traits such as curiosity and stubbornness but also circumstances of the moment, such as what progress you make, how much time and effort it is taking, and whether it stays interesting or gets boring. Just as inclination sustains engagement in thinking, sensitivity continues to operate midcourse in thinking, to register opportunities and traps of the main line of your thought that you might easily pass by. These points underscore the stochastic character of dispositions. Having a general sensitivity or an inclination does not guarantee that a person will notice every occasion or engage it. "Sensitive to" and "inclined to" mark trends, not inevitabilities.

The three-way analysis also does not imply that sensitivity, inclination, and ability always operate in sequence. At the very moment you read about the correlation between sleep and health, you might find yourself silently saying, "Wait a minute, I hope they're not suggesting that sleeping less is good for our health, because there are lots of possible reasons for that correlation, for instance sick people needing more sleep." In such a case, there is no distinct moment of detection, then of investment, and then thinking through the matter, although, from a functional standpoint, detection, investment, and engagement have occurred.

With these qualifications about the complex, stochastic, and sometimes merged nature of sensitivity, inclination, and ability, one might wonder about the advantages of identifying the triad at all. However, it has proven to be a useful construct, logically clarifying because detection, investment, and thinking through are conceptually distinct matters, and empirically clarifying, because, as will be seen, the three are empirically separable. The triad gives a richer picture of the dynamics of thinking, especially when circumstances call for thinking with a soft voice rather than a loud one.

With this as a backdrop, let us turn to a body of empirical research based on the dispositional triad.

HOW MUCH DOES WHEN COUNT?

Speaking of turbulent rivers, one such is the gap between a plausible framework and empirical test. The triadic analysis of thinking behavior may make philosophical sense and appeal to common sense, but it leaves open a question of magnitude. Sensitivity and inclination might turn out to be negligible influences on effective thinking compared to ability.

Research cited earlier suggested that the dispositional side of thinking might contribute substantially to good thinking. For example, Norris (2002) found that offering clues to take the place of missing dispositions boosted performance on a critical thinking instrument by 60%. Stanovich and West (1997), controlling for cognitive capacities, found that dispositional factors identified by self-rating influenced argument evaluation. Both need for cognitive closure and need for cognition have been shown to influence cognitive performance independent of cognitive abilities (Cacioppo & Petty, 1982; Webster & Kruglanski, 1994). This sets the stage for examining the contribution of dispositions to thinking within the triadic model.

An Early Study

This issue became the focus of a series of empirical studies carried out over a number of years. The first investigation occurred in the early 1980s, piggy-backed on a large-scale investigation of the impact of formal education on everyday reasoning (Perkins, 1985, 1989; Perkins, Allen, & Hafner, 1983; Perkins, Farady, & Bushey, 1991). It predated the triadic framework outlined here and motivated our later investigations of dispositions. The main focus of this work was the impact of conventional formal education at the high school, college, and graduate level on everyday reasoning, and the principal finding was that schooling enhanced students reasoning outside their areas of study only very slightly (Perkins, 1985). However, of concern here is a comparison between subjects' competence and their performance imbedded in the methodology.

The method employed one-on-one interviews. An interviewer posed to a subject an issue current at the time (for example, "Would a nuclear disarmament treaty reduce the likelihood of world war?" or "Would a bottle deposit law in the state of Massachusetts reduce litter?") and asked the subject to reason about it. Pretesting had yielded a set of issues that people saw as vexed. Subjects leaned one way about as often as the other, could argue from several standpoints, and did not vary much in actual expertise, so the issues brought commonsense reasoning to the fore. A subject could take a yes or no position or come down in the middle. Most subjects adopted positions and piled up reasons on their preferred side of the case with little attention to the other side of the case or to possible flaws in their own arguments, a well-known trend sometimes called my-side bias.

The methodology also employed a short-form IQ test. IQ correlated with number of points subjects offered on their preferred side of the case at .4 or .5, but often did not significantly correlate with number of points on the other side of the case before prompting (Perkins et al., 1991). This suggested that my-side bias reflected dispositions rather than cognitive capacity.

In later research, the interviewer pushed subjects to elaborate their arguments on both sides further. When it appeared that a subject had no more to say, the interviewer then asked the subject point blank to identify weaknesses in his or her argument and to elaborate the other side of the case. Subjects could do so readily. Most dramatically, when directly prompted, subjects increased points mentioned on the other side of the case by an average of 700% (Perkins et al., 1991). The data showed that subjects generally did not, but easily could, examine the other side of the case with care. It implicated an important role for dispositions in thinking: People in trend were capable of, but not generally disposed to, critique their own arguments or examine the other side of the case. Similar results have been found by Baron, Granato, Spranca, and Teubal (1993). Stanovich (1994) generalized the phenomenon to refer to *dysrationalia*: "The key diagnostic criterion for dysrationalia is a level of rationality, as demonstrated in thinking and behavior, that is significantly below the level of the individual's intellectual capacity" (p. 11).

A Methodology for Examining Sensitivity, Inclination, and Ability

Years later, we and our colleagues began an extended program of research on dispositions guided by the triadic model, a program that continues today. We developed a methodology to distinguish between the contributions of sensitivity, inclination, and ability to thinking. We focused on intermediate-level elementary school students. The developed procedure used brief stories with embedded shortfalls in thinking. For example, one story concerned a Mrs. Perez who finds that the company she works for plans to relocate to another city. Mrs. Perez explains the situation to her daughter and concludes that they have to move: "I have no other choice. There's no other decision I can think of in this situation." Mrs. Perez's daughter is in the last half of her final year of high school. She is disappointed to leave her friends and miss graduation. The shortfall lies in Mrs. Perez's statement that there's no choice. There are several alternatives. For example, Mrs. Perez might get another job, or negotiate to stay behind for a few months as part of a mop up operation, or arrange for her daughter to stay with friends for the last few months of high school (Perkins & Tishman, 2001; Perkins et al., 2000).

Several stories concerning decision making, problem solving, and causal explanation were employed, with shortfalls of failing to search for options, considering only one side of the case, and more. To confirm that the shortfalls written into the stories could be detected by discerning readers, we gave a broad sample of the stories to several individuals involved professionally in the critical thinking movement. They all easily identified the shortfalls.

The basic experimental procedure differed somewhat from study to study but broadly took the form of an escalating scaffold. An experimenter invited a subject to read, for instance, the story of Mrs. Perez. Then, in step 1, the experiment asked what the subject thought of the thinking in the story. Occasionally, subjects would say, "Well, but Mrs. Perez does have choices. For instance . . ." More commonly, a subject did not identify any particular problems with the thinking. In that case, the experiment advanced to step 2 with statements like this: "Some of Mrs. Perez's friends think she should have tried to find more options. Other friends believe she tried hard enough to find options. Suppose you were in Mrs. Perez's place. What would your thinking be like?"

At this point, the subject might agree that Mrs. Perez had not examined the options and identified some alternatives. However, maybe not, in which case the interviewer advanced to step 3, asking point blank for options and discovering whether or not the subject was able to devise them.

This three step procedure for the Perez story and a number of others reflects the dispositional triad. Step 1, a test of sensitivity, gives a chance for the subject to recognize a thinking shortfall on his or her own and respond to it. Step 2, a gauge of inclination, alerts the subject to the potential shortfall and determines whether the subject thinks it's worth attention. Step 3 probes ability directly by asking the subject to generate options.

A number of interesting findings have emerged from this series of studies. Details are reported in Perkins and Tishman (2001) and Perkins et al. (2001). Here the trends are summarized.

Measuring the Contribution of Sensitivity and Inclination

The most important finding, confirmed over and over again in our work, showed that dispositional considerations more than abilities limited thinking. Sensitivity was by far the greatest bottleneck, followed by inclinations. One index of this looked at the successful response rate at step 1 versus step 2 versus step 3. To derive a score, the simple comment that a situation called for attention (e.g. "Mrs. Perez should have considered other options") counted as one hit, with each mention of an option or possible solution or pro or con, depending on the kind of story, counting as one more.

One study involved 64 eighth graders responding to four stories, each with two thinking shortfalls embedded in them for eight shortfalls in all. Two of the stories concerned decision making and two problem solving, and the shortfalls, distributed over the stories in a counterbalanced way, concerned looking for alterative options and examining the other side of the case. Thus, the Perez story included a shortfall of failing to seek alternative options in the context of decision making.

Analysis based on the scoring system mentioned earlier showed that by step 3 most subjects could identify some alternative options or other-side arguments. For instance, subjects offered the sorts of options for the Mrs. Perez story mentioned above. The analysis also examined the distribution of when subjects responded with awareness of the thinking shortfall and alternative options or other-side reasons—at step 1, step 2, or step 3. If the dispositional contribution to thinking were small, those subjects who performed at all well would do so right away at step 1. Frequencies of response would fall off sharply from step 1 to 2 and step 2 to 3.

In fact, the findings revealed just the opposite. For alternative options shortfalls, scores at step 1 averaged only .1 hits; at step 2, 1.6; and at step 3, 2.1. For other side of the case shortfalls, scores at step 1 averaged again about .1 hits, at step 2 about 3.0, and at step 3 about 2.9. In other words, very few subjects detected the shortfalls at step 1, showing hardly any sensitivity to the shortfalls. When, at step 2, the possibility of a shortfall was pointed out, only about half the subjects agreed that this was a shortfall. Yet, as gauged by step 3, almost everyone, whether they noticed the shortfall initially or thought it was a shortfall, could devise alternative options and other-side reasons.

This was strong support for the importance of the dispositional side of thinking. It also challenged the common presumption that dispositions were mostly a matter of motivation. To be sure, inclination proved an important factor in accord with the step 2 scores. However, by far the greatest bottleneck was sensitivity—failure to notice at all what needs thoughtful attention.

A second study streamlined the procedures previously described, which involved one-on-one or small group administration. This version allowed paper administration in large groups. The study eliminated step 2, focusing on the contrast between sensitivity and abilities. The study employed shorter and more stories, a body of 18 stories spanning three kinds of thinking—decision making, problem solving, and explanation—and embodying shortfalls in seeking options and looking for reasons on both sides of a matter as before. Ninety-four sixth graders responded to all 18 stories. Scoring for each response was done with a 6-point Likert scale, the low end representing no or sparse responses, the high end richly articulated responses. After some practice, strong interjudge reliability was achieved.

The findings mirrored those from the previous study. If dispositions contributed little to performance, students would easily notice and attend to the thinking shortfalls at step 1, although their comments on the shortfalls might be shallow. Scores for step 1 and (skipping step 2) step 3 would be about the same, because subjects would already have done well on step 1, perhaps mentioning one or two more responses on step 3. In fact, step 3 performance was far superior to step 1. Composite scores for each subject were created for step 1 and for step 3 by summing ratings across stories. The mean composite score for step 1 ($x = 2.12$) was over one standard deviation lower than that for step 3 ($x = 2.98$, $p < 0001$).

The results were also analyzed in terms of hits and misses, the style of the previous study, by establishing a threshold on the Likert scales for steps 1 and 3 for what constituted a hit. For both options and other-side reasons, subjects showed a mean hit percentage at step 1 of about 10% and at step 3 of about 70%. These rates did not vary appreciably with the kinds of stories in which the shortfalls were imbedded—decision making, problem solving, and explanation.

Examining the Causes of Low Sensitivity

Because dispositions contributed so much to performance, a further study was designed to examine why. The study compared three possible explanations for subjects' difficulties: (a) subjects lacked the knowledge necessary to make the proper discriminations between shortfalls, even though they could produce other-side reasons, options, and such on demand; (b) subjects had the appropriate knowledge, but simply did not approach the situation with an alertness to the shortfalls; and (c) the shortfalls were difficult to detect even with the appropriate knowledge and alertness.

The investigation focused on step 1 of the method described previously: Subjects were asked to read stories with imbedded thinking shortfalls and comment on the thinking. The investigation compared the three hypotheses by including scaffolds for saliency and knowledge in a counterbalanced fashion. To increase saliency, for two conditions key sentences where the shortfall appeared were underlined, but not otherwise explained. To support knowledge, for two conditions, subjects received a crib sheet of five kinds of shortfalls to look for, for instance "this is a place where it is important to look for an alternative explanation," and "this is a place where it is important to make a plan."

The subjects included 105 eighth graders, each reading eight 1-page stories across which were distributed 30 thinking shortfalls. The subjects were divided into four gender-balanced groups: no crib sheet and no underlining, crib sheet but no underlining, no crib sheet but underlining, and both crib sheet and underlining. The experimenters evaluated subjects' responses in two ways. Detection meant that a subject detected a shortfall by marking it. This was relevant only in the no-underlining conditions because in the underlining conditions detection came free. Explanation meant that a subject explained a shortfall appropriately, either after detecting it or coming across it underlined. This was relevant in all conditions, because having the crib sheet still did not tell a subject which shortfall applied.

First consider detection, only relevant in the not-underlined conditions. The results showed little impact of providing the crib sheet. Subjects detected about 41% of the targets without standards and 38% with, a negligible and nonsignificant contrast. This argued against hypothesis 1, that subjects lacked the knowledge, and against hypothesis 2, that subjects had the knowledge but lacked alertness, since the crib sheet both provided knowledge and alerted subjects about what to look for.

Now consider explanation. When subjects detected a shortfall in the not-underlined conditions, they offered a satisfactory explanation 88% and 81% of the time with no crib sheet and crib sheet respectively, another nonsignificant contrast. The crib sheet had more impact in the underlined conditions. Without the crib sheet, subjects offered satisfactory explanations about 67% of the time but with the crib sheet 86%, a statistically significant contrast. However, arguably this was to a considerable extent an artifact of the method, since the crib sheet reduced the interpretation of an underline to a multiple choice problem with a 1-in-5 probability of getting it right by luck. The pattern of findings provides further evidence against hypothesis 1, that subjects lacked the knowledge, because providing knowledge via the crib sheet did not enhance explanations much.

In summary, providing knowledge of what to look for did not help subjects to detect shortfalls nor help subjects much to explain them. Saliency, on the other hand, allowed most subjects to go on and explain the shortfalls. The results favored the third hypothesis, that shortfalls were difficult to detect in the midst of the stories despite appropriate knowledge and priming. This is in keeping with the perceptual overtones of the notion of sensitivity, suggesting a pattern recognition process that goes beyond simply knowing about shortfalls in principle and searching for them systematically.

Conclusion

In general, then, this series of studies provided strong support within the methodology adopted for the importance of the dispositional side of thinking. People often do not perform nearly as well as they might in situations that call for thinking principally because they miss the situations altogether and secondarily because they fail to engage the situations thoughtfully. This challenges the hegemony of abilities-centric accounts of thinking and indeed intelligence.

DISPOSITIONS AS TRAITS

The work previously outlined focused on the relative contribution of sensitivity, inclination, and ability to intellectual performance. Another question concerns the extent to which sensitivity and inclination are trait-like constraints independent of ability. In particular, (a) are such candidate traits stable across time and task; (b) are they more domain general or domain specific; (c) are they statistically independent of ability measures; and (d) what dispositional traits are there—one or many and which ones? Such questions were not the central focus of this program of inquiry, but they were addressed from time to time and research from other quarters speaks to them.

Stability Across Time and Task

Research on constructs such as need for cognition (Cacioppo et al., 1996) and need for closure (Kruglanski, 1990) has demonstrated test-retest reliability. The present program examined test-retest correlations on sensitivity scores for detecting thinking shortfalls and found correlations of about .8 for a ninth-grade sample and .6 for a fifth-grade sample.

As to stability across tasks, these studies also involved several different kinds of thinking trouble spots—neglecting alternative options, my-side bias, and more—imbedded in different problem situations—decision making, problem solving, and explanation. Factor analyses of the influence of trouble spots and story types generally yielded single sensitivity and inclination factors despite the differences in trouble spots and story types. In other words, subjects performed consistently across these variations (Perkins et al., 2000; Perkins & Tishman, 2001).

Domain Generality

Related to stability across time and task is the matter of domain generality. Whether a cognitive skill is relatively domain general (roughly, operative over a wide range of settings and disciplines), or relatively domain specific (operative only in particular domains where the individual has a well-developed knowledge base and a version of the skill adapted to the domain) is a complex and controversial issue (Anderson, Reder, & Simon, 1996; Brown, Collins, & Duguid, 1989; Lave & Wenger, 1991; Perkins & Salomon, 1989). Although we have argued here that thinking dispositions complement thinking skills rather than reducing to them, much the same question arises for dispositions. For example, if one is disposed to think about the other side of the case or to scrutinize sources of information for potential bias, does this tendency figure broadly and generally in one's cognition or only in scattered domains where one is especially knowledgeable and well-practiced?

A full examination of this challenging issue is beyond the scope of the present treatment, but several observations are in order:

1. In principle, some dispositions are domain general and some more restricted—for instance the general disposition to look for evidence on both sides of a matter versus a lawyer's specific disposition to look for legal precedents.

2. However, a disposition general in principle may not operate in a general way, even when the person possesses the relevant knowledge. For example, one of our early studies (Perkins et al., 1991) examined student lawyers' disposition to examine the other side of the case on everyday issues and found them on the average just as subject to my-side bias as other populations.

3. Those who do not exhibit the general form of a disposition may display a more local form. For example, we presume (this was not tested) that, in the context of planning a legal case, the student lawyers' training would lead them to consider how the other side might argue.

4. Moreover, a disposition general in principle is likely to operate that way for some people. For example, as noted earlier, we validated our instruments on several experts in critical thinking, all of whom performed vary well across our diverse stories. They proved generally alert to a number of traps that caught most of our subjects.

5. However, a disposition even if operative in general form is not likely to serve well when a person's domain knowledge is sparse. For example, one of our critical thinking experts would certainly seek to examine the other side of a legal case, but would likely lack the legal knowledge to do so well.

In summary, it is much too sweeping to ask whether dispositions are domain general or domain specific, yes or no. They may be relatively general or relatively specific in principle, and when more general in principle may actually operate fairly generally or in more restricted ways depending on individual development.

Relationship to Abilities

In studies of such dispositional constructs as need for cognition (Cacioppo et al., 1996) and incremental versus entity learning (Dweck, 1975, 1999), researchers have often found a low or negligible correlation between the disposition and intellectual aptitude as conventionally mentioned. Our studies occasionally examined this question. First of all, the investigation from the 1980s showed no correlation between my-side bias and IQ (Perkins et al., 1991).

In the study of 94 sixth graders described earlier, the experimenters gathered grade point averages for the students as a rough proxy for intellectual aptitude (permission for a short-form vocabulary test could not be obtained) and examined the relationships among the sensitivity measure, ability on the task at hand in the sense of step 3 performance, and grade point average. Sensitivity correlated with step 3 performance at .72 but with grade point average at only .36. However, step 3 performance correlated with academic standing at .61. The pattern of results suggests that sensitivity depends on somewhat different cognitive resources than intellectual aptitude as reflected in school grades (Perkins et al., 2000; Perkins & Tishman, 2001).

In the study of causes of low sensitivity, permission was obtained to use a short-form vocabulary test as a proxy for intellectual aptitude. Detection plus explanation in the conditions without underlining seemed the best gauge of sensitivity, since this showed that subjects detected shortfalls without help and understood what they had noticed. The correlations between detection plus explanation scores and vocabulary scores were .32 without the list of standards and .26 with the list, neither significant at the .05 level. Although the study included no step 3 condition in the sense outlined earlier, the underlined conditions were more abilities-centered, because they did not ask the subject to detect but simply to explain a shortfall of thinking in the story. In the underlined conditions, the correlations were .45 without the list of standards and .44 with, both significant at the .05 level. Although the differences are hardly dramatic, this again suggests that sensitivity is somewhat less related to intellectual aptitude as usually measured than are tasks that directly pose a problem to be solved (Perkins et al., 2000; Perkins & Tishman, 2001).

Distinct Dispositional Traits

What distinct dispositional traits are there? This question is particularly challenging given the present state of research. Many of the investigations have addressed isolated dispositional constructs, such as need for cognition, and their contrast with intellectual aptitude as conventionally conceived. Research of this sort does not propose complementary sets of dispositions.

Other scholars have advanced lists of complementary thinking dispositions (see Ritchhart, 2002 for a full review of lists of dispositions). For example, Ennis suggested a list of 14 critical thinking dispositions, including seeking and offering reasons, seeking alternatives, and being open-minded (Ennis, 1986). Facione and Facione (1992; Facione et al., 1995) proposed a list of seven, including open-mindedness, inquisitiveness, systematicity, analyticity, truth-seeking, critical thinking self-confidence, and maturity. We and our colleagues synthesized several sources in the literature to suggest a list of seven (Perkins et al., 1993):

1. The disposition to be broad and adventurous
2. The disposition toward wondering, problem finding, and investigating
3. The disposition to build explanations and understandings
4. The disposition to make plans and be strategic
5. The disposition to be intellectually careful
6. The disposition to seek and evaluate reasons
7. The disposition to be metacognitive

These and other lists certainly articulate dispositional traits that appear to be conceptually distinct. Whether they are psychometrically distinct is another matter. Recall that our factor analyses of performance across types of shortfalls and types of stories yielded single factors for sensitivity and inclination. Most of these lists were constructed conceptually rather than empirically. The Faciones based their list on a factor analysis. However they employed not subjects' performance on tasks but subjects' self-ratings of a long list of traits such as: We can never really learn the truth about most things, and the best argument for an idea is how you feel about it at the moment.

Therefore, their list most likely represents subjects' conceptual groupings rather than performance factors.

It is not necessarily surprising that conceptually distinct dispositions would merge into a single factor. The same is true of much of human knowledge and skill, simply because most people learn the same things at about the same time. Whether or not such lists ultimately prove to reflect distinct factors based on performance rather than self-rating tasks, they do guide the construction of studies and can inform instruction designed to cultivate dispositions, a matter addressed later.

WHAT KIDS KNOW ABOUT WHEN

As noted earlier, one should not view sensitivity and inclination as monolithic traits. They are better treated as complex processes, with measurements of sensitivity and inclination only extracting broad trends. They involve the alert use of knowledge about when—about thinking traps such as neglecting the other side of the case and thinking opportunities such as looking for tacit assumptions when a problem proves difficult. To be sure, knowledge is at best a necessary condition. As noted before, knowing about something does not guarantee its active use, the problem of inert knowledge. Nonetheless, it is of some interest to examine youngsters' knowledge of the traps and opportunities of thinking.

Accordingly, we interviewed students informally to explore what they knew about the whens of thinking. The interviews were part of an investigation into how teachers and schools might best foster thinking dispositions. The interviewees were students in grades four through eight at schools in both the United States and in Sweden. The interviews took the form of informal classroom discussions. They centered on three important areas of thinking: seeking truth, evaluating fairness, and directing one's own thinking.

Three questions organized these discussions. In the case of truth, the investigator would begin with "Sometimes it's hard to know whether or not something is true. When are some times when that happens?" (An equivalent phrase for fairness was "sometimes it's hard to know whether something is fair" and for directing your thinking "sometimes it's hard to direct your thinking"). Student wrote responses before sharing them with the class. With examples shared and captured on the blackboard, the investigator took a further step: "When it is hard to know whether or not something is true, what can you do about it?" Students shared their ideas here as well and the investigator recorded them on the blackboard. The investigator then asked a third question, sometimes on a later day because of time, following the same procedure: "It's often hard to investigate the truth of something. When is it worth the trouble?"

Clearly this procedure is limited. Discussions in this style give a collective but not an individual sense of what students know. Students' reflections reveal only what they think about thinking, not how they perform in real situations. Nonetheless, much of interest emerged. The discussions revealed what knowledge students have about when thinking becomes challenging, which is relevant to sensitivity. The discussions exposed the repertoire of strategies students possess around truth and other areas of thinking, which is relevant to their ability. Finally, the discussions led students to recount what motivational factors made thinking more or less worthwhile, relevant to inclination.

Students' Thinking About Truth

In general, students' reflections on truth proved much more advanced than one might anticipate. Although they did not use sophisticated terminology, they brought forward many basic and sometimes nuanced dilemmas of seeking truth.

Students showed an awareness that the truth is often ambiguous and must be investigated. Across all ages, students indicated that information can not be equally trusted from all sources. Fourth graders and eighth graders alike noted that books, news accounts, and the conversations of peers may not always be true—"It's not always easy to know the truth about things someone tells you or what you read in the newspaper." However, younger students more readily accepted truth from expert sources they knew personally, such as peers or parents. Older students showed more awareness of multiple perspectives and the need to synthesize. Furthermore, older students saw that issues of truth go beyond mere facts, including the challenge of self-knowledge ("It's hard to know the truth about your own opinion and feelings sometimes"), ethical issues ("It can be hard to know the truth about what is right and wrong in a situation"), larger epistemic issues ("Scientific theories like the Big Bang can be hard to know the truth about"), and issues of faith ("It's hard to know things about God").

Pondering what is worth thinking about, younger students focused on the importance of the truth to them personally at that moment. If there were no immediate consequences for them, they often signaled that it was not a strong priority. Not surprisingly, older students recognized the impact of the truth on others and distinguished between personal relevance and larger societal relevance. Addressing the latter, students evaluated worth based on their ability to contribute to the truth. Knowing the truth about chemical weapons in Iraq might be very important, but it was not worth their time personally. Besides potential to contribute, students also identified curiosity as a motivation. Although they might not need to know whether cola drinks break down tooth enamel, it might be fun to find out, particularly if the investment in finding out was not too taxing.

When it comes to strategies for investigating truth, students at least talked a good game. For younger students, strategies often took the form of simple information gathering from more reliable sources: Look in a book, check the internet, ask the person, etc. Older students saw a need to combine information from multiple sources, assess the motives and bias of those sources, and synthesize this information. These students were also more likely to see themselves as important judges of truth in some situations: "You need to try it out for yourself. You should gather your own evidence. You need to look within yourself."

This data, informal as it is, suggests that students know a remarkable amount about issues of truth, when it becomes problematic, what one might do about it, and when it is worth the bother. Though students had never had these discussions before, the readiness of their responses showed knowledge rather close to the surface and readily uncovered.

Students' Reflections on Issues of Fairness

Students generally showed great familiarity and indeed passion for issues concerning fairness. All of these discussions were spirited: What is fair and unfair is of great interest to students. In addition to the usual discussions about "When is it hard?" "What can you do when it is hard?" and "When is it worthwhile?" our colleague Bermúdez conducted an extensive analysis of 61 Massachusetts fifth graders' recognition of instances of unfairness in their lives and their subsequent assessments of those events. The investigator asked students to rate the unfairness of the described situations on a continuum from "highly unfair" to "only a little bit unfair" and to justify those rankings, revealing how these students reasoned about issues of fairness and what variables they paid attention to in making their assessment.

The fifth graders demonstrated an understanding of fairness as an issue of equity or balance among competing claims, interests, values, or opportunities. The most prevalent type of unfair situation students identified, accounting for 37% of the 323 responses generated, involved equity in the distribution of goods, opportunities, or responsibilities. "My brother ate the bigger half of the bagel. I got the small half and didn't get to eat as much as him," was an example of unfair goods. "My baseball coach put the older players on the field more than the younger players. The older kids get to play more than the younger kids" was an instance of unfair opportunity. "I always have more homework than my sister" was an example of unfair responsibilities.

Students mentioned several other kinds of situations frequently: consistency ("When my older brother was little he had a later bedtime than my older sister. But now I have the same bedtime as my younger brother. I think I should have a later bedtime."); actions based on false information ("My brother threw a ball and it hit the lamp and broke, and he said that I did it, and I got in trouble."); not having one's say ("We had a group project. The teacher told us to agree on a topic. The group chose a topic I didn't like and I didn't agree on."); reciprocity ("I was mean to an old friend and she was being nice to me."); undeserved burdens ("I threw my toy down the toilet and my parents had to pay for something I did."); promised outcomes ("Yesterday my mom promised me we could play a game and then she said I had to go to bed."); relationships ("I left a friend out of our project and made fun of her behind her back. I am sorry! I used to be best friends and then we kind of grew apart. It wasn't right."); human rights–social justice ("When people kill other people on the street, because people lose their lives."), and action against one's wants ("My mom didn't let me finish my project because it was too late. It was unfair because I need to do my homework.")

As these examples show, students readily recognized many kinds of unfairness, noticing different types of inequity and imbalance in their lives. Further, in making judgments about how unfair these situations were and explaining them, students showed that they were not taking absolute stances toward these situations but could recognize aggravating and mitigating factors. In particular, students paid attention to issues of need, who was first, age, capability, ownership, intention, relationship to the person, and the amount of burden in deciding how unfair a situation was. These nuanced assessments show that students bring a wealth of awareness with them to the spotting of occasions.

Students' Understanding of Self-Direction

One would not expect students to know as much about self-direction as about truth and fairness. The term self-direction certainly is not part of students' everyday speech—indeed we were not able to locate a vernacular term for self-direction in either English or Swedish—and the construct itself is not always easy to grasp. Accordingly, the investigator began with conversations about what it might mean to manage or be in charge of one's own thinking. Students responded with ideas related to reflecting on ideas and action, checking over one's thoughts to make sure they were right, controlling one's mood, considering consequences, giving oneself time to think, and evaluating one's thoughts. Building on students' ideas, the investigator then introduced a simple four-part framework for self-direction that included: thinking ahead, taking on the right attitude, checking in, and reflecting back. Each of these areas was explored in turn, and students identified instances of when and how they might be used. These tasks laid the groundwork for discussions of when self-direction of one's thinking is a problem and what you can do about it.

As to when it is a problem, students overwhelmingly mentioned factors related to mood, attitude, and one's physical state: "It's hard when you are in a bad mood. When you don't care. When you have no energy left." Their strategies for dealing with such situations were limited, even simplistic: "Get more sleep; take a break; think about something fun." They often passed the responsibility on to another: "Ask the teacher for help; have the coach check in with you; ask someone who has already done it."

Though this data is informal and one should not make too much of it, the contrast with the same students' understanding of issues of fairness and truth was striking. Both spotting occasions and suggesting remedies, even in the reflective sense probed through discussion, seemed impoverished when it came to self-direction. This is understandable. The concept of self-direction does not receive as much natural play in students' social interactions as does truth or fairness. Furthermore, the metacognitive demands of self-direction make it more complex. Students do not encounter such situations in the same kind of direct way they do issues of fairness and truth. Therefore, the consequences of poor self-direction and the sense that one could do better may be less acutely felt than matters of fairness and truth.

HOW SETTINGS CAN DEVELOP GOOD THINKERS

The notion that thinking can be taught is as old as the Greek rhetoriticians, who systematically cultivated the art of argument albeit not always for noble ends. Today a number of approaches to teaching thinking of various sorts thrive, with diverse philosophies, frameworks, and track records. Although the prospects of teaching thinking have been challenged from several quarters, there is clear evidence that at least some interventions are effective—see for example the reviews in Grotzer and Perkins (2000), Nickerson (1989), Nickerson, Perkins, and Smith (1985), Perkins (1995), and Perkins and Grotzer (1997).

That said, most programs do not attend directly and systematically to dispositional aspects of thinking, although they may foster dispositions as a side-effect. In the context of the present discussion, it becomes important to ask: What might instruction designed to cultivate the dispositional side of thinking look like?

One view of this argues that culture is the best teacher of dispositions (cf. Dewey, 1922, 1933; Tishman et al., 1993, 1995; Vygotsky, 1978). Plainly people pick up much of their general alertness and attitudes from the culture around them, as part of becoming streetwise about whatever streets one walks. A culture in the classroom, the family, or the workplace that foreground values of thinking and encouraged attention to thinking would likely instill street wisdom about thinking. Moreover, an enculturative approach helps to avoid a dilemma inherent in the concept of dispositions: They cannot be taught as directly as skills because dispositions are not procedural. Students cannot straightforwardly practice up values and commitments that motivate thinking and alert states of mind that favor detecting thinking opportunities. Enculturation suggests a kind of osmosis that avoids this dilemma.

However, just how does this osmosis operate? How can settings, in particular classroom settings, nurture students' sensitivity and inclination toward thinking as well as their ability? One place to look for answers to these questions is in classrooms where such work is currently taking place, environments in which teachers are establishing a classroom culture rich in thinking.

Ritchhart (2002) conducted a year-long qualitative study of six such classrooms, focusing on urban, suburban and private school settings at the middle school level. These case studies proved rich in the particulars of how teachers establish cultures of thinking and develop students' thinking in their settings and subject areas. At the same time, the cases revealed common trends. The teachers studied did not treat thinking as content to be covered but used the culture of the classroom to instill it. They created settings where thinking was welcome, where there were many attractive whens—occasions when thinking was appropriate and incentives to undertake it.

Making Room for Thinking

What does it mean for a teacher to provide students with thinking opportunities? Ritchhart's (2002) research found that such patterns of practice focused on big ideas, included occasions for student choice and self-direction, encouraged students' intellectual independence or autonomy, and provided time for thinking. There was much worthwhile to think about, indeed that required thinking, as well plenty of room to notice and develop one's own ideas.

For one specific practice, teachers based their instruction on guiding questions such as "What does it mean to 'come of age' and how does it differ across culture, time, and gender?" Such questions not only focus the curriculum, but also provide a daily touch point for class reflections. Furthermore, such questions call in a rather loud voice for thinking. For other practices, teachers made time for thinking in several ways. Teachers followed their questions with considerable wait time, often fostered extended discussions, and framed homework and tests to explore a few questions or issues deeply.

Besides making room for thinking, teachers' formal and informal interactions with students encouraged and guided students in when and how to think. One can examine their practices through the dispositional triad.

Developing Ability: Creating Spaces and Structures for Thinking

While the classrooms studied made ample room for thinking, students still need to know how to think—the abilities issue. These teachers did not teach thinking skills directly. They relied on the incorporation of what we call thinking routines (Ritchhart, 2002). Like other classroom routines (Lein-hardt & Greeno, 1986; Leinhardt, Weidman, & Hammond, 1987), thinking routines become part of the way students do things in the classroom. They are simple procedures or practices that see frequent use.

Brainstorming is a good example of a thinking routine. It is a simple pro-cedure designed to promote a specific type of thinking (openness and flexibil-ity) with wide applicability across subjects and grade levels. It works well at the group level, and individuals can also use it. Brainstorming and other practices functioned as routines, rather than simply strategies, because they became regular features of classroom learning. Routines operate at the socio-cultural level, first experienced and learned in group settings and gradually internalized as patterns or habits of thinking.

Besides brainstorming, the teachers developed routines for discussing and exploring ideas, such as the "why?" routine in which students were regularly asked to explain the thinking and reasoning behind their ideas or the "take a stance" routine in which students had to defend a position. There were rou-tines for managing and documenting thinking, such as using journals for reg-ular reflections. Finally, there were routines for exploring ideas, which might involve a specific process for the making of interpretations or writing as a means of exploring what one knows and thinks.

Nurturing Inclination: Conveying the Value of Thinking

During the first days of school, the teachers Ritchhart (2002) studied con-veyed their values to students both explicitly through their talk of expecta-tions and implicitly through their actions. For instance, teachers talked with students about the importance of curiosity, inquiry, and playing with ideas as part of the work of the classroom. In addition, they probed students' re-sponses in a Socratic manner that let them know the importance of justifying one's responses and engaging in dialogs that build understanding. These early steps go a long way toward cultivating students' inclination toward thinking in the classroom setting.

Teachers' ongoing actions also supported inclination. Teachers honored students' disposition toward thinking by recognizing their thoughtful contri-butions and demonstrating genuine interest in students' ideas, sending the message that thinking is valued. By helping students to experience cognitive emotions, such as the joy of verification, surprise at unexpected outcomes, and the thrill of discovery, teachers led students to see not only that thinking is important in the given situation but that thinking has intrinsic rewards and benefits. Teachers' modeling of their own thinking revealed what prompts them to think and the paths that thinking can take, helping students to see the whens of thinking. However, the kind of modeling most often observed was not direct demonstration of a certain type of thinking behavior, metacognition, for example, but the regular day-to-day demonstration of the teacher's curiosity, reasoning, and reflection. This kind of modeling, the kind that just comes up, seemed to be a powerful force in maintaining a classroom culture of thinking.

Cueing Awareness: Starting and Sustaining Thinking

It is axiomatic that to spot opportunities for thinking, the opportunities must be there. A prerequisite for developing students' awareness of occasions for thinking is a classroom rich in thinking opportunities. However, even in such a culture many thinking opportunities are likely to go unnoticed. When opportunities do get detected, students still have to match them with an appropriate type of thinking: Is this a moment to consider other perspectives, weigh alternatives, or seek clarification? Clearly, opportunities are not sufficient to ensure that students will find and exploit them.

The teachers studied used a variety of means to make occasions for thinking more salient for students. These means were generally so subtle and ingrained that the teachers themselves were often unaware of them. One means was the teachers' use of the language of thinking (Tishman & Perkins, 1997)—process terms such as reflecting, product terms such as hypothesis, stance terms such as agreeing or disagreeing, and state terms such as clarity or confusion. The language of thinking was rich in these classrooms, and it was the extensive use of product and stance words that especially stood out. For instance, in one math classroom students were always being asked to produce conjectures, form hypotheses, and take stances toward others' ideas. Such words may be particular useful because they call for an outcome that can be observed and thus prompt the desired action.

Sensitivity toward particular occasions of thinking also can be cued more directly. Just as a writer uses foreshadowing to heighten a reader's awareness of future events, the teachers sometimes cued students to anticipated occasions for certain types of thinking. Such cues were most often general in nature. They acted as sensitivity boosters rather than explicit commands to think in a certain way. For instance, an English teacher engaged students in a discussion of the meaning of power and then told them, "This is the kind of thinking you can be doing as you're reading." As students engaged tasks rich with thinking opportunities, many would still pass them by. When this happened, teachers scaffolded thinking by pushing students to the next level. For instance, in a discussion of citizenship requirements in a history class, students reacted to a proposal emotionally in terms of whether they liked it or disliked it. The teacher then raised expectations, stating, "Okay, now that we are past your personal feelings, let's go to the next level. What is the intent in requiring something like this?"

A Vygotskian Perspective

This discussion of classroom cultures of thinking suggests a learning process with a distinctly Vygotskian cast. In the social setting of the classroom, teachers foster values, practices, and foci of attention that play out in public ways—in the language used, the kinds of verbal and written products produced, the small-group and whole-class conversations held, and so on. These make up the warp and weft of the classroom culture. Students' participation in that culture engenders a process of orientation and internalization that advances their individual skills and dispositions as thinkers.

The notion of creating a culture around students certainly has not passed educational developers by. It figures prominently in some approaches to cultivating thinking and thoughtful learning—for example, the *Philosophy for Children* program developed by Lipman and colleagues (Lipman, 1988; Lipman, Sharp & Oscanyon, 1980), which foregrounds Socratic discussion, and the *Knowledge Forum* developed by Scardamalia and Bereiter (1996, 1999), which engages learners in collectively building online knowledge webs through inquiry processes scaffolded online by the language of thinking.

Veterans of several program development initiatives in thinking: see for example *Odyssey* (Adams, 1986), *The Thinking Classroom* (Tishman et al., 1995), *Keys to Thinking* (Perkins, Tishman, & Goodrich, 1994), and *Thinking Connections* (Perkins, Goodrich, Tishman, & Owen, 1994). We and our colleagues are currently using the idea of thinking routines in the design of a program to support students' dispositional development. While routines provide an important avenue for teaching thinking skills and strategies, thus fostering students' ability, their presence as routines and not merely isolated strategies offers other benefits. Because thinking routines constitute ways of doing things in a particular subculture, they can help to engrain patterns of behavior, support the development of students' inclination toward thinking, and increase sensitivity to opportunities for using the routines to engage in thinking.

Initial results indicate that teachers find such routines easy to integrate into their instruction and curriculum and that students quickly pick up the pattern of thinking encouraged through a routine. This can be seen in students using the "what makes you say that?" routine. This simple prompt asks students to give evidence for inferences they have made about an object, picture, or story they have encountered. Students quickly catch on to the idea of supporting their assertions with reasons and evidence and begin to do so even without prompting. Furthermore, they internalize the idea that opinions, inferences, and claims need supporting evidence and often ask for such evidence from others.

BEYOND ABILITIES

Both folk psychology and a good deal of academic psychology give abilities center stage in explaining good and not-so-good thinking. This becomes especially evident in testing practices. To gauge how well people think, we give them problems to solve and motivate them to do well. The idea behind all this is simple and plausible: How well you think when pressed to perform explains and predicts how well you will do out there in the world when you need to think. Along with this abilities-centric view of thinking comes an abilities-centric view of what it is to teach thinking: To get people to think better, improve their abilities—teach problem solving skills, learning skills, self-management skills, and so on.

All this certainly has value as far as it goes. However, the arguments advanced here question the completeness of the storyline. They challenge whether perform-on-demand tasks are a good model of how thinking works in everyday life. An abilities-centric account of thinking leaves out the matter of when. The same common-sense folk psychology that places abilities in the center also and paradoxically makes room for and considers important various traits of intellectual character—curiosity, persistence, open-mindedness, due skepticism, and so on (a luxury of folk psychology is that it need not be consistent). As a matter of logic, accepting an intellectual challenge implies dealing with the when—Is this a problem here and one worth engaging? While some situations, such as taking a test, call for thinking with a loud voice, others do not. One might easily miss a deceptive point in a politician's speech or a decision point one should treat thoughtfully rather than by default.

Empirical research underwrites the importance of the when of thinking. As reviewed earlier, research on a variety of dispositional constructs—for instance, need for cognition (Cacioppo & Petty, 1982), need for cognitive closure (Kruglanski, 1990), entity versus incremental learning (Dweck, 1975, 1999)—has shown substantial influence on performance. Moreover, such traits generally correlate weakly or not at all with typical measures of cognitive ability. Our and our colleagues' research on sensitivity, inclination, and abilities has provided evidence that sensitivity to occasions that invite thinking is a major bottleneck, a factor that more than anything else may undermine thoughtfulness in day-to-day matters.

A devotee of abilities-centric theories might dismiss such arguments as follows: "Well, of course motivation matters. Motivation matters throughout human behavior. All such research really shows is that motivation matters to performance and we never doubted that." However, this response reduces the dispositional view to a straw man. The dispositional view has much more depth and nuance. For one point, the dispositional side of thinking involves not just motives, which may be transient, but stable intellectual values and habits of mind. For another, research from our group emphasizes that a large part of the dispositional side of thinking does not straightforwardly concern motive in any sense but rather sensitivity to occasion.

With a dispositional view of thinking comes a different approach to the teaching of thinking. Whether thinking can be taught at all in any general sense is somewhat controversial, although surveys cited earlier have revealed what appear to be clear positive instances. In any case, efforts to do so are generally abilities-centric, as noted earlier. A dispositional view suggests that efforts to teach thinking should give substantial attention to cultivating values and commitments associated with thinking, as well as alertness to the subtle signs of occasions for thinking that might pass one by. Since neither values and commitments nor alertness can be practiced in a straightforward sense, this in turn looks toward enculturative styles of teaching and learning, where learners internalize values and patterns of practice from the classroom, family or workplace culture around them. To be sure, abilities-centric interventions may accomplish some of this in any case, simply through putting thinking in the foreground and treating it seriously and attentively. Nonetheless, it seems likely that deliberate attention to the dispositional side of thinking from an enculturative perspective would add value.

In *Cognition in the Wild*, one of the notable books about cognition in recent years, Edwin Hutchins (1996) related his studies of crewmen on U.S. Navy ships coping with the many complexities of navigation. Hutchins emphasized how different the work of cognition looked in this setting from the mind-with-a-pencil model that seems so prominent in typical laboratory research on cognition. Hutchins noted how cognitive work was socially distributed across team members at various levels of command and physically distributed across various instruments and notational systems.

Another characteristic of the wild—whether on a Navy ship or on the playground or in a work setting—is the great range in how loudly or softly circumstances call for thinking. When, in one incident Hutchins reported, a ship suddenly loses all power and steerage while underway, everyone knows there is a problem to be solved, especially since a large vessel can coast for miles under its own momentum and thereby end up in disastrous places. There is little doubt that this is a when for quick thinking and quick action. However, often we do not know whether there is a problem or whether it is worth addressing. Only when the when of good thinking takes its place beside the what are we likely to have a rich explanation of how and how well people think in the wild.

ACKNOWLEDGMENTS

Some of the ideas and research reported here were developed with much-appreciated support from the Stiftelsen Carpe Vitam Foundation and the John D. and Catherine T. MacArthur Foundation. The positions taken by the authors are of course not necessarily those of the foundations. We also thank our principal colleagues and coresearchers in this endeavor Angela Bermúdez, Lotta Norell, Patricia Palmer, Ylva Telegin, and Shari Tishman.

REFERENCES

Adams, M. (Ed.) (1986). *Odyssey: A curriculum for thinking*. Watertown, MA: Mastery Education Corporation.

Anderson, J. R., Reder, L. M., & Simon, H. A. (1996). Situated learning and education. *Educational Researcher, 25*(4), 5–11.

Aristotle (350 B. C. E). *Prior analytics* (A. J. Jenkinson, Trans.). Available: http://classics.mit.edu/Aristotle/prior.html

Bacon, F. (1878). *Novum organum* (T. Fowler, Ed.). Oxford, England: Clarendon Press. (Original work published 1620)

Baron, J. (1985). *Rationality and intelligence*, New York: Cambridge University Press.

Baron, J., Granato, L., Spranca, M., & Teubal, E. (1993). Decision-making biases in children and early adolescents: Exploratory studies. *Merrill-Palmer Quarterly, 39*(1), 22–46.

Basseches, M. (1984). *Dialectical thinking and adult development.* Norwood, NJ: Ablex.

Bransford, J. D., Franks, J. J., Vye, N. J., & Sherwood, R. D. (1989). New approaches to instruction: Because wisdom can't be told. In S. Vosniadou & A. Ortony (Eds.), *Similarity and analogical reasoning* (pp. 470–497). New York: Cambridge University Press.

Brody, N. (1992). *Intelligence*. New York: Academic Press.

Brown, J. S., Collins, A., & Duguid, P. (1989). Situated cognition and the culture of learning. *Educational Researcher, 18*(1), 32–42.

Cacioppo, J. T., & Petty, R. E. (1982). The need for cognition. *Journal of Personality and Social Psychology, 42*, 116–131.

Cacioppo, J. T., Petty, R. E., Feinstein, J. A., & Jarvis, W. B. G. (1996). Dispositional differences in cognitive motivation: The life and times of individuals varying in need for cognition. *Psychological Bulletin, 119*(2), 197–253.

Case, R. (1992). *The mind's staircase: Exploring the conceptual underpinnings of children's thought and knowledge*. Hillsdale, NJ: Lawrence Erlbaum Associates.

Dewey, J. (1922). *Human nature and conduct*. New York: Holt.

Dewey, J. (1933). *How we think: A restatement of the relation of reflective thinking to the educative process*. Boston: D. C. Heath and Company.

Dweck, C. S. (1975). The role of expectations and attributions in the alleviation of learned helplessness. *Journal of Personality and Social Psychology, 31*, 674–685.

Dweck, C. S. (1999). *Self-theories: Their role in motivation, personality, and development*. Philadelphia: Psychology Press.

Elgin, C. Z. (1996). *Considered judgment*. Princeton, NJ: Princeton University Press.

Ennis, R. H. (1986). A taxonomy of critical thinking dispositions and abilities. In J. B. Baron & R. S. Sternberg (Eds.), *Teaching thinking skills: Theory and practice* (pp. 9–26). New York: Freeman.

Facione, P. A., & Facione, N. C. (1992). *The California critical thinking dispositions inventory.* Millbrae, CA: The California Academic Press.

Facione, P. A., Sanchez, C. A., Facione, N. C., & Gainen, J. (1995). The disposition toward critical thinking. *Journal of General Education, 44*(1), 1–25.

Fiske, D. W. (1949). Consistency of the factorial structures of personality ratings from different sources. *Journal of Abnormal and Social Psychology, 44*, 329–344.

Grotzer, T. A., & Perkins, D. N. (2000). Teaching intelligence: A performance conception. In R. J. Sternberg (Ed.), *Handbook of intelligence* (pp. 492–515). New York: Cambridge University Press.

Herrnstein, R. J., & Murray, C. (1994). *The bell curve: Intelligence and class structure in American life.* New York: The Free Press.

Honderich, T. (1995). *The Oxford companion to philosophy.* New York: Oxford University Press.

Hutchins, E. (1996). *Cognition in the wild.* Cambridge, MA: MIT Press.

Inhelder, B., & Piaget, J. (1958). *The growth of logical thinking from childhood to adolescence.* New York: Basic Books.

Jensen, A. R. (1980). *Bias in mental testing.* New York: The Free Press.

Jensen, A. R. (1998). *The g Factor: The science of mental ability.* Westport, CT: Praeger.

Kant, I. (1994). Fundamental principles of the metaphysics of morals (Thomas K. Abbott, Trans.). Upper Saddle River, NJ: Prentice Hall. (Original work published in 1785)

Kruglanski, A. W. (1990). Motivations for judging and knowing: Implications for causal attribution. In E. T. Higgins & R. M. Sorrentino (Eds.), *The handbook of motivation and cognition: Foundation of social behavior* (Vol. 2, pp. 333–368). New York: Guilford.

Kruglanski, A. W., & Freund, T. (1983). The freezing and unfreezing of lay inferences: Effects of impressional primacy, ethnic stereotyping, and numerical anchoring. *Journal of Experimental Social Psychology, 19*, 448–468.

Langer, E. J. (1989). *Mindfulness.* Menlo Park, CA: Addison-Wesley.

Lave, J., & Wenger, E. (1991). *Situated learning: Legitimate peripheral participation.* New York: Cambridge University Press.

Leinhardt, G., & Greeno, J. (1986). The cognitive skill of teaching. *Journal of Educational Psychology, 78*(2), 75–95.

Leinhardt, G., Weidman, C., & Hammond, K. M. (1987). Introduction and integration of classroom routines by expert teachers. *Curriculum Inquiry, 17*(2), 135–175.

Lipman, M. (1988). *Philosophy goes to school.* Philadelphia: Temple University.

Lipman, M., Sharp, A., & Oscanyon, F. (1980). *Philosophy in the classroom.* Philadelphia: Temple University.

Maw, W. H., & Magoon, A. J. (1971). The curiosity dimension of fifth-grade children: A factorial discriminant analysis. *Child Development, 42*, 2023–2031.

Murray, H. A. (1938). *Explorations in personality.* New York: Oxford University Press.

Nickerson, R. S. (1989). On improving thinking through instruction. *Review of Research in Education, 15*, 3–57.

Nickerson, R., Perkins, D. N., & Smith, E. (1985). *The teaching of thinking.* Hillsdale, NJ: Lawrence Erlbaum Associates.

Norris, S. P. (2002). The meaning of critical thinking test performance: The effects of abilities and dispositions on scores. In D. Fasco Jr. (Ed.), *Critical thinking: Current research, theory, and practice* (pp. 315–330). Cresskill, NJ: Hampton Press.

Paul, R. (1986). Dialogical thinking: Critical thought essential to the acquisition of rational knowledge and passions. In J. B. Baron & R. J. Sternberg (Eds.), *Teaching thinking skills: Theory and practice* (pp. 127–148). New York: Freeman.

Paul, R. (1990). *Critical thinking: What every person needs to survive in a rapidly changing world.* Rohnert Park, CA: Center for Critical Thinking and Moral Critique, Sonoma State University.

Paul, R. (1993). *Critical thinking: What every person needs to know to survive in a rapidly changing world.* Santa Rosa, CA: Foundation for Critical Thinking.

Paul, R., & Elder, L. (1997). The role of affect in critical thinking. In S. Tishman & D. N. Perkins (Eds.), *The dispositional side of thinking*. Manuscript submitted for publication.

Perkins, D. N. (1985). Postprimary education has little impact on informal reasoning. *Journal of Educational Psychology, 77*(5), 562–571.

Perkins, D. N. (1989). Reasoning as it is and could be. In D. Topping, D. Crowell, & V. Kobayashi (Eds.), *Thinking: The third international conference* (pp. 175–194). Hillsdale, NJ: Lawrence Erlbaum Associates.

Perkins, D. N. (1995). *Outsmarting IQ: The emerging science of learnable intelligence*. New York: The Free Press.

Perkins, D. N., Allen, R., & Hafner, J. (1983). Difficulties in everyday reasoning. In W. Maxwell (Ed.), *Thinking: The frontier expands* (pp. 177–189). Hillsdale, NJ: Lawrence Erlbaum Associates.

Perkins, D. N., Farady, M., & Bushey, B. (1991). Everyday reasoning and the roots of intelligence. In J. Voss, D. N. Perkins, & J. Segal (Eds.), *Informal reasoning* (pp. 83–105). Hillsdale, NJ: Lawrence Erlbaum Associates.

Perkins, D. N., Goodrich, H., Tishman, S., & Owen, J. N. (1994). *Thinking connections: Learning to think and thinking to learn*. Reading, MA: Addison-Wesley.

Perkins, D. N., & Grotzer, T. A. (1997). Teaching intelligence. *American Psychologist, 52*(10), 1125–1133.

Perkins, D. N., Jay, E., & Tishman, S. (1993). Beyond abilities: A dispositional theory of thinking. *The Merrill-Palmer Quarterly, 39*(1), 1–21.

Perkins, D. N., & Salomon, G. (1989). Are cognitive skills context bound? *Educational Researcher, 18*(1), 16–25.

Perkins, D. N., & Tishman, S. (2001). Dispositional aspects of intelligence. In S. Messick & J. M. Collis (Eds.), *Intelligence and personality: Bridging the gap in theory and measurement* (pp. 233–257). Mahwah, NJ: Lawrence Erlbaum Associates.

Perkins, D. N., Tishman, S., & Goodrich, H. (1994). *Keys to thinking*. Johannesberg, South Africa: UPTTRAIL Trust.

Perkins, D. N., Tishman, S., Ritchhart, R., Donis, K., & Andrade. A. (2000). Intelligence in the wild: A dispositional view of intellectual traits. *Educational Psychology Review, 12*(3), 269–293.

Ryle, G. (1949). *The concept of mind*. London: Hutchinson House.

Ritchhart, R. (2002). *Intellectual character: What it is, why it matters, and how to get it*. San Francisco: Jossey-Bass.

Scardamalia, M., & Bereiter, C. (1996). Adaptation and understanding: A case for new cultures of schooling. In S. Vosniadou, E. DeCorte, R. Glaser, & H. Mandl (Eds.), *International perspectives on the design of technology-supported learning environments* (pp. 149–163). Mahwah, NJ: Lawrence Erlbaum Associates.

Scardamalia, M., & Bereiter, C. (1999) Schools as knowledge-building organizations. In D. Keating & C. Hertzman (Eds.), *Today's children, tomorrow's society: The developmental health and wealth of nations* (pp. 274–289). New York: Guilford.

Scheffler, I. (1991). In praise of cognitive emotions. In I. Scheffler, (Ed.), *In praise of cognitive emotions* (pp. 3–17). New York: Routledge.

Schrag, F. (1988). *Thinking in school and society*. New York: Routledge.

Schunk, D. H., & Zimmerman, B. J. (Eds.). (1994). *Self-regulation of learning and performance: Issues and educational applications*. Hillsdale, NJ: Lawrence Erlbaum Associates.

Siegel, H. (1997). *What (good) are thinking dispositions?* Unpublished manuscript.

Stanovich, K. E. (1994). Reconceptualizing intelligence: Dysrationalia as an intuition pump. *Educational Researcher, 23*(4), 11–22.

Stanovich, K. E. (1999). *Who is rational? Studies of individual differences in reasoning*. Mahwah, NJ: Lawrence Erlbaum Associates.

Stanovich, K. E., & West, R. F. (1997). Reasoning independently of prior belief and individual differences in actively open-minded thinking. *Journal of Educational Psychology, 89*(2), 342–357.

Sternberg, R. J., & Wagner, R. K. (Eds.). (1986). *Practical intelligence: Nature and origins of competence in the everyday world.* New York: Cambridge University Press.

Tishman, S. (1994, April 4–8). *Thinking dispositions and intellectual character.* Paper presented at the 1994 Annual Meeting of the American Educational Research Association, New Orleans, LA.

Tishman, S. (1995, October). High-level thinking, ethics, and intellectual character. In *Think: The magazine on critical and creative thinking* (pp. 9–14).

Tishman, S., Jay, E., & Perkins, D. N. (1993). Thinking dispositions: From transmission to enculturation. *Theory Into Practice, 32*(3), 147–153.

Tishman, S., & Perkins, D. N. (1997). The language of thinking. *Phi Delta Kappan, 78*(5), 368–374.

Tishman, S., Perkins, D. N., & Jay, E. (1995). *The thinking classroom.* Boston: Allyn and Bacon.

Toulmin, S. E. (1958). *The uses of argument.* Cambridge, England: Cambridge University Press.

Von Neumann, J., & Morgenstern, O. (1944). *Theory of games and economic behavior.* Princeton, NJ: Princeton University Press.

Vygotsky, L. S. (1978). *Mind in society: The development of higher psychological processes.* Cambridge, MA: Harvard University Press.

Wagner, R. K., & Sternberg, R. J. (1985). Practical intelligence in real-world pursuits: The role of tacit knowledge. *Journal of Personality and Social Psychology, 49*, 436–458.

Wagner, R. K., & Sternberg, R. J. (1990). Street smarts. In K. E. Clark & M. B. Clark (Eds.), *Measures of leadership* (pp. 493–504). West Orange, NJ: Leadership Library of America.

Webster, D. M., & Kruglanski, A. W. (1994). Individual differences in need for cognitive closure. *Journal of Personality and Social Psychology, 67*(6), 1049–1062

Wertheimer, M. (1945). *Productive thinking.* New York: Harper.

Whitehead, A. N. (1929). *The aims of education and other essays.* New York: Simon & Schuster.

14
▼▼▼▼▼▼▼

Thought and Affect in American and Chinese Learners' Beliefs About Learning

Jin Li
Brown University

Kurt W. Fischer
Harvard University

FRANCIS BACON AND LIU XIANG: WESTERN AND CHINESE VISIONS OF LEARNING

In 1605, Francis Bacon wrote the following in his renowned *The Advancement of Learning*:

> . . . God has framed the mind of man as a mirror or glass, capable of the image of the universal world, and joyful to receive the impression thereof, as the eye joyeth to receive light; and not only delighted in beholding the variety of things and vicissitude of times, but raised also to find out and discern the ordinances and decrees, which throughout all those changes are infallibly observed . . . For that nothing parcel of the world is denied to man's inquiry and invention, . . . ; for all knowledge and wonder (which is the seed of knowledge) is an impression of pleasure itself . . . let men endeavour an endless progress or proficience in both [God's word and God's works] . . . ; only let men beware that they apply both to charity, and not to swelling; to use, and not to ostentation. . . . (1952, pp. 3–4)

Bacon addressed this book to the king of his time in an attempt to persuade him (thereby outline an agenda of learning) to engage his people and his kingdom in scientific inquiry based on the new methodology Bacon himself advanced. Carrying on the profound interest in nature manifest at least since Greek antiquity, Bacon emphasized five essential ideas: (a) Inquiry is an enterprise on which human beings are destined to embark; (b) the human mind is supreme in carrying out this inquiry; (c) scientific discovery requires active engagement of the learner; (d) one derives intrinsic enjoyment and pleasure by participating in this process; and (e) knowledge as produced by such learning must be put to ethical use. It does not require a stretch of imagination to find affinity between Bacon's vision of learning and modern principles of academic learning and intellectual functioning in the West. In Peltonen's (1996) evaluation, "there remains today much that Bacon would recognize as part of the [scientific] program he inaugurated" (pp. 23–24).

In a much earlier period (77–6 B.C.), also articulating the Confucian conception of learning, the proliferate Chinese writer and historian Liu Xiang (Wang &Wang, 1992) told a story in his book *Shuo Yuan (On Royal Gardens)*, written also to give advice to his king:

> The king of Jin, Ping Gong, asked his blind musician Shi Kuang "I am already seventy. I'd like to learn, but I am afraid it's too late." Shi Kuang replied "Why not light a candle?" Ping Gong was offended "How could a subject ridicule his king?" Shi Kuang responded "How dare I, a blind subject?! I have only heard that love for learning in young age is like the light from the rising sun; love for learning in adult prime age is like the bright sunlight at noon; and love for learning in old age is like the light from the candle. Lighting the candle or groping in darkness, which one is better?" Ping Gong brightened "How marvelous!" (p. 124)

This story is still widely read and told by Chinese people (Wang, 1992). The appeal of the story resides less in what the blind musician said to the king than in the fact that a powerless subject dared to challenge his king on the topic of learning. His persuasion manifests itself in the process of how an arrogant king was transformed and enlightened by the love for learning. Like Bacon's passage, this story also reveals five essential ideas about learning in the Chinese tradition: (a) A person without the desire to learn is one without aim and power; not even the king can be exempt; (b) the pursuit of learning enables and dignifies powerless individuals (to the degree that they are legitimized to challenge the otherwise powerful); (c) learning is a lifelong process; (d) love for and commitment to learning are sine qua non for lifelong learning; and (e) the purpose of learning is not to produce objective knowledge but to cultivate/perfect oneself morally.

The two visions of learning articulated by both Bacon and Liu Xiang are what we term cultural beliefs about learning. Cultural beliefs about learning include ideas about purposes and processes of learning as well as related affects, which are necessarily a part of motivation for learning. We focus on Western and Chinese cultural beliefs about learning because these two cultures (despite diversity within the West) have very different value systems, histories, and developments, even though both emphasize learning. In spite of dramatic historical changes, both Western and Confucian beliefs have enjoyed enduring influence in their respective cultures (Li, 2003a, 2003b; Tweed & Lehman, 2002). Even after more than a century's frequent interactions between the West and the East, the fundamentals of their respective beliefs, surprisingly, remain distinctly their own (Li, 2003a; Nisbett, 2003).

Since intellectual functioning is at the heart of learning, especially academic learning in formal settings, cultural beliefs about learning are central to intellectual functioning. Cultural beliefs about learning play an indispensable role in how learners think and feel about learning, how they approach learning, and ultimately how they achieve learning. In other words, such beliefs affect important aspects of learning such as what to learn, how to learn, what enables one to learn, for what purposes one learns, what would happen to oneself if one fails to learn well, and so forth. They also influence how these various aspects are related in learners and how they as a whole function in their actual learning and achievement. Therefore, regardless of individual cognitive styles, personal propensities, and learning strategies, children growing up in different cultures are bound to be shaped by their culture's beliefs about learning.

In this chapter, we examine thought and affect and their relationship to the two cultures' beliefs about learning. We argue, based on recent empirical research, that people's learning in these cultures cannot be fully understood without considering the influence of their cultures' beliefs. To do so, we first review research literature on learning and culture in general. Next, we present our own research on U.S. and Chinese cultural beliefs about learning. We then elaborate specifically on how purposes, processes, achievement, and affects (including both positive and negative) may be integrated differently in U.S. and Chinese learners. We conclude by discussing some new directions for research in this area.

RESEARCH ON LEARNING IN CULTURAL CONTEXTS

Human learning as a vast topic has been approached from a great many perspectives. However, cultural variations were not studied until recently. Since the 1980s, the field has witnessed an increasing attention to culture as an important source of variation in human learning. Three areas are of particular relevance to individual intellectual functioning: (a) intelligence, (b) achievement and its motivation, and (c) learning styles and strategies.

Intelligence

As found across cultures, intelligence assumes central importance in human learning. However, the meaning of intelligence can vary from culture to culture. In the West, intelligence, often used interchangeably with the concepts of ability and competence, thrives on its century-long theoretical and psychometric tradition of IQ testing. It stresses mental functioning that mostly involves logical-mathematical and verbal skills. Despite expanded delineations of intelligence in recent decades (Gardner, 1983; Sternberg, 1985; Vernon, 1969), intelligence is undoubtedly understood as a property of the mind, which enables humans to learn things other species are incapable of learning (Pinker, 1997).

Yet, different cultures have views that diverge from this Western concept. For example, African conceptions of intelligence focus on wisdom, trustworthiness, and social attentiveness (Dasen, 1984; Serpell, 1993; Super 1983; Wober, 1974). Japanese conceptions elaborate on different kinds of social competence such as one's ability to sympathize with others (Azuma & Kashiwagi, 1987). Similarly, Chinese notions of intelligence also emphasize, in addition to general cognitive ability, effort, a sense of humility, and moral self-striving (Li, 2002a; Yang & Sternberg, 1997). Within the United States, ethnic groups also have different views of intelligence; for example, Latinos regard social-competence as part of intelligence more than their Anglo counterparts whereas Cambodians stress hard work and observance of school rules (Okagaki & Sternberg, 1993).

Different cultural meanings and beliefs about intelligence can influence the role intelligence plays in learning. Thus, intelligence in the West is often believed to be the cause of learning and academic achievement. Those who possess a higher level of intelligence, however measured, are generally believed more capable of learning and achieving (Covington, 1992; Nicholls, 1984; Varenne & McDermott, 1998). Recent research indeed documents the positive impact of Westerners' belief in their ability on their persistence, as well as performance of academic tasks (Heine et al., 2001).

In general, research is scarce on how various views of intelligence from diverse cultures and ethnic groups may influence individuals' learning. Nevertheless, there is some research indicating that Western style educational systems in Africa (e.g., Zambia) do not accommodate the learning of local children who hold different views of intelligence (Serpell, 1993). Also compared to their Western counterparts, Japanese students who believe in increasing their ability through effort (i.e., incremental theory of intelligence, Dweck, 1999) have been shown to persist longer after failure (Heine et al., 2001). Similarly, Chinese adults and children are more inclined to view ability as something that they achieve through personal effort and social factors rather than something that causes achievement per se (Li, 2001, 2003b, 2003c).

Achievement and Its Motivation

Much cross-cultural research focuses on children's school achievement, particularly on comparing Asian and Western children. It has been widely documented that Asian children achieve highly, most notably in math and science

(Coley, 2002; Harmon et al., 1997; Stevenson & Stigler, 1992). Research on a broad spectrum of factors (e.g., school attendance, teaching, and parental expectations) has been offered to account for this so-called learning gap (Stevenson & Stigler, 1992). However, achievement motivation that directly links individuals' learning behavior to their achievement remains a key psychological domain that continues to generate across-cultural research on learning.

Achievement motivation was originally defined in the West as a personality trait based on one's sense of independence. Many non-Western cultures (e.g., Latino, Indian, and Chinese) measured by this concept were once claimed to lack achievement motivation (McClelland, 1961). However, research since has challenged this initial claim (Suárez-Orozco & Suárez-Orozco, 1995). Whereas achievement motivation has extended into a very large area of research, cross-cultural research, for the most part, has examined two essential aspects: (a) belief in ability versus effort and (b) intrinsic versus extrinsic motivation.

With regard to the former, extensive research shows that Western learners believe more in ability than effort because ability is viewed as a person's invariant dispositional quality that underlines one's learning and achievement (Ruble, Eisenberg, Higgins, 1994; Stevenson & Stigler, 1992). When Western learners are asked to explain their success and failure, they attribute these opposite outcomes differently: success to their ability and failure to lack of effort or task difficulty. Moreover, while one's ability is seen as a stable factor, one's effort is regarded as unstable, fluctuating from situation to situation (Weiner, 1986). Finally, a consistent developmental trajectory of these beliefs has emerged indicating that Western preschool children do not differentiate ability and effort in influencing one's performance of tasks (i.e. smart people work hard, and hardworking people are smart). However, upon entry into school, children develop the belief, through self-other perceptions involved in social comparisons, that their ability determines their learning outcome more than effort, especially for demanding tasks (Covington, 1992; Nicholls, 1984, Ruble et al., 1994, Stipek & Mac Iver, 1989).

Cross-cultural research indicates that Asian learners hold the opposite belief from Western learners. They believe more in effort than ability (Stevenson & Stigler, 1992), even though Asian learners are, counter to popular claims, also keenly aware of individual differences in intelligence.[1] There are indeed few who endorse the idea that one's ability is fixed (Hong, Chiu, & Dweck, 1995). Even when they appeal to ability for interpreting their achievement outcomes, ability, as previously noted, can have very different

---

[1]However, it is erroneous to assume that Asians do not recognize individual differences in their natural ability such as memory, speed of information processing, and math ability, just because they believe more in effort. The difference appears to be the weight they attach to what determines learning outcome (see Li, 2002a for more discussion on this point).

meanings than those of their Western peers (Li, 2002a). Converging evidence also indicates that, instead of viewing ability as an invariant dispositional quality of a person, Asian learners regard the self as malleable, capable of improvement through one's effort (Heine et al, 2001). However, effort (Chinese attach the term personal to it, so personal effort to indicate that it is a dispositional quality of a person) is not seen as an unstable, situation-dependent factor, but a personal quality that one always needs and exerts for any learning task regardless of the situation (Hau & Salili, 1991; Li, 2002a). Finally, Asian children's development of their differing beliefs in ability and effort also charts a divergent path. Preschool children appear to share with their Western peers similar beliefs about nonability factors to account for achievement (e.g., effort and good learning behavior) as enabling one to achieve (Li & Wang, in press). However, unlike their Western peers who may diverge from their early concepts, older Asian children develop even stronger beliefs in those nonability factors (Biggs, 1996; Li & Yue, 2003; Stevenson, 1992).

With regard to intrinsic versus extrinsic motivation, it has been assumed and empirically tested in the West that intrinsic motivation promotes learning and achievement whereas extrinsic motivation undermines them. This is so because extrinsic rewards can be perceived as a means of control, thus threatening one's sense of agency and autonomy (deCharms, 1968; Deci & Ryan, 1985). Although there is research on different forms of intrinsic motivation, most empirical research has focused on the human need to make choices and to be autonomous in learning and achievement situations in order to exercise personal control. Accordingly, when experiencing personal choice and autonomy, Western learners show more engagement, better performance, and more creativity in learning (Hennessey & Amabile, 1998; Lepper & Malone, 1987). Conversely, when experiencing lack of choice and autonomy, learners suffer from detrimental effects on those learning outcomes (Conti, Amabile, & Pollack, 1995; Deci & Ryan, 1985).

While intrinsic motivation continues to enjoy its across-cultural efficacy and appeal, some recent research has cast double on its universal applicability. Iyengar and Lepper (1999) found that personal choice may not be as essential to Asian-American children's intrinsic motivation, due to their social orientation. Euro-American children consistently showed their strongest intrinsic motivation for academic enjoyment, learning, and performance as a function of personal choice. By contrast, Asian-American children showed strongest motivation for these same outcomes not as a function of their own choice but those made by their trusted others such as mothers and class peers. Yu and Yang also argue that Chinese achievement motivation is primarily socially rather than individually oriented (Yu, 1996; Yu & Yang, 1994), which echoes a more general distinction between self-oriented versus other-oriented learning (Bransford, Brown, & Cocking, 2000).

Research by Chao (1994, 2001) further posed challenges to the established universal claim that the so-called authoritative parenting style produces well-adjusted and well-achieving children, whereas authoritarian parenting style is associated with maladjusted and low-achieving children. Ironically, Chinese-American children's ratings consistently place their parents high on traditional authoritarian measures, an outcome that purportedly undermines intrinsic motivation for learning and achievement. Yet, these children achieve well despite their parents' authoritarian style. According to Chao's analysis of cultural values, Chinese-American children may perceive their parents' intense routine monitoring and nudging as care and love instead of interference with their personal choice or the so-called fear of academic failure associated with authoritarian parenting as claimed by Steinberg, Dornbush, and Brown (1992) and Eaton and Dembo (1997). The Chinese-American parenting style cannot be made to fit the framework of the authoritative versus authoritarian dichotomy. Instead, it may be a culturally based style of their own, which manages to motivate Chinese-American children to learn and to achieve well.

Learning Styles and Strategies

Differences in learning styles and strategies were once thought of as an exclusive domain of individual differences (Slavin, 1999). However, recent research has shown some marked, consistent differences at least between Western and Asian cultures (Watkins & Biggs, 1996). Two areas have received more research attention: (a) approaches to academic tasks and (b) the role of verbal expression.

With respect to approaches to academic tasks, researchers have noted that Western learners take steps that are organized around the notion of task efficiency (Brophy & Good, 1986; Hess & Azuma, 1991; Smith & Caplan, 1988). The idea is to complete the task at hand at a fast pace using effective strategies so that the learner can move on to the next task. This style is believed effective in managing tasks, organizing time, and getting the job done while keeping oneself on the task, avoiding boredom, even increasing fun and interest one may experience in learning. These aspects also belong to the general notion of self-regulated learning (Pintrich & de Groot, 1990). Western learners also frequently display a higher level of creativity in their approaches to learning tasks (Gardner, 1989). Western teaching, as well as pedagogical materials, are designed to foster this style of learning (Brophy & Good, 1986; Stigler & Hiebert, 1999).

Asian learners have been observed to take a slower and more thorough approach to learning. They spend more time focusing on each component of a task, practicing a skill repeatedly and meticulously until they master it (Gardner, 1989; Hess & Azuma, 1991; Singleton, 1998). Asian learners were once believed to engage in rote learning, not to learn for understanding, but for high examination grades. However, scholars have pointed out the impossibility of rote learning leading to high achievement among Asian learners, which is a fundamental paradox begging for explanation (Watkins & Biggs, 1996, 2001). Recent research indicates that Chinese learners aim at deeper understanding despite their memorization (Marton, Dall'Alba, & Kun, 1996; Volet & Renshaw, 1996). It appears that memorization is used as a strategy, instead of the end of learning, to lay a factual foundation for understanding of the creative aspects of an original work, for example, (e.g. a poem or an essay). After this initial step, learners move on to seek connections and deeper meanings of the work (Li, 1997; Marton et al., 1996; Pratt, Kelly, & Wong, 1999).

The role of verbal expression is of central importance to Western learners. First, as discussed earlier, verbal ability constitutes one of the two key dimensions of the Western conception of intelligence (logical-mathematical intelligence is the other). Second, verbal skills, ranging from reading, speaking, writing, and other literacy skills, are significant achievements to be marked in formal education, as well as in people's careers. Third, verbal skills are necessary tools for communication at all levels in society. Therefore, Western learners engage intensely in learning how to read, talk, and write from early on (Snow, Burns, & Griffin, 1998). As a related but a more demanding process of learning in the Western intellectual tradition, learners are frequently encouraged to participate in discussions and debates whereby they question and challenge not only each other but authorities as well (Barnes, 1965; Gardner, 1999; Hunt, 1993; Miller, 1981; Nisbett, 2003; Tweed & Lehman, 2002).

Asian learners have been observed to be less verbal in learning. Even though they are attentive and work hard, they tend to be quiet in class (Duncan & Paulhus, 1998; Kim & Markus, 2002; Winner, 1989). This tendency has often been interpreted as a sign of obedience, docility, and lack of inquisitiveness, creativity, and imagination. This passivity is believed due to Asian cultures' emphasis on deference toward authority (Ouyang, 2000; Tweed & Lehman, 2002). Whereas some Asian educational observers concur with the previous characterization, others are reluctant to embrace such interpretations. For example, Kim (2002) in experimental studies found Euro-Americans more likely to think verbally and to believe that talking is conducive to thinking; however, Asian-Americans did not due to their cultural belief that talking may interfere with their thinking. Furthermore, Inagaki, Hatano, and Morita (1998) studied Japanese school children's participation in scientific inquiry and found that even though many children were overtly quiet, they were just as actively engaged as their verbal peers. Counterintuitively, these children did many of the inquisitive activities, such as questioning, disagreeing, and taking sides covertly, for example, in journals or essays. Similarly, Pratt et al. (1999) also found a different learning approach among Chinese learners that may help explain their reluctance to verbalize their thoughts *in medias res*: They initially commit the material to memory; next they seek to understand the intention, style, and meaning of the material. They then try to apply their understanding to situations that call for use of such knowledge, and finally they enter a deeper level of questioning and modification of the original material. Whereas the last step in their approach is verbally interactive by nature, the first three steps may call for more solitary learning and contemplation (which is an important aspect of Chinese intellectual tradition, de Bary, 1983). Clearly, this style is not bound by the immediate verbal exchange at the moment but can extend over a period of days, weeks, months, and in some cases even several years (as a doctoral student may publish a paper to challenge his or her mentor's ideas with which the student disagreed several years earlier)!

CULTURAL BELIEFS ABOUT LEARNING: A NEW WINDOW

The previous brief review shows a rich body of research on learning and culture even though the bulk of research focuses on Western-Asian comparisons. This research has begun to chart important cultural differences in specific thinking and behavior in learning. However, as a whole, research also faces some common barriers that prevent us from achieving greater understanding of learning in cultural contexts. Two barriers are particularly striking. The first is our persistent reliance on the use of existing Western conceptions to study learning across cultures. While these etic (the outside views) are necessary for cross-cultural understanding and communication, emic notions (views of those being studied) are equally essential, therefore must be considered in research. The latter has not received adequate attention. Second, bearing on the central theme of this volume, research has been favoring mental processes. The purposive, affective, and moral aspects have not been studied in sufficient detail, let alone well integrated with mental processes. If our purpose is to understand intellectual functioning as a whole, then we must also include these other aspects.

U.S. AND CHINESE BELIEFS: INTEGRATING PURPOSES, PROCESSES, ACHIEVEMENT, AND AFFECT

In an attempt to address these inadequacies, Li (2001, 2002a, 2002b, 2003b, 2003c, 2004) conducted a number of studies on U.S. and Chinese cultural beliefs about learning. By using open-ended empirical approaches, her data contained rich details of thoughts regarding intelligence, ability, skill, knowledge, and mental processes, or the plain side of learning. Yet these data also revealed purposes, personal significance, and emotions (both positive and negative), or the colored side of learning. It was clear that the two sides were expressed not as separate but as intertwined processes such that stressing only one side would lead to misunderstanding and distortion of people's beliefs (Fischer, Shaver, & Carnochan, 1990). We review two studies that focused on adult or developed beliefs. In addition, we briefly refer to two further studies on children's developing beliefs. In doing so, we attempt to retain the integrative nature of each culture's beliefs about learning.

In her first study, Li (2003b) asked U.S. (middle class Euro-American—the term "U.S." is used for convenience hereafter) and Chinese college students to free-associate the English term learn–learning and its Chinese equivalent "xuexi" after ascertaining their high similarity in meaning through word frequencies and a cross-translation procedure (see Li, 2003b for more detail). She initially collected nearly 500 terms from each culture. By using a rating procedure for relevance to learning, she obtained 205 English and 225 Chinese terms as the core list for each culture, respectively. These core items were then given to college students in their own culture to sort, based on similarity in meaning, into groups. With cluster analyses, the sorted groups finally resulted in each culture's conceptual map of learning as shown in Figs. 14.1 and 14.2.

Whereas these maps contain much detailed information, it suffices to highlight the most relevant features to this chapter. The U.S. map (Fig. 14.1) focuses on learning processes (with the majority of terms) on one side and learning content (with fewer terms) on another. Within the learning processes, a great many more terms fall within learner characteristics than within social context. The two most significant dimensions are under learner characteristics: (a) specific learning processes elaborating on active learning, thinking, inquiry, and communicating; and (b) individual characteristics stressing cognitive skills, motivation, open mind, and intelligence.

The Chinese map (Fig. 14.2) focuses on desirable versus undesirable approaches to learning with the majority of terms falling on the desirable side, which contains two further distinctions: seeking knowledge (also process-oriented but with heightened personal agency) and achievement categories and standards. Under seeking knowledge, the most significant groups are (a) heart and mind for wanting to learn, which includes lifelong pursuit, a set of learning virtues (diligence, endurance of hardship, steadfast perseverance, and concentration), humility, and desire; (b) purpose of learning containing three essential ideas—learning as an end in itself, status, and contributions to society. Under achievement there is one significant dimension: kinds of achievement emphasizing breadth and depth of knowledge, abilities, unity of knowing and morality, and originality.

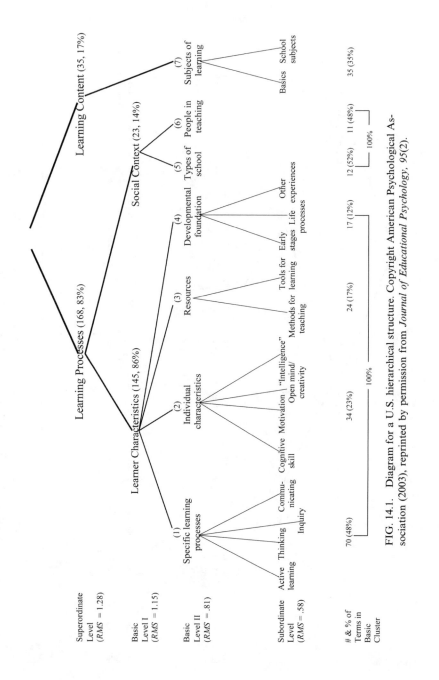

FIG. 14.1. Diagram for a U.S. hierarchical structure. Copyright American Psychological Association (2003), reprinted by permission from *Journal of Educational Psychology*, 95(2).

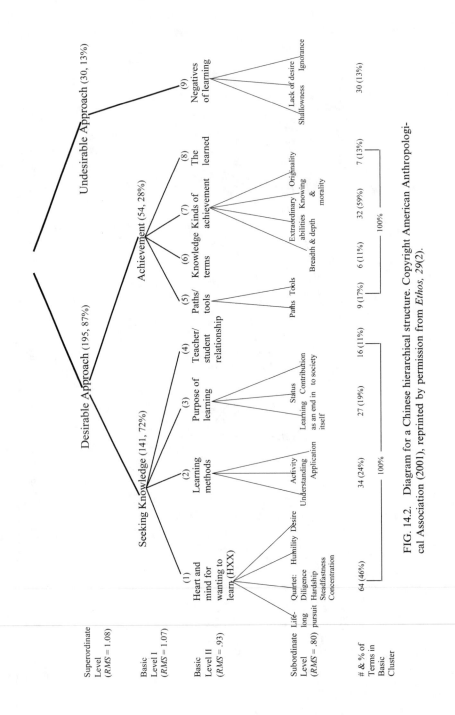

FIG. 14.2. Diagram for a Chinese hierarchical structure. Copyright American Anthropological Association (2001), reprinted by permission from *Ethos*, 29(2).

In the second study, Li (2002a) asked U.S. and Chinese college students to describe their ideal learners in order to access a fuller account of learning images as embodied in real people in addition to language expressions that she utilized in her first study. She probed four specific dimensions: (a) ideal learners' thinking on the nature of knowledge, purposes and processes of learning, and views of intelligence and excellence; (b) their understanding of the relationship between learning and one's moral development; (c) their learning behaviors in routine situations such as facing high achievement, high intelligence, failure, not understanding concepts, inability to learn despite effort, and boredom; and (d) their emotional patterns associated with good or poor learning. The written descriptions of each of these dimensions were analyzed qualitatively first and then later quantitatively (see Li, 2002a for more details). These procedures yielded four profiles corresponding to the four probed dimensions of the ideal learner for each culture.[2]

The basic findings from the two studies converge to two comprehensive pictures of the two cultures' beliefs about learning. Table 14.1 summarizes the components and dimensions of these two different belief systems. There are at least four large common component headings across the two cultures: purpose, process, achievement (excellence of learning), and affect. The specific items within each component were decided on the frequency of the number of each culture's respondents who referred to these ideas as well as the presence of these components on the two cultural maps of learning beliefs as derived from learning related terms. Purpose contains beliefs about personal meanings, significance, value, and regard people attach to learning. Process includes conceptions regarding how learning takes place, what enables a person to learn, what role inherent ability, the mind, and personal effort play, what preferred activities are, what course of action to take, and so forth. Achievement refers to views of what counts as worthy levels of learning achievement and the standards people strive for. Finally, affect encompasses emotional and attitudinal aspects that exist and function dynamically in the various components and their relations. Affect also includes both positive and negative valences that serve either to promote or discourage learning.

Figure 14.3 indicates how purpose, process, and achievement might be integrated for both cultures. Since affect is present in every main component, which is necessary for the belief system to be activated in learning, we placed it at the center of the system. In the following, we discuss each culture's system by describing each component. Then we attempt to draw relationships between these components and affect while highlighting similarities and differences between the U.S. and Chinese beliefs.

---

[2]The Chinese data have been fully analyzed and published, but the U.S. data are still being analyzed. The presentation of the U.S. data is based on preliminary analysis.

TABLE 14.1

Components and Dimensions of U.S. and Chinese Beliefs About Learning

U.S.	Chinese
Purpose of Learning	
Cultivate the mind–understand the world	Perfect oneself morally–socially
Develop one's ability–skill	Acquire knowledge–skills for self
Reach personal goals	Contribute to society
Process of Learning	
Engage actively	Resolve
Think	Diligence
Inquire	Endurance of hardship
Communicate	Perseverance
	Concentration
	(Learning virtues)
Kinds of Achievement	
Understanding of essentials–expertise	Breadth-depth–mastery of knowledge
Personal insights–creative problem solving	Application of knowledge
Being the best one can be	Unity of knowledge and moral character
Affect	
Positive	Commitment ("establish one's will")
Curiosity–interest–motivation	Love–passion–thirst (may not favor intrinsic
Intrinsic enjoyment	source, but cultivated affect, including per-
	sonal, social, spiritual, or moral)
Challenging attitudes	Respect
Pride for achievement	Calmness–humility for achievement
Negative	
Indifference–boredom	Lack of desire
Extrinsic motivation	Arrogance
Disappointment–low self-esteem for failure	Shame–guilt for failure

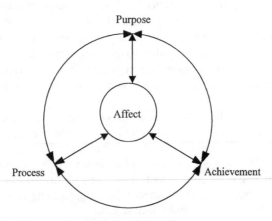

FIG. 14.3. Diagram for dynamic relationships among purpose, process, achievement, and affect in beliefs about learning.

U.S. Beliefs About Learning

Purpose of Learning. As indicated in Table 14.1, three main U.S. purposes emerged from Li's data: (a) Cultivate the mind–understand the world, (b) develop one's ability–skill, and (c) reach personal goals. The most frequent reference to purpose of learning among U. S. respondents is cultivating one's mind and understanding the world. As an essential part of the Western intellectual tradition, also explicitly articulated in Bacon's vision, the mind is assumed to have most importance in human intellectual functioning. As discussed earlier, the notion of intelligence as a capacity lies centrally in the mind. The mind enables one to learn, but it also develops or becomes sharpened as a result of exposure to stimulating environment that demands its proper use. Understanding of the world is not limited to certain aspects of the world but all that can be known by the mind or all that the person desires to know such as the physical, social, moral, psychological, and spiritual, disciplined knowledge, even common sense. In describing her model learner, one respondent wrote:

> His purpose of learning is to understand as much of the world as possible. He is intrigued by everyone and everything in his environment, and he wishes to know why people act the way they do, why things work the way they do, and how to live his life best as he can.

The second large purpose of learning is developing one's ability and skills that one needs to be a fully functioning member of one's society. Important skills include those for a successful career, one's self-sufficiency and independence, as well as knowledge that enables one to solve problems in life, to help one maintain social relations, to be effective as a person, and to take control of one's life and surroundings.

The third purpose of learning is to reach one's personal goals. Even though personal goals may include developing one's ability and skill as presented in the second purpose, they more often refer to notions of self-fulfillment, personal happiness, a well-rounded person, spiritual quest, or any personal goals individuals may desire and pursue. In the words of one respondent:

> One learns to gain a better knowledge of self and one's own place within the world. Learning justifies, deepens, challenges, or changes personal belief . . . The model learner sees learning as the fundamental function of growing up, and never becomes so "adult" that they stop actively seeking brain stimulation.

These three large types of purposes are inherently related. While the mind plays a central role in learning, it also needs cultivation. This very process is also one by which a person develops various abilities and skills in order to reach personal goals in life.

Process of Learning.   Data analysis yielded four main processes all of which find affinity to the basics of Western learning tradition hinted at in Bacon's passage. First is active engagement, centering around the notion that learning is a process in which a person needs to be actively involved. This active nature of learning emphasizes hands on activities, learning by doing, interaction with people, and participation in other activities both inside and outside the classroom. A respondent described her model leaner thus: "most of his learning comes from practicing, for example building things, fixing things, and changing things through manipulations that involve action, and trial and error."

The second process is captured in the idea of thinking, which is what the mind does and does best. Thinking concerns the whole spectrum of mental processes that are involved in learning. This spectrum includes multiple levels and dimensions. Within levels, for example, one could move from lower-order differentiations of objects to higher-order synthesis of systems or relations. Within dimensions, for example, one could engage in rigorous deductive logic or inductive reasoning, or, as a different sort, analytical or critical reasoning. Still more, one is free to reflect or contemplate on anything of personal interest. The following are statements respondents made about the importance of thinking involved in learning: "how to think, keeping an open mind, new perspectives, arguments, and reasoning," "thinking about things in different ways," and "thinking independently."

Inquiry, the quintessential process underlying Western scientific development, is the third kind mentioned by respondents. Also as a central focus of Bacon's advocacy, inquiry stresses that learning is also discovering the unknown and inventing the new. In this process, one seeks to find out about things in the world through a variety of routine but disciplined activities of research. Key to this process is one's engagement in challenging existing canons of thought and claims, finding new problems, searching for creative solutions, and imagining the unimaginable. Many respondents mentioned the ideas of inquiry such as "finding out how things work," "learning through inquisitive questions," and "she openly questions society and why things are the way they are . . . to gain many different points of view about things learned."

Finally, the fourth process, communication, emphasizes the communicative aspect as an integral part of learning. Communication serves both as learning itself and a form of dissemination of one's knowledge and discoveries. For learning itself, one participates in oral, as well as written forms of social interactions. In these communications, one not only shares and exchanges ideas with others but also discusses, critiques, or argues with others in order to achieve better understanding of a subject, using reasoning tools such as logic, evidence, and devil's advocacy. For dissemination purposes, one presents, explains, demonstrates one's views, positions, or research findings, often using visual forms and technical devices to reach audiences.

Like the purposes, these four processes of learning are also linked coherently even though they each have distinct emphases. Active learning not only ensures fuller engagement of the mind but also maximal and effective participation with all of one's senses. The active nature of involvement promotes thinking in all levels, forms, and dimensions, which facilitates inquiry. Communication is a natural part of active learning given its interactive nature, which in turn can lead to more active engagement, thinking, and inquiry. These four processes are therefore better conceptualized as belonging to a larger system.

Kinds of Achievement. There were also three main kinds of achievement or forms of excellence of learning as shown in Table 14.1: (a) Understanding of essentials–expertise, (b) personal insights and creative problem solving, and (c) being the best one can be. Whereas understanding of essentials is not limited to a particular field of study but includes anything deemed worthy of learning by the person, expertise is a notion that applies only to an area of study or practice such as math, art, or business. Given that the purpose of learning is to understand the world, the standard for gauging achievement is sensibly the extent to which a person gains better understanding of a subject or a practice. Many respondents inserted that excellence of learning does not rest on knowing facts but deeper underlying principles of things or knowledge of how various elements are related. For example, "excellence is truly seeing and understanding 'deep' or underlying 'truth' beneath superficial things . . . the perception of the most 'truth', the perception with the least biases, and learning that displays the most wisdom."

The second standard for achievement is personal insight and creative problem solving. This standard goes beyond understanding and requires that one put one's knowledge to solving problems, as well as to creative use in new situations. This kind of achievement displays one's brilliance and creativity. Respondents gave ample testimonies for such achievement, for example: "excellence is the ability to grasp an idea or topic and think about it creatively from many different perspectives" and "excellence is just above and beyond doing something that has never been done . . . when he succeeds in applying his knowledge to discover, uncover, or invent something new."

The third kind of achievement addresses being the best one can be in learning. Compared to the first two standards that also imply social recognition, the third standard is a more intra-personal delineation of "being one's best." One sets his or her own goal of achievement and strives for it. As respondents articulated, "excellence comes from pursuing your own learning" and "striving to be your best academically, making the most of your life circumstances."

Of these three kinds of achievement, the first two are more closely related with one another than with the third one although when striving to be one's best is aligned with understanding the world, developing expertise in a field, and applying one's knowledge and skill creatively to solving problems, the three kinds of standards are synergistically linked and inform each other.

Affect.   Affects imbued in purposes, processes, and achievement within the U.S. learning beliefs contain both positive and negative valences. As Table 14.1 shows, three positive affects in both purposes and processes of learning were salient: (a) curiosity, interest, and motivation for learning; (b) intrinsic enjoyment; and (c) challenging attitudes. For achievement, pride was found as one general affect. Two negative affects were found for purposes and processes: (a) indifference and boredom, and (b) extrinsic motivation. For lack of achievement, there was also only one general negative affect of disappointment and low self-esteem.

As discussed earlier, respondents did not make statements about purposes, processes, and achievement apart from affect. Instead, they frequently described their model learners with their affects intimately intertwined with their thoughts and understanding. With respect to curiosity, interest, and motivation, respondents presented integrative descriptions of these elements: "his purpose of learning is to understand more about the world, to find something that excites and intrigues him" and "just that, to learn more, this person is fascinated with many things, with almost everything." Regarding intrinsic enjoyment, examples of statements include "the most important thing is that this person enjoys learning . . . if he is presented with a topic he is especially interested in, he goes the extra mile to learn the material." Challenging attitudes, as shown earlier, are deeply rooted in the Western learning tradition that is clearly demonstrated in all four processes noted earlier. This integration is well expressed in the words of a participant: "having interest in learning more and a passion for discovery, and an intelligence that makes it possible to continue to think critically and pursue further inquiry."

It is worth pointing out that these affects mirror the fascination, wonder, and intrinsic passion about the world, as well as the inquisitive and critical spirit that characterize great scientists in the West (Csikszentmihalyi, Rathunde, & Whalen, 1993). These affects are also eloquently expressed by Bacon himself.

The general positive affect associated with U.S. model learners' achievement is pride that they display in themselves. Such pride is an expression for self-acknowledgement and self-esteem. These positive feelings about oneself in turn motivate the person to learn further. One respondent indicated that "he would see it as a source of pride. He does not mind when people praise his intelligence—he smiles."

With regard to negative affect, these data showed that model learners also encounter these feelings when the learning task is perceived as uninteresting or boring. When this happens, learners were described usually as not giving up, but continuing to learn the materials, especially if the materials are still required or important or useful knowledge. Still, they would not display intrinsic motivation and enjoyment. Instead, they would persist with some level of indifference, tepidity, boredom, even dread. Many respondents also acknowledged that these learners would stop investing time and effort into the materials if they are deemed less essential. For example, "he'd plow through it with boredom," "she would feel dread doing it," and "procrastinate from studying and complain about the materials."

Related to these negative affects, respondents also referred to extrinsic motivation as antithetical to natural curiosity, interest, and enjoyment. For example, "he would not spend time on it because the acquisition of knowledge must be an interesting and fulfilling process for him to want to pursue it. Learning to impress, or for money, or for other external rewards is not enough."

When model learners experience failure, they were described to feel a number of related negative emotions such as sadness, frustration, anger (at self), shame, low self-esteem, and depression. Naturally, these emotions stand in sharp contrast to those associated with high achievement. For example, "she would be frustrated . . . , embarrassed about her ignorance" and "he would lose his confidence and be nervous around others when engaging in conversations." However, these negative emotions were not described as having a devastating effect on these learners. Quite the contrary, model learners were believed to be able to bounce back, change their course of action, and aim at doing better next time. These positive attitudes were described as necessary and conducive to their personal goals, as well as processes of learning.

Chinese Beliefs About Learning

Purpose of Learning. Similar to the U.S. learners, also three main purposes emerged from the data: (a) Perfect oneself morally–socially, (b) acquire knowledge–skills for self, and (c) contribute to society (Table 14.1). With respect to the first, the most significant, Chinese respondents described the purpose of their model learners as a need to perfect themselves morally and socially. This purpose is deeply influenced by Confucian teaching of *ren*, a lifelong striving to become the most genuine, sincere, and humane person one can become (Tu, 1979). Ren is regarded as the highest purpose of human lives. However, a person is not born but learns to become ren. Therefore, the first and foremost purpose of learning is to engage in this process of one's own moral and social development, which is the tenet of Liu Xiang's story. Such learning is called the great learning, as opposed to narrowly defined skill learning (Li, 2003a). Respondents wrote: "the purpose of learning is by no means just to gain knowledge itself; more importantly it is to reach self-fulfillment and self-perfection," and "learning perfects his character. Through learning he is morally elevated. Learning increases one's knowledge and experience and strengthens one's ability to discriminate right from wrong."

It is worth noting here that some of the U.S. model learners also held self-fulfillment and self-actualization as their personal purposes of learning. However, they more emphasized being one's best through learning academic subjects rather than to cultivate themselves morally as defined in Confucian terms. Interestingly, the term learning was not defined, but left for respondents to construe. Whereas U.S. respondents interpreted it as falling within the realm of learning about and understanding the world, their Chinese counterparts took it to connote moral and social self-perfection in addition to academic learning (Li, 2002a).

The second purpose, acquiring knowledge and skills for self, is reminiscent of the U.S. second purpose, developing one's ability and skill, although Chinese respondents seemed to stress mastery of knowledge more whereas the U.S. respondents elaborated more on developing ability. For Chinese model learners, knowledge and skill are also needed for survival, self-sufficiency, and successful careers. Similarly, these skills are seen as enabling and empowering them to solve problems, maintain satisfying social relations, and reach their personal goals.

The third purpose is contributing to society. Again, contributing one's knowledge and skill back to society has been a consistent call of the Confucian learning model that inspires Chinese learners. This call functions not only to validate individuals' self-perfection and their pursuit of knowledge, but also to bind it to a higher moral and social obligation. Learning, thus, is no longer delineated as an individual and personal matter; it is also linked to society and the commonwealth of which one is a part (Cheng, 1996; Li, 2002a; Wu & Lai, 1992). This emphasis may differ from U.S. learning purposes. In the words of respondents, "he hoped to give his knowledge back to the human world," "his purpose of learning is to serve his people," and "his purpose is to become a journalist so that he could help correct society's wrong doings and expose society's dark side."

Like the U.S. purposes, these Chinese purposes are inherently related. All of these purposes have been explicitly part of Confucian beliefs about learning and are actively promoted by families, communities, schools, and society at large (Cheng, 1996; Lee, 1996; Yu, 1996). Accordingly, one needs to engage in personal skill learning and moral development before one can meaningfully contribute to society. However, one's moral self-cultivation and skill acquisition are not conceptualized as separate or sequential but simultaneous processes. They take place not as a one-time deed, but continuously from early on throughout life.

Admittedly, many U.S. model learners also harbored the desire to make a difference in the word, relieve suffering, and help others. However, this purpose was not as strongly and prevalently expressed as by their Chinese peers.

Process of Learning. When Chinese respondents were asked to describe how their model learners learn (i.e., what they do, what steps they take, how they behaved when they encountered difficulties, failure, etc.), they surprisingly did not describe much that would be considered learning processes per se as those described by their U.S. peers. Instead, they wrote extensively about what Li termed learning virtues, which were also found as central notions of Chinese learning beliefs in Li's first study (see "quartet" in Fig. 14.2). The term learning virtues was used because these aspects emphasize a morally good and desirable dispositional quality that underlies personal agency, action, even the use of learning strategies that are integral parts of learning processes. Five such virtues emerged.

The first is the notion of resolve (*fen or fafen*). This concept specifies the determination or strong decision the learner makes so as to come to a course of action and a high degree to which he or she is prepared to follow through his or her commitment. Fen is believed necessary to ensure one's clarification of intention, desire, or goal; the course of action one must take to realize one's desire and goal; and a way to hold oneself accountable for one's own temptation to stray from the course of action, to stop midway, or simply to give up in the face of obstacles. Frequently, upon making the resolve, the person shares his or her fen with his or her family or close friends who serve as witnesses. Such witnesses are invited to monitor, to watch for, and even to demand consistency between one's resolve and follow-up action. Respondents wrote: "he made his *fen* and forces himself to learn no matter what difficulties he may bump into" and "nothing can stop her, no matter what obstacles; this has to do with her determination."

The second virtue is diligence (*qin*), which refers to frequent studying behavior. The emphasis, therefore, falls on much learning and much time spent on learning. If one is to show some action upon personal resolve, diligence is the immediate measure and manifestation of resolve. Therefore, resolve and diligence go hand in hand, thus the combined term in Chinese *qinfen*. However, psychologically there are two steps even though behaviorally only diligence is observable. Diligence apart from resolve is also believed necessary because frequent learning could ensure familiarity, which in turn opens opportunities for mastery (Li, 2001; Wu & Lai 1992). Descriptions offered by respondents include: "he works twice as much. When other people are not studying, he is. Diligence can compensate for one's natural weaknesses" and "in learning you got to do plenty of reading, plenty of listening, plenty of asking questions, plenty of doing, and plenty of thinking."

The third virtue is endurance of hardship (*keku*), which focuses on over-coming difficulties and obstacles one is bound to encounter in learning. Respondents referred to three kinds of difficulties: (a) physical drudgery and poverty, (b) difficult knowledge and learning tasks, and (c) lack of natural ability. First, physical drudgery and poverty are considered hardships because they have been an unavoidable living condition throughout Chinese history. Even though life standards have been improved in recent decades, in much of China, physical labor and poverty remain the harsh reality for many. Furthermore, difficulty in understanding particular academic concepts is a routine encounter for any learner. Finally, respondents were very clear about individual differences in their natural capacity and acknowledged the impact of such differences on people's learning. However, there was also consensus that these obstacles are not reasons for not learning. Instead, model learners developed the virtue of endurance of hardship, which they believe would enable them to face and combat these hardships. Thus, in terms of poverty, "her family was poor, and she couldn't go to school cause they needed her to work in the fields. But she'd learned words from kids who went to school. It was hard, but she learned many Chinese characters that way." For difficult learning tasks, "no difficulty can scare him away. He'd do everything humanly possible to endure hardship." Finally, for less natural ability, "she has no choice but to force herself to spend more time studying than others; yes, using her strengths (spending more time) she can make up for her weakness."

The fourth virtue is perseverance (*hengxin*) that addresses a general attitude toward learning and behavioral tendency in a person's life course. The importance of perseverance is due to the belief that there is no shortcut to learning. Knowledge does not come about overnight, but through a bit-by-bit, accumulative process over a long period of time, a process fraught with obstacles and distractions. Perseverance is believed potent in helping a person stay on the task from the beginning to the very end no matter how long it takes. It is a virtue required to achieve any serious learning (Huang & Peng, 1992; Lee, 1996; Li, 2001, Liu 1973). One respondent wrote that "poverty cannot block his learning. As long as he still breathes, he will continue. As long as he has enough food, he will not give up because learning is part of his belief system."

The final virtue is concentration (*zhuanxin*). Concentration reminds one of the concept of mindfulness or being engrossed in something that can refer to specific tasks. However, concentration in Chinese is used more often to describe a general learning behavior, not necessarily related to specific tasks. Concentration emphasizes studying with consistent focus and dedication without ever swerving from it. It also includes earnestness, carefulness, and thoroughness of learning. Concentration is believed to be an essential quality of the learner because this disposition would allow the full engagement of one's mind and heart in study. Without such engagement, there would be no true understanding, no mastery, let alone application of knowledge (Li, 2001, 2002b). In the words of respondents, "he is very careful and thorough in how he goes about each worthy step of study" and "she is oftentimes so involved as to forget to eat and sleep."

These five learning virtues are clearly related to form a whole in intellectual functioning. They all presume a desire to learn because, without it, these learning processes and behaviors cannot be sustained. Without resolve and its resultant commitment, diligence, endurance of hardship, and persistence may be limited to sheer situational factors. Likewise, if concentration can be halted by hardship or if one lacks perseverance, one's resolve may be aborted half-way.

Chinese respondents also revealed other learning processes and activities similar to those revealed by their U.S. peers, such as thinking, participation in social activities, and talking to people. However, compared to their U.S. respondents, they mentioned those categories less. Similarly, whereas U.S. respondents also acknowledged their model learners' hard work and persistence, their reference to these learning virtues was less consistent.

Kinds of Achievement.   As Table 14.1 shows, there were also three general kinds of achievement for which Chinese model learners aimed and against which they are measured. The first one, depth and breadth, mastery of knowledge, or both is also captured in Fig. 14.2 under "kinds of achievement." Whereas breadth refers to one's extensive knowledge of different disciplines or subjects, depth concerns one's deep understanding of a subject or genuine scholarship. Moreover, the integration of breadth and depth is also emphasized. Even though the notion of mastery may not highlight breadth and depth, it nevertheless stresses ownership of knowledge, and by implication the broader and deeper such ownership, the better. This achievement standard seems sensible considering that the ultimate goal is self-perfection, which is open-ended and lifelong in nature. Pursuing knowledge for a life's course could make breadth and depth and related mastery obtainable even though knowledge is boundless. Respondents described that "it's not the perfect score on an exam but deep and broad knowledge that can lead to original work in one's field."

The second standard is application of knowledge. Although application of knowledge is reminiscent of the U.S. personal problem solving, the Chinese emphasis falls on the use of what one has learned in real life situations. The conceptual distinction lies in book knowledge versus knowledge in use. Whether such use is personal or social in origin matters less. This standard thus includes application of knowledge that may not be deemed as creative in any sense (e.g., use math to verify a bank transaction), personal creative problem solving and insight (similar to the U.S. standard), and genuine advancement of one's field or historical impact of the whole society. One respondent expressed that "it's more important to use one's knowledge. Like a physics student with perfect exam scores is not as excellent if he doesn't know how to fix electronics as someone who has his exam scores but also can fix electronics."

The third standard is unity of knowledge and moral character, which is also shown as one of the four kinds of achievement in Fig. 14.2. Consistent with the purposes of moral and social self-perfection, acquisition of knowledge for self, and contribution to society, achieving the unity of the cognitive–intellectual with the social–moral is only natural. Respondents articulated that "excellence must include both the moral character and knowledge of the learner because one's moral character is more important" and "a well rounded person with her moral character placed before intellectual and physical development."

As alluded to previously, these achievement standards are inherently related to each other. Acquisition of depth and breadth of knowledge can enable the person to better apply such knowledge, which in turn can broaden and deepen one's knowledge. So long as the learner also continues to self-perfect morally and socially, he or she will likely continue to seek breadth and depth of learning, which loops back to his or her ability to use his or her knowledge in life.

Affect.   Like affect in U.S. beliefs, Chinese affect also showed both positive and negative types. Four most commonly mentioned positive affects were found: (a) commitment (establish one's will); (b) love, passion, and thirst for learning; (c) respect embedded in expressions of purposes and learning processes; and (d) calmness and humility for achievement. Two negative affects were found for purposes and learning processes: (a) lack of desire and (b) arrogance. For lack of achievement, there was also only one general negative affect of shame and guilt.

Similar to their U.S. counterparts, Chinese respondents did not present purposes, processes, and achievement apart from feelings and emotions. Instead, they provided well-integrated descriptions. The notion of commitment, *lizhi* (establish one' will) in Chinese, is part of one's learning purpose. This concept aims at helping the learner, often during secondary school, to start pondering about his or her life's purposes in order to come to a clear personal vision (*zhixiang* or *baofu*). This process is deliberately designed and practiced to lead the learner to imagine or envision something greater than his or her current (temporal sense) and own (individual sense) life. It is orienting oneself in learning toward one's future (parents and teachers frequently engage adolescent children in this discussion). In doing so, Chinese learners believe that they will not only find a more specific path to focus on (e.g., I want to help relieve human physical suffering), but also know to what path to attach their energy, dedication, emotion, and action (e.g., therefore I will study medicine and all knowledge I need to achieve this goal). Therefore, the process of lizhi is a spiritually uplifting and emotionally positive process. In the words of respondents, "she had a far-reaching ambition for her lifelong learning, that is, to help human beings achieve true equality," "he established a will to become a political leader; learning then became an internalized obligation for him. He couldn't stop learning from that point on."

Notice that lizhi is not to be confused with career goal setting, although it may coincide with it, but searching for an inspirational purpose in the large framework of the three purposes discussed earlier in order to channel one's lifelong learning. Here, Liu Xiang's story sets a good example of lizhi for the king to start to self-cultivate even at age seventy.

Some U.S. respondents also touched on personal ambitions. However, such cases were not described consistently as a deliberate and socially concerted process where the learner is urged to search for a purpose and to establish commitment to reaching that goal for life.

Love, passion, and thirst were described similarly as enjoyment among U.S. model learners for both purposes and processes of learning. However, a significant difference lies in the source of such affect between the two cultures' learners. Whereas for the U.S. learners, intrinsic enjoyment, curiosity, and motivation were described as essential, this intrinsic source was not emphasized by Chinese respondents. In fact, many of the respondents acknowledged that their model learners were initially not motivated or interested in learning when they were young, but they developed love and passion once they realized the importance of learning for their lives or once their parents and teachers guided them into the process. Much like Liu Xiang's king, his love for learning initially lay dormant or perhaps didn't exist; it was his subject who awakened or helped generate his love. One respondent gave the following testimony:

> He actually was a naughty kid when he was young. He didn't like to learn. But his parents demanded that he learn. His teachers also had high expectations of him and helped him. By and by, his attitude improved, and he began tasting the joy of learning. Probably in high school he realized that learning is his need to self-perfect, and after that he always has passion for learning.

This kind of formation of love and passion as cultivated and fostered by one's social world parallels the recent work on intrinsic motivation as less essential for Asian-American children for school learning by Iyengar and Lepper (1999).

Respect is another distinct affect that Chinese model learners express toward knowledge and teachers in the form of humility. Because learning in the

Confucian persuasion is not limited to academic learning but more importantly social and moral learning, respect toward knowledge and teachers (that ideally embody the self-perfecting process) is sensible and expected. However, this general attitude of respect among Asian learners has been taken as a sign of obedience and lack of critical thinking (Keats, 1982; Tweed & Lehman, 2002). As discussed earlier, this is a misunderstanding (Inagaki et al., 1998; Li, 2003a; Pratt et al., 1999). Asian learners' deference toward teachers does not stem from their fear or blind acceptance of authority but from their deep sense of humility. Instead of treating humility as a personal weakness, they regard it a personal strength and courage because those who are humble are willing to self-examine, admit their inadequacies, and self-improve. Moreover, humility also leads one to want to learn from others regardless of their social status. Therefore, respect and humility go hand in hand. In these processes, one's ego or self-esteem generated by lack of competence is not seriously threatened and in need of protection as may be the case among U.S. learners (Brickman & Bulman, 1977; Ruble et al., 1994). Chinese learners believe that one can always self-improve so long as one learns humbly and respectfully from others (Li & Wang, in press).

Respondents wrote that "one needs to respect one's teachers because one has something to learn from them" and "she'd listen to her teachers; then she'd apply what she learned in real life, which may lead her to discover new problems. Then she'd go back to her teachers and raise questions; she'd learn from everyone humbly."

As alluded to earlier, Chinese learners' respect and humility may be very different from U.S. learners' challenging attitude, especially in the form of immediate verbal exchange in the midst of a class or a discussion. It was generally the case that Chinese respondents made few references to such challenging attitudes toward teachers and experts even though their model learners did engage in discussions and debates with their peers. However, as mentioned earlier, this does not mean that Chinese learners do not challenge. In fact, many respondents wrote that challenging old knowledge or advancing new knowledge was an important goal for learners in the end. Yet one is reluctant to engage in challenges until one has thoroughly understood the knowledge in question or mastered one's field. This finding concurs with the finding by Pratt et al. (1999). Still, as Liu Xiang's story illustrates, a learned person in Chinese culture is enabled, dignified, and legitimized to challenge the otherwise powerful, despite his or her powerless status (de Bary, 1983). Chinese learners understand this cultural spirit well and use it judiciously.

For achievement, Chinese learners generally do not display pride although they may be happy themselves (Li, 2002a). This tendency is different from their U.S. peers who usually feel proud of themselves and like to share their joy with others (Mascolo, Fischer, & Li, 2003). Chinese model learners were described as feeling a need to remain calm and humble. Related to the forgoing discussion of respect and humility, the need to be humble stems from the same recognition that learning is a lifelong journey. Although others may acknowledge one's achievement publicly, focusing on celebration for oneself may be perceived as a negative tendency that pulls one away from further self-perfection. For example, "facing achievement he would show humility" and "she would not be too proud of herself; she'd remain calm. She'd reflect on her purpose and tell herself that she needs to make more progress."

The two negative affects associated with purpose and processes of learning are lack of desire and arrogance. The former shows some affinity to the U.S. indifference and boredom. Lack of desire is the opposite of a heart and mind for wanting to learn (Li, 2001). Many Chinese learning related words and phrases refer to this state as lying in the heart of any motivational problem. By hearing or using these words, learners sense disapproval and concern from their social world because, as Liu Xiang's story alerts us, a person without the desire to learn is one without aim and real power; not even the king can be exempt.

Arrogance is also an affect that refers to complacency, conceitedness, and hubris, which is the opposite of humility. Learners who achieve highly are believed to be vulnerable to this inflated sense of oneself. Given the importance of humility in Chinese learning beliefs, there is little wonder why pride/arrogance is a great concern among learners. As respondents wrote, "she would not be complacent and conceited for achievement because she knows the meaning of 'arrogance leads one to fall.' "

Similar to their U.S. peers, Chinese model learners were described to feel a number of related negative emotions such sadness and pain when they experience failure. The most frequently revealed emotions are shame and guilt both in terms of learners facing themselves as well as their families (Li, 2002a). Shame is a powerful and prevalent emotion in Chinese culture (Li, 2002a; Li, Wang, & Fischer, in press). Even though shame in Chinese culture is an emotion of disgrace or humiliation as in most cultures, it is also a moral discretion and sensibility that people desire to develop (Fung, 1999; Fung & Chen, 2001). Thus, the meanings of shame and guilt shade into each other. Together they function to direct people into self-examination in social situations in order to recognize their own wrong doings, as well as to motivate people to improve themselves. One respondent revealed that "he would feel guilty toward his family. They provided all help he needed at all costs, but he failed to learn with his heart and mind. How can he face his family? He'd hurry to change himself!"

SUMMARY OF THE TWO CULTURES' BELIEFS

Based on the forgoing findings and analyses, U.S. beliefs center around a set of purposes that focus on the finely differentiated functions of the mind in order to understand the world, developing personal skills, and realizing personal goals. Personal curiosity about and interest in the world are very much part of these purposes. To pursue these purposes, one is actively engaged in a broad range of activities and experiences. Thinking in all forms, levels, and dimensions assumes key importance, and inquiry guides one to examine and question the known and to explore and discover the new. In these processes, one also needs to communicate in order to understand as well as to make others understand one's own learning results. Curiosity and interest continue to sustain these learning processes. Yet intrinsic enjoyment and challenging attitudes also accompany the learner throughout these processes. Such learning leads to achievement that aims at understanding the essentials of a given topic, developing expertise in a field, personal insights and creative problem solving in real life, being the best one can be, or all of the above. When these goals are realized, one feels proud of oneself. However, when experiencing failure, one feels disappointment and low self-esteem.

Chinese beliefs elaborate on perfecting oneself morally and socially, acquiring knowledge and skill for oneself, and contributing to society. Embedded in these purposes are commitment and passion which may or may not be intrinsic in origin as understood in the West. To pursue those purposes of learning, one needs to develop the so-called learning virtues of resolve, diligence, endurance of hardship, perseverance, and concentration. These virtues are seen as more essential than actual learning activities such as reading, thinking, asking questions, or doing research. Chinese learners believe that once the learning virtues are there, one can apply them to all learning activities and processes. Because these virtues are by nature volitional attitudes, affect is already in every element. An additional affect in the learning processes is respect for knowledge and teaching authority, which does not mean obedience and blind acceptance of what is taught. Such learning aims at breadth and depth or mastery of knowledge, application of knowledge to real life situations, and unity of one's knowledge and moral character. When learners achieve learning, they remain calm and humble; they also watch out for signs of complacency and arrogance in order to continue self-perfecting. When encountering failure, they feel shame and guilt not only themselves but also in reference to those who nurtured them, which in turn motivates them to self-improve.

CONCLUSION

In this chapter, we have presented a view of beliefs about learning as an important topic in intellectual functioning and illustrated with empirical findings how thought and affect among U.S. and Chinese learners are intertwined in their beliefs (Fischer et al., 1990). However, a discussion of integration between thought and affect involving two cultural groups of learners cannot proceed without examining related cultural values and beliefs in the first place. Based on our analyses, individuals' beliefs are far from being just individual; they are deeply informed by the basic orientations of their culture's beliefs and values regarding learning. These cultural forces help define what purposes learning serves, how learning takes or should take place, what kind of achievement is worthy of pursuing, and what emotions and attitudes are involved in all of these dimensions. Despite changes throughout history, these basic cultural orientations tend to be persistent. The profound interest in nature and understanding of the world among the Greeks that is well reflected in Bacon's thinking continues to inspire contemporary learners in the West. Likewise, the passion for moral and social self-perfection among Confucian scholars that echoes well in Liu Xiang's writing finds enthused learners among the present-day Chinese. Consequently, the particular thoughts and affects in the two cultures' learners are configured differently, and are therefore bound to shape their intellectual functioning differently as well.

Thus, one might expect that because of the emphasis on the mind, inquiry, and accompanying intrinsic motivation and pride, Western learners learn best when the task matches their purposes and skill level on the one hand and engages them with enjoyment and pride on the other. The concept of flow (Csikszentmihalyi, 1990) may indeed be an optimal state of such intellectual functioning. However, when such a balance is not achieved, learners may face frustration, boredom, or anxiety. Due to the emphasis on moral–social purposes, learning virtues, and accompanying passion and humility, Chinese learners learn best when they have clear long-term goals, rather than being prompted by individual learning tasks; when they can continuously exercise their learning virtues for a length of time, rather than relying on their mental feats at hand, and when they feel humble rather than proud. Even though their learning beliefs may better equip them to face motivational problems, they may still feel perplexed in orientation if they are confronted with Western style learning (as the case with many Asian children in American classrooms).

The above thought-affect configurations in learning are meant to illustrate cultural norms. In individual functioning, variability and overlap are likely the case, especially considering the significant cultural exchanges and profound changes that have occurred and are still underway in today's world. Still, taken as a whole, these cultural patterns are distinguishable, and they are also likely to persist. These tendencies show affinity to what Bruner (1996) discussed as cultural canonical approaches to learning.

Given the vast topic of cultural beliefs about learning and the dearth of research, the research presented in this chapter was only an initial step. Much remains to be studied. We venture to point out some directions. As hinted earlier, Li's study dealt with ideal learners and group consensus of beliefs at the cultural level. Individual learners' own thoughts and emotions need to be examined. As an ongoing investigation, Li and Yue (2003) collected written data from nearly 2000 Chinese elementary and secondary school children across several regions on their own beliefs about learning. Preliminary data analysis (Li, 2003, April) indicates that these children's own beliefs resemble their culture's beliefs. As a further empirical effort, actual processes involving both thoughts and affect need to be examined as learners engage in learning.

If research is generally scarce on cultural beliefs about learning, there is even less attention to how these beliefs are developed in children. To begin exploring this topic, Li also examined U.S. (again middle class Euro-American) and Chinese preschool children's stories about learning (Li, 2002b, 2003d; Li & Wang, in press). As predicted, children in their respective cultures begin to develop beliefs about learning early on. Their beliefs resemble each culture's adult beliefs. This trend becomes clearer when children get older. Developmental research focusing on socialization processes at home and school as well as children's own constructions of various beliefs will illuminate more the pathways of such development (Fischer et al., 1990).

Although there is more research on learning in the West and Asia, there is less on other cultures. As research by Delgado-Gaitan (1988), Gallimore and Reese (1999), and Serpell (1993) demonstrated, Latino and African cultures also have different beliefs about learning and these differences may provide important clues for children's formal learning in school and their development in this domain.

Finally, today's world is witnessing ever more intense interactions among cultures. More and more children grow up bilingual and bicultural, which presents even greater challenges to research in this area. For example, how do children from Asia deal with both systems of beliefs when they immigrate to a Western culture? Are there new forms of integration between thought and affect? How do these new forms function in children's learning?

These and many more questions only attest to the need for more research. Our chapter has fulfilled its goal if our research and analyses have helped generate more research questions on thought and affect in intellectual functioning across cultures.

REFERENCES

Azuma, H., & Kashiwagi, K. (1987). Descriptors for an intelligent person: A Japanese study. *Japanese Psychological Research, 29,* 17–26.

Bacon, F. (1952). Advancement of learning. In R. M. Hutchins (Ed.), *Great books of the Western world.* Chicago: Encyclopedia Britannica. (Original work published in 1605)

Barnes, H. E. (1965). *An intellectual and cultural history of the Western world.* London: Dover.

Biggs, J. B. (1996). Western misperceptions of the Confucian-heritage learning culture. In D. A. Watkins & J. B. Biggs (Eds.), *The Chinese learner* (pp. 45–67). Hong Kong: Comparative Education Research Centre.

Bransford, J. D., Brown, A. L., & Cocking, R. R. (Eds.). (2000). *How people learn: Brain, mind, experience, and school.* Washington, DC: National Academy Press.

Brickman, P., & Bulman, R. J. (1977). Pleasure and pain in social comparison. In J. M. Suls & R. L. Miller (Eds.), *Social comparison processes: Theoretical and empirical perspectives* (pp. 149–186). Washington, DC: Hemishpere.

Brophy, J., & Good, T. L. (1986). Teacher behavior and student achievement. In M. C. Wittrock (Ed.), *Handbook of research on teaching* (3rd ed., pp. 328–375). New York: Macmillan.

Bruner, J. (1996). *The culture of education.* Cambridge, MA: Harvard University Press.

Chao, R. K. (1994). Beyond parental control and authoritarian parenting style: Understanding Chinese parenting through the cultural notion of training. *Child Development, 65,* 111–1119.

Chao, R. K. (2001). Extending research on the consequences of parenting style for Chinese American and European Americans. *Child Development, 72*(6), 1832–1843.

Cheng, K.-M. (1996). *The quality of primary education: A case study of Zhejiang Province, China.* Paris: International Institute for Educational Planning.

Coley, R. J. (2002). *An uneven start: Indicators of inequality in school readiness.* Princeton, NJ: ETS.

Conti, R., Amabile, T. M., & Pollack, S. (1995). Enhancing intrinsic motivation, learning, and creativity. *Personality and Social Psychology Bulletin, 21,* 1107–1116.

Covington, M. V. (1992). *Making the grade.* New York: Cambridge University Press.

Csikszentmihalyi, M. (1990). *Flow: The psychology of optimal experience.* New York: Harper & Row.

Csikszentmihalyi, M., Rathunde, K, & Whalen, S. (1993). *Talented teenager: The roots of success and failure.* New York: Cambridge University Press.

Dasen, P. R. (1984). The cross-cultural study of intelligence: Piaget and the Baoulé. *International Journal of Psychology, 19,* 407–434.

de Bary, W. T. (1983). *The liberal tradition in China.* New York: Columbia University Press.

deCharms, R. (1968). *Personal causation.* New York: Academic.

Deci, E. L., & Ryan, R. M. (1985). *Intrinsic motivation and self-determination in human behavior.* New York: Academic.

Delgado-Gaitan, C. (1988). The value of community: Learning to stay in school. *Anthropology and Education Quarterly, 19,* 354–381.

Duncan, J., & Paulhus, D. L. (1998, August). *Varieties of shyness in Asian- and European-Canadians.* Paper presented at the 106th Annual Convention of the American Psychological Association, San Francisco, CA.

Dweck, C. S. (1999). *Self-theories.* Philadelphia: Psychology Press.

Eaton, M. J., & Dembo, M. H. (1997). Differences in the motivational beliefs for Asian-American and Non-Asian students. *Journal of Educational Psychology, 89*(3), 433–440.

Fischer, K. W., Shaver, P. R., & Carnochan, P. (1990). How emotions develop and how they organise development. *Cognition & Emotion, 4*(2), 81–127.

Fung, H. (1999). Becoming a moral child: The socialization of shame among young Chinese children. *Ethos, 27,* 180–209.

Fung, H., & Chen, E. C.-H. (2001). Across time and beyond skin: Self and transgression in the everyday socialization of shame among Taiwanese preschool children. *Social Development, 10*(3), 420–437.

Gallimore, R., & Reese, L. J. (1999). Mexican immigrants in urban California: Forging adaptations from familiar and new cultural sources. In M. C. Foblets & C. L. Pang (Eds.), *Culture, ethnicity and migration* (pp. 245–263). Acco, Belgium: Leusden.

Gardner, H. (1983). *Frames of mind.* New York: Basic Books.

Gardner, H. (1989). *To open minds.* New York: Basic Books.

Gardner, H. (1999). *The disciplined mind: What all students should understand.* New York: Simon & Schuster.

Harmon, M., Smith, T. A., Martin, M. O., Kelly, D. L., Beaton, A. E., & Mullis, I. V. S. (1997). *Performance assessment in IEA's Third International Mathematics and Science Study (TIMSS).* Chestnut Hill, MA: TIMSS International Study Center, Boston College.

Hau, K. T., & Salili, F. (1991). Structure and semantic differential placement of specific causes: Academic causal attributions by Chinese students in Hong Kong. *International Journal of Psychology, 26,* 175–193.

Heine, S. J., Kitayama, S., Lehman, D. R., Takata, T., Ide, E., Leung, C., & Mtsumoto, M. (2001). Divergent consequences of success and failure in Japan and North America: An investigation of self-improving motivations and malleable selves. *Journal of Personality and Social Psychology, 81,* 599–615.

Hennessey, B. A., & Amabile, T. M. (1998). Reward, intrinsic motivation, and creativity. *American Psychologist, 53,* 674–675.

Hess, R. D., & Azuma, M. (1991). Cultural support for schooling: Contrasts between Japan and the United States. *Educational Researcher, 20*(9), 2–8.

Hong, Y., Chiu, C., & Dweck, C. S. (1995). Implicit theories of intelligence: Reconsidering the role of confidence in achievement motivation. In M. H. Kernis (Ed.), *Efficacy, agency, and self-esteem* (pp. 197–216). New York: Plenum.

Huang, D. Y., & Peng, H, J. (1992). *San zi jing* [Three character classic]. Taipei, Taiwan: Ruisheng Book & Magazine Publishing House.

Hunt, M. (1993). *The story of psychology.* New York: Doubleday.

Inagaki, K., Hatano, G., & Morita, E. (1998). Construction of mathematical knowledge through whole-class discussion. *Learning and Instruction, 8,* 503–526.

Iyengar, S. S., & Lepper, M. R. (1999). Rethinking the value of choice: A cultural perspective on intrinsic motivation. *Journal of Personality and Social Psychology, 76,* 349–366.

Keats, D. (1982). Cultural bases of concepts of intelligence: A Chinese versus Australian comparison. In Proceedings of Second Asian Workshop on Child and Adolescent Development (pp. 67–75). Bangkok, Thailand: Behavioral Science Research Institute.

Kim, H. S. (2002). We talk, therefore we think? A Cultural analysis of the effect of talking on thinking. *Journal of Personality and Social Psychology, 83,* 828–842.

Kim, H., & Markus, H. R. (2002). Freedom of speech and freedom of silence: An analysis of talking as a cultural practice. In R. Shweder, M. Minow, & H. R. Markus (Eds.), *Engaging cultural differences: The multicultural challenge in liberal democracies* (pp. 432–452). New York: Russell Sage Foundation.

Lee, W. O. (1996). The cultural context for Chinese learners: Conceptions of learning in the Confucian Tradition. In D. A. Watkins & J. B. Biggs (Eds.), *The Chinese learner* (pp. 45–67). Hong Kong: Comparative Education Research Centre.

Lepper, M. R., & Malone, T. W. (1987). Intrinsic motivation and instructional effectiveness in computer-based education. In R. E. Snow & M. J. Farr (Eds.), *Aptitude, learning, and instrunction: Conative and affective process analysis, Vol. 3.* (pp. 255–286). Hillsdale, NJ: Lawrence Erlbaum Associates.

Li, J. (1997). Creativity in horizontal and vertical domains. *Creativity Research Journal, 10,* 107–132.

Li, J. (2001). Chinese conceptualization of learning. *Ethos, 29,* 111–137.

Li, J. (2002a). A cultural model of learning: Chinese "heart and mind for wanting to learn." *Journal of Cross-Cultural Psychology, 33*(3), 248–269.

Li, J. (2002b). Models of learning in different cultures. In J. Bempechat & J. Elliott (Eds.), *Achievement motivation in culture and context: Understanding children's learning experiences, New Directions in Child and Adolescent Development* (pp. 45–63). San Francisco: Jossey-Bass.

Li, J. (2003a). The core of Confucian learning. *American Psychologist, 58,* 146–147.

Li, J. (2003b). United States and Chinese cultural beliefs about learning. *Journal of Educational Psychology, 95,* 258–267.

Li, J. (2003c). "I learn and I grow big:" Chinese preschoolers' purposes for learning. Manuscript submitted for publication.

Li, J. (2004). High abilities and excellence: A cultural perspective. In M. Ferrari & L. V. Shavinina (Eds.), *Beyond knowledge: Extracognitive aspects of developing high ability* (pp. 187–208). NJ: Lawrence Erlbaum Associates.

Li, J., & Wang, Q. (in press). United States and Chinese preschool children's perceptions of achievement and their achieving peers. *Social Development*.

Li, J., Wang, L., & Fischer, K. W. (in press). The organization of Chinese shame concepts. *Cognition and Emotion*.

Li, J., & Yue, X.-D. (2003). Learning conceptions, desires, and actions among Chinese school children. Manuscript submitted for publication.

Liu, Z. (1973). *Shi dao* [Principles of teacherhood]. Taipei, Taiwan: Chung Hwa Book Company.

Marton, F., Dall'Alba, G., & Kun, T. L. (1996). Memorizing and Understanding: The keys to the paradox? In D. A. Watkins & J. B. Biggs (Eds.), *The Chinese learner* (pp. 69–83). Hong Kong: Comparative Education Research Centre.

Mascolo, M. F., Fischer, K. W., & Li, J. (2003). The dynamic construction of emotions in development: A component systems approach. In N. Davidson, K. Scherer & H. Goldsmith (Eds.), *Handbook of affective science* (pp. 375–408). New York: Oxford University Press.

McClelland, D. C. (1961). *The achieving society*. New York: Van Nostrand.

Miller, G. A. (1981). *Language and speech*. San Francisco: Freeman.

Nicholls, J. G. (1984). Achievement motivation: Conceptions of ability, subjective experience, task choice, and performance. *Psychological Review, 91*(3), 328–346.

Nisbett, R. E. (2003). *The geography of thought*. New York: Simon & Schuster.

Okagaki, L., & Sternberg, R. J. (1993). Parental beliefs and children's school performance. *Child Development, 64*, 36–56.

Ouyang, H.-H. (2000). One way ticket: A story of an innovative teacher in mainland China. *Anthropology and Education Quarterly, 31*, 397–425.

Peltonen, M. (1996). Introduction. In M. Peltonen (Ed.), *The Cambridge comanion to Bacon* (pp. 1–24). Cambridge, England: Cambridge University Press.

Pinker, S. (1997). *How the mind works*. New York: Norton.

Pintrich, P. R., & de Groot, E. V. (1990). Motivatinal and self-regulated learning components of classroom academic performance. *Journal of Educational Psychology, 1*, 33–40.

Pratt, D. D., Kelly, M., & Wong, K. M. (1999). Chinese conceptions of "effective teaching" in Hong Kong: Towards culturally sensitive evaluation of teaching. *International Journal of Lifelong Learning, 18*, 241–258.

Ruble, D. N., Eisenberg, R., & Higgins, E. T. (1994). Developmental changes in achievement evaluations: Motivational implications of self-other differences. *Child Development, 65*, 1095–1110.

Serpell, R. (1993). *The significance of schooling: Life journeys in an African society*. New York: Cambridge University Press.

Singleton, J. (Ed.). (1998). *Learning in likely places*. Cambridge, England: Cambridge University Press.

Slavin, R. E. (1999). *Educational psychology: Theory and practice* (6th ed.). Boston: Allyn & Bacon.

Smith, J. D., & Caplan, J. (1988). Cultural differences in cognitive style development. *Developmental Psychology, 24*, 46–52.

Snow, C. E., Burns, M. S., & Griffin, P. (1998). *Preventing reading difficulties in young children. National Research Council*. Washington, DC: National Academy Press.

Steinberg, L., Dornbusch, S., & Brown, B. (1992). Ethnic differences in adolescent achievement: An ecological perspective. *American Psychologist, 47*, 732–729.

Sternberg, R. J. (1985). *Beyond IQ: A triarchic theory of human intelligence*. New York: Cambridge University Press.

Stevenson, H. W. (1992). Learning from Asian schools. *Scientific American, 267*, 70–76.

Stevenson, H. W., & Stigler, J. W. (1992). *The learning gap*. New York: Simon & Schuster.

Stigler, J. W., & Hiebert, J. (1999). *The teaching gap: Best ideas from the world's teachers for improving education in the classroom*. New York: The Free Press.

Stipek, D., & Mac Iver, D. (1989). Developmental change in children's assessment of intellectual competence. *Child Development, 60,* 521–538.

Suárez-Orozco, C., & Suárez-Orozco, M. (1995). *Trans-formations: Immigration, family life, and achievement motivation among Latino adolescents.* Stanford, CA: Stanford University Press.

Super, C. M. (1983). Cultural variation in the meaning and uses of children's intelligence. In J. B. Deregowski, S. Dziurawiec, & R. C. Annis (Eds.), *Expiscations in cross-cultural psychology* (pp. 199–212). Lisse, Holland: Swets & Zeitlinger.

Tu, W. M. (1979). *Humanity and self-cultivation: Essays in Confucian thought.* Berkeley, CA: Asian Humanities Press.

Tweed, R. G., & Lehman, D. R. (2002). Learning considered within a cultural context: Confucian and Socratic Approaches. *American Psychologist, 57*(2), 89–99.

Varenne, H., & McDermott, R. (1998). *Successful failure: The school America builds.* Boulder, CO: Westview.

Vernon, P. E. (1969). *Intelligence and cultural environment.* London: Methuen.

Volet, S. E., & Renshaw, P. D. (1996). Chinese students at an Australian university: Adaptability and continuity. In D. A. Watkins & J. B. Biggs (Eds.), *The Chinese learner* (pp. 205–220). Hong Kong: Comparative Education Research Centre.

Wang, Y. (1992). Forward. In Y. Wang & T.-H. Wang (Eds.), *Complete translation of Shuo Yuan* (pp. 1–10). [in Chinese]. Guizhou, China: Guizhou People's Publishing House.

Wang, Y., & Wang, T.-H. (1992). *Complete translation of Shuo Yuan.* [Shuo Yuan quanshi]. Guizhou, China: Guizhou People's Publishing House.

Watkins, D. A., & Biggs, J. B. (Eds.). (1996). *The Chinese learner: Cultural, psychological, and contextual influences.* Hong Kong: Comparative Education Research Centre.

Watkins, D. A., & Biggs, J. B. (Eds.). (2001). *Teaching the Chinese learner: Psychological and pedagogical perspectives.* Hong Kong: Comparative Education Research Centre.

Weiner, B. (1986). *An attributional theory of motivation and emotion.* New York: Springer-Verlag.

Winner, E. (1989). How can Chinese children draw so well? *Journal of Aesthetic Education, 23*(1), 65–84.

Wober, M. (1974). Towards an understanding of the Kiganda concept of intelligence. In J. W. Berry & P. R. Dasen (Eds.), *Culture and cognition: Readings in cross-cultural psychology* (pp. 261–280). London: Methuen.

Wu, S.-P., & Lai, C.-Y. (1992). *Complete text of the four books and five classics in modern Chinese.* [in Chinese]. Beijing, China: International Culture Press.

Yang, S.-Y., & Sternberg, R. J. (1997). Taiwanese Chinese people's conceptions of intelligence. *Intelligence, 25*(1), 21–29.

Yu, A. B. (1996). Ultimate life concerns, self, and Chinese achievement motivation. In M. Bond (Ed.), *The handbook of Chinese psychology* (pp. 227–246). Hong Kong: Oxford University Press.

Yu, A. B., & Yang K. S. (1994). The nature of achievement motivation in collectivist societies. In U. Kim, H. C. Triandis, C. Kagitcibasi, S. C., Choi, & G. Yoon (Eds.), *Individualism and collectivism: Theory, method, and applications* (pp. 239–250). Thousand Oaks, CA: Sage.

EPILOGUE
Putting It All Together:
Some Concluding Thoughts

David Yun Dai
University at Albany, State University of New York

In his seminal work, Newell (1988, 1990) envisioned a unified theory of cognition that is based on the human cognitive architecture as we know of, and fully testable by way of computational formalism. In the process of "putting it all together" (Newell, 1988, p. 428), however, motivation is hinted (e.g., deliberate acts at the rational-level, thinking as action, progressive deepening; see Newell, 1990) but not explicated in the architecture; emotion seems to be completely left out (cf. Norman, 1980). We have argued in this volume that putting it all together means treating cognition not as a neutral system of perception and thinking with invariant properties, but rather, as always embedded in specific functional contexts, directed, tinted or otherwise altered by motivation and emotion, for good or ill. We see a different kind of putting it all together in the preceding chapters, a more functionalist (and presumably more realistic) view of how the human mind works under adaptive challenges and in striving toward goals of personal and cultural values.

Despite diverse perspectives presented in this volume, signs of convergence are evident. We have witnessed much cross-talk, explicit and implicit, beyond and across the disciplinary boundaries of differential, developmental, social-cultural, motivational and cognitive traditions, encompassing the whole spectrum of neurobiological, psychological-behavioral, and phenomenological levels of analysis. In the following section, I make some further observations and extrapolations.

DIVERSITY OF HUMAN BIOLOGY
AND FUNCTIONAL CONTEXTS:
THE ISSUE OF ECOLOGICAL NICHES

The diversity of human biology, as well as human functional contexts, is a pervasive theme. First, consider human biology. Affective and cognitive differences are evident in a century of research on human development from infancy on, as well as current research on human genomes (Kagan, 2001; Posner & Rothbart, 1998). We cannot ignore vast individual differences in terms of how people respond to challenging developmental tasks and sustain (or fail to sustain) their goal-directed efforts (Kosslyn, Cacioppo, Davidson, Hugdahl, Lovallo, Spiegel, & Rose, 2002). This said, humans as living, adaptive, and open systems also make self-regulatory changes (Ford, 1992), and develop new patterns of behavior, skills, self-perceptions, values, dispositions, in response to adaptive pressures (Matthews & Zeidner, chap. 6; Zimmerman & Schunk, chap. 12). Such development is the basis for intellectual growth.

Besides biological variations that greatly enhance our chance of survival as a species, the diversity of human functional contexts is equally striking. We define functional context in terms of values, goals, opportunities, and constraints a situation affords at any given moment to an organism. For humans, a functional context can be social and practical (e.g., business and law) or academic (e.g., sciences and humanities); formal (e.g., disciplinary inquiry; Wineburg, 1991) and informal (e.g., everyday cognition; Rogoff & Lave, 1984; see also Perkins & Ritchhart, chap. 13); group-based, such as navigation (Hutchins, 1995) or collaborative scientific inquiry (Dunbar, 1997), or individual-based, such as chess (de Groot, 1978) or creative writing (Amabile, 2001); involving dynamic changes and time pressure (e.g., business or military operations; Klein, 1998) or permitting prolonged deliberation and scrutiny (e.g., scientific research; Neisessian & Thagard, 1999).

A functional context can be primarily learning or performance. To be sure, any authentic activity or performance involves learning one way or another (Lave, 1993). Performance often engenders new learning or new demands for learning, and learning involves performance (e.g., problem solving). Nevertheless, the distinction is still important because the lack of proper knowledge and strategies to tackle specific problems (i.e., the learning condition) indicates a distinct constraint on intellectual functioning with profound ramifications for motivation and social and technical support (Bandura, 1986; Vygotsky, 1978; see also Zimmerman & Schunk, chap. 12, for a discussion of a shift of focus between process and outcome as one gains competence).

Given the diversity of human functional contexts, the issue becomes that of sensibility and adaptivity of a person in fitting in, and sometimes carving out, an appropriate ecological niche[1] for himself or herself, which is the essence of successful intelligence (Sternberg, 1996). The inner resources required for meeting adaptive challenges include motivational, emotional, and cognitive ones. At the same time, social and cultural capital provides necessary tools, support, as well as incentives, thus modulating to some extent how individuals growing up and living in a specific culture or subculture cultivate their potential.

Duality of Attention and Processing: The Task and the Self

What is striking in the preceding chapters is that, one way or another, the authors point to a fundamental duality of processing in intellectual functioning, for example, cognitive engagement and coping (Matthews & Zeidner, chap. 6), maintaining positive affect and meeting new intellectual challenges (Labouvie-Vief & Gonzalez, chap. 9), improving oneself and an incremental view of ability versus proving oneself and an entity view of ability (Dweck, Mangels, & Good, chap. 2). Other models have addressed the same phenomena (e.g., learning vs. coping mode, Boekaerts, 1993; action vs. state orientations, Kuhl, 1985; task vs. ego involvement, Nicholls, 1984; processing of task-related information and self-related or motivational information, Rigney, 1980; Winne & Marx, 1989; text comprehension and the self, Kintsch, 1998; see Apter, 2001, for a comprehensive treatment of the duality of mental life).

Duality of attention and processing is based on the fact that a human agent can perform a task (object 1) and at the same time have self-awareness that he or she is performing a task at hand and that how he or she feels about the task or content involved (object 2). This is the doer–watcher duality pointed out by James (1950). Piaget (1950, 1981) conceptualized the interplay of cognition and affect in terms of this duality. Besides primary action that defines an enactive agent (subject) and an impinging environment (object), with cognition as instrument and affect instigating action, there is secondary action, the agent's reaction to his or her own action. This reaction takes the form of feeling or affect (emotion), and regulates primary action by assigning meaning and valence to the task, and subsequently prioritizing personal goals (see also Simon, 1967, 1994). Damasio (1999, 2000) also sees this duality as critical for understanding the nature of extended consciousness and the phenomenal self.

From a functional point of view, the duality of attention and processing constitutes one of the most important dimensions of the ecology of human functioning. Many theoretical models, such as attention allocation model of

---

[1]We use the term ecological niches to indicate the person–environment fit in a psychological and functional sense; no evolutionary meaning is intended.

the effects of depression on cognitive processes (Ellis & Ashbrook, 1988), stress and cognitive performance (Mandler, 1984), goal orientation theory (e.g., Nicholls, 1984) are predicated on the assumption of how attention can be preempted by interfering emotions to the detriment of task focus and performance.

The duality of attention and processing highlights the importance of emotional self-regulation and control of attention. Success and failure of self-regulation have profound consequences on intellectual functioning and development. On the negative side, intellectual functioning can become degraded (Labouvie-Vief & Gonzalez, chap. 9); one is switching to a coping mode. On the positive side, one can reach complete identification with the object of interest, leading to the merge of self and action or the object in an optimal state of flow (Csikszentmihalyi, 1996). From a developmental point of view, a person can tune in or tune out of a specific developmental task as a result of identification or disidentification (Snow, 1992).

Another duality of processing, conscious, effortful, serial (capacity-limited) versus largely unconscious, automatic, parallel-distributed processing (see Simon, 1994) also deserves mention (see also Kahneman, 2003, for a discussion). Although beyond the scope of this volume, the relevance of the integration of motivation, cognition, and affect to this duality issue becomes clear when the outcome of parallel processing often emerges as affective experiences (Barnes & Thagard, 1996; Iran-Najad, Clore, & Vondruska, 1984; see also Kihlstrom, 1999, for a discussion of the cognitive, emotional, and motivational unconscious). For example, in the creativity research, the mind-popping or sudden-insight phenomenon has puzzled psychologists for decades (Sternberg & Davidson, 1995). Very few would put the insight phenomenon in the context of motivated reasoning and problem solving. However, as Miller (1996) conjectured in his historical research on scientific discovery:

> Activation is maintained in the unconscious as the result of intense conscious desire to solve the problem at hand. This activation can spread in the unconscious in ways that might not have been possible with the confines of conscious thought. (p. 337)

This example demonstrates the power of motivation in cognitive transformation beyond those changes pointed out by cognitive psychologists (e.g., with practice, one can circumvent limits of the working memory capacity, Ericsson, 1998). It also shows yet another example of embodied cognition about which we still do not know much as to its exact mechanisms at the psychological and neurological levels (but see Gruber, 1995, for a discussion of affect and creative insight; Thagard, 2002, for an account of largely parallel processes of constraint satisfaction in scientific discovery).

The Temporal Dimension of Intellectual Functioning:
An Ever Changing Dynamic

The ongoing, temporal nature of intellectual functioning, as well as its psychological properties, its rich associations to the past and projections to the future in the individual or collective memory is another critical dimension of intellectual functioning (Newell, 1990). The very notion of the duality of attention and processing, of self-regulation, or of progressive deepening, all depends on an understanding of the temporal unfolding of a transactional event. It is this temporal dimension that unifies intellectual functioning and development. As demonstrated in several chapters (e.g., Alexander, chap. 10; Labouvie-Vief & Gonzalez, chap. 9), intellectual functioning and development are not inherently separate phenomena but rather two sides of the same coin. One's intellectual competence is evolving along the way of performing an intellectual task (see Sternberg, 1999, on intelligence as developing expertise). Thus, we can meaningfully discuss a functioning-development isomorphism at the microdevelopmental (e.g., children's problem solving, Siegler, 2002; see Granott & Parziale, 2002) as well as macrodevelopmental level (e.g., intentional conceptual change and scientific discovery; Neisessian & Thagard, 1999).

Temporal dimension implies a changing dynamics because the timescale of an act places additional constraints on performance. Consider two experimental conditions: a social judgment task used by social psychologists, and a text comprehension or mathematical problem solving task. High workload of a task demands more time to reach a satisfactory solution. The longer it takes to think through a problem, the more likely one will experience a cognitive overload (Just & Carpenter, 1992), or distress and disengagement responses (Matthews & Zeidner, chap. 6), since one has to hold all relevant information in working memory and update information on a continual basis (see also Linnenbrink & Pintrich, chap. 3, for a discussion). To offset this constraint, humans also improve their mental fitness with practice and organization, and continually relegate part of cognitive control to the unconscious through automaticity (Sternberg, 1985) and shorthand retrieval structure (Ericsson & Kintsch, 1995). More importantly, with developing competencies come new affordances in meaning and action, all the way to the point where an expert chess player like Kasparov can generate a move in a split second that will take years for a novice to figure out (see Newell, 1990, for a discussion of the preparation–deliberation trade-off). A challenge for researchers is to understand how an initially conceptually demanding task becomes almost a perceptual one, as one develops expertise (de Groot, 1978), and more importantly, how expert knowledge is represented in such an embodied way that feeling, intuition, and visceral reaction (gut feeling) become integral part of expertise

(Speelman, 1998). It is not trivial to note that Kasparov characterized his match with Deep Junior as "intuition versus the brute force of calculation" (Sieberg, 2003, p. 1).[2]

Integration of Neurobiological, Psychological-Behavioral (Functional), and Phenomenological Levels of Analysis: Emergentism, Reductionism, and Interactionism

As discussed earlier, integrative efforts can be seen as operating with three distinct epistemological stances or levels of analysis: neurobiological, psychological-behavioral, and phenomenological. Unifying these approaches would mean forging a marriage between the sciences of the biological and "the sciences of the subjective" (Bruner, 1996, p. 12), with the sciences of functional behavior in-between. No wonder why some would question whether such a marriage is a possible, or even desirable, one (Kendler, 1987; Shweder, 2001). However, the dream of putting it all together, of forging the unity or consilience of the natural and human sciences, is very much alive and well (e.g., Damasio et al., 2001). According to Sternberg and Grigorenko (2001), a unified psychology is possible if we (a) focus on psychological phenomena rather than compartmentalizing psychology into isolated components, and (b) use convergent operations rather than insulated single research paradigms. Dweck's (1999; Dweck et al., chap. 2) work provides a good example. Dweck's theory (1999) has a distinct interpretive component: people's implicit theories of intelligence, which belongs in the sciences of the subjective. However, her theory is also grounded in empirical work searching for causal patterns of motivation, emotion, cognition, and observable behaviors, a behavioral-functional level integration. Also, the social-cognitive approach she adopts does not prevent her from exploring measurable physiological differences of individuals with different goal orientations in addition to behavioral analyses (see Dweck et al., chap. 2). Thus, the use of multimethods and convergent operations, and the flexible shift of epistemological stances (from a more or less positivist stance to an interpretive stance) have enhanced our understanding of the phenomenon in question.

---

[2]Of course, whether human expert intuition is the result of computation at the unconscious level, analogous to that of artificial neural networks (ANNs), is an empirical question. Our hunch is that the human capability of pattern recognition and analogical mental modeling enables such a quick insight without going through the lengthy, inefficient, rule-based iteration of a computer program such as Deep Blue (see Klein, 1998). It is possible that more embodied cognitive modeling such as dynamic systems approaches (Port & Gelder, 1995) may better approximate the underlying mechanisms of human intuition and perception. On the other hand, one should also be open to the possibility that some mental processes and events are fundamentally noncomputational (see Edelman, 1989).

At a metatheoretical level, interlevel integration poses challenges. The critical issue is whether and to what extent the mind is divisible and decomposable. Emergentism argues that higher levels of organization of the mind have emergent properties, such as molar-level mental states or intentionality that cannot be understood at the lower levels of its components (see Cornwell, 1995). Reductionism, on the other hand, holds that phenomena as complex as mind (with all its properties such as cognition, affect, and conation) can be understood through interlevel reduction, from the mental to the neuronal (e.g., Churchland & Churchland, 1995). It appears that from a structural point of view, cognition and emotion, and emotion and motivation, can be distinguished from each other. For example, separation of emotion and cognition is evident in brain structures and functions (M. Posner, personal communication, May 12, 2003; see also Dai & Sternberg, chap. 1). With functional neuroimaging techniques available now, we are able to find neuronal concomitants of many mental processes, such as emotion (Damasio, 1999), attentional orienting (Derryberry & Tucker, 1994), consciousness (Meltzinger, 2000), and even volition or attentional control (Posner & Peterson, 1990), so that psychological constructs of the motivational, emotional, and cognitive nature can be more precisely defined, and indeed more embodied in the exact sense of the word. The mind–brain mapping of cognitive, motivational, and emotional processes can become difficult, however, if complex cognitive tasks are involved. Using the timescales of intellectual functioning again, we suspect that the shorter the timescale (e.g., word recognition), the more likely specific neuronal mechanisms and functions can be pinpointed. Yet as the complexity of a task and the corresponding timescale of an intellectual act increase (e.g., lengthy text comprehension tasks), the difficulty localizing precise neuropsyiological mechanisms can increase. Measurable increases in activation in multiple parts of the brain can be obtained, indicating intensified cognitive efforts (Carpenter, Just, Keller, Eddy, & Thulborn, 1999; Just, Carpenter, Maguire, Diwadkar, & McMains, 2001). However, here motivation and cognition cannot be teased apart as separate processes at the brain level. As Kagan (2002) suggested, "a psychological phenomenon is the result of a cascade of many brain events that occurs over intervals usually ranging from a quarter-second to several seconds" (p. 21). The mind–brain relation is likely to be a highly complex, reciprocal (i.e., top-down and bottom-up), part–whole relation (e.g., how individual neural circuits are integrated or coordinated to support certain mental structures and functions), rather than a unidirectional, linear, one-to-one process. In the case of Carpenter, Just, and colleagues' research cited above, intensified brain activity or motivated cognition is a function of increasing task demands and workload. One should also espouse the possibility that the content of a person's intention (e.g., specific objectives in mind), as well as specific content knowledge a person activates in problem solving is fundamentally unmappable (Kagan, 2002), because of its semantic nature, and its intentionality (Searle, 2001).

At the phenomenological level, psychologists will continue to experience ambivalence as to how to confront consciousness and its subjective content head-on, because traditionally psychological researchers are not trained to be cognitive anthropologists or cultural psychologists of some sort. However, if we do not deal with this layer of human psychology, we may miss an essential constituent of mind that enables intellectual functioning (Bruner, 1990, 1997). It is important to note that at this level, the epistemic stance is largely interpretive (i.e., concerning intentionality and meaning) rather than explanatory (i.e., concerning causal structures and relations). (See Geertz, 1973, for a discussion of interpretive sciences; Dennett, 1987, for intentional stance).

Ultimately, we might still have to resort to psychological-behavioral (functional level) explanations because it is at the this level that the person as an intentional agent is interacting with a task environment, and the locus of personal agency cannot be reduced to some activated brain circuits (Kagan, 2002; see also Bandura, 1986, for a delineation of reciprocal causation of environment, behavior and internal processes), nor to some sheer subjectivity. However, without an understanding of neurobiological substrates of human functioning, and the phenomenology of human meaning systems, psychological-behavioral analyses may have limited power in explaining intellectual phenomena as complex as text comprehension, scientific problem solving, or creative insights.

Strategies for Integration: Local and Global Theories

Integration can be done in various ways. Yet they seem to fall into a continuum from the most local to the most global scales (e.g., comparing Abelson, 1963, with Tomkins, 1963). The local approach focuses on specific psychological phenomena, and conceptualize ways that specific cognitive processes involved can be related to motivational and affective processes or put in proper social or cultural contexts, what Greeno (2003) called situative analysis.

Some examples of such local integration include motivation and students' conceptual change (Pintrich, Marx, & Boyle, 1993; see also Sinatra & Pintrich, 2003), motivated reasoning in social argumentation (Kunda, 1990), emotion in social decision making (Damasio, 1994), affect infusion model for social judgment (Forgas, 1995), affect in mathematical problem solving (Goldin, 2000; see also Linnenbrink & Pintrich, chap. 3), emotion in scientific cognition (Thagard, 2002), and task and ego goal conditions and cognitive processes (Graham & Golan, 1991; see also Dweck et al., chap. 2).

In contrast to local integration efforts, global integration is more ambitious and involves formulating unified frameworks for integration efforts, that is, how human intelligent systems operate in general, and why motivation or emotion should be considered in such a system. The global approaches often consider complex psychological and social organization of intellectual functioning. These approaches often posit hierarchically organized functioning systems (Demetriou, Kazi, & Georgiou, 1999; Greeno, 2003; Stanovich, 1999), different levels of functioning, such as operation, action, and activity (Leont'ev, 1978), multiple-component functioning system (e.g., Perkins's triadic model of thinking; Perkins & Ritchhart, chap. 13; Ford's theory of living systems; Ford, 1992). In local integration, traditional conceptual foundations often remain intact, although motivation and emotion are conceptually and empirically infused or reinstated as missing links. In contrast, global integration efforts often call for the overhaul of the entire system of language and the change of the entire way of thinking. One example is to conceptualize person–situation as an indivisible unit of analysis for the aptitude research (see Snow, 1992; see also Lohman, 2001). Similarly, the conception of distributed intelligence (Pea, 1993), which combines the ecological psychology of affordances and the motivational theory of desire, challenges the conventional definition of intelligence as a property of the mind. Also, if cognition as fundamentally situated, embodied, and cannot be separated from one's goals, actions, emotions, and feelings (Bruner, 1994; Glenberg, 1997; Reed, 1997), then the traditional distinction between cognition and emotion, thinking and action becomes problematic, and the entire conceptual edifice starts to crumble. Time will tell whether more modest, local approaches or more ambitious, global restructuring approaches to integration will bear more fruition.

To end these concluding thoughts, regardless of whether we will eventually reach a reunion, a unified psychology that puts it all together in a coherent way, whether the natural and social sciences will find a convergent point in psychology (Driver-Linn, 2003), we hope that this volume represents a step in the right direction in the dialectical process of scientific discourse on psychology in general and intellectual functioning in particular.

ACKNOWLEDGMENT

This work was made possible by a grant from the National Science Foundation (#0296062).

REFERENCES

Abelson, R. P. (1963). Computer simulation of "hot" cognition. In S. S. Tomkins & S. Messick (Eds.), *Computer simulation of personality: Frontier of psychological theory* (pp. 277–298). New York: Wiley.

Amabile, T. M. (2001). Beyond talent: John Irving and the passionate craft of creativity. *American Psychologist, 56,* 333–336.

Apter, M. J. E. (2001). *Motivational styles in everyday life: A guide to reversal theory.* Washington, DC: American Psychological Association.

Bandura, A. (1986). *Social foundations of thought and action: A social cognitive theory.* Englewood Cliffs, NJ: Prentice Hall.

Barnes, A., & Thagard, P. (1996). Emotional decisions. In Cognitive Science Society (Ed.), *Proceedings of the eighteenth Annual Conference of the Cognitive Science Society* (pp. 426–429). Mahwah, NJ: Lawrence Erlbaum Associates.

Boekaerts, M. (1993). Being concerned with well-being and with learning. *Educational Psychologist, 28,* 149–167.

Bruner, J. (1990). *Acts of meaning.* Cambridge, MA: Harvard University Press.

Bruner, J. (1994). The view from the heart's eye: A commentary. In P. M. Miedenthal & S. Kitayama (Eds.), *The heart's eye: Emotional influences in perception and attention* (pp. 269–286). San Diego, CA: Academic Press.

Bruner, J. (1996). *The culture of education.* Cambridge, MA: Harvard University Press.

Bruner, J. (1997). Will cognitive revolution ever stop? In D. M. Johnson & C. E. Erneling (Eds.), *The future of the cognitive revolution* (pp. 279–292). New York: Oxford University Press.

Carpenter, P. A., Just, M. A., Keller, T. A., Eddy, W., & Thulborn, K. (1999). Graded funcitonal activation in the visualspatial system with the amount of task demand. *Journal of Cognitive Neuroscience, 11,* 9–24.

Churchland, P. M., & Churchland, P. S. (1995). Intertheoretic reduction: A neuroscientist's field guide. In J. Cornwell (Ed.), *Nature's imagination: The frontiers of scientific vision* (pp. 64–77). Oxford, England: Oxford University Press.

Cornwell, J. (Ed.) (1995). *Nature's imagination: The frontiers of scientific vision.* Oxford, England: Oxford University Press.

Csikszentmihalyi, M. (1996). *Creativity: Flow and the psychology of discovery and invention.* New York: HarperCollins.

Damasio, A. R. (1994). *Descartes' error: Emotion, reason, and the human brain.* New York: Avon Books.

Damasio, A. R. (1998). *The feeling of what happens: Body and emotion in the making of consciousness.* New York: Harcourt Brace & Company.

Damasio, A. R. (2000). A neurobiology for consciousness. In T. Metzinger (Ed.), *Neural correlates of consciousness* (pp. 111–120). Cambridge, MA: The MIT Press.

Damasio, A. R., Harrington, A., Kagan, J., McEwen, B. S., Moss, H., & Shaikh, R. (Eds.). (2001). *Unity of knowledge: The convergence of natural and human science (Annals of the New York Academy of Sciences, Vol. 935).* New York: The New York Academy of Sciences.

de Groot, A. D. (1978). *Thought and choice in chess* (2nd ed.). The Hague, Netherlands: Mouton.

Demetriou, A., Kazi, S., & Georgiou, S. (1999). The emergent self: The convergence of mind, personality, and thinking styles. *Developmental Science, 2,* 387–409.

Dennett, D. (1987). *The intentional stance.* Cambridge, MA: Bradford Books/MIT Press.

Derryberry, D., & Tucker, D. M. (1994). Motivating the focus of attention. In P. M. Miedenthal & S. Kitayama (Eds.), *The heart's eye: Emotional influences in perception and attention* (pp. 167–196). San Diego, CA: Academic Press.

Driver-Linn, E. (2003). Where is psychology going? Structural fault lines revealed by psychologists' use of Kukn. *American Psychologist, 58,* 269–278.

Dunbar, K. (1997). How scientists think: On-line creativity and conceptual change in science. In T. B. Ward, S. M. Smith, & J. Vaid (Eds.), *Creative thought: An investigation of conceptual structures and processes* (pp. 461–493). Washington, DC: American Psychological Association.

Dweck, C. S. (1999). *Self theories: Their role in motivation, personality, and development.* Philadelphia: Psychology Press.

Edelman, G. M. (1989). *The remembered present: A biological theory of consciousness.* New York: Basic Books.

Ellis, H. C., & Ashbrook, P. W. (1988). Resource allocation model of the effects of depressed mood states on memory. In K. Fiedler & J. Forgas (Eds.), *Affect, cognition, and social behavior* (pp. 25–43). Toronto, Canada: Hogrefe.

Ericsson, K. A. (1998). Basic capacities can be modified or circumvented by deliberate practice: A rejection of talent accounts of expert performance. *Behavioral and Brain Sciences, 21,* 413–414.

Ericsson, K. A., & Kintsch, W. (1995). Long-term working memory. *Psychological Review, 102,* 211–245.

Ford, M. E. (1992). *Motivating humans: Goals, emotions, and personal agency beliefs.* Newbury, CT: Sage.

Forgas, J. P. (1995). Mood and judgment: The affect infusion model (AIM). *Psychological Bulletin, 117,* 39–66.

Geertz, C. (1973). *The interpretation of cultures: Selected essays.* New York: Basic Books.

Glenberg, A. M. (1997). Mental models, space, and embodied cognition. In T. B. Ward, S. M. Smith, & J. Vaid (Eds.), *Creative thought: An investigation of conceptual structures and processes* (pp. 495–522). Washington, DC: American Psychological Association.

Goldin, G. A. (2000). Affective pathways and representation in mathematical problem solving. *Mathematical Thinking and Learning: An International Journal, 2,* 209–219.

Graham, S., & Golan, S. (1991). Motivational influences on cognition: Task involvement, ego involvement, and depth of information processing. *Journal of Educational Psychology, 83,* 187–194.

Granott, N., & Parziale, J. (2002). Microdevelopment: A process-oriented perspective for studying development and learning. In N. Granott & J. Parziale (Eds.), *Microdevelopment: Transition processes in development and learning* (pp. 1–28). Cambridge, England: Cambridge University Press.

Greeno, J. (2003, April). *Integration of cognitive and social perspectives.* Speech presented at the annual meeting of the American Educational Research Association, Chicago.

Gruber, H. E. (1995). Insight and affect in the history of science. In R. J. Sternberg & J. E. Davidson (Eds.), *The nature of insight* (pp. 397–431). Cambridge, MA: The MIT Press.

Hutchins, E. (1995). *Cognition in the wild.* Cambridge, MA: The MIT Press.

Iran-Nejad, A., Clore, G. L., & Vondruska, R. J. (1984). Affect: A functional perspective. *The Journal of Mind and Behavior, 5,* 279–310.

James, W. (1950). *The principles of psychology* (Vol. 1). New York: Dover Publications.

Just, M. A., & Carpenter, P. A. (1992). A capacity theory of comprehension: Individual differences in working memory. *Psychological Review, 99,* 122–149.

Just, M. A., Carpenter, P. A., Maguire, M., Diwadkar, V., & McMains, S. (2001). Mental rotation of objects retrieved from memory: A functional MRI study of spatial processing. *Journal of Experimental Psychology: General, 130,* 493–504.

Kagan, J. (2001). Biological constraint, cultural variety, and psychological structures. In A. R. Damasio, A. Harrington, J. Kagan, B. S. McEwen, H. Moss, & R. Shaikh (Eds.), *Unity of knowledge: The convergence of natural and human science (Annals of the New York Academy of Sciences, Vol. 935)* (pp. 177–190). New York: The New York Academy of Sciences.

Kagan, J. (2002). *Surprise, uncertainty, and mental structures.* Cambridge, MA: Harvard University Press.

Kahneman, D. (2003). A perspective on judgment and choice: Mapping bounded rationality. *American Psychologist, 58,* 697–720.

Kendler, H. H. (1987). A good divorce is better than a bad marriage. In A. W. Staats & L. P. Mos (Eds.), *Annals of theoretical psychology* (Vol. 5, pp. 55–89). New York: Plenum.

Kihlstrom, J. F. (1999). The psychological consciousness. In L. A. Pervin & O. P. John (Eds.), *Handbook of personality: Theory and research* (pp. 424–442). New York: The Guilford Press.

Kintsch, W. (1998). *Comprehension: A paradigm for cognition*. Cambridge, England: Cambridge University Press.

Klein, G. (1998). *Sources of power: How people make decisions*. Cambridge, MA: MIT Press.

Kosslyn, S. M., Cacioppo, J. T., Davidson, R. J., Hugdahl, K., Lovallo, W. R., Spiegel, D., & Rose, R. (2002). Bridging psychology and biology. *American Psychologist, 57*, 341–351.

Kuhl, J. (1985). Volitional mediators of cognition-behavior consistency: Self-regulatory processes and action versus state orientation. In J. Kuhl & J. Beckmann (Eds.), *Action control: From cognition to behavior* (pp. 101–128). Berlin: Springer.

Kunda, Z. (1990). The case for motivated reasoning. *Psychological Bulletin, 108*, 480–498.

Lave, J. (1993). The practice of learning. In S. Chaiklin & J. Lave (Eds.), *Understanding practice: Perspectives on activity and context* (pp. 3–32). Cambridge, England: Cambridge University Press.

Leont'ev, A. N. (1978). *Activity, consciousness, and personality*. Englewood Cliffs, NJ: Prentice-Hall.

Lohman, D. F. (2001). Issues in the definition and measurement of abilities. In J. M. Collis & S. Messick (Eds.), *Intelligence and personality: Bridging the gap between theory and measurement* (pp. 79–98). Mahwah, NJ: Lawrence Erlbaum Associates.

Mandler, G. (1984). *Mind and body: Psychology of emotion and stress*. New York: Norton.

Meltzinger, T. E. (2000). *Neural correlates of consciousness: Empirical and conceptual questions*. Cambridge, MA: The MIT Press.

Miller, A. I. (1996). *Insights of genius: Imagery and creativity in science and art*. New York: Springer-Verlag.

Neisessian, N. J., & Thagard, P. (Eds.). (1999). *Model-based reasoning in scientific discovery*. New York: Kluwer/Plenum Publishers.

Newell, A. (1988). Putting it all together. In D. Klahr & K. Kovovsky (Eds.), *Complex information processing: The impact of Herbert A. Simon* (pp. 399–440). Hillsdale, NJ: Lawrence Erlbaum Associates.

Newell, A. (1990). *Unified theories of cognition*. Cambridge, MA: Harvard University Press.

Nicholls, J. G. (1984). Achievement motivation: Conceptions of ability, subjective experiences, task choice, and performance. *Psychological Review, 91*, 328–346.

Norman, D. A. (1980). Twelve issues for cognitive science. *Cognitive Science, 4*, 1–32.

Pea, R. D. (1993). Practices of distributed intelligence and designs for education. In G. Salomon (Ed.), *Distributed cognitions: Psychological and educational considerations* (pp. 47–87). Cambridge, England: Cambridge University Press.

Piaget, J. (1950). *The origins of intelligence in children*. New York: International University Press.

Piaget, J. (1981). *Intelligence and affectivity: Their relationship during child development*. Palo Alto, CA: Annual Reviews Inc.

Pintrich, P. R., Marx, R. W., & Boyle, R. A. (1993). Beyond cold conceptual change: The role of motivational beliefs and classroom contextual factors in the process of conceptual change. *Review of Educational Research, 63*, 167–199.

Port, R. F., & van Gelder, T. E. (1995). *Mind as motion: Explorations in the dynamics of cognition*. Cambridge, MA: The MIT Press.

Posner, M. I., & Peterson, S. E. (1990). The attention system of the human brain. *Annual Review of Neuroscience, 13*, 25–42.

Posner, M. I., & Rothbart, M. K. (1998). Attention, self regulation and consciousness. *Philosophical Transactions of the Royal Society of London B, 353*, 1915–1927.

Reed, E. (1997). The cognitive revolution from an ecological point of view. In D. M. Johnson & C. E. Erneling (Eds.), *The future of the cognitive revolution* (pp. 261–273). New York: Oxford University Press.

Rigney, J. W. (1980). Cognitive learning strategies and dualities in information processing. In R. E. Snow, P.-A. Federico, & W. E. Montague (Eds.), *Aptitude, learning, and instruction*

(Vol. 1: Cognitive process analysis of aptitude, pp. 315–343). Hillsdale, NJ: Lawrence Erlbaum Associates.

Rogoff, R., & Lave, J. (1984). *Everyday cognition.* Cambridge, MA: Harvard University Press.

Searle, J. R. (2001). Chinese Room Argument. In R. A. Wilson & F. C. Keil (Eds.), *The MIT encyclopedia of the cognitive sciences* (pp. 115–116). Cambridge, MA: The MIT Press.

Shweder, R. A. (2001). A polytheistic conception of the sciences and the virtues of deep variety. In A. R. Damasio, A. Harrington, J. Kagan, B. S. McEwen, H. Moss, & R. Shaikh (Eds.), *Unity of knowledge: The convergence of natural and human science* (pp. 217–232). New York: The New York Academy of Sciences.

Sieberg, D. (2003). Kasparov: "Intuition versus the brute force of calculation." *CNN/ACCESS.* Retrieved February 24, 2003, from http://www.cnn.com/2003/TECH/fun.games/02/08/cnna. kasparov/index.html

Siegler, R. S. (2002). Microgenetic studies of self-explanation. In N. Granott & J. Parziale (Eds.), *Microdevelopment: Transition processes in development and learning* (pp. 31–58). Cambridge, England: Cambridge University Press.

Simon, H. A. (1967). Motivational and emotional controls of cognition. *Psychological Review, 74,* 29–39.

Simon, H. A. (1994). The bottleneck of attention: Connecting thought with motivation. In W. D. Spaulding (Ed.), *Nebraska Symposium on Motivation, Vol. 41: Integrative views of motivation, cognition, and emotion* (pp. 1–21). Lincoln, NE: University of Nebraska.

Sinatra, G. M., & Pintrich, P. R. (Eds.). (2003). *Intentional conceptual change.* Mahwah, NJ: Lawrence Erlbaum Associates.

Snow, R. E. (1992). Aptitude theory: Yesterday, today, and tomorrow. *Educational Psychologist, 27,* 5–32.

Speelman, C. (1998). Implicit expertise: Do we expect too much from our experts? In K. Kirsner, C. Speelman, M. Maybery, A. O'Brien-Malone, M. Anderson, & C. MacLeod (Eds.), *Implicit and explicit mental processes* (pp. 135–147). Mahwah, NJ: Lawrence Erlbaum Associates.

Stanovich, K. E. (1999). *Who is rational? Studies of individual differences in reasoning.* Mahwah, NJ: Lawrence Erlbaum Associates.

Sternberg, R. J. (1985). *Beyond IQ: A triarchic theory of human intelligence.* Cambridge, England: Cambridge University Press.

Sternberg, R. J. (1996). *Successful intelligence.* New York: Simon & Schuster.

Sternberg, R. J. (1999). Intelligence as developing expertise. *Contemporary Educational Psychology, 24,* 359–375.

Sternberg, R. J., & Davidson, J. E. E. (1995). *The nature of insight.* Cambridge, MA: The MIT Press.

Sternberg, R. J., & Grigorenko, E. L. (2001). Unified psychology. *American Psychologist, 56,* 1069–1079.

Thagard, P. (2002). The passionate scientist: Emotion in scientific cognition. In P. Carruthers & S. Stich (Eds.), *The cognitive basis of science* (pp. 235–250). New York: Cambridge University Press.

Tomkins, S. S. (1963). Simulation of personality: The interrelationships between affect, memory, thinking, perception, and action. In S. S. Tomkins & S. Messick (Eds.), *Computer simulation of personality: Frontier of psychological theory* (pp. 3–57). New York: Wiley.

Vygotsky, L. S. (1978). *Mind in society: The development of higher psychological processes.* Cambridge, MA: Harvard University Press.

Wineburg, S. S. (1991). On the reading of historical texts: Notes on the breach between school and academy. *American Educational Research Journal, 28,* 73–87.

Winne, P. H., & Marx, R. W. (1989). A cognitive-processing analysis of motivation within classroom tasks. *Research on motivation in education. Vol. 3: Goals and cognitions* (pp. 223–257). New York: Academic Press.

Author Index

Subject Index